SEA-LEVEL FLUCTUATION AND COASTAL EVOLUTION

Based on a Symposium in Honor of William Armstrong Price

Sponsored by the Society of Economic Paleontologists and Mineralogists

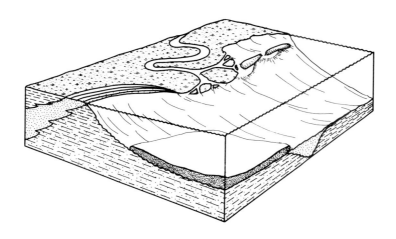

Edited by

Dag Nummedal, Department of Geology and Geophysics
Louisiana State University, Baton Rouge, Louisiana

Orrin H. Pilkey, Department of Geology
Duke University, Durham, North Carolina

and

James D. Howard, Skidaway Institute of Oceanography
Savannah, Georgia

Barbara H. Lidz, Editor of Special Publications
Special Publication No. 41

Tulsa, Oklahoma, U.S.A.   *December 1987*

A PUBLICATION OF

THE SOCIETY OF ECONOMIC PALEONTOLOGISTS AND MINERALOGISTS

ISBN # 0-918985-71-4

© 1987 by
Society of Economic Paleontologists and Mineralogists
P.O. Box 4756
Tulsa, Oklahoma 74131

Printed in the United States of America

PREFACE

This special publication is the result of a symposium in honor of W. Armstrong Price held at the first SEPM Midyear Meeting at San José, California, on August 12, 1984. Some papers were added after the symposium. The participation of Dr. Price in that symposium added greatly to its value and provided a sense of historical continuity to SEPM's role as the leading professional society for the study of sediments and sedimentary rocks. Armstrong Price has been a long-term SEPM member and a leading investigator of modern sedimentary processes. Thirty years before "process-response" models became customary, Armstrong Price applied fundamental physical principles in his analysis of the sedimentary deposits on the south Texas coastal plain.

The factors controlling relative sea-level change along our shores are varied and, at best, imperfectly understood. Yet, the relative rate of change is what controls shoreline erosion, the arrangement of sedimentary facies of the coastal zone, and the character of disconformities within the coastal stratigraphic record. Therefore, these papers address sea-level changes, shoreline responses, and the controls on the three-dimensional geometry of the consequent lithosomes; in short, the architecture of the coastal depositional systems.

Part 1 specifically considers changes in sea level in historical time and includes discussions of our present understanding of the causes of those changes. Gornitz and Lebedeff present a thorough statistical analysis of global tide-gauge data to substantiate their proposed 1.2 mm/yr "eustatic" sea-level rise. By further focusing on the North American part of that data set, they have derived accurate regional maps of local relative sea-level change.

Komar and Enfield present an interesting review of oceanographic factors known to cause short-term changes in sea level. In fact, many of the annual and decadal variations seen in Gornitz and Lebedeff's sea-level curves are explicable in terms of variations in the strength of ocean currents, breakdowns in global circulation patterns such as the El Niño, and latitudinal displacements of principal storm tracks. Much of this short-term sea-level variability is considered "noise" in the longer record; but, as Komar and Enfield express it, "one person's noise is another's key to a better understanding of nature."

Focusing on eastern North America, Braatz and Aubrey conclude that regional differences in relative sea-level change reflect postglacial adjustments in the land surface. It is also of great interest to see that Braatz and Aubrey's time series analysis reveals an increase in the rate of sea-level rise since the mid-1930s.

In part 2 the focus is on environmental and engineering concerns about the effects of the present rise of sea level. This concern is particularly relevant in view of current debate about the possibility of accelerated sea-level rise in response to a global greenhouse warming. If, as currently believed by many panels of the National Research Council, eustatic sea level will rise 75 cm over the next century, it is imperative that we conduct comprehensive research on the "engineering implications" of such a rise.

This effort has already begun. The two papers by Everts and by Pilkey and Davis, included in this part of the book, and the papers by Wells and Kraft and co-authors in part 4, significantly advance our current predictive capabilities. The actual numbers for shoreline retreat rates in Virginia and North Carolina are, of course, important. The primary reason for including the papers in this volume, however, is to stimulate greater efforts among coastal geologists and engineers to use our communal knowledge to develop methodologies of increasingly greater reliability.

Part 3 presents studies of areas with a highly variable Holocene sea-level history, either due to postglacial isostatic adjustments and forebulge migration, or to localized faulting. Along coastal Maine, Belknap and co-authors reconstruct a Holocene sea-level history with a highstand of relative sea level about 13 ka, a lowstand from 10 to 9 ka and a relative rise with accompanying coastal onlap since.

Scott and co-authors document that postglacial sea-level history and sedimentation patterns in Canada's Maritime Provinces are directly controlled by position relative to the forebulge at maximum glaciation. Observed sea-level histories support the predicted theoretical pattern for crustal response to deglaciation, they constrain geophysical estimates of the late Wisconsinan ice thickness, and they offer explanations for a complex landward succession of coastal and shallow marine facies.

Newman and co-authors apply a different perspective by analyzing, first, the regional response to deglaciation—the southward tilting of an early postglacial datum—and second, the impact of local faulting on the sea-level history of the lower Hudson Valley. The conceptual approach to the analysis of local tectonic effects is particularly valuable and could with great benefit be applied to sea-level curves elsewhere.

The interpretation of the sedimentary geological record has been greatly stimulated over the past few years by rapid conceptual advances in "sequence stratigraphy," i.e., the attempt to analyze stratigraphic successions in terms of genetically related packages of strata. The value of the concept of a "depositional sequence" lies both in the recognition of a consistent three-dimensional arrangement of facies within the sequence, the facies architecture, and the regional (and inter-regional) correlation of the sequence boundaries. It has also been argued that many sequence boundaries are correlatable globally, and that they reflect periods of sea-level lowstand, i.e., sequence boundaries are subaerial erosion surfaces.

The majority of the papers in this book has been assembled to document, in great detail, the actual stratigraphy and architecture of depositional systems of the coastal and shallow marine components of the most recent depositional sequences, those of late Quaternary age. The book, therefore, complements another SEPM Special Publication which is focused on the ancient geological record: *Sea Level Changes—An Integrated Approach*. Only a few papers in this book go back beyond the late Quaternary, and when they do it is to use the older rock record to develop further the concepts initiated in studies of Quaternary strata.

Part 4 consists of five papers which focus on the evolution of coastal depositional systems during the late Holocene. The first one documents that Holocene sea level has not been uniformly rising across the globe. In a fascinating paper on the deltas of the Brazilian coast, Dominguez and his co-authors document that sea level there has dropped about 5 m over the last 5,000 yrs causing extensive strand-plain progradation. The sea-level fall was not uniform; short-term periods of rise produced a series of internal unconformities within the strand-plain sequence.

Concurrent with this episode of sea-level fall, local relative sea level along the United States east coast and other mid-latitude coasts undeniably rose. Two papers from the United States mid-Atlantic region document the Holocene sedimentary response to this sea-level rise. For coastal Delaware, Kraft and co-authors document the significance of the antecedent topography (the sea-level lowstand surface) on the preservation potential of the transgressive coastal stratigraphic sequence. Their paper is also of value in erosion studies because they document many of the short-comings of the simple Bruun Rule for prediction of shoreline retreat. Specifically, the three-dimensional paths of sediment dispersal in the coastal zone and the grain-size composition of the eroding shoreface need to be considered in calculations of beach retreat.

Finkelstein and Ferland have analyzed a series of vibracores from the back-barrier environments of the Atlantic coast of Virginia and conclude that these extensive areas have evolved from large open lagoons, via tidal flats, into today's marshes. Consequently, extensive lithosomes with a fining-upward textural sequence have developed during the Holocene transgression of that coast. This is in distinct contrast to the more common coarsening-upward sequences in neighboring coastal Delaware, which are dominated by flood-tidal deltas and washover fans.

The Gulf Coast basin is characterized by very high rates of sediment supply, subsidence and relative sea-level rise. This setting has produced numerous regressive deposits during the late Holocene Epoch in spite of local relative sea-level rise. Wells' paper documents the evolution of the most recent example of these regressive deposits, the Atchafalaya delta. This delta is, in itself, a fascinating study of the initial phase of development of Mississippi subdeltas. It also serves as a timely reminder that one cannot assume, as has often been done in modeling of ancient depositional sequences, that sediment supply is constant during the buildup of a sequence.

The final paper on coastal depositional systems evaluates the relative preservation potential of wave-dominated and tide-dominated deposits along coastlines undergoing transgressions or regressions. As expected, Davis and Clifton find overwhelming evidence that regressive sequences have a higher preservation potential, and that preservation of transgressive facies successions is higher in tide- than in wave-dominated settings.

Part 5 expands the scale of investigations from the de-

positional systems of part 4 to the larger, unconformity-bounded depositional sequences. Both papers address the Quaternary sequences in the Gulf Coast basin. Morton and Armstrong Price present an integrated account of the late Quaternary geology of the Texas coastal plain and shelf, a fitting statement to Dr. Price's life-long devotion to the Texas coast. The paper emphasizes the structural control on the arrangement of the depositional systems and the diversity of facies within individual depositional sequences in response to their location relative to major depocenters.

Suter and co-authors document the late Quaternary seismic stratigraphy of the western Louisiana continental shelf. Multiple episodes of sea-level lowstand have caused extensive dissection of the Louisiana shelf by channels of the Mississippi and Red rivers, as well as smaller coastal plain streams. During lowstand, the rivers built major prograding shelf-edge deltas. During subsequent sea-level rise, the entrenched valleys filled with bay-fill facies of great diversity. Also, the depth of transgressive truncation of individual sequences varies greatly, perhaps as a function of the rate of relative sea-level rise.

Part 6 contains two papers which focus equally on the boundaries of the depositional sequences and their internal architecture. These studies are particularly relevant to studies attempting to derive Phanerozoic sea-level histories from sequence-bounding unconformities. Demarest and Kraft argue convincingly that a differentiation of the transgressive ravinement surface and the "basal" sequence boundary (the late Wisconsinan lowstand surface in their example) is essential in order to infer correctly whether the transgressive or regressive hemi-sequence accounted for the majority of the deposits in a given depositional sequence. Because of the distinct lithologic contrast across the ravinement surface, this erosional surface is often misidentified as the sequence boundary.

Nummedal and Swift emphasize some basic principles which control the architecture of the transgressive part of coastal and shallow marine depositional sequences. Data for this analysis come from numerous Late Quaternary and Cretaceous examples. Significant emphasis is placed on erosional surfaces within the coastal and shallow marine sequences. It becomes clear that significant thicknesses of coastal plain fluvio-deltaic strata, and many continental shelf sandstones, are of transgressive origin. The paper also identifies sedimentological criteria which permit recognition of changes in water depth on continental shelves.

It is our intent in this book to present a comprehensive and timely account of the present understanding of how sea-level changes controlled the formation of unconformities, facies and depositional systems in coastal plains and shallow marine settings. Moreover, we feel that the contributions truly reflect an approach to coastal sedimentological research pioneered by William Armstrong Price.

For the editors,
Dag Nummedal

CONTENTS

A TRIBUTE TO W. ARMSTRONG PRICE (1889–1987)

A Tribute . . .

Paying tribute to a legendary figure is, on the one hand, a very great honor, and on the other, a very great responsibility. This volume, dedicated to William Armstrong Price, will, by association with the topics and authors contained therein, provide some measure of the importance of Professor Price in the development of coastal geology not only as a field unto itself but as a genuine application of Uniformitarianism, however literally one chooses to define the term, to interpretation of the geologic record. To those of us who have had the privilege of knowing him as a mentor, colleague and friend, his impact on our thinking and work ethic has been profound.

In March of this year, Armstrong celebrated his 97th birthday, a day which found him working as usual at his desk and map table, and wearing his house slippers and green eyeshade, pencil in one hand and artgum eraser in the other—exactly as I remember him in September 1953 when I came to the Texas A & M College Department of Oceanography as his research assistant. I have never witnessed before or since an office so filled with maps, reprints and manuscripts or a person with such zeal and exuberence for his work. And, I might add, a person so patient and understanding of the ignorance that I presented to him.

He corresponded with everyone. He was the great communicator. He still is. I have an entire file drawer of his letters and messages written on post-cards, hotel stationery, backs of envelopes and 3 × 5 cards. Some of his most important comments were hand-written in the margins and between the lines of type, obviously as afterthoughts following the original text. He solicited advice and information from multitudes, particularly his students.

His field trips to the coast were buffets of geology, Indian lore and Texas and Mexican history—and, if he was driving the carryall, often terrifying. He would tell of the vicissitudes associated with field work on horseback and on foot in West Virginia, Texas and Out West. His anecdotes were as instructive as they were delightful. I hesitate to name the geologists, now pre-eminent in their field, on whom his papers and his personal contact or correspondence had such a mighty impact, for fear of omission of many—but they know who they are.

He was asked in 1984 which of his published papers he liked the most. He suggested that the paper "Development of the Basin-In-Basin Honeycomb of Florida Bay and the Northeastern Cuban Lagoon," given at the GCAGS Meeting in Mexico, must have been of importance to some. This modest man didn't mention such classic papers as the "Role of Diastrophism in the Corpus Christi Area, South Texas" (AAPG v. 17, 1933); "Lissie Formation and Beaumont Clay in South Texas" (AAPG v. 18, 1934); "Equilibrium of Form and Forces in Tidal Basins of the Coasts of Texas and Louisiana" (AAPG v. 31, 1947); "Geomorphology of Depositional Surfaces" (AAPG v. 31, 1947); "Barrier Island, Not Offshore Bar" (Sci. v. 113, 1951); and his publications and reports concerning the development and classification of coasts based on wave energy and offshore bottom conditions from work sponsored by the Office of Naval Research during the period 1954–1956.

The breadth of his geological interests can be appreciated only by examining his bibliography which begins with his Ph.D. dissertation on the "Pennsylvanian Fauna of Maryland" (Johns Hopkins University, 1913) and currently ends with citation number 156 as an abstract with R. A. Morton on the "Influence of Sea Level on Erosional, Depositional and Submergence Patterns of the Texas Coast," presented at the 1984 SEPM Midyear Meeting in San José. The variety of topics so astutely discussed in those intervening decades are simply too many to describe here.

In 1973, Armstrong was awarded the Society of Economic Paleontologists and Mineralogists Francis P. Shepard Medal for his contributions to the field of coastal and marine geology. This honor was particularly fitting because these two gentlemen of science were of similar vintage and character and laid the foundations upon which we and our younger colleagues build today. Always ready and eager to challenge dogma and stagnant thought, Papa Price is truly a man for all seasons.

Vernon J. Henry
Department of Geology
Georgia State University
Atlanta, Georgia

October 1986

PART I
RECENT SEA-LEVEL RISE

GLOBAL SEA-LEVEL CHANGES DURING THE PAST CENTURY

VIVIEN GORNITZ

Lamont-Doherty Geological Observatory and Goddard Space Flight Center, Institute for Space Studies, New York, New York 10025

AND

SERGEJ LEBEDEFF

CENTEL Sigma Data Services, Goddard Space Flight Center, Institute for Space Studies, New York, New York 10025

ABSTRACT: An updated and expanded data base of tide-gauge measurements and late Holocene sea-level indicators is used to obtain a revised global average sea-level rise, corrected for long-range glacio-isostatic and/or tectonic trends. The global average is determined using two methods: (1) the arithmetic mean of all stations, and (2) a new technique which weights contributing stations by distance from a given cell and relative coastal area. A least-squares regression line is then fitted to the composite regional sea-level curve. In the second method, the global average is derived by averaging 11 regional sea-level curves, weighting each region equally, and also according to the relative reliability of the regional data. This latter step is designed to reduce the influence of regions with few stations or poor data.

The "corrected" average eustatic sea-level rise for both methods is 1.2 ± 0.3 and 1.0 ± 0.1 mm/yr, respectively. Weighting for regional reliability does not alter the global average significantly. The results agree with those of previous studies and provide an independent verification for a global increase in sea level during the past century. The closeness in values between the two averaging methods used here and those of earlier studies suggests that the observed change represents a true eustatic sea-level rise in spite of noisy data, geographic bias, and differences in approach and techniques.

Sea level, corrected for long-term movements, is found to be rising in all but three regions, which have small station populations, sparse long-range data or are tectonically active. Along the east coast of North America, an apparent maximum sea-level rise is observed in both tide-gauge and late Holocene sea-level indicators between Chesapeake Bay and New Jersey ($36°–40°N$). This enhanced mid-Atlantic subsidence, possibly indicating neotectonic activity or sediment loading, has persisted for at least the last 7,000 yrs. Subsidence of northern New England-Maritime Canada ($44°–46°N$) may be caused by a migrating crest of the peripheral forebulge at the edge of formerly glaciated areas. Sea-level changes in western North America show greater spatial variations than for the east coast, which can be related to more active tectonism in California and British Columbia and to strong, localized isostatic rebound in Alaska.

Most of the recent sea-level rise can be accounted for in terms of the thermal expansion of the upper layers of the ocean and by melting of alpine glaciers.

INTRODUCTION

The recent history of sea-level change arouses considerable interest because of its potential sensitivity to climate change and its effects on shoreline erosion. The strong likelihood of a global warming produced by anthropogenic addition of CO_2 to the atmosphere (Hansen and others, 1981; National Academy of Sciences/National Research Council, NAS/NRC, 1979, 1982) could enhance melting of continental and alpine glaciers and cause thermal expansion of the upper layers of the oceans, which in turn, could increase sea level by 70 to 200 cm within the next century (Revelle, 1983; Hoffman, 1983). These projected rates are an order of magnitude higher than those of the past century (Gornitz and others, 1982; Barnett, 1983, 1984). Even current rates of sea-level rise may produce world-wide coastal erosion (Kerr, 1981; Geotimes, 1981), although offshore currents and construction of dams and jetties may also contribute to shrinkage of beaches (Gribbin, 1984; Galvin, 1983). It is thus essential to continue monitoring sea level to allow detection of any acceleration of the current rate of change.

World-wide secular changes in sea level are caused by several processes (Table 1). Among the most important, on time scales of thousands of years or more, are *glacio-eustatic* variations in the ocean volume, due to melting and growth of ice sheets (Fairbridge, 1961; Donovan and Jones, 1979), and *glacio-isostatic* changes, due to adjustments of the earth's lithosphere to changes in ice and water loads (Clark and others, 1978; Peltier, 1980). Over millions of years, changes in seafloor spreading rates, the volume of the ocean ridge system and subsidence of passive margin oceanic lithosphere (Pitman, 1978; Watts, 1982) can also significantly affect sea level (Hallam, 1984).

On a shorter time scale (decades or centuries), local tectonic movements could also generate sea-level trends comparable in magnitude to eustatic and isostatic changes. Sea level could also be affected partly by subsidence caused by pumping of oil or groundwater withdrawal (as in Galveston; Aubrey and Emery, 1983), or by shifts in prevailing wind patterns and ocean currents (Rossiter, 1962). Finally, sea-level rise due to sedimentation, although significant near river deltas, is negligible on a global scale. The global sea-level rise corresponding to the deposition of the suspended sediment load from the world's siltiest rivers amounts to only around 0.02 mm/yr (Holeman, 1968).

Previous estimates of sea-level changes over the past century range between 1 and 3 mm/yr (Table 1, *in* Barnett, 1983). Fairbridge and Krebs (1962) and Barnett (1983) used single, widely spaced stations, assuming that they were representative of large regions. Subsequently, Barnett (1984) expanded his coverage to 155 stations (excluding those of strong isostatic uplift) grouped into six regions, using empirical orthogonal function analysis to obtain regional averages. Aubrey and Emery (1983) used eigenanalysis methods to define spatial and temporal patterns of sea-level variability in the United States and are extending this approach to other regions as well.

In our previous paper (Gornitz and others, 1982), we obtained a global sea-level trend of 1.2 mm/yr by averaging 14 regional averages, weighting each region equally. Stations from known strongly seismic or anomalously subsiding localities and isostatically rising Fennoscandia were excluded as well as those with record lengths under 20 yrs. A minimum length of 20 yrs was chosen in order to minimize the effects of the 18.6-yr lunar nodal cycle. In addition, we also removed the effects of long-range trends

TABLE 1.—CAUSES OF SEA-LEVEL CHANGE

Process	Rate
1. Glacio-eustatic changes in volume of ocean water	10 mm/yr, over 7,000 yrs following deglaciation
2. Glacio-isostatic changes in volume of ocean basins	1–10 mm/yr
3. Seafloor spreading; cooling and subsidence of oceanic lithosphere; change in volume of ocean floor	0.01 mm/yr
4. Sediment accumulation, global; local river deltas	0.02 mm/yr 1–3 mm/yr
5. Tectonic uplift/subsidence	1–3 mm/yr

(≤6,000 yrs), which are predominantly glacio-isostatic in origin (Clark and others, 1978; Peltier, 1980; Wu and Peltier, 1983) but may also include tectonic movements.

In the present paper, we use a different averaging procedure to reevaluate the estimate of relative sea-level change over the past century. This new technique, initially developed for climate studies, produces a composite regional average sea-level curve from the tide-gauge data of individual stations. Late Holocene sea-level indicators are used to compensate for the effects of glacio-isostasy and long-term tectonism. Several regions are studied more extensively to ascertain causes of variability in sea-level trends, among these the east coast of North America, which is tectonically relatively stable and has abundant long-term data. The geometry of this coastline is also reasonably simple. The west coast is examined in some detail, as an example of a region where tectonic processes are important.

PROCEDURE

The introduction clearly indicates that the determination of the global eustatic sea-level signal is a complex problem. Two possible approaches may be used to extract the global eustatic sea-level signal from tide-gauge data: (1) stations with known isostatic or tectonic movements can be excluded, and (2) long-range isostatic and/or tectonic trends obtained from independent data sources can be removed. The first approach gives a measure of the total sea-level change, but subjectively eliminates unstable stations, which may otherwise contain long, continuous records. In the second approach, the recent sea-level change obtained may still contain components due to local short-term tectonic and/ or climatic processes. These residual short-term elements, however, are essentially random on a global scale. The influence of these random fluctuations can be reduced by selecting an appropriate measure of central tendency, such as the mean or the median. A measure of central tendency minimizes the sum of the absolute values or of the squares of the deviation (Ostle, 1963). Therefore, it represents an estimate of common change of sea level over the regions considered. The arithmetic mean is preferred because the frequency distribution of sea-level trends is symmetrical (see below) and also because the mean lends itself more readily to statistical manipulation.

Tide-gauge measurements from the Permanent Service for Mean Sea Level, Bidston Observatory, Birkenhead, England, have been expanded and updated through 1982. This data base contains over 800 stations (Fig. 1); however, most tidal records are still too short or too broken to be

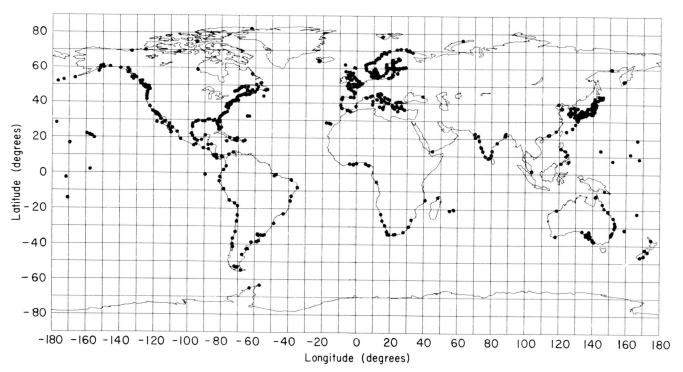

FIG. 1.—Index map showing the location of all tide-gauge stations.

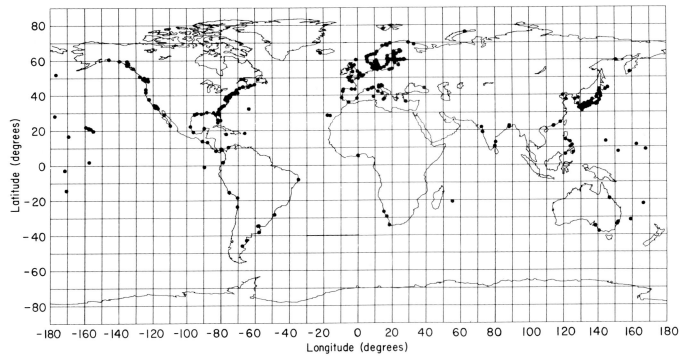

FIG. 2.—Map showing the location of tide-gauge stations with record lengths ≥20 years.

useful. Furthermore, there is a strong geographic bias toward the northern hemisphere. One means of reducing this bias is to divide the tide-gauge stations into a number of regions, based on geographic proximity, and weighting each region equally, to obtain a "global" average. It has been pointed out, however, that this procedure gives equal weight to both regions with many well-recorded stations and with a few (possibly poor) stations. To overcome this bias, we also introduce a weighting factor for each region, based on the relative reliability of the data. The weights used are the normalized inverse of $\sigma/\sqrt{n-1}$ for each geographic region, where σ = standard deviation of the slopes and n = number of stations in a region.

To allow comparison with previous results, least-squares regression lines of sea-level position as a function of time (SL trends) have been fitted to *all* tide-gauge stations with a record length of 20 yrs or greater (Fig. 2), from which the global arithmetic mean is computed (Table 2,a). In order to ascertain the effect of isostatic rebound on the global average, the calculation is repeated, excluding 54 stations in Fennoscandia (Table 2,b).

We also correct for long-term isostatic and tectonic factors by subtracting long-range (usually ≤6,000–7,000 yrs) sea-level trends which are still present in the corresponding station data (Gornitz and others, 1982). We use a greatly expanded compilation of ^{14}C-dated Holocene sea-level indicators, such as mollusks, corals and brackish-water peats (over 4,000 entries, Fig. 3; W. S. Newman, pers. commun.; Marcus and Newman, 1983). This data set was supplemented by Bloom (1977 and references cited therein), Mörner (1980) and Clague and others (1982). The ^{14}C dates

were corrected to the 5,730-yr half-life (Godwin, 1962) and recalibrated to account for past atmospheric ^{14}C fluctuations (Suess, 1978).

A substantial fraction of the late Holocene data could not be used, because (a) a large number of points were too far from any tide-gauge station, (b) the dates were too old, and (c) the scatter of data points at several localities was too great to yield a reliable SL curve. Sources of error include uncertainties in estimating the past tidal ranges, the relation of the dated material to sea level, differences in definition of sea-level position, and dating errors (Kidson, 1982). Examination of sea-level indicators within specified geographic cells, however, did not reveal any systematic differences related to the nature of the material dated. Shells are often considered to be less reliable SL indicators than basal salt marsh peats. Yet in many cases, shells were found

TABLE 2.—SUMMARY OF AVERAGE SEA-LEVEL CHANGES OVER THE LAST CENTURY

	Arithmetic Average mm/yr	Average of Regional Cell Averages mm/yr
a. All* tide-gauge stations ≥20 yrs	0.6 ± 0.4†	0.71 ± 0.1
b. All** tide-gauge stations of (a) except Fennoscandia	1.7 ± 0.3	1.7 ± 0.4
c. Tide-gauge stations*** with long-range trends removed	1.2 ± 0.3	1.0 ± 0.1

*A total of 292 stations, from which six with trends > |10| have been excluded.
**231 stations, excluding 56 from Fennoscandia and five with trends > 3σ. (The latter five stations are among the six excluded above).
***130 stations.
†95% confidence interval.

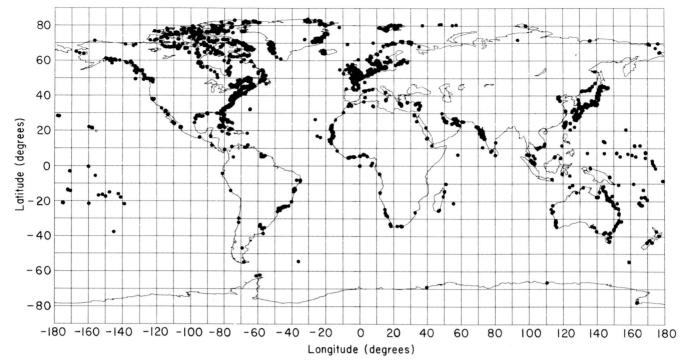

FIG. 3.—Index map showing the location of all ^{14}C-dated Holocene sea-level indicators (from W. Newman, pers. commun.).

to fall on the same SL curve as the other SL indicators, whereas conversely, some peat samples were occasionally way off.

The long-range data were sorted into cells, selected to be sufficiently small to have undergone a fairly uniform isostatic or tectonic change, yet large enough to collect a sufficient number of data points for a reasonably smooth sea-level curve, representative examples of which are shown in Figure 4. A simple linear regression fit was used for most cells, although quadratic and even higher order polynomial curve fits were employed in a few cases. The 6,000- to 7,000-yr interval was the greatest length that could be approximated by a linear fit, without approaching the period of rapid sea-level rise following the deglaciation of the Laurentide and Fennoscandian ice sheets. The error (as given by the 95% confidence interval) was found to be relatively large in several cells because of scatter in the data for reasons discussed above, or an insufficient number of points. Cells for which the ratio of the error to the slope exceeded 35% were discarded, leaving a total of 71 cells (Fig. 5).

After correction of sea levels for long-range trends, as described above, a global average was obtained in two ways. For the first method, the long-range trend derived for data points within each cell was subtracted from all tide-gauge stations lying entirely within the cell or within several tenths of a degree latitude or longitude from the cell boundary. The arithmetic mean was then computed for 130 tide-gauge stations.

In the second method, a new technique has been developed (J. Hansen and others, pers. commun.; Rind and Lebedeff, 1984) to combine time series of variable length and with discontinuities, such as those represented by tide-gauge records, into an average, composite, time series within a given cell of arbitrary size. Each individual cell is first subdivided into a large number of subcells. The average sea-level trend of each cell is obtained as a distance-weighted average of the tide-gauge data from surrounding stations. The weight, w, is assumed to be a linear function of d, the distance between the center of a subcell and that station.

$$w = \begin{cases} 1 - d/d_0 & \text{for} \quad d < d_0 \\ 0 & \text{for} \quad d > d_0. \end{cases}$$

The distance, $d_0 = 250$ km, was estimated from the extent of correlation among tide-gauge records from surrounding stations, as described by Rind and Lebedeff (1984). Calculations were repeated using $d_0 = 100$ km to assess the sensitivity of the cell average to changes in distance. Long-range trends, derived as described above, are subtracted from the average sea-level trend of the cell. A digitized $1° \times 1°$ Rand topographic map is used to obtain the area of those subcells that lie within 1° latitude and longitude from the shore. The area along the shore determined in this manner for each cell is then combined with the coastal areas for several cells grouped into larger regions, outlined in Figure 5, to obtain a composite, coastal area-weighted average sea-level curve before obtaining a least-squares fit slope for the region. Finally, the global sea-level change is obtained by averaging the 11 regional sea-level curves, weighting each region equally. The global average is also computed using weights based on the relative reliability of the data from each region.

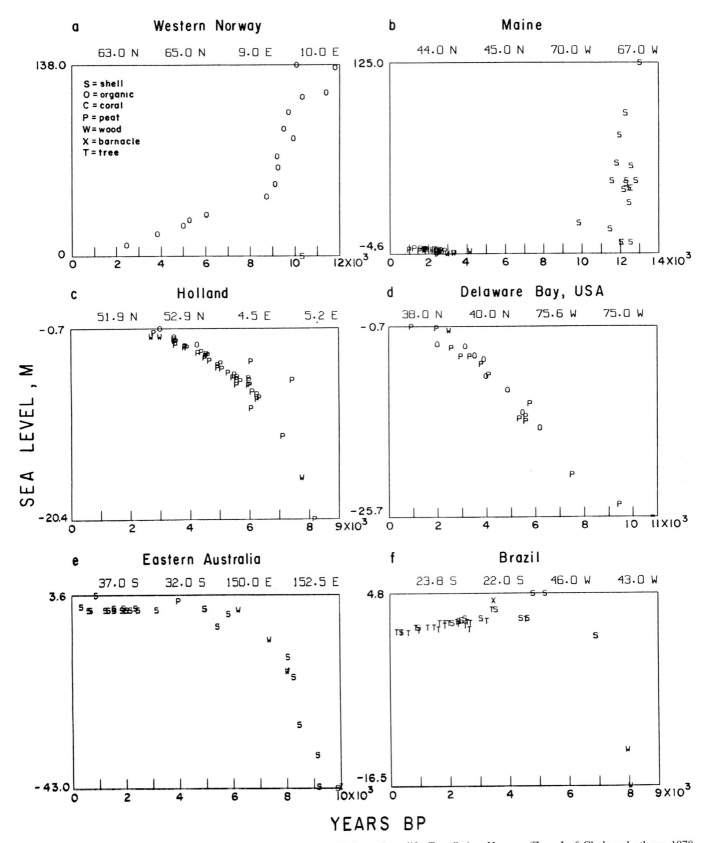

FIG. 4.—Representative examples of long-range sea-level curves. (a) Isostatic uplift, Trondheim, Norway (Zone I of Clark and others, 1978; Peltier, 1980). (b) Initial isostatic uplift followed by subsidence, transitional area, (Zone I-II), Maine. (c) Continuous subsidence, collapsing peripheral bulge (Zone II), Holland. (d) The same as (c), from Delaware Bay, eastern United States. (e) Little coastal movement over the past 6,000 yrs, eastern Australia. (f) Mid-Holocene emergent shoreline, Rio de Janeiro, Brazil.

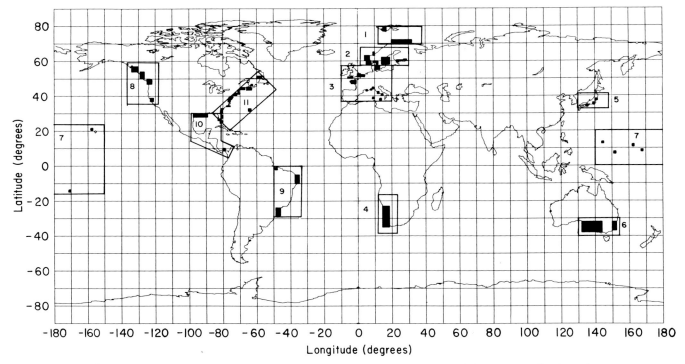

FIG. 5.—Locations of cells (black) and regions (outlined) used in obtaining global average sea-level trend.

RESULTS

The arithmetic mean of 286 tide-gauge stations with record lengths ≥ 20 yrs, uncorrected for long-range trends, is 0.6 ± 0.4 mm/yr (Table 2,a). The histogram in Figure 6A illustrates the spatial variability among all stations; the time variability of the tide-gauge data is neglected. The wide scatter reflects diverse geologic processes, such as isostatic uplift in Fennoscandia, leading to negative SL trends, and subsidence due to tectonism (Japan) or a migrating forebulge (eastern North America), leading to high positive SL trends (Fig. 6A). If Fennoscandian stations are excluded, the global mean rises to 1.7 ± 0.3 mm/yr (Table 2,b), a value similar to that obtained by Barnett (1983, 1984).

The arithmetic mean for sea-level data, corrected for long-range trends, is 1.2 ± 0.3 mm/yr (Table 2,c; Fig. 6B). The negative trends of Fennoscandia have become positive; the large positive slopes for Japan and eastern North America and the Gulf coast are reduced substantially. The distribution of sea-level slopes on uncorrected data (Fig. 6C) is compared with the identical subset of corrected stations (Fig. 6B). The comparison shows that the spread of sea-level slopes is significantly reduced after long-range trends have been subtracted. This result supports our contention that long-term trends contribute to the scatter and that their removal will improve the estimation of eustatic sea-level change.

The results of the second averaging method agree well with the preceding one (Table 2). The global mean sea-level change, with all regions weighted equally, is 1.0 ± 0.1 mm/yr after long-range trends are subtracted. This is slightly below the global arithmetic mean sea-level change

(Method I) but still within the uncertainty. After introducing weighting factors for regional reliability, the global average becomes 0.9 ± 0.1 mm/yr, which is not significantly different from using equal weights. Therefore, the bias introduced by averaging each region equally is not serious.

The regional breakdown of sea-level changes is presented in Table 3 and Figure 7. These values were obtained, using a distance, $d_0 = 250$ km, in weighting the contribution of tide-gauge data from stations surrounding each cell. Decreasing d_0 to 100 km did not alter the global or most regional means substantially, except for that for the Arctic, which has a low station population. Therefore, $d_0 = 250$ km is used in the remainder of this paper.

Sea level, corrected for long-term movements, is found to be rising in all but three regions. Whereas small station populations or sparse long-range data may account for the anomalous trends of the Arctic or Pacific islands, tectonic movements may, in part, be responsible for the erratic trend of western North America (Aubrey and Emery, 1983). This latter region will be described in greater detail in the next section. Other factors responsible for the large observed regional variability, including changes in ocean circulation, will also be examined further.

The suggestion that the rate of sea-level rise may have increased during the last 50 yrs, relative to the preceding 50 yrs (Barnett, 1984), is now examined. Globally, the rate of sea-level rise (corrected) has increased by 0.6 mm/yr between 1932–1982 relative to 1880–1931 (Fig. 7). In eastern North America, the corrected SL trend has increased by 1.7 mm/yr between 1932–1982 relative to 1880–1931, supporting Barnett's suggestion. Similar increases for the second period over the first occur in western North

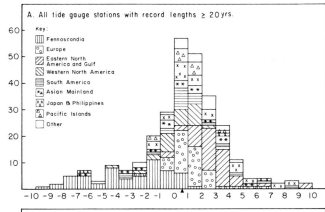

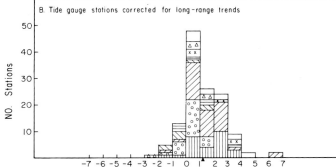

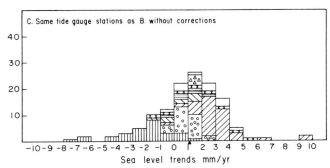

FIG. 6.—Histogram of number of stations versus sea-level trends. (A) All tide-gauge stations with record lengths ≥20 yrs. (B) The same, for tide-gauge stations from which long-range trends have been subtracted. (C) Same subset of stations as (B); long-range trends included.

TABLE 3.—AVERAGE SEA-LEVEL CHANGES BY REGION

Regional Mean	Long-Range Trends Removed			
	$d_0 = 250$ km		$d_0 = 100$ km	
	Trend mm/yr	95% Confidence interval	Trend mm/yr	95% Confidence interval
1. Arctic	−0.1	0.8	0.6	1.2
2. Fennoscandia	1.5	0.3	1.8	0.3
3. Europe	0.6	0.1	0.5	0.1
4. Africa	1.9	1.0	2.0	1.0
5. Japan	2.5	0.6	2.4	0.6
6. Australia	1.5	0.3	1.5	0.3
7. Pacific Island	0.1	0.4	0.1	0.3
8. W. North America	0.0	0.2	−0.1	0.2
9. E. South America	1.2	1.2	1.3	1.5
10. Gulf of Mexico + Caribbean	2.4	0.4	2.5	0.4
11. E. North America	1.3	0.2	1.3	0.2
Global mean (all regions weighted equally)	1.0	0.1	1.0	0.1
Global mean (with weighting factors)	0.9	0.1	1.0	0.1

First, the uncertainty in the slope, expressed by the 95% confidence limit, is associated with the time variability of the tidal records. Sources of temporal variation include changes in atmospheric pressure, wind stress and ocean circulation (Lisitzin, 1974; Rossiter, 1962). Sea-level changes on a very short time scale (several years) largely reflect atmospheric/oceanic interactions, such as the El Nino/southern oscillation or variations in the Kuroshio current or Gulf Stream (see Komar and Enfield, this vol). For example, the mean winter sea-level height increased by 5.6 cm in southern California within a single decade, due to an ocean warming related to reduced north-south wind stress (Namias and Huang, 1972). Another source of variation is fluctuation in annual river runoff, which may account for 7 to 21% of the total variation in mean annual sea level along the east coast of the United States (Meade and Emery, 1971). The 18.6-yr lunar nodal cycle also introduces periodic noise in the sea-level trends. Amplitudes may range to as much as 9 mm at 65° latitude (Rossiter, 1962; Lisitzin, 1974). Stations with short time series show a proportionally greater sensitivity to the lunar cycle. The lunar effect is largely removed by employing record lengths ≥20 yrs.

Second, sea-level trends may vary from station to station because of tectonic movements, localized subsidence caused by river sedimentation, or groundwater withdrawal. On a larger spatial scale, one possible explanation for the high observed inter-regional variability may be related to changes in ocean circulation induced by an expected decrease in wind stress accompanying climatic warming. The observed inter-regional pattern of sea-level rise is qualitatively consistent with first-order predictions from simple barotropic calculations, which indicate greater sea-level rise along the northwestern ocean coasts (i.e., Japan and eastern North America, with SL rises of 2.5 ± 0.6 mm/yr and 1.3 ± 0.2 mm/yr, respectively) than the eastern ocean coasts (western North America, 0.0 ± 0.2 mm/yr and Europe, 0.6 ± 0.1 mm/yr; Table 3). Mid-ocean islands are anticipated to show small changes (e.g., Pacific Islands, 0.1 ± 0.4 mm/yr).

America (1.6 mm/yr) and the Gulf of Mexico (1.7 mm/yr). Other regions, however, show substantially different behavior: decreases of −0.6, −0.1, and −0.7 mm/yr for Fennoscandia, Europe and Australia, respectively. Since inter-regional variability is great, and the error on the slope increases proportionally by dividing the record length into two parts, the significance of this result is open to question.

DISCUSSION

Sources of variability in sea level data.—

Large regional variations in sea level remain, even after subtraction of long-range trends (Table 3). Two types of uncertainty contribute to the variability of sea-level trends.

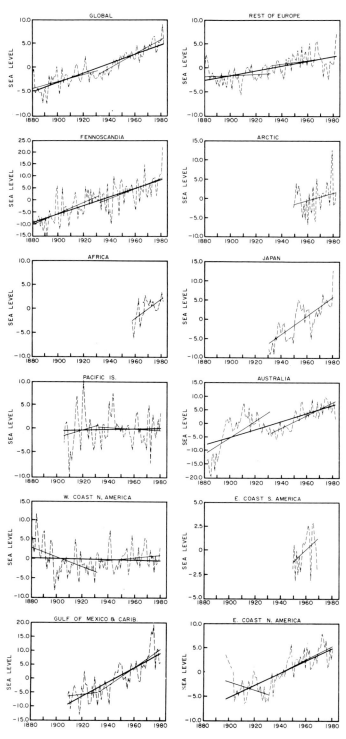

FIG. 7.—Sea-level curves, 1880–1980. Units are in centimeters. Heavy line represents least-squares slope for the past century. Lighter lines represent slopes for the intervals 1880–1931 and 1932–1980.

Intraregional variations in sea level—eastern and western North America as test cases.—

A more detailed investigation into possible causes of intraregional variability in mareograph records will now be presented for both the east and west coasts of North America. The location of individual stations along the east coast is indicated on Figure 8, together with the short-range (tide-gauge) and long-range sea-level trends. Three stations show anomalous mareograph trends relative to adjacent stations: Fernandina, Florida (FERN, -0.90 mm/yr), Richmond, Virginia (RICH, -0.46) and Buzzard's Bay (BUZZ, 0.52). All three stations have very short record lengths (20–26 yrs). Our record for Fernandina only covers 1898 to 1923, although Hicks and others (1983) present data for this station from 1898–1924 and 1939–1980. The slope changes abruptly between these two intervals. Furthermore, the older interval pre-dates coverage from most other stations and therefore introduces a divergent trend. Both Richmond and Buzzard's Bay have very short and noisy records. These three stations have therefore been deleted. The arithmetic mean for the 37 remaining stations between Key West, Florida, and St. John's Newfoundland, is 3.0 ± 0.8 mm/yr.

Long-term ($\leq 7,000$ yrs) sea-level data for eastern North

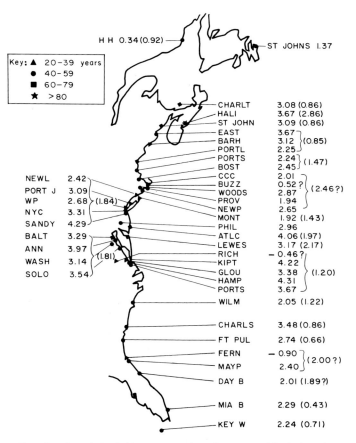

FIG. 8.—Location of tide-gauge stations for eastern North America. Number on left represents the sea-level trend from tide-gauge data (mm/yr); number on right is the corresponding long-range trend for each cell.

America, grouped into 20 cells (Fig 5; region 11), have been compared with the tide-gauge data (Fig. 8). Anomalously high long-range trends between Daytona Beach and Fernandina (Fig. 8) are probably unreliable due to a limited number of data points. The United States east coast arithmetic average SL rise (long-range trends removed) is 1.6 ± 0.8 mm/yr.

The slopes of tide-gauge (short-range) and long-range data are plotted as a function of latitude on Figure 9A and B, respectively. Error bars represent 95% confidence limits on the slopes. Whereas errors are relatively large in both cases, surprisingly, they are higher for the mareograph data. The

errors on the sea-level trends are approximately inversely proportional to the tide-gauge record lengths. Both plots of short-term (tide-gauge) and long-term sea-level trends as a function of latitude show an apparent maximum between 36° and 40° N. This spatial pattern becomes more pronounced for tide-gauge stations with record lengths ≥45 yrs (Fig. 10A, B). Because error estimates on the stations with longer record lengths are correspondingly lower, the enhanced peak in sea-level trends between 36° and 40° N is therefore likely to be real. The present data are consistent with the observation of Hicks (1972, 1981) and Aubrey and

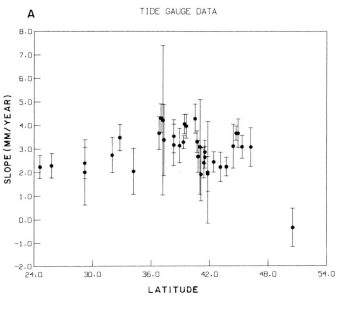

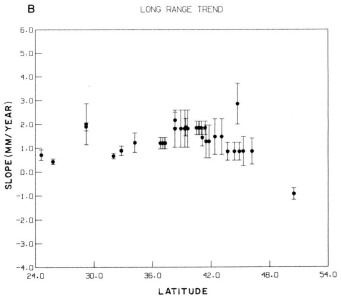

FIG. 9.—Plot of United States east coast sea-level trends as a function of latitude. Error bars represent 95% confidence limits on the slopes. (A) Tide-gauge data. (B) Late Holocene sea-level indicators.

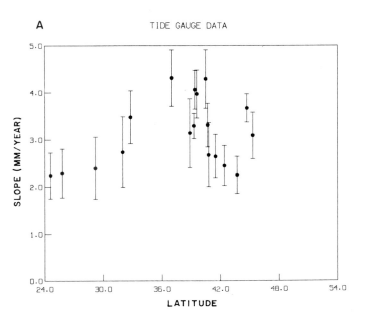

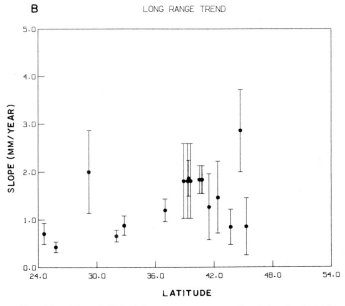

FIG. 10.—Plot of United States east coast sea-level trends. (A) The same as Figure 9A, but for tide-gauge stations with record lengths ≥45 yrs. (B) The same as Figure 9B, but for locations corresponding to the stations of Figure 10A.

Emery (1983) that sea-level trends increase systematically between Portland, Maine, and Portsmouth, Virginia, reaching a maximum in the Chesapeake Bay area. The higher than average sea-level trends between Delaware Bay and New Jersey may be caused by river sediment loading (Newman and others, 1980). Around Chesapeake Bay, neotectonic subsidence may dominate (Brown, 1978; Holdahl and Morrison, 1974). Anomalous subsidence of the northern New England-Maritime Canada area (44°–46° N) may result from migration of the crest of the peripheral forebulge at the edge of formerly glaciated regions (Quinlan and Beaumont, 1981, 1982; see Scott and others, this volume). A local minimum SL slope at Wilmington, North Carolina, (Fig. 8) may be real, reflecting upwarp of the Cape Fear arch (Brown, 1978), but there are too few data points in that area to draw definitive conclusions. Long-range trends in excess of 1.8 mm/yr are concentrated between New York City and the upper Chesapeake Bay (Fig. 8), suggesting that enhanced subsidence of the mid-Atlantic coast has continued throughout the Holocene.

A basic assumption in this paper is that subtraction of long-range trends from individual tide-gauge stations will provide an estimate of the eustatic sea-level rise over the past century. This assumption is tested for the relatively quiescent United States east coast, with the relation:

$$t_{m,n} = s + l_n + \epsilon_{m,n}$$

where $t_{m,n}$ is the sea-level slope of the tide-gauge station, m, in the nth cell, l_n is the long-range trend for cell n, s is the eustatic sea-level trend, and $\epsilon_{m,n}$ is the residual error. If we assume that the mean value of $\epsilon_{m,n} = 0$, then $\bar{s} = \overline{(t_{m,n} - l_n)}$. The errors, $\epsilon_{m,n}$, are found to be random and normally distributed. Only three out of a total of 36 stations examined have errors that lie outside the 95% confidence limit of the combined tide-gauge and long-range trends. The data, therefore, show a uniform difference between short- and long-term records over the whole east coast, which most likely represents the eustatic change. Furthermore, the similar spatial variations in both tide-gauge and long-range data (Fig. 9A, B) suggest that these intraregional differences are not solely caused by recent (≤100 yrs) neotectonic movements, but rather are part of geologic processes continuing throughout the late Holocene and Recent epochs, which include neotectonism, shelf warping due to river sedimentation, and residual glacio-isostatic adjustments.

Sea-level trends along the west coast display a much more erratic spatial distribution, largely because of active tectonism. Thus, the corrected regional average SL trend deviates further from those of most regions (Table 3). Some of these geologic processes are now examined more closely. The locations of tide-gauge stations along the west coast are shown in Figure 11.

Stations from Yakutat to Juneau exhibit strongly negative trends. The strongly negative SL trends near Juneau represent the effects of localized isostatic uplift, following deglaciation around Glacier Bay (Hicks and Shofnos, 1965). In addition to isostatic movements, the SL trend at Yakutat may include recent tectonic uplift after the 1899 earthquake (Aubrey and Emery, 1983).

The variability of sea-level trends on Vancouver Island and around the Strait of Georgia illustrates the interplay of complex geologic processes. Leveling surveys as well as sea-level measurements indicate a pattern of recent uplift along the coasts of southern Vancouver Island and the Olympic Peninsula, coupled with subsidence farther inland, producing a regional eastward tilt (Ando and Balazs, 1979). Thus, sea-level trends at Neah Bay, Fulford Harbor, Victoria and Friday Harbor are either negative or close to zero, whereas those at Point Atkinson and Seattle farther eastward are positive (Fig. 11, inset). This pattern of deformation is linked to ongoing subduction of the Juan de Fuca plate beneath the North American Continent. Radiocarbon-dated materials suggest, however, that sea levels have differed from present levels by less than 2 m over the last 5,000–6,000 yrs (Clague and others, 1982). Therefore, long-range (late Holocene) trends for this area are taken as 0 ± 0.3 mm/yr. The late Holocene sea-level history for this area stands in sharp contrast to that following the rapid deglaciation 13.0 to 10.0 ka, during which period sea-level trends along the inner and outer coasts diverged strongly due to differences in position with respect to the glacial rebound.

The cause for the difference in relative SL trends between San Francisco and Alameda (near Oakland) is not clearly understood, but may reflect a minor E-W regional tilt accompanying the dominantly horizontal right-lateral shear along the San Andreas, Hayward and related fault systems.

Fairly high uplift rates (1–6 mm/yr) have been determined by amino acid-dating of marine terraces along the Santa Barbara-Ventura coast (Wehmiller and others, 1979). These rates decrease toward Los Angeles. The SL trend at Santa Monica (1.95 mm/yr) indicates subsidence. Wood and Elliott (1979) found, by comparing tide-gauge readings, that Los Angeles is rising relative to San Diego. The low SL trend at San Diego (0.2 mm/yr; Fig. 11) may be erroneous. The Bidston data between 1906–1925 are anomalously high relative to the subsequent series, which is identical to that of Hicks and others (1983). Therefore, the value of 1.9 mm/yr reported by Hicks and others (1983) is probably correct and agrees more closely with that at nearby La Jolla (1.75 mm/yr). Avila and Newport Bay are stations with short and noisy records (22 yrs each).

The regional uncorrected arithmetic mean for stations lying between Ketchican and Ensenada (Fig. 11) is 0.6 ± 1.3 mm/yr (21 stations). Correction for long-range trends lowers this to 0.04 ± 1.2 mm/yr (11 stations).

Causes of recent (≤100 yrs) sea-level rise.—

It is tempting to ask whether the recent rise in sea level is one of the first manifestations of the expected global warming produced by manmade addition of CO_2 to the atmosphere (Hansen and others, 1981; NAS/NRC, 1979, 1982). Other potential indicators of global warming include a reduction in summer Antarctic pack ice within the last decade (Kukla and Gavin, 1981), dilution of North Atlantic deep-water salinity within the last 20 yrs, possibly from melting Greenland glaciers (Brewer and others, 1983; Swift, 1984), and increased growth rates of subarctic trees over

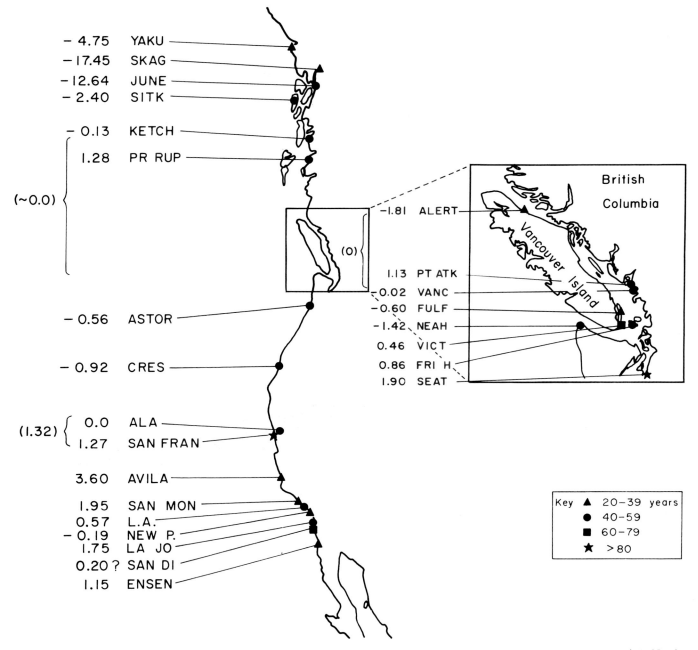

FIG. 11.—Location of tide-gauge stations for western North America. Numbers represent sea-level trends from tide-gauge data (mm/yr). Numbers in parentheses represent corresponding long-range trends.

the last century (G. C. Jacoby, pers. commun.).

The correlation coefficient between the global sea-level trend and surface air temperature curve for the past century (Hansen and others, 1981) is 0.6 (annual mean curve). The correlation coefficient increases to 0.8 when 5-yr running means are used for both quantities (Gornitz and others, 1982). Thermal expansion of the upper layers of the oceans could account for a significant fraction of the observed sea-level rise. Depending on the equilibrium sensitivity used, between 0.14 and 0.45 mm/yr can be attributed to thermal expansion (Gornitz and others, 1982). Direct observations

of the Greenland and Antarctic ice sheet mass balance are not yet sufficiently accurate to establish the sign of any trend. The suggestion that the earth's rotation has decreased as a result of transfer of polar ice to the world's oceans (Etkins and Epstein, 1982) is not supported by observations (Hansen and others, 1983; Barnett, 1983). Recent measurements from the Lageos satellite (Yoder and others, 1983) suggest a non-tidal acceleration of the earth's rotation, attributed to continuing glacio-isostatic lithospheric readjustments. On the other hand, mass balance calculations of climatically more sensitive alpine glaciers over the last century imply a melting rate equivalent to a sea-level rise of 0.46 ± 0.26 mm/yr (Meier, 1984).

Modeling calculations by Lambeck and Nakiboglu (1984) indicate that between 30 and 50% of the current sea-level rise may be caused by readjustments of the crust to melting of the Pleistocene ice sheets. This basically agrees with our findings, if one compares the average global sea-level trend (excluding Fennoscandia) from tide gauges with the average obtained by subtracting the long-range trends, which largely represent glacio-isostatic movements (see Table 2,b and c). The observation of Lambeck and Nakiboglu (1984) provides additional justification for our procedures. Thus, the "corrected" trend indicates the true short-term eustatic sea-level rise.

Another possible cause of sea-level change is anthropogenic modification of the hydrologic cycle. Groundwater withdrawals in the United States in 1980 (1.23×10^2 km³/yr; Table 18 *in* Solley and others, 1983) are equivalent to a sea-level rise of 0.3 mm/yr. If the ratio of groundwater to total water withdrawal, 0.20 (from Solley and others, 1983, Table 14), in the United States is representative of consumptive water use globally, then out of the 2,405 km³ of total annual global water consumption (L'vovich, 1979, Table 32, p. 329), 481 km³ comes from groundwater, which is equivalent to a sea-level rise of around 1.3 mm/yr. On the other hand, replenishing of the water table by deep seepage from reservoirs and irrigation (550 km³/yr; Fowler and Helvey, 1974) would reduce sea level by 1.5 mm/yr. Furthermore, water stored in reservoirs is equivalent to an additional sea-level reduction of 0.5 to 1.0 cm over the past century (L'vovich, 1979; The World Almanac Book of Facts, 1983). Thus, these anthropogenic effects will probably cancel out and will not contribute significantly to sea-level changes.

Continued rise of sea level is likely in the near future if predictions of global warming prove to be correct (Hansen and others, 1981; NAS/NRC, 1979; 1982). Thermal expansion of sea water could increase sea level by 20 to 30 cm in the next 70 to 100 yrs (Gornitz and others, 1982; Revelle, 1983) and an additional 40 cm could come from polar ice-sheet melting, yielding an estimated 70 cm during the next 100 yrs (Revelle, 1983). This estimate may represent a lower limit, however. The Environmental Protection Agency (Hoffman, 1983) projects an increase of between 144 and 217 cm by the year 2100, depending on the rate of increase of CO_2. The Atlantic and Gulf coasts of the United States are especially vulnerable to enhanced shoreline erosion and the damaging effects of storm surges. Within the last three decades, the duration and frequency of storms generating high waves, and the length of the winter storm season have increased substantially along the mid-Atlantic coast (Hayden, 1975). Environmental and economic impacts of projected sea-level trends due to the greenhouse warming are discussed further by Barth and Titus (1984).

SUMMARY AND CONCLUSIONS

The global mean sea-level rise, corrected for long-range trends, yields values of 1.0 and 1.2 mm/yr over the past century, using two different averaging procedures. These values are consistent with previous results (Gornitz and others, 1982; Barnett, 1983, 1984; Lisitzin, 1974; Fairbridge and Krebs, 1962) and provide additional independent corroboration for an increase in sea level. The global average sea-level rise (summarized in Table 2) depends less on the averaging procedures used than on sampling or on correction for long-range trends. This finding suggests that the simple arithmetic average of the best-fit regression slopes (Method I) is a good representation of the central tendency of the data, and compares reasonably well with the more complex averaging scheme (Method II). Introduction of a weighting factor for relative regional reliability does not appear to affect the global mean significantly (Table 3). This suggests that the global mean SL change is not too sensitive to the number of stations in a region or to the intra-regional variability. The estimate of eustatic mean sea-level rise, however, remains unavoidably biased toward the Northern Hemisphere (given the geographical limitations of the present data base). Errors in mareograph data could be improved in future studies by removing the noise due to changes in atmospheric pressure, wind stress, and river runoff. The error bars in long-range data could be reduced by additional dating of sea-level indicators spanning the last few thousand years.

The noisiness of long-range data could introduce additional errors into the "corrected" trends. Yet, in at least one region (eastern North America), where good data sets exist on both short and long time scales, errors, although relatively large for both data sets, are higher in the tide-gauge data (Fig. 9A, B).

After removal of long-range trends, sea level is found to be increasing in all but three regions. These three have relatively few stations, poor long-term records or active tectonics (Table 3, Fig. 7). Considerable differences remain among the regional means even in "corrected" data. Changes in oceanographic circulation could contribute, in part, to the intraregional variability in sea-level rise. The greater observed sea-level increases along northwestern coasts of oceans (e.g., Japan and eastern North America) than along eastern shorelines (Europe and western North America) are qualitatively consistent with first-order predictions from simple barotropic calculations of wind stress (H. E. Brooks, pers. commun.). Two of these regions lie along plate boundaries, however, and therefore effects of recent tectonism cannot be ruled out.

Intra-regional variability represents a complex interplay among diverse factors, including tectonism, shelf loading due to river sedimentation, runoff, local groundwater or petroleum removal, and glacio-isostasy (the latter effect largely removed by subtracting late Holocene trends).

In the Chesapeake Bay-New Jersey area, tide-gauge records indicate enhanced subsidence due to possible neotectonic activity (Brown, 1978; Holdahl and Morrison, 1974) or river sediment loading (Newman and others, 1980). The Maritime Provinces of Canada also exhibit greater subsidence than the regional average (Figs. 9A, 10A). Long-range data show that above-average subsidence of the mid-Atlantic coast has continued during the Holocene (Figs. 9B,

10B). In the Maritime Provinces, increased subsidence may result from a migrating collapsed forebulge (Quinlan and Beaumont, 1981, 1982).

In western North America, tide-gauge data record high isostatic uplift in Alaska, especially around Glacier Bay (Hicks and Shofnos, 1965). Farther south, a pattern of sea-level fall along Vancouver Island and rise farther inland probably reflects ongoing subduction of the Juan de Fuca plate beneath North America, which produces an eastward tilt (Ando and Balazs, 1979). Still farther south, in south-central California, complex variations in sea level result from localized uplift or subsidence in response to north-south crustal shortening near the "big bend" in the San Andreas fault, superimposed on the dominantly horizontal movements of the prevailing right-lateral strike-slip fault system (Wehmiller and others, 1979, Wood and Elliott, 1979).

Most of the observed sea-level rise over the past century can be ascribed to thermal expansion of the upper layers of the ocean and to melting of alpine glaciers, and may thus be an early response to global warming (Hansen and others, 1981). The role of the Greenland and Antarctic ice sheets remains to be determined. Anthropogenic processes, such as groundwater withdrawal, dam building, irrigation, etc., tend to cancel, and thus are not likely to contribute significantly to sea-level change.

ACKNOWLEDGMENTS

This research was carried out under National Aeronautics and Space Administration Cooperative Agreement NCC5-29 (Task A). We thank Professor W. Newman, Queens College, New York, for making available his compilation of Holocene sea-level indicators; Dr. D. T. Pugh, Director, Permanent Service for Mean Sea Level, Bidston Observatory, Birkenhead, England, for sending us an updated computer tape of tide-gauge records; and Dr. J. Hubbard, National Ocean Service, National Oceanic and Atmospheric Administration, Rockville, Maryland, for providing tide-gauge records for the United States. We benefited from interesting discussions with Professor L. Zobler of Barnard College and Dr. W. R. Peltier of the University of Toronto.

REFERENCES

ANDO, M., AND BALAZS, E. I., 1979, Geodetic evidence for aseismic subduction of the Juan de Fuca plate: Journal of Geophysical Research, v. 84, p. 3023–3028.

AUBREY, D. G., AND EMERY, K. O., 1983, Eigenanalysis of recent United States sea levels: Continental Shelf Research, v. 2, p. 21–33.

BARNETT, T. P., 1983, Recent changes in sea level and their possible causes: Climatic Change, v. 5, p. 15–38.

———, 1984, The estimation of "global" sea level change: a problem of uniqueness: Journal of Geophysical Research, v. 89, p. 7980–7988.

BARTH, M. C., AND TITUS, J. C., eds., 1984, Greenhouse Effect and Sea Level Rise, A Challenge for this Generation: Van Nostrand Reinhold Co., New York, 325 p.

BLOOM, A. L., ed., 1977, Atlas of Sea Level Curves: International Geological Correlation Program, Project 61 (not consecutively paginated).

BREWER, P. G., BROECKER, W. S., JENKINS, W. J., RHINES P. B., ROOTH, C. G., SWIFT, J. H., TAKAHASHI, T., AND WILLIAMS, R. T., 1983, A climate freshening of the deep North Atlantic (north of 50° N) over the past 20 years: Science, v. 222, p. 1237–1239.

BROWN, L. D., 1978, Recent vertical crustal movement along the east coast of the United States: Tectonophysics, v. 44, p. 205–231.

CLAGUE, J., HARPER, J. R., HEBDA, R. J., AND HOWES, D. E., 1982, Late Quaternary sea levels and crustal movements, British Columbia: Canadian Journal of Earth Sciences, v. 19, p. 597–618.

CLARK, J. A., FARRELL, W. E., AND PELTIER, W. E., 1978, Global changes in post-glacial sea level: a numerical calculation: Quaternary Research, v. 9, p. 265–287.

DONOVAN, D. T., AND JONES, E. J. W., 1979, Causes of world-wide changes in sea level: Geological Society of London Journal, v. 136, p. 187–192.

ETKINS, R., AND EPSTEIN, E. S., 1982, The rise of global mean sea level as an indication of climatic change: Science, v. 215, p. 287–289.

FAIRBRIDGE, R. W., 1961, Eustatic changes in sea level, in Ahrens, L. H., Press, F. Rankama, K., and Runcorn, S. K., eds., Physics and Chemistry of the Earth: Pergamon Press, London, v. 4, p. 99–185.

———, AND KREBS, D. A., JR., 1962, Sea level and the southern oscillation: Geophysical Journal of the Royal Astronomical Society, v. 6, p. 532–545.

FOWLER, W. B., AND HELVEY, J. D., 1974, Irrigation as a potential for climatic modification: Environmental Conservation, v. 1, p. 204.

GALVIN, C., 1983, Sea level rise and shoreline recession, in Proceedings of the Third Symposium on Coastal and Ocean Management: American Society of Civil Engineers, p. 2684–2705.

GEOTIMES, 1981, Along U.S. Coasts, Old Solutions Fail to Solve Beach Problem: December 1981 issue, p. 18–22.

GODWIN, H., 1962, Half-life of radiocarbon: Nature, v. 195, p. 984.

GORNITZ, VIVIEN, LEBEDEFF, SERGEJ, AND HANSEN, JAMES, 1982, Global sea level trend in the past century: Science, v. 215, p. 1611–1614.

GRIBBIN, J., 1984, The world's beaches are vanishing: New Scientist, no. 1409, p. 30–32.

HALLAM, A., 1984, Pre-Quaternary sea level changes: Annual Review of Earth and Planetary Sciences, v. 12, p. 205–243.

HANSEN, JAMES, JOHNSON, D., LACIS, ANDREW, LEBEDEFF, SERGEJ, LEE, P., RIND, DAVID, AND RUSSELL, GARY, 1981, Climate impact of increasing atmospheric carbon dioxide: Science, v. 213, p. 957–966.

———, GORNITZ, VIVIEN, LEBEDEFF, SERGEJ, AND MOORE, ELIZABETH, 1983, Global mean sea level: indicator of climate change?: Science, v. 219, p. 996–997.

HAYDEN B. P., 1975, Storm wave climates at Cape Hatteras, N.C.: recent secular variations: Science, v. 190, p. 981–983.

HICKS, S. D., 1972, Vertical crustal movements from sea level measurements along the east coast of the United States: Journal of Geophysical Research, v. 77, p. 5930–5934.

———, 1981, Long-period sea level variations for the United States through 1978: Shore and Beach, p. 26–29.

———, DEBAUGH, H. A., JR., AND HICKMAN, L. E., JR., 1983, Sea level variations for the United States 1855–1980: U.S. Department of Commerce, National Oceanic and Atmospheric Administration, National Ocean Service, Rockville, Maryland, 170 p.

———, AND SHOFNOS, W., 1965, The determination of land emergence from sea level observations in southeast Alaska: Journal of Geophysical Research, v. 70, p. 3315–3320.

HOFFMAN, J. S., 1983, Projecting future sea level rise, methodology, estimates to the year 2100, and research needs: Office of Policy and Resource Management, Environmental Protection Agency, EPA 230-09-007, Washington, D.C., 121 p.

HOLDAHL S. R., AND MORRISON, N. L., 1974, Regional investigations of vertical crustal movements in the U.S., using precise relevelings and mareograph data: Tectonophysics, v. 23, p. 373–390.

HOLEMAN, J. N., 1968, The sediment yield of major rivers of the world: Water Resources Research, v. 4, p. 737–747.

KERR, R. A., 1981, Whither the shoreline: Science, v. 214, p. 428.

KIDSON, C., 1982, Sea level changes in the Holocene: Quaternary Science Reviews, v. 1, p. 121–151.

KUKLA, G., AND GAVIN, J., 1981, Summer ice and carbon dioxide: Science, v. 214, p. 497–503.

LAMBECK, K., AND NAKIBOGLU, S. M., 1984, Recent global changes in sea level: Geophysical Research Letters, v. 11, p. 959–961.

LISITZIN, E., 1974, Sea level changes: Elsevier, New York, 286 p.

L'VOVICH, M. I., 1979, World Water Resources and Their Future: Translation Board, American Geophysical Union, Washington, D.C., 264 p.

MARCUS, L. F., AND NEWMAN, W. S., 1983, Hominid migrations and the eustatic sea level paradigm: a critique, *in* Masters, P. M., and Fleming, N. C., eds., Quaternary Coastlines and Marine Archaeology: Academic Press, London, p. 63–85.

MEADE, R. H., AND EMERY, K. O., 1971, Sea level as affected by river runoff, eastern United States: Science, v. 173, p. 425–427.

MEIER, M. F., 1984, Contribution of small glaciers to global sea level: Science, v. 226, p. 1418–1421.

MÖRNER, N. A., ed., 1980, Earth Rheology, Isostasy and Eustasy: John Wiley, New York, 599 p.

NAMIAS, J., AND HUANG, J. C. K., 1972, Sea level at southern California: A decadal fluctuation: Science, v. 177, p. 351–353.

NATIONAL ACADEMY OF SCIENCES/NATIONAL RESEARCH COUNCIL (NAS/NRC), 1979, Carbon Dioxide and Climate, A Scientific Assessment: National Academy Press, Washington, D.C., 22 p.

——, 1982, Carbon Dioxide and Climate, A Second Assessment: National Academy Press, Washington, D.C., 72 p.

NEWMAN, W. C., CINQUEMANI, L. J., PARDI, R. R., AND MARCUS, L. F., 1980, Holocene delevelling of the United States' east coast, *in* Mörner, N. A., ed., Earth Rheology, Isostasy and Eustasy: John Wiley, New York, 449–463.

OSTLE, B., 1963, Statistics in Research: Iowa State University Press, 585 p.

PELTIER, W. R., 1980, Models of glacial isostasy and relative sea level, *in* Ball, A. W., Bender, P. L., McGetchin, T. R., and Walcott, R. I., eds., Dynamics of Plate Interiors: Geodynamics Series, American Geophysical Union, v. I, p. 111–127.

PITMAN, W. C., III, 1978, Relationship between eustasy and stratigraphic sequences of passive margins: Geological Society of America Bulletin, v. 89, p. 1389–1403.

QUINLAN, G., AND BEAUMONT, C., 1981, A comparison of observed and theoretical postglacial relative sea level in Atlantic Canada: Canadian Journal of Earth Sciences, v. 18, p. 1146–1163.

——, AND ——, 1982, The deglaciation of Atlantic Canada as reconstructed from the postglacial relative sea level record: Canadian Journal of Earth Sciences, v. 19, p. 2232–2246.

REVELLE R. R., 1983, Probable future changes in sea level resulting from increased atmospheric carbon dioxide, *in* Changing Climate: Report of the Carbon Dioxide Assessment Committee, National Academy of Sciences/National Research Council, National Academy Press, Washington, D.C., p. 433–448.

RIND, DAVID, AND LEBEDEFF, SERGEJ, 1984, Potential climatic impacts of increased atmospheric CO_2 with emphasis on water availability and hydrology in the United States: Environmental Protection Agency, EPA 230-04-84-006, 96 p.

ROSSITER, J. R., 1962, Long-term variations in sea level, *in* Hill, N. M., ed., The Sea: Interscience, New York, p. 590–610.

SOLLEY, W. B., CHASE, E. B., AND MANN, W. B., IV, 1983, Estimated use of water in the U.S. in 1980: U.S. Geological Survey Circular 1001, 56 p.

SUESS, H. E., 1978, La Jolla measurements of radiocarbon in tree-ring dated wood: Radiocarbon, v. 20, p. 1–18.

SWIFT, J. H., 1984, A recent θ-S shift in the deep water of the northern Atlantic, *in* Hansen, J. E., and Takahashi, T., eds., Climate Processes and Climate Sensitivity: MAURICE EWING Series, v. 5, Geophysical Monograph 29, American Geophysical Union, Washington, D.C., p. 39–47.

WATTS, A. B., 1982, Tectonic subsidence, flexure and global changes of sea level: Nature, v. 297, p. 469–474.

WEHMILLER, J. F., SARNA-WOJCICKI, A., YERKES, R. F., AND LAJOIE, K. R., 1979, Anomalously high uplift rates along the Ventura-Santa Barbara Coast, California, tectonic implications: Tectonophysics, v. 52, p. 380.

WOOD, S. H., AND ELLIOTT, M. R., 1979, Early 20th Century uplift of the northern Peninsular Ranges Province of southern California: Tectonophysics, v. 52, p. 249–265.

THE WORLD ALMANAC AND BOOK OF FACTS, 1983, Newspaper Enterprises Association, New York, p. 147.

WU, P., AND PELTIER, W. R., 1983, Glacial isostatic adjustment and the free air gravity anomaly as a constraint on deep mantle viscosity: Geophysical Journal of the Royal Astronomical Society, v. 74, p. 377–449.

YODER, C. F., WILLIAMS, J. G., DICKEY, J. O., SCHUTZ, B. E., EANES, R. J., AND TAPLEY, B. D., 1983, Secular variation of earth's gravitational harmonic J_2 coefficient from Lageos and nontidal acceleration of earth rotation: Nature, v. 303, p. 757–762.

SHORT-TERM SEA-LEVEL CHANGES AND COASTAL EROSION

PAUL D. KOMAR AND DAVID B. ENFIELD

College of Oceanography, Oregon State University, Corvallis, Oregon 97331

ABSTRACT: Investigations of the role of sea level in producing coastal erosion have focused mainly on the long-term rise due to melting of glaciers and thermal expansion of sea water. There are, however, additional shorter term changes in the local sea level produced by a variety of ocean processes. Variations in the coastal currents, for example, can alter the water level at the shoreline due to the geostrophic balance between the current and the offshore sea-surface slope. Other factors which may alter local sea level include changes in atmospheric pressure, winds blowing either in the longshore or cross-shore directions, and the occurrence of upwelling. Because the inclined continental shelf and slope act as a wave guide, the fluctuations often become trapped and propagate over longshore distances beyond where they are actually generated. In that many of these processes are typically seasonal, the responding sea level also has a pronounced seasonal cycle, but frequently there can be significant fluctuations at periodicities of several days to a few weeks. The magnitudes of such changes vary considerably with coastal location but are typically on the order of 10 to 30 cm, achieving a maximum of about 100 cm in the Bay of Bengal.

The occurrence of an El Niño in the equatorial Pacific is known to have considerable impact on the erosion of the coasts of California and Oregon. This occurs because associated with an El Niño are shifts in the storm paths and a temporary rise in sea level. An El Niño is a breakdown of the normal equatorial wind and current patterns. This breakdown releases water which is normally set up in the western Pacific by the trade winds. The release creates a "wave" of sea-level rise, which first propagates eastward along the equator and then poleward along the eastern ocean margin. Such "waves" have been measured in the tide records of the western United States, amounting to some 20 to 60 cm and lasting for several months. Such transient sea-level changes have likely played an important role in coastal erosion.

INTRODUCTION

The long-term and progressive rise in sea level has been cited justifiably as a major cause of erosion along our coastlines. Analyses of tide-gauge records from "stable" regions throughout the world place this eustatic rise at about 15 cm/century (Hicks, 1978) to 23 cm/century (Barnett, 1984). Any assessments of sea level determined from tide gauges show a great deal of variability, especially from week to week but even when yearly averages are being compared in attempts to determine such long-term trends. Thus, in the curves of annual sea-level changes (for example, those of Hicks, 1978, Gornitz and others, 1982 and Barnett, 1984), superimposed upon the long-term trend of generally rising sea levels are many irregularities and even some reversals. In those studies such fluctuations are considered to be unwanted "noise," but one person's "noise" is another's key to a better understanding of nature. In this case, physical oceanographers, in particular, have utilized short-term variations in coastal water levels as measured at tide gauges to advance our knowledge concerning the variability of major ocean currents and even to investigate global-scale responses of the ocean/atmosphere system.

Although the long-term sea-level rise of 15 to 23 cm/century undeniably plays an important role in causing coastal erosion, the shorter term sea-level changes might also contribute to erosion. The seasonal cycle typically accounts for water-level rises on the order of 10 to 30 cm and in unusual cases to as much as 100 cm, so that they equal or greatly exceed the long-term rise that has been the focus of most of our explanations for sea-level effects on coastal erosion. Unfortunately, in many cases little is known about the coastal response to these shorter term changes, although there are qualitative correlations which suggest their significance.

The principal objectives of this paper are to review what is known concerning the physical processes causing these shorter term sea-level fluctuations and to consider their possible role in producing coastal erosion.

SEASONAL CYCLES OF SEA LEVEL

The most obvious of the shorter term sea-level variations at nearly all coastal sites is the seasonal cycle. Examples are shown in Figure 1 for several locations around the coasts of the United States. A global summary of the month-by-month sea-level changes has been compiled by Pattullo and others (1955) and is discussed further by Pattullo (1966). She found that the seasonal variations range from only a few centimeters in the tropics to amounts on the order of 20 cm or more at higher latitudes. The largest change occurs in the Bay of Bengal, where the water-level variation regularly exceeds 100 cm within a year. Over most of the world the lowest sea level in the annual cycle occurs during the spring, the highest being in the fall (Fig. 1). This is true of both hemispheres, the Northern and Southern hemispheres oscillating in opposite directions according to the seasons. Although this is the average seasonal pattern of sea-level variability, there are many exceptions as to its exact timing which depends on local oceanic and atmospheric cycles.

Interpretations of the seasonal cycle of sea level are difficult because most of the driving mechanisms are seasonal and highly coherent, that is, exactly in phase with one another. Thus, at a specific coastal site, the sea level will be responding to the atmospheric pressure and its variability, local coastal winds, the currents they may generate (including coastal upwelling), and even rainfall. In that the atmospheric pressures, winds, rain and currents are all coupled, it is readily apparent that separating their comparative influences on the changing sea level will be difficult.

A significant portion of the annual change in sea level can be ascribed to variations in atmospheric pressure. Over the open ocean, sea level will respond as an inverse barometer to changes in the atmospheric pressure, that is, the sea surface is depressed 1 cm for each millibar of increased atmospheric pressure so that the net bottom pressure remains constant (Robinson, 1964). In the first detailed anal-

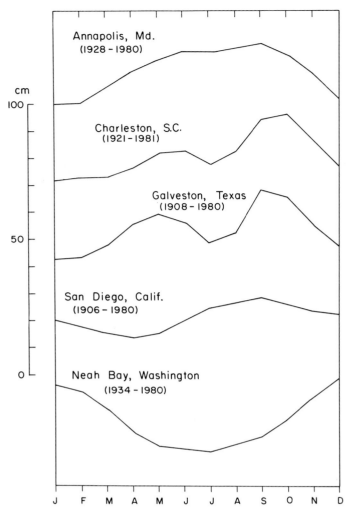

FIG. 1.—Examples of annual cycles of sea-level changes determined from tide gauges, based on the measurements of Hicks and others (1983). In each example the years given denote the time period over which the averaged results are based.

ysis of monthly sea-level variations along the west coast of the United States, Roden (1960, 1966) found that, as expected, there is a strong inverse relationship with the local barometric pressure, but the response was some one to two times greater than accounted for by the inverse-barometric effect alone. Apparently, other factors that affect sea level were coupled with the atmospheric pressure. Also examining sea level on the west coast, Saur (1962) similarly noted responses greater than the theoretical inverse barometric value, finding that the departure was associated with stronger winds from the south which correlated with the atmospheric pressure. Such southerly winds likely cause a piling up of water along the coast due to Ekman mass transport induced by the winds. In the Northern Hemisphere this water drift is to the right of the wind direction due to the Coriolis force. In a recent study, Chelton and Davis (1982) analyzed 29 yrs of tide-gauge records from Mexico to Alaska in order to examine more closely the several factors involved in producing the sea-level variability over time scales of months

to years. They concluded that north of San Francisco 50 to 60% of the sea-level variability reflects the simple inverse barometric response to local atmospheric pressure, whereas this effect accounts for only 10 to 15% of the variance at stations to the south. In the north this inverse-barometer response represents a nearly uniform rise or fall of sea level all along the coast of the North Pacific, not being simply a local response.

Nearly all of the annual variations of sea level at tide stations on the Atlantic and Gulf coasts of the United States have their maxima between June and October, the minima occurring during the cold months of December through March (Fig. 1). Montgomery (1938) was the first to attribute this directly to thermal effects, pointing out that a typical increase in temperature from 8° to 18° C distributed over 100 m of water depth would raise sea level by 19 cm, nearly the rise observed. He further pointed out, however, that thermal effects cannot be the only factor involved, since the maximum in water level generally occurs somewhat later in the year than the observed maximum in water temperature.

LaFond (1939) investigated the causes for seasonal sea-level changes off California, shown in Figure 2, the total annual range being some 25 cm. After examining a number of possible causes, LaFond determined that it is produced by cyclic variations in the surface water density. This change in density is brought about mainly by variations in the water temperature; salinity had only a secondary effect. The temperature variations are in turn produced by offshore currents, not simply being a warming and cooling of the water from the annual changes in solar radiation. Off California the Davidson Current flows from north to south, nearly parallel to the coast, driven by winds from the north. In this case Ekman mass transport produces a seaward drift of the surface waters and its replacement by an upwelling of cold deeper water. This cold water near the coast has a greater density so that sea level is lowered. Upwelling off California is at a maximum in the spring, and this accounts for the reduced sea level at that time (Fig. 2). As upwelling wanes throughout the summer, the coastal water is progressively heated by solar radiation and the sea level rises, reaching a maximum in about September. The temperature changes are not sufficient to account for the total variation in water level, however, so additional factors must again be involved.

Direct rainfall and river runoff may be significant factors in changing sea level along some coasts. Rainfall and runoff are a major effect in producing the 100-cm sea-level variation observed in the Bay of Bengal. Meade and Emery (1971) examined their role in affecting sea level along the coasts of the eastern United States and Gulf of Mexico. They concluded that variations in annual river inflow account for 7 to 21% of the total sea-level variations from one year to the next along those coasts. This includes the long-term rise in sea level; if this latter variation is excluded, river runoff accounts for 20 to 40% of the remaining variations.

The seasonal cycle in sea level is seen to occur in response to a complex interaction of physical processes: atmospheric pressure, coastal winds, the wind-generated cur-

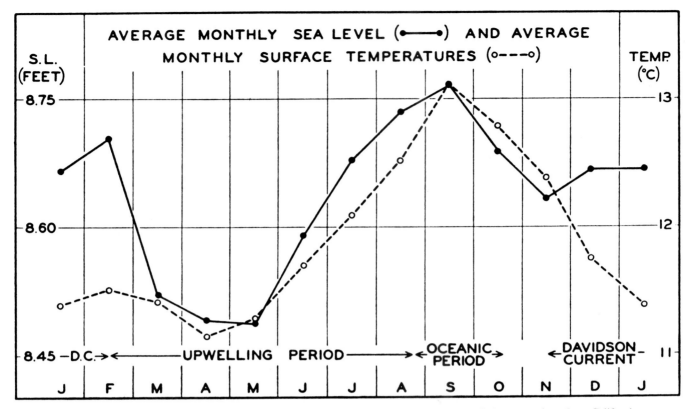

FIG. 2.—Annual cycles of sea level and water temperature measured by LaFond (1939) off the coast of southern California.

rents, upwelling, water temperature changes, rainfall and river discharges. It is apparent that most of the processes are inter-related so that, in general, it is not possible to separate their relative contributions to the observed total sea-level change.

DAILY TO WEEKLY SEA-LEVEL VARIATIONS

Individual storms can produce localized changes in the sea level which persist for only a short time. This sea-level change is caused principally by the low-pressure center of the storm and its winds, the extreme case being a storm surge. In addition, ocean waves generated by the storm can produce a setup along the coast, a rise in water level amounting to tens of centimeters (Holman and Sallenger, 1985). These combined effects are observed in the tide-gauge record.

Early observations of the response of sea level to atmospheric low pressure systems of storms were obtained by Hamon (1962, 1966) along the east coast of Australia, observations which indicated that although the initial effects on sea level were local, the disturbed sea level thereafter propagates in the longshore direction as a wave. Such "shelf waves" are trapped over the continental margin by the offshore slope of the continental shelf. The shelf acts as a wave guide, much as edge waves are trapped on a sloping beach. The physics of shelf waves and edge waves are very similar, the primary difference being that shelf waves typically have periods of some 3 to 50 days so their motions

are affected by the Coriolis force. This Coriolis influence limits the occurrence of shelf waves such that in the Northern Hemisphere they must propagate with the coast on their right, on their left in the Southern Hemisphere. Propagation speeds on the order of 150 to 300 km/day have been measured, so that a sea-level disturbance produced by some local effect such as a storm system can alter the level along a considerable length of coast, the influence acting for tens of days and commonly amounting to a sea-level change of 10 to 30 cm. Hence, many significant fluctuations in sea level are remotely forced and cannot be readily associated with local effects. In the United States, the greatest attention to such coastal-trapped waves as observed in "sea-level" records has been on the west coast, the studies by Wang and Mooers (1977), Romea and Smith (1983) and Enfield and Allen (1983) being examples.

SEA-LEVEL VARIATIONS DUE TO MAJOR OCEAN CURRENTS

Ocean currents can produce sea-level changes as measured at coastal stations in that established flows are usually in geostrophic balance with the offshore sea-surface slope at right angles to the flow direction. In the Northern Hemisphere this slope is upward to the right when viewed in the direction of current flow. A steady-state condition is reached when the higher water on the right opposes and balances the Coriolis force, tending to turn the current to the right. Even the major ocean currents have variations in their discharges and mean velocities, however, and this change in current flow will alter the cross-flow sea-surface slope and thus change sea level as recorded on opposite sides of the flow. An increase in flow velocity will increase the cross-flow slope, and as a result this factor alone would produce a sea-level rise to its right, while at the same time lowering sea level to its left. Thus, it is the fluctuations in these currents that are observed in the coastal tidal records. In most cases these fluctuations are seasonal, so we have still another process contributing to the annual cycle of sea level.

Physical oceanographers have utilized tide-gauge records as a tool for monitoring the adjacent ocean currents. Such records are far more continuous and of longer duration than possible by more direct measurements of the currents. Of particular interest are locations where major currents are in close proximity to the land, having a significant effect on the coastal sea level. Very convenient for such a study is the narrow Straits of Florida (Fig. 3), where the Florida Current-Gulf Stream system flows between the Florida peninsula on its left with Cuba and the Bahamas on its right. Sea level can thereby be monitored on both sides of this major ocean current and the results utilized to infer fluctuations in the flow. This site was in fact the first to be utilized in such an analysis; Montgomery (1938) compared sea-level variations at Bermuda with the east coast tide gauges at Key West and Miami, Florida and at Charleston, South Carolina. The differences in sea level between Bermuda on one side of the current with the mainland stations on the other side showed that the cross-flow water slope is greatest in July and least in October. Similar analyses have been undertaken by Stommel (1953) and Wunsch and others (1969), who compared tide-gauge records at Key West and Miami on the mainland with those at Havana, Cuba, and Cat Cay, Bahamas, thereby providing a better examination of the current as it passes through the Straits of Florida (Fig. 3A). The comparison between Miami and Cat Cay is shown in Figure 3B. The seasonal variations at both locations show maxima toward the fall season, that at Cat Cay being slightly earlier than at Miami. These individual cycles may be influenced by a number of factors, but their difference indicates changes in the water-surface slope across the Straits of Florida, which probably mainly reflect variations in the strength of the Florida Current. The results again show a maximum in July to August with a minimum in October to November, in agreement with data of Montgomery (1938). These slopes imply a maximum current flow in mid-summer, the lowest flow being in the fall, results that are largely confirmed by direct measurements of the Florida Current (Fuglister, 1951; Niiler and Richardson, 1973). Blaha (1984) and Maul and others (1985) provide more recent analyses of fluctuations in the Florida Current-Gulf Stream system based on tide-gauge records of sea level, including more detailed considerations of other factors such as monthly changes in coastal winds and water temperature.

Such analyses of tide-gauge records from opposite sides of an ocean current indicate changes in the cross-flow sea-surface slope, but not in the absolute values of the slopes. Fluctuations in the currents can thereby be inferred, but not their actual magnitudes. This problem may be solved by utilizing satellite altimetry. Fu and Chelton (1984) have used

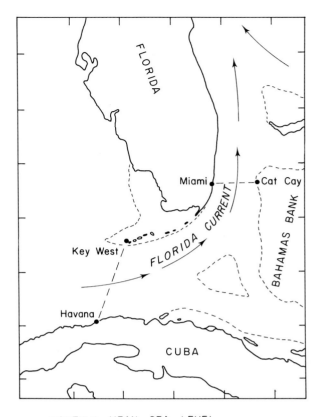

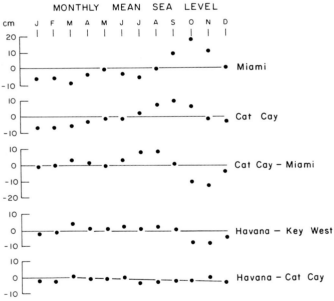

Fig. 3.—Annual cycles of sea level on opposite sides of the Florida Current, the differences Cat Cay—Miami and Havana—Key West reflecting fluctuations in the strength of the current. The data come from Pattullo and others (1955); the analysis is that of Stommel (1953).

sea-level measurements by the Seasat altimeter to study the flow of the Antarctic Circumpolar Current, obtaining a series of sea-level profiles across the current. It can be expected that such analyses will become more common in the future.

A particularly interesting example of the relationship between coastal sea level and adjacent currents occurs in the Pacific Equatorial Current system studied by Wyrtki (1973). He focused on the Pacific Equatorial Countercurrent which flows from west to east across the entire ocean, confined mainly between 4°N and 10°N latitudes (Fig. 4). This flow is in approximate geostrophic balance, the cross-flow slope producing a ridge in sea level near 4°N and a trough near 10°N. The difference in the height of sea level between the ridge and trough varies between about 10 and 30 cm. This countercurrent and its associated cross-flow water slope affect sea level differences between pairs of islands situated north and south of the current. Again, the greater the current velocity, the greater the surface slope. In Figure 5 it is seen that Christmas and Canton islands, both nearly on the equator, have almost identical annual cycles of sea level but differ from those at Truk and Kwajalein to the north of the current. This is the expected pattern of sea-level changes responding to the varying flow of the countercurrent. When the flow increases, the cross-flow water slope increases, the water level is rising to its right at the equator (Christmas and Canton islands), while simultaneously dropping on its left (Truk and Kwajalein). Just the opposite occurs when the current slows down. The sea-level difference between Christmas and Kwajalein (Fig. 5), relative to an arbitrary zero level, exhibits a marked seasonal variation with an annual cycle of about 18 cm. This seasonal variation in cross-flow slope as deduced from the sea levels at the islands, reflecting the strength of the countercurrent flow, is seen in Figure 5 to agree with measurements of the flow obtained by other methods. As expected, the maximum sea-level difference corresponding to the highest cross-flow water slope occurs when the flow is greatest. Based on such a correlation, Wyrtki went on to utilize the tidal records to compute the monthly mean discharge in the countercurrent for the prior 21 yrs of available records in order to examine long-term variability. Periods of exceptionally high transport in the countercurrent were found to coincide with the

occurrence of El Niño events, to be discussed in the next section.

SEA LEVEL DURING EL NIÑO EVENTS

Certainly one of the most intriguing changes in sea level within the Pacific Ocean is that associated with El Niño. It is of particular relevance here in that it likely played a role in the extensive erosion along the coasts of California and Oregon during 1982–83, the most recent occurrence of this atmospheric and oceanic phenomenon. El Niño represents an anomalous oceanic event characterized by the sudden appearance of abnormally warm surface waters off the coasts of Peru and Ecuador. This region is normally characterized by coastal upwelling, the cold nutrient-rich water supporting an abundant fishery which is largely destroyed by the influx of warm water associated with El Niño.

For many years it was thought that the onset of El Niño was caused by the breakdown of the local coastal winds which produce upwelling off Peru. This view changed considerably about a decade ago. First, direct observations showed that our conventional ideas were wrong; the local coastal winds do not necessarily diminish during an El Niño. Wyrtki (1975) showed that El Niño is instead triggered by the breakdown of the trade wind system in the central and western Pacific, far away from the Peruvian coastal waters where its chief impact is felt. Wyrtki concluded that during normal periods of strong southeast trades, there is a sea-level setup in the western equatorial Pacific with an overall west-to-east downward slope of the sea surface along the equator. When the trade winds subsequently relax, the potential energy of this sloping water surface is released, and it is this release that produces the variety of observations associated with an El Niño. Wyrtki argued that during the relaxation, the accumulated warm water in the western Pacific propagates eastward in the form of a baroclinic disturbance, much like an equatorially trapped internal Kelvin wave. The sea surface would bulge up at the equator as a moving rise in sea level, the thermocline beneath being de-

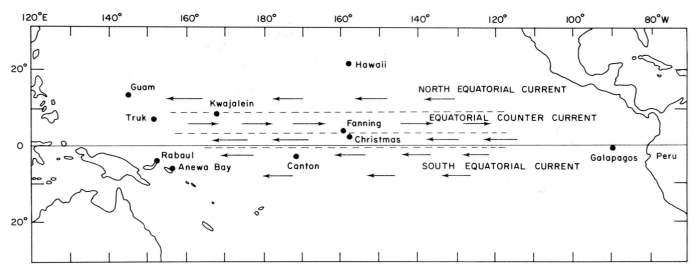

FIG. 4.—The major ocean currents in the equatorial Pacific and the islands where tide-gauge records have been utilized to monitor the current strengths and El Niño sea-level disturbances.

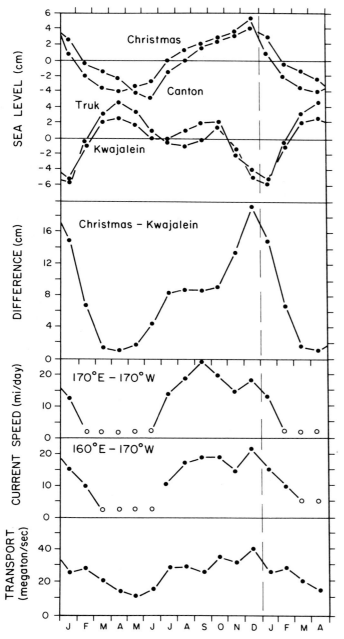

FIG. 5.—Sea levels at islands in the equatorial Pacific (Fig. 4) which are influenced by the strength of the equatorial countercurrent, analyzed by Wyrtki (1973), the difference Christmas—Kwajalein reflecting the cross-flow sea-surface slope. Also shown for comparison are current strengths as measured by drifting ships and by hydrographic sections.

warmer water, the aspect of El Niño that is detrimental to the Peruvian fisheries. The equatorially trapped sea-level "wave" splits when it reaches the coast, propagating both to the north and south as coastally trapped internal Kelvin waves held by the inclined continental shelf and slope. It is the sea-level change associated with these propagating shelf waves that is of particular interest here, as the waves likely have played a role in beach erosion along the North American west coast.

Wyrtki (1977) documented sea-level changes associated with the 1972 El Niño at several equatorial islands. Figure 6 contrasts the records obtained at Anewa Bay, Solomon Islands, in the far western Pacific, and at Baltra in the Galapagos Islands. In 1971 before El Niño, sea level was high at Anewa Bay and low at Baltra, shown by Wyrtki to be associated with unusually intense trade winds. From May 1971 sea level dropped in the west, first slowly, later rapidly, reaching a low in January 1973. In contrast, sea level at Baltra did not start to rise until December 1971, when it rose rapidly until April 1972, dropped slightly, and then reached a second peak in December 1972. Thereafter, sea level at both locations returned to near normal. Although somewhat complicated in its variations, it is apparent that this pattern of west-to-east sea-level changes parallel to the equator is consistent with the dynamic wave concept of Wyrtki (1975). It should be further noted that the sea-level changes involved are large, some 50 cm total at Anewa Bay and 35 cm at Baltra in the Galapagos. Similarly, rapid changes in sea level were observed at the other Pacific islands; the drop in sea level at Guam amounted to 38 cm in 4 months, having catastrophic consequences on the marine life (Yamaguchi, 1975).

Sea levels at stations along the coast of Peru and Ecuador follow closely the same pattern as that at Baltra in the Galapagos (Wyrtki 1975), representing the arrival of the sea-level "wave" at the eastern boundary of the ocean. The subsequent north and south progression of the now coastally trapped Kelvin waves has been documented by Enfield and Allen (1980), who analyzed 25-yr time series (1950–1974) of monthly-averaged sea-level anomalies along the Pacific eastern boundary from Yakutat, Alaska (59°N) to Valparaiso, Chile (33°S). It is evident in Figure 7 that there is a strong visual coherence of the high sea-level anomalies associated with El Niño events (e.g., 1957–58, 1965, 1969, and 1972–73). Spectral analyses of the records showed that the sea-level fluctuations at North American stations have consistent phase lags with alongshore distance, demonstrating a sense of poleward propagation at a phase speed of 75 km/day. This rate is consistent with the theoretical rate of baroclinic wave propagation and is much faster than could be explained as having been caused by purely advective processes. Of particular interest, a noteworthy feature of Figure 7 is that the El Niño-related sea-level anomalies appear to be only slightly smaller in amplitude along the coast of California and Mexico than along the Peruvian coast. Although one might expect some height loss as energy is "leaked" offshore in the form of Rossby waves, the poleward migration causes the remaining fraction to be confined to a narrower coastal band due to the latitude-dependence of the Coriolis force. There is also some indication

pressed. Coriolis forces both to the north and south of the equator act to confine the wave to the equatorial zone, preventing its dissipation by expansion to the north and south. Computer simulations of the process depict such a progressive disturbance or sea-level "wave," also indicating that it would require about two months for passage across the Pacific (O'Brien and others, 1981). Upon arrival of the disturbance on the coast of South America, there would be a deepening of the thermocline and a massive influx of

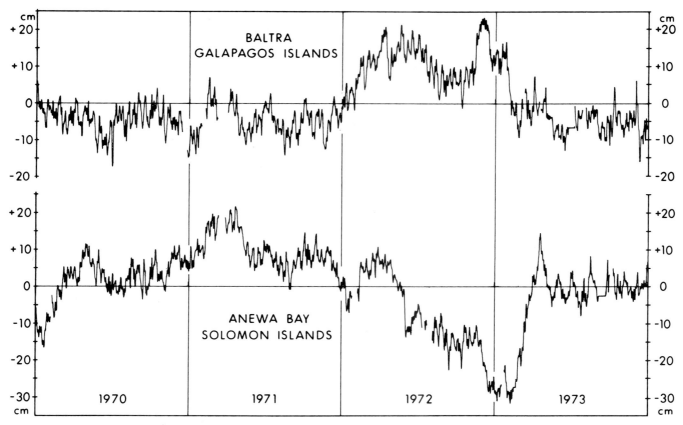

FIG. 6.—Sea levels measured at tide gauges in the Solomon and Galapagos islands (Fig. 4), showing variations of as much as 50 cm, most of which represent the progression of a sea-level "wave" along the equator associated with the 1972 El Niño (Wyrtki, 1977).

in Figure 7 that the sea-level amplitudes decrease faster with latitude south of the equator than to the north, a hemispheric asymmetry in the effectiveness of poleward propagation. Rather than resulting from different rates of wave damping in the two hemispheres, it is probable that in the Northern Hemisphere the sea-level signal is enhanced by southward-displaced winter storms which raise the coastal sea levels.

In summary, one aspect of the atmospheric and oceanic phenomenon known as El Niño is the generation of a significant sea-level anomaly, which takes the form of a wave which first propagates eastward along the equator, splitting into poleward-propagating waves when it reaches the eastern margin of the Pacific. These basin-wide responses involve several months of wave transit time, and at any given coastal site, the sea-level wave may raise the water level for tens of centimeters over a period of some 6 months to a year (Fig. 7).

The most recent El Niño, 1982–83, inspired considerable news media attention due to its unusual intensity and apparent association with such diverse phenomena as draughts in Australia, floods in the Western Hemisphere, and severe erosion along the coast of California. By most measures, this El Niño was probably the strongest episode within the past century. The earliest signs of the developing El Niño came in June 1982 as the southeast trade winds began to

break down, the collapse being complete by July when the normal trades were replaced by winds from the west, a condition which persisted until December 1982. October marked the onset of El Niño conditions on the coast of Peru, where there were profound biological consequences (Barber and Chavez, 1983).

The 1982–83 El Niño also attracted considerable scientific interest and as a result is the most thoroughly documented event of its kind to date. Although much of the accumulated data remains to be analyzed, a number of papers have already appeared: the February 1983, October 1983 and November 1984 issues of *Tropical Ocean-Atmosphere Newsletter* are devoted to this topic, the three articles by Cane (1983), Rasmusson and Wallace (1983) and Barber and Chavez (1983) in a special issue of *Science* offer good reviews, and the summer 1984 issue of *Oceanus* presents a series of popular articles.

Sea-level records during the 1982–83 El Niño are, for the most part, consistent with the notion that breakdown of the trade winds releases an equatorially trapped Kelvin wave which propagates across the Pacific (Wyrtki, 1983, 1984; Enfield and others, 1983). Sea level at Rabaul in the western Pacific (Fig. 8) reached a peak in March or April and then began to drop. In a typical year it rises again to a second peak in the fall, the peak which is normally associated with El Niño events, but in 1982 the sea level con-

SEA LEVEL

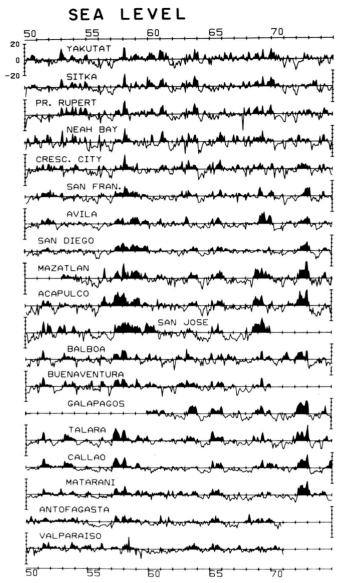

FIG. 7.—Sea-level anomalies along the eastern margin of the Pacific, associated with El Niño events such as those of 1957–58, 1965, 1969 and 1972–73. Analyses by Enfield and Allen (1980) demonstrate that these anomalies propagate poleward away from their equatorial origin, apparently as coastally trapped Kelvin waves.

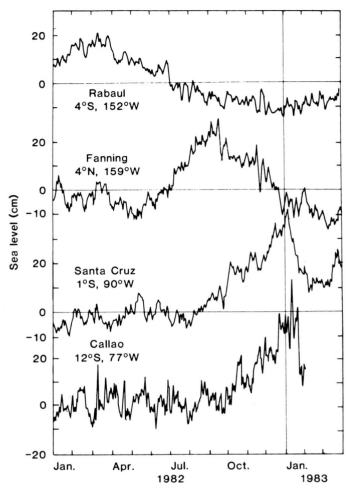

FIG. 8.—The equatorially trapped sea-level "wave" associated with the 1982–83 El Niño, shown in the analyses of tide-gauge records by Wyrtki (1983) from islands (Fig. 4) and from Callao on the coast of Peru.

tinued to drop throughout the year. The drop was especially sharp at the end of June when the trade winds decreased, falling by 12 cm at Rabaul within a few days. In the mid-Pacific at Fanning Island due south of Hawaii, sea level was near normal into June but then began to rise rapidly (Fig. 8), reaching a maximum in September which was some 30 to 40 cm higher than 6 months earlier. On the Peruvian coast at Callao, the rise did not begin until late September, reaching a maximum in January 1983, a rise in excess of 50 cm (Fig. 8).

The progression of a sea-level rise along the equator continued north as a coastally trapped Kelvin wave, similar to

the waves of Figure 7 studied by Enfield and Allen (1983). Figure 9 shows the monthly mean sea levels at Newport, Oregon for 1982–83 (Huyer and others, 1983). Sea level there reached a maximum in February 1983, nearly 60 cm higher than the level in May 1982, 9 months earlier. The thin solid line in the figure is the 10-yr means and the dashed lines give the previous maxima and minima for that period; it is readily apparent that the 1982–83 sea levels were exceptional, reaching some 10 to 20 cm higher than previous maxima, about 35 cm above the normal winter level.

These abnormally high sea levels along the west coast of the United States certainly played a role in the severe 1983 beach erosion in Oregon and California. There were other El Niño-related meteorological and oceanographic changes, however, which made significant contributions to this erosion. The entire northern Pacific meteorological patterns shifted farther south than usual. The jet stream in the subtropical Pacific not only moved southward during the El Niño, but also intensified to record strength. Storm tracks entering North America from the Pacific were displaced hundreds of miles to the south; storm systems which nor-

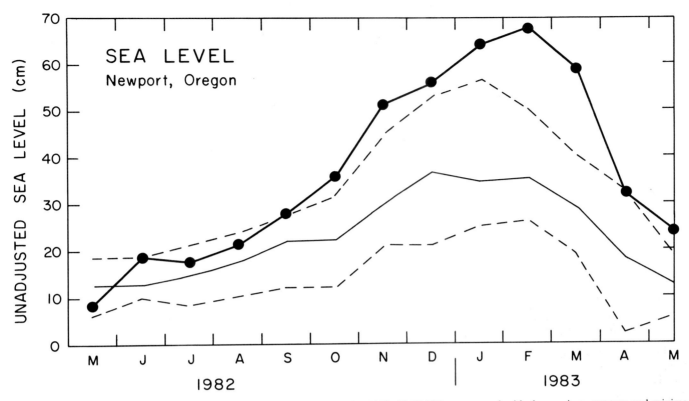

FIG. 9.—The monthly-averaged sea levels at Newport, Oregon, during the 1982–83 El Niño, compared with the maxima, average and minima previously measured, demonstrating the exceptional levels reached by the most recent El Niño sea-level "wave" (Huyer and others, 1983). Extensive erosion occurred along the Oregon coast during this period of high-water levels.

mally cross the Oregon-Washington coast to produce the severe wave conditions characteristic of that region were instead directed at the coast of California with devastating results.

El Niño conditions, which have their origins in equatorial regions, thereby have a direct consequence on erosion along the west coast of North America. This impact comes from both high wave energies produced by the intense storms and by a significant rise in sea level. The timing of the sea-level rise is such that it reaches the west coast of the United States during the winter months (Fig. 9) of maximum wave activity and reduced beach buffering, thus guaranteeing a role in the coastal erosion processes.

SUMMARY AND DISCUSSION

We have seen in this review that sea level as determined from tide gauges shows a considerable variability on time scales ranging from days to years with water-level changes typically in the range 10 to 30 cm, in some cases exceeding 100 cm. These are known to have a number of atmospheric and oceanic causes, including variations in the atmospheric pressure, wind strengths and directions, water temperatures, and coastal currents. The principal problem faced in analyzing the sea-level response to these several factors is that they are commonly coherent, that is, they are closely in phase with one another. In spite of such problems, there is now a reasonable understanding of the physical processes

responsible for the observed fluctuations in coastal sea levels.

More poorly understood is the response of beaches to such sea-level variations, as there have been few studies focusing on this question. Sea-level changes associated with El Niño most certainly must be an important factor in producing coastal erosion, the 1982–83 shoreline erosion in California and Oregon being a graphic example, but even here it is unclear how much of this erosion can be directly attributed to the sea-level rise (of some 60 cm) versus the intensified storm systems with higher wave energies.

The principal variation in sea level at most coastal sites is seasonal, and one might thereby expect to see a parallel change in the beaches. LaFond (1938) has demonstrated a remarkable correspondence (Fig. 10) between the monthly sea level at La Jolla, California, and the level of the beach close to the shore. It is seen that the changing sand level, amounting to some 90 cm, almost exactly parallels the 30-cm variation in sea level. A rise in sea level, however, corresponds with a rise in sand level, opposite to the expected erosion of the beach under higher water levels. It is very probable that the correspondence seen in Figure 10 is coincidental. This change in beach level at La Jolla is typical for the seasonal cycle in beach profiles, the beach being cut back during winter storms (Komar, 1976). The annual cycle in wave energy is more likely the cause of the changes in beach sand level, not the parallel variations in the mean sea level. Here again, we have the problem that the most im-

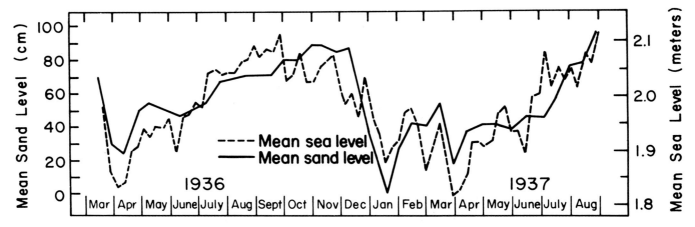

FIG. 10.—A remarkable correspondence between the monthly sea level measured by LaFond (1938) at La Jolla, California, and the level of the beach near the shoreline.

portant processes act in phase, so that it will be a challenge to devise experiments to detect the effects of seasonal sea-level fluctuations on coastal changes, including beach erosion.

The study which provides the clearest correlation between beach cycles and sea-level fluctuations is that of Clarke and Eliot (1983), made possible because they focused on cycles that are longer period than the seasonal variations. Their analyses of a 16-yr record of beach-width changes on the west coast of Australia revealed a cycle of 3.5 yrs as well as the annual cycle. Sea-level spectra showed the same periodicity, leading the beach response by approximately one-tenth of a cycle, a 1-cm rise in water level producing an approximate 100-cm retreat of the shoreline. It is likely that the many short-term variations in sea level, those reviewed in this paper, have similar beach erosion responses.

ACKNOWLEDGMENTS

This work is a result of research sponsored by the U.S. Department of Commerce, National Oceanic and Atmospheric Administration Office of Sea Grant, under Grant NA81AA-D-00086 (Project No. R/CP-20) and by the NOAA Eastern Pacific Ocean Climate Studies program under Grant NA84RAD05043. The U.S. Government is authorized to produce and distribute reprints for governmental purposes, notwithstanding any copyright notation that may appear hereon.

REFERENCES

BARBER, R. T., AND CHAVEZ, F. P., 1983, Biological consequences of El Niño: Science, v. 222, p. 1203–1210.
BARNETT, T. P., 1984, The estimation of "global" sea level change: a problem of uniqueness: Journal of Geophysical Research, v. 89, no. C5, p. 7980–7988.
BLAHA, J. P., 1984, Fluctuations of monthly sea level as related to the intensity of the Gulf Stream from Key West to Norfolk: Journal of Geophysical Research, v. 89, no. C5, p. 8033–8042.
CANE, M. A., 1983, Oceanographic events during El Niño: Science, v. 222, p. 1189–1195.
CHELTON, D. B., AND DAVIS, R. E., 1982, Monthly mean sea-level variability along the west coast of North America: Journal of Physical Oceanography, v. 12, p. 757–784.
CLARKE, D. J., AND ELIOT, I. G., 1983, Mean sea-level and beach-width variations at Scarborough, western Australia: Marine Geology, v. 51, p. 251–267.
ENFIELD, D. B., AND ALLEN, J. S., 1980, On the structure and dynamics of monthly mean sea level anomalies along the Pacific coast of North and South America: Journal of Physical Oceanography, v. 10, p. 557–578.
————, AND ————, 1983, The generation and propagation of sea level variability along the Pacific Coast of Mexico: Journal of Physical Oceanography, v. 13, p. 1012–1033.
————, SMITH, R. L., AND HAYES, S. P., 1983, Sea level variability at the eastern equatorial Pacific boundary in 1982: Tropical Ocean-Atmospheric Newsletter, no. 21, p. 13–14.
FU, L. -L., AND CHELTON, D. B., 1984, Temporal variability of the Antarctic Circumpolar Current observed from satellite altimetry: Science, v. 226, p. 343–346.
FUGLISTER, F. C., 1951, Annual variations in current speeds in the Gulf Stream system: Journal of Marine Research, v. 10, p. 119–127.
GORNITZ, V., LEBEDEFF, L., AND HANSEN, J., 1982, Global sea level trend in the past century: Science, v. 215, p. 1611–1614.
HAMON, B. V., 1962, The spectrums of mean sea level at Sydney, Coff's Harbour, and Lord Howe Island: Journal of Geophysical Research, v. 67, p. 5147–5155.
————, 1966, Continental shelf waves and the effects of atmospheric pressure and wind stress on sea level: Journal of Geophysical Research, v. 71, p. 2883–2893.
HICKS, S. D., 1978, An averave geopotential sea level series for the United States: Journal of Geophysical Research, v. 83, no. C3, p. 1377–1379.
————, DEBAUGH, H. A., JR., AND HICKMAN, L. E., JR., 1983, Sea level variations for the United States, 1855–1980: U.S. Department of Commerce, NOAA, National Ocean Service, Rockville, Maryland, 170 p.
HOLMAN, R. A., AND SALLENGER, A. H., 1985, Set-up and swash on a natural beach: Journal of Geophysical Research, v. 90, no. C1, p. 945–953.
HUYER, A., GILBERT, W. E., AND PITTOCK, H. L., 1983, Anomalous sea levels at Newport, Oregon during the 1982–83 El Niño: Coastal Oceanography and Climatology News, v. 5, no. 4, p. 37–39.
KOMAR, P. D., 1976, Beach Processes and Sedimentation: Prentice-Hall, Englewood Cliffs, New Jersey, 429 p.
LAFOND, E. C., 1938, Relationship between mean sea level and sand movements: Science, v. 88, p. 112–113.
————, 1939, Variations of sea level on the Pacific coast of the United States: Journal of Marine Research, v. 2, p. 17–29.
MAUL, G. A., CHEW, F., BUSHNELL, M., AND MAYER, D. A., 1985, Sea level variation as an indicator of Florida Current volume transport: comparisons with direct measurements: Science, v. 227, p. 304–307.
MEADE, R. H., AND EMERY, K. O., 1971, Sea level as affected by river runoff, eastern United States: Science, v. 173, p. 425–427.
MONTGOMERY, R.B., 1938, Fluctuations in monthly sea level on eastern U.S. coast as related to dynamics of western North Atlantic Ocean: Journal of Marine Research, v. 1, p. 165–185.

NIILER, P. P., AND RICHARDSON, W. S., 1973, Seasonal variability of the Florida Current: Journal of Marine Research, v. 31, p. 144–167.

O'BRIEN, J. J., BUSALACCHI, A., AND KINDLE, J., 1981, Ocean models of El Niño, *in* Glantz, M. H., ed., Resource Management and Environmental Uncertainty: John Wiley & Sons, New York, p. 159–212.

PATTULLO, J., 1966, The principal factors influencing the seasonal oscillation of sea level, *in* Hill, M. N., ed., The Sea, v. 2: Interscience, New York, p. 485–496.

————, MUNK, W., REVELLE, R., AND STRONG, E., 1955, The seasonal oscillation in sea level: Journal of Marine Research, v. 14, p. 88–155.

RASMUSSON, E. M., AND WALLACE, J. M., 1983, Meteorological aspects of the El Niño/Southern Oscillation: Science, v. 222, p. 1195–1202.

ROBINSON, A.R., 1964, Continental shelf waves and the response of sea level to weather systems: Journal of Geophysical Research, v. 69, p. 367–368.

RODEN, G.I., 1960, On the nonseasonal variations in sea level along the west coast of North America: Journal of Geophysical Research, v. 65, p. 2809–2826.

————, 1966, Low-frequency sea level oscillations along the Pacific coast of North America: Journal of Geophysical Research, v. 71, p. 4755–4776.

ROMEA, R. D., AND SMITH, R. L., 1983, Further evidence for coastal-trapped waves along the Peru coast: Journal of Physical Oceanography, v. 13, p. 1341–1356.

SAUR, J. F. T., 1962, The variability of monthly mean sea level at six stations in the eastern North Pacific: Journal of Geophysical Research, v. 67, no. 7, p. 2781–2790.

STOMMEL, H. M., 1953, Examples of the possible role of inertia and stratification in the dynamics of the Gulf Stream system: Journal of Marine Research, v. 12, p. 184–195.

WANG, D-P., AND MOOERS, C. N. K., 1977, Long coastal-trapped waves off the west coast of the United States, summer 1973: Journal of Physical Oceanography, v. 7, p. 856–864.

WUNSCH, C., HANSEN, D. V., AND ZETLER, B. D., 1969, Fluctuations of the Florida Current inferred from sea level records: Deep Sea Research, v. 16, suppl., p. 447–470.

WYRTKI, K., 1973, Teleconnections in the equatorial Pacific Ocean: Science, v. 180, p. 66–68.

————, 1975, Fluctuations of the dynamic topography in the Pacific Ocean: Journal of Physical Oceanography, v. 5, p. 450–459.

————, 1977, Sea level during the 1972 El Niño: Journal of Physical Oceanography, v. 7, p. 779–787.

————, 1983, Sea level in the equatorial Pacific in 1982: Tropical Ocean-Atmosphere Newsletter, no. 16, p. 6–7.

————, 1984, The slope of sea level along the equator during the 1982/1983 El Niño: Journal of Geophysical Research, v. 89, no. C6, p. 10,419–10,424.

YAMAGUCHI, M., 1975, Sea level fluctuations and mass mortalities of reef animals in Guam, Mariana Islands: Micronesica, v. 11, p. 227–243.

RECENT RELATIVE SEA-LEVEL CHANGE IN EASTERN NORTH AMERICA[1]

BARBARA V. BRAATZ AND DAVID G. AUBREY

Woods Hole Oceanographic Institution Woods Hole, MA 02543

ABSTRACT: Eigenanalysis of tide-gauge records between 1920 and 1983 in eastern North America reveals highly variable spatial and temporal patterns of relative sea-level change. Auxiliary data from numerical modeling suggest that much of the long wavelength (thousands of kilometers) spatial patterns of sea-level change are due to postglacial isostatic adjustment of the land surface. Filtering the isostatic component from the rates of relative sea-level movement yields residual rates that fluctuate about a coastal mean of 1.0–1.5 mm/yr during this 64-yr time interval. This mean rate is within the range of previous estimates of mean rate of eustatic rise in sea level during the past century. Some residual fluctuations (wavelengths of tens to hundreds of kilometers) correlate with tilts of the land surface revealed by geodetic leveling transects, and appear to be related to regional geology (i.e., basement structures and tectonic provinces in Florida, Georgia, the Carolinas, and the Chesapeake Bay area; fault reactivation in northern New England and the Maritime Provinces). These results suggest that tide-gauge data can be used to determine neotectonic movements along this coastline. Analysis of the temporal patterns of relative sea-level change reveals a gradual increase in the rate of rise centered at about 1934, which may be due to steric expansion of the ocean. Broad peaks in the spectrum of temporal sea-level fluctuations at 3-, 6-, and 20-yr periodicities (significant at the 80 percent level) may be a reflection of oceanographic, atmospheric, and lunar forcing.

INTRODUCTION

The CO_2 content of the atmosphere has risen approximately 20 percent since the Industrial Age (Hoffman and others, 1983). Most of this increase has been due to burning of fossil fuels and clearing of forested areas. Current projections estimate a doubling of pre-industrial age atmospheric CO_2 by 2050 to 2080 (Berger, 1984), and an associated increase in global average surface air temperature of 1.5–4.5° C (National Research Council, 1979) due to the "greenhouse" effect (tropospheric warming caused by increased absorption of the long wave radiation emitted by the earth's surface). Such warming, by thermally expanding the oceans and melting continental and alpine glaciers, would cause a rapid eustatic (i.e., global, although not necessarily globally equivalent) sea-level rise. Estimates of this rise range from 38 cm in the next century, to 5 m in the next 40 yrs (Mercer, 1978; Hoffman and others, 1983; Revelle, 1983). These estimates, as well as estimates of other aspects of the atmospheric-biospheric-oceanic response to increased atmospheric CO_2 and other gases, are subject to much debate (e.g., Perry, 1983; Berger, 1984; Kondratyev, 1984). Adverse impacts of higher sea levels include shoreline retreat, erosion, flooding, destruction of coastal structures, and saltwater instrusion of bays, rivers, and aquifers.

To predict future changes in sea level accurately, we must assess the past response of the oceans to atmospheric change. If atmospheric CO_2 has increased by 20 percent since the Industrial Revolution, what has been the associated increase in eustatic sea level? Is this rate of sea-level rise increasing? Various estimates of this rate have been made (Table 1). Agreement between the estimates is surprisingly good, given the different data sets and methods of analysis. Results from some of these studies suggest that the rate of sea-level rise has increased during the past century (Thorarinsson, 1940; Gutenberg, 1941; Fairbridge and Krebs, 1962; Emery, 1980; Barnett, 1984), although the timing of this increase varies between studies. The most recent comparison of average global sea-level rise over different time periods (Barnett, 1984) revealed little or no trend between

1881–1920, but a positive trend between 1920–1980 (22.7 ± 2.3 cm per century for the period 1930–1980).

Tide-gauge data are complicated, because coastlines along which sea level is measured do not maintain constant elevation. Factors such as isostatic adjustment due to glacial and hydrostatic loading and unloading, tectonic movements, sediment loading and flexure, pore-fluid removal, and sediment compaction affect relative sea levels with varying magnitudes over the globe. Oceanographic and atmospheric factors, such as the El Niño-Southern Oscillation, meanders and eddies of western boundary currents such as the Gulf Stream and the Kuroshio, and changes in wind stress and atmospheric pressure, also have varying effect in space and in time on sea-level elevation.

For these reasons, recent studies (Aubrey and Emery, 1983, 1986; Emery and Aubrey, 1985) have examined relative sea-level (RSL) change on a regional basis. Results from these studies indicate that in some regions RSL is dominated by factors other than pure eustacy. In Japan, the spatial structure of RSL rise can be explained by subduction of the Pacific and Philippine plates beneath the Japanese islands, and the higher frequencies of the temporal fluctuations in RSL probably are related to shifts in the position of the Kuroshio (Aubrey and Emery, 1986). Isostatic rebound clearly explains the concentric pattern of RSL lowering seen in the Fennoscandian region (Emery and Aubrey, 1985). RSL along the coast of the east Asian mainland appears to be controlled by geologic structure (Emery and Aubrey, 1986a). These studies demonstrate the variability, both in time and in space, of the rate and magnitude of RSL change. To quantify the eustatic sea-level rise during the past century, the magnitude of these tectonic, isostatic, and oceanographic effects on RSL in different regions around the world must be determined.

Empirical orthogonal function analysis of tide-gauge data from the coastlines of the United States (Aubrey and Emery, 1983) revealed a highly variable spatial record of RSL change over the 40-yr period 1940–1979, which is probably a result of a number of factors. Along the United States east coast, three distinct regions were identified, each with a consistent sea-level trend. From Pensacola to Cape Hatteras the rate of RSL rise increases; from Cape Hatteras to Boston the rate decreases; and from Boston to Eastport the rate

[1]Woods Hole Oceanographic Institution Contribution Number 6205.

TABLE 1.—ESTIMATES OF MEAN EUSTATIC SEA-LEVEL INCREASE (AFTER BARNETT, 1983)

Author	Rate (cm/century)	Method
Thorarinsson (1940)	>5	Cryologic Aspects (ice budget data from 6 glaciers, extrapolated for global estimate)
Gutenberg (1941)	11	Tide Gauges (69 stations, 1880's–~1939)[A]
Kuenen (1950)	12–14	Tide Gauges (11 Dutch stations, 1832–1942)[B]
Lisitzin (1958)	11.2 ± 3.6	Tide Gauges (5 N. European & 1 Indian station, 1800's–1943)[C]
Fairbridge & Krebs (1962)	12	Tide Gauges (1900–1950)[D]
Emery (1980)	30	Tide Gauges (247 stations, ~1850–1979)[E]
Gornitz and others (1982)	12	Tide Gauges (193 stations, ~1900–1979)[F]
Barnett (1983)	15.1 ± 1.5	Tide Gauges (9 stations, 1903–1969)[G]
Barnett (1984)	14.3 ± 1.4	Tide Gauges (155 stations, ~1880–1980)[H]
Aubrey & Emery (Aubrey, 1985)	0–30	Tide Gauges[I]

[A]Stations in regions of known postglacial uplift omitted.

[B]Rate includes correction for "secular sinking of crust" determined from geologic, archeologic, and leveling data.

[C]Rate includes correction for secular relative sea-level movement.

[D]Stations in regions of known postglacial uplift, orogenic activity, and sediment compaction omitted.

[E]This rate is based on values for continental stations which record relative sea-level rise; if the continental stations which record a relative sea-level fall are also included, the resulting rate is ~15 cm/century.

[F]Stations in regions of known postglacial uplift, orogenic activity, and sediment compaction omitted; if corrections for secular relative sea-level change, determined from ^{14}C-dated shoreline indicators, are included, Gornitz and others obtain a global rate of 10 cm/century.

[G]Each station chosen as a "stable" regional representative to obtain equal-area weighted global average.

[H]Quasi equal-area weighting scheme, stations with anomalous vertical motion deleted.

[I]These rates based on separate studies of different regions, over different intervals of time.

increases again. Aubrey and Emery (1983) suggested isostatic rebound as an explanation for the trend in the most northern region, but found no tectonic or geologic reasons to explain the remainder of the east coast signal. A comparison between the mean annual RSL and depth to shelf break along the east coast was made with the hypothesis that if RSL trends had persisted for a long period of time, the trends would be reflected in the depth to shelf break. Lack of correlation between the two data sets led the authors to conclude that segmentation of RSL along the east coast may be due to oceanographic and atmospheric forcing.

A number of previous analyses of different data sets (geodetic leveling; archeology; radiocarbon dating of terraces, beaches, and peat bogs; oceanographic temperature and salinity measurements) have demonstrated this spatial and temporal variability in rate of RSL change along the United States east coast (Wunsch, 1972; Winker and Howard, 1977; Brown, 1978; Newman and others, 1980; Bloom, 1983, among many others). The abundance of these studies, as well as the good coverage by tide gauges along the United States east coast compared to other regions, justifies further analysis of RSL trends. The purpose of this study is to expand the United States east coast portion of Aubrey and Emery's (1983) analysis of United States tide-gauge records to include additional years of record and additional stations in the United States and Canada that were not previously analyzed, and then use related studies to determine how eustatic, isostatic, geologic, and oceanographic factors produce the spatial and temporal variability in RSL in eastern North America.

METHODS

Data for this study are yearly mean sea levels from tide-gauge stations, from 1920 through 1983, provided by the Permanent Service for Mean Sea Level (United Kingdom) and the National Ocean Service (United States). Each sea-level series was plotted and visually inspected for discontinuities or jumps that could be the result of movement of the tide gauge or datum, or simply a data entry error. Stations located on large rivers also are suspect. Meade and Emery (1971) found that variations in annual river runoff can account for 7–21 percent of the total variation in sea level along the United States east coast. The entire record at Richmond, on the James River, was deleted for this reason. Stations having less than 20 yrs of data, from the period 1920–1983, inclusive, were also deleted, leaving a total of 44 stations to be analyzed (Fig. 1, Table 2). Aubrey and Emery (1983) analyzed 26 stations along the United States east coast over the 40-yr time span between 1940 and 1979.

Empirical orthogonal function analysis, or eigenanalysis, was applied to sea-level records to determine the dominant temporal and spatial structure of the data. Advantages of eigenanalysis over averaging and linear or non-linear regression techniques are outlined in Aubrey and Emery (1983). Briefly, eigenanalysis separates a data set into orthogonal spatial and temporal modes that most efficiently describe the variability of the data set (see Appendix of Aubrey and Emery, 1986). No preconceived subjective models are fit to the data, as in regression techniques. Eigenanalysis usually is applied to over-lapping time series (equal and concurrent duration), and any stations having gaps are excluded. In order to use all available data without interpolation or extrapolation, a modified eigenanalysis (Aubrey and Emery, 1986; Aubrey and Welch, in prep.) was employed. Station means were removed, and each station variance was set to unity before the eigenvalues and eigenvectors were calculated to minimize dominance by any single energetic sea-level station. Linear regressions of the 1920–1983 portions of each station's record were computed to determine anomalous yearly means and to compare with eigenanalysis results. RSL rates are presented as positive for RSL rise and negative for RSL fall. Finally, spectral analysis was used on the temporal eigenfunctions to determine the dominant frequencies of sea-level change.

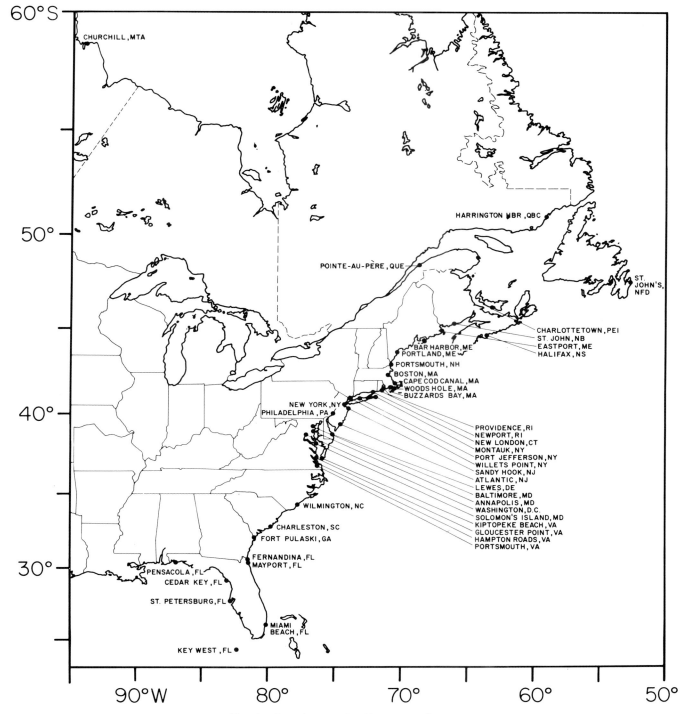

FIG. 1.—Location map for tide-gauge stations.

RESULTS

Eigenanalysis of tide-gauge data yields both spatial and temporal functions ranked to explain sequentially diminishing amounts of the total variation in the records. Each spatial function has a corresponding temporal function which explains the same amount of the variance (Figs. 2, 3). Most (81.2%) of the total sea-level variance is explained by the first three eigenfunctions (the first, second, and third functions account for 69.6, 6.4, and 5.2%, respectively, of the true variance of the data set).

An F-test was used to determine if the slopes of the temporal eigenfunctions were statistically significant at the 95% level. The first temporal function (Fig. 3) has a significant

TABLE 2.—TIDE-GAUGE STATION LOCATIONS AND RATES OF RSL MOVEMENT*

Station Name	Location (latitude, longitude)	Synthetic Rate (mm/yr)	Model Estimate (mm/yr)	Residual Rate (mm/yr)
Pensacola, FL	30°24.2'N, 87°12.8'W	2.0 ± .4	0.6?	1.4 ± .4
Cedar Key, FL	29°08.1'N, 83°01.9'W	1.2 ± .2	0.4?	0.8 ± .2
St. Petersburg, FL	27°46.4'N, 82°37.3'W	1.6 ± .3	0.2?	1.4 ± .3
Key West, FL	24°33.2'N, 81°48.5'W	1.9 ± .4	−0.1	2.0 ± .4
Miami Beach, FL	25°46.1'N, 80°07.9'W	1.6 ± .3	0.0	1.6 ± .3
Mayport, FL	30°23.6'N, 81°25.9'W	1.9 ± .4	0.3	1.6 ± .4
Fernandina, FL	30°40.3'N, 81°28.0'W	1.8 ± .3	0.4	1.4 ± .3
Fort Pulaski, GA	32°02.0'N, 80°54.1'W	2.1 ± .4	0.6	1.5 ± .4
Charleston, SC	32°46.9'N, 79°55.5'W	2.8 ± .5	0.8	2.0 ± .5
Wilmington, NC	34°13.6'N, 77°57.2'W	1.8 ± .3	1.2?	0.6 ± .3
Portsmouth, VA	36°49.3'N, 76°17.6'W	2.9 ± .5	1.7	1.2 ± .5
Hampton Roads, VA	36°56.8'N, 76°19.8'W	3.5 ± .7	1.8	1.7 ± .7
Gloucester Point, VA	37°14.8'N, 76°30.0'W	3.2 ± .6	1.8?	1.4 ± .6
Kiptopeke Beach, VA	37°10.0'N, 75°59.3'W	2.8 ± .5	1.8?	1.0 ± .5
Solomon's Island, MD	38°19.0'N, 76°27.2'W	2.4 ± .5	1.9	0.5 ± .5
Washington, D.C.	38°52.5'N, 77°01.4'W	2.6 ± .5	1.8	0.8 ± .5
Annapolis, MD	38°59.0'N, 76°28.8'W	2.6 ± .5	1.8	0.8 ± .5
Baltimore, MD	39°16.0'N, 76°34.7'W	2.8 ± .5	1.8	1.0 ± .5
Lewes, DE	38°46.9'N, 75°07.2'W	3.0 ± .6	2.1	0.9 ± .6
Atlantic City, NJ	39°21.3'N, 74°25.1'W	3.0 ± .6	2.1	0.9 ± .6
Philadelphia, PA	39°57.1'N, 75°08.4'W	2.6 ± .5	1.8	0.8 ± .5
Sandy Hook, NJ	40°28.0'N, 74°00.1'W	3.2 ± .6	1.7	1.5 ± .6
New York, NY	40°42.0'N, 74°05.5'W	2.7 ± .5	1.6	1.1 ± .5
Willets Point, NY	40°47.6'N, 73°46.9'W	2.2 ± .4	1.6	0.6 ± .4
Port Jefferson, NY	40°57.0'N, 73°04.6'W	2.8 ± .5	1.6?	1.2 ± .5
Montauk, NY	41°02.9'N, 71°57.6'W	1.7 ± .3	1.6?	0.1 ± .3
New London, CT	41°21.3'N, 72°05.2'W	1.8 ± .3	1.5	0.3 ± .3
Newport, RI	41°30.3'N, 71°19.6'W	2.1 ± .4	1.6	0.5 ± .4
Providence, RI	41°48.4'N, 71°24.1'W	1.9 ± .4	1.5	0.4 ± .4
Woods Hole, MA	41°31.5'N, 70°40.4'W	2.2 ± .4	1.7	0.5 ± .4
Buzzards Bay, MA	41°44.5'N, 70°37.1'W	0.8 ± .2	1.7?	−0.9 ± .2
Cape Cod Canal, MA	41°46.3'N, 70°30.4'W	1.8 ± .3	1.7?	0.1 ± .3
Boston, MA	42°21.3'N, 71°03.0'W	1.9 ± .4	1.2	0.7 ± .4
Portsmouth, NH	43°04.9'N, 70°44.7'W	1.6 ± .3	0.9	0.7 ± .3
Portland, ME	43°39.4'N, 70°14.8'W	2.2 ± .4	0.7	1.5 ± .4
Bar Harbor, ME	44°23.5'N, 68°12.3'W	2.0 ± .4	0.8?	1.2 ± .4
Eastport, ME	44°54.2'N, 66°59.1'W	2.2 ± .4	0.9	1.3 ± .4
St. John, NB	45°16.0'N, 66°04.0'W	2.1 ± .4	0.9?	1.2 ± .4
Halifax, NS	44°40.0'N, 63°35.0'W	2.6 ± .5	1.6?	1.0 ± .5
Pointe-au-Père, QUE	48°31.0'N, 68°28.0'W	0.5 ± .1	−2.2?	2.7 ± .1
Charlottestown, PEI	46°14.0'N, 63°70.0'W	1.4 ± .3	0.6?	0.8 ± .3
Harrington Hbr, QUE	50°30.0'N, 59°29.0'W	−0.1 ± .0	−1.4?	1.3 ± .0
St. John's, NFD	47°34.0'N, 52°43.0'W	1.1 ± .2	0.4?	0.7 ± .2
Churchill, MTA	58°46.0'N, 94°11.0'W	−2.2 ± .4	−10.0?	7.8 ± .4

*Synthetic rates of RSL movement generated using eigenanalysis of tide-gauge data between 1920 and 1983; model estimates of isostatic adjustment from Peltier (1986) (? = interpolation from contour map, otherwise directly from table, see text); residual rates of RSL movement equal synthetic rate minus model estimate.

positive trend, of 0.0053/yr (in dimensionless units); the second function has no statistically significant trend; and the third function displays large amplitude fluctuations about a significant positive trend of 0.0084/yr. The first function shows a distinct change in slope, from a flat trend during the early portion of the time series to a positive trend during the later portion. Based on the best fit (in a least-squares sense) of a two-segment line, this change in slope is centered at 1934/1935. Linear regression slopes for both the 1920–1934 (−0.0037 mm/yr) and for the 1935–1983 (0.0057) segments are significant at the 95% level. This change in slope of the first function could have been a result of either a low sampling density before 1934 or bias introduced by the eigenanalysis, so a comparison was made between the first temporal eigenfunction computed using only those stations in operation before 1935, and the first temporal eigenfunction computed using all of the data. This comparison yielded negligible differences (Fig. 4), indicating the change in slope centered around 1934/1935 is neither an artifact of a lower sampling density during the

early period (26 of the 44 stations began operation before 1935), nor of bias introduced by the eigenanalysis, but represents an actual change in the rate of RSL movement for stations along the east coast of North America. This change in rate of RSL movement was not observed in Aubrey and Emery (1983), because they analyzed the United States east coast data from only 1940 to 1979.

Linear regression slopes of these temporal eigenfunctions were combined with the spatial eigenfunctions to produce synthetic rates of RSL movement for each station (Fig. 5). The 1935–1983 portion of the first temporal eigenfunction was used to produce the synthetic RSL curve. The slopes of the 1935–1983 portion of both the second and third temporal eigenfunctions were not significant. Error bars for the synthetic rates of RSL change for each station (Table 2, Fig. 5) were derived from the expected deviation in slope of the 1935–1983 portion of the first temporal eigenfunction, using a t-test at the 95% significance level.

Synthetic RSL rates (Fig. 5) are highly variable along the coast. Rate of RSL rise increases northward from about

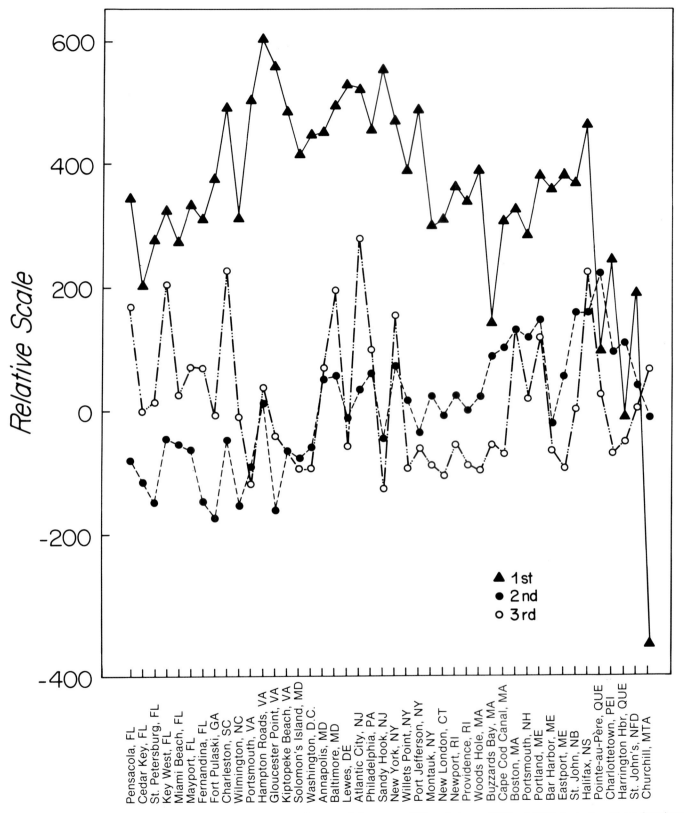

FIG. 2.—First three spatial eigenfunctions for the 44 stations having records in excess of 20 yrs between 1920 and 1983, inclusive. These functions account for 69.6, 6.4, and 5.2 percent, respectively, of the true variance of the records.

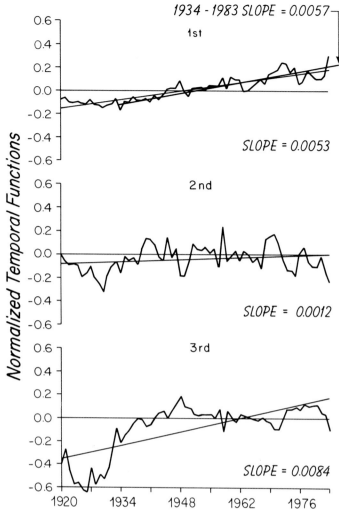

FIG. 3.—First, second, and third temporal eigenfunctions. These functions account for 69.6, 6.4, and 5.2 percent, respectively, of the true variance of the records. Units are dimensionless and normalized. Based on a best fit of a two-segment line, there is a change in trend in the first eigenfunction centered at 1934/1935. The 1920–1934 portion has a slope of -0.0037, and the 1935–1983 portion has a slope of 0.0057. This is not an artifact of lower sampling density between 1920 and 1934 or of the analysis technique (see text).

1.2 to 2.0 mm/yr at the Florida stations to a maximum of 3.5 mm/yr at Hampton Roads. North of Hampton Roads, rate of RSL rise follows a general decreasing trend with fluctuations, to 1.6 mm/yr at Portsmouth, New Hampshire. Stations north from Portsmouth to Halifax display an increase in rate of RSL rise. From Halifax to Churchill, the decrease in rate of RSL rise is dramatic, from 2.6 mm/yr at Halifax to -2.2 mm/yr at Churchill, and highly variable. A comparison between the synthetic rates of RSL rise and linear regressions (Fig. 6) shows a good one-to-one correspondence, except at Churchill where the synthetic rate is less than half the regression trend.

Spectral analysis of the temporal eigenfunctions was made, after detrending, to determine dominant frequencies in time

scales of RSL movement (Fig. 7). None of the spectral estimates are significant at the 90% level, but the first and second functions show slightly significant energy at the 80% level in the low frequencies. In the first function there are peaks at both 20- and 6-yr periods, whereas in the second function, there is a broad peak between periods of 4 and 20 yrs, and a peak at about 3 yrs. The third function shows higher energy at the lower frequencies, but no significant peaks of energy at the 80% level. Short record length and nonstationary forcing combine to lower the significance of the spectral estimates.

DISCUSSION

Spatial Fluctuations

Spatial fluctuations in rates of RSL movement (Fig. 5) can be discussed in terms of two spatial scales: long wavelength (order of thousands of kilometers) and short wavelength (order of tens to hundreds of kilometers). Ice sheets that covered the Northern Hemisphere during the Pleistocene were large enough to cause elastic and plastic deformation of the lithosphere, having wavelengths of thousands of kilometers. The maximum southeastern extent of these ice sheets along the east coast of North America is marked by Long Island, yet geologic evidence and modeling results indicate the isostatic effects of these ice sheets (crustal rebound from glacial depression, forebulge relaxation, hydrostatic depression) have extended great distances from the margins of ice sheets, and continue to influence vertical land motion today (e.g., Walcott, 1972a; Farrell and Clark, 1976; Clark and others, 1978; Quinlan and Beaumont, 1981). Shorter wavelength RSL movements could be caused by regional land warping due to tectonic movements, subsidence due to groundwater withdrawal or sediment loading, seismic activity, etc.

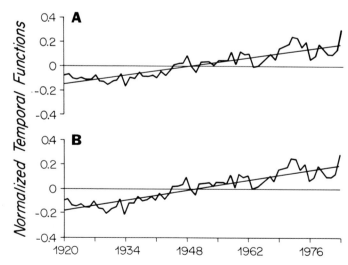

FIG. 4.—(A) The first temporal eigenfunction computed from all 44 stations used in this study. (B) The first temporal eigenfunction computed from the 26 stations which were in operation before 1935. There is almost no difference between the two results, indicating that the change in slope of the first temporal eigenfunction at 1934 is not an artifact of lower sampling density between 1920 and 1934, nor is it a bias resulting from the analysis (see text).

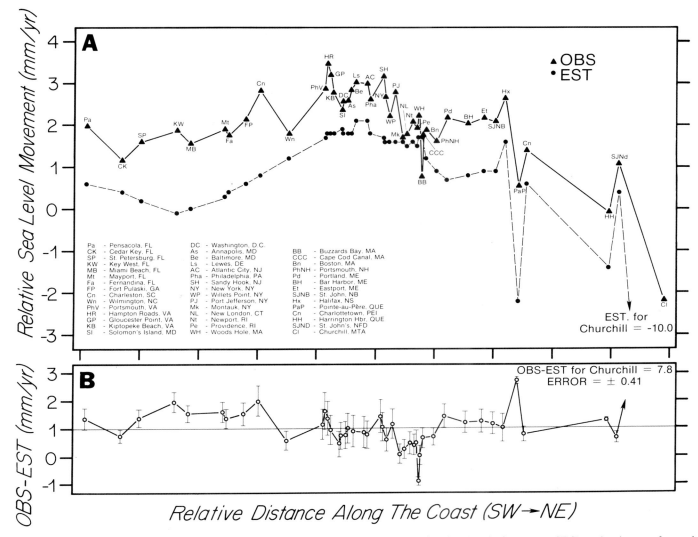

FIG. 5.—(A) Mean annual RSL movement for 1920–1980 from reconstructed eigenfunction data (synthetic rates, or OBS), and estimates of annual RSL movement due to postglacial isostatic adjustment (EST, Peltier, 1986), plotted in a relative sense along the coastline. These relative distances are obtained by drawing perpendiculars from the stations to lines drawn approximately parallel to the coastline. From Pensacola to Key West, this line trends 146° measured clockwise from true north; from Key West to St. John's, Newfoundland, the line trends 40° measured clockwise from true north. Churchill, located along the west central coast of the Hudson Bay, is placed at an arbitrary distance from St. John's. (B) Residual annual RSL movement, i.e., synthetic (OBS) minus estimated (EST) isostatic adjustment. Error bars are derived as discussed in the text.

Oceanographic and atmospheric influence.—

Changes in the density of the water column, atmospheric pressure, wind velocity, and oceanic circulation all can affect tide-gauge measurements at different spatial scales. Strong interseasonal changes and small but measurable decadal changes in air pressure, wind stress, and Ekman upwelling over the North Atlantic have been documented (Thompson and Hazen, 1983). Unfortunately, studies of meteorological effects on sea-level variation have concentrated on the Pacific and have been over time scales too short to be useful in this study (e.g., Pattullo, 1960; Lisitzin and Pattullo, 1961). Similar problems exist with oceanographic data. Variations in transport of the Florida Current, the portion of the Gulf Stream system flowing through the

Florida Straits northward to the point where the flow leaves the continental slope, could have a measurable effect on tide-gauge records south of Cape Hatteras (Iselin, 1940; and see Komar, this volume). Studies of the transport of the Gulf Stream, however, have also been on time scales too short to be applicable here (e.g., Niiler and Richardson, 1973). For these reasons, atmospheric and oceanographic effects on the spatial variation RSL movement will not be discussed further.

Glacio-isostatic influence.—

Estimates of current glacio-isostatic vertical land movement at different tide-gauge stations can be obtained from RSL curves generated from ^{14}C-dated shoreline indicators

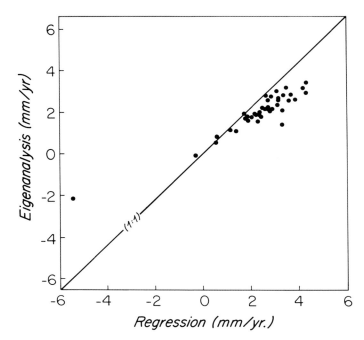

FIG. 6.—Scatter diagram of rates of change in RSL at individual stations obtained by both eigenanalysis and regression.

structure have been successively refined by fitting these various models to different sets of geophysical data. Data consist of different manifestations of the earth's response to the loading and unloading of the Pleistocene ice sheets: postglacial (18 to 1 ka) variations in relative sea level, free air gravity anomalies over present areas of rebound, and anomalies in the earth's rotation (non-tidal acceleration of rotation and secular drift of the rotation pole revealed by the International Latitude Service pole path). All of these models use a radially stratified viscoelastic representation of the earth. One of the most recent refinements of this representation used ^{14}C records of postglacial relative sea levels in North America and Europe and strandline tilts in the Great Lakes (Peltier, 1986). The resultant model (elastic model 1066B with a 196.6-km-thick lithosphere, upper mantle viscosity of 10^{21} P and a lower mantle viscocity of 2×10^{21} P) was then used to filter the glacio-isostatic portion of the recent (1940–1980) RSL signal recorded by 26 tide gauges along the United States east coast and 12 tide gauges along the United States west coast. The mean of the residual at the east coast stations (secular trend recorded by

(e.g., Gornitz and others, 1982) and also from geophysical models of the response of the earth to glacial unloading and meltwater loading (e.g., Peltier, 1986). Both methods have their weaknesses. The ^{14}C method is constrained by a small amount of data from the last few thousand years. Therefore, linear rates based on a few data points over thousands of years must be used to represent the last 100 yrs or so of RSL change, when RSL curves are known to be nonlinear (e.g., Bloom, 1967). Geophysical models can be adjusted to generate sea-level curves for shorter intervals of time, but the models are only as good as the parameters used to construct them, and many of these parameters are poorly constrained. There is considerable debate about the space and time scales of loading and unloading of the Pleistocene ice sheets, as well as the vertical structure and rheology of the earth. Variations in these parameters yield quite different model results (e.g., Clark and others, 1978; Peltier, 1984, 1986). Also, these models do not account for lateral inhomogeneities in the earth, such as variations in lithology and structure, so local records of RSL variation, as determined from ^{14}C dates, tide-gauge records, geodetic leveling, etc., can be expected to depart from model RSL curves. Another factor which is not accounted for in these models is a eustatic rise in sea level that may have occurred during the past century due to the "greenhouse" effect. Keeping these simplifications in mind, results of one of these models are used to assess the isostatic part (due to Pleistocene deglaciation) of RSL movement recorded by tide gauges.

In a series of papers over the past decade (e.g., Peltier and Andrews, 1976; Clark and others, 1978; Peltier and others, 1978; Peltier and Wu, 1982; Wu and Peltier, 1983, 1984; Peltier, 1984, 1986), models of earth rheology and

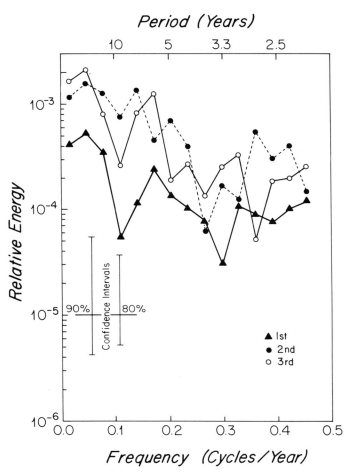

FIG. 7.—Spectra of the first, second, and third temporal eigenfunctions. Estimates have four degrees of freedom. Energy units are relative. All three eigenfunctions display high energy in the low frequencies (4- to 20-yr periodicities).

tide gauges minus the predicted present rate of RSL movement determined by modeling isostatic adjustment) was 1.1 mm/yr. If the residual were due to a purely eustatic sea-level signal, this residual would be fairly uniform along this coastline. The residual shows a great deal of variability about its mean, however, indicating that other mechanisms of RSL movement are influencing the tide-gauge records.

A similar residual was calculated here, by subtracting Peltier's (1986) estimates of isostatic adjustment from synthetic rates of RSL movement constructed from eigenanalysis (Fig. 5). Present rates of isostatic adjustment are given in Peltier (1986) for only 26 of the 44 tide-gauge stations analyzed here; rates for the remaining 18 stations were interpolated from a contour map of predicted rates of present vertical glacio-isostatic motion for North America (Peltier, 1986, Fig. 12). Subtracting the isostatic portion of RSL movement from the RSL curve results in a residual RSL curve (Fig. 5), from which most of the long-wavelength component of the RSL curve has been removed (ignoring Buzzards Bay, Pointe-au-Père, and Churchill, the filtering results in a reduction in variance by more than a factor of two). The equally weighted average of the resultant residual is 1.2 mm/yr. Residual rates at Buzzards Bay, Pointe-au-Père, and Churchill are questionable, for reasons to be discussed later; removing these results yields an equally weighted mean residual of 1.0 mm/yr. By averaging tide-gauge results from eight regions of equal length along the coast, the distance-weighted mean residual rate of RSL rise is 1.5 mm/yr (1.2 mm/yr if residuals at Churchill, Pointe-au-Père, and Buzzards Bay are not included). This may be a more accurate estimate of mean residual RSL rise. Other weighting schemes, equally plausible and defensible, yield similar results.

If the variability is due to more local events along the coastline, i.e., seismic movements, subsidence and warping of the land surface, etc., one would expect fluctuations to occur about a mean close to zero (assuming Peltier's 1986 estimates of current isostatic adjustments are not uniformly low along the entire coastline). A non-zero mean residual rate of RSL movement that is close to previous estimates of the mean rate of eustatic sea-level rise over the past century (Table 1) suggests that this mean residual rate of 1.0–1.5 mm/yr may approximate the eustatic component of RSL change. This suggestion is questionable, however, for three reasons: (1) the global tide-gauge network is heavily skewed toward the Northern Hemisphere, particularly the North Atlantic. Many long-term stations are in a zone of glacio-isostatic submergence (e.g., Walcott, 1972a). Therefore, the estimates shown in Table 1 may be biased by RSL rise due to land submergence, although most of the studies in Table 1 attempted some correction for this effect. (2) The mean residual rate of RSL change determined in this study may result from large-scale (margin-wide) tectonic movement of the coastline (i.e., subsidence of the coastal plain), although the change in rate of RSL rise, from a small negative to a larger positive rate (revealed by the first temporal eigenfunction) argues against a geologic cause (see section on temporal fluctuations). (3) The glacio-isostatic model may underpredict present rates of adjustment.

Geologic influence.—

Shorter wavelength variations in RSL movement appearing as fluctuations about the mean residual rate may be due to lateral compositional inhomogeneities and structural discontinuities in the lithosphere not accounted for in Peltier's (1986) model (e.g., crustal thinning and faults). Geodetic leveling studies, geologic structure, and records of seismic activity along this coastline provide an indication of where these may be affecting local RSL.

Precise geodetic leveling surveys conducted during the past century by the National Geodetic Survey provide estimates of relative vertical land movements. Absolute rates of crustal movement can be determined only if the leveling net is tied into a fixed frame of reference, usually tide-gauge stations (e.g., Holdahl and Morrison, 1974; Vaníček, 1975, 1976). Leveled surfaces are warped to fit the tide-gauge data, which can introduce errors due to nonsynchronous leveling and tide-gauge data, as well as excessive smoothing (Brown and Oliver, 1976). For these reasons, and since it would be inconsistent to use leveling results fit to tide-gauge data then to analyze tide-gauge data, only relative movements determined by leveling studies are used here.

Leveling data are not without error. Constant relative movement over the time interval between relevelings is assumed, although various studies have shown that this assumption is not always correct (e.g., Brown and Oliver, 1976; Brown, 1978). Time frames of leveling studies must be matched to those of the tide-gauge data as closely as possible. Also, as discussed by Brown (1978), leveling surveys are susceptible to error from local effects (variations in atmospheric pressure, rapid pressure gradients, expansion or contraction of the ground due to temperature changes, frost heaving, and near-surface ground water variations), as well as systematic influences (unequal refraction, tidal attraction, ocean loading, and unequal lighting). Also, recently a magnetic error associated with the Zeiss Ni-1 level instrument, which was used between 1972 and 1979, was discovered in the United States leveling net (S. R. Holdahl, pers. commun.). On average, vertical error due to this instrument is 0.8 mm/km. Large (hundreds of kilometers) north-south tilts in the United States leveling net, which indicate movement down to the north, are probably a result of this error and will not be used in this study.

Additional confusion results from the use of relative, instead of absolute, geodetic measurements since some vertical land movements due to isostatic adjustments will be apparent in relative geodetic leveling results and others will not. For example, if the vertical rise or fall of the land surface at a hypothetical station A is equivalent to that at another hypothetical station B over the time interval between levelings, then the relative movement recorded by the levelings between these two stations would be zero. The equivalent vertical movement at the two stations, however, will be apparent in the tide-gauge data, and if the movement is due to postglacial isostatic adjustment, it should appear in Peltier's data. On the other hand, unequal vertical movement at stations A and B *will* be recorded as non-zero relative movement by geodetic levelings, the tide-gauge data, and Peltier's data (if applicable).

The geology of the study area (Fig. 8) also helps interpret local deviations from the coastal mean rate of RSL rise. In the north, Precambrian metamorphic and plutonic infracrustal rocks of the Canadian Shield are exposed (King, 1970, and references therein). These rocks are overlain by younger platform deposits to the south (the Interior Platform), and also to the north, along the southeastern side of Hudson Bay (the Hudson Bay Platform). Along the southeastern side of North America, and running seaward to the northeast of Newfoundland, is the Appalachian foldbelt, composed of geosynclinal deposits that were highly deformed, faulted, and metamorphosed during the Taconian, Acadian, and Alleghenian orogenies of the Paleozoic era. Smaller units of Precambrian unaltered geosynclinal sedimentary and volcanic rocks, as well as metamorphic and plutonic infracrustal rocks, occur within this foldbelt. Less deformed, post-orogenic strata (Carboniferous and Triassic in age) are present in the Appalachian foldbelt as well. The Carboniferous rocks have undergone moderate to steep compressional folding; the Triassic rocks are tilted, warped, and block-faulted. The Appalachian foldbelt is overlain along its southern and southeastern flanks by platform deposits of the Gulf and Atlantic coastal plains. These platform deposits are composed of thick sequences of Jurassic, Cretaceous, and Cenozoic marine and non-marine sediments.

From south to north, the tide-gauge stations from Pensacola (Florida) to Sandy Hook (New Jersey), as well as those on Long Island and Cape Cod, are located on the coastal plain. Tide-gauge stations between, and including, New York and Halifax (Nova Scotia), and also Pointe-au-Père (Quebec), are in the Appalachian foldbelt. Newport and Providence (Rhode Island), Boston (Massachusetts), St. John (New Brunswick), and Charlottetown (Prince Edward Island) are in Carboniferous basins within the foldbelt. St. John's (Newfoundland) is on a terrane of Precambrian sedimentary and volcanic rocks, overlain by Cambrian and younger shallow-marine sediments (the Avalon terrane). Harrington Harbor (Quebec) is in the Canadian Shield, and the northernmost station, Churchill (Manitoba), is on Paleozoic and younger, relatively flat-lying, platform deposits overlying Precambrian basement (the Hudson Bay Platform).

Seismic data also can be used to interpret the variability in the rates of RSL movement along the coast. In areas of major earthquakes such as California and Japan, rapid horizontal and vertical crustal movements occur 10 to 20 yrs to a few hours prior to an earthquake and continue for as long as a few months after the earthquake (Scholz, 1972). Unfortunately, earthquakes and crustal displacements due to earthquakes are not as well understood in eastern North America (e.g., Kerr, 1981). Surface rupturing due to an earthquake has never been observed in this area, and leveling studies have not been made often enough to document movements due to specific earthquakes. Until recently, the density of seismograph stations in eastern North America has been low (spacing between stations is typically ~300 km), so earthquake epicenters could not be determined with much accuracy, and correlations between specific earthquakes and geologic or geophysical features have been difficult. Zones of seismic activity following geologic and geophysical trends, however, have been delineated in eastern North America (e.g., Woollard, 1958; Fletcher and others, 1978; Sykes, 1978). Although a comparison between seismicity and land displacements determined by leveling along the entire United States east coast showed a poor correlation (Brown, 1978), a correlation between anomalous RSL movement recorded by tide-gauge data and a zone of high seismic activity may be significant.

Starting at the southwestern end of the residual RSL curve (Fig. 5), residual rates of RSL rise equal to or greater than 1 mm/yr occur between Pensacola, Florida, and Kiptopeke Beach, Virginia, except at Cedar Key, Florida (residual rate = 0.8 mm/yr) and Wilmington, North Carolina (residual rate = 0.6 mm/yr). Assuming the coastal mean residual rate of ~1.0 mm/yr represents a eustatic signal or a margin-wide tectonic signal, these fluctuations about the mean indicate that all the stations are undergoing subsidence, except at Cedar Key and Wilmington, which are undergoing uplift. Analysis of leveling surveys perpendicular to the coasts shows generally consistent tilt downward toward the ocean along the Gulf and Atlantic coastal plains (Brown and Oliver, 1976). This oceanward increase in subsidence correlates in general with an oceanward increase in sediment thickness (Murray, 1961; Brown and others, 1972), although the tilt rates are too high to be explained by sediment compaction alone (Brown and Oliver, 1976). Nevertheless, if this tilt is real and not due to geodetic leveling error, it is consistent with most of the tide gauges along this coastline.

Analyses of leveling transects parallel to the coast, from Cedar Key, Florida, southward to Key West, Florida, and then northward to Charleston, South Carolina, yield results grossly inconsistent with tide-gauge data (Holdahl and Morrison, 1974; Brown, 1978). The sense of movement revealed by residual RSL rates, however, is in agreement with the sense of past movement revealed by basement structural features of the area. The tide gauge at Cedar Key, which shows a relative dip in the residual RSL curve (Fig. 5), is located just west of a basement structure known variously as the Central Georgia uplift, the Peninsular arch, and the Ocala uplift (Fig. 8). The Central Georgia uplift-Peninsular arch represents the late Paleozoic and Mesozoic axes of maximum upwarping; the Ocala uplift represents the center of Cenozoic unwarping, subparallel to and west of the Peninsular arch (Murray, 1961). Releveling data suggest this westward migration of the axis of maximum uplift in northern Florida continues today (Holdahl and Morrison, 1974; Brown and Oliver, 1976). This upwarping would explain the drop in the residual RSL curve at Cedar Key, relative to points north and south. The remaining stations in Florida, Georgia, and South Carolina are all located near or in structural lows. Pensacola is located west of the Southwest Georgia, or Apalachicola, embayment, a basin filled primarily with late Mesozoic and Cenozoic sediments (Murray, 1961). St. Petersburg, Key West, and Miami Beach are located in the South Florida basin, a post-Paleozoic northwest-southeast-trending basin that dominates the structure of peninsular Florida south of the Ocala uplift (Fig. 8). Mayport, Fernandina, Fort Pulaski, and Charleston are located in the Southeast Georgia, or Savannah, embay-

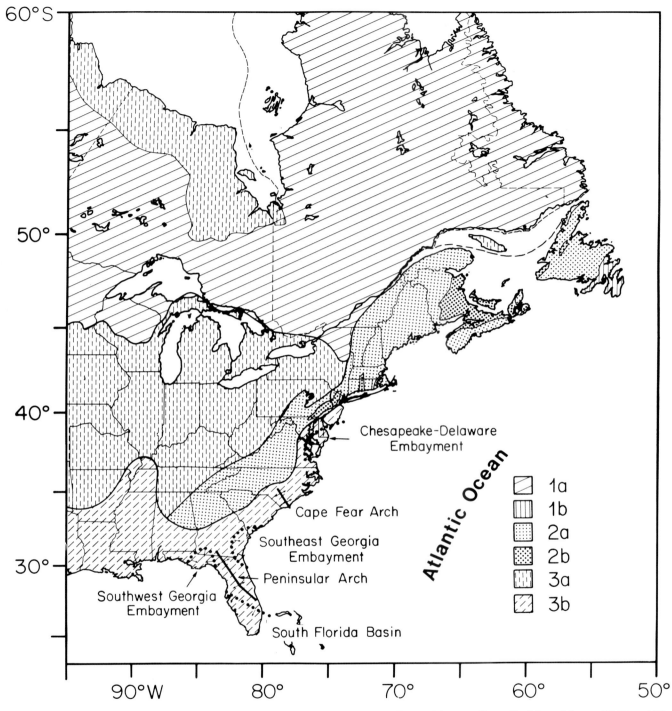

FIG. 8.—Tectonic map of eastern North America, provinces and structural features discussed in text. Generalized from Murray (1961) and King (1969, 1970). Key: (1) Precambrian rocks (metamorphic and plutonic): (a) Canadian Shield, (b) Avalon terrane; (2) Appalachian foldbelt: (a) geosynclinal deposits, (b) post-orogenic deposits (Carboniferous and Triassic); (3) Paleozoic and younger platform deposits: (a) on Precambrian basement (Interior and Hudson Bay Platforms), (b) on Paleozoic basement (Gulf and Atlantic coastal plains).

ment, an asymmetric shallow syncline north of the Ocala uplift (Fig. 8). Deformation of ancient shorelines across the Southeast Georgia basin suggests that warping of this area has continued through the Pleistocene (Winker and Howard, 1977).

Beneath these basement features in Florida are older lithotectonic units bounded by basement hinge zones and fracture zones, which resulted from early Mesozoic rifting of the North American from the South American/African plates. The basement hinge zone, which represents the block-faulted edge of the North American plate, separates Paleozoic and older crustal rocks to the northwest from Jurassic rifted crust beneath marginal basins to the southeast (Klitgord and others, 1984). This hinge zone intersects the west Florida coast at St. Petersburg. Key West and Miami are located in the Jurassic marginal rift basin to the southeast. Cutting across peninsular Florida, from southeast to northwest, is a broad Jurassic transform zone that intersects the west Florida coast at Cedar Key. The Southwest and Southeast Georgia embayments to the north both overlie Jurassic sedimentary basins and late Triassic rift zones. All tide-gauge stations in Florida, Georgia, and South Carolina that record residual rates of RSL rise higher than the coastal mean are in regions underlain by Jurassic rift basins.

Some subsidence at Fort Pulaski also may be due to groundwater withdrawal. Leveling around Savannah, 20 km west of Fort Pulaski, indicates the land within a 5-mi (8 km) radius of the city has subsided more than 20 mm between 1933 and 1955 (Davis and others, 1963). This subsidence has been due primarily to the decline in artesian pressure head which has resulted from groundwater withdrawal in the Savannah area (Davis and others, 1963). Groundwater withdrawal has been shown to cause substantial subsidence (tens to hundreds of millimeters) in many areas of the continental United States, but the effects are usually quite local (Chi and Reilinger, 1984). Subsidence around Savannah probably is due to compaction of the deposits comprising the artesian aquifer as well as underdrainage and compaction of the overlying confining unit (Davis and others, 1963). Fort Pulaski has undergone a concurrent decline in pressure head (20 ft or 6 m between 1935 and 1955, compared to 40 to 100 ft or 12 to 30 m around Savannah; Davis and others, 1963). Releveling between Savannah and Savannah Beach, along a line passing about 1.5 km south of the tide gauge at Fort Pulaski, indicates subsidence south of Fort Pulaski of ~10 mm between 1935 and 1955. This subsidence is local, however, affecting only about 11 km of the transect, which is on the opposite side of the Savannah River from the tide gauge.

At Charleston, South Carolina, the rate of residual RSL rise is 0.4 to 0.6 mm/yr higher than the residual rates at the other stations in the Southeast Georgia embayment. Mayport and Fernandina are located on the southwestern flank of the syncline, Charleston on the northeastern flank. Either the northeastern flank is subsiding faster than the southwestern, resulting in a higher residual RSL rate at Charleston than at the other stations in this basin, or local subsidence is occurring around Charleston. The first option is unlikely, since the southwestern flank is steeper and more pronounced than the northern and northeastern flanks (Murray, 1961). Charleston, however, is located in a region of high seismic activity relative to the rest of the southeastern United States (e.g., Bollinger, 1973). The Charleston earthquake of 1886 (magnitude ~7; Kerr, 1981) is one of the few major United States earthquakes to have occurred outside the Pacific coast region. During the last century, there have been two additional intervals of high seismicity (based on the number of earthquakes greater than magnitude 3): one between 1912 and 1917, and the other between 1958 and 1962 (Seeber and others, 1982). Many thrust and normal faults have been mapped in this area, but the fault or faults responsible for the earthquakes have not been identified, nor has fault displacement been measured (Bollinger, 1973; Kerr, 1981). Epicenters of the Charleston earthquakes lie along a zone extending from Charleston northwest into Tennessee (Bollinger, 1972, 1973). Perhaps the subsidence indicated by residual RSL movement at the Charleston tide gauge is due to vertical crustal movement associated with stress release along this zone.

At Wilmington, North Carolina a sizeable relative drop in the residual RSL curve (Fig. 5) indicates local uplift. Wilmington lies along the crest of the Cape Fear arch, a northwest-southeast trending basement ridge extending under the continental shelf and slope at the southeast end, and gradually surfacing near the western edge of the Atlantic coastal plain at the northwest end (Bonini, 1955; Murray, 1961). Leveling transects indicate present dome-like uplift of this structural high centered offshore (Brown and Oliver, 1976; Brown, 1978). Brown (1978) suggests the movement recorded here by the relevelings may be associated with a Triassic basin located seaward of the Cape, near the inferred center of uplift. The basin, a zone of weakness in the crust, could be responding to contemporary regional stress.

Residual rates of RSL movement at tide-gauge stations around Chesapeake Bay (Portsmouth, Virginia northward to Philadelphia, Pennsylvania) fluctuate about the coastal mean of 1.0 mm/yr. This entire region is deeply embayed, indicating long-term relative land subsidence and sea-level encroachment. The basement structure is dominated by the Chesapeake-Delaware embayment (Fig. 8), a major northwest-southeast-trending feature underlain by Triassic basins (Bayley and Muehlberger, 1968; Klitgord and Hutchinson, 1985). Geodetic leveling from Norfolk, Virginia (next to Portsmouth) to Philadelphia indicates a broad downwarping in the Chesapeake region relative to points to the north and south (Brown, 1978). This leveling transect crosses the Delmarva Peninsula, however, from Norfolk to the southern tip of the peninsula (Kiptopeke Beach), and then northward to Philadelphia, whereas all of the tide-gauge stations in this region, except Kiptopeke Beach and Lewes, are on the opposite (western) side of Chesapeake Bay. Residual rates of RSL movement at three stations located at the mouth of Chesapeake Bay (Portsmouth, Hampton Roads and Gloucester Point) suggest local subsidence, although not of the magnitude indicated by the leveling survey (residual RSL rates suggest subsidence of 0.2–0.7 mm/yr, whereas the leveling suggests relative subsidence of as much as 3 mm/yr across the Delmarva Peninsula). Residual rates of RSL movement at the other tide-gauge stations in this region (Kiptopeke Beach to Philadelphia) indicate no anomalous rates of subsidence; in fact, there may be some uplift occurring at Solomon's Island. While tide gauges along this section record some of the highest rates of RSL rise along the east coast of North America, this region is also the area of the highest present rates of isostatic forebulge relaxation (Fig. 5; Peltier, 1986). All RSL movement recorded by tide gauges between Kiptopeke Beach and Philadelphia (except at Solomon's Island) can be accounted for by isostatic relaxation and a hypothesized eustatic sea-level rise. These results indicate the large tilt rates of the Chesapeake Bay region recorded by leveling surveys are due primarily to high rates of isostatic adjustment, although the magnitude of movement indicated by the leveling is high compared with tide-gauge results.

The residual rate at Sandy Hook suggests local subsidence, in addition to isostatic adjustment and eustatic sea-level rise. Recent publications have stated that the Sandy Hook data are erroneous or unreliable due to localized subsidence (Hicks, 1972; Brown, 1978), although no evidence is given for these statements. Hicks (1972) states that Sandy Hook is a station of "independently known local subsidence" but gives no support for this statement. Citing Hicks (1972), Brown (1978) states that the Sandy Hook tide gauge is "unreliable" since it is "affected by very localized, nontectonic subsidence." Citing Minard (1969), Brown (1978) also suggests local groundwater withdrawal and rapid spit buildup nearby are probably responsible for subsidence at Sandy Hook. Although Minard (1969) states that the Sandy Hook quadrangle is a region of heavy industrial use of groundwater and is an active recurved spit, however, no mention is made of local subsidence. Heavy industrial use of groundwater in this region may be causing localized subsidence, although leveling surveys in areas of equivalent water withdrawal along the eastern United States coastline show no effects of fluid withdrawal except at Savannah, Georgia. The amount of sediment compaction and surface subsidence due to fluid withdrawal is difficult to predict. The location of the tide gauge at Sandy Hook, on the northwestern side of a spit composed primarily of fine-to-coarse sand with relatively thin layers of clay and clayey sand (Minard, 1969, see Geologic Map and Section), argues against land subsidence due to groundwater withdrawal.

Residual rates of RSL movement at tide-gauge stations from New York northward to Portsmouth, New Hampshire, are all lower than the coastal mean of 1.0 mm/yr, except for the rates at New York and Port Jefferson, which are both close to the coastal mean (1.1 and 1.2 mm/yr, respectively; Table 2, Fig. 5). These results indicate that isostatic adjustment, plus a eustatic sea-level rise, explain the RSL movement recorded by tide gauges at New York and Port Jefferson, whereas at Willets Point, Montauk, New London, Newport, Providence, Woods Hole, Buzzards Bay, Cape Cod Canal, Boston, and Portsmouth, crustal uplift, in addition to isostatic adjustment and eustatic sea-level rise, may be occurring.

The large discrepancy in the rates of residual RSL movement (1.1 mm/yr) between the two stations on Long Island (Port Jefferson and Montauk) is surprising, since both Montauk and Port Jefferson are underlain by Upper Cretaceous and Quaternary coastal plain deposits that show no evidence of deformation (Fisher and others, 1971). Residual rates suggest that except for postglacial adjustments, Port Jefferson is stable, while Montauk is undergoing uplift. High-resolution seismic reflection profiles across the New York Bight have delineated a north-northeast-trending fault (the New York Bight fault) which may continue northward underneath Long Island (Hutchinson and Grow, 1985). The fault runs along the western edge of a Mesozoic rift basin (the New York Bight basin) that was mapped using mag-

netic data (Klitgord and Hutchinson, 1985). This basin appears to continue northward across Long Island and Long Island Sound and to connect with the Hartford basin onshore.

Displacement along the New York Bight fault is down to the west. This sense of movement is consistent with the differential movement between Port Jefferson and Montauk, although evidence for Quaternary activity along the fault is ambiguous. An earthquake (magnitude ~2) was recorded near Port Jefferson during the period 1928–1959 (Smith, 1966), and there was another of about the same magnitude centered ~10 km to the west of the fault in the New York Bight in 1976 (Kafka and others, 1985). The trend of the fault and the basin, however, indicates that they would pass very close to Port Jefferson, so any vertical motion associated with these features would occur near Port Jefferson instead of near Montauk, as indicated by the rates of residual RSL rise at these two stations.

Residual RSL rates at the remaining stations between New York and Portsmouth are all below the coastal mean. Uplift recorded at Willets Point may be related to seismic activity which has been historically and instrumentally recorded in the greater New York city area (Smith, 1966; Kafka and others, 1985). If seismic activity is affecting RSL movement at Willets Point, however, it is not clear why the station at New York would not be affected as well, since both stations are located on the same geologic "province" of crystalline Paleozoic and Precambrian rocks known as the Manhattan Prong (Kafka and others, 1985).

Leveling transects between Willets Point and Portsmouth suggest a crustal tilt downward toward the northeast (Brown, 1978), as do RSL rates at the eastern end of this section of coastline (New London to Portsmouth). The strongest signature in the leveling transect is a sharp change in relative crustal movement as the leveling profile crosses the Hartford basin (Brown, 1978), a Triassic graben filled with sedimentary rocks dipping to the east. Leveling results indicate the same sense of movement. Historical and instrumentally recorded earthquakes have been reported in the vicinity of this graben, particularly along the eastern border fault (Yang and Aggarwal, 1981). Seismic activity also has been noted in southeastern Connecticut, attributed to strain release along the Honey Hill thrust fault, a northward-dipping zone of highly strained rock (Lundgren and Ebblin, 1972; Block and others, 1979). The sense of motion is southeastward thrusting of the northern blocks. Measurements of offsets along a single thrust plane suggest recently active faulting (Block and others, 1979). New London is located ~50 km east of the eastern (normal) border fault of the Hartford basin and ~15 km south of the Honey Hill thrust fault. Crustal movement due to strain release along these fault systems may be affecting RSL at New London.

A sharp drop in the residual rate at Buzzards Bay, Massachusetts (to −0.9 mm/yr) indicates an anomalous amount of uplift here relative to surrounding tide gauges (Fig. 5). This anomalous result is probably due to the short record length at this station (20 yrs of data, the minimum used in this study). Such a short record may not reflect all the time scales of RSL motion along the coastline, particularly the long period fluctuations indicated by spectral analysis (Fig.

7) to be an important part of the temporal structure of the data. Cape Cod Canal, however, located approximately 10 km northeast of the Buzzards Bay station, also has a very short, concurrent record (20 yrs). It is not clear why the rates of RSL movement at these two stations are so different. Tide-gauge records at both stations are smooth, with no extreme outliers. Unfortunately, no detailed analyses of leveling transects in this region exist.

Between Boston and Portland, residual rates of RSL rise increase from 0.7 mm/yr at Boston and Portsmouth to 1.5 mm/yr at Portland, suggesting crustal uplift at Boston and Portsmouth and crustal subsidence at Portland. Vertical motion at these stations may be associated with seismic activity. Boston and Portsmouth are located in a zone of seismic activity similar to that passing through Charleston, South Carolina. This seismic belt trends northwest from Boston and Portsmouth through Ottawa, Ontario (Sbar and Sykes, 1973), although seismic activity may not be continuous along this zone (e.g., Yang and Aggarwal, 1981). Relative crustal movement between Portsmouth and Portland is also apparent in leveling transects, although leveling suggests a higher differential. Leveling between Portsmouth and Portland in 1923 and 1966 shows Portsmouth rose relative to Portland at a rate of 1.1 mm/yr (Brown, 1978), whereas tide-gauge data suggest Portsmouth rose relative to Portland at a lower rate of 0.6 mm/yr.

Rates of RSL rise from Portland northeast to Halifax, Nova Scotia, are fairly constant between Portland and St. John (2.0–2.2 mm/yr), increasing at Halifax to 2.6 mm/yr (Table 2, Fig. 5). Residual rates of RSL rise at these stations reveal that isostatic adjustment and a eustatic sea-level rise, or coastal submergence, fully account for the RSL movement at Halifax, whereas between Portland and St. John, northeasterly decreasing amounts of subsidence are occurring, from 0.5 mm/yr at Portland to 0.2 mm/yr at St. John. Previous studies of sea-level trends in Maine have considered the rate of RSL rise in the northernmost Maine station of Eastport anomalously high (Hicks, 1972; Anderson and others, 1984). Regional trends of RSL along the northeast coast of North America, however, determined using the most recent tide-gauge data, demonstrate that the movement recorded at Eastport is not anomalously high but is consistent with data points to the north and south.

The fairly constant rates of RSL rise in Maine are not reflected in geodetic leveling studies, which indicate that northeastern Maine is subsiding relative to southern Maine (Brown, 1978; Tyler and Ladd, 1980; Anderson and others, 1984). Anderson and others (1984) state that releveling data show Eastport to be subsiding by as much as 9 mm/yr. This rate, however, taken from Tyler and Ladd (1980), is the rate of movement at Eastport relative to Calais (~40 km northwest of Eastport), and therefore cannot be interpreted as an absolute rate. Geodetic leveling between Portland and Eastport indicates Eastport subsided relative to Portland at a rate of 1.8 mm/yr between 1926 and 1966/67, and at a rate of 7.8 mm/yr between 1942 and 1966/67 (Brown, 1978). Levelings between Bangor (~65 km northwest of Bar Harbor) and Calais show Calais subsided with respect to Bangor at an average rate of 1 mm/yr between 1926 and 1966/67, and at 8 mm/yr between 1942

and 1966/67 (Brown, 1978). Anderson and others (1984) suggest that this increase in rate of crustal movement may be related to a post-1940 increase in New England seismic activity (Shakal and Toksoz, 1977).

Since no definitive evidence of Cenozoic faulting has been found in Maine, it is not possible to unravel the discrepancy between the leveling and the tide-gauge data. Both data sets, however, indicate crustal movement in Maine and New Brunswick, possibly due to reactivation of Triassic fault systems (apparent in the leveling transects across the Hartford basin). The Gulf of Maine and the Bay of Fundy are heavily dissected with Triassic horsts and grabens, similar tectonically to Triassic grabens on land (Ballard and Uchupi, 1975). *In situ* measurements of stress in this region suggest a greatest principal stress direction similar to that inferred from Triassic-Jurassic block faulting in the Gulf of Maine (Anderson and others, 1984). The coastline surrounding the Gulf of Maine and Bay of Fundy has been, and is, seismically active (Smith, 1966; Lepage and Johnson, 1983; Anderson and others, 1984). Stress release along these fault systems also may be causing crustal movement from Portland to New Brunswick.

The remaining tide-gauge station situated in the Appalachian foldbelt is Pointe-au-Père, Quebec. Disjointed, releveled segments from northern New Brunswick to Halifax indicate Pointe-au-Père is rising relative to St. John and Halifax (Vaníček, 1976; Grant, 1980; note that Vaníček has warped the releveled network to fit tide-gauge data). Broad intertidal platforms, however, cut into sedimentary rocks near Pointe-au-Père (Grant, 1980), indicate RSL has been static at this location for some time. Crustal deformation due to seismic activity may be occurring at Pointe-au-Père, an area with a high density of recorded earthquakes (Smith, 1966; York and Oliver, 1976). Historically, the most active seismic region in eastern Canada is centered ~150 km southwest of Pointe-au-Père (the Charlevoix region northeast of Quebec City). It is unlikely, however, that seismic activity has caused ~2.7 mm/yr of RSL rise over the past 64 yrs. Peltier's (1986) estimate of the current rate of isostatic adjustment for Pointe-au-Père (−2.2 mm/yr) seems excessive, particularly since the tide gauge and local geomorphology indicate high amounts of uplift have not been occurring here. Also, the residual rate at Pointe-au-Père (2.7 mm/yr) is higher than Peltier's estimate of isostatic adjustment. It is unlikely that non-isostatic crustal movement is occurring here at a rate which is greater than the amount attributable to isostatic adjustment, since Pointe-au-Père is located in the region once covered by Pleistocene ice sheets.

Rates of residual RSL movement at Charlottetown, Harrington Harbor, and St. John's fluctuate within 0.3 mm/yr of the coastal mean. Charlottetown is located in a post-orogenic (Carboniferous) basin in the Appalachian Province; Harrington Harbor is located on Precambrian infracrustal rocks of the Canadian Shield; and St. John's is located on the Avalon terrane (believed to be a separate crustal block from the rest of Newfoundland, unrelated to Appalachian tectonics; Keen and others, 1986). Residual rates of RSL rise suggest that, in addition to isostatic adjustment and a eustatic sea-level rise, Charlottetown and St. John's are undergoing slight subsidence, while Harrington Harbor is undergoing slight uplift. Unfortunately, geodetic leveling transects are sparse in Canada and systematic relevelings are sparser still (Lambert and Vaníček, 1979). Most analyses of relevelings in eastern Canada have warped the leveling data to fit tide-gauge trends (e.g., Vaníček, 1976), so the results cannot be used as an independent means to determine vertical crustal motion.

The residual rate of RSL rise at Churchill, located on the Hudson Bay Platform, suggests that in addition to glacio-isostatic adjustment and eustatic sea-level rise, crustal uplift of 7.8 mm/yr is occurring. As at Pointe-au-Père, this rate seems unreasonably high. Glacio-isostatic adjustment should be dominating any vertical crustal motion here. Churchill is located 500–1,000 km northwest of what has been the center of glacio-isostatic uplift in Canada over the past 7,000 yrs (Walcott, 1972b), and free-air gravity anomalies in this region are close to the largest in eastern Canada (~30–40 milligals over Churchill). These anomalies are probably due to incomplete recovery from ice-load depression (Walcott, 1970, 1972b), indicating that the area of largest overcompensation in Canada, and by inference, the area of highest isostatic adjustment, is located here.

Some of the discrepancy between tide-gauge results and Peltier's results at Churchill may be due to eigenanalysis. A comparison of the results of eigenanalysis and linear regression (Fig. 6) indicates a one-to-one correspondence does not exist at Churchill. The discrepancy is partly an artifact of eigenanalysis. Most (95%) of the stations with positive rates of RSL movement lie below the line of 1:1 correspondence on the scatter plot (Fig. 7); the one station with a high negative rate of RSL movement (Churchill) lies substantially above this line. The offset of these two data sets about the line of 1:1 correspondence indicates RSL movements recorded at Churchill are not coherent (in time) with the rest of the east coast data. A residual rate of RSL rise at Churchill, however, determined using linear regression (4.6 mm/yr), is still less than half of the estimate of isostatic adjustment (10 mm/yr). The average rate of RSL fall at Churchill over the past 2,000 yrs, determined from radiocarbon-dated organic materials (Walcott, 1972b), is the same rate as Peltier's (1986) estimate. RSL curves derived from both radiocarbon-dated materials and geophysical models, however, indicate the rates of glacio-isostatic adjustment have slowed with time. If tide-gauge data at Churchill are accurate, results indicate RSL fall has slowed here over the past 2,000 yrs, and Peltier's estimate of present glacio-isostatic adjustment is too large.

TEMPORAL FLUCTUATIONS

The first temporal eigenfunction (Fig. 3) documents the rate of RSL movement along the east coast of North America, changing from a shallow, decreasing trend (just barely significant) to a steeper, increasing trend. This change in rate is centered around 1934. Analysis of tide-gauge records of western North America revealed a similar change in slope of the first temporal eigenfunction, from a nearly flat trend before 1935, followed by an increasing trend (Emery and Aubrey, 1986b). Barnett's (1984) analysis of global tide-gauge data also showed an increase in rate of RSL rise centered around 1930. It is difficult to imagine

any geologic or tectonic processes that could explain this change in rate of RSL movement. Given the varied geologic structure of this coastline, it is difficult to conceive of any coherent tectonic movement that could cause this change in slope, although its occurrence in tide-gauge data from both coasts of North America suggests that isostatic adjustments may be involved since the effect of the Pleistocene ice sheets was continent-wide.

Oceanographic factors may also be involved in this change in slope. A reoccupation (1957, 1981) of two zonal North Atlantic oceanographic sections (24°30'N and 36°6'N) documented a significant warming of an ocean-wide band between 700- and 3,000-m depths (Roemmich and Wunsch, 1984). This warming resulted in a 2–3 cm steric expansion of the water column between 700 to 3,000 m. If this expansion were basin-wide, it would explain a large part of the RSL rise along the east coast of North America. Unfortunately, no similar reoccupations are available to determine if this steric expansion was global. The consistency of the mid-depth warming observed between 24° and 36°N, as well as its magnitude (roughly an order of magnitude greater than the perturbation of temperature profiles attributable to short time-scale eddies), suggest that the signal is not due to eddy noise. Moreover, the depth at which warming occurred implies local air-sea interactions were not important since the characteristics of mid-depth and deep waters are controlled by processes at middle and high latitudes.

To determine the time scale of the observed temperature changes at 24° and 36°N, Roemmich and Wunsch (1984) analyzed data from the Panulirus station (Bermuda, 32°N) for comparison. These data consist of temperature and salinity measurements taken twice monthly between 1954 and 1981, the longest continuous time series of hydrographic measurements available. Roemmich and Wunsch (1984) examined the depth change (with time) of the 4° C isotherm, because of its large observed displacement (100 m) between 1957 and 1981 at 24° and 36°N. The mean annual depths of the 4° C isotherm at the Panulirus station showed a clear trend, increasing approximately 100 m over the past 25 yrs, supporting their hypothesis that the data at 24° and 36°N are part of a long-term (in an oceanographic sense) warming in the oceans. In a later study, Roemmich (1985) showed the warming trend below 700 m at 24° and 36°N was also apparent at the Panulirus station (below 1,000 m) over the 22 yrs of record.

Based on the results of the reoccupation study, Roemmich and Wunsch (1984) suggested steric expansion of the oceans is responsible for some or all of the observed RSL rise occurring over the globe during the past century (Table 1). Another study, however, in which hydrographic data from various regions of the globe were analyzed, found no significant trends in dynamic height over the past century (Barnett, 1983). Only data from the upper ocean were examined, however, and the studies discussed previously (Roemmich and Wunsch, 1984; Roemmich, 1985) have shown that long-term steric changes in the ocean are not confined to the upper layers of the ocean. More long-term, shallow- to deep-water oceanographic data are clearly needed before a steric rise in sea level over the past century can be identified unambiguously.

Spectral analysis of the temporal eigenfunctions reveals significant energy at periods of about 6 and 20 yrs in the first function (which accounts for 69.6 percent of the sea-level variance) and at 3 yrs, and in a broad band between periods of 4 to 20 yrs in the second function (which accounts for 6.4 percent of the sea-level variance). The highest energy in the third function is in the lower frequencies, but there are no significant peaks. These periods are suggestive of oceanographic and atmospheric processes. Unfortunately, there are few long-term oceanographic time series that can be analyzed for dominant periodicities longer than 1 yr. A 9- to 10-yr periodicity is apparent (by visual inspection) in the 27 yrs of record of the mean annual depth of the 4° C isotherm at the Panulirus station (Roemmich and Wunsch, 1984), whereas 5-yr running mean averages of surface temperature at the Panulirus station between 1957 and 1967 display a 6-yr half-cycle of a 12-yr period (Pocklington, 1972). Both of these series are too short and too local to reach any significant conclusions. They do suggest, however, that more than one oceanographic process is responsible for the broad bands of energy in the 6- to 20-yr periodicities indicated by spectral analysis.

The high energy around a 20-yr periodicity may be a reflection of the 18.6 lunar nodal cycle (a wobble of the plane of the moon's orbit around the earth). This cycle has been shown to affect annual mean sea-level curves, although rather weakly (Kaye and Stuckey, 1973).

The shorter 3-yr periodicity in the spectrum of the first eigenfunction, significant at the 80% level, may be related to the Southern Oscillation. This alternation of regional pressure anomalies between the Indian and southeast Pacific oceans has a period of 2 to 3 yrs (Fairbridge and Krebs, 1962). Even though global mean annual sea-level oscillations have been correlated with the Southern Oscillation (Fairbridge and Krebs, 1962), however, teleconnections between the Pacific and the Atlantic oceans are not understood. This 3-yr periodicity has appeared in spectra of RSL movement (along both the east and west coasts of North America) that have been corrected for barometric pressure fluctuations (Vaníček, 1978), suggesting the 3-yr periodicity is due to some phenomenon other than the Southern Oscillation.

CONCLUSIONS

Eigenanalysis of tide-gauge data along the east coast of North America reveals a highly variable record of RSL change. The segmentation of this coastline observed by Aubrey and Emery (1983) is a result of more than isostatic and oceanographic factors. Estimates of RSL movement based on numerical models of postglacial isostatic adjustments indicate more than half of the variance of RSL movement determined from the eigenanalysis of the tide-gauge data is due to isostatic adjustment. The mean of the residual RSL movement along the entire coastline (tide-gauge rates minus isostatic adjustment rates), 1.0–1.5 mm/yr, may approximate the present eustatic sea-level rise. Leveling surveys, geologic structure, and seismic data indicate that much of the shorter wavelength features of RSL movement are due to various amounts of crustal movement. These results suggest that tide-gauge data, in addition to providing information on movements of the sea surface, also can be used as an indicator of neotectonic movements along the coastline.

Tide-gauge stations from Florida northward to New Jersey are located along the Gulf and Atlantic coastal plains, across which geodetic leveling surveys have shown a consistent tilt downward toward the ocean. This subsidence is reflected in all tide-gauge results from Pensacola to Gloucester Point, except at Cedar Key and Wilmington. Uplift is occurring at these two stations, both located in structural highs (the Pensacola arch and the Cape Fear arch, respectively). Pensacola, St. Petersburg, Key West, Miami Beach, Mayport, Fernandina, Fort Pulaski, and Charleston are all located in, or near, structural lows (the Southwest Georgia embayment, the South Florida basin and the Southeast Georgia embayment), and are underlain by Jurassic rift basins. Seismic activity may also be contributing to the subsidence recorded at Charleston. High rates of RSL rise recorded by tide gauges around Chesapeake Bay, as well as the high rates of crustal subsidence measured by leveling transects in this region, are primarily due to high rates of isostatic adjustment. Tectonic subsidence also appears to be occurring at the mouth of the bay.

The remaining stations, except Harrington Harbor and Churchill, are located in the northern Appalachian foldbelt. Residual rates of RSL movement at these stations suggest crustal movements here are associated with pre-existing faults and basins, particularly ones that were active during the Mesozoic. Seismic activity in New England demonstrates contemporary stress release, which may be related to crustal movement recorded by tide gauges. Different rates of RSL movement across Long Island (between Port Jefferson and Montauk) are probably due to movement associated with the New York Bight fault and basin (structures which appear to be related to the Hartford basin on land). Subsidence along the New York, Connecticut, and Rhode Island coasts may be related to movement along existing faults and the Hartford basin. A major seismic zone intersects the coast at Boston and Portsmouth (New Hampshire). Subsidence at these stations, as well as uplift to the north at Portland, may be related to this seismic activity. Subsidence at Pointe-au-Père, located in another zone of densely recorded earthquakes, may also be related to seismic activity. Subsidence around the Gulf of Maine and the Bay of Fundy (in Maine and the Maritime Provinces) may be associated with movement along Triassic horsts and grabens which dissect the offshore region. RSL movement at the remaining stations is dominated by isostatic adjustment; tide-gauge data suggest that estimates of current glacio-isostatic adjustment at Pointe-au-Père and Churchill (Peltier, 1986) are too high.

The temporal structure of the data shows that an increase in rate of RSL rise occurred along the east coast of North America centered near 1934. This increase may be due to a change in rate of isostatic adjustment over the continent, or steric expansion of the mid- to deep depths of the oceans. Further analysis, as well as more oceanographic data, are needed to evaluate these suggestions. Dominant periodicities of sea-level movement are indicative of oceanographic, atmospheric, and lunar cycles.

ACKNOWLEDGMENTS

This research was funded by the National Oceanic and Atmospheric Administration National Office of Sea Grant under Grant No. NA83-AA-D-0049, by the National Science Foundation under Grant No. OCE-8501174, and by the Woods Hole Oceanographic Institution's (W.H.O.I.) Coastal Research Center. Support for B. Braatz was supplied by the W.H.O.I. education program. We thank W. R. Peltier for supplying us with the isostatic adjustment data, and E. Uchupi and K. O. Emery for reviewing the manuscript.

REFERENCES

ANDERSON, W. A., KELLEY, J. T., THOMPSON, W. B., BORNS, H. W., JR., SANGER, D., SMITH, D. C., TYLER, D. A., ANDERSON, R. S., BRIDGES, A. E., CROSSEN, K. J., LADD, J. W., ANDERSEN, B. G., AND LEE, F. T., 1984, Crustal warping in coastal Maine: Geology, v. 12, p. 677–680.

AUBREY, D. G., 1985, Recent sea levels from tide gauges: Problems and prognosis, *in* Glaciers, Ice Sheets, and Sea Level: Effect of a CO_2-Induced Climatic Change: National Academy Press, Washington, D.C., p. 73–91.

———, AND EMERY, K. O., 1983, Eigenanalysis of recent United States sea levels: Continental Shelf Research, v. 2, p. 21–33.

———, AND ———, 1986, Relative sea levels of Japan from tide-gauge records: Geological Society of America Bulletin, v. 97, p. 194–205.

BALLARD, R. D., AND UCHUPI, E., 1975, Triassic rift structure in Gulf of Maine: American Association of Petroleum Geologist Bulletin, v. 59, no. 7, p. 1041–1072.

BARNETT, T. P., 1983, Recent changes in sea level and their possible causes: Climate Change, v. 5, p. 15–38.

———, 1984, The estimation of "global" sea level change: a problem of uniqueness: Journal of Geophysical Research, v. 89, p. 7980–7988.

BAYLEY, R. W., AND MUEHLBERGER, W. R., 1968, Basement Rock Map of the United States: U.S. Geological Survey, Washington, D.C.

BERGER, A., 1984, Book reviews of carbon dioxide and climate: a second assessment and the long-term impacts of increasing atmospheric carbon dioxide levels: Transactions, American Geophysical Union, EOS, v. 65, p. 53–54.

BLOCK, J. W., CLEMENT, R. C., LEW, L. R., AND DE BOER, J., 1979, Recent thrust faulting in southeastern Connecticut: Geology, v. 7, p. 79–82.

BLOOM, A. L., 1967, Pleistocene shorelines: a new test of isostasy: Geological Society of America Bulletin, v. 78, p. 1477–1494.

———, 1983, Sea level and coastal changes, *in* Wright, H. E., Jr., ed., Late-Quaternary Environments of the United States, The Holocene: University of Minnesota Press, Minneapolis, v. 2, p. 42–51.

BOLLINGER, G. A., 1972, Historical and recent seismic activity in South Carolina: Bulletin of Seismological Society of America, v. 62, p. 851–864.

———, 1973, Seismicity of the southeastern United States: Bulletin of the Seismological Society of America, v. 63, p. 1785–1808.

BONINI, W. E., 1955, Seismic-refraction studies of geologic structure in North Carolina and South Carolina (abs.): Geological Society of America Bulletin, v. 66, p. 1532–1533.

BROWN, L. D., 1978, Recent vertical crustal movement along the east coast of the United States: Tectonophysics, v. 44, p. 205–231.

———, AND OLIVER, J. E., 1976, Vertical crustal movement from leveling data and their relation to geologic structure in the eastern United States: Reviews of Geophysics and Space Physics, v. 14, p. 13–35.

BROWN, P. M., MILLER, J. A., AND SWAIN, F. M., 1972, Structural and stratigraphic framework, and spatial distribution of permeability of the Atlantic Coastal Plain, North Carolina to New York: U.S. Geological Survey Professional Paper 796, Washington, D.C., 79 p.

CHI, S. C., AND REILINGER, R. E., 1984, Geodetic evidence for subsidence due to groundwater withdrawal in many parts of the United States of America: Journal of Hydrology, v. 67, p. 155–182.

CLARK, J. A., FARRELL, W. E., AND PELTIER, W. R., 1978, Global changes in post-glacial sea level: A numerical calculation: Quaternary Research, v. 9, p. 265–287.

DAVIS, G. H., SMALL, J. B., AND COUNTS, H. B., 1963, Land subsidence related to decline of artesian pressure in the Ocala Limestone at Savannah, Georgia, *in* Trask, P. D., and Kiersch, G. A., eds., Engineering Geology Case Histories, no. 4: Geological Society of America, Boulder, p. 1–8.

EMERY, K. O., 1980, Relative sea levels from tide-gauge records: Proceedings of the National Academy of Science, v. 77, p. 6968–6972.

———, AND AUBREY, D. G., 1985, Glacial rebound and relative sea levels in Europe from tide-gauge records: Tectonophysics, v. 120, p. 239–255.

———, AND ———, 1986a, Relative sea-level changes from tide-gauge records of eastern Asia mainland: Marine Geology, v. 72, p. 33–45.

———, AND ———, 1986b, Relative sea-level change from tide-gauge records of western North America: Journal of Geophysical Research, v. 91, no. B14, p. 13,941–13,953.

FAIRBRIDGE, R. W., AND KREBS, O. A., JR., 1962, Sea level and the Southern Oscillation: Geophysical Journal of the Royal Astronomical Society, v. 6, p. 532–545.

FARRELL, W. E., AND CLARK, J. A., 1976, On postglacial sea level: Geophysical Journal of the Royal Astronomical Society, v. 46, p. 647–667.

FISHER, D. W., ISACHSEN, Y. W., AND RICKARD, L. V., 1971, Generalized tectonic-metamorphic map of New York: New York State Museum and Science Service, Map and Chart Series No. 15.

FLETCHER, J. B., SBAR, M. L., AND SYKES, L. R., 1978, Seismic trends and travel-time residuals in eastern North America and their tectonic implications: Geological Society of America Bulletin, v. 89, p. 1656–1676.

GORNITZ, V., LEBEDEFF, S., AND HANSEN, J., 1982, Global sea level trend in the past century: Science, v. 215, p. 1611–1614.

GRANT, D. R., 1980, Quaternary sea-level change in Atlantic Canada as an indication of crustal develeling, *in* Mörner, N.-A., ed., Earth Rheology, Isostasy, and Eustasy: John Wiley and Sons, Ltd., New York, p. 201–214.

GUTENBERG, B., 1941, Changes in sea level, postglacial uplift and mobility of the earth's interior: Geological Society of America Bulletin, v. 52, p. 721–772.

HICKS, S. D., 1972, Vertical crustal movements from sea level measurements along the east coast of the United States: Journal of Geophysical Research, v. 77, p. 5930–5934.

HOFFMAN, J. S., KEYES, D., AND TITUS, J. G., 1983, Projecting future sea level rise, methodology, estimates to the year 2100, and research needs: U.S. Environmental Protection Agency Report no. 230-09-007, 121 p.

HOLDAHL, S. R., AND MORRISON, N. L., 1974, Regional investigations of vertical crustal movements in the U.S., using precise relevelings and mareograph data: Tectonophysics, v. 23, p. 373–390.

HUTCHINSON, D. R., AND GROW, J. A., 1985, New York Bight fault: Geological Society of America Bulletin, v. 96, p. 975–989.

ISELIN, C.O'D., 1940, Preliminary report on long-period variations in the transport of the Gulf Stream System: Papers in Physical Oceanography and Meteorology, v. 8, no. 1, 40 p.

KAFKA, A. L., SCHLESINGER-MILLER, E. A., AND BARSTOW, N. L., 1985, Earthquake activity in the greater New York City area: magnitudes, seismicity, and geologic structures: Bulletin of the Seismological Society of America, v. 75, no. 5, p. 1285–1300.

KAYE, C. A., AND STUCKEY, G. W., 1973, Nodal tidal cycle of 18.6 yr: its importance in sea-level curves of the east coast of the United States and its value in explaining long-term sea-level changes: Geology, v. 1, p. 141–144.

KEEN, C. E., KEEN, M. J., NICHOLS, B., REID, I., STOCKMAL, G. S., COLMAN-SADD, S. P., O'BRIAN, S. J., MILLER, H., QUINLAN, G., WILLIAMS, H., AND WRIGHT, J., 1986, Deep seismic reflection profile across the northern Appalachians: Geology, v. 14, p. 141–145.

KERR, R. A., 1981, Assessing the risk of eastern U.S. earthquakes: Science, v. 214, p. 169–171.

KING, P. B., 1969, Tectonic map of North America: U.S. Geological Survey map, scale 1:5,000,000.

———, 1970, Tectonics and geophysics of North America, *in* Johnson, H., and Smith, B. L., eds., The megatectonics of continents and oceans, New Brunswick, Rutgers University Press, 282 p.

KLITGORD, K. D., AND HUTCHINSON, D. R., 1985, Distribution and geophysical signatures of early Mesozoic rift basins beneath the U.S. Atlantic continental margin, *in* Robinson, G. R., Jr., and Froelich, A. J., eds., Proceedings of the Second U.S. Geological Survey Workshop on the Early Mesozoic Basins of the Eastern United States: U.S. Geological Survey Circular 946, Chapter 9.

————, POPENOE, P., AND SCHOUTEN, H., 1984, Florida: a Jurassic transform plate boundary: Journal of Geophysical Research, v. 89, p. 7753–7772.

KONDRATYEV, K. YA., 1984, Book Review of Carbon Dioxide Review: 1982: Transactions, American Geophysical Union, EOS, v. 65, p. 382.

KUENEN, PH. H., 1950, Marine Geology: John Wiley & Sons, Inc., New York, 568 p.

LAMBERT, A., AND VANICEK, P., 1979, Contemporary crustal movements in Canada: Canadian Journal of Earth Science, v. 16, p. 647–668.

LEPAGE, C. A., AND JOHNSON, R. A., 1983, Earthquakes in Maine: October, 1975 to December, 1982: Maine Geological Survey Open-File Map 83-2.

LISITZIN, E., 1958, Le niveau moyen de la mer: Bulletin d'Information, Comité d'Oceanographie et d'Etudes des Cotes, v. 10, p. 254–262.

————, AND PATTULLO, J. G., 1961, The principal factors influencing the seasonal oscillation of sea level: Journal of Geophysical Research, v. 66, p. 845–852.

LUNDGREN, L., AND EBBLIN, C., 1972, Honey Hill fault in eastern Connecticut-regional relations: Geological Society of America Bulletin, v. 83, p. 2773–2794.

MEADE, R. H., AND EMERY, K. O., 1971, Sea level as affected by river runoff, eastern United States: Science, v. 173, p. 425–428.

MERCER, J. H., 1978, West Antarctic ice sheet and CO_2 greenhouse effect: A threat of disaster: Nature, v. 271, p. 321–325.

MINARD, J. P., 1969, Geology of the Sandy Hook quadrangle in Monmouth County, New Jersey: U.S. Geological Survey Bulletin, v. 1276, 43 p.

MURRAY, G. E., 1961, Geology of the Atlantic and Gulf Coastal Province of North America: Harper & Brothers, New York, 692 p.

NATIONAL RESEARCH COUNCIL, 1979, Carbon Dioxide and Climate: A Scientific Assessment: National Academy Press, Washington, D.C., 496 p.

NEWMAN, W. S., CINQUEMANI, L. J., PARDI, R. R., AND MARCUS, L. F., 1980, Holocene deleveling of the United States east coast, *in* Mörner, N.-A., ed., Earth Rheology, Isostasy, and Eustasy: John Wiley and Sons, Ltd., New York, p. 449–463.

NIILER, P. P., AND RICHARDSON, W. S., 1973, Seasonal variability of the Florida Current: Journal of Marine Research, v. 31, p. 144–167.

PATTULLO, J. G., 1960, Seasonal variation in sea level in the Pacific Ocean during the International Geophysical Year, 1957–1958: Journal of Marine Science, v. 18, p. 168–184.

PELTIER, W. R., 1984, The thickness of the continental lithosphere: Journal of Geophysical Research, v. 89, p. 11,303–11,316.

————, 1986, Deglaciation induced vertical motion of the North American continent: Journal of Geophysical Research, v. 91, p. 9099–9123.

————, AND ANDREWS, J. T., 1976, Glacial-isostatic adjustment—I. The forward problem: Geophysical Journal of the Royal Astronomical Society, v. 46, p. 605–646.

————, FARRELL, W. E., AND CLARK, J. A., 1978, Glacial isostasy and relative sea level: a global finite element model: Tectonophysics, v. 50, p. 81–110.

————, AND WU, P., 1982, Mantle phase transitions and the free air gravity anomalies over Fennoscandia and Laurentia: Geophysical Research Letters, v. 9, p. 731–734.

PERRY, A. M., 1983, Estimating the greenhouse effect: Transactions, American Geophysical Union, EOS, v. 222, p. 1072.

POCKLINGTON, R., 1972, Secular changes in the ocean off Bermuda: Journal of Geophysical Research, v. 77, p. 6604–6607.

QUINLAN, G., AND BEAUMONT, C., 1981, A comparison of observed and theoretical postglacial relative sea level in Atlantic Canada: Canadian Journal of Earth Science, v. 18, p. 1146–1163.

REVELLE, R. R., 1983, Probable future changes in sea level resulting from increased atmospheric carbon dioxide, *in* Changing Climate, Report of the Carbon Dioxide Assessment Committee: National Academy Press, Washington, D.C., p. 433–448.

ROEMMICH, D., 1985, Sea level and the thermal variability of the ocean, *in* Glaciers, Ice Sheets, and Sea Level: Effect of a CO_2-Induced Climatic Change: National Academy Press, Washington, D.C., p. 104–115.

————, AND WUNSCH, C., 1984, Apparent changes in the climatic state of the deep North Atlantic Ocean: Nature, v. 307, p. 447–450.

SBAR, M. L., AND SYKES, L. R., 1973, Contemporary compressive stress and seismicity in eastern North America: an example of intra-plate tectonics: Geological Society of America Bulletin, v. 84, p. 1861–1882.

SCHOLZ, C. H., 1972, Crustal movements in tectonic areas: Tectonophysics, v. 14, p. 201–217.

SEEBER, L., ARMBRUSTER, J. G., AND BOLLINGER, G. A., 1982, Large-scale patterns of seismicity before and after the 1886 South Carolina earthquake: Geology, v. 10, p. 382–386.

SHAKAL, A. F., AND TOKSOZ, M. N., 1977, Earthquake hazard in New England: Science, v. 195, p. 171–173.

SMITH, W. E. T., 1966, Earthquakes of eastern Canada and adjacent areas 1928–1959: Dominion Observatory Publications 32, Ottawa, Ontario, p. 87–121.

SYKES, L. R., 1978, Intraplate seismicity, reactivation of preexisting zones of weakness, alkaline magmatism, and other tectonism postdating continental fragmentation: Reviews of Geophysics and Space Physics, v. 16, p. 621–688.

THOMPSON, K. R., AND HAZEN, M. G., 1983, Interseasonal changes of wind stress and Ekman upwelling: North Atlantic, 1950–1980: Canadian Technical Report of Fisheries and Aquatic Science, no. 1214, 175 p.

THORARINSSON, S., 1940, Present glacier shrinkage and eustatic changes in sea level: Geografiska Annaler, v. 12, p. 131–159.

TYLER, D. A., AND LADD, J. W., 1980, Vertical crustal movement in Maine, *in* Thompson, W. B., ed., New England Seismotectonic Study Activities in Maine during Fiscal Year 1980: Maine Geological Survey Report to U.S. Nuclear Regulatory Commission, p. 99–153.

VANIÇEK, P., 1975, Vertical crustal movements in Nova Scotia as determined from scattered geodetic relevelings: Tectonophysics, v. 29, 183–189.

————, 1976, Pattern of recent vertical crustal movements in Maritime Canada: Canadian Journal of Earth Science, v. 13, p. 661–667.

————, 1978, To the problem of noise reduction in sea-level records used in vertical crustal movement detection: Physics of Earth and Planetary Interiors, v. 17, p. 265–280.

WALCOTT, R. I., 1970, Isostatic response to loading of the crust in Canada: Canadian Journal of Earth Science, v. 7, p. 716–727.

————, 1972a, Past sea levels, eustasy and deformation of the earth: Quaternary Research, v. 2, p. 1–14.

————, 1972b, Late Quaternary vertical movements in eastern North America: quantitative evidence of glacio-isostatic rebound: Reviews of Geophysics and Space Physics, v. 10, p. 849–884.

WINKER, C. D., AND HOWARD, J. D., 1977, Correlation of tectonically deformed shorelines on the southern Atlantic coastal plain: Geology, v. 5, p. 123–127.

WOOLLARD, G. P., 1958, Areas of tectonic activity in the United States as indicated by earthquake epicenters: Transactions, American Geophysical Union, EOS, v. 39, p. 1135–1150.

WU, P., AND PELTIER, W. R., 1983, Glacial isostatic adjustment and the free air gravity anomaly as a constraint on deep mantle viscosity: Geophysical Journal of the Royal Astronomical Society, v. 74, p. 377–449.

————, AND ————, 1984, Pleistocene deglaciation and the earth's rotation: a new analysis: Geophysical Journal of the Royal Astronomical Society, v. 76, p. 753–791.

WUNSCH, C., 1972, Bermuda sea level in relation to tides, weather, and baroclinic fluctuations: Reviews of Geophysics and Space Physics, v. 10, p. 1–49.

YANG, J.-P., AND AGGARWAL, Y. P., 1981, Seismotectonics of northeastern United States and adjacent Canada: Journal of Geophysical Research, v. 86, p. 4981–4998.

YORK, J. E., AND OLIVER, J. E., 1976, Cretaceous and Cenozoic faulting in eastern North America: Geological Society of America Bulletin, v. 87, p. 1105–1114.

PART II
PREDICTING SHORELINE RETREAT

CONTINENTAL SHELF EVOLUTION IN RESPONSE TO A RISE IN SEA LEVEL

CRAIG H. EVERTS

Moffatt & Nichol, Engineers, 250 W. Wardlow Road, Long Beach, California 90807

ABSTRACT: As the shoreface part of the inner continental shelf retreats, its trailing edge forms a new surface which becomes an extension of the ramp. Waves are primarily responsible for shaping the concave shoreface at the shallow, most landward part of the shelf. Shoreface retreat occurs because of sand losses and/or sea-level rise. The ramp, located seaward of the shoreface, is usually a planar feature with a seaward inclination. Its slope, γ, at the time it is formed is dependent upon the long-term average retreat rate of the shoreface, $\bar{s}$, and the long-term average rate of sea-level rise relative to the shoreface, $\bar{a}$. The shoreface and ramp usually join asymptotically between 1 and 5 km from shore. Retreat of the shoreface may occur without a significant change in shape. Shoreline retreat on the order of kilometers is almost always the response of the shoreface to a long-term rise in sea level.

Recent shoreline retreat rates measured over a short time period (10^1 to 10^2 yrs) can be compared to long-term average past rates (10^3 to 10^4 yrs) to forecast shoreline behavior in the future, unless sedimentation or tectonism altered the ramp slope formed in the past. The recent shore retreat rate, s_p, for a given recent sea-level rise rate, a_p, is compared to the present average slope of the ramp, γ_p, where γ_p is assumed equal to $\bar{a}/\bar{s} = \gamma$. If $\gamma_p >> a_p/s_p$, the present shore retreat rate is probably anomalously large compared to the long-term average rate for the reach of coast being considered. If $\gamma_p << a_p/s_p$, the present shore retreat rate is probably anomalously small compared to the long-term average rate for that reach. The future shore retreat rate, s_f, can consequently be expected to increase rather than decrease in a trend more consistent with $s_f = a_f/\gamma_p$. When the reason for present anomalous rates is established, a more definitive projection of the future rate can be made.

A test of the relationship of γ_p to a_p/s_p was made at five barrier island sites along the mid-Atlantic coast of the United States. At Smith and Assawoman Islands in Virginia, present shoreline retreat rates are similar to the long-term shoreline retreat rates of the past when referenced to the same relative sea-level rise rates. These islands are migrating landward (i.e., both ocean and lagoon shorelines are moving away from the ocean at about the same rate) as littoral sand is transported landward by overwash and tidal inlet processes. At Ocean City, Maryland; Sandbridge, Virginia, and a portion of the Outer Banks, North Carolina, the present shore retreat rate is anomalously low when compared to the present relative rate of sea-level rise. These islands are narrowing (i.e., ocean and lagoon shorelines are moving toward each other). When the islands reach a critical width (perhaps 350 m), island migration will begin and the ocean shore retreat rate will likely increase to five to eight times the present rate.

INTRODUCTION

The surface of the inner continental shelf is characterized by two first-order geometric features (Price, 1954). The shoreface is the concave-up and landward-steepening part closest to shore; the ramp is the seaward-dipping, relatively planar part adjacent to the shoreface. In plan, the ramp is usually the largest feature. It joins the shoreface asymptotically, generally at a depth of 5 to 20 m (Everts, 1978). One of the most diagnostic elements of the ramp surface is its slope (rise/run) normal to the shoreline.

This paper describes the mechanism by which the ramp surface is formed. A comparison of the slope of the ramp forming today with the average slope of the ramp formed in the past provides a clue to the causes and relative magnitude of past shoreline retreat rates and to trends in future shoreline behavior.

MECHANISM OF RAMP FORMATION

The ramp surface forms as the shoreface retreats. Smith Island, Virginia, a barrier island located immediately north of the entrance to Chesapeake Bay (Fig. 1), is one of the few areas where the historic shoreline retreat rate has been large enough and sufficient shallow-water bathymetric surveys have been made over a time period long enough (1852–1980) to illustrate the evolution of the ramp. Figure 2 shows the relationship between the movement of the shoreface (shoreline) and the landward elongation of the ramp at Smith Island. Profiles were obtained using bathymetric data from the archives of the National Oceanic and Atmospheric Administration. The following conclusions can be drawn from the data illustrated in the figure: (1) a new portion of the ramp formed at the trailing edge of the retreating shoreface. (2) The ramp which existed seaward of the shoreface prior to 1852 was extended landward about 700 m as a planar surface. (3) Shoreface shape remained constant, within survey tolerances, as the shoreface moved landward. This dynamic equilibrium of shoreface shape suggests waves and currents did not change greatly when averaged over 100 yrs. (4) Vertical changes in the pre-1852 ramp surface were minimal and within survey tolerances during the period the new ramp surface formed, indicating that shoreface retreat had little effect on the shape or slope of the pre-existing ramp. Sediments that eroded from behind the shoreface as it retreated were not deposited on either the newly formed ramp surface or the pre-existing ramp surface.

A ramp can form as either an erosional or depositional surface. Along a coast fronted by barrier islands, the shoreface is the seaward boundary of a relatively "recent" sediment deposit whose volume can either decrease, remain unchanged (Fig. 3), or increase as it migrates landward with sea-level rise. Ramp formation is considered to be (1) accompanied by deposition when recent sediments are deposited above pre-recent sediments as the shoreface retreats; (2) accompanied by erosion when the prerecent sediments are scoured as the shoreface retreats; or (3) accompanied by neither (Fig. 3) when deposition or scour is absent.

DETERMINATION OF RAMP SLOPE

The slope, γ of a ramp segment is the ratio of the height, $\bar{a}$, of sea-level rise on the shoreface and the length, $\bar{s}$, of shoreface retreat that accompanied formation of that segment (Fig. 3), or

$$\gamma = \frac{\bar{a}}{\bar{s}}. \tag{1}$$

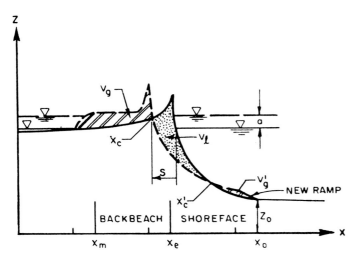

FIG. 4.—Changes that occur as a new ramp segment forms during a rise in sea level (slope of pre-existing ramp is less than slope of new ramp).

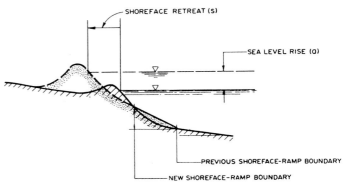

FIG. 5.—Ramp surface formed by deposition (slope of pre-existing ramp less than slope of new ramp).

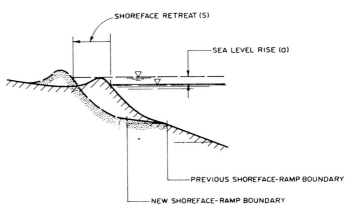

FIG. 6.—Ramp surface formed by erosion (slope of pre-existing ramp greater than slope of new ramp).

lagoon increases, i.e., deposition of fine-grained sediment in the lagoon does not keep up with sea-level rise.

The shape of the equilibrium shoreface profile must be considered when sediments that will not be stable on the shoreface are liberated as the shoreface retreats. When the value of k is less than 1, the scour region, V_1, must be treated separately (equation 3). Sediment deposited in the V_g and V_g' regions is assumed to be that which would be stable on the shoreface, usually of sand size or greater.

Slope of new ramp segment.—

The newly created ramp segment, $j(x)$, left behind as the shoreface profile retreats (equation 3), is expressed

$$j(x) = \frac{a}{s}(x - x_o) + z_o \qquad (4)$$

in which z_o equals elevation of the shoreface/ramp intersection above zero reference (Fig. 4). This new ramp segment of slope, a/s, will be a seaward-dipping straight line as long as the sea-level rise rate and rate of sand loss or gain, V_o, remain reasonably constant.

Type of new ramp surface.—

When the slope of the new ramp surface, $\gamma_n = a/s$, is greater than the seaward, adjacent, pre-existing ramp slope, γ, deposition will produce the profile between x_o and $x_o + s$ (shore retreat) as shown in Figure 5. This could occur because of either an increase in the sea-level rise rate, a decrease in the V_o loss rate, or both. Material is required at the base of the shoreface to maintain a profile in equilibrium with the sea surface. Since the shoreface steepens in a landward direction, the required volume of sediment, V_g', will generally be small compared to V_g. When a/s is less than the preexisting ramp slope, erosion will produce the new ramp profile shown in Figure 6.

EXAMPLES OF RAMP SEGMENTS FORMING TODAY

Five examples illustrate the relative importance of present processes involved in the formation of new ramp segments. All are located adjacent to mid-Atlantic barrier islands (Fig. 1). At each site, equation 3 was solved by trial and error for shoreline change as a function of V_o, k, a, and the average shape of the shoreface profile $f(x)$. Integrations were made by approximation using the trapezoidal rule. A more complete discussion of the calculation procedure and assumptions is given by Everts (1985a).

Ocean City, Maryland.—

This 14-km-long, highly developed portion of a barrier island (Fig. 7) is located north of Ocean City inlet (Fig. 1). Island width exceeds 0.75 km in most places. Because of its developed nature, eolian sand transport and ephemeral inlet openings and closings are not factors in sediment transport away from the shoreface. The small quantity of sediment recently transported by overwash was returned to the beach. The major loss of sand between 1930 and 1980 was caused by alongshore transport to Ocean City inlet. Perhaps 20,000 m³/yr were also lost at the base of the shoreface (Everts, 1985b); this quantity produced elongation of shore-connected linear shoals as the shoreface retreated. Since 1930, about 1 million m³ of sand have been artificially placed on the beach. Sand constitutes about 75% of the sediment landward and above the base of the shoreface at a depth, z_o, of -8.5 m. The remainder is mud- and silt-size material that would not be stable on the shoreface. The rate of sea-level rise at Ocean City has averaged 3.6 mm/yr since 1930 (Hicks and others, 1983).

Shoreline retreat, when averaged for the entire reach, was about 1.2 m/yr. About 80% of that retreat can be accounted for by sand losses; about 20% of the retreat was the result of relative sea-level rise. The effect of a on s was obtained using equation 3 with $V_o = 0$; the effect of V_o on s was calculated using $a = 0$; all other parameters remained unchanged. If the shoreface was backed entirely by sand, the calculated shoreline retreat would have been about 20% less. The slope of the newly formed ramp is 0.003.

Assawoman Island, Virginia.—

This narrow, undeveloped, low-lying, 5-km-long barrier island (Fig. 8) is located 60 km north of the Chesapeake Bay entrance (Fig. 1). A 2-km-wide marsh backs the northern half of the island, and shallow Kegotank Bay lies landward of the southern half. Sediments behind the shoreface contain approximately 25% sand-size components (unpub-

lished vibracore data, Finkelstein, 1983, pers. commun.), with most of the remainder being in the silt-size ($k = 0.25$) range. Thickness of the surface sand layer on the shoreface at depths below about -3 m is 0.3 m or less. At $z_o = -8.5$ m, the base of the shoreface, the sand thickness above silty lagoonal sediments, was only about 6 mm in 1980, based on short cores collected by divers. Hardly any sand-size material apparently passes seaward of this depth.

Longshore sediment transport from north to south is the main transport process that affects V_o seaward of the shoreline. In 1860, the development of Fishing Point 15 km north of Assawoman Island interrupted the supply of sediment to the south. Since that time, islands to the south have been rapidly retreating toward the mainland. At about the same time, Fishermans Island, at the south end of the system, began expanding at a rate of about 200,000 m³/yr. When the loss of this volume of sand is applied uniformly to all islands in the system south of Fishing Point except at inlet reaches, the longshore loss rate becomes approximately -2.5 m³/m/yr. Sand losses to inlets are assumed to be zero, because the sounds appear to be expanding rather than filling. Overwash is also a major factor in sand losses from the shoreface.

Fig. 7.—Ocean City, Maryland, view to the southwest in 1980.

FIG. 8.—Marsh deposits composed mainly of silt on the beach at Assawoman Island, Virginia.

Sea-level rise relative to the shoreface has been 2.8 mm/yr for the past 60 yrs, based on tide data obtained at Hampton, Virginia (Hicks and others, 1983) and adjusted National Geodetic Survey relevelings near Assawoman Island (Holdahl and Morrison, 1974). The shoreline has been retreating at a relatively constant rate of 4.3 m/yr for the past 130 yrs, as indicated by a comparison of historic United States Coast and Geodetic T-sheets. Calculations using equation 3 suggest that (1) sea-level rise accounts for about 60% of the retreat, (2) sand losses by longshore transport account for about 30%, and (3) overwash losses produce approximately 10% of the retreat. Overwash and the creation of ephemeral inlets maintain an island that averages 350 m wide as it migrates to the west (Fig. 8). Since 1850, about 560 m of new ramp have been formed with a slope of 0.00065.

Smith Island, Virginia.—

Smith Island is a low, narrow, 11.5-km-long barrier island located just north of the Chesapeake Bay entrance (Fig. 1). It is a part of the same undeveloped barrier island chain that includes Assawoman Island. Sand is lost from the shoreface to a depth of −7 m by two transport processes.

About 29,000 m³/yr (2.5 m³/m/yr) are lost by longshore transport. An additional 6,000 m³/yr are moved landward by ephemeral inlet and overwash processes (Fig. 9). This volume maintains the central 60% of the island width at about 350 m. Smith Island has been the site of an anomalously low relative sea-level rise in the last 60 yrs. Based on adjusted relevelings and tidal records in the vicinity of the entrance to Chesapeake Bay, Holdahl and Morrison (1974) report the vertical velocity of sea level relative to the island at +2.2 mm/yr. A k value of 0.36 is used based on an analysis of 23 sediment samples extracted from shoreface cores taken by divers (Everts, 1985a).

Shoreline retreat has averaged 5.6 m/yr since at least 1852. Sea-level rise accounts for approximately 50% of the total shore retreat; net sand losses account for the remainder. Net shoreline retreat would be about 1.3 m/yr if all the sediment behind the shoreface were of a size that would be stable on the shoreface. The new ramp formed since 1852 (Fig. 2) has an average slope of 0.0004.

Sandbridge, Virginia.—

This 7.3-km-long developed reach of Currituck Spit is located about 15 km south of the entrance to Chesapeake

FIG. 9.—Ephemeral inlet in 1980 near the center of Smith Island, Virginia.

Bay (Fig. 1). Its width is variable but averages about 0.75 km. A 5-m-high foredune prevents overwash in most places.

Most sand is lost by longshore transport to the north from a divergent nodal reach located near the south end of the Sandbridge reach (Everts, 1984). Net longshore losses are about 160,000 m³/yr. Sand transport landward by overwash and ephemeral inlet formation during storms is small, and losses or gains of sand at the base of the shoreface (depth about −9.5 m and 1,325 m from shore) are assumed negligible. Material landward of the shoreface is almost all sand that would be stable on the shoreface. The k value is taken as unity. Sea-level rise relative to the shoreface is 3.5 mm/yr.

Shoreline retreat since about 1920 has been 1.9 m/yr when averaged over the entire reach. The rate decreases from south to north away from the divergent nodal reach. Sea-level rise accounts for about 20% of the shoreface retreat; approximately 80% is the result of longshore transport losses. An average of about 250 m of new ramp with a slope of 0.0019 has formed off Sandbridge in the last 130 yrs.

Outer Banks of North Carolina.—

This 75-km-long ocean reach extends from Oregon Inlet, North Carolina to Cape Hatteras, North Carolina (Fig. 1).

The barrier island, which averages 1 km in width, is fronted along most of its length by a 5- to 6-m-high dune which has prevented overwash in recent times.

A k value of 0.75 is assumed from recent work north of Oregon Inlet (Riggs, pers. commun., 1983). Riggs estimated that about 50% of the Outer Banks has been cut by inlets in the past 6,000 yrs. Filled inlet channels typically contain 100% sand. Riggs also estimated that sand comprises 50% of the shoreface sediments along the remainder of the reach.

Longshore sediment transport losses at Oregon Inlet and Cape Hatteras appear to be the only significant factor in the V_o term. By balancing the volume of littoral sediments lost from adjacent reaches and the volume gained in the migrating flood-tidal shoals of the inlet, Everts and others, (1983) concluded that very little sediment bypasses the inlet. Even though the net transport is to the south, about 150,000 m³/yr enters from beaches south of the inlet during periods when transport is to the north. The region north of Cape Hatteras is retreating in a way that suggests transport is southward at a rate of 110,000 m³/yr. This loss varies with distance from the Cape. Combined with the losses at Oregon Inlet, the average net loss from the reach was −2.6 m³/m/yr.

The rate of shoreline change is −1.4 m/yr. The effect of relative sea-level rise (3.6 mm/yr) accounts for about 90% of the shore retreat (Everts, 1985a). Alongshore losses to Oregon Inlet and Cape Hatteras account for the rest. The slope of the 220-m-wide ramp developed between 1850 and 1980 was 0.0025.

DISCUSSION

The present first-order slope of any ramp surface is produced by one or more of three factors: (1) the initial slope created by the retreat of the shoreface, (2) possible post-formation crustal deformation, and (3) possible post-formation changes in surface morphology resulting from the addition, removal, or redistribution of sediment on the ramp.

Sediment can be added or removed from the ramp surface in a number of ways. If $k < 1$ (equation 2), some or all of the silt- and mud-size material liberated during shoreface retreat may be carried seaward and deposited on the ramp; some may be carried through inlets into lagoons. Sediments that can be stable on the shoreface may also be carried to the ramp after it forms. Currents directed offshore, for example, can play a significant role in moving sand seaward in some areas. Nevertheless, most post-formation changes in surface morphology, with or without an addition of sediment, produce second-order features, such as sand ridges, with wave lengths considerably smaller than the 10- to 200-km total width of the ramp. For this reason, they probably have a negligible effect on modifying the ramp slope.

Post-formation changes in ramp slope caused by crustal deformation, however, can be significant. For the United States Atlantic coast, Heller and others (1982) note that post-deformation slope changes are probably small, compared to the γ produced as a result of shore retreat in the past 10^4 yrs, and that shore-normal subsidence on the passive Atlantic margin is generally decreasing. They suggest that cooling and thickening of the lithosphere are the primary subsidence mechanism. Conversely, Clark (1981) argues for long-term alongshore deformation, which is supported by recent variations in relative sea level obtained from tide records (Hicks and others, 1983). Changes in γ caused by crustal deformation are assumed equal to zero in the following discussion.

Everts (1978) found that the ramp surface to 30.5 km from shore off the United States Atlantic coast is best depicted by a single sloping straight line, although the slope at different locations varies considerably. This shape suggests that the relationship between γ and $\bar{a}/\bar{s}$ represents the long-term average condition of shore retreat at a site in response to a rise in sea level. The ramp slope averages 0.00041 with a range of 0.0000 to 0.00098. If large, long-term fluctuations in $\bar{a}/\bar{s}$ had occurred, the ramp would have developed other shapes. A step would have formed if the rise in sea level had been anomalously large with respect to shoreline retreat. A step does not form during a sea-level still-stand. A jagged ramp profile would have formed as a result of alternating periods of high rates of sea-level rise and low rates of shore retreat (high-gradient slope) on one hand, and stillstands or low rates of sea-level rise accompanied by moderate to high rates of shoreface retreat (low-gradient ramp slope) on the other. Neither sea-level stillstand without shoreline retreat, nor a sea-level decline accompanied by a progradation of the shore can be inferred from the slope of the ramp surface. A concave-up ramp forms when the $\bar{a}/\bar{s}$ ratio is progressively increasing. A convex-up ramp forms when the sea-level rise rate drops and the sand loss rate remains constant.

Present shore retreat rates measured over a short-time period (10^1 to 10^2 yrs), when compared with long-term average past rates (10^3 to 10^4 yrs), provide a means to estimate shore retreat trends in the future. If $\gamma_p >> a_p/s_p$, the present shore retreat rate is probably anomalously large with respect to the long-term average rate for the reach of coast being considered, if γ_p is assumed equal to $\bar{a}/\bar{s}$. If $\gamma_p << a_p/s_p$, the present shore retreat rate is probably anomalously small with respect to the long-term average rate for that reach. The future shore retreat rate, s_f, can be expected to increase rather than decrease in a trend more consistent with $s_f = a_f/\gamma_p$, where the subscript f denotes future conditions.

A comparison of the relationship of γ_p to a_p/s_p was made at the five barrier island sites (Table 1). At Smith and Assawoman Islands, Virginia, present shoreline retreat rates are similar to long-term rates when referenced to sea-level rise rates. These islands are presently migrating landward (i.e., ocean and lagoon shorelines are both moving away from the ocean at about the same rate) as much littoral sand is transported landward by overwash and tidal inlet processes. At Ocean City, Maryland; Sandbridge, Virginia, and a portion of the Outer Banks, North Carolina, the present shore retreat rate is anomalously low with respect to the present relative rate of sea-level rise. These islands are narrowing (i.e., ocean and lagoon shorelines are moving toward each other). When the islands reach a critical width (perhaps 350 m), island migration will begin and the ocean shore retreat rate will likely increase to five to eight times the present rate.

Note that the first-order ramp slope, γ_p, is similar at all sites (Table 1) except at Sandbridge, Virginia, where the slope is influenced by processes at the entrance to Chesapeake Bay. The ramps at all five sites appear to have been formed primarily by island migration; island narrowing, such as is presently occurring at three of the five sites, is probably not a common condition during a period of ramp formation.

TABLE 1.—SUMMARY OF RAMP DATA FOR FIVE MID-ATLANTIC COASTAL SITES (FIG. 1)

Location	Recent Shoreface Retreat Rate, S_p, m/yr	Recent Relative Sea-Level Rise Rate, a_p, mm/yr	a_p/s_p	γ_p
Ocean City, Maryland	1.2	3.6	0.00300	0.00045
Assawoman Island, Virginia	4.3	2.8	0.00065	0.00049
Smith Island, Virginia	5.6	2.2	0.00040	0.00051
Sandbridge, Virginia	1.9	3.5	0.00200	0.00026
Outer Banks, North Carolina	1.4	3.6	0.00250	0.00050

CONCLUSIONS

General

The ramp portion of the continental shelf forms as the shoreface retreats. This process usually occurs during a period of relative sea-level rise. The slope of a newly formed ramp segment is the ratio of sea-level rise, a, to shoreline retreat, s. The ramp forms by deposition if the slope is greater than the slope of the seaward-adjacent ramp slope, and by erosion if the seaward-adjacent ramp slope is greater.

Assessment of Present Conditions

(1) Present shoreline retreat rates at Assawoman Island and Smith Island are large compared to the other three sites, because the islands are migrating and the portions of sediment that are both stable on the shoreface and contributed by shoreface erosion are small.

(2) At Ocean City, Sandbridge, and the Outer Banks, the portion of sandy sediments landward of the shoreface is large. At those sites, the rate of shore retreat is anomalously low compared to past rates because the islands are presently narrowing.

(3) That portion of the present rate of shoreline retreat caused by sea-level rise at Ocean City and Sandbridge is small (about 20%), because sand losses from the shoreface, V_o, by alongshore transport are large. Conversely, at the Outer Banks, where sand losses are relatively small, the effect of sea-level rise is presently accounting for almost 90% of the shoreface retreat rate. At Assawoman Island and Smith Island, sea-level rise is responsible for slightly over half the shoreline retreat.

(4) At Assawoman and Smith Islands, the present ratio of sea-level rise to shore retreat is similar to that which occurred over a long time period in the past (when crustal deformation following ramp formation is assumed negligible). The ramp formed mainly when the barrier islands were migrating toward the mainland as they are today. In the past, as today, these islands were probably backed by lagoonal muds and silts rather than sand. The sand loss rate apparently increases as the sea-level rise rate increases, i.e., the a/s ratio remains constant when the rate of sea-level rise increases. The sand loss increase can reasonably be expected to result from increased overwash and inlet transport from the shoreface to the lagoon.

Prediction of Future Shoreline Retreat

(1) If the present narrowing rate continues at Ocean City, Sandbridge, and the Outer Banks, and no measures are taken to mitigate it, the islands will reach a critical average width of perhaps 350 m in about 200 yrs. At that time, island migration will commence, driven by overwash and inlet transport processes. Ocean shoreline retreat rates will then probably increase to from five to eight times the present rate. Human intervention in the form of artificial dunes constructed of local beach sand would initially maintain the present rate, but the islands would continue to narrow without replenishment sand from outside the island-shoreface system. In time (perhaps an additional 100 yrs), the islands could cease to exist, i.e., they could drown in place.

(2) Predictions of the rate of shoreline retreat for the future and hindcasts of shoreline retreat rates in the past can be made using the ramp slope relationship, $\gamma = \bar{a}/\bar{s}$, when postformation crustal deformation is assumed to be equal to zero and the ramp is assumed to be formed by shoreface migration.

ACKNOWLEDGMENTS

Moffatt & Nichol, Engineers, provided time and resources to complete this study. Boat sheets to test the equilibrium profile assumptions were provided by the National Ocean Service, National Oceanic and Atmospheric Administration. Andrew Gram of Moffatt & Nichol, Engineers, developed a computer code to solve equation 3. Field data at Assawoman Island were collected while the author was employed at the Coastal Engineering Research Center, Fort Belvoir, Virginia. Kathryn Everts edited the manuscript.

REFERENCES

BRUUN, P., 1962, Sea Level Rise as a Cause of Shore Erosion: American Society of Civil Engineers, Proceedings, Journal of the Waterways and Harbors Division, v. 88, p. 117–130.

———, 1983, Review of conditions for uses of the Bruun Rule of erosion; Coastal Engineering, v. 7, p. 77–89.

CLARK, J. A., 1981, Comment and reply on Late Wisconsin and Holocene tectonic stability of the United States mid-Atlantic coastal region: Geology, v. 9, p. 438.

EVERTS, C. H., 1978, Geometry of Profiles Across Some Inner-Continental Shelves of the United States: TP 78-4, U.S. Army Corps of Engineers, Coastal Engineering Research Center, Fort Belvoir, Virginia, 92 p.

———, 1984, Yearly Maintenance Requirements for Fill Material at Sandbridge, Virginia: unpublished report prepared for Norfolk District, Corps of Engineers, 19 p.

———, 1985a, Sea Level Rise Effects on Shoreline Position; American Society of Civil Engineers, Journal of Waterways, Port, Coastal and Ocean Engineering Division, v. 111, no. 6, p. 985–999.

———, 1985b, Effect of Sea Level Rise and Net Sand Volume Change on Shoreline Position at Ocean City, Maryland; unpublished draft report prepared for the Environmental Protection Agency, 41 p.

———, BATTLEY, J. P., AND GIBSON, P. N., 1983, Shoreline Movements, Cape Henry, Virginia, to Cape Hatteras, North Carolina, 1849–1980; Technical Report, CERC-83-1, U.S. Army Corps of Engineers Waterways Experiment Station, Vicksburg, Mississippi, 111 p.

HELLER, P. L., WENTWORTH, C. M., AND POAG, C. W., 1982, Episodic postrift subsidence of the United States Atlantic continental margin; Geological Society of America Bulletin, v. 93, p. 379–390.

HICKS, S. D., DEBAUGH, H. A., JR., AND HICKMAN, L. H., JR., 1983, Sea Level Variations for United States, 1855–1980, U.S. Department of Commerce, National Ocean Service, National Oceanic and Atmospheric Administration, Rockville, Maryland, 170 p.

HOLDAHL, S. R., AND MORRISON, N. L., 1974, Regional investigations of vertical crustal movements in the U.S. using precise relevelings and mareograph data: Tectonophysics, v. 33, p. 373–390.

PRICE, W. A., 1954, Correlation of shoreline type with offshore condition in the Gulf of Mexico: Proceedings of Second Coastal Geography Conference, National Academy of Sciences, National Research Council, p. 11–30.

AN ANALYSIS OF COASTAL RECESSION MODELS: NORTH CAROLINA COAST

ORRIN H. PILKEY AND THOMAS W. DAVIS

Department of Geology and Marine Laboratory, Duke University, Durham, North Carolina 27708

ABSTRACT: Using the North Carolina barrier island shoreline as the test area, a variety of simple geometric recession models has been applied to predict shoreline erosion rates for various sea-level rise scenarios. All sea-level rise scenarios assume no acceleration in rate of rise. South of Cape Lookout, the Bruun Rule, Generalized Bruun Rule and the slope of the migration surface all lead to similar recession predictions. North of Cape Lookout, the slope of the migration surface predicts a much greater recession than Bruun-related models. This suggests the possibility that the islands are in an "out-of-equilibrium position" with respect to present sea level. If this is the case, the possibility exists that very rapid migration of the northern islands will soon occur.

The assumptions used in the present mathematical models depicting shoreline retreat are generally weak. Better models are needed, especially for shorelines where recession is part of the barrier island migration process. The large number of types of islands in a wide variety of geologic and oceanographic settings makes a universally applicable model difficult, if not impossible, to formulate.

INTRODUCTION

The response of the open-ocean sandy shoreline to a rising sea level is one of the most important applied problems facing coastal geologists today. Predictions of greenhouse-related sea-level rise vary considerably, but all agree that acceleration is likely. The Environmental Protection Agency projects that future sea-level rise on a world-wide basis will range from 0.52 to 3.45 m by 2100 A.D. (Hoffman and others, 1983). The Committee of the National Research Council on Carbon Dioxide Assessment suggests a rate of 0.70 m/century by the year 2100 (Revelle, 1983). Discussions of sea-level rise and related phenomena are presented by several authors in this volume (e.g., Braatz and Aubrey, Gornitz and Lebedeff, and Komar and Enfield) and will not be addressed here.

The purpose of this paper is to test several shoreline recession models by applying them to the entire open-ocean North Carolina barrier island coast. The models applied include the Bruun Rule (Bruun, 1962), the Edelman rule (Edelman, 1968, 1970) and the Generalized Bruun Rule (Dean and Maurmeyer, 1983). In addition, rates of shoreline movement due to a sea-level rise are predicted on the basis of slope of the ravinement surface or barrier island migration surface (Swift, 1976a,b). Finally, present erosion rates (Kochel and others, 1983; Benton, 1983) are extrapolated.

The Bruun, Edelman and Modified Bruun rules are briefly outlined below. For more detailed discussions of these models, the reader is referred to the original papers and to Dean and Maurmeyer (1983).

The Bruun Rule (Bruun, 1962) is the basis for all other erosion models that are presently used. It is still the most widely used and recognized method of calculating shoreline change. Bruun maintained that the shoreface profile reacts to a sea-level rise by simply retreating landward and upward such that the profile remains constant relative to sea level down to the depth of effective wave motion. This depth is assumed to be 10 m for the purposes of this study. The active profile in Bruun's equation essentially corresponds to the shoreface. The Bruun Rule is stated as:

$$R = \frac{L}{(B + h)} S = \frac{1}{\tan \theta} S \qquad (1)$$

where R = recession due to sea-level rise; S = sea-level rise; B = berm height; θ = active profile slope; h = depth of active profile base; and L = width of active profile.

It is assumed that there is no net loss of sediment due to longshore transport, and that the amount of sand eroded from the subaerial portion of the profile will roughly equal the volume deposited on the lower shoreface. From the equation, it can be seen that R is directly proportional to S, and the amount of recession is larger than the amount of sea-level rise by an amount proportional to the tan θ term. Therefore, according to the Bruun Rule, gentle beaches will recede faster than steep beaches for a given sea-level rise.

Rosen (1978) applied the Bruun Rule to eroding shorelines of Chesapeake Bay. He concluded that, in the particular circumstances of the bay shorelines, the Bruun Rule accurately characterized and predicted shoreline recession rates for known rates of sea-level rise.

In 1968 Edelman developed a model for quantifying shoreline response, based on profiles of the Dutch coast, and concluded that the equilibrium profile approximates a constant at any one instant and is of uniform slope. In addition, Edelman concluded that for a given storm surge, higher dunes will recede less than lower dunes.

Edelman's second model is much more innovative than his first and actually provides a numerical answer to the dune erosion question (Edelman, 1970). The assumption that changes of profile keep pace with rising sea level makes this model more realistic than the first. The Edelman II model is as follows:

$$R = L \ln \left(\frac{hb_o + hd_o}{hb_o + hd_o - S} \right) \qquad (2)$$

where R = recession due to sea-level rise; L = width of active profile; S = sea-level rise; hb_o = depth of active profile base; and hd_o = height of dunes.

The two main assumptions behind equation 2 are the constancy of wave conditions throughout the time period analyzed, and the direct relationship between sea-level rise and the speed of profile migration, resulting in proportional rates of movements for the two processes. The sole difference between the Edelman and Bruun models is the allowance for a reduction in dune height through time when using the Edelman II model. This allowance causes the Edelman II model to yield slightly greater recession values than those found by using the Bruun Rule.

Dean and Maurmeyer (1983) have modified the Bruun Rule, adopting it for usage in predicting the recession/migration of a retreating beach which is part of a larger barrier island system. Their model, which they call the Generalized Bruun Rule, is as follows:

$$R = \frac{S(L_o + W + L_l)}{(B_o + hb_o) - (B_l + hb_l)} \quad (3)$$

where R = recession due to sea-level rise; S = sea-level rise; L_o = width of oceanside active profile; L_l = width of lagoon-side active profile; hb_o = depth of base of active zone; hb_l = depth of base of active zone of lagoon side; B_o = open-ocean berm height; B_l = lagoon berm height; and W = width of the barrier island.

The main assumptions associated with the use of this model are the constancy of island width W through time by the overwash of sand, and the vertical growth of the entire island at the same rate as sea level rises. This diversion of island sand from the shoreface causes the Generalized Bruun Rule to predict a higher recession value than the Bruun Rule does for the same setting. As will be discussed more fully subsequently, this is a logical outgrowth of the different rates of shoreline movement for migrating barrier islands compared to islands which are merely experiencing shoreline recession without significant overwash.

Recently, Everts (1984 and this volume) developed a model for shoreline recession differing from Bruun's work in several important ways. As Everts states (p. 998), his model "is not constrained to the singular movement of sediment in an offshore direction; it accounts for changes in sand volume within a shoreline reach, including that caused by alongshore and cross-shore transport, transport into inlets, overwash, beach nourishment, sand mining, and others; it allows for barrier island preservation during a rising sea level; and it treats sediment movement in a more analytical way." These developments are very important because they address many, if not all, of the weaker aspects of the Bruun Rule. Conversely, Everts' model is similar to Bruun's in other ways, namely, that the shoreface is assumed to be in equilibrium with sea level and will thus translate vertically an amount equal to the rise in sea level. This means that, as in any model, sand redistribution is needed to maintain the equilibrium profile.

Unfortunately, the Everts' model could not be applied to the coast in this study because of the lack of the requisite accurate nearshore and shoreface profiles. (See Everts, this volume, for application of his model to other coastal areas.)

MODEL-CALCULATED RECESSION

The Bruun Rule, Generalized Bruun Rule and Edelman II models were applied as shoreline recession predictors for the entire North Carolina coast (Fig. 1). Most of the data used in this study are measurements obtained from the U.S. Geological Survey topographic quadrangle maps and National Ocean Service charts available along the 92 transects shown in Figure 2. A number of assumptions were used in the models where profile data were incomplete or not sufficiently detailed.

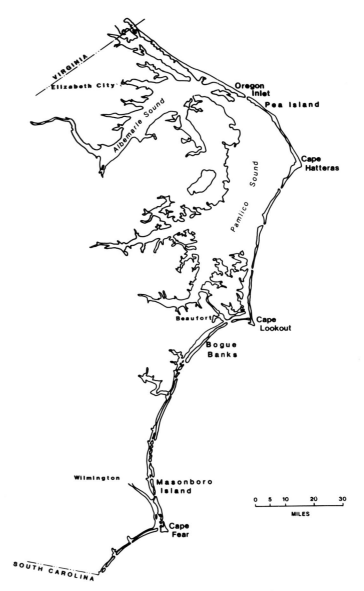

FIG. 1.—Index map of the North Carolina study area.

Sea level, unless stated otherwise, is assumed to be rising at the rate of 23 cm/century. No acceleration of sea-level rise is assumed. The depth of the base of the active profile, equivalent to the shoreface, is assumed to be 10 m for all of the North Carolina coast. For Bruun Rule calculations, berm height, B, is assumed to be 1 m above mean sea level. For the Generalized Bruun Rule the open-ocean berm height is assumed to be 1 m, the lagoonal berm height 0.5 m, the depth of significant sediment movement on the lagoon side 1 m, and the width of the zone of active sediment movement in the lagoon 20 m. Dune height for use in the Edelman II model calculation is either 1 m, 3 m or 5 m, depending upon the dune height classification of Kochel and others (1983).

Edelman II model results are not plotted in Figure 3, because the results are essentially the same as Bruun Rule

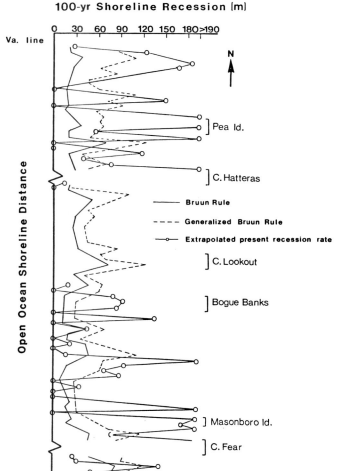

FIG. 3.—Comparison of expected 100-yr shoreline recession rates in meters calculated using the Bruun Rule and the Generalized Bruun Rule. Shown also is the extrapolated present rate of erosion. Calculations are based on an assumed sea-level rise of 23 cm/100 yrs.

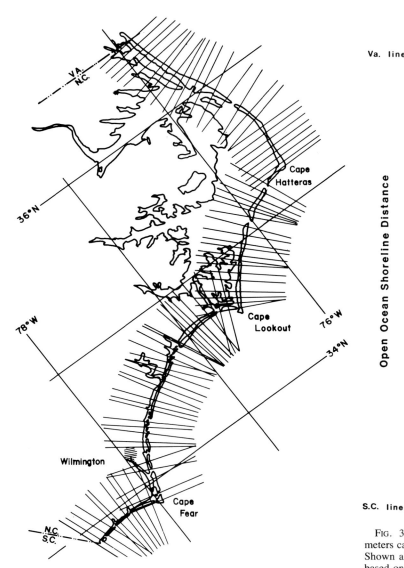

FIG. 2.—Map of the study area showing transect lines along which model calculations were made.

calculations. The circles shown on Figure 3 are 100-yr extrapolations of present erosion rates which average 0.631 m/yr (May and others, 1982).

The trends of Bruun Rule- and Generalized Bruun Rule-calculated erosion rates are more or less parallel throughout the study area (Fig. 3). Some of the variability in predicted rates of shoreline movement is due to shoreface-connected ridges and other features which locally affect calculation of the slope of the shoreface. The average erosion rates for the coast predicted by these two models is typically between 40 to 60 m per 100 yrs. Rates predicted by both models for the cape regions are anomalously high due to the effect of the offshore sand shoals on apparent shoreface slopes. Only Cape Lookout recession values are plotted on Figure 3.

The Generalized Bruun Rule consistently predicts more recession than the Bruun Rule. This is because the Generalized Bruun Rule requires the entire island profile, from the base of the shoreface to the landward limit of the lagoon's active profile, to remain constant throughout time, whereas the Bruun Rule requires profile maintenance only from the base of the shoreface to the top of the first dune (or berm). The need for more sand to maintain the entire island profile results in larger recession rates.

In should be noted that the Bruun and Generalized Bruun predictions (Fig. 3) are both conservative in that they assume that only sand is being bypassed through the shoreface. It is possible to use a "sediment compatibility factor" (Dean and Maurmeyer, 1983) to take into account that mud may also be bypassed. The basic assumption is that island and shoreline recession rates are directly proportional to the percentage of mud in shoreface-bypassed material. The "sediment compatibility factor" was not applied in this study because more studies, such as that of Hine and Snyder (1985) are needed to determine the grain size of barrier island shorefaces of North Carolina islands.

Extrapolation of present rates of erosion (not available on national seashores) produced highly variable recession rates for the next 100 yrs (Fig. 3). Zero recession rates shown on Figure 3 usually represent shoreline areas presently experiencing accretion. Most often such areas are near inlets, and accretion rates cannot be considered good indications of future shoreline movement. Overall, the extrapolated recession values have no clear relation to the rates of model-calculated recession. Furthermore, in most cases, extrapolations of present recession rates are higher than those predicted by the models, assuming a 23 cm/century sea-level rise rate.

Why the difference between extrapolated and predicted rates of erosion? At this point, one can only list possibilities, which include the fact that: (1) many factors other than sea-level rise, including a regional sand deficit, may cause shoreline retreat, (2) extrapolation of short-term data is meaningless and does not lead to meaningful long-term values of shore retreat, (3) the predictive models are unrealistic, or (4) some combination of all of the above.

It is useful to emphasize again that all of the model-predicted values shown in Figure 3 are based on the assumption that there will be no acceleration in the rate of sea-level rise. Since this is a poor assumption, all shoreline recession values shown in Figure 3 are minimum values.

RECESSION PREDICTED BY MIGRATION SURFACE SLOPE

If the sea level were to rise 10 m in the next decade, the shoreline would be inland at the 10-m contour line. The scenario which would correctly predict shoreline position of this highly unlikely event is the migration surface slope model, which is based on the assumption that the extent of shoreline retreat is a function of the slope of the lower coastal plain.

There is no question that this is a valid model for large and rapid sea-level rises. For example, the slope of the barrier island migration surface must have been the major control of shoreline position during the times represented by

TABLE 1.—DEFINITION OF THE VARIOUS MIGRATION SURFACE SLOPES USED TO CALCULATE RECESSION RATES. LOCATION OF THE VARIOUS SLOPES ON A TYPICAL LOWER COASTAL PLAIN CROSS SECTION IS SHOWN IN FIGURE 4

Slope A = Difference in elevation of a point 2 km inland from the lagoon shoreline and base of shoreface ÷ horizontal distance between above points.
Slope B = Difference in elevation of points 30 km landward and 30 km seaward from shoreline ÷ horizontal distance between above points (60 km).
Slope C = Difference in elevation of shoreline and base of shoreface (10 m) ÷ horizontal distance between above points.
Slope D = Difference in elevation of a point 20 km landward from lagoon shoreline and base of shoreface ÷ horizontal distance between above points.
Slope E = Elevation of a point 2 km landward of the lagoon shoreline ÷ 2 km.

the steeper portions of the Holocene sea-level curve (e.g., Blackwelder and others, 1979). The more difficult question is, what role does migration surface slope play in determining shoreline position in a shorter term sea-level rise of 0.2 or 1 m?

A wide variety of migration surface slopes can be chosen, each resulting in different "rise to run" ratios and consequently a wide variety of retreat rates. The five slopes chosen for this study are shown in Figure 4 and Table 1. The slope-calculated rates of shoreline recession, assuming a 1-m rise in sea level, are shown in Figure 5 for five representative coastal localities.

The extreme recession of more than 5,000 m predicted for a 1-m sea-level rise for slopes A and D at Cape Hatteras are due to Diamond Shoals. This large sand body, extending more than 20 km seaward at the cape, produces an apparent, very gentle migration surface and consequently very large recession predictions. Since the shoal is a body of sand restricted to the continental shelf or a shoal retreat massif (Swift, 1976b), it is not part of the regional barrier

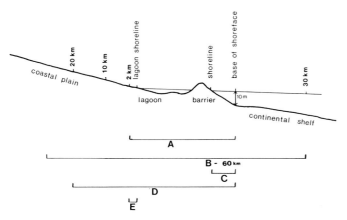

FIG. 4.—A diagrammatic cross section of the lower coastal plain and barrier island system showing the reaches over which the various migration surface slopes used in Table 1 are defined.

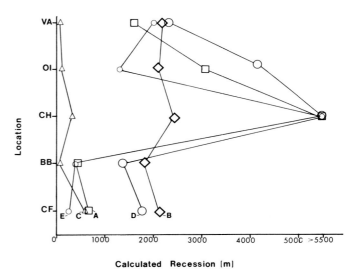

FIG. 5.—Expected shoreline recession as a result of a 1-m sea-level rise, assuming that recession is controlled only by migration surface slopes. The various slopes used are shown in Figure 4 and Table 1. Key to localities is as follows: Va = Virginia line, OI = Oregon Inlet, CH = Cape Hatteras, BB = Bogue Banks, CF = Cape Fear. Localities are shown in Figure 1.

island migration surface, and the predicted Cape Hatteras retreat is meaningless.

Slopes *B* and *C* are unaffected by the presence of Diamond Shoals. Slope *C* extends from the barrier island shoreline to a depth of 10 m (Fig. 4). Basically, this is the shoreface slope. Using slope *C* nearly always produces the least amount of predicted recession, reflecting the fact that the shoreface is the steepest portion of the lower coastal plain of North Carolina. It is also not a reasonable approximation of the barrier island migration surface slope, because the shoreface is, in itself, a migrating feature.

Slope *B* usually covers the greatest horizontal distance of any of the alternative slopes chosen. It extends 30 km seaward and landward of the barrier island shoreline. The distance on which this slope is based is so large that it effectively minimizes the size of the barrier island perched on it and also is unaffected by the cape-associated shoal. Recession rates obtained using this slope are typically among the highest. Most often a 1-m sea-level rise will cause a shoreline retreat in excess of 2,000 m, if slope *B* is assumed to be the best predictor (Fig. 5). The uniformity of predicted recession values is due to the fact that this regional slope averages out numerous coastal morphologic irregularities, such as shoals and estuaries. Slope *B*, because of its regional nature and the consequent smoothing out or elimination of local topographic variations, may be the best migration surface slope to predict average regional shoreline recession rates.

Slopes *A*, *D* and *E* predict much more variable rates of shoreline recession than do slopes *C* and *B*. In Figure 5 it can be seen that slopes *A* and *D* predict relatively high shoreline recession rates, especially for the northern half of the state, and that slope *A*, which extends 2 km onto the mainland, consistently predicts less recession (by 500 to 1,000 m) than slope *D*.

Figure 6 depicts the amount of shoreline recession which can be expected from 1-m and 6-m sea-level rises calculated for slopes *A* and *B*. The amount of recession ranges from 1 km to nearly 18 km with a 6-m sea-level rise. The greatest amounts of recession are predicted at the capes, but these are likely to be unrealistically high for the reasons just discussed.

North of Cape Hatteras, slopes *A* and *B* predict roughly comparable recessions of 1 km for a 1-m sea-level rise and 6 km for a 6-m sea-level rise. South of Cape Hatteras, slope *B* again yields about a 1 km recession for a 1-m rise and a 6-km shoreline retreat for a 6-m sea-level rise. The use of slope *A* for the same rise, however, predicts only a 1-km recession for a 6-m rise.

The more regional slope *B* generally predicts significantly greater recession than slope *A* for a given sea-level rise. A few notable exceptions to this are north of Cape Hatteras, where extensive coastal zone swamps cause slope *A* to be more gentle than slope *B*.

COMPARISON OF MODEL AND SLOPE PREDICTIONS

Figure 7 presents a comparison of the 100-yr recession of the North Carolina shoreline based on slope *A* and on the Generalized Bruun Rule, assuming a sea-level rise of 23 cm/100 yrs. Results of extrapolation of present rates for 100 yrs are also shown as unconnected circles.

North of Cape Lookout, slope *A* predicts a much greater recession rate than the Generalized Bruun Rule. We believe this is a result of the very gentle migration surface produced by wide back-barrier lagoons. South of Cape Lookout, the difference between the two models is slight. The two produce impressively similar recession rates.

It is suggested that the close correspondence between slope- and model-predicted recession rates for the southern part of the study area (which exhibits a relatively steep migration surface) indicates that a sort of equilibrium has been achieved. That is, the shoreline is more or less in its equilibrium position with relation to the level of the sea. From another viewpoint, if the Bruun model has any natural basis, model-predicted retreat cannot be greatly different from that predicted by the slope of the land.

On the other hand, the great difference in predicted rates of shoreline retreat north of Cape Hatteras may indicate that the present islands are in an out-of-equilibrium position with the level of the sea. If this is the case, the possibility exists that very rapid migration of the northern islands will soon occur. Possibly, this out-of-equilibrium situation could lead to overstepping of the island chain.

TOWARD BETTER MODELS?

The results of applying models and migration slope data to projections of shoreline recession for a rising sea level are difficult to evaluate. We know (as did the authors of the models) that the models do not include many of the fundamental evolutionary concepts that are well established by coastal recession/island migration studies. The number of environmental parameters is large, and the relative importance of the various parameters is highly variable for different shoreline locations. Perhaps the situation is so complex that a generally applicable and accurate model for shoreline recession in a rising sea level is an impossibility. One hopes this is not the case, because accurate prediction of short-range recession rates in a rising sea level has important societal and geological ramifications. Problems include the following. (1) The number of variables affecting shoreline recession is very large. Probably all such variables have not yet been recognized. (2) The variables are often difficult, if not impossible, to quantify in any meaningful way. (3) The relative importance of these variables varies widely over short distances. (4) The relative importance of these variables varies through time as, for example, the slope of the shoreface changes or the position of a shore-connected ridge changes during a storm. (5) Even if all variables are known and quantified, our understanding of shoreline processes is as yet too meager to know precisely how they act and interact in the shore environment.

If one takes the broad view and considers the response of shorelines to a rising sea level to be a problem in barrier island migration, a whole new set of variables and assumptions comes into play. (See the discussion by Everts, this volume.) Some of them are listed and briefly discussed here.

(1) The more gentle the migration surface (lower coastal

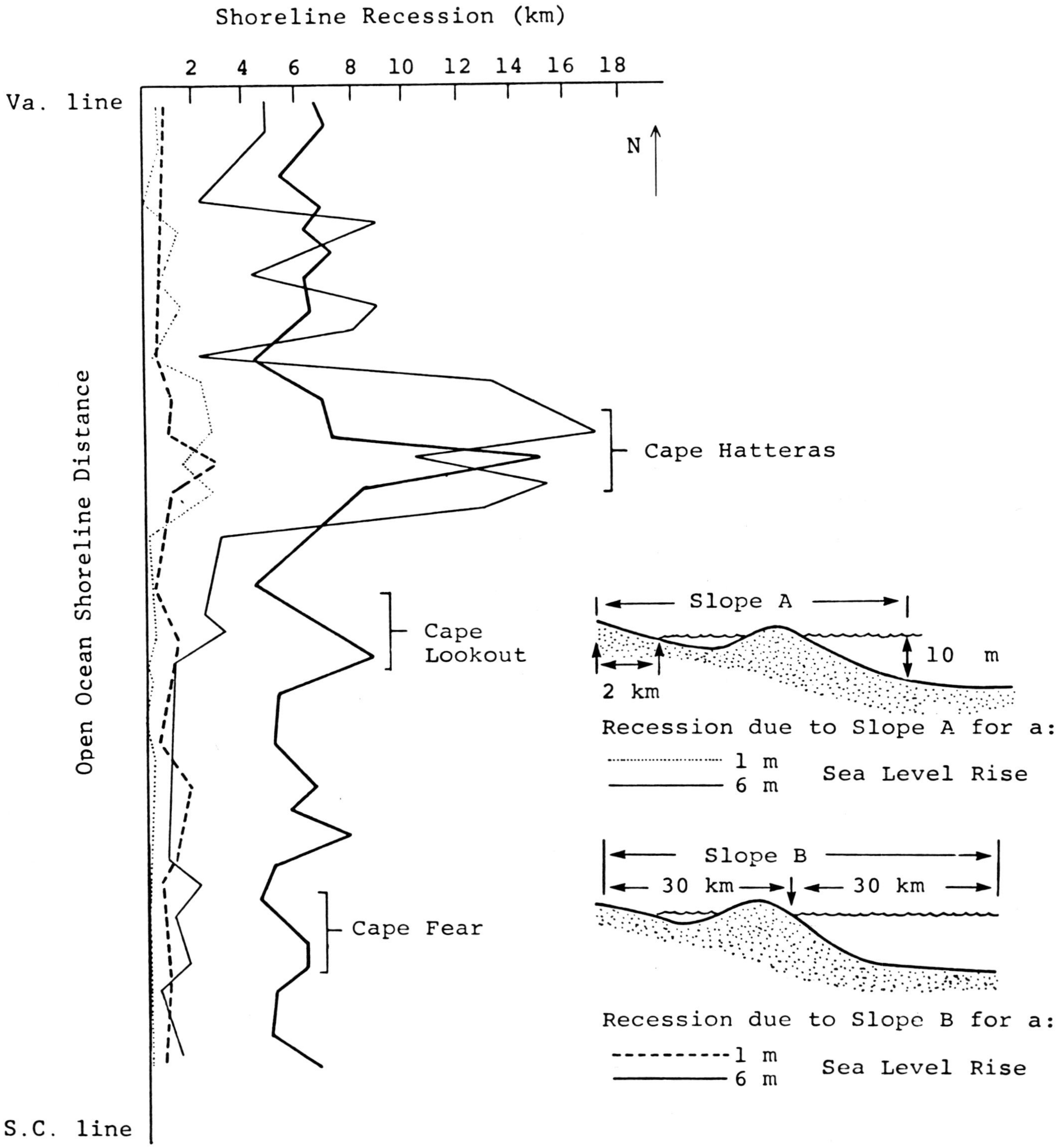

FIG. 6.—Graph showing the amount of shoreline retreat in kilometers due to 1-m and 6-m sea-level rises and assuming that migration surface slope is the only factor in control of recession. Slopes *A* and *B* are defined in Table 1.

plain slope), the greater the amount of recession from a given rate of sea-level rise.

(2) Prior to island migration, large amounts of sediment may be moved through existing tidal inlets and deposited in lagoons (Everts and others, 1983). Deposition in tidal deltas may represent a major sand sink during periods of extended sea-level stillstand. During island migration in response to a sea-level rise, the flood-tidal delta may be a

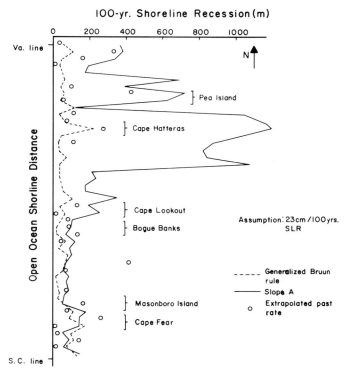

FIG. 7.—Comparison of shoreline recession (in meters) in the next 100 yrs predicted by the Generalized Bruun Rule and by the slope of the migration surface (slope *A*). The dots show recession rates extrapolated over the next 100 yrs from present erosion rates.

major sand source briefly slowing down shoreline recession.

(3) The latest stillstand, lasting possibly as long as 5,000 yrs, has allowed some barrier islands to prograde (Everts, 1984; Heron and others, 1984) and also to increase the volume of their dunes, thereby increasing the supply of sediment potentially available for incorporation into the early stages of the migration process.

(4) Most barrier islands in North Carolina will continue to lose land mass in a rising sea level, through shoreline recession on both sides until efficient overwash begins, allowing island migration to commence. The critical width of an island necessary for efficient overwash to proceed may vary significantly depending upon wave climate.

(5) Accompanying the transition from island thinning to island migration by storm overwash will be a reduction in shoreface slope (Swift, 1976a). Everts (1984) estimates that once the critical width is reached, the rate of shore movement will increase from four to eight times the rate for a thinning island, since essentially all available sand will move through overwash and inlet transport processes, reducing the amount available for shoreface maintenance.

(6) Other things being equal, the steeper the shoreface, the greater the initial rate of migration/recession. Once a more gentle shoreface profile has been reached as a result of the rapid recession of the upper shoreface, there will be a relative increase in the sediment supply, since fair weather-wave onshore transport will be more effective. This, in turn, will reduce the shoreline recession rate, beginning the process of steepening the shoreface again (Moody, 1964).

(7) Finally, barrier island migration models must be able to account for the variations in shoreline erosion caused by the incorporation of shoreface-bypassed sediment, which is not compatible with that needed for preservation of the shoreface slope. Mud is of no value in maintaining a shoreface in all but the gentlest of wave regimes, so a shoreface which is backed by fine-grained sediment can become sand-starved, receding at a much faster rate than when sand is available (Swift, 1976a; Dean and Maurmeyer, 1983; Everts, 1984).

NORTH CAROLINA ISLAND SCENARIOS (100–200 YRS)

The following are four possible short-range scenarios of barrier island response to sea-level rise (Fig. 8). These are additional illustrations of the fact that different types of islands respond at different rates and by different mechanisms. They are also indications of the fact that the various recession models applied in this paper are very simple approximations at best. The scenarios are based on a number of assumptions, most of which have been discussed in the preceding section and are discussed also by other authors in this volume.

Scenario #1: regressive barrier island without back-barrier marsh.—

Bogue Banks, North Carolina, is a 19-km-long, east-west trending barrier island. Except for its central portion, it is a wide beach-ridge island. It is also a regressive island (Heron and others, 1984) and contains a larger volume of sand than any other North Carolina island. The back-barrier lagoon is open, i.e., it is not filled with salt marsh, and fringing marshes are narrow to non-existent. At the present time, both open-ocean and lagoonal shorelines are actively retreating where not stabilized by man.

With continued and accelerating rise in sea level, the island can be expected to continue to thin until the critical width is achieved that will allow overwash-deposited fans to extend into the back-barrier lagoon. At that point, true island migration will commence (Fig. 8A). Shoreline retreat on both sides of the island prior to overwash dominance will be relatively slow because of the large volume of sand stored in the high beach-ridge system of this island. The island-thinning process will also be slowed, because of the lack of mud and the preponderance of sand-size material being supplied to the eroding system by shoreface bypassing.

Once migration begins, it will occur at a slow rate because sand-size material will continue to be furnished through shoreface bypassing. The dominance of coarse material is assumed by the lack of salt marsh on the lagoon side of this island. Island migration and the accompanying initial loss of large volumes of sand across the island can be expected to cause the shoreface to become more gentle. This, in turn, should cause a slight reduction in island migration rates with time (Fig. 8).

Scenario #2: narrow transgressive island with marsh filled lagoon.—

Masonboro Island, North Carolina, is an example of a transgressive island backed by a salt marsh-filled lagoon.

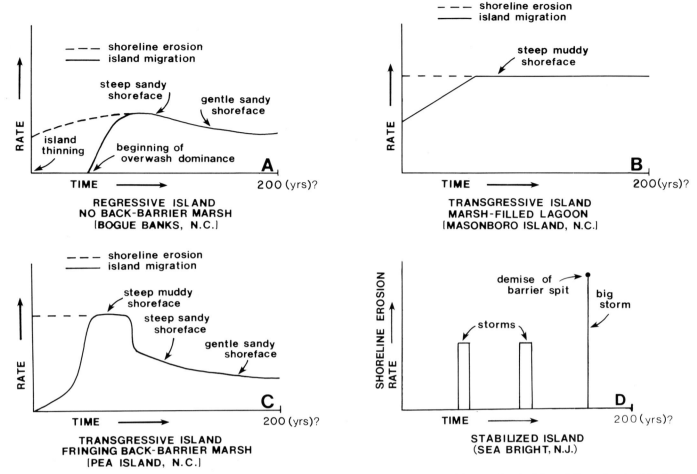

Fig. 8.—Four possible scenarios showing 100- to 200-yr(?) histories of the response to a rising sea level of four different barrier islands.

At present, this 8-mi-long (13 km), narrow, undeveloped low island is subject to frequent overwash, some of which crosses the entire island. In recent years, the island's sand supply has been strongly reduced by the Masonboro Inlet jetties at the north end of the island. In 1986, 800,000 cu yds (611,680 cu m) of sand were pumped onto the island to prevent shoreline retreat from flanking the jetties and exposing adjacent Wrightsville Beach to storm waves approaching from the southeast.

A possible scenario of island migration in a rising sea level is shown in Figure 8B. This scenario assumes that there will be no sand replenishment in the future. Initially, the rate of island migration is moderate because, at present, most overwash remains on the island. At the point of island narrowing, with cross-island overwash becoming a frequent event, rapid and steady migration will ensue. The rate of migration will be enhanced by the large mud component in the sediment arriving via shoreface bypassing.

Scenario #3: narrow island with fringing marsh.—

Pea Island, North Carolina, is a relatively narrow island which is presently thinning by erosion on both front and back sides (Jarrett, 1983). In most locations, the island is backed by a substantial fringing salt marsh. At present, overwash seldom crosses the entire island, even in locations where an artificial dune line, constructed by the National Park Service in the 1930s and 1940s, has been breached.

After initial thinning, rapid island migration should ensue due to the bypassing of muddy sediment on the shoreface. It is assumed (in Fig. 8C) that migration will be sufficiently rapid to prevent re-establishment of the fringing marsh. If this is the case, the rate of migration should abruptly decrease as fine but sandy floor sediments in Pamlico Sound replace the muddier, fringing marsh-lagoon sediments at the bypassing interface on the shoreface.

Scenario #4: the stabilized island.—

A digression from the general scope of this paper, but of considerable practical interest, is the response of a stabilized island to sea-level rise. A good example of such an island is Sea Bright, New Jersey.

Sea Bright is a north-south trending barrier spit, long subjected to heavy development pressure. Both open-ocean and back-barrier shorelines are totally stabilized. Little visible recreational beach remains and the shoreface has steepened considerably. Offshore bar formation or beach flattening can no longer occur in response to storm waves. The future scenario of Sea Bright evolution in an accelerating rise in sea level depends on natural processes as much as on governmental decisions regarding the priority of the funding of future sea wall maintenance and repair.

A possible scenario is shown in Figure 8D. The spit will thin slightly in step-like fashion as the result of sea wall failure in future storms, followed by wall reconstruction. By this time, the barrier spit will resemble a fortress atop a narrow sand ridge with a non-existent system for sand transfer in any direction except offshore. A "very large" storm can be expected to destroy much of the sea wall. After such an event, flattening of the oversteepened shoreface could result in total loss of the barrier spit, since shoreline retreat would be too rapid for island migration to occur.

BARRIER ISLAND SCENARIOS, 1,000–2,000 YRS

Figure 9 shows two scenarios of barrier island response viewed in a longer term sense, perhaps on the order of 1,000–2,000 yrs. In the case of a very rapid rise in sea level of the sort that typifies the steep part of the Holocene sea-level curve, the migration rate of islands, and the recession rate of shorelines, would be identical and both would be a direct function of coastal plain slope (Fig. 9A).

In the case of an accelerating sea level, island migration and shoreline recession both accelerate together. At some point, if acceleration continues, either mainland welding or island overstepping will occur (Fig. 9B). In any event, the island disappears, at least temporarily.

DISCUSSION AND SUMMARY

The generalizations discussed in this paper apply specifically to the North Carolina barrier island shoreline. To some extent the principles developed have application to all barrier islands, but it is important to emphasize that all discussion and data have been concerned with open-ocean unconsolidated shorelines. Little relevance is assumed or expected for non-barrier and especially for rocky shorelines.

Clearly, a very large number of process and product variables is involved in the response of barrier island shorelines to a rising sea level. This fact alone makes the formulation of a universally applicable model for predicting shoreline retreat highly unlikely. What makes the possibility of an accurate model a virtual impossibility is that even if we could measure shoreline process variables in any meaningful way, we could not analyze the data accurately because how the processes interact is not fully understood.

On unconsolidated shorelines, one obvious factor that complicates predictions of shoreline response is the ease by which the shape of the sea floor can change. Typically, the most rapid changes in the shape of the shoreface occur as a result of emplacement of structures such as jetties. Such stabilization structures cause a readjustment of sources and sinks of shoreface sediment which, in turn, profoundly affect nearshore wave patterns and sediment transport. The changes on natural shorelines are perhaps less spectacular and more gradual, but it is clear that a single event such as

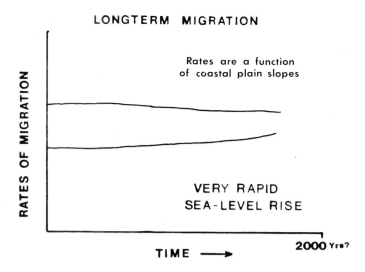

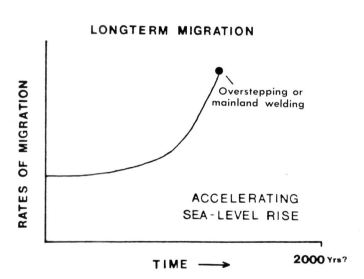

FIG. 9.—Two possible scenarios showing 1,000- to 2,000-yr(?) responses to a rapid sea-level rise and an accelerating sea level.

a storm can cause important and lasting changes (e.g., Moody, 1964).

If the perfect answer is not available, then we should attempt to look for predictive tools that come closest to the truth. If all variables that affect shoreline retreat cannot be measured, we should learn to estimate the most important ones.

How meaningful or accurate are the results of this study, particularly the plots of model-predicted recession and slope-predicted recession? Are the predicted recession rates realistic? First of all, long-range shoreline recession predictions by models cannot be drastically different from slope-predicted rates. There is no question that, if shorelines are retreating up a slope, the geometry of the slope will be a factor in determining rate and distance of translation. Slope is a "real world" factor.

The fact that from Cape Lookout south, the Generalized

Bruun Rule and slope *A* predicted similar recession rates (Fig. 6) affords some degree of mutual credibility for both approaches. Comparison of Generalized Bruun Rule and Slope *A* recession rates with the extrapolation of present rates of erosion, again for the stretch south of Cape Lookout, also shows some similarities. That is, 100-yr extrapolated erosion rates, although highly variable, are mostly within 100 m of the other predictors and sometimes much closer. The numerous factors other than sea-level rise which are involved in control of local erosion rates are undoubtedly responsible for the high variability of extrapolated rates of erosion.

North of Cape Lookout, a different situation prevails. A very large difference in shoreline recession is predicted by migration slope and by the Generalized Bruun model. The principal reason for the high slope-predicted recession value can be construed to be the anomalously large lagoons (Pamlico and Albemarle sounds) behind the Outer Bank barrier chain. Swift (1976a, p. 276) suggests that the Outer Banks are a "near stillstand coastal sector with effect of rising sea level compensated by sand surplus associated with coastwise sand flux." There is no field evidence, as yet, to support or deny Swift's contention, but if it is true, the stillstand of the shoreline is certainly a temporary one. The presumed surplus of sand absorbed by the shoreface has held the Outer Bank's shoreline in place sufficiently long for this shoreline position to be out of equilibrium with the present level of the sea. As discussed earlier, the difference in predicted recession rates may also be a measure of shoreline stability or vulnerability to future sea-level changes.

ACKNOWLEDGMENTS

This study was supported by the Donner Foundation and the North Carolina Geological Survey. We are grateful to Dag Nummedal, John Wells, Thomas Johnson, Jamie Camp and David Bush for reading early drafts of this manuscript. Steve Benton of the North Carolina State Division of Coastal Management furnished valuable erosion rate data and offered a number of useful suggestions.

REFERENCES

BENTON, S., 1983, Average annual long-term erosion rate update: Memorandum to the North Carolina Coastal Resources Commission, March 10, 6 p.

BLACKWELDER, B. W., PILKEY, O. H., AND HOWARD, J. D., 1979, Late Wisconsinan sea levels on the U.S. Atlantic shelf based on in-place shoreline indicators: Science, v. 204, p. 618–620.

BRUUN, P., 1962, Sea-level rise as a cause of shore erosion: Proceedings of the American Society of Civil Engineers, Journal of the Waterways and Harbors Division, v. 88, no. WWI, p. 117–130.

DEAN, R. G., AND MAURMEYER, E. M., 1983, Models for beach profile responses, *in* Komar, P. D., ed., Handbook of Coastal Processes and Erosion: Chemical Rubber Company Press, p. 151–166.

EDELMAN, T., 1968, Dune erosion during storm conditions: Proceedings, 11th International Conference on Coastal Engineering, American Society of Civil Engineers, New York, p. 719–723.

———, 1970, Dune erosion during storm conditions: Proceedings, 12th International Conference on Coastal Engineering, American Society of Civil Engineers, New York, p. 1305–1307.

EVERTS, C. H., 1984, Sea level rise effects on shoreline position: American Society of Civil Engineers, Journal of Waterway, Port, Coastal and Ocean Engineering, vol. 111, no. 6, November, 1985, p. 985–999.

———, BATTLEY, P. P., AND GIBSON, P. N., 1983, Shoreline movements, report 1, Cape Henry, Virginia, to Cape Hatteras, North Carolina, 1849–1980: Technical Report CERC-83-1, U.S. Army Corps of Engineers, Waterways Experiment Station, Vicksburg, Mississippi, 111 p.

HERON, S. D., MOSLOW, T. F., BERELSON, W. M., HERBERT, J. R., SKELE, F. A., AND SWANSON, K. R., 1984, Holocene sedimentation of a wave dominated barrier island shoreline: Cape Lookout, North Carolina, *in* Greenwood, B., and Davis, R. A., eds., Hydrodynamics and Sedimentation in Wave Dominated Coastal Environments: Marine Geology, v. 60, no.. 1, p. 413–434.

HINE, A. C., AND SNYDER, S. W., 1985, Coastal lithosome preservation: evidence from the shoreface and inner continental shelf off Bogue Banks, North Carolina: Marine Geology, v. 63, p. 307–330.

HOFFMAN, J. S., KEYES, D., AND TITUS, J. G., 1983, Projecting Future Sea Level Rise: Methodology, Estimates to the Year 2100, and Research Needs: U.S. Environmental Protection Agency, 2nd edition, 121 p.

JARRETT, J. T., 1983, Changes of some N. Carolina barrier islands since the mid-19th century, *in* Magoon, O. T., and Converse, H., eds., Coastal Zone '83, Proceedings of the 3rd Symposium on Coastal and Ocean Management: American Society of Civil Engineers, p. 641–661.

KOCHEL, R. C., KAHN, J. H., DOLAN, R., HAYDEN, B. P., AND MAY, P. F., 1983, Mid-Atlantic Microtidal Barrier Coast Classification: Classification of Coastal Environments: Technical Report 27, Department of Environmental Science, University of Virginia, Office of Naval Research, Coastal Sciences Program, 86 p.

MAY, S.. K., KIMBALL, W. H., GRANDY, N., AND DOLAN, R., 1982, CEIS: The Coastal Erosion information system: Shore and Beach, Jan., p. 19–25.

MOODY, D. W., 1964, Coastal morphology and processes in relation to the development of submarine sand ridges off Bethany Beach: Unpublished Ph.D. Dissertation, The Johns Hopkins University, Baltimore, 167 p.

REVELLE, R. R., 1983, Probable future changes in sea level resulting from increased atmospheric carbon dioxide, *in* Changing Climate: National Research Council Report, National Academic Press, Washington, D.C., p. 433–448.

ROSEN, P. S., 1978, A regional test of the Bruun Rule on shoreline erosion: Marine Geology, v. 26, p. M7–M16.

SWIFT, D. J. P., 1976a, Coastal sedimentation, *in* Stanley, D. J., and Swift, D. J. P., eds., Marine Sediment Transport and Environmental Management: John Wiley and Sons, New York, p. 127–158.

SWIFT, D. J. P., 1976b, Continental shelf sedimentation, *in* Stanley, D. J., and Swift, D. J. P., eds., Marine Sediment Transport and Environmental Management: John Wiley and Sons, New York, p. 311–350.

PART III
RESPONSE TO DEGLACIATION

LATE QUATERNARY SEA-LEVEL CHANGES IN MAINE

DANIEL F. BELKNAP
Department of Geological Sciences and Center for Marine Studies, University of Maine, Orono, ME 04469

BJORN G. ANDERSEN
Institute for Quaternary Studies, University of Maine, Orono, ME 04469

R. SCOTT ANDERSON
Department of Botany, University of Maine, Orono, ME 04469

WALTER A. ANDERSON
Maine Geological Survey, State House Station 22, Augusta, ME 04333

HAROLD W. BORNS, JR.
Department of Geological Sciences and Institute for Quaternary Studies, University of Maine, Orono, ME 04469

GEORGE L. JACOBSON
Department of Botany and Institute for Quaternary Studies, University of Maine, Orono, ME 04469

JOSEPH T. KELLEY
Department of Geological Sciences and Institute for Quaternary Studies, University of Maine, Orono, ME 04469
and Maine Geological Survey, State House Station 22, Augusta, ME 04333

R. CRAIG SHIPP
Center for Marine Studies, University of Maine, Orono, ME 04469

DAVID C. SMITH
Department of History and Institute for Quaternary Studies, University of Maine, Orono, ME 04469

ROBERT STUCKENRATH, JR*
Radiocarbon Laboratory and Smithsonian Environmental Research Center, Rockville, MD 20852-1773

WOODROW B. THOMPSON
Maine Geological Survey, State House Station 22, Augusta, ME 04333

AND

DAVID A. TYLER
Department of Civil Engineering, University of Maine, Orono, ME 04469

ABSTRACT: On the Maine coast, evidence of local relative sea level 12.5 ka is now exposed 60–80 m above present sea level. At that time, eustatic sea level was at least 70 m below present in most parts of the world. The difference is due to isostatic depression of the Maine coast by the weight of glacial ice. During deglaciation, the sea advanced inland in contact with the retreating margin of the marine-based ice sheet. Due to isostatic rebound and the contours of the land, the ice sheet grounded as much as 150 km inland of the present coast, glaciomarine deltas formed, and the transgression reached a stillstand at what is termed the upper marine limit. Due to differential tilting during rebound, this marine limit is now over 132 m in elevation at its farthest inlet extent. As rebound became dominant, sea level reached to 65 m below present at about 9.5 ka. At that time rebound slowed to about the same rate as that of eustatic sea-level rise. Shorelines were cut and deltas were formed at this lower marine stillstand position. Subsequently, eustatic rise became the predominant mode. Radiocarbon dates on fossil marine mollusks provide timing for this onlap and offlap.

From 7.0 ka to the present, radiocarbon dates on wood and salt marsh peats provide a relatively precise sea-level curve. During the period 4.2–1.5 ka, sea level rose at 1.22 m/1,000 yrs. Before that period, it may have risen more than twice as fast. After 1.5 ka, it slowed to half the mid-late Holocene rate. Recent tide-gauge records show an acceleration in rate to 2–3 mm/yr for the past 40 yrs. Releveling, tide gauges, and other evidence (Anderson and others, 1984) suggest that the coast is being warped downward to the east, possibly due to non-glacially induced neotectonics.

INTRODUCTION

Relative sea-level changes in Maine have been rapid and of large magnitude over the past 14,000 yrs. Glacio-isostatic depression and rebound of the land has had the largest relative effect, with glacio-eustatic changes becoming dominant after retreat of the Wisconsinan Laurentide ice sheet. Continuing slower sea-level rise is indicated by drowned tree stumps, peats, archeological sites, historic structures, and by tide gauges (summarized by Anderson and others, 1984). There is also evidence for neotectonic warping along the coast from releveling studies (Tyler and Ladd, 1980). The work presented in this paper represents contributions by a working group of the University of Maine at Orono and the Maine Geological Survey, supported by the United States Nuclear Regulatory Commission. This group has been studying crustal warping in coastal Maine for the past 6 yrs. In addition, the first author has received support for independent but related studies from the National Science Foundation. This paper summarizes current thinking in an ongoing project on sea-level changes during the late Quaternary, based on that group effort as well as other related work. Further explanation of this group effort is provided in the acknowledgments. A complete presentation of the results of the overall project is presently in preparation as a Maine Geological Survey Bulletin. The purpose of this paper is to examine existing and new sea-level data and model sea-level curves, which include the effects of glacial eustasy and isostasy.

Geologic implications of these profound relative sea-level changes include effects on coastal processes, land-use planning, and identification of geologic resources and hazards.

---

*Present Address: Radiocarbon Dating Laboratory University of Pittsburgh Applied Research Center, Pittsburgh, Pennsylvania 15238.

To understand effects of sea-level change as distinct from shorter term wave and tidal processes, it is useful to study the Holocene stratigraphic record along the coast, as well as to compare areas possibly undergoing modern rates of rise differing by a factor of three. The natural rate of rise may be coupled with possible tidal range effects from proposed tidal barrages in the Bay of Fundy (Greenberg, 1979; Larsen and Topinka, 1984). There may also be accelerated rates of rise due to CO_2 greenhouse effects (Barth and Titus, 1984; Etkins and Epstein, 1982; Hoffman, 1982; Hoffman and others, 1983).

Another geologic effect of the late Quaternary sea-level fluctuations is found in the southern part of Maine, where a coastal strip as much as 100 km wide (Fig. 1) was cov-

ered by a rapid marine transgression during deglaciation. This allowed deposition of a glaciogenic rock-flour marine mud, the Presumpscot Fm (Bloom, 1960, 1963). Subsequently, there was a rapid regression into the Gulf of Maine. This coastal strip has a surficial geology dominated by the Presumpscot Fm, till, and sand-and-gravel outwash deposits. Muds of the Presumpscot Fm, which were a historically important brick-making material, are also a geohazard, with frequent slumps in gulleys and coastal bluffs (Thompson, 1979; Novak and others, 1984).

Finally, understanding the shape of Maine's local relative sea-level curves will aid in models of isostatic rebound (Bloom, 1963; Newman and others, 1980; Grant, 1980), mantle rheology (Cathles, 1980; Clark, 1980; Fastook and

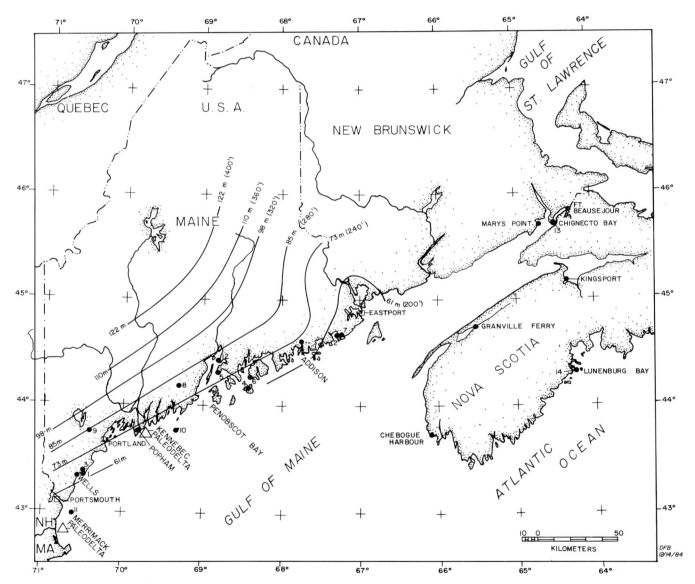

FIG. 1.—Location map for Maine and adjacent areas. Localities of radiocarbon-dated sites are indicated by numbers (Table 1; Fig. 5) for Pleistocene and by name for Holocene localities (Table 2; Figs. 3, 5, 6). Tide gauges are shown as squares, and the lowstand paleodeltas as triangles. The isolines are elevation contours for marine limit glaciomarine deltas, recontoured from data in Thompson and others (1983) and Thompson and Borns (1985).

Hughes, 1979) and Wisconsinan ice sheet reconstruction (Peltier and Andrews, 1976; Grant, 1977; Hughes, 1981a, b). Some of this work has focused on Atlantic Canada (Quinlan and Beaumont, 1981, 1982) with extrapolations into Maine on the basis of limited data.

GEOLOGIC SETTING

Maine is part of the northern Appalachian mountain belt, with Paleozoic rocks ranging from highly deformed high-grade metamorphic rocks in the southwest to low-grade metavolcanics and metasediments in the north and east, all intruded by Paleozoic and Mesozoic igneous bodies (Osberg and others, 1985).

Erosion has resulted in a low rolling topography in the coastal lowlands. Denny (1982) suggests that most of this topographic expression is pre-glacial. The Wisconsinan glaciation (and at least one and probably many previous glaciations) caused streamlining and abrasion of the rock terrain, with differential erosion controlled by structures and rock type, creating a terrain known as fjard* coast in Scandinavia. This surface is mantled by discontinuous units of varying thickness (Thompson and Borns, 1985), such as till, stratified drift, and glaciomarine mud—the Presumpscot Fm. Below the upper marine limit, the P esumpscot Fm is widespread in valleys. Reworking during the fall of sea level from its late glacial highstand caused stripping from the highs and wave winnowing of till and outwash in a thin surficial zone. Thompson (1979, 1982) has summarized the surficial deposits of the coastal lowland, whereas Belknap and others (1987) have discussed the Quaternary units of the nearshore Gulf of Maine and adjoining estuaries.

The Holocene coastal environments experience active processes which vary in their effects in diverse coastal geomorphological settings. Maine's coast is divided into four main geomorphic zones: southwestern sandy arcuate embayments, west-central structure-controlled rocky peninsulas and muddy embayments, east-central large embayments and granitic pluton islands, and northeastern fault-controlled straight-cliffed coast (Kelley, 1987). Maine tides range from 2.4 m in the south to nearly 7 m in the northeast, with mean breaker heights of 45 cm (U.S. Army Coastal Engineering Research Center, 1973) making the coast a mixed-energy to tide-dominated coast in the model of Hayes (1979). The Maine coast is rocky, but also has extensive tidal flats, marshes, estuaries and neutral embayments (no freshwater input), and a few sand and gravel beaches. Kelley (1987) has classified the relative importance of each of these environments and has also proposed a model in which the site of deposition of sediments within embayments migrates headward with Holocene sea-level rise and transgression, with efficient internal recycling of Holocene and Pleistocene sediments within the embayment.

---

*fjard: small, narrow, irregular inlet, or submerged glacial valley on a flat rocky coast; shorter, shallower and broader in profile than a fjord. AGI Glossary of Geology, 2nd ed., 1980.

QUATERNARY SEA LEVELS

The local relative sea-level curve is of fundamental importance to understanding the Quaternary evolution of the Maine coast. Clark and others (1978) have shown that geoidal warping requires examination of local relative sea-level curves, rather than an unavailable "eustatic curve." In addition, the isostatic effects of the Wisconsinan glacier have caused major excursions of sea level in Maine. Only recently have the data allowed evaluation of the relative contribution of glacio-isostasy, eustasy, and (Anderson and others, 1984) possible neotectonic warping. The advance of glacial ice warped the crust well below sea level even as eustatic sea level lowered; then, as ice retreated, the "DeGeer Sea" (Lougee and Lougee, 1976) flooded the depressed coast. Subsequent rebound caused rapid fall of sea level to a lowstand in the Gulf of Maine, after which eustatic rise dominated to the present. The rate, timing and magnitude of these fluctuations are becoming more precisely determined through recent work.

Previous studies.—

It has long been recognized that Maine has a drowned coast (Shaler, 1874, 1875; Davis, 1910; Johnson, 1925), but only with the advent of ^{14}C dating could sea-level curves be quantified. Hussey (1959, 1970) used radiocarbon dates on tree stumps in the Wells area to evaluate coastal evolution. Newman and others (1980) also used stump data for a relative curve for the Maine coast (Fig. 2). Thompson (1973), however, showed that stumps are not reliable indicators of sea-level position in Maine. During the 1960s and 1970s, sea-level curves were developed for southern New England* (e.g., Bloom and Stuiver, 1963; Kaye and Barghoorn, 1964; McIntire and Morgan, 1964; Fairbridge and Newman, 1968; Redfield, 1972) and for Atlantic Canada (Grant, 1970). Most recently, Oldale (1985) has summarized the southern New England curves at a common scale. Little was done in Maine until Thompson (1973) dated salt marsh peats in Addison, Maine. Timson (1978) and Nelson (1979) dated a few salt marsh peats in southern Maine, which showed a much slower apparent rate of rise than those of Thompson (1973) for northeastern coastal Maine.

During this period, the late Pleistocene received closer scrutiny. Bloom (1960, 1963), using dates from marine shells from the Presumpscot Fm, suggested a sea-level and crustal rebound curve (Fig. 2). Later refinement of that information and extensive new dating by Stuiver and Borns (1975) on shells and seaweed provided a clearer timing of the Presumpscot marine submergence and emergence. Smith (1985) has continued this dating, providing more detailed information on ice-front and shoreline positions on time-distance diagrams, but he did not attempt to construct a sea-level curve. Schnitker (1974) used the limited ^{14}C data then available, coupled with seismic profiling in west-central coastal Maine, to produce a sea-level curve with an inferred lowstand of 65 m below present (Fig. 2). Although undated, this lowstand was based on apparent subaerial ero-

---

*See Dix Lisle (1982) for an annotated bibliography.

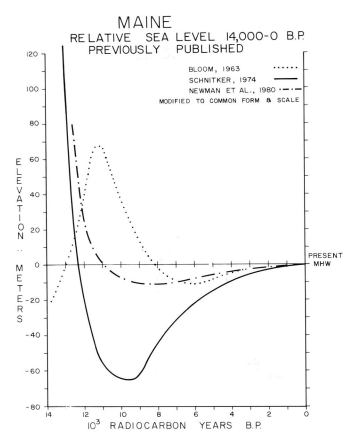

MAINE
RELATIVE SEA LEVEL 14,000-0 B.P.
PREVIOUSLY PUBLISHED

BLOOM, 1963 ......
SCHNITKER, 1974 ———
NEWMAN ET AL., 1980 ·—·—
MODIFIED TO COMMON FORM & SCALE

FIG. 2.—Previously published Maine local relative sea-level curves. Those of Bloom (1963) and Schnitker (1974) have been transformed from crustal rebound curves relative to an absolute elevation to a frame of reference relative to a coastal position at present sea level.

sion of Pleistocene sediments to that level. Belknap (1985) and Belknap and others (1987) interpreted the seismic facies in the same area with new data, showing a paleodelta of the Kennebec River constructed at lowstand, adjacent to deep, glacially scoured valleys filled with Pleistocene Presumpscot Fm muds, overlain by natural gas-rich estuarine and marine mud of Holocene age. Despite different interpretations of the seismic facies, Belknap and others (1986) found the same suggestion of lowering to −65 m as Schnitker. Kelley and Kelley (1985), Kelley and others (1986) and Shipp (1985) show similar lowstands in Saco Bay, Casco Bay, and Wells Bay in southern Maine. Oldale and others (1983) found a 47-m lowstand on the Merrimac River paleodelta off Massachusetts, Birch (1984) suggested a 30-m lowstand in New Hampshire, and Knebel and Scanlon (1985a) suggested a 40-m lowering in Penobscot Bay based on channels cut into the Presumpscot Fm. The date of this lowstand is not directly known but is most likely in the range of 10.0 to 8.0 ka.

The late Holocene sea-level record has come under intensive study from the late 1970s to present, as the apparent mismatch between southern and northeastern Maine sea-level curves became evident. A Nuclear Regulatory Commission-funded study of neotectonic warping contributed new data in Addison and elsewhere along the coast (Anderson

and Race, 1981; Anderson and Borns, 1983; Anderson and others, 1984; Belknap and others, 1985). The data were somewhat ambiguous in places, perhaps due to tidal range, ice rafting, and slumping in marshes, and possibly due to the earlier coring techniques. The present study includes a continuation of the NRC project, re-examining the Addison data with new techniques, and using an interdisciplinary approach to integrate archaeologic, historic, and releveling data of the NRC project with the longer term salt marsh radiocarbon-dating information.

Similar studies of salt marshes in the Bay of Fundy and Nova Scotia were used to infer an increase in tidal range from about 7.0 ka to present and sea-level curves of remarkable constancy around the Bay (Fig. 3; Scott and Medioli, 1978; Scott and Greenberg, 1983).

A final body of information is provided by the tide-gauge studies of Hicks and others (1983; pers. commun., 1984). Linear regression of these data apparently shows a distinct, statistically significant ($p < 0.05$) difference in rates of relative rise for the 1940–1982 period among Portsmouth, New Hampshire; Portland, Maine; and Eastport, Maine (Fig. 4). There are complex problems, however, of smoothing of daily data to monthly means, filtering, and assimilating local meterological effects which must be considered in order to make this a valid analysis. Neotectonic warping of the coast has been suggested as the cause of this apparent difference (Tyler and Ladd, 1980; Anderson and others, 1984). Tyler and Ladd (1980) used first-order releveling surveys to support this neotectonic warping concept, but found vertical velocities three times as great as those suggested by the tide gauges, although in the same sense of motion. Brown (1978)

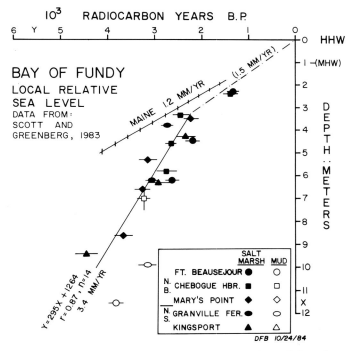

FIG. 3.—Radiocarbon-dated salt marsh and organic mud dates from the Bay of Fundy (data from Scott and Greenberg, 1983). Their five curves have been combined on one axis, with a linear regression fitted to salt marsh data points (filled symbols) older than 2.0 ka.

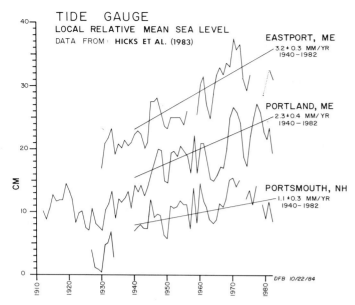

FIG. 4.—Local tide-gauge information (data from Hicks and others, 1983; pers. commun., 1984). Linear regression lines fit to annual means for the years 1940–1982. The vertical scale is arbitrary with respect to initial level.

of deglaciation and offlap, but are somewhat speculative as to timing for the period of lowstand and early rise. Using available ^{14}C dates from the Presumpscot Fm and contemporaneous moraines (Table 1, after Smith, 1985; and Thompson and Borns, 1985) elevations were projected to a common value of rebound, the 73-m contour of Figure 1. Only coastal dates (locations given in Fig. 1) were projected. This contour is parallel to and nearly at the present coast between Portland and Addison, and the tilt of the plane here is about 0.7 m/km. Thus, the relative sea-level curve is representative of only the mid-coastal region. The warp of the plane is distorted in eastern Maine, in the same sense as the releveling and tide-gauge data. It has been suggested that this is a neotectonic warping (Anderson and others, 1984), or it may represent local variations in ice thickness at the time of Presumpscot deposition, as suggested by Quinlan and Beaumont (1982, Fig. 3). Timing of the retreat of the Wisconsinan ice is provided by radiocarbon dates in marine sediments interfingering with till (nos. 1, 2, and 3, Table 1; Fig. 1). These represent the fluctuating grounding line of a marine-based ice sheet (Stuiver and Borns, 1975; Smith, 1985) which reached the southwest coast about 13.8 ka and the northeast coast about 500 yrs later. Minor fluctuations may have occurred at the Kennebunk and Pineo

has discussed the uncertain relationship between releveling and tide gauge records on the United States east coast.

Latest Pleistocene to mid-Holocene sea-level curve.—

Construction of a sea-level curve for the time of deglaciation, deposition of the Presumpscot Fm, and the subsequent sea-level fall requires data which constrain the plane of sea level at various times in a geographically widespread area to account for later isostatic warping during rebound. Thompson and others (1983) have measured the elevations of foreset-topset contacts on glaciomarine deltas, which are thought to represent maximum submergence. These deltas probably were formed at the transgressive marine limit, since none show evidence of deposition of glaciomarine mud or extensive marine reworking on their tops. They are also assumed to have been deposited within a relatively brief time span (about 500 yrs), but much more work needs to be done to extend the limited radiocarbon control of this interval. The level of this assumed horizontal plane has been uplifted differentially to the northwest by isostatic rebound. Figure 1 includes a recontour of the delta elevation data from Thompson and others (1983, fig. 1), Anderson and others (1984, fig. 3) and Thompson and Borns (1985). It represents an interim compilation, since more data are currently being collected and analyzed, but the general pattern is unlikely to change greatly. To construct a valid latest Pleistocene sea-level curve, the warp of this surface must be included. We have not yet attempted to include the New Brunswick glaciomarine data except in the immediate vicinity of the Maine border, but Rampton and others (1984, fig. 24) show a sea-level curve quite similar to the Maine data.

Figure 5 is the local relative sea-level curve for the period 14.0 ka to present. The data are quantified for the period

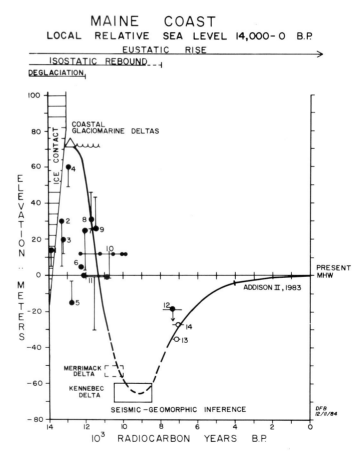

FIG. 5.—Local relative sea-level changes from 14.0 ka to present. Data are listed in Table 1. Filled circles are Maine data; open circles are data from Nova Scotia.

TABLE 1.—MAINE COAST DEGLACIAL TO EARLY TRANSGRESSION SEA-LEVEL DATA

No.	Lab Number	Location	Source	Material	Interpretation	Radiocarbon Age (yrs)	Elevation (m)	Normalized to 73-m isoline** (m)
1.	QL-192	Great Hill, Kennebunk	a*	Marine shells between tills	Ice grounding line	13,830 ± 100	5	14
2.	Y-2217	Pond Ridge moraine, Cutler	b*	Seaweed in end moraine	Ice grounding line	13,320 ± 200	5	30
3.	Y-2208	Kennebunk moraine	b*	Marine shells in deformed glaciomarine	Ice grounding line	13,200 ± 120	12	20
4.	SI-4651	Swans Island	a*	Marine shells in glaciomarine	Onlap	12,905 ± 110	49	60
5.	Y-2214	Cape Rosier, Brooksville	b*	Barnacles on bedrock, buried by glaciomarine	Onlap	12,780 ± 160	−3	−15
6.	Y-2206	Tremont	b*	Marine shells in glaciomarine	Offlap	12,250 ± 160	2	3
7.	Y-2201a	Machias Bay, Cutler	b*	Marine shells in glaciomarine	Offlap	12,020 ± 120	3	25
	Y-2201b	Machias Bay, Cutler	b*	Seaweed in glaciomarine	Offlap	12,080 ± 250	3	25
8.	DIC-1599	Whitney Corner, Warren	a*	Marine shells in glaciomarine	Offlap	11,720 ± 125	46	31
9.	SI-4747	Little Falls, Gorham	c*	Marine shells in glaciomarine	Offlap	11,450 ± 90	43	26
10.	SI-2714a SI-2710a SI-2711a SI-2713a SI-2712a	Monhegan Island	d*	Marine shells in sand and gravel, base of bog	Offlap	9,835 ± 90 10,020 ± 105 10,565 ± 110 11,215 ± 85 12,280 ± 100 mean: 10,783 ± 994	−13 (controlling sill depth −1 m)	12
11.		Isles of Shoals	h*	Peat in estuarine mud	Offlap?	12,080 ± 400 10,820 ± 400	−30 −31	0 −1
12.	W-1306	Penobscot Bay	e*	Wood in sand, on unconformity	Emerged upland	7,390 ± 500	−18	—

Other possibly relevant samples: Nova Scotia and New Brunswick, Canada.

No.	Lab Number	Location	Source	Material	Interpretation	Radiocarbon Age (yrs)	Elevation (m)	Normalized
13.	GX-4939	Chignecto Bay, New Brunswick	f*	Salt marsh peat	Holocene transgression	7,140 ± 160	−35	—
14.	GX-6490	Lunenburg Bay, Nova Scotia	g*	Salt marsh peat, not in place?	Holocene transgression?	7,070 ± 300	−27	—
	GS-6491	Reworked salt marsh peat			Holocene transgression	6,945 ± 190		

*Sources: a. Thompson and Borns, 1985
            b. Stuiver and Borns, 1975
            c. Crossen, 1983
            d. Bostwick, 1978
            e. Ostericher, 1965
            f. Scott and Greenberg, 1983
            g. Scott and Medioli, 1982
            h. Collins, 1985 and pers. commun.

**Normalized elevations: removal of relative isostatic tilt of 0.7 m/km normal to +73 m (240 ft) datum of Thompson and others (1983); see also Anderson and others, 1984; Fig. 3), oriented N63°E (N10°E in Machias).

Ridge moraines. The significance of the Pineo Ridge event is still controversial (Smith, 1985; Borns and Hughes, 1977).

Onlap of the sea occurred in contact with the ice and may be represented by points 4 and 5 on Table 1. The remainder of the Presumpscot Fm shell dates (nos. 6–10, Table 1) represents offlap and shoaling. The Monhegan Island dates (no. 10) are of uncertain reliability, probably not in-place. The final dates in this range are from peats near the Isles of Shoals (Collins, 1985 and pers. commun.). They represent offlap, but also warmer, conditions. Schnitker (1975) also found evidence of warming conditions in Stellwagen Basin between 14.0 and 8.0 ka, the local maximum warming, before increased tidal mixing with sea-level rise caused cooling of the Gulf of Maine. These data constrain the lowstand to below their level. The normalization of rebound suggested in Table I may be excessive here, an extrapolation to where the degree of isostatic depression and re-

bound would have been less. For example, Kaye and Barghoorn (1964) discuss the Boston Clay IV, an analogue of the Presumpscot Fm found only up to elevations of about 20 m.

The depth below present to which sea level dropped (Fig. 5) is based on less firm evidence: interpretation of high-resolution seismic profiles over the Kennebec paleodelta (Belknap, 1985; Belknap and others, 1987) and apparent shoreline features in the range of 50 to 70 m below sea level in Wells Bay (Shipp, 1985), Saco Bay (Kelley and Kelley, 1985), Casco Bay (Kelley and others, 1986) and in several areas to the northeast (Belknap and others, 1987). Examination of Figure 1 suggests that the −45-m level cited by Knebel and Scanlon (1985) and Knebel (1986) is a reasonable value when compared to the −65-m level of the Kennebec paleodelta, due to the rebound tilt. The Merrimac paleodelta value of −47 m (Oldale and others, 1983) may also be comparable due to earlier deglaciation to the south and less rebound there at that time. The Birch (1984) value of −30 m may be only a maximum level. The consequences of a decreasing rate of rebound and a eustatic rise in sea level are a period of time in which the two motions would be equal. This would result in a relative stillstand. The shorelines and deltas could have been produced during this time of relative stability. Since they are prominent and not found as well developed at other levels when sea level would have been rising or falling rapidly, they seem to represent this turn-around in relative sea level.

Timing of the early Holocene sea-level rise is constrained by few firm dates. Ostericher (1965) radiocarbon-dated wood on the basal Holocene unconformity at 7.39 ± 0.5 ka (no. 12, Table 1), but this is only an approximation of the maximum level of the sea at that time. Three other points from New Brunswick and Nova Scotia (nos. 13 and 14, Table 1) by Scott and Greenberg (1983) and Scott and Medioli (1982) may also represent the early Holocene transgression. Would isostatic warping change the level at these points? Andrews (1970) suggests that by 8.0 ka this region would be rebounding less than 1 m per century. Calculations of simple exponential rebound also suggest that most of the rebound would have been accomplished by 7.0 ka (Appendix A). For example, using Dillon and Oldale's (1978) sea-level curve, a value of −70 m was chosen for sea level 12.5 ka, implying that the coastal deltas were depressed a total of 143 m (Appendix A). Using a simple exponential rebound calculation with a 1,500-yr half-life (Andrews, 1968; Stuiver and Borns, 1975), 95% of the rebound, or all but 7 m, would have been accomplished by 6.0 ka. Using a half-life of 700 yrs (Ten Brink and Weidick, 1974), 95% of rebound would have been accomplished by 9.5 ka. If the marginal bulge hypothesis is correct (Walcott, 1970), rebound would have been less in Massachusetts, whereas several hundred kilometers south of the ice margin (i.e., Delaware to Long Island) the margin would have experienced subsidence. Quinlan and Beaumont (1981) present one model of numerical calculations of this effect. Belknap and Kraft (1977) and Dillon and Oldale (1978) discuss warping of the margin south of New England.

Comparing the proposed relative sea-level curve for Maine (Fig. 5) to the Bermuda sea-level curve (Redfield, 1967; Neumann, 1969; Hine and others, 1979) shows that the Maine coast was approximately 15 m lower 7.0 ka. If Bermuda can be considered as a relatively stable reference point, a more delayed rebound than that of the simple exponential calculations, or a deeper lowstand, is implied. In any case, it is clear that most of the rebound was completed at this time, and the dates from Nova Scotia and Maine may be comparable within 5 to 10 m.

Quinlan and Beaumont (1981, 1982) calculate rebound for eastern Canada based on similar data but different assumptions of the extent of the ice sheet. They use two reconstructions of maximum extent of the ice sheets, the "minimum" model of Grant (1977), and the "maximum" model of Peltier and Andrews (1976). It should be noted that the "maximum" model of Hughes and others (1981) is more extensive than the latter. The Quinlan and Beaumont (1982, fig. 10) reconstruction for paleosea levels between

13.0 and 7.0 ka is strongly at odds with the delta and marine shell information in Maine. The curve of Newman and others (1980) for coastal Maine shows a drop in sea level to a lowstand only 10 m below present, similar to the Quinlan and Beaumont (1982) reconstruction for Boston. If the 65-m lowstand for Maine is correct, the assumptions of those models will need to be re-examined. The approach of these authors, and workers such as Clark and others (1978), Grant (1980) and Cathles (1980) is valid, but the assumptions of ice extent and mantle rheology may need adjustment. Fastook and Hughes (1982) have examined ice margins in the Gulf of Maine in a numerical model of retreat, and when they encompass simultaneous rebound into the model, it may be possible to delimit more accurately the effects of isostatic rebound on the coast of Maine (T. J. Hughes, pers. commun.).

Late Holocene sea level.—

The late Holocene record of sea level in Maine is most reliably examined through basal salt marsh peats. Previous studies have used a variety of materials and sampling techniques, but for new data we have used a vibracorer to obtain undisturbed samples. Figure 6 is a plot of all available Holocene salt marsh sea-level data for Maine, including the 1983–1984 data. There is an obvious spread of points. There are several reasons for this. First, there may be along-coast variations of rate of relative sea-level change, as suggested by the tide-gauge, releveling, and delta evidence (Anderson and others, 1984). Thus, the Popham and Wells data from southwestern Maine may differ from the Deer Isle and Newcastle data from the central coast and from the Addison

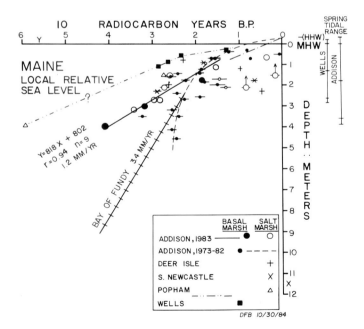

Fig. 6.—Late Holocene radiocarbon-dated salt marsh peats. Data from Timson (1978) for Wells, Nelson and Fink (1978) for Popham, Anderson and Race (1981) for Deer Isle and South Newcastle, Thompson (1973) and Belknap and others (1985) for Addison. Linear regression is for Addison II 1983–1984 data older than 1.5 ka. Bay of Fundy curve from Figure 3.

data on the northeast coast (Fig. 1). Second, some of the data are basal salt marsh peats (solid symbols) on a noncompatible substrate, whereas others are within the sediment column and may have been displaced by compaction. Third, only the Addision 1983–1984 data were collected with a 7-cm-diameter continuous pipe vibracorer, which minimizes contamination problems. This core can be examined for hiatuses and evidence of slumping or ice rafting. Some of the earlier data points may have been contaminated during sampling, especially the Davis cores. Thompson (1973) cited at least two cases of this problem in his study. Fourth, the large tidal range (noted on the

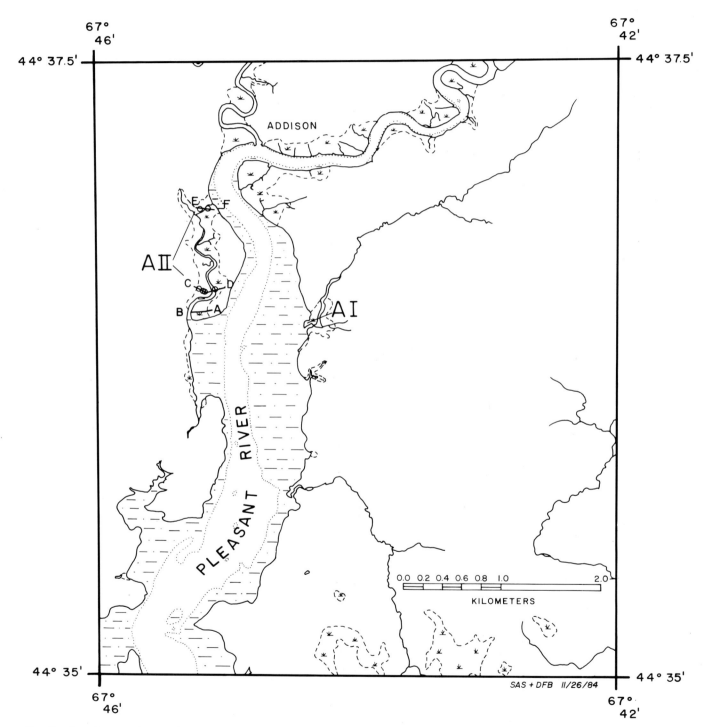

Fig. 7.—Location map for Addison salt marshes. Based on U.S. Geological Survey 7.5′ topographic maps for Addison, Maine and Harrington, Maine.

vertical axis, Fig. 6) provides a potential for disruption of the record through slumping into tidal creeks and ice rafting onto the marsh surface. Finally, the material dated must be representative of sea level. Wood and other debris collect as flotsam at the high tide line in a marsh, but this debris may be considerably older than the marsh surface. The approach of Scott and Medioli (1978) is to date this wood; we would avoid such material.

The primary focus of the 1983–1984 study was re-examination of the Addision II (AII) marsh (Belknap and others, 1985). Figure 7 is the location map, with the transects from Thompson (1973) which were re-examined. Figure 8 is cross section C-D in AII, along the deepest and widest peat section. The cross section shows a tidal estuarine channel colonized by salt marsh, which migrates landward and upward through the past 4,000 yrs. The channel narrowed to a tidal marsh creek and migrated from west to east more than 100 m during the past 1,000 yrs. The present setting is that of a broad, mature, high salt marsh, dominated by *Spartina patens*, with *Juncus gerardii* on the higher high marsh

and *Spartina alterniflora* on the creek margins. Figure 9 is a plot of the Addison radiocarbon dates with elevations based on leveling. Linear regression of the 1983–1984 data older than 1.5 ka clearly defines a straight line rising at 1.22 m/yr from 4.2 to 1.5 ka. Points younger than 1.5 ka have been affected by the rapid sedimentation and/or slumping during migration of the tidal creek near AII-VC-2. Re-examination of Thompson's (1973) data suggests that his two deepest points (queried, below −4 m, Fig. 9) are slump blocks into the channel on transect A-B. This would have been difficult to determine with a Davis corer. Other points which can be excluded are the wood and total organic carbon (TOC) data, and the two queried points that Thompson (1973) suggested were contaminated in the field. Other data points may also be questioned, because they were amalgamated samples of three or four Davis corer penetrations.

AII peats prior to 1983 were taken from a black basal unit which is heavily contaminated with humic acids. NaOH soluble fractions of these samples (Belknap and others, 1985) showed wide variations from the insoluble fraction. The

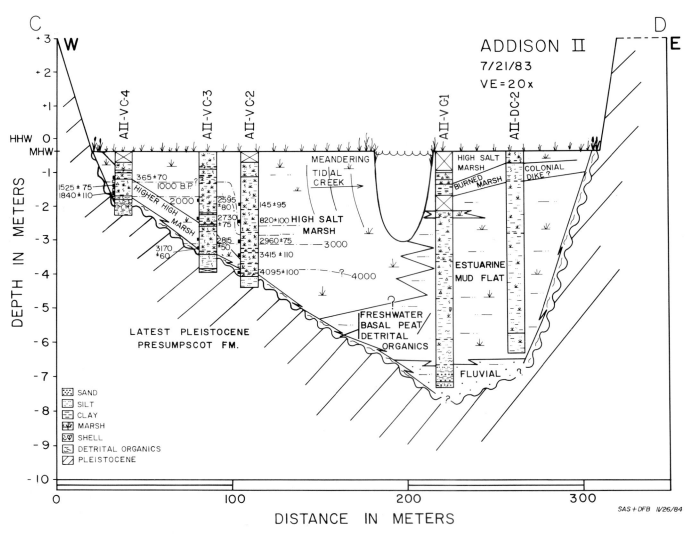

FIG. 8.—Cross section C-D, Addison II marsh. Based on sedimentologic interpretations and 12 radiocarbon-dated peats in four vibracores and one "Dutch" core (Eijkelkamp gouge auger).

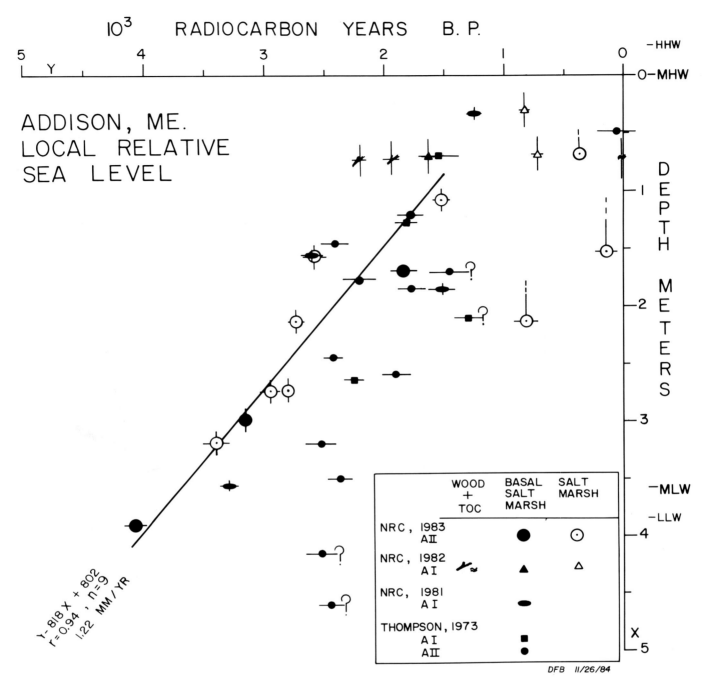

FIG. 9.—Addison sea-level data: radiocarbon-dated peats, wood and total organic carbon, from studies by Thompson (1973), Anderson and Race (1981), and Belknap and others (1985). Linear regression based on Addison II 1983–1984 data (larger symbols), pre-1.5 ka.

1983–1984 data (Table 2) were taken from a layer about 10 cm above the black basal unit, in a brown peat with few detrital contaminants. This material was prepared in the same fashion, to remove NaOH soluble material (Table 2). Macroscopic examination of the peat allowed identification of plant species, by comparison to modern examples of rhizomes and other parts. Dated samples were primarily *Juncus gerardii* and *Spartina patens*. Anderson and Race (1981)

used salt marsh foraminifera, following the method of Scott (1977) and Scott and Medioli (1978), to determine marine from non-marine sections of the same marsh. The rapid influx of foraminifera always occurs within the basal black peat.

Due to the limitations of accuracy inherent to salt marsh sea-level data, we have not attempted to define short period fluctuations in the rate of rise. As pointed out by Belknap

TABLE 2.—ADDISON ¹⁴C DATES: 1982–1983

Sample	Material	Depth MHW (cm)	NaOH Insoluble Corrected Age (yrs)	δ¹³C	NaOH Soluble Corrected Age (yrs)	δ¹³C
Addison I Marsh: Eroding face on Pleasant River, 1982						
82-1	(W)	74	2,220 ± 50	—	—	
82-2	(W)	73	1,945 ± 60	—	—	
82-3	(SM)	70	1,635 ± 50	−27.7	1,595 ± 70	−25.2
82-4	(TOC)	71	20 ± 80	−27.9	865 ± 75	−29.2
82-5	(SM)	30	815 ± 45	−24.4	760 ± 60	−25.0
82-6	(SM)	62-75	720 ± 45	−23.7	955 ± 65	−23.0
Addison II Marsh: Vibracores, 1983						
Vibracore 2 SI-						
6203	(SM)	150–155	145 ± 95	−19.6	910 ± 95	−20.1
6202	(SM)	210–215	820 ± 100	−15.3	4,415 ± 220	−15.7
6201	(SM)	270–275	2,960 ± 75	−21.1	2,815 ± 155	−20.3
6200	(SM)	315–320	3,415 ± 110	−23.4	110% modern	−23.4
6199	(SM)	384–393	4,095 ± 100	−23.0	3,850 ± 70	−22.0
Vibracore 3						
6203	(SM)	152–157	2,595 ± 80	−18.5	137% modern	
6206	(SM)	209–214	2,730 ± 75	−17.9	1,810 ± 130	−18.3
6205	(SM)	269–274	2,815 ± 50	−18.8	1,885 ± 100	−19.3
6204	(SM)	295–300	3,170 ± 60	−26.6	3,145 ± 85	−25.9
Vibracore 4						
6210	(SM)	65–70	365 ± 70	−22.8	1,040 ± 65	−20.6
6209	(SM)	105–110	1,525 ± 75	−28.2	550 ± 145	−27.7
6208	(SM)	165–170	1,840 ± 110	−26.9	2,170 ± 80	−27.2

Linear regression for AII dates >1.0 ka (Insol.) for x = depth (cm); y = age (yrs); $y = 8.18 \times + 802$; $r = 0.94$; $n = 9$; <0.01 slope = 1.22 mm/yr; 88% of variance explained. Material: W = Wood, SM = Salt Marsh Peat, TOC = Total Organic Carbon

and Kraft (1977) and Belknap and Hine (1983), the data limitations are better handled by statistical regression analysis to determine long-term rates.

It has long been clear that salt marshes in Maine are usually less than 5 m thick (Davis, 1910; McIntire and Morgan, 1964). Redfield (1967) suggested a slowing in rate of sea-level rise 4.0 ka, which first allowed broad marshes to accumulate here. We agree with this possibility, but are continuing to explore for submerged marshes in the nearshore area (Belknap and others, 1987).

The comparison between the 1983–1984 sea-level data and previous work shows a tighter clustering of the new data (88% of the variance explained by a linear distribution). The differences may be due to the sampling techniques. There may be a slowing in the rate of rise at Addison after 2.0 ka, but the peat dates cannot yet resolve this problem. On the other hand, the tide-gauge information (Fig. 4) suggests that presently sea level is rising two to three times faster than the long-term late Holocene trend. This is a common situation along most of the United States east coast (Brown, 1978; Belknap and Kraft, 1977).

We are presently evaluating similar data from central and southern Maine which will address the postulated neotectonic warping. In addition, several more samples have been taken to enhance the Addison II curve. Despite limitations imposed by tidal range, ice rafting, and lack of marshes thicker than about 5 m, we expect to answer the question of long-term along-coast warping initially posed by the NRC study.

As for the short-term, latest Holocene record, a combination of archeologic, historic, seismic and releveling measurements suggests that the eastern Maine coast near Eastport has undergone differential downwarping (Anderson and others, 1984). The lack of archeological sites older than about 2.5 ka, drowning of colonial dikes and later wharves, the differential warping indicated by precise first-order re-

leveling of bench marks, and the tide-gauge evidence (Fig. 4) all suggest that eastern coastal Maine is undergoing neotectonic warping of relatively recent origin or sporadic activity.

CONCLUSIONS

Relative sea-level changes in Maine have been extreme and rapid over the past 14,000 yrs. They have been caused by a combination of isostatic movements of the land and eustatic sea-level changes. The best evidence for the highstand of marine onlap is from marine mollusk shells in the Presumpscot Fm glaciomarine mud and intefingering coarser units. These data are not precise indicators of sea level but track deglaciation, trangression and regression. The best indicators for the level of the highstand at +73 m along the coast, about 13.0 to 12.5 ka, are glaciomarine deltas. The lowstand at −65 m (possibly about 9.5 ka) is best indicated by seismic reflection profiles over shorelines and deltas now submerged in the Gulf of Maine. The subsequent transgression is tracked by a few dates from the lowstand to 7.0 ka, but only the late Holocene from 4.0 ka to present has adequate data coverage. From 4.2 to 1.5 ka, sea level rose nearly linearly 1.22 m/1,000 yrs. It may then have slowed to about half that rate until very recently.

We cannot yet evaluate the precise relative contributions of isostasy and eustasy, but the Maine coast was dominated by isostatic warping from before 14.0 ka until about 9.5 ka. The period of 10.0 to 9.0 ka was a relative balance between eustatic rise and isostatic rebound, causing a near stillstand of sea level. This was the period in which the −65-m shorelines and deltas were constructed. Although slow rebound continued, eustatic sea-level rise and onlap occurred from 9.5 ka to the present.

The coast may be experiencing neotectonic warping, as indicated by a variety of data (Anderson and others, 1984).

This is presently being tested in the longer term time frame with multiple late Holocene sea-level curves.

ACKNOWLEDGMENTS

This work was supported by a contract from the United States Nuclear Regulatory Commission to the Maine Geological Survey and through the National Science Foundation EPSCOR program Grant PRM-80-11448. In a multidiscipline, multiworker project, it is sometimes difficult to acknowledge contributions by everyone completely. This paper is primarily geologic in scope, but the opportunity for interdisciplinary exchanges with archeologists, civil engineers, and historians has strengthened the project. The responsibility for conclusions reached in this paper rests with the first author, but the credit for the work done must be shared with the group. During the course of the present study, field and laboratory assistance was provided by students Cloe C. Caputo, Bradley W. B. Hay, Sarah B. Miller, Stephanie A. Staples, and Captain Mike Dunn of the R/V LEE. Special thanks are due David Sanger of the University of Maine at Orono Anthropology Department. Other facets of the larger project have included student assistance from Anne E. Bridge, Kristine J. Crossen, Douglas C. Kellogg, Jonathan W. Ladd, and Charles D. Race. The pioneering efforts by Stuart N. Thompson, Detmar Schnitker, Bruce W. Nelson, L. Kenneth Fink, Jr., Barry S. Timson, and Arthur M. Hussey II were an important starting point for this study. The paper was improved by review from Walter S. Newman.

REFERENCES

ANDERSON, R. S., AND BORNS, H. W., JR., 1983, Evidence for Late Holocene sea-level rise in New England: a summary of available data derived from salt marshes and other organic materials, in Thompson, W. B., and Kelley, J. T., eds., New England Seismotectonic Study Activities in Maine During Fiscal Year 1982: Maine Geological Survey Report to U.S. Nuclear Regulatory Commission, Augusta, p. 121–136.

————, AND RACE, C. D., 1981, Evidence for Late Holocene and recent sea-level rise along coastal Maine utilizing salt marsh data, in Thompson, W. B., ed., New England Seismotectonic Study Activity in Maine During Fiscal Year 1981: Maine Geological Survey Report to U.S. Nuclear Regulatory Commission, Augusta, p. 79–96.

ANDERSON, W. A., KELLEY, J. T., THOMPSON, W. B., BORNS, H. W., JR., SANGER, D., SMITH, D. C., TYLER, D. A., ANDERSON, R. S., BRIDGES, A. E., CROSSEN, K. J., LADD, J. W., ANDERSEN, B. G., AND LEE, F. T., 1984, Crustal warping in coastal Maine: Geology, v. 12, p. 677–680.

ANDREWS, J. T., 1968, Pattern and cause of variabilty of post-glacial uplift and rate of uplift in Arctic Canada: Journal of Geology, v. 76, p. 404–425.

————, 1970, Present and postglacial rates of uplift for glaciated northern and eastern North America derived from post-glacial uplift curves: Canadian Journal of Earth Science, v. 7, p. 703–715.

BARTH, M. C., AND TITUS, J. G., eds., 1984, Greenhouse Effect and Sea Level Rise, a Challenge for this Generation: Van Nostrand Reinhold Company, New York, 325 p.

BELKNAP, D. F., 1985, The submerged glaciofluvial paleodelta of the Kennebec River, west-central Maine coast: Geological Society of America, Abstracts with Programs, v. 17, p. 4.

————, AND HINE, A. C., 1983, Evidence for a sea level lowstand between 4500 and 2400 years B.P. on the southeast coast of the United States—discussion: Journal of Sedimentary Petrology, v. 53, p. 679–685.

————, KELLEY, J. T., AND SHIPP, R. C., 1987, Quaternary stratigraphy of representative Maine estuaries: initial examination by high-resolution seismic reflection profiling, in FitzGerald, D. M. and Rosen, P. S., eds., Treatise on Glaciated Coasts: Academic Press, New York, p. 177–207.

————, KELLEY, J. T., BORNS, H. W., JR., SHIPP, R. C., JACOBSON, G. L., JR., AND STUCKENRATH, R., JR., 1985, Sea-level curves for coastal Maine: Maine Geological Survey Report to U.S. Nuclear Regulatory Commission, Crustal Warping Studies in Maine, Fiscal Year 1983, 33 p.

————, AND KRAFT, J. C., 1977, Holocene relative sea-level changes and coastal stratigraphic units on the northwest flank of the Baltimore Canyon trough geosyncline: Journal of Sedimentary Petrology, v. 47, p. 610–629.

————, SHIPP, R. C., AND KELLEY, J. T., 1986, Depositional setting and Quaternary stratigraphy of the Sheepscot estuary, Maine: a preliminary report: Geographie physique et Quaternaire, v. 40, p. 55–69.

BIRCH, F. S., 1984, A geophysical study of sedimentary deposits on the inner continental shelf of New Hampshire: Northeastern Geology, v. 6, p. 207–221.

BLOOM, A. L., 1960, Late Pleistocene changes of sea level in southwestern Maine: Maine Geological Survey, Augusta, 143 p.

————, 1963, Late-Pleistocene fluctuations of sea level and postglacial crustal rebound in coastal Maine: American Journal of Science, v. 261, p. 862–879.

————, AND STUIVER, M., 1963, Submergence of the Connecticut coast: Science, v. 139, p. 332–334.

BORNS, H. W., JR., AND HUGHES, T. J., 1977, The implications of the Pineo Ridge readvance in Maine: Geographie Physique et Quaternaire, v. 31, p. 203–206.

BOSTWICK, L. G., 1978, An environmental framework for cultural change in Maine: pollen influx and percentage diagrams from Monhegan Island: Unpublished M.S. Thesis, Institue for Quaternary Studies, University of Maine, Orono, 67 p.

BROWN, L. D., 1978, Recent vertical crustal movement along the east coast of the United States: Tectonophysics, v. 44, p. 205–231.

CATHLES, L. M., 1980, Interpretation of postglacial isostatic adjustment phenomena in terms of mantle rheology, in Morner, N. A., ed., Earth Rheology, Isostasy, and Eustasy: John Wiley and Sons, New York, p. 11–44.

CLARK, J. A., 1980, A numerical model of worldwide sea level changes on a viscoelastic earth, in Mörner, N. A., ed., Earth Rheology, Isostasy, and Eustasy: John Wiley and Sons, New York, p. 525–534.

————, FARRELL, W. E., AND PELTIER, W. R., 1978, Global changes of post-glacial sea level: a numerical calculation: Quaternary Research, v. 9, p. 265–287.

COLLINS, D. W., 1985, Biostratigraphy of post-glacial sediments from the Isles of Shoals, New Hampshire: Geological Society of America, Abstracts with Programs, v. 17, p. 12.

CROSSEN, K. J., 1983, Glaciomarine deltas and moraines, Sebago Lake region, Maine: Guidebook for Field Trip 12, Geological Society of Maine, July 31, 1983, 19 p.

DAVIS, C. A., 1910, Salt marsh formation near Boston and its geological significance: Economic Geology, v. 5, p. 623–639.

DENNY, C. S., 1982, The geomorphology of New England: U.S. Geological Survey Professional Paper 1208, 18 p.

DILLON, W. P., AND OLDALE, R. N., 1978, Late Quaternary sea-level curve: reinterpretation based on glaciotectonic influence: Geology, v. 6, p. 56–60.

DIX LISLE, L., 1982, Annotated bibliography of sea-level changes along the Atlantic and Gulf coasts of North America: Shore and Beach, v. 50, no. 7, p. 24–33.

ETKINS, R., AND EPSTEIN, E. S., 1982, The rise of global mean sea level as an indication of climate change: Science, v. 215, p. 287–289.

FAIRBANKS, R. G., AND MATTHEWS, R. R., 1978, The marine oxygen isotope record in Pleistocene corals, Barbados, West Indies: Quaternary Research, v. 10, p. 181–196.

FAIRBRIDGE, R. W., AND NEWMAN, W. S., 1968, Postglacial crustal submergence of the New York area: Annals of Geomorphology, Neue Folge Band 12, v. 3, p. 296–317.

FASTOOK, J. L., AND HUGHES, T. J., 1982, A numerical model for reconstruction disintegration of the late Wisconsin glaciation in the Gulf of Maine, in Larson, G. L., and Stone, B. D., eds., Late Wisconsinan Glaciation of New England: Kendall/Hunt Publishing Company, Dubuque, Iowa, p. 229–242.

GRANT, D. R., 1970, Recent coastal submergence of the Maritime Provinces: Canadian Journal of Earth Science, v. 7, p. 676–689.

———, 1977, Glacial style and ice limits, the Quaternary stratigraphic record, and changes of land and ocean level in the Atlantic Provinces, Canada: Geographie Physique et Quaternaire, v. 31, p. 247–260.

———, 1980, Quaternary sea-level change in Atlantic Canada as an indication of crustal develeling, in Morner, N. A., ed., Earth Rheology, Isostasy and Eustasy; John Wiley and Sons, New York, p. 201–214.

GREENBERG, D. A., 1979, A numerical model investigation of tidal phenomena in the Bay of Fundy and Gulf of Maine: Marine Geodesy, v. 2, p. 161–187.

HAYES, M. O., 1979, Barrier island morphology as a function of tidal and wave regime, in Leatherman, S. P., ed., Barrier islands from the Gulf of St. Lawrence to the Gulf of Mexico: Academic Press, New York, p. 1–27.

HICKS, S. D., DeBAUGH, H. A., JR., AND HICKMAN, L. E., JR., 1983, Sea level variations for the United States 1855–1980: Tides and Water Levels Branch, National Ocean Service, National Oceanic and Atmospheric Administration, Rockville, Maryland, 170 p.

HINE, A. C., SNYDER, S. W., AND NEUMANN, A. C., 1979, Coastal plain and inner shelf structure, stratigraphy, and geologic history: Bogue Banks area, North Carolina: Final Report to North Carolina Science and Technology Committee, October, 1979, 3 parts (not consecutively paginated).

HOFFMAN, J. S., 1984, Estimates of future sea level rise, in Barth, M. C., and Titus, J. G., eds., Greenhouse Effect and Sea Level Rise: A Challenge for this Generation: Van Nostrand Reinhold Company, New York, p. 79–103.

———, KEYES, D., AND TITUS, J. D., 1983, Projecting Future Sea Level Rise: Methodology, Estimates to the Year 2100, and Research Needs: second revised edition, Office of Policy and Resource Management, U.S. Environmental Protection Agency, GPO No. 055-000-00236-3, Washington, D.C., 121 p.

HUGHES, T. J., 1981a, Lithosphere deformation by continental ice sheets: Proceedings of the Royal Society of London, v. 378, p. 507–527.

———, 1981b, Numerical reconstruction of paleo-ice sheets, in Denton, G. H., and Hughes, T. J., eds., The Last Great Ice Sheets: John Wiley and Sons, New York, p. 222–274.

———, DENTON, G. H., ANDERSEN, B. G., SCHILLING, D. H., FASTOOK, J. L., AND LINGLE, C. S., 1981, The last great ice sheets: a global view, in Denton, G. H., and Hughes, T. J., eds., The Last Great Ice Sheets: John Wiley and Sons, New York, p. 275–318.

HUSSEY, A. M., II, 1959, Age of intertidal tree stumps at Wells Beach and Kennebunk Beach, Maine: Journal of Sedimentary Petrology, v. 29, p. 464–465.

———, 1970, Observations on the origin and development of the Wells Beach area, Maine: Maine Geological Survey Bulletin 23, Augusta, p. 58–68.

JOHNSON, D., 1925, The New England-Acadian Shoreline: facsimile edition, Hafner Publishing Company, New York, 1967, 608 p.

KAYE, C. A., AND BARGHOORN, E. S., 1964, Late Quaternary sea-level change and crustal rise at Boston, Massachusetts, with notes on the autocompaction of peat: Geological Society of America Bulletin, v. 75, p. 63–80.

KELLEY, J. T., 1987, Sedimentary environments along Maine's estuarine coastline, in FitzGerald, D. M. and Rosen, P. S., eds., Treatise on Glaciated Coasts: Academic Press, New York.

KELLEY, J. T., AND KELLEY, A. R., 1985, The sedimentary framework of Saco Bay, Maine: Geological Society of America, Abstracts with Programs, v. 17, p. 28.

———, BELKNAP, D. F., AND SHIPP, R. C., 1986, Variability in the evolution of two adjacent bedrock-framed estuaries in Maine, in Wolfe, D. A., ed., Estuarine Variability: Academic Press, Orlando, Florida, p. 21–42.

KNEBEL, H. J., 1986, Holocene depositional history of a large glaciated estuary, Penobscot Bay, Maine: Marine Geology, v. 73, p. 215–236.

———, AND SCANLON, K. M., 1985, Sedimentary framework of Penobscot Bay, Maine: Marine Geology, v. 65, p. 305–324.

LARSEN, P. F., AND TOPINKA, J. A., eds., 1984, Fundy Tidal Power Development: Preliminary Evaluation of its Environmental Consequences to Maine: Report to Maine State Planning Office, Technical Report 35, Bigelow Laboratory for Ocean Science, West Boothbay Harbor, 136 p.

LOUGEE, R. J., AND LOUGEE, C. R., 1976, Late-Glacial Chronology: Vantage Press, New York, 553 p.

McINTIRE, W. G., AND MORGAN, J. P., 1964, Recent geomorphic history of Plum Island, Massachusetts and adjacent coasts: Coastal Studies Series No. 8, Louisiana State University Press, Baton Rouge, 44 p.

NELSON, B. W., 1979, Shoreline changes and physiography of Maine's sandy coastal beaches: Unpublished M.S. Thesis, Department of Oceanography, University of Maine, Orono, 303 p.

———, AND FINK, L. K., JR., 1978, Geological and botanical features of sand beach systems in Maine: Maine Critical Areas Program, Maine State Planning Office Planning Report No. 54, Augusta, 269 pp.

NEUMANN, A. C., 1969, Quaternary sea level data from Bermuda (abs.): 8th International Quaternary Association Congress, Paris, p. 228–229.

NEWMAN, W. S., CINQUEMANI, L. J., PARDI, R. R., AND MARCUS, 1980, Holocene develeling of the United States' east coast, in Mörner, N. A., ed., Earth Rheology, Isostasy and Eustasy: John Wiley and Sons, New York, p. 449–463.

NOVAK, I., SWANSON, M., AND POLLOCK, S., 1984, Morphology and structure of the Gorham, Me., landslide: Geological Society of America, Abstracts with Programs, v. 16, p. 53–54.

OLDALE, R. N., 1985, Late Quaternary sea-level history of New England: a review of published data: Northeastern Geology, v. 7, p. 192–200.

———, AND O'HARA, C. J., 1980, New radiocarbon dates from the inner continental shelf off southeastern Massachusetts and a local relative sea-level-rise curve for the past 12,000 years: Geology, v. 8, p. 102–106.

———, WOMMACK, L. E., AND WHITNEY, A. B., 1983, Evidence for postglacial low relative sea-level stand in the drowned delta of the Merrimack River, western Gulf of Maine: Quaternary Research, v. 33, p. 325–336.

OSBERG, P. H., HUSSEY, A. M., II, AND BOONE, G. M., 1985, Bedrock Geologic Map of Maine: Maine Geological Survey, 1:500,000, Augusta.

OSTERICHER, C., 1965, Bottom and subbottom investigations of Penobscot Bay, Maine: U.S. Naval Oceanographic Office Technical Report 173, 177 p.

PATTERSON, W. S. B., 1981, The Physics of Glaciers: second edition, Pergamon Press, Oxford, 380 p.

PELTIER, W. R., AND ANDREWS, J. T., 1976, Glacial-isostatic adjustment—I. the forward model: Geophysical Journal of the Royal Astronomical Society, v. 46, p. 605–646.

QUINLAN, G., AND BEAUMONT, C., 1981, A comparison of observed and theoretical postglacial relative sea level in Atlantic Canada: Canadian Journal of Earth Science, v. 18, p. 1146–1163.

———, ———, 1982, The deglaciation of Atlantic Canada as reconstructed from the postglacial relative sea-level record: Canadian Journal of Earth Science, v. 19, p. 2232–2246.

RAMPTON, V. N., GAUTHIER, R. C., THIBAULT, J., AND SEAMAN, A. A., 1984, Quaternary Geology of New Brunswick: Canadian Geological Survey, Memoir 416, 69 p.

REDFIELD, A. C., 1967, Postglacial changes in sea level in the western North Atlantic Ocean: Science, v. 157, p. 687–692.

———, 1972, Development of a New England salt marsh: Ecological Monographs, v. 42, p. 201–237.

SCHNITKER, D., 1974, Postglacial emergence of the Gulf of Maine: Geological Society of America Bulletin, v. 85, p. 491–494.

———, 1975, Late glacial to recent paleoceanography of the Gulf of Maine: Maritime Sediments, Special Publication 1, p. 385–392.

SCOTT, D. B., 1977, Distributions and population dynamics of marsh-estuarine foraminifera with applications to relocating Holocene sea-level: Unpublished Ph.D. Dissertation, Department of Geology, Dalhousie University, 207 p.

———, AND GREENBERG, D. A., 1983, Relative sea-level rise and tidal development in the Fundy tidal system: Canadian Journal of Earth Science, v. 20, p. 1554–1564.

———, AND MEDIOLI, F. S., 1978, Vertical zonations of marsh foraminifera as accurate indicators of former sea levels: Nature, v. 272, p. 528–531.

———, ———, 1982, Micropaleontological documentation for early Holocene fall of relative sea level on the Atlantic coast of Nova Scotia: Geology, v. 10, p. 278–281.

SHACKLETON, N. J., 1977, The oxygen isotope record: stratigraphic tool and palaeoglacial record (abs.): 10th International Quaternary Association, Congress, Birmingham, p. 415.

SHALER, N. S., 1874, Preliminary report on the recent changes of level on the coast of Maine: Memoirs Boston Society of Natural History, v. 2, p. 321–340.

———, 1875, Remarks on the geology of the coast of Maine, New Hampshire and that part of Massachusetts north of Boston: U.S. Coast Survey, Coast Pilot for the Atlantic Sea-Board: Gulf of Maine and its Coast from Eastport to Boston (1874), p. 321–340.

SHIPP, R. C., 1985, Late Quaternary evolution of the Wells Embayment, southwestern Maine: Geological Society of America, Abstracts with Programs, v. 17, p. 63.

SMITH, G. W., 1985, Chronology of Late Wisconsinan deglaciation of coastal Maine, in Borns, H. W., Jr., LaSalle, P., and Thompson, W. B., eds., Late Pleistocene History of Northeastern New England and Adjacent Quebec: Geological Society of America Special Paper 197, p. 29–44.

STUIVER, M., AND BORNS, H. W., JR., 1975, Late Quaternary marine invasion in Maine: its chronology and associated crustal movement: Geological Society of America Bulletin, v. 86, p. 99–104.

TEN BRINK, W., AND WEIDICK, A., 1974, Greenland ice sheet history since the last glaciation: Quaternary Research, v. 4, p. 429–440.

THOMPSON, S. N., 1973, Sea-level rise along the Maine coast during the last 3,000 years: Unpublished M.S. Thesis, Department of Geological Sciences, University of Maine, Orono, 78 p.

THOMPSON, W. B., 1979, Surficial Geology Handbook for Coastal Maine: Maine Geological Survey, Augusta, 68 p.

———, 1982, Recession of the Late Wisconsinan ice sheet in coastal Maine, in Larson, G. J., and Stone, B. D., eds., Late Wisconsinan Glaciation of New England: Kendall/Hunt Publishing Company, Dubuque, Iowa, p. 211–228.

———, AND BORNS, H. W., JR., 1985, Surficial Geological Map of Maine: Maine Geological Survey, 1:500,000, Augusta.

———, CROSSEN, K. J., BORNS, H. W., JR. AND ANDERSEN, B. G., 1983, Glacial-marine deltas and late Pleistocene-Holocene crustal movements in southern Maine, in Thompson, W. B., and Kelley, J. T., eds., New England Seismotectonic Study Activities in Maine during Fiscal Year 1982: Maine Geological Survey Report to the U.S. Nuclear Regulatory Commission, Augusta, p. 153–171.

TIMSON, B. S., 1978, New carbon-14 dates: The Maine Geologist, v. 4, p. 6.

TYLER, D. A., AND LADD, J. W., 1980, Vertical crustal movement in Maine, in Thompson, W. B., ed., New England Seismotectonic Studies in Maine During Fiscal year 1980: Maine Geological Survey Report to U.S. Nuclear Regulatory Commission, Augusta, p. 99–153.

U.S. ARMY COASTAL ENGINEERING RESEARCH CENTER, 1973, Shore Protection Manual: U.S. Government Printing Office, Washington, D.C. (not consecutively paginated).

WALCOTT, R. I., 1970, Isostatic response to loading of the crust in Canada: Canadian Journal of Earth Science, v. 7, p. 716–734.

APPENDIX A

The relative importance of isostatic warping and eustatic sea-level change must be determined by comparison of local data to "stable" localities and by models of rheological response to ice loading. Clark and others (1978) have shown that there are no truly stable areas on earth; far-field isostatic warping of 8 m or more is expected well away from ice sheets.

In order to determine rebound in Maine, several assumptions must be made. Glaciomarine delta foreset-topset contacts are used as an elevation marker for the marine limit approximately 12.5 ka. They are assumed to be synchronous and deposited in an approximately horizontal plane with respect to one another (Thompson and others, 1983). There is no evidence that they were overtopped. There is good evidence that the features were in contact with the ice, and we will assume here for illustrative purposes only that the area was in isostatic equilibrium at 12.5 ka. Using these simplifying assumptions, Figure A-1 represents the ice

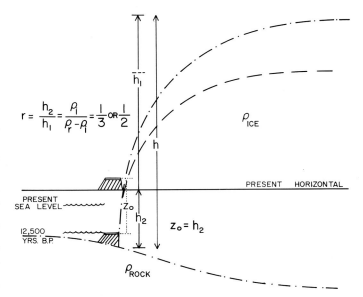

FIG. A-1.—Schematic diagram of deformation of coastal Maine deltas by glacio-isostatic loading.

margin at the time of delta formation and also the present setting of the deltas. In order to model isostatic rebound, we must know the depth of depression of the region. The ratio of thickness of ice below the present horizontal plane, h_2, to that above, h_1, is related to the density of ice, ρ_i, and rock, ρ_r, by the ratio:

$$r = \frac{h_2}{h_1} = \frac{\rho_i}{\rho_r - \rho_i} = \frac{1}{3} \text{ or } \frac{1}{2}. \qquad (1)$$

Hughes and others (1981) suggest that the ratio 1/3 holds, considering a visco-plastic lithosphere deformation (Hughes, 1981a, b). Patterson (1981) uses the ratio 1/2, considering only the crust. The next assumption requires an absolute value for sea level 12.5 ka. Such a value is ambiguous. We use the Dillon and Oldale (1978) curve from the southern New England-New York Bight shelf (Fig. A-2) as a reasonable approximation, a value of −70 m. Hughes and others (1981, table 6-3) have calculated a maximum eustatic drop in sea level of 91 to 117 m 18.0 ka, in agreement with estimates from oxygen isotope records for ice volume change (after accounting for seafloor hydro-isostatic response, Shackleton, 1977; Fairbanks and Matthews, 1978). The Dillon and Oldale (1978) curve corresponds with the 91-m estimate for 18.0 ka. If the deeper value is correct, their curve may be too shallow by 26 m or so in its earlier portions, which is just the amount they removed to "correct" actual data to account for a postulated deformation of the shelf. If not corrected, the "eustatic" value 12.5 ka might be −90 m.

Using the −70-m value, the total downwarp of deltas in Maine would be 143 m. The −90-m value would give 163 m of downwarp. If we consider that no significant uplift is occurring now, then h_2 = 143 or 163 m, thus:

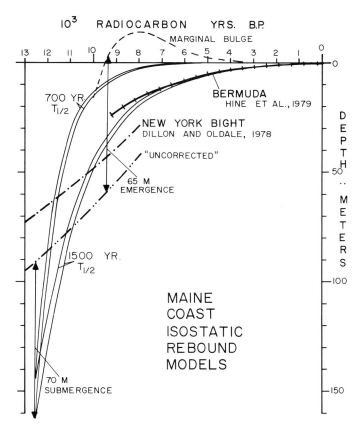

FIG. A-2.—Maine coast isostatic rebound models, based on simple exponential rebound with half-lives of 1,500 and 700 yrs, and initial values of 143 and 163 m of depression. These are compared to the Dillon and Oldale (1978) New York Bight Curve, both corrected and uncorrected for subsidence, to illustrate the 70-m submergence 12.5 ka and the 65-m emergence 9.5 ka (Fig. 5). A marginal bulge (Walcott, 1970) may explain part of the emergence. Later stages of rebound are compared to the Bermuda curve of Hine and others, 1979.

$$h_1 = \frac{h_2}{r} \tag{2}$$

and

$$h = \text{total ice thickness} = h_1 + h_2 \tag{3}$$

so:

$$\text{if } h_2 = 143 \text{ m}, \ r = \frac{1}{3}, \ h_1 = 429 \text{ m}, \ h = 572 \text{ m}$$

$$r = \frac{1}{2}, \ h_1 = 290 \text{ m}, \ h = 433 \text{ m}$$

$$\text{if } h_2 = 163 \text{ m}, \ r = \frac{1}{3}, \ h_1 = 489 \text{ m}, \ h = 652 \text{ m}$$

$$r = \frac{1}{2}, \ h_1 = 326 \text{ m}, \ h = 489 \text{ m}$$

So, ice thickness was about 1/2 km. To determine a simple exponential decay curve (Fig. A-2):

$$z = z_0 e^{-\lambda t} \tag{4}$$

with a decay constant determined from the half-life:

$$\frac{1}{2} z_0 = z_0 e^{-\lambda t_{1/2}} \tag{5}$$

$$\ln\left(\frac{1}{2}\right) = -\lambda t_{1/2}$$

$$\lambda = \frac{\ln 2}{t_{1/2}} = \frac{0.693}{t_{1/2}} \tag{6}$$

Using a half-life for decay of rebound of 1,500 yrs (Andrews, 1968):

$$t_{1/2} = 1,500 \text{ yrs}, \quad \lambda = 4.62 \times 10^{-4} \text{ yr}^{-1} \tag{7}$$

Using a half-life of 700 yrs (Ten Brink and Weidick, 1974):

$$t_{1/2} = 700 \text{ yrs}, \quad \lambda = 9.90 \times 10^{-4} \text{ yr}^{-1} \tag{8}$$

z_0 is either -143 or -163 m.

The four resulting curves are plotted in Figure A-2. Using equation 7, 95% of the rebound is accomplished by 6.0 ka. Using equation 8, 95% is accomplished by 9.5 ka. To check this simple model in another way, we compare it to the Bermuda curve of Hine and others (1979). At 7.0 ka the Maine local relative sea-level curve is at -27 m, whereas the Bermuda curve is at -12 m, suggesting a slow half-life or delayed rebound, such as would be caused by the marginal bulge. At 3.0 ka the Maine Curve is at -2.8 m and the Bermuda curve is at -1.8 m, a reasonable agreement, suggesting that most of the rebound is over by this time. The Oldale and O'Hara (1980) curve for southern Massachusetts is at -19 at that time, an intermediate value.

The depth of fall of sea level 9.5 ka is the most difficult feature to accommodate with these models. A fall to -65 m requires a rapid rebound and the deeper assumption to modify the Dillon and Oldale (1978) curve. The rate of offlap required by dates in the Presumpscot Fm (Smith, 1985), however, requires either the 1,500-yr half-life or delay in rebound. The decay of a marginal bulge might also cause a more rapid rebound several thousand years after retreat of the ice front.

The assumption of isostatic equilibrium is an oversimplification. Stuiver and Borns (1975, equation 1) have calculated the effects of a retreating ice front, out of equilibrium. More complete numerical modeling, such as the work by Fastook and Hughes (1982) and Quinlan and Beaumont (1981, 1982), is required to resolve the problem. Hopefully, future modeling can be better constrained by the new data.

GEOPHYSICAL MODELS

The quantitative model developed by Peltier and Andrews (1976) for the earth's response following deglaciation described a "peripheral bulge" occurring along former ice margins. This bulge is created as the ice load forces mantle material out from underneath it to the periphery of the ice sheet, and this extra mantle material creates an uplift along the ice margin. As the ice sheet retreats, the peripheral bulge retreats with it. Quinlan and Beaumont (1981) used this model to simulate RSL changes that may have occurred in Atlantic Canada, given different ice configurations. They proposed dividing the region into RSL zones. Zone D was entirely beyond the periphery of the former ice sheet and past the crest of the peripheral bulge; only RSL rise occurred here, because the crest of the peripheral bulge migrated inward and away from this area as the ice sheet retreated. Second is zone C, just inside the former ice margin and inside the crest of the peripheral bulge. This zone experienced early RSL fall and later RSL rise which drowned any early raised marine features. Third was zone B, an area farther inside the former ice margin and subject to substantial elastic rebound as well as the migration of the peripheral bulge. This area had substantial RSL fall with late RSL rise and was characterized by an abundance of raised marine features. Fourth was zone A, an area close to the former ice center which experienced only RSL fall until present. Quinlan and Beaumont (1981) present two possible situations: a maximum ice model (from Peltier and Andrews, 1976) and a minimum ice model (Grant, 1977). The two ice configurations indicate substantial differences in the locations of the zonal boundaries. With the RSL observations in this paper, we define which model best conforms to the field data. Zonal boundaries for the maximum ice load configuration are presented in Figure 1.

SEA LEVEL OBSERVATIONS

Atlantic coast of Nova Scotia.—

We present two curves here, one from Sable Island (Scott and others, 1984; Fig. 2A) and one composite curve from the Atlantic coast area circled in Figure 1 (Scott and Medioli, 1982; Miller and others, 1982; Fig. 2B). The curve from Sable Island shows continuous RSL rise over at least the last 7.0 ka at what appears to be a uniform rate. This is a typical zone D curve. The composite curve from the coast of Nova Scotia indicates a different situation with an undetermined amount of RSL fall prior to 7.0 ka (Scott and Medioli, 1982) but RSL rise since. This is a typical zone C curve. We do not know the amplitude of the early RSL fall, except that it was less than the subsequent RSL rise, since there are no subaerial, early Holocene marine features on the Nova Scotia coastline.

Nova Scotia-New Brunswick border.—

The curve shown in Figure 2C is a composite of RSL rise (Scott and Greenberg, 1983) and RSL fall curves from the same area (Scott and Medioli, 1980b). In this area, we were fortunate that a core collected offshore contained a sequence in which we could identify the reversal from RSL

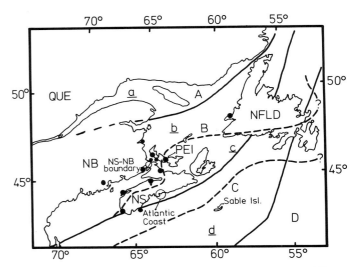

FIG. 1.—Theoretical sea-level zones predicted by Quinlan and Beaumont's (1981) maximum ice load configuration (solid lines, capital letters) with modifications based on field observations (dashed lines, small letters). Three composite RSL curves are presented later (Sable Island, Atlantic coast, NS-NB border), but additional curves are available from sites marked by solid dots. The Quebec-New Brunswick border is the dashed line that extends the A-B boundary.

fall to rise at about 7.0 ka. Actual reversal points are difficult to find because a specific sedimentary sequence is required to verify the points. This sequence, which must consist of a salt marsh subject to both regression and transgression, is only rarely preserved at offshore sites (e.g., Lunenburg Bay, Scott and Medioli, 1982). The highest raised marine features at this site are 10 m above present sea level. Farther south along the New Brunswick coast, raised marine features of the same age are observed as much as 75 m above present sea level (Scott and Medioli, 1980b) with correspondingly less subsequent RSL rise. These are all typical zone B curves.

Prince Edward Island.—

There are four RSL curves from Prince Edward Island, but they only represent the last 3,000 yrs (Scott and others, 1981). They do indicate, however, that the east end of the island has RSL rise rates twice as high as the west end (15 cm/100 yrs vs. 8 cm/100 yrs). This indicates the scale of the observed changes and shows that relatively large differences can be observed over a small distance (in this case 60 km). Raised marine features are observed on the west end but not in the east (Prest, 1973). The west end, therefore, is in zone B, whereas the east end is in zone C.

Newfoundland.—

One RSL curve recently published from western Newfoundland (Brookes and others, 1985) places western Newfoundland firmly within zone B. The curve is a composite and indicates marine features raised 35 to 40 m above present sea level 13.0 to 14.0 ka, with RSL falling until 6.0 ka to a level about 15 m below present and subsequently rising to its present level.

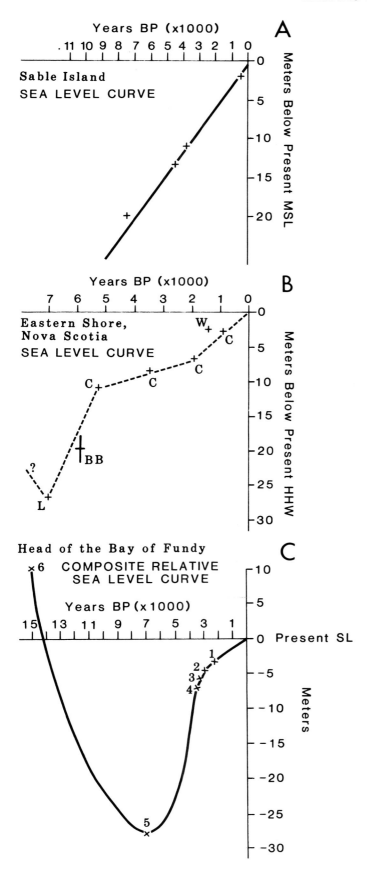

Northern New Brunswick and Quebec.—

All published curves from west of the Quebec-New Brunswick border (the zone A-B boundary in Fig. 1) suggest continuous RSL fall following deglaciation (e.g., Dionne, 1972). Varying RSL fall rates have occurred since the retreat of the Champlain Sea 12.0 ka (Cronin, 1977). Maximum RSL fall in Quebec appears to be between 100 and 200 m (Dionne, 1972). Dionne (1985) recently reported a short RSL rise period along the north shore of the St. Lawrence but this appears to be localized. RSL fall rates of 1 m/century are common, but few workers can present precise curves since RSL points are based on uplifted terrace dates with high error margins. This is a typical zone A response.

COMPARISON OF OBSERVATIONS TO THE MODEL

The field observations support the sea-level zones proposed by Quinlan and Beaumont (1981) in a general sense. Their geophysical model does provide the most plausible explanation for the regional differences in the observed data. The observations allow us to calibrate the model more closely. Quinlan and Beaumont (1981) have two possible ice configurations: minimum and maximum. The maximum ice model places 1,000 m of the ice over a large part of Atlantic Canada with an abrupt thinning to the ice margins on the continental shelf. This model also places a large amount of ice in the Gulf of St. Lawrence (Quinlan and Beaumont, 1981, fig. 3). The minimum ice model was adapted from Grant (1977) and locates the ice margins close to the present shorelines. The minimum model estimates from 250 to 500 m of ice thickness in Atlantic Canada (Quinlan and Beaumont, 1981, fig. 4). The zonal boundaries shown in Figure 1 correspond to the maximum ice model. The boundaries for the minimum model are so out of line with the observations that they are not shown, i.e., the A-B boundary for the minimum model would be off the map of Figure 1. Our data suggest a different position of the C-D boundary which we place between Sable Island and the present coastline. Based on field data, the B-C boundary cuts through the center of Nova Scotia, along the Nova Scotia-New Brunswick border, through the center of Prince Edward Island and across the southern coast of Newfoundland. We place the A-B boundary where Quinlan and Beaumont (1981) show it, near the Quebec-New Brunswick border.

Although the observations fit fairly closely with the predictions of the maximum ice model, we know that the Late Wisconsinan ice margins were located close to those of the minimum model because of direct geological evidence (e.g., Grant, 1977; King, 1980). Quinlan and Beaumont (1981)

· FIG. 2.—Composite observed RSL curves (curves drawn using data from more than one site) for Atlantic Canada from several sources. (A) Sable Island, zone D (Scott and others, 1984). (B) Atlantic coast, Nova Scotia, zone C (C points from Scott, 1977; W point, unpublished; BB point, Miller and others, 1982; L point, Scott and Medioli, 1982). (C) NS-NB border, zone B (points 1–5, Scott and Greenberg, 1983; point 6, Scott and Medioli, 1980b).

suggest that the large displacement in sea-level change zones between the minimum and maximum models are a result of ice thickness differences rather than ice marginal positions and imply that small-scale changes in the location of the ice margin will not change the zonal boundaries as much as changes in the ice load. The amplitudes of observed RSL change fall between those predicted for the two models, suggesting that there were more than 500 m of ice but probably less than 1,000 m covering most of Atlantic Canada during the late Wisconsinan.

SEDIMENTATION RESPONSE TO CHANGES IN RELATIVE SEA LEVEL

Zone D: Sable Island Bank.—

Observed and predicted sea levels for a zone D location like Sable Island (Figs. 1, 3) indicate a transgression since around 15.0 ka and predict a resulting coastal/marine sediment sequence. Few data are available from boreholes on the outer Scotian shelf. Our data consist primarily of seismic stratigraphy from Sable Island Bank and data of Scott and others (1984) from boreholes on Sable Island itself.

Quaternary sediments under Sable Island are at least 260 m thick (Hardy, 1974), indicating a location near the margin of at least one and perhaps several Pleistocene glacial advances. The late Quaternary pattern of sedimentation on Sable Island Bank is interpreted to consist of a proglacial or subglacial channel sequence extending down to a late Wisconsinan sea-level lowstand near the present shelf break at depths of 65 to 90 m below present sea level. A stratified, seaward-thickening wedge of sediment below −85 m (vertical bar pattern on Fig. 4) appears to represent a shallow marine accumulation at the distal end of the channel sequence. This sedimentation pattern of channeled continental shelf and shelf-edge deposition is consistent with other exposed continental margins during Pleistocene lowstands of sea level (e.g., the Gulf of Mexico; Suter and Berryhill, 1985).

As RSL rose at the beginning of the Holocene transgression, the shallow marine shelf-edge deposits briefly onlapped the channel sequence before giving way to a shoreface retreat style of transgression which reworked the underlying channel sequence. The northward migration of the shoreface produced a regional flat-lying acoustic reflector (Fig. 4), interpreted as the erosional unconformity at the base of the Holocene transgression. After the shoreface migrated through the area, a shoreface-connected ridge system evolved on the shallow inner shelf of Sable Island Bank (Fig. 3) in much the same fashion as the Middle Atlantic Bight regions of the United States east coast (Swift and Field, 1981). Substantial erosion was associated with shoreface retreat, resulting in the production of large sediment volumes which were transported northward to accumulate in the Holocene sand body of Sable Island Bank. Above the regional unconformity in the south lies a shore-

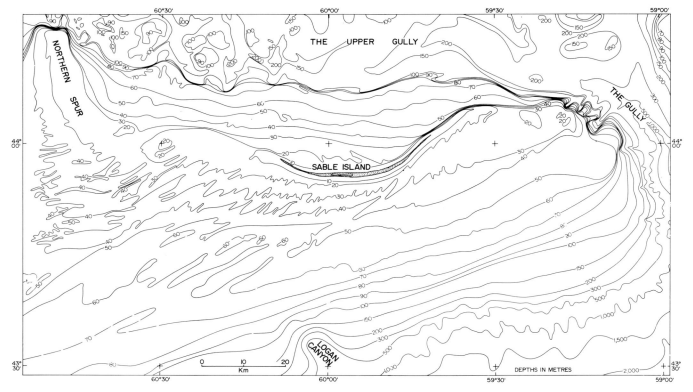

FIG. 3.—Sable Island is located in zone D on the outer Scotian shelf, over 200 km from the Nova Scotian coast. The sediment-abundant Sable Island Bank displays a characteristic transgressive morphology dominated by shoreface-detached ridge systems. Sable Island is part of a Holocene shelf sand body as much as 85 m thick which stretches 150 km from Northern Spur to the Gully (redrawn from a Geomarine Associates map based on Canadian Hydrographic Service field surveys).

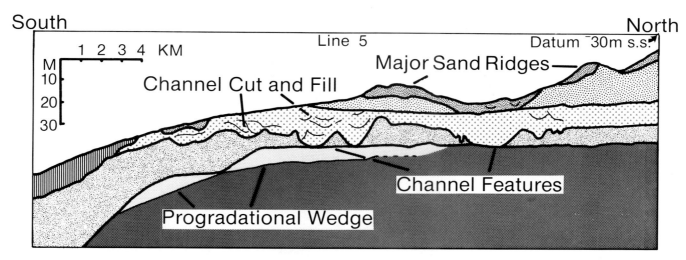

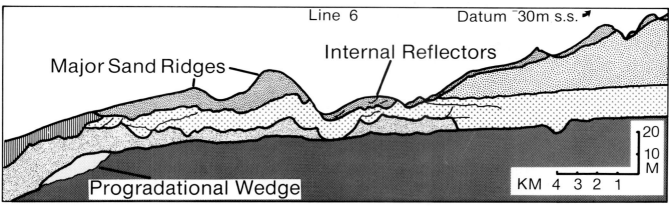

FIG. 4.—Digitized seismic lines 10 km apart and running from Logan Canyon (Fig. 3) to the west tip of Sable Island. The flat, horizontal reflector at −65 m is interpreted to represent a transgressive unconformity at the Holocene-Pleistocene boundary. Above this reflector (shaded dot pattern) lies the Holocene Sable Island shelf sand body and its associated shoreface ridge system. Below the −65m reflector is a Pleistocene sequence characterized by channeled units and progradational wedges formed during sea-level lowstands.

face-detached ridge system varying in thickness from 0 to 15 m (Fig. 3). Our RSL curve (Fig. 2A) indicates that the upper 25 m of this sand body accumulated in the last 8,000 yrs. Because of the location of Sable Island on an isolated topographic high, the thick Holocene sand body is likely to be preserved *in situ* at the completion of transgression.

Zone C: Atlantic coast of Nova Scotia.—

In zone C, RSL initially fell as the forebulge approached. Thereafter, sea level continued to rise until the present time. The initial period of RSL fall was short and is interpreted to have occurred prior to 7.0 ka (Fig. 2B). Any surficial evidence of this regressive phase has been removed during the subsequent transgression, except for isolated deposits (Scott and Medioli, 1982).

The sedimentation pattern on the Atlantic coast of Nova Scotia can be summarized in a six-stage evolutionary model (Boyd and others, in prep.) developed for the Eastern Shore region (Fig. 5). In Stage 1, Pleistocene glaciation produced NW-to-SE elongate scours in the Meguma Group metasedimentary bedrock. This glaciation also locally deposited a

10- to 20-m-thick drumlin till and a thinner, more widespread, lodgment or ablation till. After forebulge passage, rising RSL produced the Stage 2 transgression, which removed most evidence of RSL fall except in protected basins. Elongate bedrock scours were transformed into estuary systems. Concurrently, the relatively high-energy wave climate of the Eastern Shore began reworking the till deposits into baymouth barrier systems.

During the past 7,000 yrs, barrier evolution has followed a cyclic trend of generation, retreat, destruction and landward migration prior to re-establishment. Initially, during Stage 3, where sediment supply from drumlin or older barrier sources exceeded the rate of RSL rise, the barriers prograded, many forming beach-ridge plains. Later, during Stage 4, as drumlin sediment supply diminished, barrier retreat ensued in response to ongoing sea-level rise. Sediment was moved landward during Stage 4, infilling estuaries with flood-tidal deltas, tidal channels and marsh sediments. The loss of shoreline sediments to estuaries eventually resulted in barrier destruction (Stage 5) and the subsequent landward migration of the remnant barrier. The evolutionary cycle

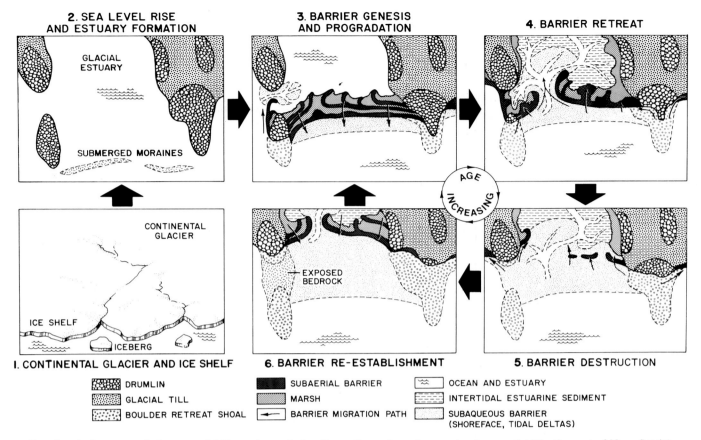

FIG. 5.—A six-stage evolutionary model illustrating typical sedimentation patterns for a region in zone C (Atlantic coast of Nova Scotia).

was completed in Stage 6 at a new, landward location, where fresh drumlin sediments, together with reworked remnants of the former barriers, combined in a new phase of barrier genesis and progradation.

In summary, Holocene sedimentation in zone C was characterized by glacial scouring to bedrock and subsequent deposition of thin but widespread ground moraine, lodgment and ablation tills. The glacial sediment was reworked during the transgression and was preserved only as coastal deposits within the topographically low estuarine systems. Inner-shelf bathymetry (Fig. 6) and seismic data show the transgressed surface to consist of exposed bedrock and truncated drumlin shoals and ridges, separated by relatively flat valley systems, oriented perpendicular to shore at the sites of former estuaries. Within the valley systems, the preserved sequence consists of Pleistocene till overlying Paleozoic bedrock with an uppermost unit of transgressive Holocene sediments deposited in estuarine and coastal barrier environments. The entire sequence of unconsolidated Quaternary sediment accounts for less than 30 m of thickness but more often is only 0–10 m thick (Hall, 1985).

Zone B: Bay of Fundy, western Prince Edward Island, eastern New Brunswick and western Newfoundland.—

The RSL response to deglaciation in zone B produced inundation of coastal areas previously loaded by ice. As these regions subsequently rebounded, they also experienced forebulge passage, resulting in major regression back from a "marine limit" (Fig. 7). Finally, in regions closer to the original ice margin (e.g., farther southeast), a second transgression followed the passage of the forebulge crest.

The sedimentation response below the "marine limit" was to accumulate saline glaciomarine deposits (e.g., Presumpscot Fm in Maine; Buzas, 1965). These glaciomarine sediments are composed of gray sandy silts; they are homogenous, non-bioturbated and contain foraminifera. The following regression deposited beach and delta sediments at old shoreline positions (Swift and Borns, 1967). After the regression, most zone B sedimentation was confined to lacustrine basins. Freshwater muds accumulated in these basins, characterized by a vertical succession of brownish-gray, laminated, organic-rich silty clays and clayey silts with

FIG. 7.—Sea level and resulting sedimentation patterns in zone B. Rebound after deglaciation resulted in a RSL fall between 16.0 and 7.0 ka. The glacial forebulge passage followed and produced the present transgression. Areas at the former sea-level maximum exhibit raised shoreline deposits. Salt marsh and barrier deposits are found at the present transgressive shoreline. Marine deposits overlain by freshwater deposits are preserved in estuarine/lacustrine basins.

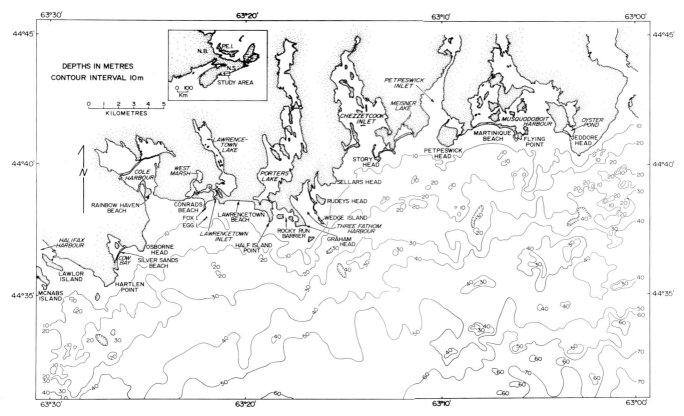

FIG. 6.—Inner-shelf morphology of the sediment-deficient eastern shore of Nova Scotia. The irregular topography of this zone C region results from exposed bedrock and till outcrops on the sea floor, such as those seaward of Jeddore Head and Three Fathom Harbour. Preservation after transgression is limited to shallow shelf valleys such as those seaward of Cole Harbour and Petpeswick Inlet. Compare this shelf topography with the zone D example in Figure 3.

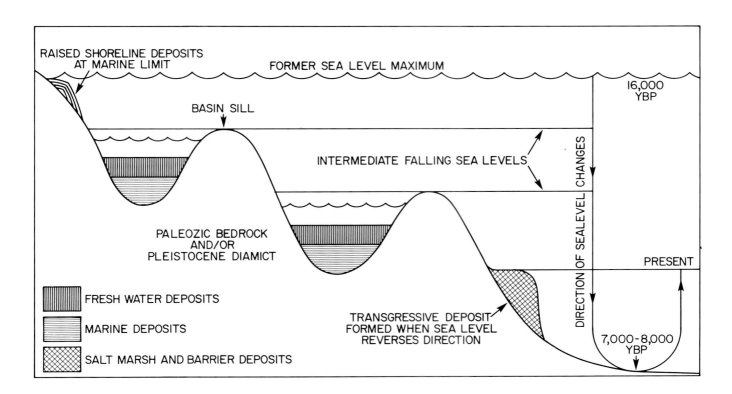

an insect fauna, overlain by brown organic muds with a characteristic thecamoebian fauna (Scott and Medioli, 1980b; Patterson and others, 1985). Along the eastern coastlines of zone B, a second marine transgression is currently in progress, producing reworked coastal barrier and estuarine sediments. These second-phase Holocene transgressive coastal deposits are well developed along the northern coast of Prince Edward Island (Dalrymple and others, 1982) and eastern New Brunswick (Reinson, 1985). They are similar in character to those described from zone C, but are more extensive and receive an additional sediment supply from eroding Carboniferous bedrock outcrops.

If preserved, a complete Wisconsinan-Holocene stratigraphic sequence in zone B would contain Carboniferous or older Paleozoic bedrock overlain in succession by glacial till, glaciomarine muds, coastal sediments, freshwater muds in lacustrine basins, and finally by estuarine/barrier deposits and marine muds.

Zone A: western New Brunswick and Quebec.—

The sedimentation history of zone A, closer to the original ice center, differs from zone B in the absence of initial and final transgression events. It consists of freshwater sedimentation in localized basins, as well as the emerged shoreline features seen also in zone B.

SUMMARY OF TRENDS NEAR THE ICE MARGIN

A distinctive pattern of sedimentation is developed close to an ice margin in response to erosion/deposition relationships and the fluctuations in RSL. Erosion predominates in subglacial environments of uplands, coastal plains and continental shelves. At these sites, deposition is only local and takes the form of material plastered over bedrock, such as drumlins or lodgment diamictites, together with lift-off moraines, eskers and recessional moraines (King, 1980; King and Fader, 1986). In contrast, the proglacial regions have abundant sediment, having received the net erosional products from source regions throughout the glacial transport path. Thick sediment sequences accumulate in glaciofluvial and glaciomarine environments (Molnia, 1983).

Depending on its location relative to the loading of the ice sheet and subsequent glacial forebulge migration, a zone near the ice sheet margin may experience sedimentation controlled by highly diverse sea-level histories, ranging from RSL rise and transgression to RSL fall and regression. In a zone D location such as Sable Island, sedimentation consists entirely of abundant trangressive coastal and marine deposits. In the path of the retreating forebulge through zones C and B, the following progression is observed: a regressive/transgressive history with thin strata containing no remaining subaerial evidence of regressive sedimentation, to a regressive/transgressive history with raised marine and coastal deposits and with a marine to freshwater sediment transition found in small lacustrine basins (Fig. 7).

In order to interpret sedimentation and RSL history in glacial regions, it is critical to locate the position of maximum glacial advance. This position of the ice margin determines whether the proglacial environment of deposition

will be concentrated in terrestrial, continental shelf or continental slope and rise environments. Along the coast of the Canadian Maritime Provinces and the adjacent continental shelf, the Wisconsinan ice margin terminated on the mid- to outer Scotian shelf (King, 1969; Grant and King, 1984). The land regions and the inner continental shelf experienced mainly erosion, whereas deposition was concentrated in the basins and on the outer banks of the Scotian shelf, the adjacent continental slope and the continental rise (King and Fader, 1986; Hill, 1983). Examples from zones B, C and D presented in this paper demonstrate the close interrelationships between glacial sediment supply, RSL and the resulting stratigraphic sequence.

DISCUSSION AND CONCLUSIONS

Although Quinlan and Beaumont's (1981) calculations do not exactly match the actual data, their model is clearly a good approximation. Part of the discrepancy is due to scale, since Quinlan Beaumont (1981) used a $1° \times 1°$ grid, and much of the variance is on a smaller scale. In a later paper, Quinlan and Beaumont (1982) have used sea-level data values with well defined amplitudes. Although the amplitudes are more in line with observations in this later paper, they are still higher than observed, particularly around Sable Island.

Peltier and Andrews (1976) originally designed their model as a way of determining mantle and crustal properties (i.e., viscosity and density), on the supposition that the postglacial sea-level movements were relatively well known and could be used to calibrate the model. In a general sense, they may have been correct. Quinlan and Beaumont (1981), however, show that in a smaller regional sense, the model variations depend more on ice configurations than mantle and crustal properties, although some gross properties can be determined for the earth's rheology as well (Cathles, 1975). There is also substantial within-zone variation, particularly in zone B, which is simply differentiated from zone C on the presence of raised marine features. For example, in New Brunswick at the NB-NS border, former RSL fall approaches zero, whereas 100 km to the southwest, there are raised marine features 75 m above sea level, although RSL rise is occurring at the present time. The combined model results and observations, however, allow the narrowing of possibilities for former ice thicknesses by eliminating the "thin ice" model suggested by Grant (1977).

Our RSL data and stratigraphic patterns demonstrate the complexity of local sea-level behavior. This has previously been recognized for broad regions of the earth. For example, the eustatic component of Holocene RSL rise slowed substantially by 6.5 ka in the South Pacific (Thom and Chappell, 1975), but because of contrasting basin dimensions, did not decrease until 3.6 ka in the Gulf of Mexico (Boyd and Penland, 1984). We have shown that strongly contrasting histories of RSL can be experienced over much shorter distances in regions close to Quaternary ice margins. This complex RSL behavior is best described through comparisons with geophysical models of glacial loading. In addition, we show a corerponding complexity in sedimentation pattern in these regions, which demonstrates the close linkage which exists between RSL history and the resulting stratigraphic sequence.

A major contrast in sedimentation style exists between subglacial and proglacial environments. In the Canadian Maritime Provinces the boundary between these two environments during late Wisconsinan time lay on the continental shelf. Subglacial regions are sediment-deficient. Diamictite, lacustrine and reworked coastal deposits characterize sedimentation on the formerly glaciated land surface. Proglacial regions are sediment-abundant, accumulating glaciofluvial deposits on raised land surfaces and thick glaciomarine deposits in shelf basins. Cross-shelf transport during sea-level lowstands develops extensive continental slope and rise sediment sequences.

ACKNOWLEDGMENTS

T. Duffett, M. Duplisea, J. Easton, G. Frotten, C. Honig, P. Lake, A. Miller, P. Workman (all from Dalhousie University) and A. Palmer (University of South Carolina) assisted in collecting sea-level data. M. Douma (Dalhousie University) compiled much of the Sable Island data. V. Baki, J. Barrett, and K. MacKinnon (Dalhousie University) assisted in completing the final manuscript. L. King, G. Fader (Atlantic Geoscience Centre), C. Beaumont (Dalhousie University) and G. Quinlan (Memorial University of Newfoundland) provided many helpful discussions over the years that led to some of the ideas in this paper. Financial support was supplied by several research agreements to Scott, Boyd, and Medioli, from the Department of Energy, Mines, and Resources of Canada. The Natural Sciences and Engineering Research Council of Canada provided individual operating grants to Scott, Boyd and Medioli.

REFERENCES

BOYD, R., AND PENLAND, S., 1984, Shoreface translation and the Holocene stratigraphic record: examples from Nova Scotia, the Mississippi delta, and eastern Australia: Marine Geology, v. 60, p. 391–412.

BROOKES, I. A., SCOTT, D. B., AND MCANDREWS, J. H., 1985, Postglacial relative sea-level change, Port au Port area, west Newfoundland: Canadian Journal of Earth Sciences, v. 22, p. 1039–1047.

BUZAS, M. A., 1965, Foraminifera from the late Pleistocene clay near Waterville, Maine: Smithsonian Miscellaneous Contributions, v. 145, 30 p.

CATHLES, L. M., III, 1975, The Viscosity of the Earth's Mantle: Princeton University Press, Princeton, 386 p.

CHALMERS, R., 1885, Preliminary report on the surface geology of New Brunswick: Geological Survey of Canada, Annual Report, new series, v. 1, p. G5-58.

———, 1890, Report on the surface geology of southern New Brunswick: Geological Survey of Canada, Annual Report, new series, v. 4, p. N5-88.

CRONIN, T. M., 1977, Late-Wisconsinan marine environments of the Champlain Valley (New York, Quebec): Quaternary Research, v. 7, p. 238–253.

DALY, R. A., 1920, Oscillations of level in belts peripheral to the Pleistocene ice caps: Geological Society of America Bulletin, v. 31, p. 303–318.

DALRYMPLE, R. W., AMOS, C. L., AND MCCANN, S. B., 1982, Beach and nearshore depositonal environments of the Bay of Fundy and southern Gulf of St. Lawrence: 11th International Congress on Sedimentology, Field Guidebook 6A, 116 p.

DIONNE, J.-C., 1972, La denominations des mers post-glaciaires du Quebec: Cahier Geographie Quebec, v. 16, no. 39, p. 483–487.

———, 1985, Evidence of a low sea level in the St. Lawrence estuary during the Holocene (abs.): Geological Association of Canada Annual

Meeting, Fredericton, New Brunswick, p. A14.

FARRELL, W. E., AND CLARK, J. A., 1976, On postglacial sea level: Geophysical Journal of the Royal Astronomical Society, v. 46, p. 647–667.

GADD, N. R., 1969, St. Stephen, New Brunswick (16/3): Geological Survey of Canada, Paper 69-1, Part A, p. 195–196.

———, 1970, Quaternary geology, southwest New Brunswick (126): Geological Survey of Canada, Paper 70-1, Part A, p. 170–172.

GRANT, D. R., 1970, Recent coastal submergence of the Maritime Provinces, Canada: Canadian Journal of Earth Sciences, v. 7, p. 676–689.

———, 1977, Glacial style and ice limits, the Quaternary stratigraphic record, and changes of land and ocean level in the Atlantic Provinces, Canada: Geographie Physique et Quaternaire, v. 31, no. 3–4, p. 247–260.

———, AND KING, L. H., 1984, A stratigraphic framework for the Quaternary history of the Atlantic Provinces, in Fulton, R. J., ed., Quaternary Stratigraphy of Canada—a Canadian Contribution to International Geological Correlation Program Project 24, Geological Society of Canada Paper 84-10, p. 174–191.

HALL, R. K., 1985, Inner shelf acoustic facies and surficial sediment distribution of the eastern shore, Nova Scotia: Unpublished M.S. Thesis, Dalhousie University, Halifax, 197 p.

HARDY, I. A., 1974, Lithostratigraphy of the Banquereau Formation of the Scotian shelf: Offshore Geology of Canada, Geological Survey of Canada, Paper 74-30, v. 2, p. 163–174.

HICKOX, C. F., 1962, Pleistocene geology of the central Annapolis Valley, Nova Scotia: Nova Scotia Department of Mines, Memoir no. 5, 36 p.

HILL, P. R., 1983, Detailed morphology of a small area on the Nova Scotian continental slope: Marine Geology, v. 53, p. 55–76.

JAMIESON, T. F., III, 1882, On the cause of the depression and re-elevation of the land during the glacial period: Geological Magazine, v. 9, p. 400–466.

KING, L. H., 1969, Submarine end moraines and associated deposits on the Scotian Shelf: Geological Society of America Bulletin, v. 80, p. 83–96.

———, 1980, Aspects of regional surficial geology related to site investigation requirements—eastern Canadian shelf, in Ardus, D. A., ed., Proceedings, Offshore Site Investigation, Geological Society of London, p. 38–59.

———, AND FADER, G. B., 1986, Wisconsinan glaciation of the Atlantic continental shelf off southeast Canada: Geological Survey of Canada Bulletin no. 363, 76 p.

MILLER, A. A. L., MUDIE, P. H., AND SCOTT, D. B., 1982, Holocene history of Bedford Basin, Nova Scotia: foraminifera, dinoflagellate, and pollen records: Canadian Journal of Earth Science, v. 19, p. 2342–2367.

MOLNIA, B. F., 1983, Glacial-Marine Sedimentation: Plenum Publishing, New York, 844 p.

PATTERSON, R. T., MACKINNON, K. D., SCOTT, D. B., AND MEDIOLI, F. S., 1985, Arcellaceans ("Thecamoebians") in small lakes of New Brunswick and Nova Scotia: modern distribution and Holocene stratigraphic changes: Journal of Foraminiferal Research, v. 15, p. 114–137.

PELTIER, W. R., AND ANDREWS, J. T., 1976, Glacial-isostatic adjustment—I. the forward problem: Geophysical Journal of the Royal Astronomical Society, v. 46, p. 605–646.

PREST, V. K., 1973, Surficial deposits of Prince Edward Island: map 1366A. Geological Survey of Canada.

QUINLAN, G., AND BEAUMONT, C., 1981, A comparison of observed and theoretical postglacial relative sea-level in Atlantic Canada: Canadian Journal of Earth Sciences, v. 8, p. 1146–1163.

———, AND ———, 1982, The deglaciation of Atlantic Canada as reconstructed from the postglacial relative sea-level record: Canadian Journal of Earth Sciences, v. 19, p. 2232–2246.

REINSON, G. E., 1985. Barrier island and associated strand plain systems, in Walker, R., ed., Facies Models, second edition: Geoscience Canada Reprint Series 1, p. 119–140.

SCOTT, D. B., 1977, Distributions and population dynamics of marsh-estuarine foraminifera with implications to relocating Holocene sea levels: Unpublished Ph.D. Dissertation, Dalhousie University, Halifax, 252 p.

———, AND GREENBERG, D. A., 1983, Relative sea-level rise and tidal development in the Fundy tidal system: Canadian Journal of Earth Sciences, v. 20, p. 1554–1564.

———, AND MEDIOLI, 1978, Vertical zonations of marsh foraminifera as accurate indicators of former sea levels: Nature, v. 272, p. 528–531.

———, AND ———, 1980a, Quantitative studies of marsh foraminiferal distributions in Nova Scotia: implications for sea level studies: Cushman Foundation, Foraminiferal Research Special Publication 17, 68 p.

———, AND ———, 1980b, Post-glacial emergence curves in the Maritimes determined from marine sediments in raised basins: Proceedings of the Canadian Coastal Conference, Burlington, Ontario, p. 428–446.

———, AND ———, 1982, Micropaleontological documentation for early Holocene fall of relative sea-level on the Atlantic coast of Nova Scotia: Geology, v. 10, p. 278–281.

———, ———, AND DUFFET, T. E., 1984, Holocene rise of relative sea-level at Sable Island, Nova Scotia, Canada: Geology, v. 12, p. 173–176.

———, WILLIAMSON, M. A., AND DUFFET, T. E., 1981, Marsh foraminifera of Prince Edward Island: their recent distribution and application for former sea-level studies: Maritime Sediments and Atlantic Geology, v. 17, p. 98–129.

SUTER, J. R., AND BERRYHILL, H. L., 1985, Late Quaternary shelf margin deltas, northwest Gulf of Mexico: American Association of Petroleum Geologists Bulletin, v. 69, p. 77–91.

SWIFT, D. J. P., AND BORNS, H. W., JR., 1967, A raised fluviomarine outwash terrace, north shore of the Minas basin, Nova Scotia: Journal of Geology, v. 75, no. 6, p. 693–710.

———, AND FIELD, M., 1981, Evolution of a classic sand ridge field, Maryland sector, North American inner shelf: Sedimentology, v. 28, p. 461–482.

THOM, B. G., AND CHAPPELL, J., 1975, Holocene sea levels relative to Australia: Search, v. 6, p. 90–93.

WALCOTT, R. I., 1972a, Late Quaternary vertical movements in eastern North America: quantitative evidence of glacio-isostatic rebound: Reviews of Geophysics and Space Physics, v. 10, no. 4, p. 849–884.

———, 1972b, Past sea levels, eustasy, and deformation of the earth: Quaternary Research, v. 2, p. 1–14.

HOLOCENE NEOTECTONICS AND THE RAMAPO FAULT ZONE SEA-LEVEL ANOMALY: A STUDY OF VARYING MARINE TRANSGRESSION RATES IN THE LOWER HUDSON ESTUARY, NEW YORK AND NEW JERSEY

WALTER S. NEWMAN[1] AND LEONARD J. CINQUEMANI
Department of Geology, Queens College of the City University of New York, Flushing, New York 11367
JON A. SPERLING AND LESLIE F. MARCUS
Department of Biology, Queens College of the City University of New York, Flushing, New York 11367
AND
RICHARD R. PARDI[2]
Radiocarbon Laboratory, Queens College of the City University of New York, Flushing, New York 11367

ABSTRACT: Eleven tidal marsh stations along the lower Hudson River estuary yield contrasting marine transgression rates: more than 2.0 m/millennium at New York City compared to about 1.0 m/millennium 100 km to the north at Marlboro near Poughkeepsie. The entire area appears to be tilting downward to the south-southeast. Three tidal marsh stations within the Ramapo Fault Zone (RFZ) yield higher transgression rates as compared to the other stations beyond the limits of the RFZ. This anomaly seems best explained by complex graben-like downfaulting, with a throw of at least 1 m having occurred within the past 2 millennia. There is also evidence, based on radiocarbon dating, of earlier fault movement after about 4.2 ka, suggesting a recurrence interval on the order of 2,000 yrs. The displacements inferred from these varying transgression rates may result from faults whose traces do not intersect the earth's surface.

INTRODUCTION

The Ramapo Fault Zone (RFZ) strikes northeast from Peapack, New Jersey, for about 100 km into and across the Hudson Highlands gorge (Fig. 1). The RFZ width ranges from less than 100 m to more than 4 km wide near the south end of the Highlands gorge (Odom and Hatcher, 1980). Seismicity suggests Holocene high-angle reverse faulting associated with the RFZ (Aggarwal and Sykes, 1978). Neither Ratcliffe (1980) nor Dames and Moore (1977), however, found evidence for Holocene fault movements within or adjacent to the RFZ in the vicinity of the Hudson valley. The absence of field evidence demonstrating recent fault movement has fueled a debate as to whether or not the RFZ has actually undergone Holocene fault movement (Seeber and Sykes, 1984; Ratcliffe, 1984).

There is a problem in attempting to relate well-defined seismic zones to field manifestations of crustal displacement. Regional vertical movements over the past century may be detected from geodetic and marigraph (tide-gauge) records. Older and less visible crustal displacement of littoral terranes may be discerned by the study of former Holocene strandlines.

Both Vita-Finzi (1975) and Huber (1975) argued that deformed and dated marine terraces can establish the nature, extent and rate of crustal movements along known or postulated faults. Taira (1975) reported stepped discontinuities of radiocarbon-dated fossil coral reefs on the Hengchun Peninsula of Taiwan, which provide evidence of as much as 10 m of fault throw for single episodes. Vita-Finzi (1975) observed that fossil beaches of the western Makran (southern Iranian coast), long suspected of reflecting repeated uplift, can serve to trace regional tectonic trends through time only if radiocarbon dating is applied to them on a massive scale.

The proximity of the Consolidated Edison Nuclear Generating Station complex to both the RFZ and the huge population concentration around New York City motivated the authors to test Vita-Finzi's argument that former Holocene strandline studies are indeed applicable to intraplate neotectonic investigations.

Tidal marshes were located which contain peat resting directly upon a compact, consolidated or bedrock substrate, and the transgressive basal peats were sampled at successively lower elevations. Marine transgression rates based on radiocarbon-dated basal peats from tidal marshes within the RFZ were then compared with tidal marshes to the north and south, presumably beyond the influence of the RFZ. Congruent transgression curves would imply little or no throw, whereas disjunct curve segments would suggest some element of vertical displacement (Fig. 2).

Radiocarbon ages for marine and/or brackish water basal peats for this region, when plotted on a time elevation diagram, usually demonstrate a continuing Holocene marine transgression over the past 6 ka (Fig. 2a). A station exhibiting a steeper transgression curve implies crustal tilting between it and neighboring stations (Fig. 2b). Two or more disjunct transgressive segments at a single station with an appreciable vertical separation (Fig. 2c) suggest a fault event. Three transgressive segments suggest two discrete fault events and enable an estimate of a recurrence interval (Fig. 2d). Finally, a station yielding a steeper transgression curve than curves for stations on either side of it may be located on an actively downfaulting block or graben (Fig. 2e). Our data indicate displacement for all three stations within the RFZ. We therefore conclude that there have been sinking fault-block movements within the RFZ over the last few millennia.

THE HOLOCENE MARINE TRANSGRESSION

In eastern North America, raised beaches and marine deposits of late Quaternary age are found throughout much of the deglaciated area, where the sea transgressed after the

---

[1]Deceased.

[2]Present address: Department of Chemistry, Physics and Environmental Science, William Paterson College of New Jersey, Wayne, New Jersey 07470.

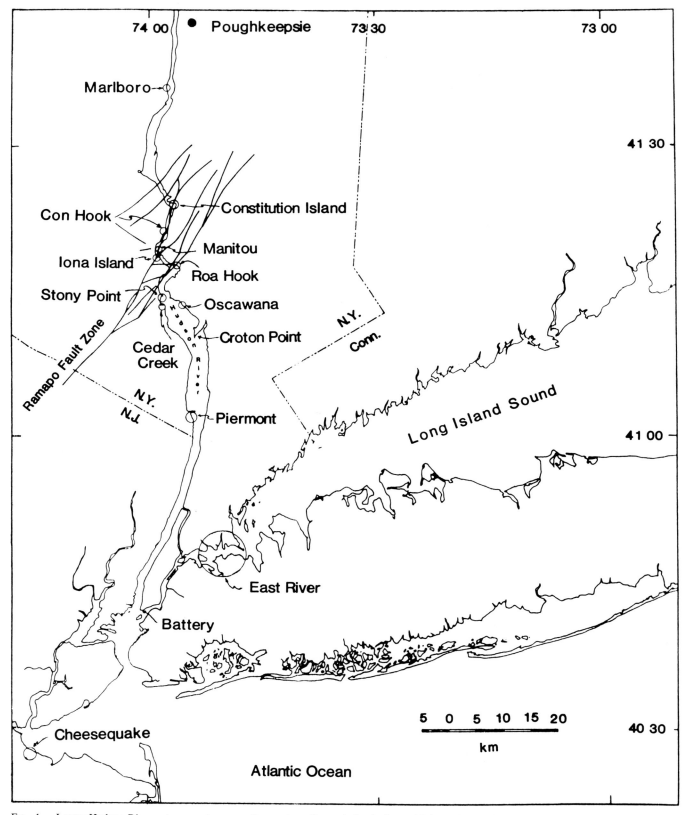

FIG. 1.—Lower Hudson River estuary and surrounding region. Open circles indicate tidal marsh sampling stations. Solid lines follow some of the fault traces associated with the Ramapo Fault Zone.

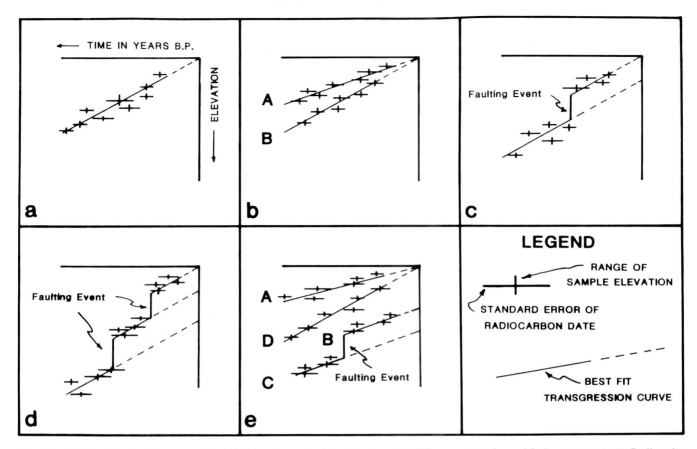

FIG. 2.—Models of sea-level curves with predictions of complications due to crustal tilting, neotectonics and fault movements. (a) Radiocarbon-dated marine and brackish water basal peats, when plotted on a time vs. elevation diagram, frequently demonstrate a smooth Holocene transgression for the northeastern United States. (b) Radiocarbon-dated marine and brackish water basal peats from two regionally adjacent tidal marshes display transgression curves with contrasting slopes due, presumably, to differential crustal tilting. The crust in the vicinity of station "B" has subsided with respect to station "A." (c) Disjunct transgressive segments at a single station with appreciable vertical separation suggest a faulting event. (d) Three transgressive curve segments suggest two discrete fault events and permit the calculation of a recurrence interval. (e) Stations yielding combinations of the above models suggest a subsiding fault-bounded crustal block with internal subsidiary faulting superimposed on regional crustal tilting.

retreat and final disappearance of the late Wisconsinan Laurentide Ice Sheet. The altitudes of these beaches and deposits display a systematic variation in age and position, indicating a continent-wide upward-doming of the land centering on Hudson Bay. Peat and other terrestrial deposits of postglacial age along the Atlantic seaboard at and beyond the margin of the deglaciated region are submerged below sea level and suggest a downward movement of the land (after allowing for possible eustatic sea-level changes) in a zone peripheral to the uplift (Newman and others, 1971; Walcott, 1972). The symmetry and geographic position of this movement generally coincide with the limits of the Laurentide Ice Sheet and are therefore believed to be largely the result of the recovery of the earth from the weight of the ice, a process termed glacial isostasy or glacio-isostatic rebound. For example, Figure 3 includes the Hudson-Champlain and St. Lawrence-Ottawa River Lowlands, where datable shoreline indicators are presumed by several investigators to mark sea level at about 12.0 ± 0.5 ka, the "Champlain Sea" datum of this paper (Newman, 1977;

Cronin, 1977; Hillaire-Marcel, 1979; Table 1). Computer-generated contours drawn on the present elevations of these former shorelines demonstrate that, since 12 ka the Montreal area has been upwarped more than 150 m with respect to New York City (Fig. 3; Clark and Karrow, 1984).

Over the past 7 millennia, sea level has been in a transgressive mode along the northeast coast of the United States south of the latitude of Boston (Cinquemani and others, 1982). For this coastal area, ancient sea levels are most frequently recorded by the radiocarbon dating of basal peats whose depths are measured from a known datum, usually the surface of a brackish or saltwater marsh, the elevation of which is at about mean high water (MHW) (Redfield, 1972). Basal peat is either "sedge peat," initially accumulated at about MHW at the inner edge of a marine or estuarine marsh, or *Spartina patens* peat, the debris of a plant that thrives only at about MHW. In either case, sea levels of the past can be properly determined by using only those basal peats deposited on a substrate that did not subsequently undergo compaction or consolidation as, for ex-

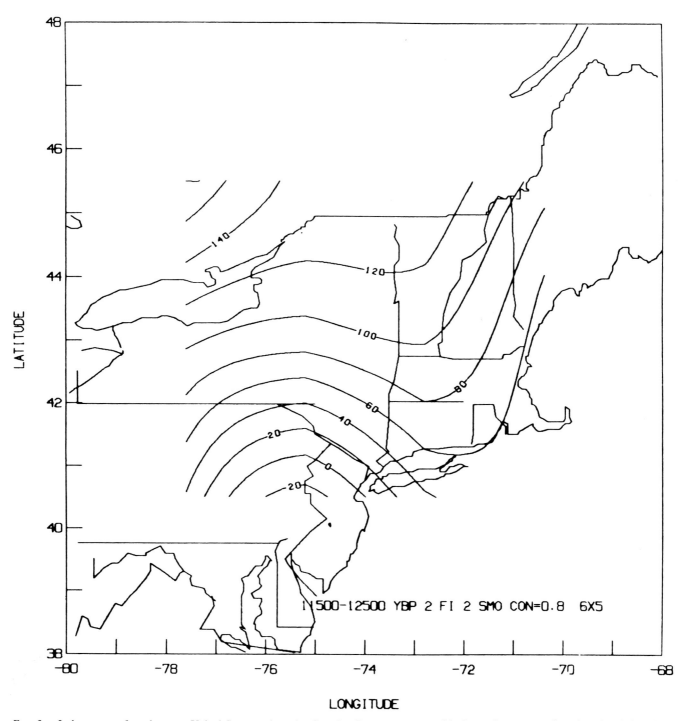

FIG. 3.—Isobase map of northeastern United States and nearby Canada. Computer-generated isobases drawn on radiocarbon-dated shoreline indicators for the interval 11.5 to 12.5 ka (Table 3) based on a 2° by 2° grid. All data from a single 2° square are averaged to arrive at a single figure. Deformation of the 12.0 ± 0.5 ka ("Champlain Sea" datum) geoid tilting down toward the southeast is easily discerned.

ample, bedrock, till, or gravel. In addition, these basal peats must be preserved by younger anaerobic sediments such as peat, clay, silt, or some composite such as organic mud. These specifications are obtained under contemporary salt and estuarine marshes. Both field observation and leveling demonstrate that high tidal marsh surfaces are about in equilibrium with contemporary MHW, thus providing a convenient local datum (Redfield, 1972). The basal peats themselves provide evidence that they were associated with the world ocean in that they contain marine and/or brackish water fossils.

Amost all of the tidal marshes investigated are (or were)

TABLE 1.—LOWER HUDSON RIVER ESTUARY RADIOCARBON-DATED BASAL PEATS

Lab#	C-14 Date	Elevation (m) local datum = MHW	Notes and Comments (dc) = diluted with dead CO_2
		MARLBORO (41.6°N, 73.9°W)	
QC-341	2230 ± 235	−3.1 to −3.3	
QC-340	3005 ± 115	−4.1 to −4.3	
QC-342	4145 ± 110	−4.8 to −5.0	
QC-705	4255 ± 125	−7.15 to −7.5	probably NOT a basal peat
QC-343	4390 ± 220	−5.8 to −6.0	
QC-686	4570 ± 105	−8.2 to −8.6	probably NOT a basal peat; brackish and freshwater diatoms
		CONSTITUTION ISLAND (41.4°N, 73.9°W)	
East side of marsh, east of Timp Fault			
QC-690	1440 ± 100	−2.1 to −2.4	freshwater diatoms only
QC-691	2320 ± 500(dc)	−1.0 to −1.3	freshwater diatoms only; date too old, benzene evaporated
QC-695	2435 ± 95	−2.9 to −3.4	
QC-696	2460 ± 105	−6.7 to −7.2	field notes suggest sediment flowed into sampler, too young
QC-693	3210 ± 110	−4.7 to −5.2	
QC-694	3760 ± 120	−6.1 to −6.6	
QC-692	4655 ± 140(dc)	−9.35 to −9.75	
Center of marsh, on trace of Timp Fault			
QC-226	2315 ± 100	−3.7 to −3.9	
QC-276	4110 ± 100	−5.95 to −6.15	
QC-227	4230 ± 120	−7.5 to −7.7	
QC-189	5710 ± 300	−9.25 to −9.45	
West side of marsh, west of Timp Fault			
QC-1039	2155 ± 125(dc)	−1.7 to −2.08	
QC-1042	4660 ± 125(dc)	−5.8 to −6.1	
QC-1040	6025 ± 285	−7.9 to −8.3	
		MANITOU (41.3°N, 74.0°N)	
QC-706	3530 ± 105(dc)	−3.65 to −4.0	
		RING MEADOW, IONA ISLAND (41.2°N, 74.0°W)	
		Northwest Transect	
QC-574	390 ± 95	−0.94 to −1.14	
QC-763	1040 ± 120	−0.6 to −1.0	
QC-575	1460 ± 90	−1.98 to −2.18	
QC-765	2135 ± 100	−2.7 to −3.0	
QC-764	2240 ± 115	−1.7 to −2.0	
L-1038B	2500 ± 250	−2.54 to −2.74	
QC-576	2830 ± 125(dc)	−3.24 to −3.44	
QC-766	2835 ± 105	−3.6 to −3.9	
QC-767	3135 ± 105	−4.9 to −5.3	
QC-1021	3425 ± 115(dc)	−2.5 to −2.75	
QC-1022	3505 ± 150(dc)	−3.41 to −3.71	
QC-274	3610 ± 120	−4.4 to −4.6	
L-1038C	4080 ± 220	−6.2 to −6.4	
QC-1019	4265 ± 260	−4.37 to −4.67	
QC-1020	4370 ± 270	−6.25 to −6.55	
QC-577	4515 ± 120	−4.89 to −5.09	
QC-1023	4795 ± 190	−5.6 to −5.85	
QC-1024	5060 ± 270	−6.6 to −6.9	
		Southeast Transect	
QC-776	2170 ± 95	−7.6 to −8.0	downfaulted block?
QC-777	2565 ± 90	−8.1 to −8.5	downfaulted block?
QC-768	2955 ± 100	−6.1 to −6.5	downfaulted block?
QC-187	3800 ± 160	−6.55 to −6.75	downfaulted block?
QC-775	3865 ± 120	−7.0 to −7.4	downfaulted block?
QC-186	3940 ± 135	−10.55 to −10.75	downfaulted block?
QC-778	4265 ± 115	−9.6 to −10.0	downfaulted block?
QC-686	4570 ± 105	−8.2 to −8.6	downfaulted block?
L-1039D	4630 ± 470	−8.02 to −8.22	downfaulted block?
		Salisbury Meadow	
L-1141	12,500 ± 600	−27.7 to −27.8	beneath causeway across Salisbury Meadow, west of Ring Meadow
		ROA HOOK (41.3°N, 73.9°W)	
		Northwest Block	
QC-511	255 ± 10	marsh surface	
QC-722	2360 ± 100	−2.3 to −2.6	
QC-569	2490 ± 120(dc)	−1.94 to −2.14	
QC-510	3140 ± 170(dc)	−4.8 to −5.0	
QC-568	3170 ± 170(dc)	−4.01 to −4.21	
QC-1041	3185 ± 160(dc)	−4.25 to −4.55	
		Southeast Block	
QC-721	3320 ± 105	−5.5 to −5.8	downfaulted block?
QC-723	3905 ± 130(dc)	−6.7 to −7.0	downfaulted block?
QC-512	4120 ± 345	−8.8 to −9.0	downfaulted block?
QC-567	4280 ± 105(dc)	−3.83 to −4.03	lab reports "result suspect"
QC-1043	4450 ± 195(dc)	−7.5 to −7.95	downfaulted block?

TABLE 1.—*Continued*

Lab#	C-14 Date	Elevation (m) local datum = MHW	Notes and Comments (dc) = diluted with dead CO_2
QC-509	4545 ± 130(dc)	−9.3 to −9.5	downfaulted block?
QC-566	4655 ± 100	−6.87 to −7.07	downfaulted block?
QC-565	5470 ± 135(dc)	−8.6 to −8.8	downfaulted block?
QC-573	6230 ± 115	−10.8 to −11.0	downfaulted block? dated wood in basal peat
		STONY POINT (41.2°N, 74.0°W)	
QC-505	3100 ± 110	−3.2 to −3.4	
QC-506	3740 ± 200(dc)	−5.8 to −6.0	
QC-469	4830 ± 105	−6.0 to −6.2	
		OSCAWANA ISLAND (41.2°N, 73.9°W)	
QC-729	330 ± 100	−5.6 to −5.9	date obviously too young
QC-228	1865 ± 90	−2.5 to −2.7	
QC-264	4500 ± 95	−6.8 to −7.0	
QC-221B	4570 ± 115	−6.6 to −6.8	
QC-221A	5145 ± 210	−7.3 to −7.5	
		CEDAR POND BROOK MARSH (41.1°N, 74.0°W)	
QC-770	795 ± 100	−0.7 to −1.0	
QC-772	1740 ± 100	−1.7 to −2.0	
QC-712	1940 ± 105	−2.5 to −2.8	
QC-709	2220 ± 120	−3.25 to −3.6	
QC-773	2650 ± 100	−2.5 to −2.8	
QC-811	2700 ± 115	−3.5 to −3.9	
QC-771	2885 ± 130	−3.1 to −3.4	NOT a basal peat; wood above QC-774
QC-810	3025 ± 100	−3.2 to −3.6	
QC-774	3085 ± 110	−3.4 to −3.7	
QC-711	3630 ± 110	−5.1 to −5.5	
QC-710	3655 ± 105	−3.85 to −4.2	
QC-812	3860 ± 150	−4.2 to −4.6	
QC-718	4400 ± 125	−6.6 to −7.0	
QC-719	5080 ± 125	−6.7 to −7.0	
		PIERMONT MARSH (41.0°N, 73.9°W)	
QC-733	modern	−0.7 to −1.0	
QC-734	1420 ± 120	−1.4 to −1.7	
QC-735	2000 ± 105	−2.8 to −3.0	
QC-211	2295 ± 160	−3.0 to −3.3	
QC-736	2545 ± 135(dc)	−4.5 to −4.8	
QC-732	2990 ± 100	−4.5 to −4.8	
QC-730	3050 ± 95	−5.2 to −5.5	
QC-738	3320 ± 140(dc)	−6.65 to −7.0	
QC-262	3460 ± 95	−4.85 to −5.05	
QC-731	3530 ± 110	−5.1 to −5.2	wood above QC-730 - NOT a basal peat
QC-737	3730 ± 200(dc)	−5.6 to −5.9	
QC-739	3790 ± 90	−7.6 to −8.0	dated wood in basal peat
QC-740	4300 ± 280	−8.6 to −9.0	
QC-261	4605 ± 115	−8.34 to −8.54	
W-3014	4620 ± 250	−7.96 to −8.16	
QC-741	4715 ± 115	−9.6 to −10.0	
QC-742	5320 ± 170(dc)	−11.1 to −11.4	
QC-808	5475 ± 135	−11.0 to −11.5	
QC-809	6840 ± 230(dc)	−11.5 to −12.0	
		EAST RIVER (40.8°N, 73.8°W)	
QC-295	1800 ± 90	−2.05 to −2.25	
L-1038A	2280 ± 250	−3.06 to −3.26	
QC-267	5650 ± 170(dc)	−12.7 to −13.0	
QC-265	6365 ± 100	−18.1 to −18.3	
L-617	6600 ± 700	−15.5 to −15.6	
QC-266	7115 ± 240(dc)	−17.7 to −18.0	
QC-306	7975 ± 390	−15.4 to −15.6	
QC-269	8100 ± 100	−19.7 to −20.1	
I-5665	9380 ± 70	−20.1 to −20.2	
L-606A	11950 ± 200	−33.0 to −33.1	
I-5663	12270 ± 180	−24.6 to −24.7	
QC-268	12400 ± 260(dc)	−20.0 to −20.3	
		WESTWAY (40.7°N, 74.0°W)	
QC-1184	5540 ± 160(dc)	−23.2 to −23.5	shell, probably incorrectly assumed to equal basal peat
QC-1029	8190 ± 130(dc)	−19.2 to −19.8	
QC-1028	8745 ± 165(dc)	−21.3 to −22.0	
QC-1026	9170 ± 225(dc)	−22.9 to −23.5	
QC-1183	9540 ± 120	−36.6 to −37.2	organic silt rather than peat
QC-1027	10500 ± 500	−22.0 to −22.6	
QC-1025	11295 ± 215(dc)	−24.8 to −25.5	
		CHEESEQUAKE MARSH (40.4°N, 74.3°W)	
QC-846	525 ± 145(dc)	−9.25 to −9.65	date obviously too young
QC-848	930 ± 170(dc)	−4.5 to −4.8	date obviously too young
QC-844	1210 ± 185(dc)	−2.6 to −2.8	
QC-847	1960 ± 130(dc)	−2.8 to −3.05	
QC-842	2080 ± 160(dc)	−3.3 to −3.5	
QC-845	4820 ± 95	−10.9 to −11.15	NOT a basal peat
QC-896	7230 ± 185	−11.8 to −12.1	

dominated by salt marsh grasses, cattails, reeds and sedges. These plants include *Spartina patens*, the common high-salt marsh plant; *Typha angustifolia*, a common cattail; the reed, *Phragmites communis*; and the bulrush, *Scirpus robustus*. These last three species are phreatophytes, and they frequently appear just above high-tide level along the shores of the estuaries. Since sea level has been demonstrably rising along the Atlantic coast and within its estuaries (Redfield, 1967), debris from these plants tends to accumulate just below mean high-tide level in an anaerobic environment where it is preserved. Plant debris accumulating above the high-tide level tends to oxidize and disappear. The accumulating phreatophyte debris forms a dark brown to black peat which has been termed "sedge peat" by Bloom (1964) and "basal peat" by some investigators including Newman and others (1969). Along the northeastern coast of Massachusetts, McIntire and Morgan (1963) have traced these basal peats from modern sea level to considerable depths downslope. In the marsh behind Plum Island, Massachusetts, McIntire and Morgan (1963, p. 23) reported that "This freshwater peat layer of varying thickness continues up the valley slope to become contiguous with modern fresh water plants which now grow slightly above high tide level."

Marsh sediments are composed of some combination of autochthonous vegetal and organic debris mixed with fine-grained allochthonous mineral material. The marsh phreatophytic plants are being and have been submerged by rising sea level and are covered with fine-grained material deposited by tidal currents. Continued submergence is usually balanced by upward growth of the marsh. The suspended fine-grained sediments are trapped and actually adhere to the culms and stalks of the marsh vegetation accumulating to MHW. The phreatophytes responsible for the upward growth of these marshes cannot grow at a level very much below MHW and are consequently restricted to an elevation at or near MHW. In effect, these phreatophytes are a sere climax assemblage, having their upper limit in a marsh at about MHW.

Redfield (1972) found that leveling across the apparently flat surface of the high marsh at Barnstable, Massachusetts, revealed a local relief of about 15 cm. Adams (1963) reported his North Carolina high tidal marsh surfaces exhibited only about 3 cm of relief. Our observations find that the Hudson estuary marshes studied were inundated only during spring tides, and then only a few centimenters of tidal water covered the marsh. Leveling at Piermont marsh showed the marsh surface to be at about equilibrium with MHW. The marsh surface exhibited a maximum relief of about 30 cm.

Tidal marshes are generally found in sheltered areas behind barrier beaches, in the estuaries of tidal rivers, and in other recesses of the upland. Their exclusion from exposed shorelines appears to depend on the instability of the substrate under wave and current action, rather than upon mechanical damage by these agents. The marshes form in protected locations along irregular and indented shorelines and estuaries. The phreatophytes are submerged by the rising sea and covered by silt and clay deposited by tides. Their buried remains record the rate of drowning of the land, because the phreatophyte inland fringe progressively migrates to higher elevations as the tides encroach upon the land. The rising sea level drowns portions of the coast and invades tributary valleys, thus forming protected reentrants suitable for tidal marsh development. It is probable that from time to time, severe storms, floods and floating ice may tear off, float and/or launch rafts of the surficial peat mat and move these "batteries" or peat hummocks (Gleason and others, 1980) to lower or higher elevations, resulting in misleading data. The rate of inundation is further complicated by changes in tidal range and local and regional neotectonics.

For any given locale, the observed relationship between radiocarbon-dated basal peats and depth is unique. This is because local sea level is a function of competing causal factors: eustasy, isostasy and regional and local tectonics. Compaction and consolidation of the substrate beneath the basal peat also play a role. Within the limits of the 100-km reach of the lower Hudson estuary, the changes of sea level over the past 7,000 yrs are reasonably well defined. After sustaining an interval of isostatic crustal rebound immediately following late Wisconsinan deglaciation (Newman, 1977), the region has been subsiding (for an expansion of this theme, see Scott and others, this volume). The rate of regional marine transgression (approximately 1.0–3.0 m/ millennium) clearly exceeds the rate of world-wide sea-level rise (about 1 m/millennium) (see Gornitz and Lebedeff, this volume). The apparent differential subsidence is greater toward the south.

Holocene warping of the North Atlantic littoral zone of the United States east coast involves more than the area actually covered by the Wisconsinan glacier. Newman and March (1968) demonstrated that the continental shelf off New York City has been differentially downwarped toward the shelf edge about 100 m or more. The total net warping of the 12 ka ("Champlain") datum from the edge of the continental shelf north to Montreal thus exceeds 250 m over the past 12 millennia (Fig. 3).

HUDSON ESTUARY TIDAL MARSHES

The eleven locations studied by the authors are located on Figure 1, whereas their geographic coordinates (latitude and longitude) are given in Table 1. The several sources of the commercially secured samples from the East River are documented in Newman (1977). The deep (L-1141) sample from Salisbury Meadow, adjacent to Iona Island, was supplied by the New York State Department of Transportation. All other basal peat samples were secured with manually-driven sampling equipment.

Earlier boring samples (through QC-577; Table 1) were obtained using a modified 2.54-cm inner diameter U.S. Geological Survey Davis peat and marl sampler (fabricated at the Queens College Physics Department Machine Shop). Later, basal peats were sampled with a 4.5-cm inner diameter "Dutch" gouge auger (manufactured by the Eijkelkamp organization of Gliesbeek, the Netherlands). We initially probed our marshes with either meter-long Lichtwardt (bayonet type) or "Dutch" auger drilling rods. Our objective was to secure basal peat samples with sufficient carbon content for radiocarbon dating. In practice, three or four 20-cm-long Davis samples had to be pooled to obtain the minimum weight of carbon for dating. Although an attempt was made to limit the gouge auger samples to a length of 20 cm, longer samples had to be used occasionally in order to obtain sufficient carbon for dating purposes.

Boring locations were sited by eye on known landmarks. Using 7.5′ topographic maps, we believe we can reoccupy our bore locations to within a distance of 50 m or less. A summary of characteristics at each study site follows.

Cheesequake marsh.—

A prominent salt marsh has formed along the south shore of Raritan Bay (Fig. 1). Data from samples obtained from below the surface of this *Spartina patens* salt marsh (Table 1) were frequently inconsistent. Cheesequake marsh was the epicenter of a magnitude 3.0 seismic event on 30 January 1979. We suspect that seismically induced liquifaction may be responsible for the aberrant data obtained from this marsh.

East River stations.—

The sea-level data from Newman (1977; see also Cinquemani and others, 1982) for stations in the vicinity of the East River (the strait between the New York City boroughs of Queens and the Bronx) were incorporated into this study. The stations include samples from Little Neck Bay, Flushing Meadow, the vicinity of Shea Stadium, the Queens Tower of the Throggs Neck Bridge, Rikers Island Bridge, the Whitestone marsh, the intersection of the Long Island and Van Wyck Expressways, and Pelham Bay Park. All of these sites are or were salt marsh deposits. The presence of *Elphidium clavatum* (Newman, 1977) indicates salinities above 14‰ (Weiss, 1974; 1976) at the time of deposition. Present salinities (where marshes still exist; many have been covered by fill) are above 14‰.

Piermont marsh.—

Piermont marsh is located on the west shore of the Hudson estuary and immediately east of the Palisades. This estuarine marsh, about 3 km in length, contains the most northerly concentration of true halophytes in the Hudson estuary (Lehr, 1967). Although dominated by cattails, the marsh does support appreciable stands of halophytes. At the west edge, it is dominated by a nearly pure stand of *Typha angustifolia*, and halophytes, such as *Spartina patens*, are increasingly evident toward the estuarine boundary of the marsh. Chapman (1960) has documented the maximal salinity tolerances of phreatophytic sedges and bulrushes. Both *Scirpus* and *Phragmites* will survive at salinities of as much as 28‰. *Typha angustifolia*, however, will only tolerate salinities of as much as 17‰. Salinities at Piermont marsh range just below that limit. The north end of the marsh abuts upon the Piermont Pier, which extends east from the west shore for about 1.5 km to nearly the center of the estuary. The pier was constructed in the middle of the 19th century and has been responsible for the increase in the area of the marsh during the past century. Our investigation indicates, however, that much of the marsh has been in existence for several thousand years. The foraminifera encountered in our bores include the typical salt marsh species *Trochammina inflata* and *Milliammina fusca*.

Cedar Pond Brook marsh.—

This tidal marsh is located at the north edge of the village of Haverstraw on the west bank of the Hudson estuary just west of the West Shore Railroad embankment and 22 km north of Piermont. Much of its north and west boundaries are bedrock, whereas the vegetation is predominately *Typha angustifolia*. The tidal marshes on the southeast side of Croton Point opposite Haverstraw were also probed and sampled, but datable material was not encountered.

Oscawana Island marsh.—

Rock-ribbed Oscawana Island lies 22 km north of Piermont marsh on the east bank of the estuary. Railroad tracks pass through a tunnel here and continue both north and south of the island by means of a combination embankment and trestle bridge. East of the railroad and the island is a small bay, which forms the drowned mouth of Furnace Brook which drains the hills immediately to the east. The shores of this small bay consist of tidal marsh deposits which comprise approximately half the total area of the embayment. The salinity of the water around the marsh is low, as indicated by the "freshwater" vegetation, including *Typha*, *Phragmites* and *Scirpus*. Bores in this marsh encountered arenaceous foraminifera, indicating that the marsh accumulated in a brackish water environment.

Stony Point marsh.—

Located 26 km north of Piermont and immediately south of the prominent west shore peninsula, Stony Point, and just east of the west shore railroad embankment, this *Typha angustifolia* marsh is bounded by bedrock on both its north and west edges. The marsh is 1.6 km north of Cedar Pond Brook marsh, and the statistics (Table 1) of these two localities are very similar.

Roa Hook (Camp Smith) tidal marsh.—

This small marsh is located 31 km north of Piermont on the east bank of the Hudson estuary just north of the entrance to the New York National Guard's Camp Smith facility. The marsh is immediately east of the Bear Mountain Bridge Road (New York Routes 6 and 202) and is almost completely surrounded by bedrock. The vegetation is again *Typha angustifolia*. Probes and bores disclosed a buried southeast-facing and northeast-striking escarpment ranging from 1 to 3 m high some 10 m southeast of the northwest shore.

This station is within the RFZ, and there are striking differences in dating results from either side of this feature (Table 2). Six of the radiocarbon-dated basal peats yielded a more or less normal transgression curve, whereas the other eight samples from this transect trace a transgression curve that is clearly disjunct, suggesting the downward movement of the southeastern block with respect to the northwestern block.

TABLE 2.—STATISTICAL SUMMARY OF ACCEPTABLE DATA*

Distance North from Piermont (km)	Location	Number of ¹⁴C Dates	Intercept (m)	Slope (m/km/yr)	Standard Deviation (m)
−58	Cheesequake	4	−0.21 ± 0.42	−1.61 ± 0.11	0.51
−25	East River	5	3.72 ± 1.67	−3.11 ± 0.33	1.55
0	Piermont	18	0.53 ± 0.56	−1.97 ± 0.14	0.95
22	Cedar Pond	13	0.41 ± 0.45	−1.39 ± 0.14	0.57
23	Oscawana	4	0.16 ± 0.40	−1.51 ± 0.10	0.24
26	Stony Point	3	0.60 ± 4.04	−1.47 ± 1.02	1.26
31	Roa Hook—all data	14	1.44 ± 0.80	−2.01 ± 0.20	1.08
	Roa Hook—southeast	8	−1.30 ± 2.04	−1.49 ± 0.44	1.05
	Roa Hook—northwest	6	0.74 ± 0.76	−1.53 ± 0.29	0.73
35	Iona—all data	27	−0.53 ± 1.18	−1.44 ± 0.34	2.07
	Iona—southeast	9	−6.28 ± 2.13	−0.51 ± 0.57	1.42
	Iona—northwest	18	0.91 ± 0.50	−1.25 ± 0.15	0.80
44	Constitution—all data	11	0.58 ± 1.17	−1.69 ± 0.29	1.18
	Constitution—east	4	4.11 ± 0.86	−2.88 ± 0.24	0.38
	Constitution—central	4	0.04 ± 1.20	−1.65 ± 0.28	0.68
	Constitution—west	3	1.56 ± 0.05	−1.61 ± 0.01	0.03
66	Marlboro	4	−0.81 ± 0.77	−1.09 ± 0.22	0.38
	ALL DATA	103	1.12 ± 0.44	−1.94 ± 0.11	1.67

*Note that the slope can also be read as the transgression rates in mm/yr. Intercepts significantly departing from the origin suggest past fault movement. Standard deviation is the estimated standard deviation of the data about the best-fit line.

Iona Island marsh.—

Iona Island lies 35 km north of Piermont. The island stands just within the southern boundary of the Highlands gorge and is separated from the west shore of the estuary by Salisbury Meadow, a tidal marsh. Iona Island is roughly U-shaped, concave toward the south. Ring Meadow, the bore site, nests within the "U" of the island. The marshes are dominated by "freshwater" species which include *Typha angustifolia*, *Phragmites communis* and others (Lehr, 1967). These marsh sediments yielded the foraminifera *Throchamina inflata* to a depth of 13 m, indicating that a brackish water environment has persisted for at least 6,000 yrs (Newman, and others, 1969). Initial results from this site were so atypical that a second transect was established about 100 m south-southeast of the first. Table 1 demonstrates the large difference between these two transects.

Manitou marsh.—

This bog lies in a bedrock channel on the east bank of the Hudson estuary just north of the Bear Mountain Bridge. It was probed and sampled by Cameron (1970), who reported peat down to a depth of at least 10 m below the marsh surface. Her site was reoccupied during this study, but peat was not found much below a depth of about 3 m. Only one basal peat sample was recovered for radiocarbon dating. The surface vegetation is mostly cattails and *Phragmities*. On the opposite bank of the estuary 2 km to the north is the rocky island of Con Hook and an adjacent marsh. The Con Hook marsh was probed to depths of more than 20 m, but peat was not encountered.

Constitution Island marsh.—

Constitution Island on the east bank of the Hudson estuary opposite West Point is a bedrock mass which partially obstructs the Hudson channel. It is located 12 km north of Iona Island and 44 km north of Piermont. The marsh lies between the island and the east shore and is now dominated by freshwater vegetation, especially *Typha angustifolia*. The presence of brackish water foraminifera in the marsh sed-

iments indicates higher salinities in the past. Our data are from three different transects: one from the east side, a second from the north-central portion of the marsh, and a third from the west side. There are notable differences in the results from these three transects (Table 1).

Marlboro marsh.—

This small tidal marsh indents the west shore of the Hudson estuary and is 66 km north of Piermont. It is confined on the east by the embankment of the West Shore Railroad. Firm substrate was lacking under much of this marsh, as noted in Table 1. The marsh vegetation consists mostly of cattail and *Phragmites*.

PALEOECOLOGY AND RADIOCARBON DATING
OF BASAL PEAT SAMPLES

Radiocarbon dating for this study was conducted at the Queens College Radiocarbon Laboratory on 118 basal peat samples (Table 1). The dated basal peat samples used in the statistical analysis are only those samples taken immediately above a firm bottom. Peat accumulated directly upon bedrock at the Constitution Island, Manitou, Ring Meadow (Iona Island), Roa Hook, Stony Point and Oscawana marshes. Peats at Cedar Pond Brook and Piermont marshes were either on bedrock or a gravel and rubble substrate. Four of the Marlboro marsh basal peat samples rested on bedrock: QC-340 through 343 (Table 1), whereas the other two samples were taken at levels where further penetration proved difficult. The substrate in this case appeared to be a consolidated organic mud, similar to the organic silt higher in the core, but more dense. The latter two samples, although dated, were not used in the analysis.

For the East River series, only sample QC-295 (Pelham Bay marsh) was directly above bedrock. The other samples in this series were immediately on top of glacial drift, usually sand. Finally, the Cheesequake marsh basal peat samples were obtained from immediately above a paleosol developed on coastal plain sediments.

Aliquots of all basal peat samples were examined for their diatom content. Only those samples containing an appreciable number of marine and/or brackish water diatom frustules were included in the statistical analyses (Table 2); excluded were dated samples which appeared to be clearly in error. Reservations concerning suspect dates are noted in Table 1. Included in the analysis, however, were 10 apparently valid dates run by other laboratories, or data previously published by other investigators.

In all, 103 radiocarbon-dated basal peat samples were used. Note that earlier studies also encountered foraminifera, mollusks and other marine and brackish water taxa at some of these stations (Newman and others, 1969; Newman, 1977).

Assuming that the sampled sediments accumulated at a rate of at least 1 m/millennium, a 20-cm length of core represents a time interval of 200 yrs or less, an additional potential source of error in the data. Although an attempt was made to standardize the radiocarbon-dated samples to a length of 20 cm, field inspection of basal peat samples suggested that some samples contained insufficient carbon for dating purposes. In these cases, the basal peat samples dated were appreciably longer than the sought-after standard of 20 cm. For example, some commercially obtained samples from the Westway Project were 60 cm long, whereas several of our own samples were as much as 50 cm long.

The ideal sample length would yield a mean radiocarbon date that is at least 100 yrs younger than the actual date of the marine transgression, assuming no other source of error. The longer samples may be as much as several hundred years younger than the date of the actual transgression, although at localities with transgression rates greater than 1 m/millennium, the error would be smaller.

Thirty-two of the samples contained insufficient carbon for dating with highest precision and were thus diluted with dead CO_2 in order to permit dating. The results, compared with undiluted samples, appeared to yield acceptable results. Note that all the dates are "conventional" ^{14}C ages (5,568-yr half-life) without MASCA corrections.

The brackish and saltwater diatom flora of the radiocarbon-dated basal peats confirms the relationship of these samples to sea level. A plot of elevation vs. radiocarbon age for the acceptable dates (Fig. 4a–c) yields a transgressive trend over the past 8,000 yrs. Data from individual stations exhibit a limited departure from a linear trend.

LOCAL AND REGIONAL NEOTECTONICS

The major neotectonic process affecting the lower Hudson estuary is postglacial isostatic rebound (Fig. 3). We have already established that the "Champlain Sea" datum, the shoreline of 12 ka, has tilted some 250 m over a distance of some 700 km, striking somewhat west of north

TABLE 3.—FORTY RADIOCARBON-DATED SHORELINE INDICATORS FOR THE TIME INTERVAL 11.5–12.5 ka LISTED IN ORDER BY AGE. THESE DATA DEFINE THE GEOIDAL DEFORMATION OF THE "CHAMPLAIN SEA" DATA, SHOWN IN FIGURE 3.

Latitude (°N)	Longitude (°W)	Lab	Lab#	Age (yrs)	Elevation (m)	Material Dated
45.4	76.5	GSC-	2269	11,500 ± 90	170.0	BONE
45.6	72.4	GSC-	475	11,530 ± 160	145.0	SHELL
41.7	70.6	Y-	1459	11,570 ± 300	−17.7	PEAT
37.1	76.1	ML-	189	11,590 ± 150	−23.0	PEAT
46.9	71.3	GSC-	1235	11,600 ± 160	176.0	SHELL
45.5	75.9	GSC-	842	11,600 ± 150	170.0	SHELL
40.7	74.0	QC-	1326	11,615 ± 200	−31.1	PEAT
44.6	69.6	W-	737	11,800 ± 240	57.0	SHELL
44.7	73.5	GSC-	2366	11,800 ± 150	96.0	SHELL
44.7	75.6	GSC-	1013	11,800 ± 210	104.0	SHELL
45.9	75.6	GSC-	2769	11,800 ± 100	182.0	SHELL
45.8	72.3	GSC-	505	11,880 ± 180	122.0	SHELL
44.6	72.5	GSC-	2338	11,900 ± 120	101.0	SHELL
45.8	75.9	GSC-	1772	11,900 ± 160	176.0	SHELL
44.7	69.8	W-	947	11,950 ± 350	76.0	SHELL
40.8	73.9	L-	606A	11,950 ± 200	−34.8	PEAT
40.7	74.0	QC-	1329	11,990 ± 220	−29.6	PEAT
45.8	72.3	GSC-	936	12,000 ± 230	122.0	SHELL
43.8	70.2	L-	678	12,100 ± 300	49.0	SHELL
44.7	67.1	SI-	1048	12,175 ± 120	39.0	SHELL
45.6	75.8	GSC-	1646	12,200 ± 160	194.0	SHELL
45.1	68.6	Y-	2205	12,210 ± 100	73.0	SHELL
43.8	70.2	Y-	1775	12,210 ± 120	49.0	SHELL
46.6	71.1	QU-	93	12,230 ± 250	104.0	SHELL
44.7	69.8	Y-	1475	12,260 ± 240	91.0	SHELL
45.3	68.6	Y-	2213	12,270 ± 120	60.0	SHELL
40.8	73.9	I-	5663	12,270 ± 180	−24.6	PEAT
42.1	70.3	W-	3380	12,320 ± 350	−57.0	PEAT
43.7	70.3	Y-	2210	12,350 ± 140	37.0	SHELL
46.8	71.3	GSC-	1533	12,400 ± 160	110.0	SHELL
40.8	73.8	QC-	268	12,400 ± 260	−20.3	PEAT
44.7	68.8	Y-	2207A	12,440 ± 120	40.0	SHELL
44.6	68.9	Y-	2203	12,450 ± 120	30.0	SHELL
41.3	74.0	L-	1141	12,500 ± 600	−27.7	PEAT
44.0	70.0	Y-	2212	12,560 ± 160	55.0	SHELL
45.0	76.0	GSC-	1859	12,800 ± 220	168.0	SHELL
44.9	69.9	Y-	1477	13,020 ± 240	125.0	SHELL
39.6	72.1	I-	2545	13,200 ± 210	−148.0	SHELL
40.1	70.5	I-	2473	13,420 ± 210	−123.0	SHELL
37.6	74.5	W-	2014	13,500 ± 350	−68.0	PEAT

from the head of the Hudson submarine canyon. The mean rate of tilting is about 36 cm/km or 3.0 cm/km/millennium. This is in contrast to the maximum warping rate of 90 cm/km over most of New England, reported by Koteff (1984) for all of postglacial time. Apparently, most of the glacial isostatic rebound occurred during the interval between deglaciation (14-12 ka) and 12 ka. Clark and Karrow (1984) found that the Champlain Sea water level in the Lake Champlain and St. Lawrence lowlands tilts upward to the north at about 1 m/km or 8.33 cm/km/millennium, a rate more than twice that of the lower Hudson estuary, but close to the figure cited by Koteff (1984). The reasons for these contrasting rates are: (1) the greater glacier thickness toward the north, (2) a more rapid rate of deglaciation in the more northerly portions of the Hudson-Champlain lowland, and (3) a greater density and larger distribution of radiocarbon-dated shorelines in that direction.

The rate of crustal tilting apparently decreased rapidly after deglaciation. On the other hand, the tilt rate for the glacial Lake Hudson strandline (which occupied the lower Hudson valley immediately after deglaciation and prior to the "Champlain Sea" marine transgression into the lower Hudson valley) is 40 cm/km (Dames and Moore, 1977), about the same rate of tilt as that of the "Champlain Sea" datum. We cannot explain this apparent contradiction. Perhaps the "Champlain Sea" transgression into the lower Hudson valley followed immediately upon the catastrophic termination of the Lake Hudson episode (Newman and others, 1969).

The slope (also the transgression rate), based on all our valid radiocarbon-dated basal peat samples, is 1.94 ± 0.11 m/millennium with the intercept at 1.12 ± 0.44 m (Table 2). Beyond the limits of the RFZ, Piermont and Cedar Pond Brook marshes provided the largest number of valid radiocarbon-dated basal peat dates (18 and 13, respectively), enabling establishment of a more or less reliable standard for the past 6,000 yrs with which the eight other stations may be compared (Fig. 4a–c). Piermont yields a mean transgression rate of 1.97 ± 0.14 m/millennium, whereas Cedar Pond Brook 22 km to the north exhibits a transgression rate of 1.39 ± 0.14 m/millennium. These two slopes are significantly different at the 0.05 level. Coupled with the apparent divergence of individual station plots back in time, as demonstrated in Figure 4, these data provide additional evidence that the axis of the Hudson estuary has tilted downward to the south. From these two stations alone, the apparent rate of southerly tilting is 2.55 ± 0.93 cm/km/millennium, significantly different from the "Champlain Sea" datum tilt rate of 3.3 cm/km/millennium.

The three stations within the RFZ yield data that contrast with those outside of the fault zone. The standard error of slope (the estimated transgression rate) is appreciably greater, the intercepts are usually greater than 1 m in absolute value, and the estimated standard deviations of the individual values about the trend line are markedly higher than for the stations to the north and south. In other words, there is a lot of scatter about the time-elevation trend for the three stations within the RFZ (Fig. 4). The lines on Figure 4 are least-square regression lines.

At Roa Hook, all 14 radiocarbon-dated basal peats yield

a transgression of rate of 2.0 m/millennium. The data from either side of the prominent scarp noted in the description of this site, however, yield transgression rates not significantly different from that obtained from the Cedar Pond Brook tidal marsh, south of the RFZ. The intercepts for the southeastern and northwestern blocks suggest that the southeastern block has sunk about 2 m relative to the northwestern block, which is on the other side of the now buried scarp. The data in Table 1 (plotted in Fig. 4a) indicate that the postulated break occurred about 3.2 ka and conforms to our model (Fig. 2c). A major caveat is that the standard error for the intercept of the Roa Hook-southeast data is 2.04 m, another indication of the large scatter of data at this station. Nevertheless, the data are consistent with downfaulting of the southeast block relative to the northwest block along the buried fault scarp under Roa Hook marsh.

The sampling locations in Ring Meadow at Iona Island were along two transects, one about 100 m south-southeast of the other. Although probings found no indication of a subsurface scarp, the data indicate that the transects are awry with respect to one another. All 27 basal peats together yield a transgression rate (1.44 ± 0.34 m/millennium) not significantly different from that of Cedar Pond Brook tidal marsh. The southeastern transect, however, has a transgression rate of about 0.5 m/millennium more than the northwestern transect. The intercepts for these two transects differ by more than 7 m (significant at the 0.05 level), the northwest transect being higher. It appears that the southeast block has dropped relative to the northwest block which, in addition, appears to have risen somewhat. Again, the caveat that the standard errors for all these data are large. Still, the data and derived statistics do not support a hypothesis of simple tilting; at the very least, one block has both rotated and dropped with respect to the other. We believe that complex faulting is responsible for the highly variable data assembled at Iona Island tidal marsh. An examination of Figure 4b indicates that the last movement occurred within the last 2,100 radiocarbon years.

The slopes for the three transects for the Constitution Island marsh exhibit considerable differences (Table 2). The mean slope for all eleven data points is 1.69 ± 0.29 m/millennium. The estimated transgression rate for the eastern transect, however, is 2.88 ± 0.24 m/millennium, more than 1 m/millennium larger than the average of the other two transects (1.63 ± 0.28) which are nearly identical. (Ratcliffe, 1980, traces the Timp Fault, one of the several constituent faults of the RFZ, north-northeast through the middle of the Constitution Island marsh; see Fig. 1.) These data indicate tilting and probably downfaulting toward the southeast. The time of faulting is difficult to estimate because of the limited data. A vertical difference of 1 m is indicated subsequent to 2.1 ka and at least 3 m of vertical separation after 4.6 ka. We require more data from Constitution Island in order to establish the times of fault movement and the recurrence interval better.

DISCUSSION

The data from stations within the RFZ appear to be anomalous when compared to stations both north and south

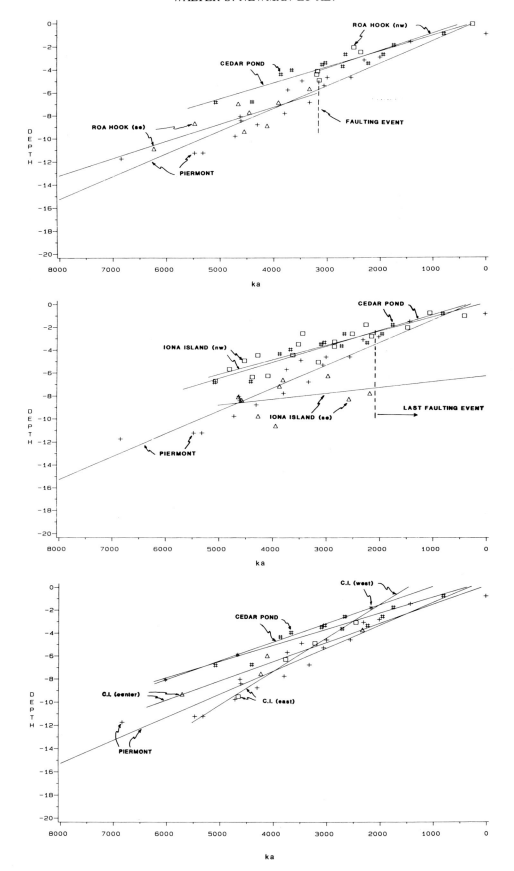

of the RFZ. The stations within the RFZ appear to be sinking with respect to those outside of the RFZ (Fig. 2e). At the Roa Hook station, a buried escarpment and the contrasting transgression intercept, but parallel transgression traces clearly indicate at least 1 m displacement along a fault. The radiocarbon dates suggest the last movement occurred about 3.2 ka.

The Iona Island transects yield similar transgression rates and slopes but are separated from one another by a meter or more. Although we are unable to demonstrate a scarp here, at the very least tilting toward the southeast is apparent. The southeastern transect reveals clear discontinuities in the transgressive trajectory subsequent to 2 ka and after 3.9 ka. These data suggest a recurrence interval on the order of 2 millennia.

Constitution Island marsh demonstrates two different patterns. The amount of data is poor, however, and permits only the notation of tilting toward the southeast, probably accompanied by downfaulting within the past 2 millennia.

The evidence for both tilting and complex faulting of blocks downward to the southeast within the RFZ seems supported by our data. The separation of the trend curves prior to about 2 ka suggests that the last fault separation occurred within the past 2 millennia. There is some suggestion that a penultimate faulting event occurred subsequent to 4 ka, thus implying a recurrence interval of the order of 2 millennia.

This study assumes an ongoing and continuous Holocene marine transgression. This assumption disagrees with those who find appreciable evidence that sea level has fluctuated within a meter or more of its present level over the past 6 ka (Fairbridge, 1961, 1976; Colquhoun and others, 1980). Although we suspect that many of these fluctuations are due to "yo-yo" tectonics, rather than eustatic fluctuations, our data are unable to resolve fluctuations of less than 1 m. The mean transgression rate of 1.99 ± 0.11 m/millennium for the region would, in any case, tend to mask any eustatic fluctuations of smaller magnitude.

Evidence for active faults is hard to find within the RFZ. For example, Ratcliffe (1980) places many of his fault traces beneath tidal marshes or the estuary itself. This item of mapping finesse is quite justifiable, but does bury the evidence. There seems no easy and inexpensive way to verify evidence (pro or con) of Holocene faulting in the field.

The major impediment to acceptance of Holocene movement at the RFZ is the absence of field evidence indicating fault movement, this after arduous and intensive exploration of the area over a considerable interval of time (Rat-

cliffe, 1980; Dames and Moore, 1977). Is the lack of Holocene surface faulting evidence a final convincing argument?

In defense of our interpretation and despite the lack of field evidence for Holocene faulting in the RFZ, we note that the 2 May 1983 Coalinga, California, earthquake (magnitude 6.5) failed to rupture through surface deposits and, instead, elastically folded the top few kilometers of the crust (Stein and King, 1984, p. 869). Crone and Harding (1984), working in the Great Basin of Utah, found that many Holocene(?) subsurface faults with substantial displacements are not associated with surface scarps. It appears that seismic events of damaging magnitude need not always manifest themselves in surface fault traces. For example, much of the Hudson Highlands may be a detached allochthonous block, and the primary fault zone may be hidden from view (Seeber and Sykes, 1984). The apparent fault throw we discerned within the RFZ may well be only a superficial manifestation of more fundamental faulting at depth whose primary trajectories do not reach the surface.

SUMMARY AND CONCLUSIONS

The "Champlain Sea" datum of 12 ka has clearly tilted along a north-northwest-striking section, upward to the north and/or downward to the south. This tilting of a former sea-level geoid has uplifted late Wisconsinan strandlines in the St. Lawrence valley to elevations of as much as 100 m or more above the present datum, whereas shorelines of similar age in the New York City region are at least several tens of meters below present sea level. Regional tilting, probably due to large lateral redistribution of mass from the time of the last glacial maximum to the present, appears to be a still ongoing phenomenon. The accumulated postglacial tilt on the "Champlain Sea" datum is about 0.36 m/km downward to the south-southeast. For the past 6,000 yrs, the apparent tilt rate for the lower Hudson estuary south of the RFZ has been about 0.16 m/km, demonstrating that the tilt rate has been declining. These contrasting rates probably represent the transition between the glacial and postglacial geoids due to mass transfers as a result of deglaciation (Fairbridge, 1961).

The contrasting transgression rates obtained from the radiocarbon dating of basal peats under tidal marshes, both within and beyond the limits of the RFZ, indicate both the sinking and rotating of blocks within the RFZ and the Hudson Highlands gorge in a complex graben-like manner within the past few thousand years. The breaks within the local transgression trajectories taken together suggest fault-block

---

FIG. 4.—Depth/time plot of Piermont marsh and Cedar Brook Pond marsh data compared with the data from within the RFZ (Ramapo Fault Zone) at Roa Hook marsh, Iona Island marsh, and Constitution Island marsh. Least-square regression lines are drawn for each station. (a) Depth/time plot of data from Table 1 for Piermont, Cedar Pond, and Roa Hook marshes. Note the divergence of 0.5 m/millennium going back in time when comparing the Piermont and Cedar Pond regression lines, a measure of crustal tilting, downward toward the south. Also note the approximately 2-m separation between the two Roa Hook traces at about 3.2 ka, presumably a faulting event corresponding to the model in Figure 2c. (b) Piermont and Cedar Pond plots as compared to the two Iona Island transects. Cedar Pond and Iona Island (nw) regression lines essentially coincide. Iona Island (se) appears to have tilted downward as compared to the other three regression lines. The last major offset of an Iona Island (se) data point suggests a faulting event within the past 2 millennia. (c) Piermont and Cedar Pond plots as compared to the three Constitution Island transects. The Constitution Island (C.I.) west transect regression line plots close to that of Cedar Pond. The C.I. (center) regression suggesting line is about a meter below that of C.I. (west), suggesting either downwarping or downfaulting of the center transect relative to the western transect. The C.I. (east) transect regression line apparently demonstrates tilting relative to the other transect regression lines.

throw with a magnitude of 1 m or more near 2, 3.2, 3.5 and 4.2 ka. Our evidence supports the argument of Aggarwal and Sykes (1978) that the RFZ has undergone fault movement during later Holocene times and is an active fault zone with a recurrence interval of from a few hundred to 2,000 yrs. Indeed, our data suggest that the RFZ will sustain a damaging movement within the next few decades.

ACKNOWLEDGMENTS

This project owes its completion to the brains and brawn of many of our past and present students. We especially single out Howard Craig, whose fine sense of humor helped us get past many a dismal moment. Also assisting us were Mike Balarazo, Larry Bruno, Fred Ciapetti, Barry Cirolli, Mark Drillings, Brian Duffy, Joe Gordon, Helene Greenberg, Jerry Greengold, John Isby, Steve Jencius, Jan Miller, Sheldon Nelson, Elizabeth Newman, Ginny Newman, Marion Newman, Bob Ortner, Jim Schneller, Kim Tessmer and Jim Wilson. Mueser, Rutledge, Johnson and DeSimone, Consulting Engineers of New York provided the bore data and samples for the Westway Project and the Whitestone-College Point tidal marsh in Queens County. The investigation was supported by National Science Foundation Grant No. EAR-7713666, U.S. Geological Survey Contract No. 14-08-0001-17729 (Earthquake Hazard Reduction Program), and several Professional Staff Congress/City University of New York Research Awards. Shaike Bornstein programmed Figure 4. An earlier version of this paper was considerably improved by the critical reviews of Don Colquhoun and Harold Wanless.

REFERENCES

ADAMS, D. A., 1963, Factors influencing vascular plant zonation in North Carolina salt marshes: Ecology, v. 44, p. 445–456.
AGGARWAL, Y. P., AND SYKES, L. R., 1978, Earthquakes, faults and nuclear power plants in southern New York and northern New Jersey: Science, v. 200, p. 425–429.
BLOOM, A. L., 1964, Peat accumulation and compaction in a Connecticut salt marsh: Journal of Sedimentary Petrology, v. 34, p. 599–603.
CAMERON, C. C., 1970, Peat deposits of southeastern New York: U.S. Geological Survey Bulletin 1317-B, 32 p.
CHAPMAN, V. J., 1960, Salt Marshes and Salt Deserts of the World: Interscience, New York, 392 p.
CINQUEMANI, L. J., NEWMAN, W. S., SPERLING, J. A., MARCUS, L. F., AND PARDI, R. R., 1982, Holocene sea level changes and vertical movements along the east coast of the United States: a preliminary report, in Colquhoun, D. J. ed., Holocene Sea Level Fluctuations, Magnitude and Causes: Department of Geology, University of South Carolina, Columbia, p. 13–33.
CLARK, PETER, AND KARROW, P. F., 1984, Last Pleistocene water bodies in the St. Lawrence Lowland, New York, and regional correlations: Geological Society of America Bulletin, v. 95, p. 805–813.
COLQUHOUN, D. J., BROOKS, M. J., ABBOTT, W. H., STAPOR, F. W., NEWMAN, W. S., AND PARDI, R. R., 1980, Principles and problems in reestablishing a Holocene sea-level for South Carolina, in Howard, J. D., DePratter, C. B., and Frey, R. W., eds., Excursions in Southeastern Geology: The Archaeology-Geology of the Georgia Coast: Guidebook 20, Geological Society of America and Georgia Geological Survey, p. 143–159.
CRONE, A. J., AND HARDING, S. T., 1984, Relationship of late Quaternary fault scarps to subjacent faults, eastern Great Basin, Utah: Geology, v. 12, p. 292–295.

CRONIN, T. M., 1977, Late Wisconsin marine environments of the Champlain valley (New York, Quebec): Quaternary Research, v. 7, p. 238–254.
DAMES AND MOORE, 1977, Geotechnical investigation of the Ramapo Fault Zone in the region of the Indian Point Generating Station: Prepared by Dames and Moore for Consolidated Edison, v. 1, March 28, 1977. Document available in Public Document Room, U.S. Nuclear Regulator Commission, 1717 H Street NW, Washington, D.C. (not consecutively paginated).
FAIRBRIDGE, R. W., 1961, Eustatic changes in sea level: Physics and Chemistry of the Earth, v. 4, p. 99–185.
———, 1976, Shellfish-eating preceramic Indians in coastal Brazil: Science, v. 191, p. 353–359.
GLEASON, P. J., PIEPGRAS, D., STONE, P. A., AND STIPP, J. J., 1980, Radiometric evidence for involvement of floating islands in the formation of Florida Everglades tree islands: Geology, v. 8, p. 195–199.
HILLAIRE-MARCEL, CLAUDE, 1979, Les mers post-glaciaires du Québec: quelques aspects: Thèse de Doctorat d'Etat es sciences naturelles, 1 Université Pièrre et Marie Curie, Paris VI, 2 vols., (not consecutively paginated).
HUBER, N. K., 1975, Marine terraces, datum planes for study of structural deformation: Earthquake Information, v. 73, p. 3–7.
KOTEFF, C., 1984, Postglacial uplift in northeastern United States, in Summaries of Technical Reports, v. XVIII: U.S. Geological Survey Open-file Report 84-628, p. 61.
LEHR, J. H., 1967, Some contributions to the floristics, plant ecology and geology of the Hudson Highlands section of the lower Hudson Valley: Sarracenia, v. 11, p. 175–189.
McINTIRE, W. G., AND MORGAN, J. P., 1963, Recent geomorphic history of Plum Island, Massachusetts and adjacent coasts: Louisiana State University Studies, Coastal Studies Series, No. 8, 44 p.
NEWMAN, W. S., 1977, Late Quaternary paleoenvironmental reconstruction: some contradictions from northwestern Long Island, New York, in Newman, W. S., and Salwen, B., eds., Amerinds and their Paleoenvironments in Northeastern North America: New York Academy of Sciences Annals, v. 288, p. 545–570.
———, FAIRBRIDGE, R. W., AND MARCH, STANLEY, 1971, Marginal subsidence of glaciated areas: United States, Baltic and North Seas, in Ters, M., ed., Etudes sur le Quaternaire dans le Monde, Union Internationale l'Etude Quaternaire, Paris, p. 795–801.
———, AND MARCH, STANLEY, 1968, The North American littoral: late Quaternary warping: Science, v. 160, p. 1110–1112.
———, THURBER, D. H., ZEISS, H. S., ROKACH, ALLAN, AND MUSICH, LILLIAN, 1969, Late Quaternary geology of the Hudson River Estuary: a preliminary report: New York Academy of Sciences Transactions, v. 31, p. 548–570.
ODOM, A. L., AND HATCHER, R. D., Jr., 1980, A Characterization of Faults in the Appalachian Fold Belt: Nuclear Regulatory Commission Report No. CR-1621, 314 p.
RATCLIFFE, N. M., 1980, Brittle faults (Ramapo Fault) and phyllonitic ductile shear zones in the basement rocks of the Ramapo seismic zones, New York and New Jersey, and their relationship to current seismicity, in Manspeizer, W., ed., Field Studies of New Jersey Geology and Guide to Field Trips: 52nd Annual Meeting of the New York State Geological Association, Geology Department, Newark College of Arts and Sciences, Rutgers University, Newark, p. 278–313.
———, 1984, Northeastern U.S. seismicity and tectonics, in Summaries of Technical Reports, v. XVIII: U.S. Geological Survey Open-File Report 84-628, p. 69–70.
REDFIELD, A. C., 1967, Postglacial changes in sea level in the western North Atlantic Ocean: Science, v. 157, p. 682–687.
———, 1972, Development of a New England salt marsh: Ecological Monographs, v. 42, p. 201–237.
SEEBER, L., AND SYKES, L., 1984, Earthquake hazard studies in the northeastern United States, in Summaries of Technical Reports, v. XVIII: U.S. Geological Survey Open-File Report 84-628, p. 16–17.
STEIN, R. S., AND KING, G. C. P., 1984, Seismic potential revealed by surface folding: 1983 Coalinga, California, earthquake: Science, v. 224, p. 869–872.
TAIRA, K., 1975, Holocene crustal movements in Taiwan as identified by radiocarbon dating of marine fossils and driftwood: Tectonophysics, v. 28, p. T1 - T5.

VITA-FINZI, C., 1975, Quaternary deposits in the Iranian Kakran: Geographical Journal, v. 141, p. 515–420.

WALCOTT, R. I., 1972, Late Quaternary vertical movements in eastern North America: quantitative evidence of glacio-isostatic rebound: Reviews of Geophysics and Space Physics, v. 10, p. 849–884.

WEISS, D., 1974, Late Pleistocene stratigraphy and paleoecology of the lower Hudson Estuary: Geological Society of America Bulletin, v. 85, p. 1561–1570.

———, 1976, Distribution of benthonic Foraminifera in the Hudson River Estuary: Maritime Sediments Special Publication 1, p. 119–129.

PART IV
HOLOCENE COASTAL DEPOSITIONAL SYSTEMS

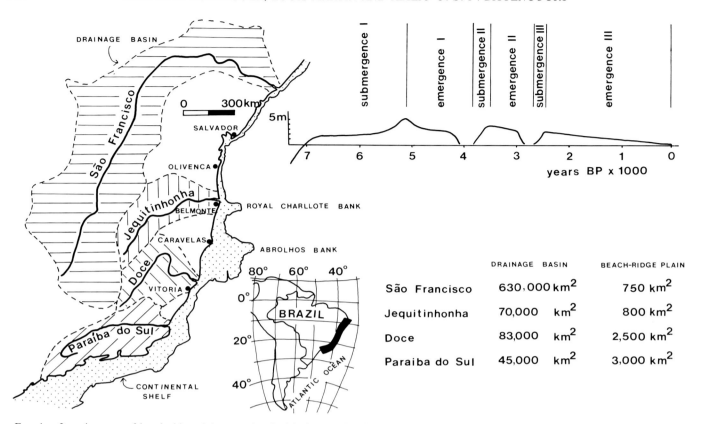

FIG. 1.—Location map of beach-ridge plains associated with the mouths of major rivers emptying onto the east-southeast Brazilian coast. Sea-level curve valid for this section of Brazilian coast is also shown. See text for details.

carbonates. Most of the inner shelf shallower than 30 m is covered by terrigenous sand (Melo and others, 1975).

Four great drainage basins nourish this stretch of the Brazilian coast: the São Francisco, Jequitinhonha, Doce, and Paraíba do Sul rivers (Fig. 1). The rocks of the São Francisco drainage basin are predominantly metasediments of Paleozoic age. By contrast, the Jequitinhonha, Doce and Paraíba do Sul basins are carved into crystalline rocks of the Precambrian basement. The hinterland for these last three basins is fairly hilly, ranging in height from 500 to 1,000 m within 100 km of the sea.

Late Pliocene alluvial fan deposits of the Barreiras Fm almost continuously fringe the entire east-southeast Brazilian coast. A line of Pleistocene cliffs carved into the sediments of this formation marks the landward limit of the Quaternary plains (Fig. 2).

The climate of a narrow belt along the coast is tropical and humid. Rainfall averages approximately 150–200 cm per year. The hinterland is rather dry with 50–100 cm of rain per year (Andrade, 1964).

Tides are semidiurnal in character. The mean tidal range decreases from north (1.5 m) to south (1.0 m). The amplitude of the spring tide is 2.3 m in the northern section of the east-southeast Brazilian coast and 1.7 m in the southern section.

QUATERNARY SEA-LEVEL OSCILLATIONS ALONG THE EAST–SOUTHEAST BRAZILIAN COAST

Two important transgressive episodes affected the east-southeast Brazilian coast during the Quaternary. The older one, named the Penultimate Transgression, reached a maximum at 120 ka when sea level was positioned 8 ± 2 m above present sea level (Martin and others, 1982). The younger episode, named the Last Transgression, reached a maximum at 5.1 ka when sea level rose 5 m above present sea level (Martin and others, 1980a; Suguio and others, 1980).

Relative sea-level curves for the last 7,000 yrs have been constructed for several sections of the Brazilian coast (Fig.

FIG. 2.—Geologic maps of the beach-ridge plains associated with the mouths of the São Francisco, Jequitinhonha, Doce and Paraíba do Sul rivers (after Dominguez and others, 1981a): (1) lake, (2) mangrove swamp, (3) freshwater swamp, (4) eolian-stabilized by vegetation, (5) eolian-active, (6) fluvial, (7) Holocene beach-ridge terrace, (8) Pleistocene beach-ridge terrace, (9) Barreiras Fm-Tertiary, (10) Precambrian basement, (11) beach-ridge alignment, (12) paleochannel, (13) Pleistocene cliff, (14) truncation in beach-ridge orientation, and (15) preferential direction of the wave-generated longshore drift.

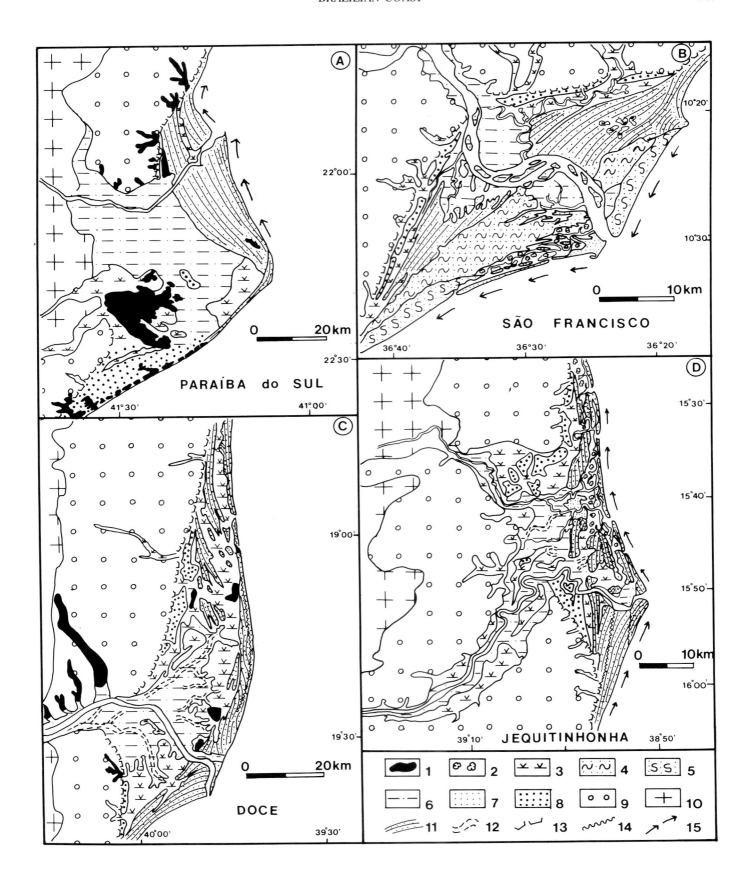

A PARAÍBA do SUL

B SÃO FRANCISCO

C DOCE

D JEQUITINHONHA

1	2	3	4	5
6	7	8	9	10
11	12	13	14	15

1) (Martin and others, 1979a; Martin and others, 1980a; Martin and others, 1980b; Suguio and others, 1980). Radiocarbon dating of samples of vermetid encrustations, calcareous algae and corals collected from above the modern life zone of these organisms were used to reconstruct ancient positions of sea level. Radiocarbon dating of beach and lagoonal deposits was also used. In this case, sedimentologic studies were necessary to determine the approximate position of mean sea level at the time these deposits were formed. These curves indicate that: (1) present mean sea level was surpassed for the first time about 6.5–7.0 ka; (2) by about 5.1 ka sea level had risen to 4–5 m above today's mean sea level; (3) at about 3.8 ka sea level experienced a lowstand and was positioned slightly below today's mean sea level; (4) at 3.5 ka sea level rose to 3.0 m above today's mean sea level; (5) at 2.7 km sea level again experienced a lowstand, dropping slightly below present mean sea level; and (6) by about 2.5 ka a third highstand was reached. At this time, sea level rose 2.5 m above today's mean sea level, and since then it has been progressively dropping.

Observations indicate that in the northern section of the east-southeast Brazilian coast, sea level first rose above today's level earlier (7.0 ka) than in the southern section (6.5 ka; Martin and others, 1980a). Also in the north, sea level rose 5 m during the maximum of the Last Transgression and in the south just 4 meters. Along the southern Brazilian coast, it was not possible to identify the lowstand at 2.7 ka. Such small discrepancies have been interpreted by some authors as the result of deformations of the geoid (Martin and others, 1980a).

In summary, it is possible to recognize along the east-southeast Brazilian coast during the Holocene three main phases of submergence (7.0–5.1 ka, 3.8–3.5 ka, and 2.7–2.5 ka) associated with three main phases of emergence (5.1–3.8 ka, 3.5–2.7 ka, and 2.5 ka to the present).

QUATERNARY DEPOSITS

Sedimentary deposits occurring on the Quaternary plains associated with the mouths of the São Francisco, Jequitinhonha, Doce and Paraíba do Sul rivers are represented by beach-ridge and fluvial terraces, lagoonal, freshwater swamp, mangrove swamp and eolian deposits (Fig. 2).

Beach-ridge terraces are the most abundant deposits on the Quaternary plains. They can be grouped into two important sets of Pleistocene and Holocene beach-ridge terraces, using as criteria their morphologic characteristics, altitude, and age (Fig. 2). The tops of the Pleistocene beach-ridge terraces reach 6 to 10 m above the present high tide level. They are normally located in a landward position on the sedimentary plains and rest directly in contact with the Pleistocene fossil cliffs of the Barreiras Fm. Pleistocene beach-ridge terraces are composed of leached sands which grade downward into a "coffee rock" cemented by humic acids and iron oxides leached from upper horizons. Sedimentary structures in most cases have been completely destroyed by pedogenic processes. Nevertheless, *Ophiomorpha* burrows associated with tabular and trough cross-stratification are sometimes found at the base of the terrace

associated with the "coffee rock." Surfaces of the Pleistocene terraces are characterized by remnants of beach ridges somewhat subdued by slope and weathering processes. Radiocarbon dates are not available for these terraces at the locations described here. In neighboring areas, however, shells collected from mud layers at the base of terraces with the same morphologic characteristics have radiocarbon ages greater than 35 ka (Martin and others, 1979b; Martin and others, 1980a; Martin and others, 1980b). At the locality of Olivenca (Fig. 1), a piece of coral collected in a reef formation underlying a beach-ridge terrace, with the characteristics described above, was dated using the Io/U method and gave an age of about 120 ka (Martin and others, 1982). This latter date suggests that these terraces were possibly formed about 120 ka, which corresponds to a well known world-wide Pleistocene highstand (Neumann and Moore, 1975; Shackleton, 1977). Some authors have reported Pleistocene beach-ridge terraces associated with a highstand in sea level about 35–40 ka (Hoyt and others, 1968; Hoyt and Hails, 1974; Moslow and Heron, 1979). This date, however, has come under much controversy because contamination of the samples with even minute amounts of modern carbon can affect the apparent radiocarbon age of dates close to the limits of the C[14] method (Mörner, 1971; Stapor and Tanner, 1973).

An ancient drainage system cut into the sediments of the Pleistocene beach-ridge terrace was observed in the Jequitinhonha River plain. Today this drainage system is filled with muds. Radiocarbon dates of wood collected in these muds gave ages of 6.18 ± 0.14 and 5.3 ± 0.14 ka (Dominguez, 1983). Similar paleodrainage systems and similar ages for the mud fillings are reported for other regions along the east-southeast Brazilian coast (Martin and others, 1980b).

The Holocene beach-ridge terraces are located seaward of those of Pleistocene age and are normally separated from the latter by a low intervening area filled with lagoonal muds (Fig. 2). These lagoonal muds are now capped by freshwater swamps. The height of the Holocene beach ridges varies from 4 m (most landward) to a few centimeters (most seaward) above present high tide. The surface of the Holocene beach-ridge terraces slopes gently seaward, which suggests that their construction took place in a period of dropping sea level.

Sedimentary structures in the beach-ridge terraces are perfectly preserved and are represented almost exclusively by beach face stratification. *Ophiomorpha* burrows were also observed, in this case associated with horizontal stratification at the base of the terraces. Landward-dipping tabular cross-stratification also occasionally occurs at the base of the terraces. At the surface, the Holocene terraces are characterized by perfectly preserved beach ridges in contrast to the eroded Pleistocene beach ridges. All radiocarbon dates for the Holocene beach-ridge terraces gave ages younger than 5 ka.

The lagoonal deposits consist of black to gray organic-rich muds with abundant wood debris and shells. Shells are mainly from marine and/or brackish environments and most of them are found in life position. Radiocarbon dates fall mostly in the range of 7–5 ka. In the Jequitinhonha plain, lagoonal sediments with radiocarbon ages varying from 7.9

to 7.0 ka were also found extending beneath the Holocene beach-ridge terrace (Dominguez, 1983). In the Doce River plain, the lagoonal sediments have two distinctive age ranges: 6–5 ka and 3.5–3.0 ka (Suguio and others, 1981).

Fluvial terraces include the coarse-grained fluvial deposits of natural levees, paleochannels, and point bar environments. Areal distribution of the fluvial terraces is primarily controlled by the evolutionary history of the Quaternary plains. In the Doce River plain, the fluvial terraces are fan-shaped (Fig. 2C), whereas in the Jequitinhonha River plain the fluvial terraces occur as individual alluvial ridges that coalesce seaward, separated by low intervening swampy areas (Fig. 2D). In the Paraíba do Sul River plain, the fluvial terrace is represented by an elongated axis of northwest-southeast orientation (Fig. 2A). In the São Francisco River plain, neither present fluvial deposits nor fluvial terraces are well developed (Fig. 2B).

Eolian deposits are found only in the São Francisco River plain where they transgress indiscriminately over all other deposits. Two generations of Holocene dunes were identified in this region (Fig. 2B), an internal one stabilized by vegetation and an external active one fringing the present coastline.

We call attention to the existence of a well marked asymmetry in facies distribution and/or progradation rates between updrift and downdrift sides of the São Francisco, Jequitinhonha and Paraíba do Sul River mouths. This asymmetry is a direct consequence of different styles of progradation (Dominguez and others, 1983). On the updrift side, progradation is promoted by the successive accretion of beach ridges which give origin to a continuous sand sheet. On the downdrift side, progradation takes place through the incorporation of sandy islands that give origin to protected environments where mangrove swamps thrive. These islands are formed in two different ways (Dominguez and others, 1983): (1) coast-ward progradation of sand spits rooted in the downdrift margin of the river mouth, and (2) wave reworking of river mouth bars. In some cases, such as in the Paraíba do Sul and Jequitinhonha River plains, an intermittent downdrift migration of the river mouth was also observed (Dominguez, 1983; Dominguez and others, 1983).

Studies carried out in the Paraíba do Sul River plain also show that the sediment characteristics are very distinctive for both sides of the river mouth (Martin and others, 1984b). These authors found that on the updrift side sand grains of the Holocene beach-ridge terrace and present beach are predominantly rounded to well rounded. On the downdrift side, sand grains of the present beach are subangular to subrounded. Sand grains on the Holocene beach-ridge terraces located downdrift of the river mouth show high variability in roundness and consist of two shapes: rounded to well rounded, and subangular to subrounded. Present river sands are characteristically subangular to subrounded.

The evidence presented above indicates that sources of sediment for progradation of the coastline are different for both sides of the river mouth. On the downdrift side, sediments are provided predominantly by the river, whereas for the updrift side longshore drift sands are more important. All this evidence suggests that the offshore buildup of the fluvial effluent acts as a jetty, trapping on the updrift

side sediments transported by the wave-generated longshore drift. Zenkovich (1967) reported similar phenomena for river mouths along the Caucasian Black Sea coast. Komar (1973), using computer simulation models, has also concluded that rivers act as a barrier to the longshore drift of sands, effectively behaving as a jetty or groin.

Although estimates of longshore transport rates and fluvial sediment discharge are not available for the areas described here, it is still possible to draw conclusions concerning the relative importance of river-borne versus longshore sediment supply during progradation of the coastline. Progradation rates, as deduced from radiocarbon dates of the Holocene beach-ridge terraces and other geomorphic evidence, indicate that the coastline in the updrift side of the river mouth progrades faster than in the downdrift side (Dominguez and others, 1983). For the Jequitinhonha and Paraíba do Sul River plains, progradation rates on the updrift side were observed to be two and one and one-half times greater, respectively (Dominguez and others, 1983). For the São Francisco, equal rates of progradation were reported for both sides of the river mouth.

Because (1) river-borne sediments are used to promote progradation only on the downdrift side of the river mouth, whereas wave-generated longshore drift supplies sediment to the updrift side, and (2) rates of progradation are normally higher for the updrift side of the river mouth, we conclude that the amount of sediment provided by longshore drift is more significant than the amount provided by the river in promoting progradation of the coastline in the river plains discussed here.

At the Doce River plain, the effects of the longshore drift in creating this asymmetry in facies distribution and progradation rates were not so pronounced, probably because of successive reversals in the longshore drift direction that affected this region during the Holocene (Dominguez and others, 1983).

QUATERNARY EVOLUTION

Integration of the regional sea-level history (Fig. 1) with detailed mapping and radiocarbon dating of the sedimentary deposits occurring in the plains associated with the São Francisco, Jequitinhonha, Doce and Paraíba do Sul River mouths indicates the existence of four main stages during the Quaternary evolution of these plains (Fig. 3; Dominguez and others, 1981a). These stages clearly show how sea-level behavior controls the styles of sedimentation in coastal regions.

Stage I—Pleistocene beach-ridge plain.—

This stage corresponds to the regressive event which followed the maximum of the Penultimate Transgression (120 ka). During this period, reworking of inner-shelf sediments as a result of dropping sea level favored progradation of the coastline through the accretion of successive beach ridges. Beach-ridge plains similar to those existing today were constructed associated with the mouths of the São Francisco, Jequitinhonha, Doce and Paraíba do Sul rivers (Fig. 3A). Remnants of these strandplains are preserved as Pleistocene beach-ridge terraces. Erosive effects triggered by the ac-

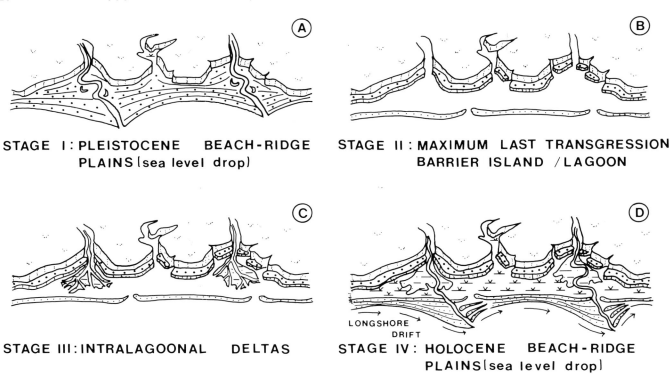

STAGE I: PLEISTOCENE BEACH-RIDGE
PLAINS (sea level drop)

STAGE II: MAXIMUM LAST TRANSGRESSION
BARRIER ISLAND / LAGOON

STAGE III: INTRALAGOONAL DELTAS

STAGE IV: HOLOCENE BEACH-RIDGE
PLAINS (sea level drop)

⅄ ⅄
⅄ ⅄   FRESHWATER SWAMP

— · —   FLUVIAL

∷∷∷∷   HOLOCENE BEACH RIDGE

∷∷∷∷   PLEISTOCENE BEACH RIDGE

FIG. 3.—Evolutionary scheme proposed for the beach-ridge plains associated with the mouths of the Sao Francisco, Jequitinhonha, Doce, and Paraiba do Sul rivers (modified from Dominguez and others, 1981a). See text for details.

centuated drop in sea level during the last glacial period favored development of a drainage network carved into the Pleistocene beach-ridge terraces. As mentioned previously, remnants of this network are still preserved, but they are filled with muds and are inactive today.

Stage II—maximum of the Last Transgression.—

The rise in sea level that followed the last glacial period partly eroded and drowned the Pleistocene plains. By the time the maximum of the Last Transgression was reached, extensive barrier island-lagoonal systems were formed at the sedimentary plains studied here, as well as along the entire east-southeast Brazilian coast (Fig. 3B). Remnants of the barrier islands are preserved today as the most landward beach ridge of the Holocene beach-ridge terraces. The paleolagoons are also well preserved today, being represented by the low-lying mud-filled areas that separate the Pleistocene from the Holocene beach-ridge terraces. The paleodrainage network carved into the Pleistocene terrace was also drowned by the Last Transgression. This explains why the muds that fill this paleodrainage network and the sediments deposited in the paleolagoons have radiocarbon ages falling within the same range (7–5 ka).

It is important to note that barrier island-lagoonal systems were established well before the maximum of the Last Transgression was reached. This is indicated by the Jequitinhonha River plain, where lagoonal sediments were found extending beneath the Holocene beach-ridge terraces. Radiocarbon dates of these sediments gave ages ranging from 7.9–7.0 ka, indicating that the barrier islands were already established by this time.

Stage III—intralagoonal delta.—

In those regions where the paleolagoons associated with the maximum of the Last Transgression reached considerable dimensions, the rivers constructed extensive intralagoonal deltas (Fig. 3C). By this time, the morphology of the east-southeast Brazilian coast was very similar to that of the United States Atlantic and Gulf coasts.

Although not active today, these intralagoonal deltas are very well preserved. This is beautifully exemplified at the Doce River plain, where the fluvial terraces have a fan-shaped spatial pattern (Fig. 2C). Intralagoonal deltas are also well developed in the Paraíba do Sul River plain, where the fluvial terraces form an elongated feature of northwest-southeast orientation (Fig. 2A). In the Jequitinhonha and

São Francisco River plains, intralagoonal deltas are not so well developed, because in these regions the paleolagoons were of reduced dimensions.

Stage IV—Holocene beach-ridge plain.—

The drop in sea level that followed the maximum of the Last Transgression favored seaward progradation of the coastline, which led to the construction of the Holocene beach-ridge terraces (Fig. 3D). This drop in sea level also exposed the estuaries and lagoons which were replaced by freshwater swamp environments. As a consequence, narrow elongated barrier islands separated from the mainland by a lagoon are virtually absent today along this section of the Brazilian coast.

It is important to note that the ultimate sediment source for the progradation of the coastline was provided by reworking of the inner-shelf sediments as a result of dropping sea level. This reworking probably took place following an inverse relationship of the Bruun coastal retreat model (Bruun, 1962). The 5-m drop in sea level along the entire east-southeast coast of Brazil has made incredible amounts of sediment available to the wave-induced longshore drift systems. Remember that most of the inner shelf shallower than 30 m is covered by terrigenous sands (Melo and others, 1975). These sediments were transported along the coast and finally came to rest in sediment "traps" such as river mouths, re-entrants of the coast, and areas protected by offshore obstacles. In fact, major Quaternary strandplains along

east-southeast Brazil are associated with just such a situation. A typical example is the Caravelas beach-ridge plain (Fig. 4), which has the same kind of sedimentary deposits found in the other beach-ridge plains described here, with the exception of fluvial deposits. Although having dimensions comparable to the Jequitinhonha beach-ridge plain, the Caravelas plain has no association with any important river course and was constructed in an area of convergence of the wave-induced longshore drift. This area is also relatively protected by the offshore reefs of Abrolhos (Fig. 4). It is clear that sediments for the progradation of the coastline in the Caravelas plain were provided by the wave-induced longshore drift of sediments. These sediments were probably made available to the longshore drift system via a falling sea level.

In this way extensive plains were constructed composed of beach-ridge, lagoonal and other coastal deposits associated with the mouths of the São Francisco, Jequitinhonha, Doce and Paraíba do Sul rivers. These plains have been previously misinterpreted as wave-dominated deltas (Baccoccli, 1971; Galloway, 1975; Coleman and Wright, 1975), because it was always believed that progradation of the coastline was controlled by river-borne sediments. This is not true, since the main sediment sources for the progradation of the coastline in these regions were apparently provided by wave-induced longshore drift of sediments reworked from the inner shelf by the fall of sea level (Bittencourt and others, 1981; Dominguez and others, 1981a;

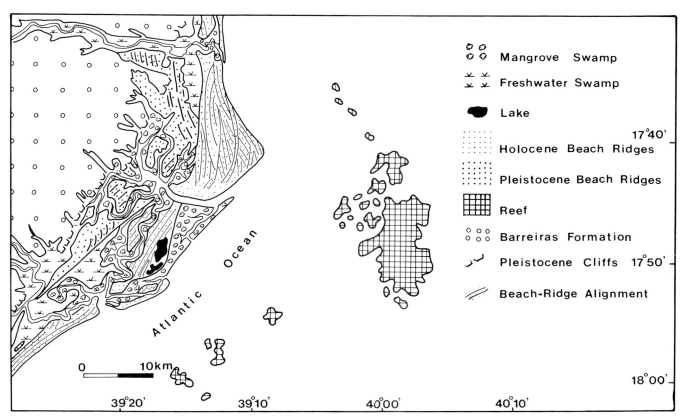

Fig. 4.—Geologic map of the Caravelas beach-ridge plain. See Figure 1 for location.

Dominguez and others, 1982; Dominguez and others, 1983; Suguio and others, 1981). In this sense, river-borne sediments played only a secondary role during progradation of the coastline.

ROLE OF THE HOLOCENE HIGH–FREQUENCY SEA-LEVEL OSCILLATIONS IN THE EVOLUTION OF THE RIVER-ASSOCIATED SEDIMENTARY PLAINS

The Holocene high-frequency sea-level oscillations were also able to produce dramatic changes in the physiography of the sedimentary plains considered here. These changes will be discussed only for the Jequitinhonha and Doce River plains, because more detailed investigations are available for these regions (Dominguez, 1983; Suguio and others, 1981) and because in these areas the high-frequency sea-level oscillations left readily interpretable records.

Jequitinhonha River plain.—

On the Jequitinhonha River plain, integration of a detailed analysis of the Holocene beach-ridge patterns, the geographic distribution of other sedimentary deposits, and radiocarbon dating has allowed the identification of six evolutionary stages during the Holocene (Fig. 5). These stages have been correlated with phases of emergence and submergence of the Holocene sea-level curve. These correlations indicate that at the Jequitinhonha River plain the short-term Holocene sea-level rises caused drowning of the river mouths and induced abrupt shifts in the lower river course. At the newly occupied river mouths, progradation resumed during the subsequent regressive events. Several lines of evidence can be pointed to in support of the above statements.

(1) Analysis of the Holocene beach-ridge orientation patterns has shown the existence of three separate beach-ridge systems, each of them associated with river mouths successively occupied by the Jequitinhonha River during the Holocene (Fig. 5B, D, F).
(2) The two previously occupied Jequitinhonha River mouths display distinct characteristics, indicating they have been drowned. The river mouth associated with beach-ridge system II (Fig. 5D), and drowned during submergence phase III (Fig. 5E), is still well preserved at the coastal plain and is easily identifiable in aerial photographs. Today, the entire central area of beach-ridge system II is occupied by a swamp environment (Fig. 5F). The fine-grained sediments deposited in these swamps partly cover the beach-ridge system II, conferring to it a drowned appearance.
(3) Associated with the three beach-ridge systems are readily identifiable belts of fluvial sediments separated from each other by intervening low swampy areas. Such a pattern shows that important shifts in the lower course of the Jequitinhonha River took place during the Holocene. These shifts are characterized by their abruptness and probably occurred through an avulsion-type process in direct relation to imbalances in the fluvial dynamics. In the Quaternary framework of the Brazilian coastal evolution, two main causes can be argued to explain these imbalances: first, the loss of the river's

transporting efficiency through an overextension of the lower river course as a result of progradation, and second, a rapid positive oscillation of sea level which, by drowning the river's mouth, reduces the river's sediment transporting efficiency. The second alternative is believed to be the more plausible one to explain the shifts observed. The systematic seaward decrease in height of the beach-ridge terrace indicates they were formed under conditions of dropping sea level, which enhances the river's transporting efficiency.

(4) A radiocarbon date of wood debris collected in the belt of fluvial sediments associated with beach-ridge system I (Fig. 5B) gave an age of 5.57 ± 0.15 ka, indicating that this is the oldest fluvial sediment belt.
(5) A radiocarbon date of a peat layer contained within the innermost beach-ridge system III gave an age of 2.57 ± 0.1 ka, which coincides with the beginning of emergence phase III of the Holocene sea-level variations curve.
(6) Radiocarbon dates of 14 wood samples collected in the fluvial sediments (mostly natural levee deposits) associated with the present lower course of the Jequitinhonha River gave ages falling in the range of 2.24 to 0.19 ka, indicating that the present lower river course was indeed occupied only after submergence phase III.

Doce River plain.—

On the Doce River plain the effects of the Holocene high-frequency sea-level oscillations were somewhat different from those on the Jequitinhonha River plain. On the Doce plain, the Holocene short-term rises in sea level caused reoccupation of ancient lagoons and drowning of the Holocene beach-ridge terrace, with subsequent development of new barrier island systems. Emergence phases of the Holocene sea-level curve are associated with periods of progradation of the shoreline. Four evolutionary stages were identified for this region during the Holocene (Fig. 6; Suguio and others, 1981).

A radiocarbon date of channel deposits associated with the north arm of the intralagoonal delta (Fig. 2C) shows that this arm was active at least until 4.25 ka. This means that the paleolagoon formed during submergence phase I had not completely emerged by this time. This is reasonable since, according to the relative sea-level curve, sea level at 4.25 ka had dropped just 1.8 m from the 5 m highstand. Also, because of the geographic position where the sample was collected (at the extremity of the north arm paleochannel), it is suggested that most of the intralagoonal delta as seen today was already constructed by that time (Suguio and others, 1981).

The main consequence of the rapid rise in sea level between 3.8–3.5 ka (submergence phase II) was the drowning of beach-ridge system I, with development of a new barrier island-lagoonal system and a partial reoccupation of the paleolagoon formed during the Last Transgression (Fig. 6C). The drowning of the first Holocene beach-ridge system gave it an aspect of large sandy islands separated from each other by low intervening swampy areas filled with lagoonal muds. Radiocarbon dates of these sediments give ages in the range of 3.5–3.0 ka. Radiocarbon dates falling

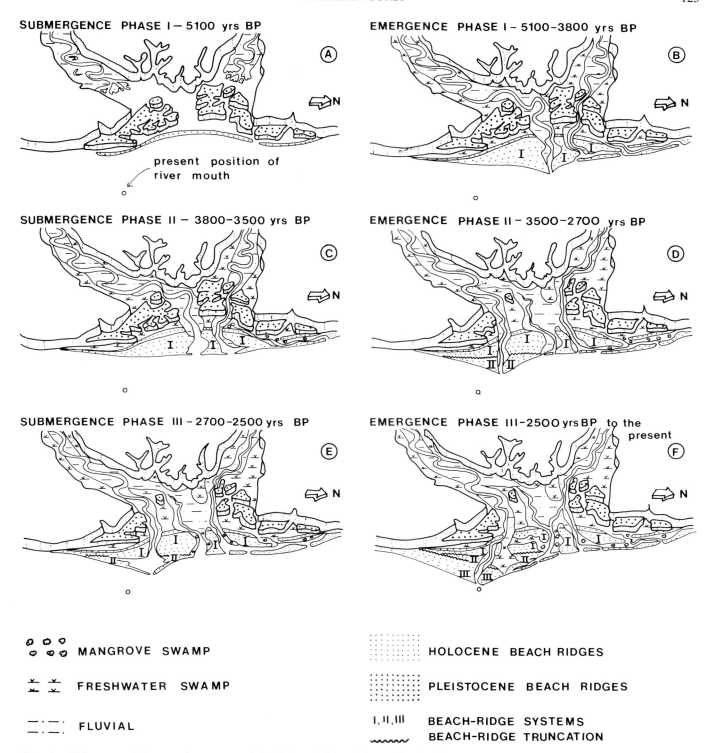

FIG. 5.—Holocene evolutionary scheme proposed for the beach-ridge plain associated with the Jequitinhonha River mouth (modified from Dominguez, 1983). Emergence and submergence phases depicted correspond to the emergence and submergence phases of the Holocene sea-level curve shown in Figure 1. See text for details.

within this same range were also found in the paleolagoon formed during the maximum of the Last Transgression, attesting to the reoccupation of this paleolagoon during submergence phase II.

For the Doce River plain, the effects of submergence phase III (2.7–2.5 ka) are difficult to identify. We suggest, however, that this event is possibly represented by an important truncation in the beach-ridge orientation of beach-ridge sys-

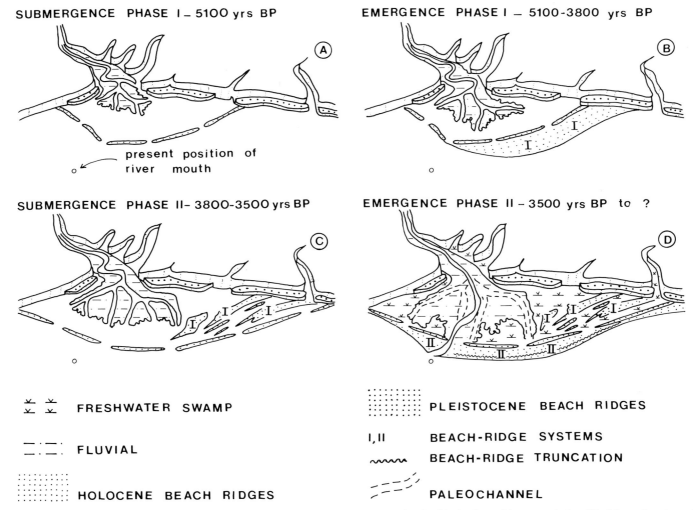

SUBMERGENCE PHASE I _ 5100 yrs BP

Ⓐ

present position of
o ↙ river mouth

EMERGENCE PHASE I _ 5100-3800 yrs BP

Ⓑ

SUBMERGENCE PHASE II _ 3800-3500 yrs BP

Ⓒ

EMERGENCE PHASE II _ 3500 yrs BP to ?

Ⓓ

⩊ ⩊
⩊ ⩊   **FRESHWATER SWAMP**

‒.‒.   **FLUVIAL**

:::::::   **HOLOCENE BEACH RIDGES**

::::::::   **PLEISTOCENE BEACH RIDGES**

I, II   **BEACH-RIDGE SYSTEMS**

⌇⌇⌇   **BEACH-RIDGE TRUNCATION**

╌╌╌   **PALEOCHANNEL**

Fɪɢ. 6.—Holocene evolutionary scheme proposed for the beach-ridge plain associated with the Doce River mouth (modified from Suguio and others, 1981). Emergence and submergence phases depicted correspond to the emergence and submergence phases of the Holocene sea-level curve shown in Figure 1. See text for details.

tem II (Figs. 2C, 6D). This truncation divides beach-ridge system II into two subsystems.

In the northern section of the Paraíba do Sul River plain, it was possible to identify a low-lying area filled with muds which separates two groups of Holocene beach ridges (Fig. 2A). Carbon-14 dating of these muds gave ages of 2.36 ± 0.18 and 2.53 ± 0.17 ka. These dates suggest that this low-lying area is probably related to submergence phase III (2.7–2.5 ka) of the Holocene relative sea-level curve.

DISCUSSION

Existing coastal sedimentation models have not properly incorporated the fundamental role of Holocene sea-level history in the development of modern coastal regions. For example, the classic work by Coleman and Wright (1975), although analyzing the influence of as many as 400 parameters on the geometry of deltaic sand bodies, did not address the effects of Holocene sea-level oscillations. Coastal sedimentation models have focused on tidal range, wave energy, and fluvial discharge as the primary controls in determining the general framework of coastal sedimentary environments (Fisher, 1969; Galloway, 1975; Hayes, 1979). It is defended here that these factors are important only in controlling aspects of the local coastal morphology. Nevertheless, it is the sea-level history which determines the general framework within which these factors act. A word of caution is needed here because sometimes huge fluvial systems (e.g., Mississippi, Amazon rivers) can completely overcome the role played by sea-level variations. It is believed, however, that for "average" coastal situations (e.g., east-southeast Brazil, United States Atlantic coast and some sections of the Gulf coast) the above statement is valid. The strong emphasis placed on factors such as wave energy, tidal range, and river discharge on elaborating coastal sedimentation models is probably the result of the general belief, which persisted until very recently, that modern sea level has been rising or at least has been stable everywhere during the last 4,000 yrs. Nevertheless, radiocarbon dating of ancient strandline indicators collected by many investigators documents varying trends of sea level for different regions of the world. Today, it is well accepted that no sea-level curve can be truly "eustatic," each having only a local validity (Newman and others, 1980). As suggested by Newman and others (1980), the Fairbridge (1961) model (Holocene sea level higher than at present) appears to describe the sea-level behavior at low latitudes, whereas the Bloom (1971) model (Holocene sea level lower than at present) best describes sea-level history in northern mid-latitudes. Possible causes for these different sea-level behaviors include, among others, sediment loading, hydro-isostasy, local and regional neotectonics, and geoidal deformation.

Under conditions of sea-level rise (Bloom model), barrier island-lagoonal systems are the dominant mode of sedimentation. Rivers do not directly reach the inner shelf but tend to construct deltas in protected environments such as lagoons, bays or estuaries. Beach-ridge plains are virtually absent. This is the morphology that characterizes, for example, the United States Atlantic and western Gulf coasts, where during the last 5,000 yrs sea level has been continuously rising. This also was the dominant mode of sedimentation along east-southeast Brazil 5 ka, during the maximum of the Last Transgression.

By contrast, sea-level fall (Fairbridge model) poses highly unfavorable conditions to the genesis and maintenance of barrier island-lagoonal systems. Lagoons and bays become emergent. Beach-ridge plains rapidly prograde, giving origin to regressive sand sheets. Rivers empty directly onto the inner shelf. This is the case of east-southeast Brazil, where narrow elongated barrier islands separated from the mainland by a lagoon are virtually absent today, although abundant in the past. These features have been replaced by extensive beach-ridge plains. Sea-level fall makes available, besides river-borne sediments, a new source of sediment for the progradation of the shoreline. This is the reworking of the inner shelf sands. These sands are incorporated into the wave-generated longshore drift systems and finally come to rest at sediment traps located along the coast, such as river mouths or any other feature that decreases the sediment transporting ability of the longshore drift systems (e.g., offshore obstacles, coastal re-entrants, etc.). Along the Brazilian coast, sediments provided in this way were more important than the fluvial input.

Finally, it is important to note that high-frequency sea-level oscillations of small amplitude (2–3 m) and short time span (200–300 yrs), such as those that affected the east-southeast Brazilian coast during the Holocene, can also cause dramatic changes in the morphology and evolution of Quaternary coastal plains, as demonstrated for the Jequitinhonha and Doce River plains. Therefore, as pointed out by DePratter and Howard (1983), it appears rather dangerous to smooth relative sea-level variation curves, a common practice in the literature. If the relative sea-level curves constructed for the east-southeast Brazilian coast and used as a basic reference in this work were to have had their format smoothed, they would indicate only a phase of submergence (5 ka) and a phase of emergence (from 5.1 ka to the present). The two high-frequency oscillations at 3.8–3.5 ka and 2.7–2.5 ka would be wiped out. These oscil-

lations have played an important role in the coastal sedimentation dynamics of these areas.

The data derived from study of the Brazilian coast strongly suggest that the most favorable setting for development of regressive sand sheets is under conditions of falling sea level. Ancient shoreline sandstone sequences, such as the Cretaceous of the Western Interior (Rice and Gautier, 1983) and the Upper Wilcox (Fisher, 1968) and Frio (Boyd and Dyer, 1964) sandstones of Texas, show in many cases toplap patterns with prograding clinoforms, interpreted as rapid excess deposition of clastic sediments representing periods of relative stillstand during a major rise in sea level (Vail and others, 1977). It is, in fact, very possible that some of these sequences were produced by small drops in relative sea level, such as that documented along the east-southeast Brazilian coast. Development of better criteria for recognizing sequences formed as a result of dropping sea level and application of these criteria to the study of ancient shoreline sandstone sequences can lead to the identification of minor regressive events superimposed on major transgressive ones and should therefore improve our knowledge of sea-level behavior in the past.

Wave-dominated delta systems and strandplain sand bodies are considered optimum hosts for high quality reservoirs because of the abundance of highly transmissive, well sorted, strike-oriented sandstone bodies (Galloway and Hobday, 1983). In fact, some of these shoreline sandstone deposits are successful oil producers (e.g., Frio of Texas, Boyd and Dyer, 1964). Conversely, it is thought that the high degree of sandbody interconnection in certain accumulations limits opportunities for stratigraphic entrapment. This opinion is mainly theoretical since the stratigraphic evolution of these shoreline sandstone sequences is rather poorly understood, particularly with respect to the influences exerted by sea-level oscillations. Broad testing of the concepts of coastal evolution that have arisen from study of the Brazilian coast will certainly result in a better understanding and utilization of stratigraphy and depositional framework so important for the success of exploration.

ACKNOWLEDGMENTS

The senior author is grateful to Harold R. Wanless for his encouragement and valuable discussions. We thank Larry Peterson, James D. Howard and an anonymous reviewer for helpful suggestions. Thanks are also extended to Dag Nummedal for inviting us to participate in this symposium volume.

Financial support for the senior author while in the United States was provided by the Coordenação de Aperfeicoamento de Pessoal de Nível Superior (CAPES-Brazil).

REFERENCES

ANDRADE, G. O., 1964, Os climas, *in* Azevedo, A., ed., Brasil a terra e o homem: 1—as bases físicas: Companhia Editora Nacional, São Paulo, Brazil, p. 397–457.

ASMUS, H. E., AND PALMA, J. C., 1973, Setor Atlantico da Geotransversal Leste-Oeste: estado atual do conhecimento (abs.): XXVIII Congresso Brasileiro de Geologia, Simposio de Geodinamica, Aracaju, Brazil, p. 42.

BACOCCOLI, G., 1971, Os deltas marinhos holocenicos brasileiros; uma tentativa de classificacão: Boletim Tecnico da Petrobras, v. 14, p. 5–38.

BITTENCOURT, A. C. S. P., DOMINGUEZ, J. M. L., MARTIN, L., AND FERREIRA, Y. A., 1981, Dados preliminares sobre a evolucão do delta do rio São Francisco (SE/AL) durante o Quaternário; influencia das variacoes do nível do mar: Atas do IV Simpósio do Quaternário no Brasil, Sociedade Brasileira de Geologia, Rio de Janeiro, p. 49–68.

BLOOM, A. L., 1971, Glacial-eustatic and isostatic controls of sea level since the last glaciation, in Turekian, K. K., ed., The Late Cenozoic Ice Ages: Yale University Press, New Haven, Connecticut, p. 355–379.

BOYD, D. R., AND DYER, B. F., 1964, Frio barrier bar system of south Texas: Gulf Coast Association of Geological Societies Transactions, v. 14, p. 309–322.

BOYER, P. R., 1969, Structure of the continental margin of Brazil, Natal to Rio de Janeiro: Unpublished Ph.D. Dissertation, University of Illinois, Urbana, 93 p.

BROECKER, W. S., AND OLSON, E. A., 1961, Lamont radiocarbon measurements III: Radiocarbon, v. 3, p. 176–204.

BRUUN, P., 1962, Sea level rise as a cause of shore erosion: American Society of Civil Engineers Proceedings, Journal of Waterways and Harbors Division, v. 88, p. 117–130.

CAMPOS, C. W. M., PONTE, F. C., AND MIURA, K., 1974, Geology of the Brazilian continental margin, in Burke, C. A., and Drake, C. L., eds., Geology of Continental Margins: Springer-Verlag, New York, p. 447–461.

COLEMAN, J. M., AND WRIGHT, L. C., 1975, Modern river deltas; variability of process and sand bodies, in Broussard, M. L., ed., Deltas, Models for Exploration: Houston Geological Society, Texas, p. 99–150.

DePRATTER, C. B., AND HOWARD, J. D., 1983, Evidence for a sea level lowstand between 4500 and 2400 years B.P. on the southeast coast of the United States—reply: Journal of Sedimentary Petrology, v. 53, p. 682–685.

DOMINGUEZ, J. M. L., 1983, Evolucão Quaternária da planície costeira associada a foz do rio Jequitinhonha (BA); influencia das variacões do nível do mar e da deriva litoranea de sedimentos: Unpublished M.S. Thesis, Universidade Federal da Bahia, Brazil, 79 p.

———, BITTENCOURT, A. C. S. P., AND MARTIN, L., 1981a, Esquema evolutivo da sedimentacão Quaternária nas feicões deltaicas dos rios São Francisco (SE/Al), Jequitinhonha (BA), Doce (ES) e Paraíba do Sul (RJ): Revista Brasileira de Geociencias, v. 11, p. 227–237.

———, ———, 1983, O papel da deriva litoranea de sedimentos arenosos na construcão das planícies costeiras associadas as desembocaduras dos rios São Francisco (SE/AL), Jequitinhonha (BA), Doce (ES) e Paraíba do Sul (RJ): Revista Brasileira de Geociencias, v. 13, p. 98–105.

———, MARTIN, L., AND BITTENCOURT, A. C. S. P., 1981b, Evolucão paleogeográfica do delta do rio Jequitinhonha durante o Quaternário; influencia das variacões do nível do mar: Atas do IV Simpósio do Quaternapio no Brasil, Sociedade Brasileira de Geologia, Rio de Janeiro, p. 69–82.

———, ———, ———, FERREIRA, Y. A., AND FLEXOR, J. M., 1982, Sobre a validade da utilizacão do termo delta para designar as planícies costeiras associadas as desembocaduras dos grandes rios da costa brasileira (abs.): XXXII Congresso Brasileiro de Geologia, Boletin 2, Resumos e Breves Comunicacões, p. 92.

FAIRBRIDGE, R. W., 1961, Eustatic changes of sea level: Physics and Chemistry of the Earth, v. 4, p. 100–185.

FISHER, W. L., 1968, Basic delta systems in the Eocene of the Gulf coast basin: Gulf Coast Association of Geological Societies Transactions, v. 18, p. 48.

———, 1969, Facies characterization of the Gulf coast basin delta systems, with Holocene analogues: Gulf Coast Association of Geological Societies Transactions, v. 19, p. 239–261.

GALLOWAY, W. E., 1975, Process framework for describing the morphologic and stratigraphic evolution of deltaic depositional systems, in Broussard, M. L., ed., Deltas, Models for Exploration: Houston Geological Society, Texas, p. 87–98.

———, AND HOBDAY, D. K., 1983, Terrigenous Clastic Depositional Systems: Springer-Verlag, New York, 433 p.

HAYES, M. O., 1979, Barrier island morphology as a function of tidal and wave regime, in Leatherman, S. P., ed., Barrier Islands from the

Gulf of St. Lawrence to the Gulf of Mexico: Academic Press, New York, p. 1–27.

HOYT, J. H., AND HAILS, J. R., 1974, Pleistocene stratigraphy of southeastern Georgia, in Oaks, R. Q., and Dubar, R. R., eds., Post-Miocene Stratigraphy, Central and Southern Atlantic Coastal Plain: Utah State University Press, Logan, Utah, p. 191–205.

———, HENRY, V. J., JR., AND WEIMER, R. J., 1968, Age of Late-Pleistocene shoreline deposits, coastal Georgia: means of correlation of Quaternary successions: Congress of the International Association for Quaternary Research, v. 8, p. 381–393.

KOMAR, P. D., 1973, Computer models of delta growth due to sediment input from the rivers and longshore transport: Geological Society of America Bulletin, v. 84, p. 2217–2226.

MARTIN, L., BITTENCOURT, A. C. S. P., AND VILAS, BOAS, G. S., 1982, Primeira ocorrencia de corais pleistocenicos na costa brasileira; datacão do máximo da Penúltima Transgressão: Revista Ciencias da Terra, v. 1, p. 16–17.

———, ———, ———, AND FLEXOR, J. M., 1980b, Texto explicativo para o mapa geológico do Quaternário costeiro do Estado da Bahia, escala 1:250,000: Companhia de Producão Mineral-Secretaria de Minas e Energia, Salvador, Brazil, 60 p.

———, FLEXOR, J. M., VILAS BOAS, G. S., BITTENCOURT, A. C. S. P., AND GUIMARÃES, M. M. M., 1979, Courbe de variations du niveau relatif de la mer au cours des 7000 dernieres annees sur un secteur homogene du littoral bresilien (nord de Salvador, Bahia), in Suguio, K., Fairchild, R. R., Martin, L., and Flexor, J. M., eds., Proceedings of the 1979 International Symposium on Coastal Evolution in the Quaternary, São Paulo, Brazil, p. 264–274.

———, SUGUIO, K., AND FLEXOR, J. M., 1979b, Le Quaternaire marin entre Cananeia (São Paulo) et Barra de Guaratinga (Rio de Janeiro), in Suguio, K., Fairchild, R. R., Martin, L., and Flexor, J. M., eds., Proceedings of the 1979 International Symposium on Coastal Evolution in the Quaternary, São Paulo, Brazil, p. 296–331.

———, ———, ———, BITTENCOURT, A. C. S. P., AND VILAS BOAS, G. S., 1980a, Le Quaternaire marin bresilien (littoral pauliste, sud-fluminense and bahianais): Cahiers Office de la Récherche Scientifique et Tecnique d'Outre-Mer, serie Geologie, v. 10, p. 95–124.

———, ———, DOMINGUEZ, J. M. L., AND AZEVEDO, A. E. G., 1984a, Evolucão da planície costeira do rio Paraíba do Sul (RJ) durante o Quaternátrio—influencia das variacões do nivel do mar: XXXIII Congresso Brasileiro de Geologia, Rio de Janeiro (RJ), Anais, p. 84–97.

———, ———, TESSLER, M. G., AND EICHLER, B. B., 1984b, Significado geológico das variacões dos graus de arredondamento das areias holocenicas da planície costeira do rio Paraíba do Sul (RJ): XXXIII Congresso Brasileiro de Geologia, Rio de Janeiro (RJ), Anais, p. 119–132.

MELO, U., SUMMERHAYES, C. P., AND ELLIS, J. P., 1975, Part IV, Salvador to Vitoria, southeastern Brazil, in Milliman, J. D., and Summerhayes, C. P., eds., Upper Continental Margin Sedimentation off Brazil: Contributions to Sedimentology, no. 4, p. 78–116.

MORNER, N. A., 1971, The position of the ocean level during the interstadial at about 30,000 B.P.—a discussion from the climatic-glaciologic point of view: Canadian Journal of Earth Sciences, v. 8, p. 132–143.

MOSLOW, T. F., AND HERON, S. D., JR., 1979, Quaternary evolution of Core Banks, North Carolina: Cape Lookout to New Drum Inlet, in Leatherman, S. P., ed., Barrier Islands from the Gulf of St. Lawrence to the Gulf of Mexico: Academic Press, New York, p. 211–236.

NEUMANN, A. C., AND MOORE, W. S., 1975, Sea level events and Pleistocene coral ages in the northern Bahamas: Quaternary Research, v. 5, p. 215–224.

NEWMAN, W. S., MARCUS, L. F., PARDI, R. R., PACCIONE, J. A., AND TOMECEK, S. M., 1980, Eustasy and deformation of the geoid: 1000–6000 radiocarbon years B.P., in Morner, N. A., ed., Earth Rheology, Isostasy and Eustasy: John Wiley and Sons, New York, p. 555–567.

RICE, D. D., AND GAUTIER, D. L., 1983, Patterns of sedimentation, diagenesis, and hydrocarbon accumulation in Cretaceous rocks of the Rocky Mountains: Society of Economic Paleontologists and Mineralogists, Short Course Notes no. 11, 279 p.

SHACKLETON, N. J., 1977, The oxygen isotope record of the Late Pleistocene: Philosophical Transactions of the Royal Society of London, series B, no. 280, p. 169–182.

STAPOR, F. W., AND TANNER, W. F., 1973, Errors in the pre-Holocene 14-C scale: Gulf Coast Association of Geological Societies Transactions, v. 23, p. 351–354.

STUIVER, M., 1980, Workshop on 14-C data reporting: Radiocarbon, v. 22, p. 964–966.

———, AND POLACH, H. A., 1977, Discussion reporting of 14-C data: Radiocarbon, v. 19, p. 355–363.

SUGUIO, K., MARTIN, L., AND DOMINGUEZ, J. M. L., 1981, Evolucão do delta do rio Doce (ES) durante o Quaternário: influencia das variacoes do nível do mar: Atas do IV Simposio do Quaternário no Brasil, Sociedade Brasileira de Geologia, Rio de Janeiro, p. 93–116.

———, ———, AND FLEXOR, J. M., 1980, Sea level fluctuations during the past 6000 years along the coast of the state of São Paulo (Brazil), *in* Morner, N. A., ed., Earth Rheology, Isostasy and Eustasy: John Wiley and Sons, New York, p. 471–486.

VAIL, P. R., MITCHUM, R. M., JR., AND THOMPSON, S., III, 1977, Seismic stratigraphy and global changes of sea level, part III; relative changes of sea level from coastal onlap, *in* Payton, C. E., ed., Seismic Stratigraphy—Applications to Hydrocarbon Exploration: American Association of Petroleum Geologists Memoir 26, p. 63–81.

ZENKOVICH, V. P., 1967, Processes of Coastal Development: Interscience Publishers, John Wiley and Sons, New York, 738 p.

THE TRANSGRESSIVE BARRIER-LAGOON COAST OF DELAWARE: MORPHOSTRATIGRAPHY, SEDIMENTARY SEQUENCES AND RESPONSES TO RELATIVE RISE IN SEA LEVEL

JOHN C. KRAFT AND MICHAEL J. CHRZASTOWSKI[1]
Department of Geology, University of Delaware, Newark, Delaware 19716
DANIEL F. BELKNAP
Department of Geological Sciences, University of Maine at Orono, Orono, Maine 04469
MARGUERITE A. TOSCANO[2] AND CHARLES H. FLETCHER, III[3]
Department of Geology, University of Delaware, Newark, Delaware 19716

ABSTRACT: Transgressive barriers of the embayed Atlantic and Gulf coast are generally similar in overall form, processes, and landward migration in response to relative sea-level rise, but they vary greatly in potential sources and volume of sand supply. Delaware's transgressive barriers vary in thickness from 25 m to less than 5 m; dunes may rise to 20 m above sea level, whereas barrier-spit and inlet sand reach depths of 10–18 m below sea level. Widths vary between 0 m at eroding headlands and 4–6 km near tidal delta and spit complexes.

A complete Holocene paralic sequence for Delaware includes a basal sand and/or gravel overlain by marsh, lagoon, and barrier lithosomes. Shoreface erosion, as the barrier lithosome moves landward, occurs to an average depth of 10 m, with about 50% of eroded sediment derived from Holocene and Pleistocene lagoonal mud outcrops. Since the suspended material is carried out of the shoreface, its removal requires a re-evaluation of the volumetric model commonly inferred from the Bruun mechanism. Also, the third dimension of longshore transport of coarse material needs to be considered.

As transgression continues, the ravinement surface exposes lagoonal sediments, marsh mud, irregularly shaped basal remnants of the Holocene barrier lithosome, or varied Pleistocene strata. These are then blanketed by varying thicknesses of inner-shelf sand. Ultimately, the transgressive barrier and associated paralic environments migrate landward to peak interglacial positions where the entire transgressive record may be preserved. A relatively complete vertical sequence of transgressive coastal lithosomes might also be preserved at the outer edge of the continental shelf at glacial sea-level minima. Thus, the optimal chance for total preservation of a transgressive coastal lithosome sequence lies at the extremes, landward at the peak interglacial when eustatic sea-level rise stops and the coastal lithosome sequences become stranded, and possibly on the outer edge of the shelf as deglaciation begins and there is rapid rate of sea-level rise.

INTRODUCTION

The coast of Delaware provides an intensively studied example of transgressive barrier-lagoon and headland beach systems. As such, it can be used to evaluate models of preservation potential, sediment budgets, and maintenance of equilibrium profile during Holocene sea-level rise. The purpose of this paper is to document the thin offshore shelf sands and to propose a model for efficient recycling of the barrier sands. Also, we will evaluate the two-dimensionsal Bruun Rule, particularly in light of a more complete description of processes of shoreface change with rising sea level, which includes grain-size and three-dimensional effects of longshore transport and antecedent topography.

Antecedent Topography and Sedimentary Infill

The Holocene sedimentary record of the Delaware coastal zone represents the transgression and sedimentary infilling of an antecedent trellis-dendritic drainage system which was tributary to a Pleistocene glacial-age Delaware River (Kraft, 1971). The course of this ancestral Delaware River corresponded approximately to that of the Delaware Shelf Valley (Fig. 1) which crosses the Atlantic inner shelf off the present coast. Seismic profiles and core data across the Delaware inner shelf allow mapping of the pre-transgression topography of the ancestral drainage system, examination of the distribution, thickness and preserved vertical sequence

of the Holocene section, and reconstruction of the Holocene transgression history of this coastal zone (Sheridan and others, 1974; Belknap and Kraft, 1985; Chrzastowski and Kraft, 1985; Chrzastowski, 1986).

The inner shelf record.—

As sea level rose during waning of the Wisconsinan glaciation, the Delaware Shelf Valley became a large estuary comparable to the present Delaware Bay (Fig. 1). Streams draining the present coastal area were tributary to this estuary and were tidally influenced. As sea level rose through the early Holocene, these stream valleys were filled with estuarine mud, fine sand and fringing marsh sequences. Approximately 7.5 ka, this estuarine coastal zone became an open-ocean coast. With continued sea-level rise, barrier systems along the open-ocean coast migrated landward and upward across these filled antecedent stream valleys to their present positions. An isopach map (Fig. 2) of the barrier-sand complex along the present coast and of the Holocene section across the inner shelf shows that maximum thickness of Holocene sediment is associated with the antecedent valleys. Shoreface erosion across the inner shelf of the present coast occurs to 10 m below mean sea level (−10 m MSL; Belknap and Kraft, 1985). Part of the Holocene sequence has been preserved along these stream valleys below the depth of shoreface erosion. Minimum thickness of the Holocene section occurs across paleo-interfluves because of lesser amounts of Holocene deposition across these areas as well as their greater susceptibility to shoreface erosion. In some areas, the Holocene section thins to 20 cm or less or is totally absent, and sediment of Pleistocene (and possibly Tertiary) age crops out across the inner shelf (Fig. 2 within the 0-m contour).

[1]Present address: Illinois State Geological Survey, Champaign, Illinois 61820; [2]Maryland Geological Survey, Baltimore, Maryland 21211; and [3]West Chester University, Department of Geology and Astronomy, West Chester, Pennsylvania 19383.

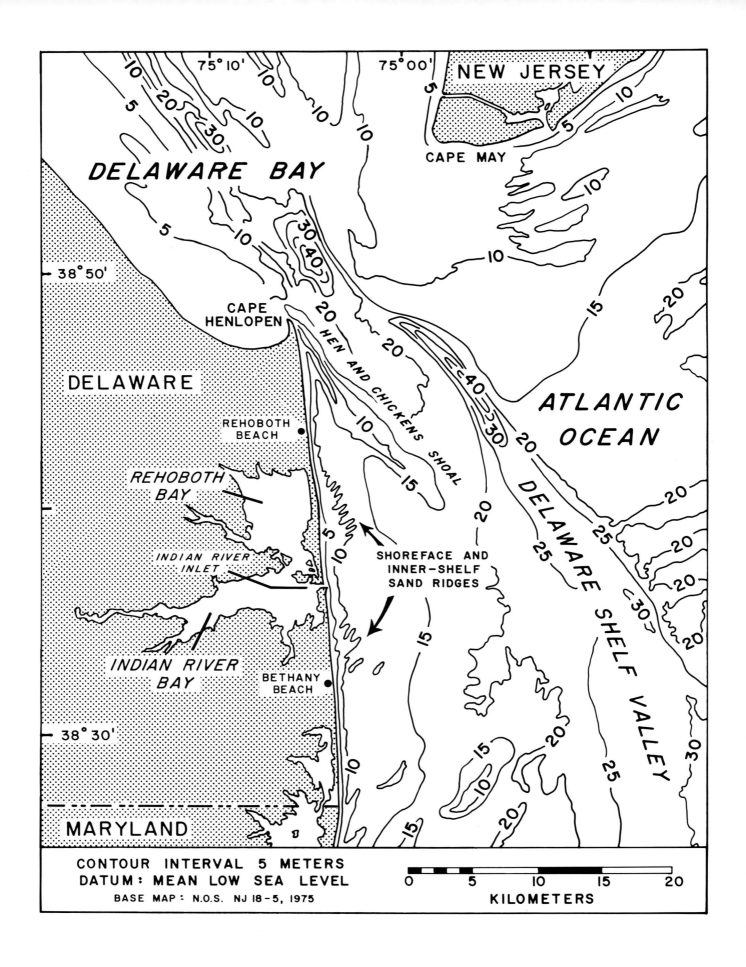

NEW JERSEY

DELAWARE BAY

CAPE MAY

ATLANTIC OCEAN

CAPE HENLOPEN

DELAWARE

REHOBOTH BEACH

REHOBOTH BAY

HEN AND CHICKENS SHOAL

INDIAN RIVER INLET

DELAWARE SHELF VALLEY

SHOREFACE AND INNER-SHELF SAND RIDGES

INDIAN RIVER BAY

BETHANY BEACH

38°30'

MARYLAND

CONTOUR INTERVAL 5 METERS
DATUM: MEAN LOW SEA LEVEL
BASE MAP: N.O.S. NJ 18-5, 1975

0   5   10   15   20
KILOMETERS

75°10'   75°00'

38°50'

The coastal record.—

Forming the shore and extending landward is the sand body of the barrier complex. The baymouth barrier at Rehoboth and Indian River bays (Fig. 2) is generally 5 m thick and reaches 10 m in thickness where the sedimentary sequence overlies antecedent valleys. Flood-tidal delta sand extends into the coastal lagoons. Beneath the lagoons at depths greater than −5 m MSL, are estuarine mud- and marsh-filled antecedent stream valleys which correspond to the landward continuation of the valleys on the inner shelf. Net littoral transport is a small closed system dominantly to the north, starting at a drift reversal at Fenwick Island on the Delaware-Maryland border (Fig. 1). The major locus of sand accumulation in this system is the Cape Henlopen spit complex which is developed at the northern terminus of this longshore transport system along the Delaware Atlantic coast. At the tip of the spit, sand has been deposited below sea level in a regressive (i.e., progradational) lithosome to become part of the sedimentary infill of an antecedent valley. The thickness, distribution and preservation potential of all these sedimentary lithosomes are directly related to the pre-transgression topography and provide a basis for interpreting the processes which have lead to the observed vertical sequences.

The shoreface.—

The shoreface is a dynamic environment wherein the barrier-lagoon sequences are modified and ultimately destroyed as the transgression continues. Shoreface erosion in Delaware is operative to −10 m MSL. It encounters sand of the Holocene barrier complex as well as sediment of the associated paralic environments, such as estuarine, lagoonal and marsh mud. Paralic (coastal) deposits of Pleistocene age are also encountered, principally at Bethany Beach and at Rehoboth Beach (Fig. 2). A coast-parallel section between these two highlands (Fig. 3) presents an overall perspective of the age, texture, thickness and distribution of sediment landward of the influences of shoreface erosion. Across the inner shelf, comparable coast-parallel stratigraphic sequences were previously planed off. For example, Figure 4 illustrates such a cross-section in the shoreface zone, which, when compared to Figure 3, shows the vertical reduction in the Holocene transgressive sequence resulting from shoreface erosion. The result of shoreface erosion is a distinct, laterally continuous erosional disconformity across the inner shelf. This type of erosional disconformity, or ravinement surface, has been described by Swift (1968), Belknap and Kraft (1985), and Demarest and Kraft (this volume). The relative positions of the ravinement disconformity and the basal unconformity determine the preservation potential of the lithosome (Belknap and Kraft, 1985, Fig. 3).

SEDIMENT SOURCES

Shoreface Erosion

The Atlantic coast of Delaware is an erosional non-deltaic coast. It does not have a continuous supply of sediment provided by rivers; therefore, storm-wave erosion of coastal highlands and erosion across the shoreface provide the principal supply of sediment to the coastal barrier system.

The supply of sediment may be divided into primary and secondary categories related to the undulating relief of the pre-transgression surface. Higher areas of the pre-transgression surface are intercepted by storm-wave erosional processes which erode these Pleistocene sediments and provide a new or primary supply of sediment to the Holocene depositional system. Where the pre-transgression surface has a lower elevation, overlying Holocene beach and shoreface sediment is recycled during storm-wave erosion and shoreface retreat to provide a secondary supply. In terms of volume, this supply of sediment may be greater than that of eroded Pleistocene material and it is "secondary" only in the sense of having been recycled. There is little net loss of material offshore or alongshore as the transgression continues, and there may be a nearly balanced sediment budget within the barrier system. Little Holocene sand is found on the shoreface, and there is an apparent conservation of the sand-size fraction via the recycling processes in the paralic zone.

The inner shelf of coastal Delaware is not considered to be a major source of sand to the barrier complex. Although some sand probably migrates from the inner shelf up the shoreface and into the littoral transport system, the inner-shelf sand sheet off the Delaware coast is thin and contains a small percentage of the present volume of the barriers in the zone from the present shoreline to 5 km offshore (five barrier widths). Core evidence shows that across broad areas this inner-shelf sand is only a veneer, and locally sand is totally absent where Holocene lagoonal and estuarine mud crops out (Sheridan and others, 1974).

Swift and others (1985) have shown that below a depth of about 15 m, normal asymmetric wave orbitals have little effect on sand motion, although some interaction of currents and symmetric orbitals can cause motion. In any case, there are no data which support a massive offshore transport of sand from the shoreface. Rather, onshore transport is dominant. Local ebb-tidal currents can create shoals, however, such as Hen and Chickens Shoal at Cape Henlopen (Fig. 1), which remove sand from the beach system. In addition, shoreface ridges form from beach sand as coastal retrogression proceeds (Swift and Field, 1981).

Volume and Grain-Size Variables

In order to investigate a sediment budget, the grain size of sediments in Pleistocene highland and interfluve areas

FIG. 1.—Bathymetry of the Atlantic inner shelf adjacent to the Delaware coastal zone. The lagoon-barrier shoreline extends along the entire coastal zone, with older Pleistocene sediments forming highlands along the coast in some areas. Present bathymetry is related to the incised valley of the Wisconsinan Delaware River now partially infilled and referred to as the Delaware Shelf Valley. Inner-shelf and shoreface sand ridges are believed to have been formed by shelf processes of waves and downwelling coastal jets (Swift and Field, 1981).

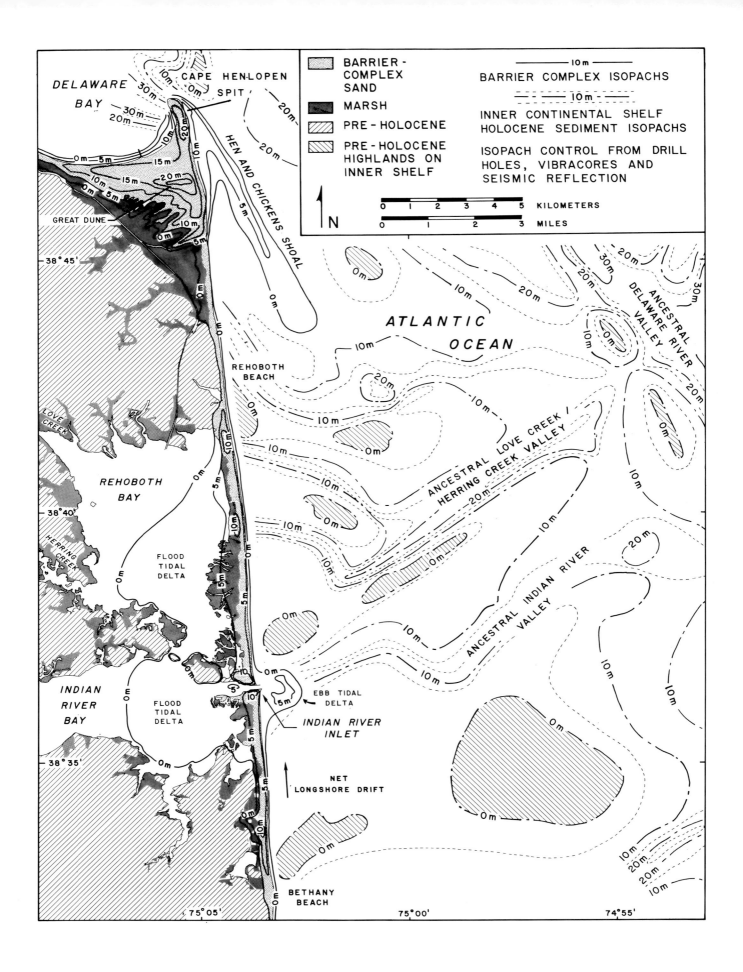

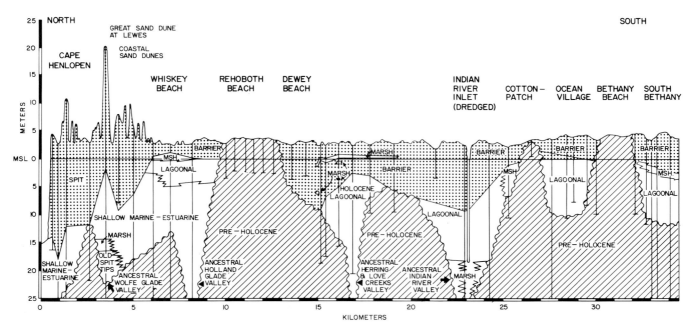

FIG. 3.—A coast-parallel cross section of the Delaware Atlantic coast showing the relationship of the Holocene section to the underlying Pleistocene paralic sediments and the antecedent trellis-type drainage system most recently incised in Wisconsinan time. The valleys have been infilled by Holocene sediments of marsh, lagoon, barrier and barrier spit depositional environments (after Kraft and John, 1979).

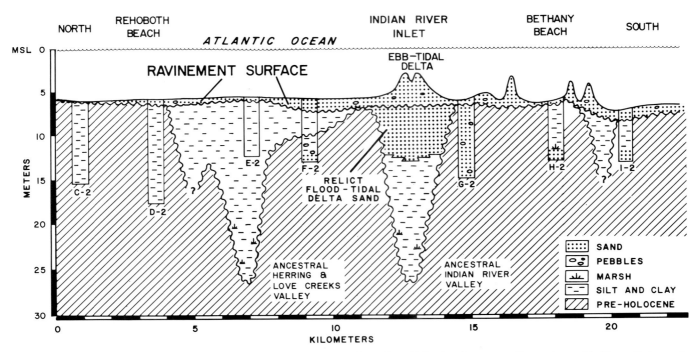

FIG. 4.—A coast-parallel cross section of the Delaware Atlantic coast along the middle shoreface zone. Comparison with Figure 3 shows the degree of shoreface erosion as the transgression proceeds, as well as the thickness and distribution of Holocene sediment preserved on the inner shelf. A result of shoreface erosion is the ravinement surface. Depending on the pre-transgression topography, the ravinement surface may correspond to or may diverge from the basal unconformity (after Belknap and Kraft, 1985).

FIG. 2.—An isopach map of the Delaware coastal barriers including the submerged flood-tidal delta elements, the barrier spit complex at Cape Henlopen, and the Hen and Chickens ebb-tidal shoal. The area of the inner shelf of the Atlantic Ocean is a contour map of the pre-transgression surface showing the trellis drainage pattern of antecedent valleys tributary to the incised valley of the ancestral Delaware River. A number of erosional sediment inliers of Pleistocene age occurs in the inner shelf (after Belknap and Kraft, 1985).

must be considered. Much of the Pleistocene sediment encountered across the shoreface consists of silt, clay and fine to very fine sand (Belknap and Kraft, 1985), not significant as a source of beach sand. These fine-grained sediments represent Pleistocene deposition in paralic units comparable to those being deposited in the present lagoon, estuary, barrier-spit and possibly inner-shelf environments. Sand and pebbly sand are common, but considering the total volume of sediment that may be eroded from the shoreface outcrops of Pleistocene material, the amount of sand or coarser material which can be added to littoral transport is limited. Shoreface erosion of Holocene material encounters sand of the barrier complex, but fine-grained material of Holocene lagoonal, estuarine and marsh environments is also encountered.

In general, shoreface erosion across major sections of Holocene or pre-Holocene lagoonal and estuarine silt, clay and very fine sand is not an anomaly along the Delaware Atlantic coast but a common occurrence. In the long-term transgression history of the barrier complex, the result is a recycling of sand-size material. Addition of new material to the sand budget occurs in a limited number of areas where shoreface erosion encounters sand-rich Pleistocene highlands.

The volume of sediment supply during stages of the transgression should be considered a continually changing quantity. At earlier stages of the Holocene transgression, the abundance and spacing of intercepted highland areas would vary depending on the antecedent topography and local relative sea level. In addition, the varying lithology of intercepted highland areas encountered at successive transgression stages would supply more or less coarse sediment suitable for beach and barrier nourishment. Unfortunately, the evidence for these changes has largely been destroyed by landward migration of the shoreface.

SEDIMENT SINKS

The sediment along the Atlantic coast of Delaware is moving in a complex system of onshore-offshore, landward, and coast-parallel transport. There is a strong component of net northward littoral transport along the portion of the coast from Bethany Beach to Cape Henlopen (Fig. 2). There is also a significant landward component of sediment transport by overwash processes and flood-tidal currents. These various sediment-transport pathways eventually terminate in sediment sinks such as spits and shoals, where large volumes of sediment temporarily reside until, with continued transgression, they may be subject to shoreface erosion and again placed into a transport system.

Cape Henlopen Spit Complex

The principal sediment sink along the Delaware Atlantic coast is the Cape Henlopen spit complex at the mouth of the Delaware estuary (Fig. 2). Here, at the northward terminus of net littoral transport, a series of recurved spits formed 0.3 to 2.0 ka and the present northward-migrating simple spit formed in the past 100 yrs. This spit complex receives the majority of sand eroded from Delaware's Atlantic coast headlands and beaches (Kraft and others, 1979).

The Cape Henlopen area is dominated by regressive (i.e., progradational) sedimentary sequences, unlike the rest of the dominantly transgressive Delaware system. Major sand accumulation occurs at the distal part of the spit where it is prograding into a 15-m-deep channel. There is also significant sand storage in the coast-parallel dune system, which averages 6–8 m in height above MSL, and a prominent coast-perpendicular dune ridge (the Great Dune at Lewes) which reaches a height of 20–22 m. Sediments emplaced in this system are continually reworked on the Atlantic coast to a depth of −10 m MSL, but the deeper portions will be preserved from continuing erosion.

Flood-Tidal Deltas

A second major sediment sink for sand-size material includes both the ancient and modern flood-tidal deltas within Rehoboth and Indian River bays (Fig. 2). The sand sheet of this delta complex extends as much as 4 km landward along a 12-km reach of the present Atlantic shoreline. The flood-tidal delta sand sheet is both the leading edge of the transgressive barrier and the base of the barrier sand lithosome. With continued sea-level rise and landward barrier migration, the emerged barrier will overlie the flood-tidal delta sand presently blanketing eastern Rehoboth and Indian River bays. Thickness ranges from 1 to 3 m within this sublagoonal sand sheet. It is thickest in its eastern part where the flood-tidal delta and washover deposits are being overridden by the emerged part of the barrier. Maximum thickness of flood-tidal delta sand is 9 m near Indian River Inlet (Fig. 3). This thickness is directly related to the antecedent topography which has accommodated long-term deposition of flood-tidal deltas into ancient tidal streams and lagoons developed along the axis of the ancestral Indian River Valley.

Nearshore and Offshore Sinks

Related to the Cape Henlopen spit complex are smaller scale sediment sinks fed by sand removed from the tip of the cape by ebb- and flood-tidal currents. Ebb currents have reworked and deposited sand onto the offshore Hen and Chickens Shoal (Fig. 2), whereas flood currents have reworked sand to form a series of shoals to the northwest and on the landward side of the cape.

Additional sediment sinks consist of the ebb-tidal delta at Indian River Inlet, which has a maximum thickness of 8 m (Fig. 2), and a series of oblique shoreface and inner-shelf sand ridges, which have a southwest-northeast orientation and a maximum thickness in the range of 5–10 m (Fig. 1). These sand ridges have been studied by Field (1980), Swift and Field (1981) and Figueiredo and others (1981). The inner shelf seaward of the 10-m contour is also a sink for a limited volume of sand-size material. The isopach map shown in Figure 2 indicates that Holocene sediment thickness across the inner shelf ranges from 20 to 25 m. The majority of this Holocene sediment, however, is marsh mud and lagoonal and estuarine mud which have filled antecedent stream valleys. These mud sequences are blanketed by a thin veneer of sand.

CHARACTERISTICS OF THE BARRIER SAND LITHOSOME

There are more than 100 cores and drill holes through the Atlantic coastal barrier of Delaware and 42 cores in the adjacent shoreface (Kraft, 1971; Kraft and Chrzastowski, 1985; Belknap and Kraft, 1985). Recent studies include the analysis of 96 cores from the Rehoboth Bay and Indian River Bay lagoon and tributary tidal streams (Chrzastowski, 1986). The following sections summarize these subsurface data and describe the three-dimensional characteristics of the barrier complex in detail.

Cross-Sectional Geometry

The barrier-sand complex consists of both subaerial (beach, dune, washover, and back-barrier marsh) and submerged (lagoonal washover and flood-tidal delta) depositional environments and facies (Kraft and others, 1979). The average thickness of the barrier sand lithosome is 8 m, in contrast to the 30- to 40-m maximum thickness of the total Holocene section. The largest volume of sediment resides in the submerged portions of the barrier, which were deposited as multiple washover fans and flood-tidal deltas during the landward migration of the barrier complex.

Figure 5 shows schematic cross sections of three variants of the barrier and associated paralic depositional units along the Delaware Atlantic coast. Figure 5A illustrates the headland beach at Rehoboth Beach. Figure 5B and C illustrate two localities of the Rehoboth Bay baymouth barrier. At Rehoboth Beach (Fig. 5A) pre-Holocene paralic sediments are undergoing erosion during extreme erosional events when beach and shoreface sand is removed by storm-wave action. Under fair weather conditions littoral transport and wave action form a beach and berm approximately 100 m wide and maintain a veneer of sand over pre-Holocene shoreface sediments. This sand veneer pinches out in the lower shoreface. A similar detachment of littoral sand from inner-shelf sand also occurs at the baymouth barrier of northern Rehoboth Bay (Fig. 5B), characteristic of the Atlantic barriers of coastal Delaware.

The barrier complex shown in Figure 5B is an example of barrier sand migrating over lagoonal and estuarine mud. These fine-grained sediments crop out in the lower shoreface, exposing a significant component of silt- and clay-size material to storm-wave and shoreface erosion. The cross section shown in Figure 5C is a contrasting example where the barrier is migrating across a topographic high of the antecedent topography. Along this line of section, there is no detachment of the barrier-sand complex from the sand sheet of the inner shelf since it occurs at the site of a former inlet-tidal delta complex, and the sands are thicker than elsewhere along the barrier. Present shoreface erosion cuts into previously deposited sand of the barrier-inlet complex. With continued shoreface retreat, however, pre-Holocene sediments will be encountered.

Vertical Sequences

The various vertical sequences are records of the sediment types and sedimentary processes of the transgressive barrier's depositional history. The base of the barrier sand lithosome can be partially or totally superimposed on the pre-transgression surface (Fig. 5C), or it may overlie variable thicknesses of lagoonal and estuarine mud (Fig. 5B). Where the barriers of the Delaware Atlantic coast have transgressed and filled antecedent stream valleys, the sand lithosome overlies as much as 10- to 25-m thick sequences of mud.

Figure 6 consists of two cross sections and vertical lithologic sequences from a series of cores drilled in the shoreface and correlated to a core drilled on a baymouth barrier (Fig. 6A) and on a headland beach (Fig. 6B). In both cases the sediments beneath the basal unconformity are Pleistocene paralic deposits. It is important to note the presence of two erosional surfaces in these sections, the basal unconformity and the ravinement surface. The Holocene/pre-Holocene unconformity varies in age from present to approximately 7.0 ka. The ravinement surface represents a composite of recent storm-wave events.

Figure 6A is a chronicle of landward barrier migration with sea-level rise. Earliest Holocene sedimentation along this line of section was deposited in a fringing salt marsh and tidal creek beginning approximately 7.0 ka, when the Atlantic barrier lay seaward and approximately 13 m below its present position. As the transgression continued, the barrier migrated landward and upward, keeping pace with local relative sea-level rise. A succession of muddy open-lagoon, silty back-barrier lagoon, and sandy flood-tidal delta facies is found in sequence in cores now seaward of the shoreline. Radiocarbon dates from core R-4101 (Fig. 6A) indicate that the leading edge of the transgressive barrier arrived at this core site after 2.78 ka. Since that time, the main body of the barrier has migrated landward, resulting in the present thickness of the barrier sand lithosome at this site.

The ravinement surface can be delineated across this line of section by sedimentologic characteristics as well as by radiocarbon dates in the underlying material, suggesting a hiatus of hundreds to thousands of years. Only a veneer of sand and silt overlies the ravinement surface across the middle shoreface (Fig. 6A). Beneath the ravinement surface, the sediment consists of fine sand and silty fine sand. Thus, shoreface erosion in this area would primarily provide suspended fine-grained sediment rather than the coarser sand typical of the beach-berm and wash-over deposits of the barrier complex. Seaward, at the edge of the inner shelf, a thin deposit of fine sand overlies the ravinement surface. This sand is likely derived from transgressive erosional processes either in the upper shoreface or from elsewhere along the coast.

Figure 6B is a line of section seaward from a headland beach at Bethany Beach which provides a contrast to the vertical sequence across the baymouth barrier. Down the shoreface and across the inner shelf, the ravinement surface and basal-transgressive unconformity occupy the same surface. The Holocene transgressive sequence is a veneer of sand and mud no more than 20 cm thick. Here again, erosion along the ravinement surface encounters predominantly fine sand and mud.

The materials affected by shoreface erosion along the lines of section in Figure 6A and B provide a minimal volume

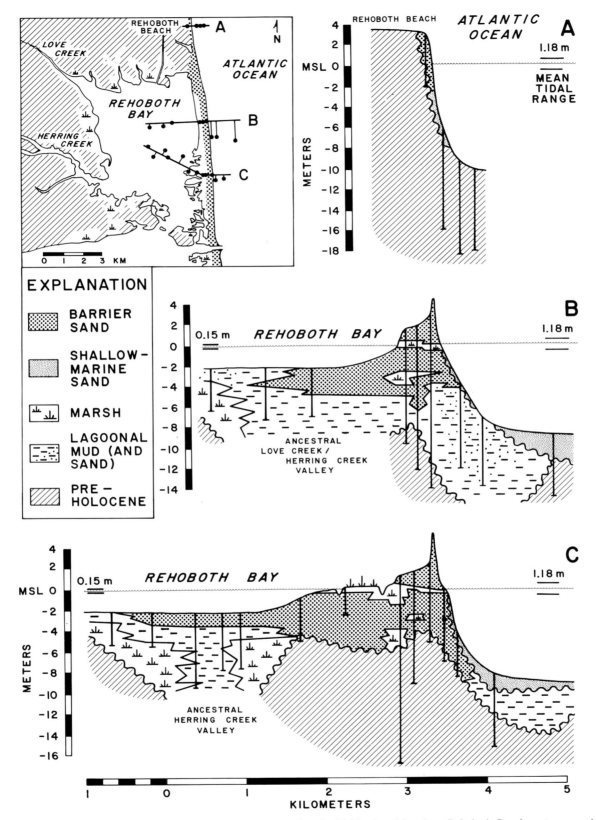

Fig. 5.—Three schematic cross sections of the Delaware coast including the highland and beach at Rehoboth Beach, a transgressive barrier overlying Holocene lagoonal muds at Rehoboth Bay, and a transgressive barrier at the site of a former inlet and tidal delta, directly overlying Pleistocene sediments along the basal transgressive unconformity (after Kraft, 1971; Kraft and John, 1979; Chrzastowski, 1986).

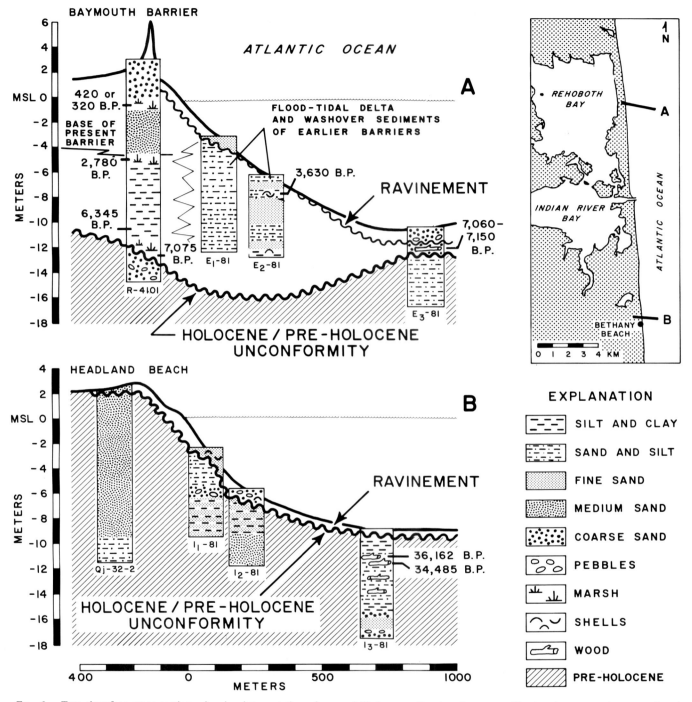

FIG. 6.—Two shoreface cross sections showing interpretation of cores drilled across the shoreface zone. The basal transgressive unconformity (Holocene/pre-Holocene) is shown and related to the ravinement surface. The two surfaces are the same in the case of erosion against a pre-existing highland of Pleistocene sediment. In the case of a lagoon-barrier cross section, the two surfaces diverge but may at some points merge. Of particular importance is the fact that very little sand-size sediment is being eroded or transported in the middle and upper shoreface (after Belknap and Kraft, 1985).

of sand for incorporation into the littoral transport system or redeposition across the inner shelf. It is likely that mud eroded in the shoreface is suspended and transported to either the middle shelf or into estuaries, lagoons or marshes along the coastal zone. Some fine-grained sediment from shoreface erosion may be transported by tidal currents through inlets to be deposited in distal flood-tidal deltas and thus incorporated into the barrier complex. Recycling of former inlet-tidal delta complexes, as shown in Figure 5C, may also supply sand to the system. In general, however, the sediment grain size supplied by shoreface erosion is too fine to be added to the barriers. In addition, littoral transport is only acting within the local cell north of Fenwick Island and is not importing sand from elsewhere. Thus, there is strong evidence of a recycling and conservation of sand and gravel in the barrier system during the landward migration.

THREE-DIMENSIONAL COASTAL SEQUENCES AND THE BRUUN RULE

Background

Bruun (1962) proposed a two-dimensional model suggesting that with sea-level rise there is a response of beach and shoreface erosion and nearshore deposition in order to maintain an equilibrium profile. Schwartz (1965) tested Bruun's model in wave-tank studies and subsequently examined the theory under carefully selected field conditions (Schwartz, 1967; Schwartz and Milicic, 1980). The model has since been referred to as "The Bruun Rule" or "Bruun's Rule."

Geologists and engineers have attempted to apply the Bruun Rule to suspected relationships between sea-level rise and coastal erosion. These investigations have tried to account for landward shifts of the shoreface and resultant deposition in the inner-shelf zone through application of the Bruun Rule, as well as to apply it to sediment budgets. The concept and laboratory and field testing of the Bruun Rule, however, are based on a two-dimensional coast-perpendicular geometry. In addition, Bruun (1983) elaborated on his original concept and noted that bottom sediment materials and bottom geomorphology are important considerations in whether or not the proposed mechanism is applicable to a particular coastal setting.

A number of researchers have noted that coast-parallel or landward sediment transport makes application of the mechanism inappropriate. For example, in an analysis of Rhode Island shoreline retreat, Fisher (1980) noted that sediment eroded from the beach and berm would not exclusively move to the nearshore zone, as predicted by the Bruun Rule. Field evidence indicated that 76% of the eroded beach material could be accounted for by material moving landward into washover, inlet, and flood-tidal deposits. Fisher (1980, p. 52) concluded that only the remaining 24% "may therefore be deposited offshore as proposed by the Bruun Rule."

Delaware Coastal Zone

Along the Delaware coast, studies of longshore transport and landward sediment transport into flood-tidal deltas suggest that the Bruun mechanism is not valid. The shoreface

core data along the Delaware Atlantic coast provide a clear example of how sediment grain-size characteristics are not compatible with the Bruun mechanism. Nearly all shoreface cores encounter lagoonal or estuarine mud and very fine to fine sand of Holocene and Pleistocene age (Belknap and Kraft, 1985). Such fine-grained sediment, when eroded, is transported in suspension to a suitable depositional site but is not deposited on the nearshore bottom as required by the Bruun Rule. The ultimate loci of deposition are not specifically known, but because the volume of fine-grained sediment may account for as much as 50% of the total eroded, the Bruun mechanism does not apply to this particular coast. Coastal settings with similar silt and clay strata in the shoreface are likewise not settings where the mechanism is applicable.

Implications

Considering the limiting factors of erosion and deposition of uniform sand-size material, and the two-dimensional basis of the Bruun Rule, there is clearly a need for conceptual and working models that have more utility, such as those of Belknap and Kraft (1981, 1985) and Kraft and others (1979). Bruun (1962) intended simply to describe a two-dimensional nearshore equilibrium profile which is maintained in response to sea-level rise. We are in agreement with Fisher (1980), Bruun (1983) and many other workers that in reality many factors should be considered other than the simplified conditions of the Bruun mechanism. For example, Figure 7 shows a hypothetical coastal setting, similar to the Atlantic coast of Delaware, with the principal variables identified which need to be considered in the relationship between sea-level rise and coastal erosion. Along the coast, shoreface erosion is intercepting sand and gravel as well as fine-grained sediments, and thus a pure-sand system is not the case. Considering the sand that is eroded in the shoreface, sediment transport pathways become important. Sediment may be transported alongshore or possibly offshore, and there is also need for consideration of sediment transport in an onshore direction. Sediment sinks are important with sand eroded in the shoreface redistributed and possibly stored in washover deposits, flood- or ebb-tidal deltas, or into spit-shoal complexes.

The cross section in Figure 7 is a first approximation of how a two-dimensional equilibrium-profile model needs to be expanded into three-dimensional components. The vertical component is a consideration of the coastal stratigraphic sequence and the variance in material size in this sequence. The longshore component is a consideration of factors such as longshore transport direction and magnitude, variance in material size along the coast, and location and characteristics of sediment sources and sinks. The shore-normal component is a consideration of onshore-offshore sediment transport, possible offshore sediment sources (or sinks), and the sediment grain-size characteristics encountered at the shoreface and how these characteristics will change as shoreline landward migration continues.

SEDIMENTARY RESPONSE TO RELATIVE SEA-LEVEL RISE

A local relative sea-level curve was constructed for the Delaware coastal zone (Kraft, 1976), based on radiocarbon

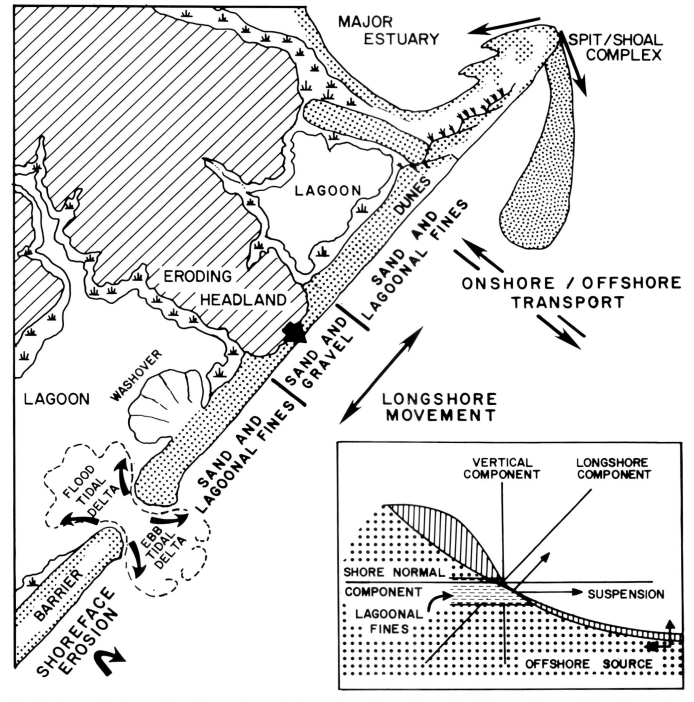

Fig. 7.—An example of topographic and process elements in the coastal zone that must be considered when creating a model to modify or replace the Bruun Rule in order to account for three-dimensional change in morphology and sediments encountered in a coastal transgression.

dates obtained from basal marsh units and other marsh deposits in the Holocene transgressive sequence. Local relative sea level was about 26 m below present mean sea level 11.0 ka (Fig. 8). During sea-level rise from this time on, coastal sedimentary environments have migrated across the continental shelf to their present position. Initially, sea-level rise was relatively rapid, rising at a rate of 29.6 cm per century before 5.0 ka. From about 5.0 to 2.0 ka, rate of sea-level rise was 20.7 cm per century. Since 2.0 ka, the rate has slowed to 12.5 cm per century, although it appears that local relative sea level is rising approximately 33 cm per century based on data over the past 50–100 yrs (Belknap and Kraft, 1977).

The present rate of sea-level rise is significantly less than

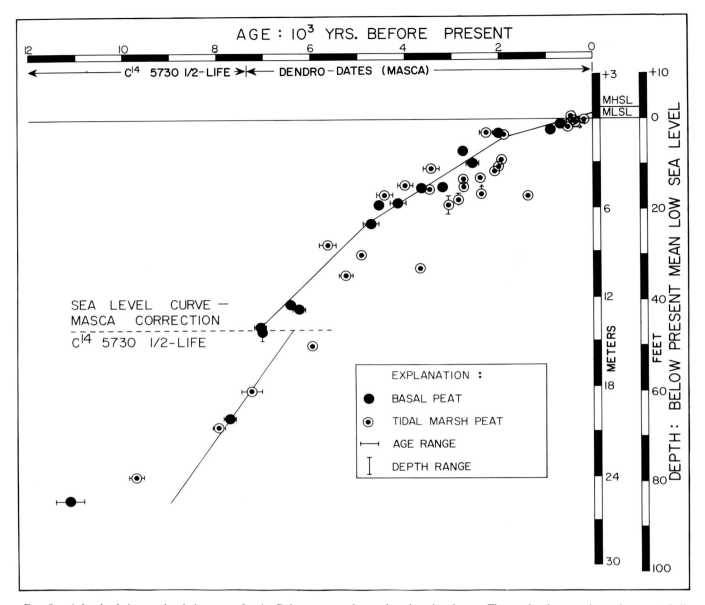

Fig. 8.—A local relative sea-level rise curve for the Delaware coastal zone based on basal peat. The sea-level curve shown is a smooth line average and is not mathematically derived. Other data from tidal marsh peaks have been used for paleogeographic reconstructions but have not been used in drawing an irregular curve based on the basal peat data shown. Dendrodate (MASCA) corrections after Ralph and others (1973; from Kraft, 1976).

that which has occurred through the majority of the Holocene transgression. We are uncertain what the short-term sedimentary response is to such slow rates of sea-level rise. On the long-term geologic average, we believe that sea-level rise is the dominant driving factor leading to a response of coastal erosion and landward migration of coastal sedimentary environments. If storm waves are the dominant factor in the erosion and redistribution of sediment across the berm, beach, and shoreface, however, then the sedimentary responses related to rising sea level are volumetrically insignificant over the short term. Therefore, in terms of sea level alone, we are observing a condition in which changes such as those addressed in two dimensions by the

Bruun Rule (Bruun, 1962; Schwartz, 1967) are, under normal wave conditions, only minor and relatively small-scale adjustments to maintain an equilibrium profile. Nevertheless, without the longer geologic time frame and relative sea-level rise, the approximately 75-km transgression of the Atlantic coast during the Holocene Epoch could not have occurred. Without sea-level rise, storm-wave erosion over the past 10,000 yrs would have been concentrated and dissipated on the Atlantic outer continental shelf. This fact is important in understanding and relating the effects of short-term processes as compared to longer term (Holocene Epoch) geologic events.

The sedimentary record on the inner shelf must also be

considered to understand better which of the shore-zone deposits might be predicted to remain below the ravinement surface as the coastal transgression continues. The Cape Henlopen spit area (Fig. 3) is a site of thick sand accumulation which extends locally to great enough depth so that part of the lower sand and gravel sequence will be below the depth of maximum shoreface erosion and will be preserved as the transgression continues. Likewise, the fairly thick accumulation of tidal-delta sand at Indian River Inlet (Fig. 3) will be, in part, below the depth of shoreface erosion and therefore will have partial preservation as a lense of sand in the inner-shelf Holocene sequence. Should the present transgression continue and the shoreline migrate several kilometers landward, it might be difficult to interpret such erosional remnants, especially when examined in ancient stratigraphic sequences. With an understanding of

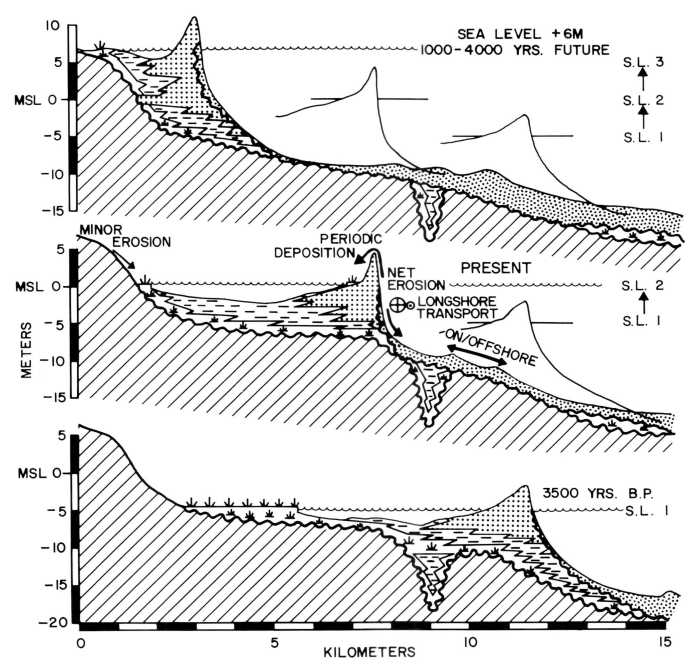

FIG. 9.—A profile projection of morphology and sedimentary environmental lithosomes, based on studies on the Delaware coastal zone. The middle profile is the present configuration. The lower profile is adjusted to a local relative sea level approximately 5 m below present about 3.5 ka. The upper profile is a projection of the coastal profile and stratigraphic sequence anticipated at a peak sea level of +6 m from 1,000–4,000 yrs in the future. The upper profile is very similar to many laterally adjacent Pleistocene stratigraphic sequences in the Delaware coastal plain, as determined by Demarest and others (1981; after Belknap and Kraft, 1985).

the paleogeography and the potential lateral and vertical sedimentary sequences, however, it might be possible to make interpretations of the origin of such remnant deposits and to project their original three-dimensional form. It is most important in interpreting such transgressive sequences to recognize and distinguish basal unconformities and ravinement surfaces, as discussed by Belknap and Kraft (1985), Demarest and Kraft (this volume), and Nummedal and Swift (this volume).

Comparison of Figures 3 and 4 illustrates that antecedent topography is a significant factor in preservation potential as shoreface erosion progresses landward. The antecedent valleys of Indian River and Love and Herring creeks contain the greatest preservation of the Holocene transgressive sequence. The rate of sea-level rise also plays an important role in preservation. For example, in the inner shelf the Holocene section is thin across paleo-interfluves, which were subject to shoreface erosion during the mid- to late Holocene when the rate of sea-level rise was slow. In contrast, maximum preservation of Holocene sediments across interfluve areas may occur along the outer shelf, where sea-level rise was rapid in the early Holocene (Belknap and Kraft, 1981).

Demarest and others (1981) have demonstrated that barrier-sand complexes may be totally or nearly totally preserved due to abandonment at maximum sea-level stands. They show examples of such highstand abandonment which occur in the Pleistocene paralic units marginal to the Delaware Atlantic coast. Using the vertical sedimentary sequences of these units as a model, we can make predictions as to the nature of the Delaware coastal zone into the short-term future as we approach a glacio-eustatic sea-level highstand.

Although predicting future erosional and depositional events is not a precise exercise, if local relative sea level continues to rise in a fashion similar to that of the past 3,000 to 5,000 yrs, then presently observed geologic sequences can be applied to projecting the positions and forms of paralic lithosomes at a future peak sea level. Figure 9 is an example of the use of present coastal stratigraphic sequences to predict transgressive sequences preserved across the inner shelf and what future paralic sedimentary environments might be abandoned at a peak interglacial sea level. It is difficult to put a precise time frame to such a projection. Based on reconstructed Pleistocene events in coastal Delaware (Demarest and others, 1981), however, we estimate that peak interglacial sea level could rise as much as 6 m above present level, as it did during isotopic stage 5e, and accompanying coastal erosion will result in as much as a 5-km landward shift of the coastline. Total preservation of these coastal sedimentary lithosomes may occur at this position of peak sea level when they are abandoned with sea-level fall, possibly at the beginning of a subsequent glacial stage (as noted by Demarest and others, 1981).

CONCLUSIONS

The transgressive barriers of the embayed Atlantic coastal zone of Delaware are products of a geomorphology that has its origins in Pleistocene Epoch transgressive events, a moderate amount of erosion of Pleistocene sediments during regressive events, and renewed transgression during the Holocene Epoch. During the ongoing transgression, sea-level rise was initially rapid, and as a result, we might expect total or near-total preservation of coastal stratigraphic sequences on the outer shelf. As the rate of sea-level rise began to slow, however, erosion of sediment of the antecedent topography became more important, as well as erosion and recycling of Holocene sediment. Such sediment eroded from the shoreface zone has been redistributed to the adjacent shelf, moved landward by overwash processes and flood-tidal delta development, and also incorporated into the littoral transport system. The result is a realignment of previously deposited sediments into dynamic coastal landforms such as barriers, barrier spits, flood- and ebb-tidal deltas, and wave-dominated depositional features across the inner shelf. Characteristics of the coastal zone erosion and deposition, sediment sources and sinks, and the sparse amount of nearshore sands suggest that sediment recycling is efficient and important in maintenance of the barrier lithosome. The Bruun Rule is clearly not effective on the Delaware coast. Three-dimensional effects of antecedent topography and longshore drift are at least as important as onshore-offshore transport in maintenance of equilibrium with rising sea level. In addition, grain size of eroded sediment must be considered. As sea level approaches and reaches its peak interglacial level, the effects of rising sea level become less pronounced, and other processes such as storm-wave erosion and tidal-current transport increase in relative importance in the redistribution of coastal zone sediments.

ACKNOWLEDGMENTS

We acknowledge the help of Mr. Daniel J. Collins in monitoring the coring process, interpreting the cores used, and providing detailed descriptive logs. We thank Mr. Kelvin W. Ramsey, who reviewed an early version of the manuscript and provided numerous suggestions and comments. This publication is the result in part of research sponsored by the National Oceanic and Atmospheric Administration Office of Sea Grant, Department of Commerce, NA80AA-D-00106 (Project Nos. R/G10 and R/G12). The United States Government is authorized to produce and distribute reprints for governmental purposes, not withstanding any copyright notation that might appear hereon. The research was also supported in part by the Department of Natural Resources and Environmental Control of the State of Delaware.

REFERENCES

BELKNAP, D. F., AND KRAFT, J. C., 1977, Holocene relative sea-level changes and coastal stratigraphic units on the northwest flank of the Baltimore Canyon trough geosyncline: Journal of Sedimentary Petrology, v. 47, p. 610–629.
———, AND ———, 1981, Preservation potential of transgressive coastal lithosomes on the U.S. Atlantic coast: Marine Geology, v. 42, p. 429–442.
———, AND ———, 1985, Influence of antecedent geology on stratigraphic preservation potential and evolution of Delaware's barrier systems: Marine Geology, v. 63, p. 235–262.
BRUUN, P., 1962, Sea level rise as a cause of shore erosion: American

Society of Civil Engineers Proceedings, Journal of Waterways and Harbors Division, v. 88, p. 117–130.

————, 1983, Review of conditions for uses of the Bruun Rule of erosion: Coastal Engineering, v. 7, p. 77–89.

CHRZASTOWSKI, M. J., 1986, Stratigraphy and geologic history of a Holocene lagoon: Rehoboth Bay and Indian River Bay, Delaware: unpublished Ph.D. dissertation, University of Delaware, Department of Geology, Newark, Delaware, 337 p.

————, AND KRAFT, J. C., 1985, Pre-transgression morphology and Holocene stratigraphy of the Delaware estuarine and Atlantic coasts: Geological Society of America, Abstracts with Programs, v. 17, p. 546.

DEMAREST, J. M., BIGGS, R. B., AND KRAFT, J. C., 1981, Time-stratigraphic aspects of a formation, interpretation of surficial Pleistocene deposits by analogy with Holocene paralic deposits, southeastern Delaware: Geology, v. 9, p. 360–365.

FIELD, M. E., 1980, Sand bodies on coastal plain shelves: Holocene record of the U.S. Atlantic inner shelf off Maryland: Journal of Sedimentary Petrology, v. 50, p. 505–528.

FIGUEIREDO, A. G., JR., SWIFT, D. J. P., STUBBLEFIELD, W. L., AND CLARKE, T. L., 1981, Sand ridges on the inner Atlantic shelf of North America: morphometric comparisons with Huthnance stability model: Geo-Marine Letters, v. 1, p. 187–191.

FISHER, J. J., 1980, Shoreline erosion, Rhode Island and North Carolina coasts—tests of Bruun Rule, in Schwartz, M. L., and Fisher, J. J., eds., Proceedings of the Per Bruun Symposium, Newport, Rhode Island, November, 1979: Bureau for Faculty Research, Western Washington University, Bellingham, Washington, p. 32–54.

KRAFT, J. C., 1971, Sedimentary facies patterns and geological history of a Holocene marine transgression: Geological Society of America Bulletin, v. 82, p. 2131–2158.

————, 1976, Radiocarbon dates in the Delaware coastal zone: Delaware Sea Grant Report DEL-SG-19-76, College of Marine Studies, University of Delaware, Newark, Delaware, 20 p.

————, ALLEN, E. A., BELKNAP, D. F., JOHN, C. J., AND MAURMEYER, E. M., 1979, Processes and morphologic evolution of an estuarine and coastal barrier system, in Leatherman, S. P., ed., Barrier Islands from the Gulf of St. Lawrence to the Gulf of Mexico, New York, Academic Press, 325 p.

————, AND CHRZASTOWSKI, M. J., 1985, Coastal stratigraphic sequences, in Davis, R. A., Jr., ed., Coastal Sedimentary Environments, second revised edition: Springer-Verlag, New York, p. 625–663.

————, AND JOHN, C. J., 1979, Lateral and vertical facies relationships of transgressive barriers: American Association of Petroleum Geologists Bulletin, v. 63, p. 2145–2163.

RALPH, E. K., MICHAEL, H. N., AND HAN, M. C., 1973, Radiocarbon dates and reality: MASCA Newsletter, Museum Applied Science Center for Archaeology, University of Pennsylvania, v. 9, p. 1–20.

SCHWARTZ, M. L., 1965, Laboratory study of sea level rise as a cause of shore erosion: Journal of Geology, v. 73, p. 528–534.

————, 1967, The Bruun theory of sea-level rise as a cause of shore erosion: Journal of Geology, v. 75, p. 76–92.

————, AND MILICIC, V., 1980, The Bruun Rule, a historical perspective, in Schwartz, M. L. and Fisher, J. J., eds., Proceedings of the Per Bruun Symposium, Newport, Rhode Island, November, 1979, Bureau for Faculty Research, Western Washington University, Bellingham, Washington, p. 6–12.

SHERIDAN, R. E., DILL, C. E., JR., AND KRAFT, J. C., 1974, Holocene sedimentary environments of the Atlantic inner shelf off Delaware: Geological Society of America Bulletin, v. 85, p. 1319–1328.

SWIFT, D. J. P., 1968, Coastal erosion and transgressive stratigraphy: Journal of Geology, v. 76, p. 444–456.

————, AND FIELD, M. E., 1981, Evolution of a classic sand ridge field, Maryland sector, North American inner shelf: Sedimentology, v. 28, p. 461–482.

————, NIEDORODA, A. W., VINCENT, C. E., AND HOPKINS, T. S., 1985, Barrier Island evolution, middle Atlantic shelf, USA. part I: shoreface dynamics: Marine Geology, v. 63, p. 331–361.

BACK-BARRIER RESPONSE TO SEA-LEVEL RISE, EASTERN SHORE OF VIRGINIA[1]

KENNETH FINKELSTEIN[2]

Virginia Institute of Marine Science, Gloucester Point, Virginia 23062

AND

MARIE A. FERLAND[3]

Coastal Engineering Research Center, U.S. Army Engineer Waterways Experiment Station, P.O. Box 631, Vicksburg, Mississippi 39180

ABSTRACT: The barrier and back-barrier environments of Virginia were examined to determine the effects of sea-level change on the resulting stratigraphy. Relative sea-level rise and/or a local sediment deficit have caused the retreat of these barrier islands during the Holocene. The results, reflected by the stratigraphy, are a narrowing of the back-barrier region, a decrease in the tidal prism with a probable constriction of inlets, and an increase in the infilling of marshes and tidal flats associated with calmer water conditions.

Core data show the progressive fine-grained infilling of the back-barrier system. As infilling proceeds, the general back-barrier environment passes from a higher energy lagoon to a lower energy salt marsh and tidal flats. The sedimentary pattern depicts a fining-upward "regressive" stratigraphy behind the receding barriers.

INTRODUCTION

Landward movement or narrowing in-place of barrier islands is occurring along many shorelines in response to a rise in relative sea level and/or a deficit of available coastal sediment (Hoyt, 1967; Dillon, 1970; Pierce and Colquhoun, 1970; Swift, 1975; Belknap and Kraft, 1977; Wilkinson and Basse, 1978; Moslow and Heron, 1979). The rise of sea level and the change in rate of that rise have had an apparent influence on barrier island translation which, in turn, has affected sedimentation in the back-barrier region. The resulting barrier and back-barrier stratigraphy thus is partially a function of the relative sea-level change and barrier island movement. Other controlling factors contributing to the depositional history of barrier systems include the pre-Holocene topography, local tectonism, glacio- and hydro-isostasy and sediment availability.

This linkage between the back-barrier stratigraphy and the geologic history of the adjacent barrier was examined in North Carolina by Berelson and Heron (1985). They related cyclic, flood-tidal delta deposits with barrier inlet dynamics. In our study, a limited sand supply, sea-level rise, and relatively rapid barrier retreat interact to create a distinctive back-barrier stratigraphy.

Specifically, this study examines the surface and shallow subsurface sediments of the barrier islands and adjacent back-barrier region of Virginia (Fig. 1). The effects of a relative Holocene sea-level rise and/or a local, net, littoral sediment deficit on the barrier islands and adjacent back-barrier environments are examined. The physical and biological characteristics of each subenvironment found within the study area are described. These include barrier islands, tidal inlets, salt marshes, subtidal lagoons, and tidal channels (Fig. 2).

Previous stratigraphic studies of this region (Newman and Munsart, 1968; Biggs, 1970; Harrison, 1972; Halsey, 1978) either have addressed specific sites or offered broad generalizations. Morton and Donaldson (1973) and Halsey (1978) determined that the present configuration of the segmented barriers of Virginia had been maintained through the Holocene transgression. Only Newman and Munsart

(1968) produced a local sea-level curve for the region. Their curve, based on only four dates, indicates a controversial relative 1.5-m drop in sea level between 5.1 and 4.4 ka. They also determined that modern marshes began to colonize about 1.0 ka.

Lucke (1934) addressed sedimentation within back-barrier regions similar to that of Virginia. He suggested that the presence of many inlets was responsible for rapid filling of lagoons far from the headland source. Meade (1982) found that the most likely sinks for river sediment along the southeast Atlantic seaboard are the extensive salt marshes that lie behind the barrier islands. Large estuaries prevent coarse-grained river sediments from reaching the back-barrier environments of the mid-Atlantic region. Kelley (1980), however, recognized that suspended sediment from Delaware Bay is deposited in southern New Jersey lagoons. Similarly, suspended sediment from Chesapeake Bay may be deposited behind the Virginia barrier islands.

Kraft (1971) and his co-workers (e.g., Kraft and others, 1979) have thoroughly documented the vertical sequence of the transgressive baymouth and estuarine barriers in nearby Delaware. The upper sediments of much of the Delaware lagoons are dominantly sand and silt. Migrating tidal deltas, overwash and eolian processes, and eroding back-barrier Pleistocene highlands contribute sand to the back-barrier region (Kraft, 1971). In Virginia, sand is much less available.

PHYSICAL SETTING

The area of investigation is on the Delmarva Peninsula south of the Maryland-Virginia State line and is commonly referred to as the eastern shore of Virginia. Limits of this study are the middle 10 barrier islands, extending from Assawoman Island in the north to Smith Island 70 km to the south, and from the mainland shoreline west of the lagoon to the lower foreshore of the barrier islands (Fig. 1). The barrier islands are approximately 5 to 20 km long and 0.3 to 2.0 km wide.

The Atlantic coast of Virginia has a semidiurnal tide with a range of about 1.0 m. The predominant and prevailing winds are from the north to northwest and south, respectively (U.S. Army Engineer District, Norfolk, 1971). Intense Atlantic storms may produce strong winds and large waves from the northeast. The dominant winds produce currents and a wave approach direction from the north, resulting in a net southerly longshore transport of sediment.

---

[1] Virginia Institute of Marine Science Contribution Number 1307.

[2] Present address: 1475 Massachusetts Ave., Lexington, MA 02173.

[3] Present address: Department of Geography, University of Sydney, New South Wales, 2006 Australia

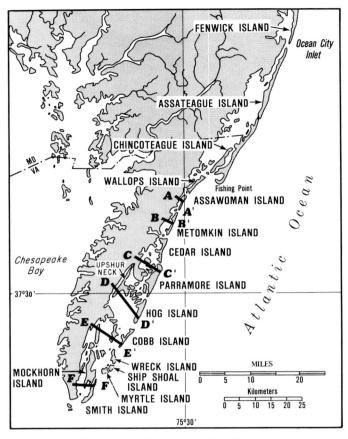

FIG. 1.—Map of the study area including vibracore transects.

FIG. 2.—Aerial view showing subenvironments of the barrier island and back-barrier complex. (A) barrier island; (B) marsh; (C) tidal channel; (D) tidal creek; (E) muddy tidal flat; (F) enclosed bay/sheltered lagoon; (G) mainland.

The primary area under consideration is the upper 10 m of unconsolidated sediments. Most Holocene and some pre-Holocene deposits occur within this depth range. Nearly all subenvironments of barrier systems are represented on the surface and/or in these sediments. Evidence of retrogradation and/or erosion is shown on many of the barrier islands by relict marsh cropping out on the lower foreshore and shoreface and washover deposits. Sand dunes are absent or discontinuous on most islands; where present, they are generally less than 2.0 m high. Multiple dune or beach-ridge systems are found, however, on a portion of three islands.

The barrier islands are separated from each other by tidal inlet channels as much as 23 m in depth and are separated from the mainland by marsh, muddy tidal flats, sheltered low-energy and open high-energy bays, and tidal creeks. Small flood-tidal deltas are presently found inside most of the barrier island inlets. Many lobes of the tidal deltas are inactive and are supporting modern salt marsh vegetation. Extensive tidal flats and shallow bays are more common along the southern half of Virginia's eastern shore, whereas the northern islands are backed predominantly by tidal marsh. The ratio of the area of open back-barrier water to the area of the entire lagoon is approximately 0.20 in the north (Biggs, 1970) compared to 0.35 in the south. The back-barrier region, whether open-water or marsh-filled, is limited by a sharp linear contact with the upland. The mainland shoreline demonstates a break in slope between the back-barrier environments and the adjacent upland. Landward of this shoreline are Pleistocene fluvial and marine silts, sands and gravels (Mixon, 1985). Pleistocene sediments as high as 4.5 m are less than 4 km from the mainland shoreline (Mixon, 1985).

METHODS

The data base for this study consists principally of vibracores from the barrier islands and back-barrier regions. Several can cores (14 × 21 × 26.5 cm) were also taken from modern environments. These data provide the means to determine the time and nature of depositional events during the Holocene evolution of the region.

The vibracorer and extraction tripod used are described by Finkelstein and Prins (1981) after Lanesky and others (1979). Thirty-four vibracores, 4 to 10 m long and 7.6 cm in diameter, were collected along six shore-normal transects. Four cores, 0.5 to 1.0 km apart, are located on transects A and B; an average of 6 cores, 1.0 to 2.0 km apart, is located on the 4 transects, C through F, that span larger back-barrier areas (Fig. 1). Transect lines and core locations were planned in the laboratory and marked in the field by stakes, with the aid of U.S. Army helicopters, prior to core collection.

All cores were split, photographed and described in detail in the laboratory. Description of each core included the major physical and biological sedimentary structures and the remains of most micro- and macro-fauna (Table 1). Sediment samples were selected toward the middle of texturally consistent units. Textural and mineralogical analyses were performed using standard techniques (Folk, 1974). X-ray radiography, following the methods of Bouma (1969)

A net deficit of sand results from much sand being trapped at Fishing Point (Fig. 1) rather than transported south to the islands (Finkelstein, 1983). Although inlet scour may provide some sand to the barrier complex, relatively little is extracted from the underlying substrate by shoreface erosion (Finkelstein, 1986).

TABLE 1.—FORAMINIFERA OF THE BACK-BARRIER COMPLEX

Calcareous Species	Agglutinated Species
Ammonia beccarii (Linné)	*Ammoastuta salsa* (Cushman and Bronnimann)
*Buccella frigida** (Cushman)	*Arenoparrella mexicana** (Kornfeld)
Elphidium discoidale (D'Orbigny)	*Haplophragmoides hancocki* (Cushman and McCulloch)
Elphidium excavatum (Terquem) = *Elphidium clavatum* (Cushman)*	*Miliammina fusca* (Brady)
Elphidium gunteri (Cole)	*Tiphotrocha comprimata* (Cushman and Bronnimann)
Haynesina paucilocula (Cushman)	*Trochammina inflata** (Montagu)

*Most Abundant.

and Howard and Frey (1975), was used to find sedimentary structures in cores containing homogeneous back-barrier sediments. Radiocarbon dates were obtained on 24 samples containing suitable organic material (Table 2).

SEDIMENTOLOGY AND STRATIGRAPHY

Sediments comprising the Virginia barrier island complex are a mixture of dominantly terrigenous sand, silt and clay. Sands are mostly quartz and may be burrowed or crossbedded. Grains of authigenic glauconite, mollusk shells and shell fragments, and microfaunal tests comprise most of the nonterrigenous component of the sediment. Lithosome identification was made on the basis of stratigraphic position, physical and biogenic sedimentary structures, texture, macrofauna, and contact characteristics. These physical parameters are nearly completely preserved in vibracores. Microfauna data were added for verification (Table 1).

TABLE 2.—RADIOCARBON AGE DATES

Core Number	Depth m (msl)	Lab Number	Type of Material	Age (yrs)
1-1	0.91	B-2659	*Spartina alterniflora*	650 ± 60
1-4	0.60	B-2660	*Spartina alterniflora*	700 ± 60
1-4	4.73	B-2661	Organic-rich muds	2,440 ± 70
1-4*	5.20	W-4789	Organic-rich muds	3,200 ± 100
1-4	5.41	B-2662	Basal peat	3,580 ± 60
2-1	1.05	B-2663	*Spartina alterniflora*	1,180 ± 60
2-2	6.60	B-1952	Basal peat	4,620 ± 80
2-3	1.68	B-1951	*Spartina alterniflora*	1,660 ± 70
2-4*	2.45	W-4788	Basal peat	2,200 ± 80
3-2*	2.13	W-4792	Oyster shell	600 ± 60
3-2	3.80	B-1954	Marsh debris in mud	3,640 ± 110
3-5	1.22	B-1955	Oyster shell	1,380 ± 90
3-5*	4.72	W-4787	Oyster shell	2,900 ± 110
4-4	0.30	B-1959	*Spartina alterniflora*	Modern
4-5	0.86	B-2664	Oyster shell	450 ± 50
4-6	0.96	B-2665	Oyster shell	890 ± 50
5-1	3.35	B-1956	Marsh debris in mud	3,160 ± 70
5-2	1.55	B-1957	Oyster shell	890 ± 60
5-4	0.30	B-2667	*Spartina alterniflora*	Modern
5-4	1.10	B-1958	Oyster shell	610 ± 70
6-5	3.90	B-1949	Sandy peat	23,350 ± 370
6-5	3.90	B-3423	Sandy peat	30,870 ± 470
6-6	0.41	B-1948	*Spartina patens*	1,430 ± 80
6-6	0.80	B-1950	Willow or tulip poplar	1,740 ± 100

*Radiocarbon dates from U.S. Geological Survey, Reston; all others from Beta Analytic, Inc., Coral Gables, Florida.

Lithosome Descriptions

Nine distinct surficial and subsurface lithosomes have been identified. They include Holocene barrier island sands, modern marsh, muddy tidal flat, mixed flat, sand flat, sheltered lagoon, back-barrier beach, basal Holocene, and one all-encompassing pre-Holocene lithosome. A description of each lithosome is summarized in Table 3.

Holocene barrier island.—

Foreshore, backshore and washover sands are grouped together as one unit, because all are only found surficially on the generally narrow barrier islands and are mostly the product of swash- and surf-zone processes. These sands are texturally and mineralogically uniform, fine-grained, and well sorted; four samples show a mean grain size ($\bar{X}$) and standard deviation (σ) of 2.40 ϕ and 0.5 ϕ, respectively. Upper foreshore sand thickness is approximately 1.0 to 2.0 m, except on Parramore and Hog islands where sands are greater than 2.0 m thick. The thin barrier islands reflect a paucity of available sand. The contact with the underlying back-barrier deposits is sharp but conformable. Planar beds dominate the unit internally. Exhumed back-barrier shells of oysters (*Crassostrea virginica*) and quahogs (*Mercenaria mercenaria*) along with Atlantic surf clams (*Spisula solidissima*) and whelks (*Busycon canaliculatum*) are common on the surface.

Modern marsh.—

Landward of and usually beneath the modern barrier islands are organic muds. Generally 0.5 to 1.0 m thick, they represent the total accumulation of late Holocene marsh sedimentation. Marshes exist principally as both large and small islands, often encroaching upon adjacent tidal flats. Marshes also fringe the landward edge of the barrier islands and the mainland shoreline. Marsh sediments contain about 15% sand, 55% silt and 30% clay (average of seven samples) but coarsen adjacent to barrier islands and back-barrier beaches. This lithosome is heavily vegetated at the surface. Total organic matter by weight ranges from almost 20% near the surface to about 7% near the bottom of the unit. Surfaces of the marsh are nearly horizontal with numerous tidal creeks and channels bisecting them. Creek channels usually exhibit a sharp, generally steep, eroding side and an accreting side with colonizing *Spartina alterniflora*. Marsh island biota include the marsh periwinkel (*Littorina irrorata*) and intertidal plants *Spartina alterniflora*, *Salicornia virginica*, and, less often, *Distichlis spicata*. The latter two grow at elevations near mean high water (MHW). Low and high marsh plants, including *Spartina patens* and *Borrichia frutescens*, are found within the fringing marshes.

Muddy tidal flat.—

The muddy tidal flat is found adjacent to and below the topographically higher marshes. The upper contact is characterized by the vegetation and finer texture of the marsh sediment, whereas the lower contact is most often with a coarser grained mixed flat. Both contacts are gradational. Thickness of this lithosome is as great as 3.0 m but aver-

TABLE 3.—SEDIMENTARY CHARACTERISTICS AND RECOGNITION CRITERIA OF IDENTIFIED LITHOSOMES

Lithosome	Texture/Lithology	Percent Sand/Silt/ Clay	Primary Sedimentary Structures	Biota
Holocene barrier island	Fine, well sorted tan sand, $\bar{X}$ = 2.40 ϕ.		Low-angle and horizontal planar beds.	Mollusk shells and foraminifera.
Modern marsh	Dark gray organic-rich mud, heavily vegetated.	15/55/30	None.	S. alterniflora, S. virginica, D. spicata. Agglutinated foraminifera.
Muddy tidal flat	Dark gray sandy mud. Oyster shells in layers as much as 2 m thick.	30/50/20	Completely bioturbated.	Many oyster shells, some articulated. Many mud snail shells (I. obsoleta). Calcareous foraminifera and ostracodes.
Mixed flat	Dark gray muddy sand.	60/30/10	Flaser, wavy, lenticular and coarsely and thinly interlayered bedding. Increased bioturbation toward top.	Some oyster shells, calcareous foraminifera, and ostracodes.
Sand flat	Gray fine to very fine sand, $\bar{X}$ = 2.90 ϕ.	95/03/02	A few round burrows, few physical structures.	A few dwarf clam shells (M. lateralis).
Sheltered lagoon	Massive mud with some plant debris.	10/55/35	Some sand laminae, mostly bioturbated.	A few ostracode spp., calcareous foraminifera, and scattered vegetation.
Back-barrier beach	Fine to medium tan sand. $\bar{X}$ = 1.75 ϕ.		Some horizontal bedding.	Mollusk shells and marsh vegetation on surface.
Basal brackish- salt marsh and peat	Brownish-gray to black organic-rich mud.	15/75/10	None.	Vegetation.
Pre-Holocene 1) Mud	Compacted blue-green to gray mud.	00/50/50	Occasional lenticular sand bed in gray muds.	None.
2) Sand	Medium ($\bar{X}$ = 1.81 ϕ) well sorted orange-tan sand or coarse sand and gravel.		Heavy mineral laminations. Planar, mostly horizontal beds. Round burrows. Coarse sands show graded bedding.	None.

ages 1.5 to 2.0 m. Eleven samples indicate an average sediment composition of about 30% sand, 50% silt, and 20% clay. The unit is extensively burrowed; thus, physical sedimentary structures are not readily preserved; few are seen even with X-radiographs. *Ilynassa obsoleta* shells are abundant. Oyster shells in layers as much as 2 m thick, but more often 0.3 to 0.5 m thick, are found in cores penetrating this lithosome. Similar to those found in South Carolina (Ruby, 1981), oyster bars in Virginia occur in a zone near the marsh-tidal flat contact. These oyster communities measure a few meters across but may be several tens of meters long.

Mixed flat.—

This lithosome is best characterized by physical sedimentary structures such as flaser, wavy, lenticular, and coarsely and thinly interlayered sand-mud bedding. Bedding results from an interplay of high-current velocity bed-load transport of sand and low-current or slack-water deposition of suspended sediment. There is a fining-upward sequence with increased bioturbation. Textural analyses of 15 samples taken perpendicular to bedding planes indicate a composition of approximately 60% sand-size material, 30% silt and 10% clay. The mixed flat lithosome usually ranges from 1.0 to 4.0 m thick and averages about 2.5 m. It is much like the high-energy lagoon of Ruby (1981). The description of this lithosome can be compared to that of Reineck and Singh (1980), who define mixed flats as those zones where sediments are deposited in transition between muddy intertidal flats near the high-water line and sandy intertidal flats near the low-water line. Similar sedimentary structures and gross sediment type may also be found in the subtidal environment (Reineck and Singh, 1980, fig. 512). Therefore, the exact location of this lithosome with respect to sea level may not be well defined. Three can cores, however, taken in 0.75 m of water (MLW) in a moderately open-water back-barrier environment just seaward of the southern tip of Mockhorn Island (Fig. 1) penetrated sediments described above. Thus, the mixed flats of this study are not intertidal but occur in the shallow subtidal environment. The mixed flat lithosome, so common at depth, probably aggraded in a vast subtidal zone during earlier, higher energy levels.

Sand flat.—

Sand flats are massive, fine to very fine-grained, slightly bioturbated subtidal sands. The silt and clay content is less than 10%. Except for the dwarf clam (*Mulinia lateralis*), there is little fauna. Unlike the previously described lithosomes, these sands are barren of foraminifera. Thickness extends to 4.0 m but averages about 1.0 m. The sand flat forms the basal portion of a continuous sequence of fining-upward subtidal to intertidal flats.

Sheltered lagoon.—

Commonly, the basal unit of the Holocene is a muddy lithosome believed to be the result of deposition in a low-energy, lagoonal environment. Modern back-barrier bays surrounded by marsh islands accumulate sediment of this type. The sediment is generally homogeneous, moderately bioturbated and fine-grained with average sand/silt/clay percentages of 10, 55 and 35, respectively (average of eight samples). Sand laminae and shell material are visible in X-radiographs. Plant remains, both as large solitary pieces and allochthonous plant detritus on bedding planes, are common. The majority of this lithosome is believed to be deposited from suspension. Flow velocities are, in most cases, probably not great enough to produce bedforms. Sand stringers are interpreted to have been deposited during storm events.

Back-barrier beach.—

Back-barrier or lagoonal washover beaches (Kraft, 1971) are often found on the mainland side of the larger back-barrier bays, where wave energy is high. Composed of coarser grained ($\bar{X} = 1.75$ ɸ) and more poorly sorted ($\sigma = 0.75$ ɸ) sand than the barrier beaches, they are surrounded by marshes which commonly encroach upon the back-barrier beaches. Sedimentary structures are rare; however, some horizontal bedding is present.

Basal Holocene.—

In the southern half of the study area, the basal Holocene facies are either the sand flat or sheltered lagoon described above. Cores here do not penetrate the pre-Holocene sediments. Cores in transects A and B (Fig. 1) penetrate older brackish-salt marshes and basal peats in several places. The name brackish-salt marsh is taken from Halsey (1978) who, on several occasions, described a lithosome of similar character. These brownish-gray organic-rich muds range in thickness between 0.3 and 0.9 m and contain a sand, silt, and clay abundance of 15, 75 and 10%, respectively (average of two samples). Thus, thickness and texture are comparable to those of the recent marshes observed higher in the sedimentary sequence. Below the brackish-salt marsh, approximately 30 cm of basal peat was penetrated. The peat is composed of *Juncus* species and is dark brown to black and richer in organics than the marsh above. The peat marks the leading edge of the Holocene transgression but is not a laterally continuous lithosome. The lower contact of the basal peat is on top of either pre-Holocene lagoonal muds or coarse sands and gravels. The brackish marsh and basal peat sediments were radiocarbon-dated as both are possible sea-level indicators.

Pre-Holocene.—

The sediments below the basal Holocene units are mostly of Pleistocene age (Halsey, 1978). These sediments, which may have been eroded, reworked, and transported during the Wisconsinan regression, have been inundated by Holocene sea-level rise. Two pre-Holocene lithosomes are identified. One is a compacted blue-green and gray mud of probable lagoonal origin composed of approximately 50% silt and 50% clay. The color, dewatered nature, and grain size provide easy recognition, contrasting sharply with the dark gray unconsolidated lagoonal and tidal flat muds of Holocene age. The other lithosome is either a coarse sand with pebbles or a medium to fine sand. The sands and pebbles overlying the pre-Holocene lagoonal mud near the mainland margin of transects B and possibly C are interpreted as fluvial deposits originating during the Wisconsinan regression. These overlie earlier transgressive sediments. Halsey (1978) found coarse sands and gravel of the Pleistocene highlands below the blue-green and gray lagoonal muds. Penetration through the compacted mud was not achieved during this study. The finer sands are iron-

stained and are interpreted as either a Pleistocene barrier island (Mockhorn Island) or a topographic high (transect E of Fig. 1). Mockhorn Island (Fig. 1) contains a sand beach unit that extends 2.0 m below mean low water. It has an orange tint, is devoid of microfossils and overlies compacted estuarine sediments. Eight foreshore samples show a medium grain size ($\bar{X} = 1.80$ ɸ) and moderate sorting ($\sigma = 0.80$ ɸ). The lagoonal deposits are, in general, similar in lithology to the pre-Holocene Diamond City Clay from North Carolina (Susman and Heron, 1979) and the Kiawah Fm from South Carolina (Moslow, 1980). All lie below Holocene back-barrier sediments and date between approximately 20 and 30 ka (Table 2).

Microfossils

Foraminifera.—

Specific foraminifera are indicative of the environment of deposition. The number and type of foraminifera in each of 36 core samples per gram (dry weight) of sediment coarser than 62 μm were recorded. All lithosomes except the barrier island and back-barrier beach sands were sampled. The foraminiferal species are listed in Table 1.

Two distinct assemblages are present. The most common is the calcareous assemblage, which occurs in subaqueous silty and sandy muds. The other is an agglutinated assemblage, which is characteristic of lower salinity environments. The latter assemblage is found in only a few samples, almost all of which are from surface or near-surface marsh sediments. The Pleistocene sediments, the basal marsh and peat deposits, and the possibly high-energy Holocene sand flat lithosome contain no foraminifera. This is attributed to either the depositional environment being unsuitable for adaptation or destruction of the tests by leaching.

The species present and the relatively low species diversity are characteristic of a marginal marine environment. There are no exotic or extinct species which might serve as natural tracers. This suggests that most of the back-barrier sediments penetrated by the cores were probably deposited under relatively uniform environmental conditions.

Ostracodes.—

Ostracodes are also useful for characterizing depositional environments. Seven core samples were analyzed for species identification and diversity. All samples except one are dominated by *Cyprideis mexicana*, a species common to brackish water lagoonal/tidal-flat environments. These six samples are from lithosomes believed to be from relatively low-energy back-barrier environments, such as muddy tidal flats or sheltered deeper water lagoons. The seventh sample, taken from a mixed flat lithosome, shows shallow marine species which provide further evidence that this lithosome occurs in a more open, unrestricted, subtidal environment.

Cross Sections

Stratigraphic cross sections are drawn from core data for all six transects shown in Figure 1. Three of these, B-B′, D-D′ and F-F′, are shown in Figures 3A, B, and C, respectively. The cross sections include radiocarbon dates; the range of error for each date is found on Table 2. The core data and the corresponding cross sections indicate no short-term oscillations in sea level.

The cross sections of this study are consistent with the hypothetical transgressive model developed by Fischer (1961). In both studies deeper water lagoonal fills are capped sequentially by tidal flat and marsh deposits. Generally, in vertical stratigraphic section, muds are found above back-barrier sands. This is attributed to a system that has become dominated by suspended sediment deposition, especially in Virginia where sand is relatively scarce.

All three cross sections exhibit a mostly fining-upward sequence, an indication of progressively more quiescent back-barrier conditions. Transect B-B' (Fig. 3A) shows the pre-Holocene units, radiocarbon-dated basal peats, and an estimate of modern marsh inception less than 2.0 m below MSL approximately 1.1 to 1.6 ka. In this region the barrier island is relatively closer to the mainland and the back-barrier is almost completely marsh-filled. For this reason, it may be considered more mature than much of the back-barrier region to the south. Transects D-D' (Fig. 3B) and F-F' (Fig. 3C) exhibit large pre-Holocene features, Upshur Neck and Mockhorn Island, that may be geomorphologically and chronologically related (Halsey, 1978). Transect D-D', landward of Hog Island (Fig. 1), provides a good example of the typical Holocene back-barrier depositional history mentioned earlier, i.e., subtidal sand flat deposition followed by mixed and muddy flats and culminating in marsh. The large open-water bay that caps part of this transect may be analogous to the back-barrier of the past with the fate of predominant marsh infilling yet to be realized.

Unlike the fining-upward sequence presented by Berelson and Heron (1985) in response to flood-tidal delta deposition, no patterns of episodic sedimentation are observed in cores from the back-barrier of Virginia. Lithosome descriptions and stationary inlets (Morton and Donaldson, 1973; Halsey, 1978) point to a continuous deposition of sediment.

The presence of a sand flat or sheltered lagoonal mud at or near the basal Holocene is probably dependent upon the pre-Holocene topography. The initial Holocene transgression invaded the deeply incised sheltered valleys, which were conducive to deposition of fine-grained sediments. Thus, the contact with the pre-Holocene probably is deeper for the sheltered lagoonal mud than for the sand flat lithosome. Where the Holocene to pre-Holocene contact is shallow, a higher energy sand flat was formed when sea level overtopped the valleys. This interpretation is consistent with the work of Halsey (1978), who found both a lower Holocene silty fine sand and a quiet water lagoonal silty clay.

SEA-LEVEL HISTORY

A relative sea-level curve for this study area is shown in Figure 4. Carbon-14 dates indicate a continued but not linear rise in sea level since 4.6 ka. There are two inflection points: the first, at approximately 3.8 ka is located between two basal peat dates and commences a time of relatively faster sea-level rise; the other is a basal peat of 2.2 ka, which begins a time of relatively slower sea-level rise.

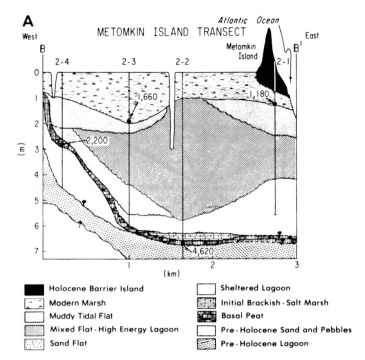

FIG. 3.—Cross sections of transects B-B' (A), D-D' (B) and F-F' (C) showing the sedimentology and stratigraphic relationships along with radiocarbon dates. Cores are shown as solid lines, numbered at top. Locations of transects are found in Figure 1. See text for discussion.

Organic materials dated include deep, organic-rich horizons identified as a basal peat or brackish-salt marsh, articulated oyster shells, wood and more recent marsh vegetation (Table 2). Two muddy, organic-rich samples from sheltered lagoon environments were also dated, but transport of vegetation into the sediment accounts for their comparatively old age. Many of these materials are useful for determining a relative sea-level curve because they are indicators of past sea levels. Because oysters in this region are found in the lower intertidal or shallow subtidal zones, the sea-level curve was drawn higher than their sampled depths. Post-depositional compaction, subsidence or tectonic uplift may disallow correlating specific dates to actual past sea levels.

Discrepancies between the sea level curve of this study and that of Newman and Munsart (1968) stem from their proposal of a relative sea-level fall or coastal uplift between 5.1 and 4.4 ka (Fig. 4). A sea-level fall is hard to establish because, other than one radiocarbon date, there is no supporting evidence from either their core data or core data from this study. They suggest the progradation of Parramore Island (Fig. 1) during this temporary emergence, using the 7.0-m-high Holocene dune ridge on the island as evidence. At 5.1 ka, however, sea level was much lower (Fig. 4) and Parramore Island would almost certainly have been in a much more seaward position. Lastly, both their 5.1 and 4.4 ka dates may be inaccurate as both are from small samples of humic acid. Regressive phases along the Atlantic coast, but at later times, have been suggested,

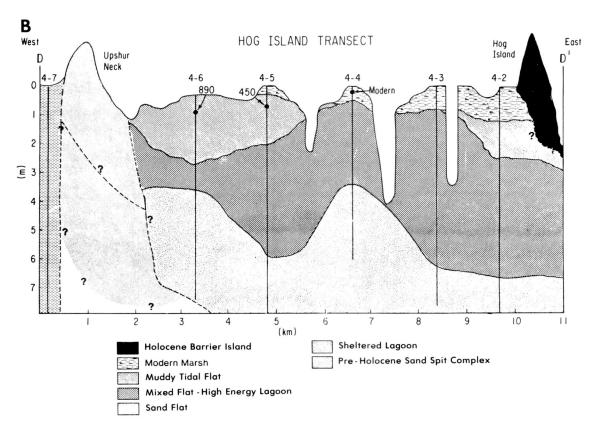

B

West

HOG ISLAND TRANSECT

Hog Island East

D

Upshur Neck

D'

4-7 4-6 890 450 4-5 4-4 Modern 4-3 4-2

(m)

0 1 2 3 4 5 6 7

? ? ? ? ? ? ?

1 2 3 4 5 6 7 8 9 10 11
(km)

■ Holocene Barrier Island
▦ Modern Marsh
▨ Muddy Tidal Flat
▧ Mixed Flat - High Energy Lagoon
□ Sand Flat

▦ Sheltered Lagoon
░ Pre-Holocene Sand Spit Complex

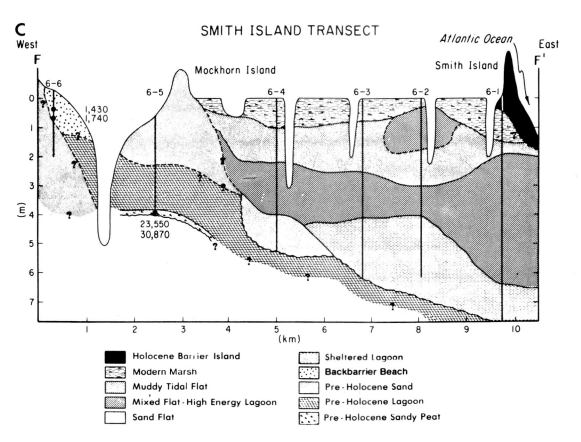

C

West

SMITH ISLAND TRANSECT

Atlantic Ocean East

F

Mockhorn Island

Smith Island

F'

6-6 1,430 1,740 6-5 6-4 6-3 6-2 6-1

(m)

0 1 2 3 4 5 6 7

23,550 30,870

? ? ?

1 2 3 4 5 6 7 8 9 10
(km)

■ Holocene Barrier Island
▦ Modern Marsh
▨ Muddy Tidal Flat
▧ Mixed Flat - High Energy Lagoon
□ Sand Flat

▦ Sheltered Lagoon
⋯ Backbarrier Beach
□ Pre-Holocene Sand
▨ Pre-Holocene Lagoon
░ Pre-Holocene Sandy Peat

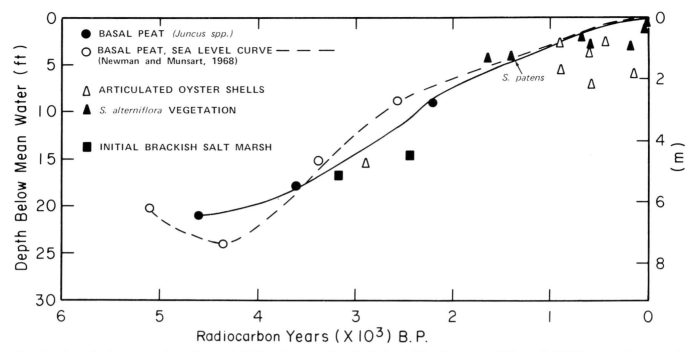

FIG. 4.—A sea-level curve for the study area (solid line) for approximately the last 4.6 ka. Newman and Munsart's (1968) sea-level curve is also shown (dashed line), although their two oldest dates, from small humic acid samples, may be inaccurate. An envelope encompassing the dates from both studies is possibly a better estimate of the local sea-level history.

however, (DePratter and Howard, 1981; Moslow and Colquhoun, 1981).

Sea-level rise for the western Atlantic slowed considerably between approximately 6.0 to 5.0 ka (Lighty and others, 1982). The data base of this study does not precede 4.6 ka, but the assumption is made that sea-level rise was then much greater. Using the age and depth of basal peats, a relatively slow rate of sea-level rise is calculated from 4.6 ka to the historical period. A more rapid rise in sea level began about 0.3 ka (Froomer, 1980). The overall sea-level rise rate is 1.5 mm/yr calculated from 4.6 ka to the present. This low rate of sea-level rise agrees with that of Belknap and Kraft (1977) for Delaware but is higher than that found in North Carolina by Heron and others (1985).

DISCUSSION

The transgressive stratigraphy of the Holocene Virginia coast points to landward movement of the barrier islands. Brackish basal peats underlying lagoonal sediments reflect the initial Holocene marine encroachment over the coastal plain and give a minimum age to the barrier islands. For example, the oldest Holocene radiocarbon date obtained in this study is 4.62 ± 0.08 ka, from a basal peat at −6.60 m in core 2-2 of transect B-B' (Figs. 1, 3A). This indicates the barrier islands were in existence at least this long and at a sea level of −6.60 m. The barrier islands would have been 4 km offshore at the −6.60-m contour, assuming no subsequent offshore sedimentation (Fig. 5). This is a minimum offshore location, as the islands at that time could have been much farther seaward and backed by a large la-

goon. Historically, the barrier islands have retreated rapidly, at mean rates ranging between 3 and 15 m/yr (Rice and others, 1976).

A general stratigraphic change from a higher to lower energy environment is found in most back-barrier cores. This probably reflects the continuous landward migration of the islands, narrowing of the lagoon and sedimentation under progressively lower energy back-barrier conditions. Since most of the back-barrier region was subaqueous 4.6 ka and barrier islands were farther offshore (Fig. 5), the narrowing and infilling of the back-barrier region over time decreased the tidal prism. In turn, the widths of the 11 principal tidal inlets probably decreased and created quieter back-barrier conditions. A positive feedback system between back-barrier restriction and inlet constriction initiated by barrier island retreat was thus set up. Suspended fine-grained sedimentation is presently replacing bedload sand influx in much of the back-barrier region. Oertel (1975) found a similar pattern in Georgia, where constriction of inlets appeared to be a response to a retreating shoreline, seasonal reversal in longshore sediment transport, localized flood channel deposits, and decreasing lagoonal tidal prism caused by marsh deposition.

Only minor inundation of the relatively steep mainland shoreline has occurred during the late Holocene. Thus, there has been little increase in lagoonal area when compared to the narrowing due to landward barrier retreat. This is demonstrated by a 4.62 ± 0.08 ka basal peat at −6.60 m in core 2-2 of transect B-B' (Fig. 3A) and a 3.58 ± 0.06 ka basal peat at the −5.41 m bottom of core 1-4 of transect A-A' (Fig. 1). The former is only 2.5 km seaward of the

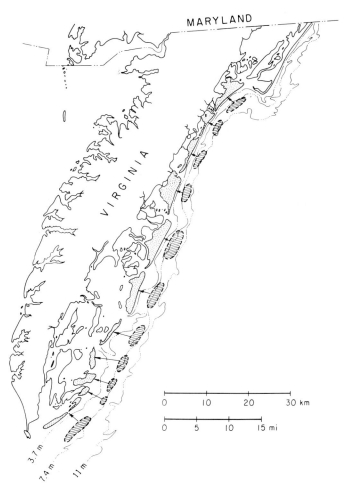

FIG. 5.—A schematic drawing depicting the suggested barrier island and back-barrier morphology and approximate location 4.6 ka (dashed islands with no back-barrier marsh islands). The locations of the islands are not absolute, but a larger lagoonal area and inlet size are proposed. The mainland shoreline has transgressed little when compared to the retrograding barrier islands; thus, the back-barrier region has become more restricted over time.

present mainland shoreline, and the latter is approximately 1.0 km seaward. Both show a thick and relatively old sequence of lagoonal deposits nearly adjacent to the mainland shoreline.

The change from higher energy to lower energy depositional conditions in the back-barrier region has created a "regressive" sequence of sedimentary deposits. As discussed by Reineck (1972), the regressive tidal flat sequence from top to bottom consists of deposits of salt marsh, mud flat, mixed flat and fine sand. A transgressive sequence would be reversed. Therefore, despite the transgressing sea and retreating barrier islands that create a transgressive coastal stratigraphy, the back-barrier region is characterized by a sequence of "regressive" deposits. This is due to sedimentation under progressively lower energy conditions. The potential for preservation of a portion of this "regressive" back-barrier sequence despite a transgressing sea should be recognized.

In contrast to the wave and flood-tidal delta-dominated Delaware system, the segmented barriers in Virginia primarily exhibit back-barrier deposition of suspended sediment. In Delaware a fining- then coarsening-upward sequence often occurs (see Demarest and Kraft, this volume); the Virginia system only fines upward. Relative to coastal Delaware, the Virginia barrier islands and adjacent back-barrier system are starved of sand. Thus, despite their close proximity, the Virginia back-barrier stratigraphic sequence differs from that found behind the Delaware baymouth barriers.

Modern marshes in this region have been reported to be 1.0 ka (Newman and Munsart, 1968). Radiocarbon dating of marsh material sampled at the deepest portion of the marsh lithosome provides dates as old as approximately 1.6 ka (Table 2). The dates are consistent with the depositional history of this region. During the time of relatively faster sea-level rise, back-barrier sedimentation occurred subaqueously. Extensive marsh growth could not occur under mostly subtidal conditions. As sea-level rise slowed after 2.2 ka, the lagoon continued to fill slowly and extensive marsh growth began as subaqueous sedimentation changed to intertidal sedimentation in many areas. This has continued to the present. Despite a more rapid sea-level rise rate of 3.6 mm/yr (Hampton Roads, Virginia) to 2.0 mm/yr (Lewes, Delaware) during the period 1940–1980 (Hicks and others, 1983), marshes continued to grow as suspended sediment deposition increased. Deforestation, which began in the Colonial period, increased stream sediment loads and introduced abundant sediment into the estuarine system (Froomer, 1980). Subsequently, because suspended sediment supply increased, marshes expanded. Maximum deposition would probably be expected in low marsh habitats (Letzsch and Frey, 1980).

The emergence and development of new marsh seem dependent only on the availability of a substrate in a low-energy intertidal environment, not on any particular grain size. Relative sea-level rise allows for continued growth. The stratigraphic sequence indicates that marshes are more abundant today than at any time during the mid- to late Holocene. In addition, the scarcity of agglutinated foraminifera below the immediate surficial layers suggests that marshes were less widely developed during accumulation of the back-barrier sediments than they are at present.

CONCLUSIONS

(1) The stratigraphic, sedimentologic, and radiocarbon age data demonstrate the landward retreat and narrowing of the back-barrier region during Holocene time. The lower Holocene lithosome is dependent on the pre-Holocene topography with subsequent units fining upward. A transition from higher to lower energy back-barrier environments over time, implying increasing back-barrier restriction, generally occurs. The barrier retreat caused a restriction of the back barrier and decreased the tidal prism, thus helping constrict the inlets. Inlet constriction assisted in further restriction of the back barrier region, thus creating a positive feedback system initiated by barrier island retreat. Presently, fine-grained suspended sediments rather than bed-

load sands are deposited in the back-barrier environment. Back-barrier bays with sand bottoms should fill with mud. Tidal flats eventually should be colonized by marsh grasses. This stratigraphy indicates continuous rather than episodic sedimentation.

(2) The fining-upward "regressive" back-barrier sequence differs from much of what is found in nearby Delaware. Deposition of suspended sediments, and sands from flood-tidal deltas and washovers dominate the upper stratigraphic sequence in Virginia and Delaware, respectively. Differences in back-barrier sedimentation between relatively sand-rich (Delaware) and sand-starved barriers (Virginia), despite their close proximity, are thus explained.

(3) A relative sea-level curve developed for the study area indicates a time of relatively faster sea-level rise between approximately 3.8 and 2.2 ka. From 2.2 ka until the past several centuries, a relatively slower sea-level rise occurred. Between the time of barrier development near the shelf edge in early Holocene or late Wisconsinan time and about 5.0 ka, sea level probably rose very rapidly. A sea-level rise of only 1.5 mm/yr is calculated from 4.6 ka to the present. This may be compared to the faster, present, local rate of sea-level rise of approximately 2.0 to 3.6 mm/yr.

(4) Extensive marsh growth occurred after approximately 1.6 ka. This reflects both the slowing of relative sea-level rise and continuous back-barrier sedimentation to intertidal levels. Despite the rapid present rise in sea level, the abundant suspended sediment provides for increased deposition. New marsh growth continues today mostly on muddy oyster-capped tidal flats but also on sandy washover fans and flood-tidal deltas.

ACKNOWLEDGMENTS

This work was carried out under the Coastal Engineering Research Center's Barrier Island Sedimentation Studies work unit. The authors express appreciation to C. H. Everts and S. K. Kimball, with whom most of this research was extensively discussed; D. F. Belknap and S. J. Williams for their technical review; A. L. Ginsburg, C. H. Hobbs, III, G. H. Johnson, T. F. Moslow, M. M. Nichols, R. C. Shipp, M. E. Wakeland, L. G. Ward, and L. D. Wright for their suggestions; J. Berg, B. Olver, and D. Prins for their field assistance; and R. Hennessey (The Nature Conservancy), who permitted access to and encouraged study of these islands. The Virginia Institute of Marine Science (VIMS) Wachapreague Laboratory provided much logistical field support; VIMS Gloucester Point provided resources and editorial assistance for the final preparation of this manuscript. Ed Meisburger did most of the foraminiferal analysis, Tom Cronin identified the ostracodes, Dick Macomber identified the basal peat flora, and the U.S. Geological Survey in Reston determined radiocarbon dates for four samples.

REFERENCES

BELKNAP, D. F., AND KRAFT, J. C., 1977, Holocene relative sea level changes and coastal stratigraphic units on the northwest flank of the Baltimore Canyon trough geosyncline: Journal of Sedimentary Petrology, v. 47, p. 610–629.

BERELSON, W. M., AND HERON, S. D., 1985, Correlations between Holocene flood tidal delta and barrier inlet fill sequences: Back Sound-Shackleford Banks, North Carolina: Sedimentology, v. 32, p. 215–222.

BIGGS, A. B., 1970, The origin and geological history of Assateague Island, Maryland and Virginia: Assateague Ecological Studies, Natural Resources Institute, University of Maryland, p. 9–41.

BOUMA, A. H., 1969, Methods for the Study of Sedimentary Structures: John Wiley and Sons, New York, 458 p.

DePRATTER, C. B., AND HOWARD, J. D., 1981, Evidence for a sea level lowstand between 4500 and 2400 years B.P.: Journal of Sedimentary Petrology, v. 51, p. 1287–1295.

DILLON, W. P., 1970, Submergence effects on a Rhode Island barrier and lagoon and inferences on migration of barriers: Journal of Geology, v. 78, p. 94–106.

FINKELSTEIN, K., 1983, Cape formation as a cause of erosion on adjacent shorelines: Proceedings of the Third Symposium on Coastal and Ocean Management, American Society of Civil Engineers, San Diego, California, p. 620–640.

————, 1986, Back-barrier contributions to a littoral sand budget: Journal of Coastal Research, v. 2, p. 33–42.

————, AND PRINS, D. A., 1981, An inexpensive, portable vibracoring system for shallow-water and land application: CETA 81-8, U.S. Army Corps of Engineers, Coastal Engineering Research Center, Fort Belvoir, Virginia, 15 p.

FISCHER, A. G., 1961, Stratigraphic record of transgressing seas in light of sedimentation on the Atlantic coast of New Jersey: American Association of Petroleum Geologists Bulletin, v. 45, p. 1656–1666.

FOLK, R. L., 1974, Petrology of Sedimentary Rocks: Hemphill, Austin, Texas, 170 p.

FROOMER, N. L., 1980, Sea level changes in the Chesapeake Bay during historic times: Marine Geology, v. 36, p. 289–305.

HALSEY, D. A., 1978, Late Quaternary geologic history and morphologic development of the barrier island system along the Delmarva Peninsula of the mid-Atlantic Bight: unpublished Ph.D. Dissertation, University of Delaware, Newark, 592 p.

HARRISON, S. C., 1972, The sediments and sedimentary processes of a Holocene tidal flat complex, Delmarva Peninsula, Virginia: Report 112, Office of Naval Research, Coastal Studies Institute, Louisiana State University, Baton Rouge, Louisiana , 107 p.

HERON, S. D., MOSLOW, T. F., BERELSON, W. M., HERBERT, J. R., STEELE, G. A., AND SUSMAN, K. R., 1985, Holocene sedimentation of a wave-dominated barrier-island shoreline: Cape Lookout, North Carolina: Marine Geology, v. 60, p. 413–434.

HICKS, S. D., DEBAUGH, H. A., AND HICKMAN, L. E., 1983, Sea level variations for the United States, 1855–1980: U.S. Department of Commerce, National Oceanic and Atmospheric Administration, National Ocean Service, 170 p.

HOWARD, J. D., AND FREY, R. W., 1975, Estuaries of the Georgia coast, U.S.A., sedimentology and biology: Senckenbergiana Maritima, v. 7, p. 1–31.

HOYT, J. H., 1967, Barrier island formation: Geological Society of America Bulletin, v. 78, p. 1125–1136.

KELLEY, J. T., 1980, Sediment introduction and deposition in a coastal lagoon, Cape May, New Jersey, in Kennedy, V., ed., Estuarine Perspectives: Academic Press, New York, p. 379–388.

KRAFT, J. C., 1971, Sedimentary facies patterns and geologic history of a Holocene marine transgression: Geological Society of America Bulletin, v. 82, p. 2131–2158.

————, ALLEN, E. A., BELKNAP, D. F., JOHN, C. J., AND MAURMEYER, E. M., 1979, Processes and morphologic evolution of an estuarine and coastal barrier, in Leatherman, S. P., ed., Barrier Islands from the Gulf of St. Lawrence to the Gulf of Mexico: Academic Press, New York, p. 149–183.

LANESKY, D. E., LOGAN, B. W., AND HINE, A. C., 1979, A new approach to portable vibracoring under water and on land: Journal of Sedimentary Petrology, v. 49, p. 654–657.

LETZSCH, W. S., AND FREY, R. W., 1980, Deposition and erosion in a Holocene salt marsh, Sapelo Island, Georgia: Journal of Sedimentary Petrology, v. 50, p. 529–542.

LIGHTY, R. G., MACINTYRE, I. G., AND STUCKENRATH, R., 1982, Acropora palmata reef framework: a reliable indicator of sea level in the western Atlantic for the past 10,000 years: Coral Reefs, v. 1, p. 125–130.

LUCKE, J. B., 1934, A study of Barnegat Inlet: Shore and Beach, v. 2, p. 45–94.

MEADE, R. H., 1982, Sources, sinks and storage of river sediment in the Atlantic drainage of the United States: Journal of Geology, v. 90, p. 235–252.

MIXON, R. B., 1985, Stratigraphic and geomorphic framework of uppermost Cenozoic deposits in the southern Delmarva Peninsula, Virginia and Maryland: U.S. Geological Survey Professional Paper 1067-G, 53 p.

MORTON, R. A., AND DONALDSON, A. C., 1973, Sediment distribution and evolution of tidal deltas along a tide-dominated shoreline, Wachapreague, Virginia: Sedimentary Geology, v. 10, p. 285–299.

MOSLOW, T. F., 1980, Stratigraphy of mesotidal barrier islands: Unpublished Ph.D. Dissertation, University of South Carolina, Columbia, 187 p.

———, AND COLQUHOUN, D. J., 1981, Influence of sea level on barrier island evolution: Oceanis, v. 7, p. 439–454.

———, AND HERON, S. D., 1979, Quaternary evolution of Core Banks, North Carolina: Cape Lookout to New Drum Inlet, *in* Leatherman, S. P., ed., Barrier Islands from the Gulf of St. Lawrence to the Gulf of Mexico: Academic Press, New York, p. 211–236.

NEWMAN, W. S., AND MUNSART, C. A., 1968, Holocene geology of the Wachapreague lagoon, eastern shore peninsula, Virginia: Marine Geology, v. 6, p. 81–105.

OERTEL, G. F., 1975, Post-Pleistocene island and inlet adjustments along the Georgia coast: Journal of Sedimentary Petrology, v. 45, p. 150–159.

PIERCE, J. W., AND COLQUHOUN, D. J., 1970, Holocene evolution of a portion of the North Carolina coast: Geological Society of America Bulletin, v. 81, p. 3694–3714.

REINECK, H. E., 1972, Tidal flats, *in* Rigby, J. K., and Hamblin, W. L., eds., Recognition of Ancient Sedimentary Environments: Society of Economic Paleontologists and Mineralogists Special Publication 16, p. 146–159.

———, AND SINGH, I. B., 1980, Depositional Sedimentary Environments with Reference to Terrigenous Clastics: Springer-Verlag, Berlin, 549 p.

RICE, T. E., NIEDORODA, A. W., AND PRATT, A. P., 1976, The coastal processes and geology, Virginia barrier islands: The Virginia Coast Reserve Study, The Nature Conservancy, p. 108–382.

RUBY, C. H., 1981, Clastic facies and stratigraphy of a rapidly retreating cuspate foreland, Cape Romain, South Carolina: Unpublished Ph.D. Dissertation: University of South Carolina, Columbia, 218 p.

SUSMAN, K. R., AND HERON, S. D., 1979, Evolution of a barrier island, Shackleford Banks, Cateret County, North Carolina: Geological Society of America Bulletin, v. 90, p. 205–215.

SWIFT, D. J. P., 1975, Barrier island genesis: evidence from the central Atlantic shelf, eastern U.S.A.: Sedimentary Geology, v. 14, p. 1–43.

U.S. ARMY ENGINEER DISTRICT, NORFOLK, 1971, Detailed project report: Chincoteague Inlet, Accomack County, Virginia: U.S. Army Corps of Engineers (unpaginated).

WILKINSON, B. H., AND BASSE, R. A., 1978, Late Holocene history of the central Texas coast from Galveston Island to Pass Cavallo: Geological Society of America Bulletin, v. 89, p. 1592–1600.

EFFECTS OF SEA-LEVEL RISE ON DELTAIC SEDIMENTATION IN SOUTH-CENTRAL LOUISIANA

JOHN T. WELLS

Institute of Marine Sciences, University of North Carolina, Morehead City, North Carolina 28557

ABSTRACT: The birth of two new deltas in Atchafalaya Bay of south-central Louisiana has provided scientists with a unique opportunity to observe and measure processes of delta growth in their incipient stages. These regressive deposits, localized along a transgressive shoreline that is characterized by low-lying marsh and eroding barrier islands, have developed in a setting in which compactional subsidence accounts for approximately 90% of the relative rise in sea level. Unlike previous Holocene deltas of the Mississippi River and its distributaries, however, the deltas in Atchafalaya Bay may soon be growing under conditions of eustatic sea-level rise that is so rapid it will exceed rates of subsidence (1–2 cm/yr).

Extrapolation of delta growth under three sea-level rise scenarios (subsidence only, 1 cm/yr, and 2 cm/yr) indicates that as rates of eustatic sea-level rise approach or exceed rates of subsidence in south Louisiana, the subaerial deltas in Atchafalaya Bay will continue to grow but at slower rates. Even at the extreme rate of sea-level rise of 2 cm/yr, sediments will accumulate subaerially for another 80–100 yrs. Perhaps contrary to expectations, the slower a delta grows, because of rising sea level, the more likely it is to be limited by inefficiency of channels and an inability to deliver sediments to its distal areas than it is to be limited by receiving basin area. Thus, a decrease in subaerial growth rate is reflected by a decrease in delta size.

In addition to producing smaller deltas, high rates of sea-level rise will affect sedimentation processes by leading to thicker sand bodies and deposition of sands farther upstream. High-energy environments of deposition, such as natural levees which grow primarily during spring floods, will keep pace with sea-level rise. Low-energy environments of deposition, such as back bar algal flats, will remain or become subaqueous as waters rise faster than sediments are introduced. Furthermore, high rates of sea-level rise will delay the extension of deltaic sediments to the continental shelf. This, in turn, will slow the growth of downdrift mudflats to the west. Accelerated growth of downdrift sediments will occur when Atchafalaya Bay becomes sediment-filled (2035–2085 A.D.), thus allowing a greater volume of sediments to enter the dynamic shelf region seaward of the bay.

INTRODUCTION

The relative stability of sea level over the last 5,000–7,000 yrs has provided an opportunity for the coastal plain of Louisiana to prograde seaward from a series of overlapping delta lobes, each with a life span of approximately 1,000 yrs (Kolb and Van Lopik, 1966; Coleman, 1976). Now, for the first time in recorded history, the cycle of delta growth is being repeated with the birth of two new deltas in Atchafalaya Bay of south-central Louisiana and the rejuvenation of downdrift mudflats along the marginal deltaic plain to the west (Fig. 1). These latest regressive deposits are localized along a transgressive shoreline that is characterized by low-lying marsh and eroding barrier islands and by variable but high subsidence rates (as much as 1–2 cm/yr).

Most of our knowledge of processes and rates of delta growth in Louisiana has been acquired previously by examination of cores and from archeological data. This latest episode of deltaic sedimentation in Atchafalaya Bay is, therefore, of broad scientific interest, because it provides us with a unique opportunity to witness delta growth in its incipient stages and to observe and measure the important geological processes contemporaneously. The accumulation of sediments into deltaic sequences is also of practical significance, primarily because of its landbuilding potential. New delta lobes are capable of adding locally 200–300 km² of subaerial land in south-central Louisiana during the next 45 yrs (Wells and others, 1984) to a coastline that is presently losing an average of 75 km² of marsh surface and barrier island sands each year (Gagliano and others, 1981).

Predictions of delta growth and the manner in which sand bodies will evolve may be complicated by future fluctuations in sea level. Although compactional subsidence in Louisiana is high by world-wide standards and accounts for approximately 90% of the relative local sea-level rise

(Swanson and Thurlow, 1973; Penland and Boyd, 1982), the input of deltaic sediments until recently has been more than sufficient to maintain a balance; the modern birdfoot delta and each of its predecessors during the last 5,000–7,000 yrs has clearly been dominated by fluvial rather than marine processes. If predictions of future rates of eustatic sea-level rise (Barth and Titus, 1984) are accurate, however, then water depths in the shallow Atchafalaya Bay may double during the next century, almost certainly altering present rates of land growth, patterns of sediment accumulation, the thickness of sand bodies, and marginal deltaic processes to the west.

The purpose of this paper is to examine how a rapid rise in sea level will affect shoreline evolution (time scale 100 yrs) when the shoreline is a regressive delta. Two broad questions are addressed. First, can deltas, composed chiefly of fine-grained sediments yet building into shallow receiving basins, continue to grow when rates of sea-level rise are on the order of 1–2 cm/yr? Second, what sedimentologic and morphologic characteristics having good preservation potential might change as rates of sea-level rise approach rates of subsidence? These questions will be examined by: (1) showing how the Atchafalaya deltas have grown subaerially during their first 10 yrs, (2) determining how fast the deltas would have grown if sea level were rising at rates of 1 and 2 cm/yr, (3) projecting these rates into the middle of the next century, and (4) extrapolating from sedimentologic data provided by cores to determine how sediments will accumulate under future conditions of sea-level rise.

GROWTH OF THE ATCHAFALAYA RIVER DELTAS

Subaqueous Infill

Evolution of the modern Atchafalaya River and its deltas is an example of the periodic diversion and potential capture of main stream flow by a distributary. The process of

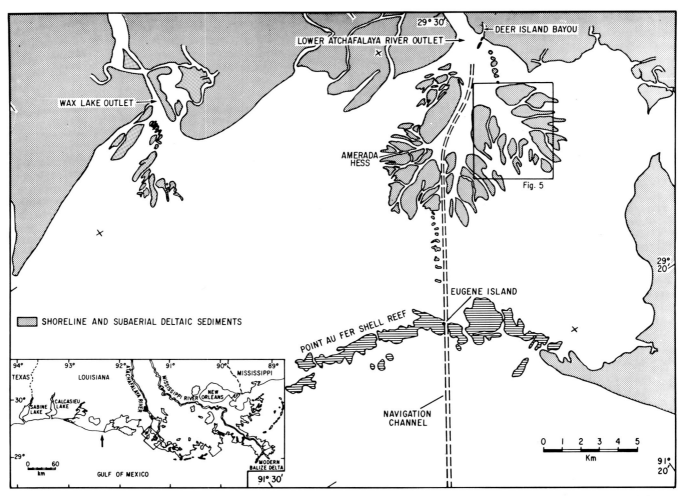

FIG. 1.—Index map to the Atchafalaya Bay of south-central Louisiana showing the Lower Atchafalaya River delta (eastern bay) and the Wax Lake delta (western bay). The arrow on the inset map shows the location of downdrift mudflats on the marginal deltaic plain (see Wells and Kemp, 1982).

channel switching or diversion in the Mississippi River is a natural one that, over the past 5,000–7,000 yrs, has resulted in the growth and deterioration of seven major delta complexes (Kolb and Van Lopik, 1966) that are sometimes further divided into 16 separate delta lobes (Frazier, 1967). Each major delta complex of the Mississippi River system remained as an active depositional site for approximately 1,000 yrs. When progradation reached the point at which gradient advantage was lost or when the river could no longer efficiently handle the water and sediment discharge, the delta commenced its abandonment stage and a new route to the sea was established by the river. The modern birdfoot delta, referred to as the Balize delta (Fig. 1, inset), has attempted during this century to relocate its site of deposition via a change in course to the Atchafalaya River, a route to the sea that is some 307 km shorter (Roberts and others, 1980).

During 400 of the last 800 yrs, a well defined sequence of events set the stage for future deltaic sedimentation in Atchafalaya Bay. According to Fisk (1952), the Atchafalaya River was a definite distributary of the Mississippi River by 1542, flowing through a broad interdistributary basin between an older course to the west (Teche) and the modern Lafourche course of the Mississippi River to the east (Fig. 1, inset). By 1940, sufficient flow had been diverted from the Mississippi River to allow a natural channel to become established. Aided by dredging, the volume of flow to the Atchafalaya River from the Mississippi River increased steadily from 13% in 1900 to nearly 30% in 1952 (Morgan and others, 1953). Until 1952, however, deltaic sedimentation was confined almost exclusively to the lakes and swamps of the Atchafalaya basin to the north.

The trapping of deltaic sediments in the Atchafalaya basin resulted in extensive lacustrine delta-fill deposits over a 50-yr period. Between 1917 and 1960, several large shallow lakes served as active traps for coarser sediments destined for Atchafalaya Bay and, by 1975, only small remnants of these lakes remained as open water (Roberts and others, 1980). The final approach to a sediment-filled state by the mid-1900s allowed prodelta clays to begin accumulating in Atchafalaya Bay. The decade 1952–1962 marked the beginning of a subaqueous delta at the mouth of the Lower Atchafalaya River Outlet.

By 1962, 0.3 m of fine-grained sediments covered 120 km² of the bay (Shlemon, 1975) in the area now shown as subaerial land in Figure 1. Although sedimentation at the Wax Lake Outlet, artificially opened in 1942, was small compared to that at the Lower Atchafalaya River Outlet, the Wax Lake Outlet carried a full 30% of the Atchafalaya River flow. Growing concern over possible abandonment of the Mississippi River in favor of the Atchafalaya River, predicted to occur by 1975 (Fisk, 1952), led to the completion of a control structure in 1963 at the Old River-Mississippi River juncture (31°00′ N). Diversion of Mississippi River flow down the Atchafalaya River was limited to approximately 30% of the combined flow from the Mississippi River and the Red River, a tributary to the Atchafalaya River course (Roberts and others, 1980).

A period of delta-front or distal-bar sedimentation (subaqueous delta deposits) occurred between 1962 and 1972, marked by the first introduction of silts and fine sands into the bay. An isopach map from Shlemon (1975) showed 285 km² of the bay covered by clay, silt, and fine-grained sand, as well as the first appearance of subaqueous distributary channels. The thickest accumulations of sediment were west of the Lower Atchafalaya River and Wax Lake outlets, reflecting partly the position of submarine spoil banks. By 1972, 1.8 m of fill had been deposited in the delta lobes of the Lower Atchafalaya River and Wax Lake outlets, and the submarine delta front had advanced to the Point au Fer shell reefs (van Heerden, 1980). The spring flood of 1973, one of the largest on record, produced the first natural land on both the east and the west sides of the Lower Atchafalaya River navigation channel. Thus, during a period of 20 yrs in which perhaps 90% of relative sea-level rise was a result of subsidence, the Atchafalaya Bay had shoaled in places from a depth of 2 m to the elevation of mean sea level.

Subaerial Growth Rates

The first step in predicting growth rates under conditions of rapidly rising sea level was to examine how the Lower Atchafalaya and Wax Lake deltas have grown under present conditions. Subaerial growth rates were determined for the period 1973–1983 by digitizing Band 7 Landsat imagery that was enlarged photographically to a scale of 1:50,000 (Fig. 2; see Wells and others, 1984 for details). Because the amount of exposed land in Atchafalaya Bay is highly dependent on water elevation (as affected by tide, river stage, barometric pressure, and wind speed and direction), it was necessary to obtain gauged water level at the time of each satellite overpass. In order to remove the effects of water elevation from actual variations in land area, a plot of the observed water elevation versus land area (Fig. 3) was made for each flood year (usually defined as April 1 through March 31). The amount of subaerial land was then determined from Figure 3 by constructing a non-linear least-squares fit to the data points for each flood year and extracting a value for subaerial land at the mean sea-level position (vertical lines).

Figure 4 shows the first 10 yrs of subaerial delta growth in Atchafalaya Bay. Each data point represents the amount of subaerial land above mean sea level for flood years as

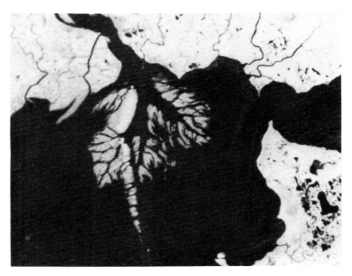

Fig. 2.—The Lower Atchafalaya River delta as shown by Landsat Band 7 image January 29, 1976.

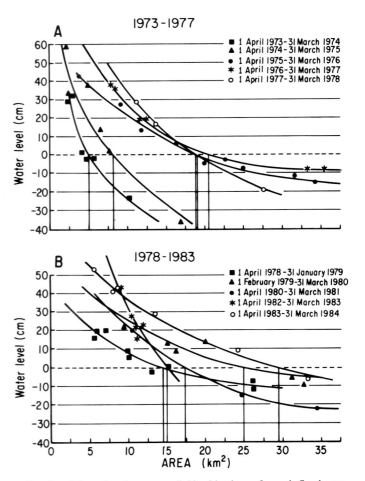

Fig. 3.—Water elevation versus digitized land area for each flood year, 1973–1983, in the Lower Atchafalaya River delta (Wax Lake delta not included). Subaerial land was determined from the non-linear least-squares best-fit curves at mean sea-level elevation.

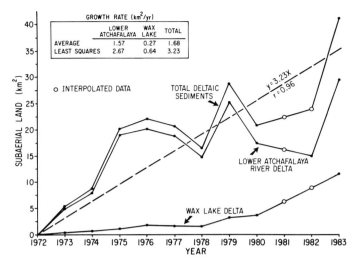

FIG. 4.—Growth curves for total subaerial land, the Lower Atchafalaya River delta, and the Wax Lake delta. Lack of sufficient clear-sky Landsat images required data points to be interpolated for 1981 and 1982.

defined in Figure 3. The pattern is clearly one of episodic growth. Major pulses of sedimentation during the first 4 yrs, during 1979, and again in 1983, can be correlated with major floods on the Mississippi and Atchafalaya rivers. In fact, three of these spring floods were among the largest on record this century (1973, 1979, 1983), Even superimposed on a recently determined relative rate of sea-level rise of approximately 0.5 cm/yr (Roberts and Wells, 1985), subaerial land is growing at 3.23 km^2/yr (using the least-squares fit) with several large, single-year pulses adding 10–15 km^2 of land per flood.

Dividing the curve for total deltaic sediments into its two components, the Wax Lake and Lower Atchafalaya River deltas, shows that progradation has been controlled by the Lower Atchafalaya River delta. The Wax Lake delta, however, increased its rate of growth in 1980 and by 1983 accounted for 30% of the total land, a value equal to the percentage of discharge carried through its outlet. The loss of subaerial land by the Lower Atchafalaya River delta during years of low spring floods has not resulted in an actual loss of sediments from the system. Rather, the passage of 10–25 cold fronts during the winter months has simply eroded and redistributed the subaerial sediments to the shallow subaqueous environment. Estimates of volume infill made from U.S. Army Corps of Engineers bathymetric and topographic survey sheets show that 140.1 × 10^{6}m^3 of sediment were deposited between 1967 and 1977 at an average rate of 14.0 × 10^{6}m^3/yr (Wells and others, 1984). These sediments, under conditions of relatively stable sea level, provide a base for future subaerial growth.

Patterns of Sedimentation

Aerial photographs and satellite images show that the deltas have grown by producing parabolic lobes of silt and fine sand that radiate out from a network of branching distributaries (Fig. 2). The delta lobes have evolved from shallow distributary-mouth bar sands, at one time mid-channel

shoals, that achieved an elevation above mean sea level during major floods. Since 1973, several levels of bifurcations have produced dozens of small, higher order distributaries.

The fundamental mechanism by which the deltas will continue to grow is by channel extension and channel bifurcation. Branching distributaries that are separated by complex delta lobes are characteristic of deltas that are frictionally dominated at the distributary mouths and are building into unstratified, low-energy, shallow-water environments (Welder, 1959; Wright, 1977). High rates of channel extension in these deltas require that the system be dominated by fluvial processes rather than marine processes. As channels extend into the bay, they are confined by their own natural levee deposits of silt and clay. With increasing channel length, slope of the energy gradient will decrease, and aggradation, splitting, or diversion of flow to new branches will be favored.

Channel extension leads to subaerial growth by two processes: (1) accretion of the subaqueous natural levees, and (2) formation of mid-channel bars, which grow vertically (Wells and others, 1984). Lateral and vertical growth of subaqueous natural levees not only adds new land to the delta lobes, but also reduces the cross-sectional area of channels (Fig. 5). This results in a tendency for channels to seal and lobes to fuse. The formation of mid-channel bars that grow laterally and vertically also reduces channel cross sections and forms bridges between adjacent delta lobes.

Figure 5 shows the pattern of growth between 1973 and 1983 in the most active part of the eastern half of the Lower Atchafalaya River delta. The processes of channel extension and lobe fusion are clearly shown. Through these processes, a large number of small delta lobes will coalesce to form a few much larger lobes. Of particular note is that during the major floods of 1979 and 1983, the delta lobes grew in upstream as well as downstream directions, thus sealing many of the smaller channels at their upstream ends. Van Heerden (1983) has suggested that upstream growth of delta lobes is the response of a mature delta and becomes dominant once bifurcation processes reach a peak.

As a generalization, progradation of the deltas in Atchafalaya Bay has led to deposition of sands over a base of silts and clays. The lowermost unit of prodelta clays is broadly continuous and has been shown to exhibit little textural variation (van Heerden and others, 1983). Overlying the prodelta facies is the coarsening-upward sequence of distal-bar sediments deposited from 1962 to 1972. Close to the distributary mouths, the distal-bar sediments become transitional to a shallower, sand-rich distributary-mouth bar facies, deposited rapidly as flow becomes unconfined at the seaward end of each distributary.

EFFECTS OF SEA-LEVEL RISE

Future Growth Rates

The Louisiana coast has entered a transgressive phase as a result of a combination of man-induced and natural causes (Craig and others, 1979; DeLaune and others, 1983; Wells and others, 1984). The Atchafalaya Bay and the eastern margin of the chenier plain are the only two segments of

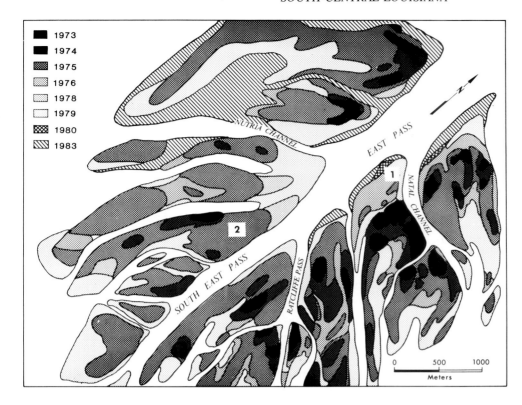

Legend:
- ■ 1973
- ■ 1974
- ▓ 1975
- ▒ 1976
- ░ 1978
- □ 1979
- ▨ 1980
- ◩ 1983

FIG. 5.—Progressive growth of delta lobes between 1973 and 1983 showing upstream and downstream extension, lobe fusion, and sealing of channels (figure modified from van Heerden, 1980). Numbers refer to locations of cores shown in Figures 8 and 9.

coast presently receiving sufficient sediments to offset the effects of subsidence and sea-level rise. Furthermore, recent estimates indicate that present rates of global eustatic sea-level rise of 10–20 cm/century (Barnett, 1984) could increase tenfold by the end of the next century (Barth and Titus, 1984). The effects of a sea-level rise of this magnitude, examined in the following paragraphs, require no assumptions about the accuracy of such predictions; rather, specific rates are applied as a means of looking at specific responses.

The three scenarios examined are a "subsidence only" generic model, which assumes no increase in rate of sea-level rise over present rates, a 1-cm/yr eustatic rise, and a 2-cm/yr eustatic rise. Projecting into the future involves two steps. First, an examination of how the deltas have grown under present conditions (Fig. 4) and second, a computation of how the deltas will grow in the future, based on life cycles of the Mississippi River subdeltas.* The generic model projections were made at 5-yr intervals, beginning in 1980, by taking the percentage of total growth expected, based on the shape of the growth curves of the four active Mississippi River subdeltas (Table 1, column 1). Then, by extrapolating from the amount of subaerial land in Atchafalaya Bay in the 1980 base year, the total amount of subaerial land was projected to future years through knowledge of what percent of growth had occurred by 1980 (see Wells and others, 1984). Using the two con-

trasting estimates for the amount of subaerial land given in Figure 4 (least squares and numerical average), a growth curve was constructed from each. The maximum amount of land in Atchafalaya Bay was achieved using the least-squares estimate for the 1980 base year; the minimum amount of land was produced using the 1980 average growth rate. Assuming the Mississippi River subdeltas to be a reasonable model, the total subaerial land at the peak of growth will be bracketed by the values 210 km^2 and 155 km^2 and will occur in the year 2035 (Fig. 6).

Growth curves under conditions of rising sea level were determined by computing the rates at which deltaic sediments would have grown subaerially from 1973–1983, if sea level had been rising at rates of 1 cm/yr and 2 cm/yr. These rates were determined from Figure 3 by finding the amount of subaerial land exposed after water levels were increased by 1 cm (or 2 cm) each year. Growth rates computed by the least-squares technique were lowered to 78.8% and 65.0% of their original rates for a sea-level rise of 1 cm/yr and 2 cm/yr, respectively; growth rates computed from numerical averaging decreased to 82.2% and 69.5% for the same 1-cm/yr and 2-cm/yr sea-level rise, respectively. The final step, extrapolation beyond the 1980 base year, was accomplished in the same manner as for the generic model approach; based on slower growth rates, the number of years to reach the percentage of total area (Table 1, column 1) was determined and the corresponding amount of land was computed.

Figure 6 shows the growth curves for the generic model, and 1- and 2-cm/yr sea-level rise scenarios. Three features are noteworthy. First, each growth curve reaches a peak and begins to deteriorate prior to the end of the next cen-

---
*The Mississippi River subdeltas were selected as a model because of their similarity to the deltas in Atchafalaya Bay and because of the excellent historical data base provided by maps and charts.

TABLE 1.—PREDICTED SUBAERIAL LAND FOR THREE GROWTH SCENARIOS

% Total Area	Generic Model		1 cm/yr		2 cm/yr	
	Upper Curve	Lower Curve	Upper Curve	Lower Curve	Upper Curve	Lower Curve
0	0	0	0	0	0	0
13.6	28.8 (8)	21.5 (8)	21.2 (10)	12.5 (10)	21.1 (12)	12.6 (12)
25.0	52.9 (13)	39.5 (13)	39.0 (16)	22.9 (16)	38.8 (20)	23.2 (19)
35.8	75.8 (18)	56.6 (18)	55.8 (23)	32.9 (22)	55.5 (28)	33.2 (26)
45.0	95.3 (23)	71.4 (23)	70.1 (29)	41.0 (28)	69.8 (35)	41.7 (33)
56.8	119.2 (28)	89.0 (28)	88.5 (35)	52.2 (34)	88.1 (43)	52.6 (40)
65.8	139.3 (33)	104.0 (33)	102.6 (42)	60.5 (40)	102.1 (51)	61.0 (48)
74.5	157.8 (38)	117.8 (38)	116.1 (48)	68.5 (46)	115.6 (58)	69.0 (55)
82.3	174.3 (43)	130.1 (43)	128.3 (54)	75.6 (52)	127.7 (66)	76.2 (62)
89.0	188.5 (48)	140.7 (48)	138.7 (60)	81.8 (58)	138.1 (74)	82.5 (69)
94.3	199.7 (53)	149.1 (53)	146.9 (67)	86.7 (64)	146.3 (81)	87.4 (76)
98.0	207.5 (58)	154.9 (58)	152.8 (73)	90.1 (70)	152.0 (89)	90.8 (84)
98.5	208.6 (63)	155.7 (63)	153.5 (79)	90.5 (76)	152.8 (96)	91.3 (91)
100.0	211.8 (66)	158.1 (66)	155.9 (83)	91.9 (80)	155.1 (101)	92.6 (95)
96.8	204.9 (68)	153.0 (68)	150.8 (86)	88.9 (83)	150.2 (105)	90.8 (98)
91.8	194.4 (73)	145.1 (73)	143.1 (93)	84.4 (89)	142.2 (112)	87.3 (105)
85.5	181.1 (78)	135.2 (78)	133.3 (99)	78.6 (95)	132.7 (120)	77.8 (112)

Note: column 1 refers to percent of subaerial land; columns 2–7 show amount of subaerial land in km² and number of years (in parenthesis) to reach that amount of land.

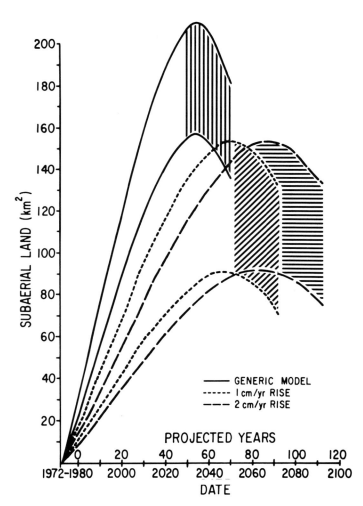

FIG. 6.—Growth-curve envelopes predicting the amount of subaerial land in Atchafalaya Bay for a "subsidence only" model and for eustatic sea-level rise of 1 cm/yr and 2 cm/yr.

tury. Second, the total amount of subaerial land is less under conditions of rapid sea-level rise than that given by the generic model. Third, an increase in rate of sea-level rise lengthens the amount of time needed to reach a peak in delta growth.

The filling of Atchafalaya Bay with deltaic sediments has an absolute subaerial limit theoretically controlled by the size of the bay. Subaerial land will emerge on the open shelf, however, and growth in Atchafalaya Bay will cease well before the bay reaches a sediment-filled condition. In fact, the Atchafalaya Bay will probably never reach a completely sediment-filled state, even without a rise in sea level, because of scour channels, very slow sedimentation in distal areas, reworking of sediment during the passage of cold fronts, subsidence, and most importantly, the selective natural sealing of the sediment delivery network.

Figure 6 shows that a rise in sea level will result in a smaller amount of subaerial land as revealed by a lower peak on the growth curves. This should be considered a reasonable consequence of rising sea level since shallow-water fluvially dominated deltas cease to grow when they develop too many small, inefficient, bifurcating distributaries, rather than when they reach a given size (Wells and others, 1984). In general, the longer and more slowly a delta grows, the more likely it is to reach a state of inefficiency with too many channels before reaching a size limited by receiving basin area. The fact that the 1- and 2-cm/yr rates of sea-level rise produce the same amount of subaerial land is not fortuitous but is a result of the computational technique utilized. Rescaling the generic model curve to represent longer periods of growth with a smaller amount of growth per unit time was undertaken such that the percent decrease in growth rates was equal to the percent increase in growth time. The rationale is that much of the sediment will be accumulating as subaqueous deposits. Perhaps the most important conclusion from Figure 6 is that, even at an extreme rate of sea-level rise of 2 cm/yr, subaerial land will continue to grow, albeit more slowly, for another 80–100 yrs.

Processes of Sedimentation

Figure 7 shows the extent, configuration, and date of maximum infilling for each set of growth curves in Figure 6. Construction of the hypothetical configuration of subaerial land was based on: (1) bathymetry of the bay to determine which areas were most likely and which were least likely to be filled, (2) patterns recognized in the previous 10 yrs of subaerial growth and 30 yrs of subaqueous growth, and (3) knowledge gained from historic maps and charts, discussed previously, that allowed application of the principles of channel extension, channel bifurcation, and lobe fusion.

The anticipated amount of land in Atchafalaya Bay could vary more than twofold, depending on which growth curve is followed. Regardless of rate of sea-level rise, however, the most important process of future subaerial growth will be fusing of small delta lobes into larger land masses, to-

gether with the sealing of distributary channels. As the bifurcation process continues, the small inefficient channels will no longer be able to deliver sediment to distal parts of the delta, and the sediment delivery network will be selectively eliminated. Because frictional resistance per unit volume of flow increases with decreasing channel size (Axelsson, 1967), much of the area shown in Figure 5 is already reminiscent of a system that is on the verge of deterioration. Closing of channels, the final step in the channel extension and bifurcation processes, effectively prevents nourishment of the delta except by overbank flooding at high river stage.

In addition to producing smaller subaerial deltas, high rates of sea-level rise will affect sedimentation processes by leading to thicker sand bodies and deposition of sands farther upstream. With open-water depths of only 1–2 m, the volume of water in Atchafalaya Bay could double within 100 yrs, and much of the sediment entering the system could be deposited subaqueously over what is now subaerial land. The result of this additional 1–2 m of water would be to allow sand bodies, which are typically 1–2 m thick, to double in thickness by the end of the next century. Because of

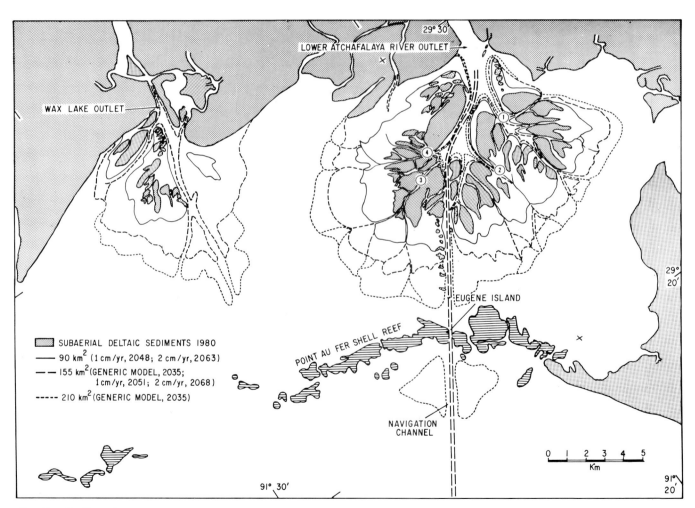

Fig. 7.—Configuration and extent of subaerial land in Atchafalaya Bay for the growth-rate scenarios given in Figure 6. Numbers enclosed by circles in the Lower Atchafalaya River delta indicate locations of major channels that will remain open at the peak of delta development; the remainder of the channel system will be sealed by levee extension and fusing of delta lobes.

rapid subsidence rates, preservation potential should be excellent. In fact, after 50–100 yrs of deterioration that will begin in the latter part of the next century, conditions in the bay could again be favorable for renewed deltaic sedimentation.

A detailed examination of hydrographic regime and sediment flux in the Atchafalaya Bay and basin (Roberts and others, 1980) has revealed a change in sediment entering the bay during the last 20 yrs from silt and clay to silt and fine sand. These coarse sediments, typically referred to as distributary-mouth bar sands, are deposited initially as subaqueous bars and mid-channel shoals at points where flow becomes unconfined, spreads, and loses velocity. Increasing water depths from sea-level rise will cause these depositional sites to move farther upstream as gradients become smaller. The natural upstream growth of delta lobes, observed by van Heerden (1983) after only 5 yrs of subaerial growth, should then accelerate. This, in turn, will force even faster sealing of channels and fusing of delta lobes; the end result will be a delta that has a lower growth-curve peak and begins undergoing deterioration with less subaerial land than its "subsidence only" counterpart (Fig. 6).

Vertical accumulation.—

Natural levee deposits form the single most significant stratigraphic unit in Atchafalaya Bay, accounting for approximately 40% of the total sedimentary sequence (van Heerden, 1983). Deposited primarily during flood stage and achieving elevations equal to those of the flood waters, subaqueous levees should easily be able to grow vertically at rates equal to rates of sea-level rise. Figure 8 shows radiographs of subaqueous levee sediments, deposited during floods between 1975 and 1981, and a typical section of a levee core as it might appear by the year 2050. Assuming a eustatic sea-level rise of 1.5 cm/yr, the total section will increase by 1.30 m over 70 yrs (1.5 cm/yr sea-level rise and 0.35 cm/yr subsidence). Silts and fine sands, deposited rapidly under high-energy conditions, will display cross laminations, climbing ripples, and scour surfaces. Although rate of deposition may average 1.85 cm/yr, thus keeping pace with subsidence and sea-level rise, the sedimentary sequence that will accumulate by the year 2050 may represent deposition only 5–10 major floods.

In contrast, the lower energy environments, such as back bar algal flats that form the interiors of delta lobes, will not keep pace with sea-level rise and subsidence. Shown in Figure 9 growing verticallly at an average rate of 1.0 cm/ yr, these environments would be covered by 0.5 m of water by the year 2050. Generally, algal flats are highly organic and consist of parallel-laminated silts and clays deposited in a more regular fashion than levee sediments. Whereas sand may enter locally from levee overtopping or from small feeder channels, these sediments are subject to scour from waves during passage of winter cold fronts. As algal flat environments are inundated by rising sea level, waves and storm currents will disperse and mix their sediments within the surrounding subaqueous environments.

Downdrift sedimentation.—

Sediment derived from the Atchafalaya Bay began forming ephemeral mudflats along the eastern margin of the

chenier plain (Fig. 1) in the late 1940s and early 1950s (Morgan and others, 1953). This new pulse of sediment, 80 km to the west, coincided with Atchafalaya basin infilling, which allowed more sediment to reach the coast and become entrained in the transport system of the Atchafalaya mudstream. Enlarging and spreading to the west, these downdrift mudflats presently form a 1–2 m thick prograding substrate for marsh grasses along 50 km of coast (Wells and Kemp, 1981, 1982).

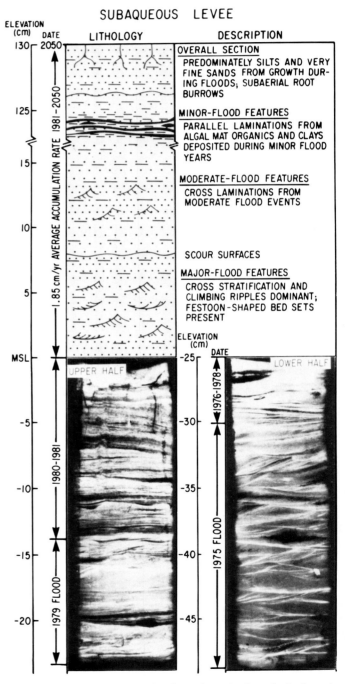

Fig. 8.—Subaqueous levee X-radiographs and a hypothesized stratigraphic column proposed for a eustatic sea-level rise of 1.5 cm/yr (location of core given in Fig. 5).

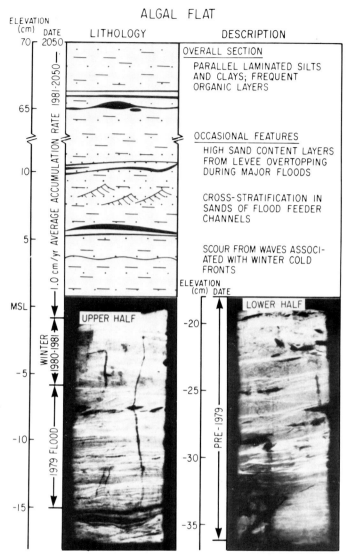

ALGAL FLAT

FIG. 9.—Back bar algal flat X-radiographs and a hypothesized stratigraphic column proposed for a eustatic sea-level rise of 1.5 cm/yr (location of core given in Fig. 5).

Rising sea level will slow delivery of sediment to the coast by trapping a greater percentage of sediment in Atchafalaya Bay. The slower growth rates shown in Figure 6 also translate into a short-term loss of sediment to the coast because of the extra time required for the growth curve to reach a peak. Filling of Atchafalaya Bay will take an additional 15–30 yrs when sea level is rising at rates of 1–2 cm/yr than when it is stable. Once the bay has reached a sediment-filled state, however, a greater volume of sediment will be transported directly to the shelf, and land in the bay will begin deteriorating as more of the sediments are passed through the system. Part of this additional sediment that reaches the shelf will be carried to the west, accelerating growth of the downdrift mudflats on the chenier plain. The time scale for accelerated chenier plain growth, dependent on rate of sea-level rise, is on the order of 50–100 yrs.

CONCLUSIONS

(1) As rates of eustatic sea-level rise approach or exceed rates of subsidence in south Louisiana, the subaerial deltas in Atchafalaya Bay will continue to grow, but at slower rates. Even at the extreme rate of sea-level rise of 2 cm/yr, sediments will accumulate subaerially for another 80–100 yrs.

(2) A decrease in subaerial growth rate is reflected by a decrease in delta size. Contrary to expectations, the more slowly a delta grows (because of a rise in sea level), the more likely it is to be limited by inefficiency of channels and an inability to deliver sediments to its distal areas than it is to be limited by receiving basin area.

(3) Rising sea level will lead to thicker sand deposits as water depths increase in the bay. An additional 1–2 m of water will allow sand bodies to double in thickness by the end of the next century. Preservation potential should be excellent because of continued high subsidence rates.

(4) Upstream growth of delta lobes will be enhanced by sea-level rise as the decrease in gradient causes the depositional sites for sands to move farther upstream. This will lead to faster sealing of channels, fusing of delta lobes, and thus a smaller subaerial delta.

(5) High-energy environments of deposition, such as natural levees which grow primarily during spring floods, will keep pace with sea-level rise. Low-energy environments of deposition, such as back bar algal flats, will remain or become subaqueous as waters rise faster than sediments are introduced.

(6) Increased rates of sea-level rise will delay the extension of deltaic sediments to the continental shelf. This, in turn, will slow the growth of downdrift mudflats to the west. Accelerated growth of downdrift sediments will occur when Atchafalaya Bay becomes sediment-filled, thus allowing a greater volume of sediments to enter the dynamic shelf region seaward of the bay.

ACKNOWLEDGMENTS

This research was funded by the U.S. Army Corps of Engineers Waterways Experiment Station in Vicksburg, Mississippi and the Louisiana Sea Grant College Program, a division of the National Sea Grant College Program. Data from Landsat images for 1981–1983 were provided by L. J. Rouse. Valuable assistance in preparing the figures for the manuscript was provided by V. Page and H. Page.

REFERENCES

AXELSSON, V., 1967, The Laiture delta: a study of deltaic morphology and processes: Geografiska Annaler, v. 49, p. 3–27.

BARNETT, T. P., 1984, The estimation of "global" sea level change: a problem of uniqueness: Journal of Geophysical Research, v. 89, p. 7980–7988.

BARTH, M. C., AND TITUS, J. G., 1984, Greenhouse effect and sea level rise: Van Nostrand Reinhold, New York, 384 p.

COLEMAN, J. M., 1976, Deltas: processes of deposition and models for exploration: International Human Resources Development Commission Publications, Boston, 102 p.

CRAIG, N. J., TURNER, R. E., AND DAY, J. W., JR., 1979, Land loss in coastal Louisiana (U.S.A.): Environmental Management, v. 3, p. 133–144.

DELAUNE, R. D., BAUMANN, R. H., AND GOSSELINK, J. G., 1983, Relationships among vertical accretion, coastal submergence, and erosion in a Louisiana Gulf coast marsh: Journal of Sedimentary Petrology, v. 53, p. 147–157.

FISK, H. N., 1952, Geological investigation of the Atchafalaya basin and the problem of Mississippi River diversion: U.S. Army Corps of Engineers, Mississippi River Commission, v. 1, 145 p.

FRAZIER, D. E., 1967, Recent deltaic deposits of the Mississippi River: their development and chronology: Gulf Coast Association of Geological Societies Transactions, v. 17, p. 287–315.

GAGLIANO, S. M., MEYER-ARENDT, K. J., AND WICKER, K. M., 1981, Land loss in the Mississippi River deltaic plain: Gulf Coast Association of Geological Societies Transactions, v. 31, p. 295–300.

KOLB, C. R., AND VAN LOPIK, J. R., 1966, Depositional environments of the Mississippi River deltaic plain, southeastern Louisiana, *in* Shirley, M. L., and Ragsdale, J. A., eds., Deltas: Houston Geological Society, Texas, p. 17–62.

MORGAN, J. P., VAN LOPIK, J. R., AND NICHOLS, L. G., 1953, Occurrence and development of mudflats along the western Louisiana coast: Coastal Studies Institute, Technical Report no. 2, Louisiana State University, Baton Rouge, 34 p.

PENLAND, S., AND BOYD, R., 1982, Assessment of geological and human factors responsible for Louisiana coastal barrier erosion, *in* Boesch, D. F., ed., Proceedings of the Conference on Coastal Erosion and Wetland Modification in Louisiana: Causes, Consequences, and Options: U.S. Fish and Wildlife Service, Report FWS/OBS-82/59, p. 14–38.

ROBERTS, H. H., ADAMS, R. D., AND CUNNINGHAM, R. H. W., 1980, Evolution of sand-dominant subaerial phase, Atchafalaya delta: American Association of Petroleum Geologists Bulletin, v. 64, p. 264–279.

———, AND WELLS, J. T., 1985, A study of sedimentation and subsidence in the south-central coastal plain of Louisiana: Summary Draft Report to U.S. Army Corps of Engineers, New Orleans District, 33 p.

SHLEMON, R. J., 1975, Subaqueous delta formation—Atchafalaya Bay, Louisiana, *in* Broussard, M. L., ed., Deltas: Models for Exploration: Houston Geological Society, Texas, p. 209–221.

SWANSON, R. L., AND THURLOW, C. I., 1973, Recent subsidence rates along the Texas and Louisiana coasts as determined from tide measurements: Journal of Geophysical Research, v. 78, p. 2665–2671.

VAN HEERDEN, I. Ll., 1980, Sedimentary responses during flood and nonflood conditions, new Atchafalaya delta, Louisiana: Unpublished M.S. Thesis, Louisiana State University, Baton Rouge, 76 p.

———, 1983, Deltaic sedimentation in eastern Atchafalaya Bay, Louisiana: Unpublished Ph.D. Dissertation, Louisiana State University, Baton Rouge, 151 p.

———, WELLS, J. T., AND ROBERTS, H. H., 1983, River-dominated suspended-sediment deposition in a new Mississippi delta: Canadian Journal of Fisheries and Aquatic Sciences, Supplement no. 1, v. 40, p. 60–71.

WELDER, F. A., 1959, Processes of deltaic sedimentation in the lower Mississippi River: Coastal Studies Institute, Technical Report No. 12, Louisiana State University, Baton Rouge, 90 p.

WELLS, J. T., AND KEMP, G. P., 1981, Atchafalaya mud stream and recent mudflat progradation: Louisiana chenier plain: Gulf Coast Association of Geological Societies Transactions, v. 31, p. 409–416.

———, AND ———, 1982, Mudflat and marsh progradation along Louisiana's chenier plain: a natural reversal in coastal erosion, *in* Boesch, D. F., ed., Proceedings of the Conference on Coastal Erosion and Wetland Modification in Louisiana: Causes, Consequences, and Options: U.S. Fish and Wildlife Service, Report FWS/OBS-82/59, p. 39–51.

———, CHINBURG, S. J., AND COLEMAN, J. M., 1984, The Atchafalaya River delta: generic analysis of delta development: U.S. Army Corps of Engineers, Technical Report HL-82-15, Vicksburg, Mississippi, 89 p.

WRIGHT, L. D., 1977, Sediment transport and deposition at river mouths: a synthesis: Geological Society of America Bulletin, v. 88, p. 857–868.

SEA-LEVEL CHANGE AND THE PRESERVATION POTENTIAL OF WAVE-DOMINATED AND TIDE-DOMINATED COASTAL SEQUENCES

RICHARD A. DAVIS, JR.
Department of Geology, University of South Florida, Tampa, Florida 33620
AND
H. EDWARD CLIFTON
U.S. Geological Survey, 345 Middlefield Road, Menlo Park, California 94025

ABSTRACT: The relative change in sea level and the rate of sediment input determine the character and the preservation potential of most coastal sequences, although wave and tidal energy, and geomorphic and geologic setting must also be considered. Progradational (regressive) coastal deposits are more likely to be fully preserved than those of transgressive coasts. Modern progradational coasts include numerous wave-dominated examples, (e.g., the Nayarit coast of Mexico, the Georgia Bight, and the Washington coast near the mouth of the Columbia River), and a few tide-dominated examples (e.g., the German Bight). In either situation, fairly complete shallowing-upward sequences of subtidal to supratidal facies are preserved, because the sedimentation rate exceeds dispersal by wave and/or tidal energy and the effect of rising or falling sea level.

Transgressive sequences, which form where relative sea-level rise exceeds net sediment accumulation, differ in degree of preservation. Wave-dominated transgressive systems include the present coast of Delaware and the outer banks of North Carolina. The Colorado River delta in the Gulf of California represents a tide-dominated transgressive coast. Under wave-dominated conditions, slow transgression with abundant sediment input and moderate or low-incident energy will allow much of the sequence to be preserved. A transgressive tide-dominated coast that is associated with low sediment influx from land is characterized by shoreward transport of subtidal sediment over the pre-existing facies. Present coastal conditions also produce geographically juxtaposed progradational and transgressive sequences, as on drumstick barriers. Such situations would generate a complicated stratigraphic record.

INTRODUCTION

Changes in sea level typically have a profound effect on coastal sedimentary environments. The influence of the Holocene transgression is readily apparent, and there is every reason to assume that periods of falling sea level would also impact on the coastal zone. Similar changes in sea level undeniably have left their mark on the stratigraphic record throughout geologic time.

From a stratigraphic standpoint, it is difficult to separate the effects of world-wide (eustatic) change in sea level from the local (regional) changes in the elevation of the land due to tectonism or to compaction of the sediment column. The focus here is on the relative change in sea level as defined by Curray (1964). Coastal deposits are most likely to be preserved within a subsiding basin, and a thick succession of coastal sediment implies that subsidence was a factor during accumulation. The average rate of subsidence, however, may be less than the rate of short-term fluctuations of relative sea level that determine both the character of the coastal sediment at a point in time and the nature of preservation within a limited amount of time. The thrust of this paper is on the consequence of these shorter term changes in sea level.

This discussion will center on the broad relationships that exist between the direction and rate of sea-level change, the available sediment supply, the dominant coastal processes, and the eventual preservation of the stratigraphic record of these coastal sequences. A general process-response model which incorporates these variables serves as the basis for estimating the effect of sea-level rise on the relative preservation potential. Specific examples are used to demonstrate various scenarios of the model.

General aspects of coastal stratigraphic sequences.—

There are three basic styles of coastal stratigraphic sequences that may accumulate over time and eventually become preserved in the stratigraphic record: (1) transgressive sequences, where sediments deposited in relatively shallow nearshore environments are progressively overlain by sediments of relatively deep, offshore environments (Fig. 1A); (2) progradational sequences, where relatively deep, offshore sediments are progressively overlain by shallower, nearshore sediments (Fig. 1B); and (3) aggradational sequences, where sediments in various environments accumulate in vertical fashion without significant spatial migration with time (Fig. 1C).

Transgressive sequences (Fig. 1A) involve the landward migration of the shoreline that typically occurs as the result of sea-level rise, but which might also occur during falling seal level if sediment supply was minimal and coastal processes were imparting high energy to the shore. During the present sea-level rise, many barrier complexes of the Atlantic and Gulf coasts are experiencing transgression.

Progradational coastal sequences (Fig. 1B) are most common during falling sea level, but they may also occur during stable or even rising sea level if sediment supply is sufficient. Such is the case presently along numerous locations of the Atlantic and Gulf coasts. The existence of transgressive and progradational sequences during the present sea-level rise demonstrates the important roles played by both sediment supply and level of wave and tide energy imparted to the coast.

The development of a truly aggradational coastal sequence (Fig. 1C) requires unlikely maintenance of a near-perfect balance between sediment supply, sea-level position and incident energy along the coast. Because of this, such coastal sequences are rare in both space and time.

Holocene sea level.—

In order to formulate a useful model of coastal sequences, which has widespread application to the rock record, it is necessary to use the recent past as the basis for

TRANSGRESSIVE

PROGRADATIONAL

AGGRADATIONAL

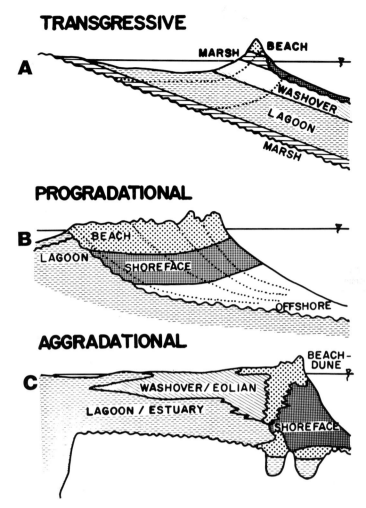

FIG. 1.—Generalized cross section showing stratigraphic relationships produced by transgression, progradation and aggradation (from Galloway and Hobday, 1983).

this model. The details of sea-level position relative to the present during the Holocene transgression are a subject of much disagreement. These points will not be debated here; however, the general patterns of sea-level change will be considered.

Regardless of when the Holocene transgression began relative to present (Curray and others, 1969), most authors agree that there was a noticeable and important decrease in the rate of sea-level rise about 7.0 ka. Another change apparently took place about 3.0–4.0 ka, but there is much disagreement about what has happened since that time. Opinions center around three possibilities: (1) sea level reached essentially its present position at that time and has been rather stable since then, (2) sea level has been fluctuating above and below its present position since then, or (3) sea-level rise slowed markedly at 3.0–4.0 ka but has steadily risen since then (Scholl and Stuiver, 1967). The latter scenario will be incorporated into the model developed here. Data from tide gauges around the world show

that at most locations sea level is rising (Hicks, 1981); however, the rate varies widely.

The rate of sea-level rise is quite important in determining the preservation of coastal stratigraphic sequences. Without varying any parameters other than sea level, it is possible to show this relationship (Kraft, 1971; Kraft and Chrzastowski, 1985). A rapid sea-level rise may result in preservation of the entire sequence (Fig. 2). As the rate of sea-level rise slows, the preservation diminishes to essentially nothing unless sediment input increases.

CONCEPTUAL MODEL

The major factors in the development and preservation of coastal sequences include changes in sea level, sediment accumulation and erosion, and the wave and tidal processes that act upon the coast. The first step in constructing a model for these sequences is to depict the spatial parameters graphically. Sea level serves as a horizontal reference datum with changes shown normal to that surface as rise or fall occurs (Fig. 3). The regional slope of the coastal area is indicated as a straight line at some acute angle with sea level. Sediment accumulation or erosion takes place in directions normal to this regional slope or land surface.

The model shown in Figure 3 is based on the same parameters, rate of relative sea-level change and rate of net deposition, used by Curray (1964) to delineate the conditions responsible for transgressions and regressions. The model presented here differs from Curray's model primarily by setting these parameters in a spatial framework that depicts a shore-normal section across a coastline and allows for visual representation of the actual nature of the shoreline changes.

By superimposing shoreline dynamics on this framework model, it is possible to assess the probability of each scenario. Below the regional slope, only erosion occurs, and the coastal depositional record is likely to be poorly, if at all, developed (Fig. 4). Above the regional slope, sedimentation occurs during retreating, stable and prograding shoreline conditions. Of these, the stable shoreline is unlikely, whereas the other two situations are common (Fig. 4).

Wave and tidal processes are more difficult to depict graphically, especially for a barrier coast. Such a complex coastal system may be wave-dominated or a combination of wave- and tide-dominated on the open-water side. The landward side of the barrier is typically tide-dominated, but extensive bays in microtidal settings may also be wave-dominated or at least be a combination of both (e.g., Pamlico Sound in North Carolina).

A reasonable approach to depicting these variables on the conceptual model (Fig. 3) is to consider one end of the regional slope as tide-dominated and the other as wave-dominated. The intersection of the regional slope with the sedimentation-erosion axis represents a balance between wave and tide domination. For purposes of the graphic conceptual model, a barrier coast will be considered as wave-dominated and a non-barrier, depositional coast will be tide-dominated. These considerations are for depositional coasts only.

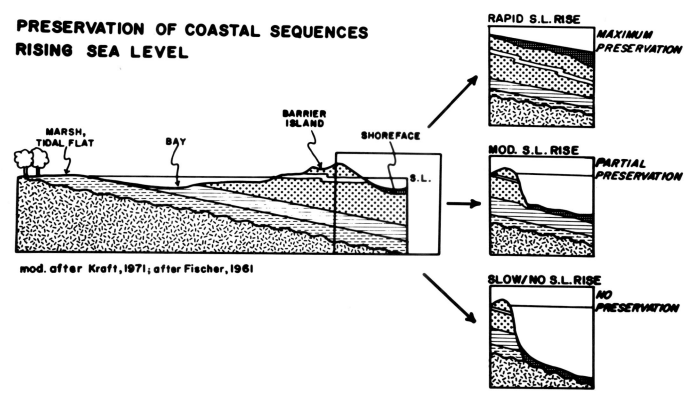

FIG. 2.—Preservation of coastal stratigraphic sequences during rising sea level (from Kraft, 1971; after Fischer, 1961).

At a given location, the combination of rate of sea-level change, sediment availability and gradient, and configuration of the coastal zone will determine the dominant coastal process and the resultant sediment body accumulations.

Some example scenarios can be used to illustrate this point. A high-relief coast with a steep inner shelf and a rapid rate of sea-level rise will result in an erosional situation. A coastal plain setting with a gently sloping inner shelf will produce a tide-dominated situation during a rapid sea-level rise due to the expected large number of estuaries developed, and as the rate of rise slows markedly or stops, then wave-dominated conditions would be expected to prevail and barrier conditions developed. Tide-dominated conditions can persist regardless of sea-level rates if tidal range is great and the shoreface gradient is low.

Summary of the conceptual model.—

Wave-dominated deposits occur throughout the coast and adjacent seaward areas. The deposits tend to be relatively more common away from the shoreline with maximum accumulation in the inner shoreface beyond the surf zone. The rate of accumulation diminishes seaward as the influence of waves on the sea floor lessens. By contrast, tide-dominated sedimentation is greatest at or near the shoreline and diminishes across the entire coastal and shoreface zones. The combination of these types of preserved sediment accumulations can be graphically shown on the conceptual model (Fig. 3). Only the relative widths of the prisms have significance.

It is appropriate to consider hypothetical examples to understand the conceptual model better. A very rapid rate of sea-level rise will result in preservation, as shown along the rise-sedimentation axes (Fig. 3). Note that in real-world situations, these axes are nearly coincidental due to the extremely gentle gradient of the regional slope. This rapid sea-level rise will result in thick sequences of wave-dom-

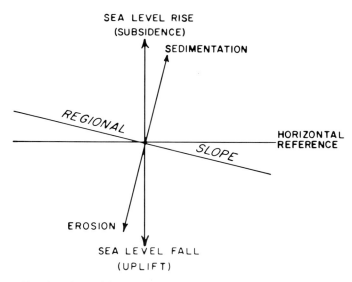

FIG. 3.—General framework for conceptual model of development of coastal sequences.

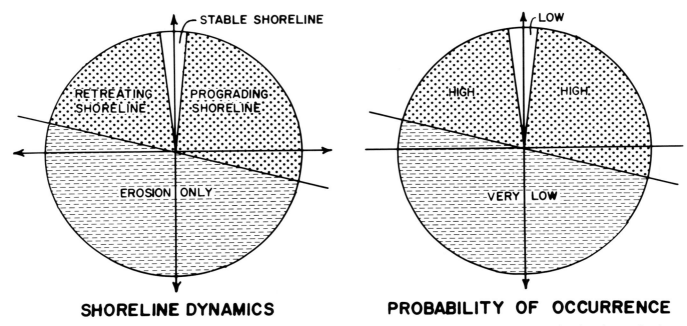

FIG. 4.—Conceptual model of shoreline dynamics and probability of occurrence for various coastal scenarios under changing sea level.

inated deposits and moderately thick tide-dominated sequences.

Very slow sea-level rise will result in thin or partially preserved sequences that will be primarily tide-dominated. Wave-dominated deposits are overwhelmed by tide-dominated deposits near the shoreline and neither are thick in the outer shoreface. The result is that with no increase in sediment availability, slow sea-level rise will result in little being preserved and that which is preserved will be primarily of a tide-dominated nature.

The rate of shoreline change depends partly on the angle of the regional slope; a steep slope will experience a slower rate of change in shoreline position than will a more gentle slope under the same conditions of sediment input and relative change in sea level. Although this model shows the slope to be uniform, a break in slope commonly occurs at the shoreline. If the offshore part of the profile is sufficiently steep, as would occur when a lowered sea level placed the shoreline at the shelf-slope break, other processes such as sediment-gravity flow may become important in removing sediment and inhibiting further progradation.

HOLOCENE EXAMPLES

One of the best ways to demonstrate the utility of the previously discussed conceptual model is to consider various examples from the stratigraphic record. Modern techniques of coring and subbottom profiling provide good stratigraphic data on Holocene sequences which can be used as such examples.

This can be summarized graphically on the framework of the conceptual model (Fig. 3) by breaking it into two parts, one to consider whether the conditions are wave- or tide-dominated along with the general rate of sedimentation, and the other to consider the displacement of the shoreline relative to the present. The latter is related to preservation potential in that rapid sea-level rise is conducive to high preservation potential and vice versa.

Four points in time are used as representative of important sea-level situations during the Holocene. The very rapid rise of the early Holocene until about 7.0 ka is represented by 12.0 ka, the more recent slow rate in sea-level rise is represented by 6.0 ka, and the present is also shown for each example. In addition, an estimate of conditions for 6,000 yrs after the present is also included. It is based on a modest increase in the rate of rise such as has been occurring during the past few decades.

Costa de Nayarit, Mexico.—

Just south of Maztalan on the west coast of Mexico is an extensive strandplain system of barriers and lagoons. Good stratigraphic and radiometric control makes this a prime example for applying the model. Holocene history is provided by Curray (1964) and Curray and others (1969).

Rapid transgression occurred from about 18.0 ka until 7.0 ka with sea level rising to about −8 m. Peats at −7 m are radiocarbon-dated at 7.0 ± 0.5 ka (Curray and others, 1969). Extensive lagoon and marsh deposits dominate the lower and landward portion of a stratigraphic section across the region (Fig. 5). The wave-dominated part of the deposit (the shoreface of the barriers that must have existed to allow the lagoons and marshes to develop) clearly had a lower potential for preservation during the transgression. The preservation of this part of the sequence began with the progradation that started at 4.75–3.60 ka at various locations along the coast.

Subsequent slowing of sea-level rise and the combination of reworking of previous sediments and addition of fluvial sediment led to a wave-dominated, progradational beach-ridge complex which has continued to the present (Fig. 5).

PROGRADING, WAVE DOMINATED COAST

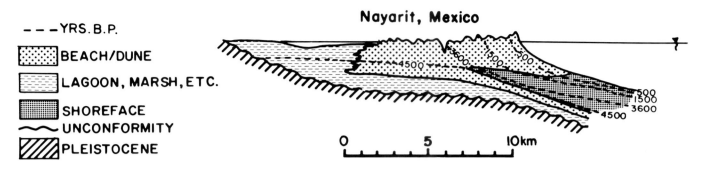

- - - YRS. B.P.

▨ BEACH/DUNE

▨ LAGOON, MARSH, ETC.

▨ SHOREFACE

〜 UNCONFORMITY

▨ PLEISTOCENE

Nayarit, Mexico

0   5   10km

FIG. 5.—General stratigraphic cross section of the Nayarit coast, Mexico, a presently prograding, wave-dominated coast (from Curray and others, 1969).

This dramatic shift from tide-dominated to wave-dominated sediment accumulation took place over a rather short period of time (Fig. 6) and is largely due to the slowing of sea-level rise. This caused the coast to return to a wave-dominated situation which will continue in the future. Seaward progradation during slowly increasing sea level is likely to be maintained unless the rate of sea-level rise increases greatly.

German Bight.—

The coast of the North Sea, which includes Denmark, West Germany and the Netherlands from northeast to southwest, is referred to as the German Bight. This is a high-energy coast with a trend of increasing tidal range and dominance toward the elbow of the coast near the mouths

of the Weser and Elbe rivers. In these areas of the West German coast, spring tidal fluctuations are in the macrotidal range and barrier islands are absent. Intertidal flats are extensive, as are subtidal, tide-dominated sediment bodies (Fig. 7).

Although stratigraphic data are limited, all indications point to a tide-dominated situation along this coast throughout the latter part of the Holocene transgression. Marsh peats along with tidal flat and estuarine muds dominate the basal Holocene units at most places (Fig. 8). Some locations contain laminated and cross-stratified shoreface sands which show significant wave influence (van Straaten, 1964; Reineck and Singh, 1980).

The sea-level curve for the adjacent Netherlands coast is similar to many of those developed for North America. There is a distinct slowing of the rise between 8.0 and 6.0 ka

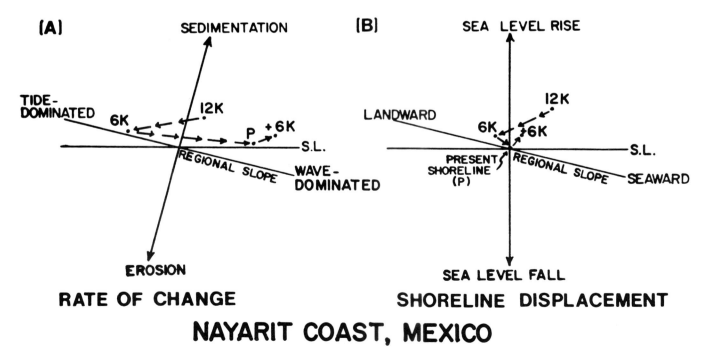

(A)

SEDIMENTATION

TIDE-DOMINATED

6K

12K

P +6K

S.L.

REGIONAL SLOPE

WAVE-DOMINATED

EROSION

RATE OF CHANGE

(B)

SEA LEVEL RISE

LANDWARD

12K

6K   6K

PRESENT SHORELINE (P)

REGIONAL SLOPE

S.L.

SEAWARD

SEA LEVEL FALL

SHORELINE DISPLACEMENT

NAYARIT COAST, MEXICO

FIG. 6.—Changes in (A) dominant conditions and (B) shoreline displacement on the Nayarit coast over the past 12,000 yrs.

PROGRADING TIDE-DOMINATED COAST

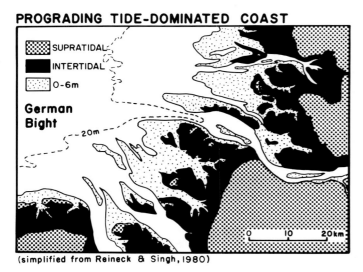

(simplified from Reineck & Singh, 1980)

FIG. 7.—Map of the coastal zone in the German Bight, a presently prograding tide-dominated coast (from Reineck and Singh, 1980).

(Jelgersma, 1961). At about 6.0 ka sea level in this area was near −7 m. This is about the time that the transgression reached the area of the present coast of the German Bight. Sediment began accumulating in a tide-dominated mode and has continued in that fashion since that time (Fig. 9). Prograding tidal flats and other tide-dominated sediment accumulations have characterized this area during the late Holocene sea-level rise, except perhaps for a period associated with the slowdown of sea-level rise as characterized by the 6.0 ka data. They will most likely continue to accumulate in the future (Fig. 9). The preservation potential of these tide-dominated deposits is quite high under such circumstances.

Washington coast, U.S.A.—

The northwestern coast of the United States can generally be considered a storm- or wave-dominated coast with a relatively high tidal range (3–4 m). There is, however, considerable variety in the distribution of the dominant physical processes along this reach of coast. This discussion will

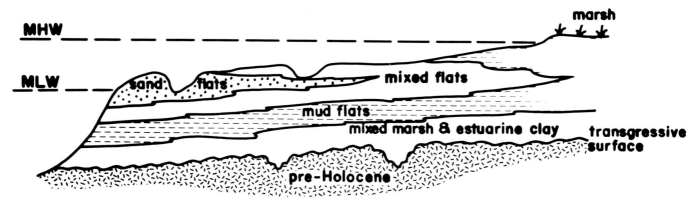

FIG. 8.—Stratigraphic cross section of the German Bight region (modified from Reineck, 1970).

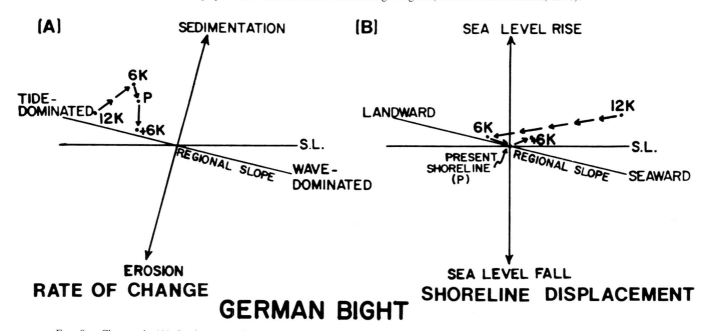

FIG. 9.—Changes in (A) dominant conditions and (B) shoreline displacement along the German Bight over the past 12,000 yrs.

focus on the area near Willapa Bay, Washington, where one of us (HEC) has conducted numerous studies over the past several years. This embayment is partially enclosed by a barrier spit which emanates from Tertiary headlands to the south (Fig. 10). The barrier spit and the non-barrier coast immediately to the north of Willapa Bay are presently wave-dominated portions of the coast. The inlet to Willapa Bay (Fig. 10) is characterized by a significantly protruding ebb delta incised by tidal channels. This portion of the coast is presently tide-dominated, whereas the coast to the north and south of the inlet is wave-dominated.

At the onset of the Holocene transgression, the coast in this area was near the present 130-m isobath with a narrow coastal plain separating the coast from the Tertiary highlands. Submarine canyons headed at the mouths of the major streams, including the Willapa River. The initial transgression may have been characterized by wave domination (Fig. 11) due to the rather sharp steepening of the

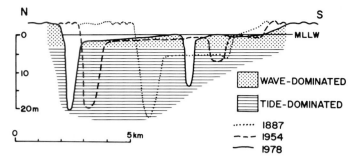

FIG. 11.—Generalized longitudinal cross section at the mouth of Willapa Bay, Washington.

gradient adjacent to the coast. Near the culmination of the rapid rise in sea level, the highly embayed coast was probably dominated by tidal processes.

As the rise in sea level slowed, discharge from the Columbia River accumulated along the coast. Wave-dominated conditions developed locally in the form of barrier spits across the tide-dominated embayments. The slowing of sea-level rise was accompanied by a reduction in the tidal prism of the embayments due to their infilling by sediment contributed both from the ocean and from streams. This situation caused the development of the wave-dominated barrier spits. Since the slowing of sea-level rise about 6.0–7.0 ka, there has been a trend toward wave domination (Fig. 12).

Except for the inlet and related tidal channels, the coast near Willapa Bay is one presently dominated by waves. A further reduction in the tidal effects can be expected as the bay fills with sediment. Ultimately, the outer part of the present ebb-tidal delta may be eroded as the coastal contours straighten in adjustment to reduced tidal flow. The tide-dominated inlet deposits will be encapsulated beneath the wave-dominated shoreface (Fig. 11).

The stratigraphic section preserved at the inlet is likely to consist of tide-dominated sediments from the base of the Holocene sequence to near present sea level. Only the upper few meters are wave-dominated barrier spit and beach sand (Fig. 11). Such sequences are only locally preserved in the embayments between the headlands of this tectonically active, high-relief coastal area. A slight tendency toward progradation may occur in the future and, along with it, a somewhat increased preservation potential.

Caladesi Island, Florida.—

Caladesi Island (Fig. 13) is a classic example of a drumstick barrier (Hayes and others, 1974). It is located near the northern end of the west peninsular Florida barrier chain. This is a microtidal, low- and mixed-energy coast (Hayes, 1979) composed of numerous drumstick barriers and tide-dominated inlets. The combination of low wave energy and small tidal range generates great variety in the dominant coastal processes along this area.

Considerable seismic profiling in the area (Davis and others, 1985; Evans and others, 1985) has shown that the pre-Holocene surface is dominated by an irregular, karstic erosion surface on the Tampa Fm (Miocene), which is locally covered by thin and discontinuous Pleistocene clays.

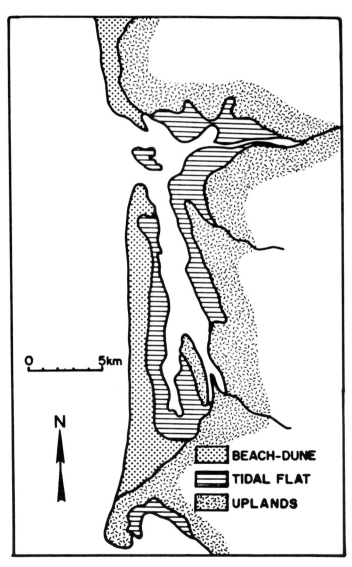

FIG. 10.—Map of general coastal environments near Willapa Bay, Washington.

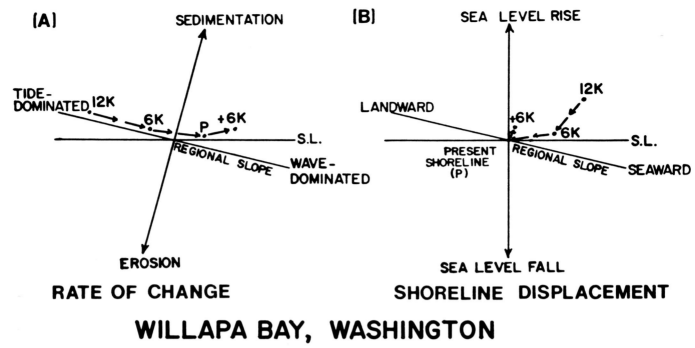

WILLAPA BAY, WASHINGTON

Fig. 12.—Changes in (A) dominant conditions and (B) shoreline displacement along the Washington coast at Willapa Bay, Washington.

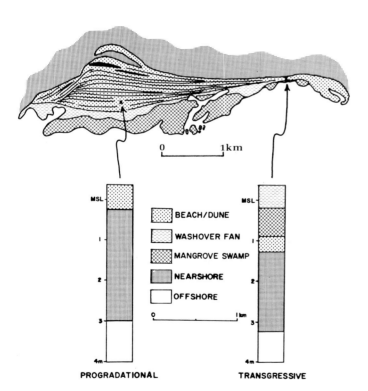

Fig. 13.—Present sedimentary environments and general Holocene stratigraphy of Caladesi Island, Florida, showing a progradational sequence in the southern (left) portion of the island and a sequence initially progradational but becoming transgressive in the northern (right) portion of the island.

Coring on Caladesi Island has demonstrated the origin of the island to be the result of emerging wave-dominated sand shoals (Davis and others, 1985).

As sea level rose during Holocene time, the broad and gently sloping coastal area in this region was characterized by tide-dominated, vegetated, paralic environments similar to those north of the present barrier system and in the Ten Thousand Islands area in south Florida near the Everglades. Salt marshes and mangrove swamps were extensive, although tidal range was probably not unlike that of today (80 cm).

The area is much like the others discussed above in that the coast changed from a distinctly tide-dominated situation at the time sea-level rise slowed greatly (Fig. 14) to one that is presently more wave-dominated. There is local variation in the dominant coastal process, so that the present time is considered as a mixed situation (Fig. 14). It is likely that the future will trend more toward wave domination due to decreasing tidal prisms, relatively slow sea-level rise and the dearth of sediment being supplied to the system.

Morphologic developments on Caladesi Island over the past several centuries serve as a good example of the local variation in preserved coastal sequences. As sea level rose through −2 m, this sequence was characterized as wave-dominated and progradational throughout the island (Fig. 13), much like that on the Nayarit coast of Mexico (Fig. 5). As sea level continued to rise slowly, the south end of the island maintained its progradational nature. By contrast, however, the north end of the island experienced transgression, as evidenced by the cores shown in Fig. 13. This is the result of abundant sediment supply at the southern, pro-

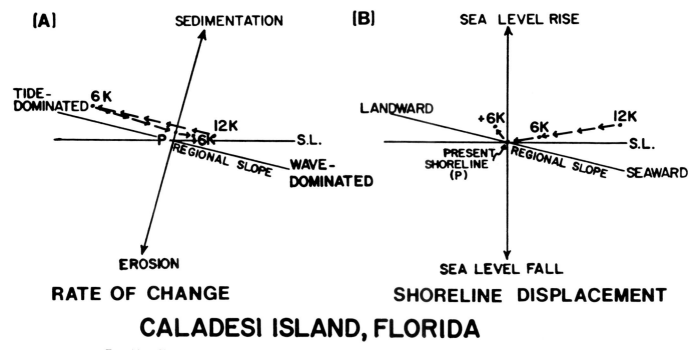

FIG. 14.—Changes in (A) dominant conditions and (B) shoreline displacement at Caladesi Island, Florida.

gradational portion of the island and a dearth of sediment in the northern transgressive end. This is testimony to the marked effect sediment supply has on coastal sequences during a rising sea level. It also demonstrates the degree of complexity that can develop over a limited reach of coast and the danger of overgeneralizing about the "dominant" coastal process. Preservation potential overall appears to be low, based on present conditions of little sediment influx and very slowly rising sea level. Increase in the rate of sea-level rise in the future may improve this situation.

INFLUENCE OF SEA-LEVEL CHANGE ON THE COASTAL STRATIGRAPHIC RECORD AND ITS PRESERVATION POTENTIAL

The foregoing section demonstrates the influence of sea-level change on present coastal sequences and their preservation potential. Similar influences have existed during the geologic past and are recorded in the stratigraphic record. For a given type of depositional setting (i.e., wave-dominated or tide-dominated), changes in sea level primarily are reflected in the nature of resulting sedimentary sequence and the degree to which they are preserved in the rock record.

For example, the nature of the wave-dominated stratigraphic sequence and its likelihood of preservation depend strongly on the balance between relative sea-level change and sedimentation rate. In general, it can be said that rapid sea-level rise results in slow rate of sediment accumulation but high preservation potential. In contrast, slowly rising sea-level conditions result in more rapid rates of sedimentation but less preservation potential.

Significant differences exist even under completely progradational situations. Three types of progradation can exist as a function of relative change in sea level. Where sea level falls, the direction of shoreline progradation is obliquely downward. An attenuated progradational sequence results, in which the stratigraphic interval between two features is less than the initial difference in water depth between the same features. Horizontal progradation occurs where sea level is essentially constant; it produces an undistorted progradational sequence in which stratigraphic intervals are equivalent to initial differences in water depth. Upward progradation results from a seaward displacement of the shoreline under conditions of rising sea level. The resulting progradational sequence is explained in the sense that stratigraphic intervals exceed the initial difference in water depth.

The identification of the vertical component of progradation may be difficult in many coastal successions. An accurate cross section (or seismic section) through a basin fill may provide an indication of the possibility of establishing an original horizontal reference. Otherwise, reliance must be placed on the thickness of specific depositional facies as compared to the estimated water depth range for the accumulation of the facies in that specific depositional setting. Such a process requires an accurate estimate of the paleo-wave regime, which commonly is a tenuous procedure. Subtle upward or downward progradations may accordingly be difficult to recognize, but sharp departure from a horizontal progradation should be fairly evident.

Preservation of wave-dominated deposits.—

Downward-prograding deposits (attenuated sequences) have the lowest potential for preservation among the wave-dominated progradational types. In addition to being thinner than other types of progradational deposits, the fall of relative sea level that attends downward progradation typically exposes the deposits to subaerial erosion. A probable example occurs in Pleistocene marine deposits exposed along Monterey Bay, California, where a continuous progradational succession 6 m thick is inferred to have developed during an interval in which sea level fell 10 m or so (Dupre, 1984).

Horizontally prograding deposits (undistorted sequences) have a relatively high potential for preservation may be fairly common in the stratigraphic record. A thick accumulation of shoreline deposits in the southern Coast Ranges of California seems to consist largely of more or less undistorted sequences (Clifton, 1981), as does a progradational Miocene deposit that formed in a narrow seaway in northern Hungary. In both cases, the inferred character of wave effects relative to water depths is consistent with horizontal progradation in the inferred paleogeographic setting.

Deposits formed by upward progradation (expanded sequences) have the greatest potential for preservation among the wave-dominated progradational types due to their greater thickness. Clearly expanded sequences, however, seem to be relatively uncommon in the geologic record. Possibly, their apparent scarcity is derived from the particularly high, and therefore generally uncommon, rate of sediment input that is required to overcome the effects of relatively rising sea level. An example is in the Pleistocene Scotia Bluffs Sandstone of northwestern California, in which stratigraphic thicknesses in part of the unit significantly exceed the depths of deposition (Bourgeois and Leithold, 1983).

A degree of upward progradation can be identified in some coastal sequences even where the sequence is not clearly expanded. The preservation of lagoonal or other subtidal embayment deposits above beach foreshore sediments in an individual sequence implies a relative rise in sea level during progradation. A few of the Miocene progradational sequences in the Caliente Range of the southern Coast Ranges show such a succession (Clifton, 1981).

Wave-dominated coastal deposits may be preserved during a transgression, but typically the landward transposition of the shoreline is attended by erosion of much of the existing shoreface (Bruun, 1962; Ryer, 1977). Commonly, the shoreface environment is represented by a few meters or less of steeply crossbedded sand and/or gravel beneath a succession that displays evidence of deposition in deeper water. Examples include the Cape Sebastian Sandstone of Late Cretaceous age in southwestern Oregon (Bourgeois, 1980), Late Cretaceous beds in the Pozo Summit-American Canyon area of the central California Coast Ranges (Howell and others, 1977), and Pleistocene marine terrace deposits on the coast of central Monterey Bay, California (Dupre, 1984).

The Dakota Sandstone (Naturita Fm) in the Cretaceous of the Colorado Plateau shows a variation on this theme. Several pulses of thin progradational barrier deposits are incorporated in an overall transgressive system during an apparent rise in sea level (Young, 1973).

Preservation of tide-dominated deposits.—

Tide-dominated deposits are typically associated with coastal embayments. They may develop within embayments such as estuaries or lagoons that lie behind a coastal barrier or form in and seaward of tidal inlets on a barrier coast. Like wave-dominated deposits, their potential for preservation depends in part on relative sea-level change and the nature of progradation and transgression.

Tide-dominated deposits that form within an estuarine setting are particularly susceptible to erosion under conditions of falling sea level because of their location in the developing fluvial valley.

Under conditions of horizontal progradation, the tidal facies of an embayment may be stranded while the barrier widens as its front shifts seaward. In such a setting the tidal influence may diminish as the embayment fills and the tidal channels become increasingly dominated by fluvial processes. Lateral migration of these developing fluvial channels may partly erode pre-existing tidal deposits. Such seems to be the case in the youngest Pleistocene terrace deposits adjacent to Willapa Bay, Washington (Clifton, 1983).

The potential for preservation of tide-dominated deposits is highest among prograding situations if the progradation has an upward component. The deposits are likely to be thicker and thus less likely to be eroded by fluvial processes. If the rate of relative sea-level rise is sufficiently high, the areas behind a prograding barrier may become drowned, thereby effectively causing a seaward transposition of the embayment facies. Such a situation would be characterized by the superposition of embayment facies without a pronounced erosional break over foreshore or eolian facies. Examples are previously described uncommon sequences in the Miocene of the Caliente Range of California (Clifton, 1981) and some of the Eocene sequences in the Hampshire basin of southern England (Plint, 1983).

The numerous tide-dominated prograding sequences that accumulated on the North American craton during the Cambrian also appear to be of this type, such as the Mt. Simon Fm in Wisconsin (Driese and others, 1981) and also the Tapeats Sandstone of Arizona (Hereford, 1977).

Unlike wave-dominated deposits, tide-dominated deposits have a high potential for preservation under conditions of transgression. Two styles of transgressive sequences may result, depending on the rates of sea-level rise and sedimentation. Conditions of slow rise and rapid sedimentation lead to stepped transgressions composed of a stacked set of shallowing-upward sequences in an overall transgressive succession. These shallowing-upward sequences may represent the fillings of individual embayments created during the transgression or the results of migrating tidal channels under conditions of slowly rising relative sea level. Examples include embayment deposits in the Merced Fm of Pliocene and Pleistocene age on the San Francisco peninsula of California (Hunter and others, 1984), successions in the Eocene Del Mar Fm and Torrey Sandstone north of La Jolla, California, in the upper Dakota Group near Denver, Colorado (Weimer and Land, 1972), and in the Almond Fm of southern Wyoming (Van Horn, 1979). Where the rate of sea-level rise is rapid relative to sediment input, the transgressive sequence may be continuous. On a barrier coastline, the landward transposition of the shoreface may cause erosion of the upper part of associated tide-dominated embayment deposits, as presently occurs on the Atlantic coast of the United States (A. C. Hine, pers. commun.).

Tidal inlet and other channel deposits may be preserved in such a situation because they extend below the depth of erosion related to the retreating shoreface. Apparent examples occur in the Cretaceous upper Almond Fm in southern Wyoming (Weimer and others, 1982) and the Mississippian Aux Vases Fm in southern Illinois (Weimer and others, 1982). In the absence of a barrier, tide-dominated deposits may simply be drowned and mantled with deeper water sediment. Such a process appears to be active in the North Sea today (Kenyon and others, 1981) and seems responsible for the preservation of such deposits as the late Miocene Santa Margarita Fm in the Santa Cruz Mountains of central California (Phillips, 1983).

SUMMARY

The effects of sea-level change are clearly evident in most stratigraphic successions of coastal deposits. The nature of the change can profoundly influence the preservation of different types of facies within these successions. A falling sea level exposes the shoreline deposits to processes of subaerial dissection. Tide-dominated facies may be particularly susceptible to erosion if an embayment in which they formed converts to a fluvial valley as a consequence of falling sea level. Under conditions of rising sea level, a shoreline will prograde if the rate of sedimentation is sufficiently high. The preservation potential of both wave- and tide-dominated facies is high under such an upward progradation. If the rate of sedimentation is less, a retrograding shoreline (marine transgression) will ensue. The potential for preserving tide-dominated facies in such a case is higher than that for wave-dominated facies.

Thick accumulations of coastal deposits exist only in areas of long-term subsidence. Therefore, most coastal deposits that are preserved in the geologic record formed under conditions of very slowly rising sea level. Relatively rapid sea-level fluctuations are likely to be superimposed on this general trend and their effects recorded in the strata.

ACKNOWLEDGMENTS

The authors are indebted to numerous workers whose previous data have served as a framework for some of the concepts and interpretations discussed herein. Both of us have benefited greatly from fruitful discussions with colleagues, especially Ralph Hunter (HEC) and Dag Nummedal (RAD). Many of the ideas incorporated in this discussion grew out of a paper presented by H. E. Clifton at the 1983 SEPM Annual Meeting in Dallas, which developed from a paper by R. A. Davis at the International Association of Sedimentologists meeting in Hamilton in 1982.

Some of the work which led to Davis's contributions to this paper was supported by the Florida Sea Grant Program. The manuscript was prepared while Davis was a visiting professor at Duke University. The facilities and support of that institution are greatly appreciated.

REFERENCES

BOURGEOIS, JOANNE, 1980, A transgressional shelf sequence exhibiting hummocky stratification: the Cape Sebastian Sandstone (Upper Cretaceous), southwestern Oregon: Journal of Sedimentary Petrology, v. 50, p. 681–702.

———, AND LEITHOLD, E. L., 1983, Sedimentation, tectonics and sea-level change as reflected in four wave-dominated shelf sequences in Oregon and California, *in* Larue, D. K., and Steele, R. J., eds., Cenozoic Marine Sedimentation, Pacific Margin, USA: Pacific Section, Society of Economic Paleontologists and Mineralogists, Los Angeles, p. 1–16.

BRUUN, PER, 1962, Sea level rise as a cause of shore erosion: American Society of Civil Engineers Proceedings, Journal of Waterways and Harbors Division, v.88, p. 117–130.

CLIFTON, H. E., 1981, Progradational sequences in Miocene shoreline deposits, southeastern Caliente Range, California: Journal of Sedimentary Petrology, v. 51, p. 165-184.

———, 1983, Discrimination of subtidal and intertidal facies in Pleistocene deposits, Willapa Bay, Washington: Journal of Sedimentary Petrology, v. 53, p. 353–369.

CLIFTON, H. E., AND HUNTER, R. E., 1980, Modern sedimentary facies of the open Pacific Coast and Pleistocene analogs from Monterey Bay, *in* Field, M. E., Bouma, A. H., Colbourn, I. P., Douglas, R. G., and Ingle, J. C., eds., Quaternary Depositional Environments of the Pacific Coast: Pacific Coast Paleogeography Symposium No. 4, Pacific Section, Society of Economic Paleontologists and Mineralogists, p. 105–120.

CURRAY, J. R., 1964, Transgressions and regressions, *in* Miller, R. L., ed., Papers in Marine Geology, Shepard Commemorative Volume: Macmillan Press, New York, p. 175–203.

———, 1969, History of continental shelves, Lecture 6, *in* The New Concepts in Continental Margin Sedimentation, Application to the Geological Record: Short Course Lecture Notes, American Geological Institute, Washington, D.C., p. JCVI-1 to JCVI-28.

———, EMMEL, F. J., AND CRAMPTON, P. J. S., 1969, Holocene history of a strand plain, lagoonal coast, Nayarit, Mexico, *in* Castanaras, A. A., and Phleger, F. B., eds., Coastal Lagoons—A Symposium: Universidad Nacional Autonoma de Mexico/UNESCO, Mexico City, p. 63–100.

DAVIS, R. A., JR., BRAME, J. W., LYNCH-BLOSSE, M. A., AND ROSEN, D. S., 1985, Caladesi Island: a classic example of a drumstick barrier, *in* Davis, R. A., Hine, A. C., and Belknap, D. F., eds., Geology of the Barrier Island and Marsh-Dominated Coast, West-Central Florida: Field Trip Guidebook, Geological Society of America Annual Meeting, Orlando, p. 35–43.

DRIESE, S. G., BYERS, C. W., AND DOTT, R. H., JR., 1981, Tidal deposition in the basal Upper Cambrian Mt. Simon Formation in Wisconsin: Journal of Sedimentary Petrology, v. 51, p. 367–382.

DUPRE, W. R., 1984, Reconstruction of paleo-wave conditions from Pleistocene marine terrace deposits, Monterey Bay, California, *in* Greenwood, B., and Davis, R. A., eds., Hydrodynamics and Sedimentation in Wave-Dominated Coastal Environments: Developments in Sedimentology, v. 39, Elsevier Publishing Co., New York, p. 435–454.

EVANS, M. W., HINE, A. C., BELKNAP, D. F., AND DAVIS, R. A., JR., 1985, Bedrock control on barrier island development; west-central Florida coast: Marine Geology, v. 63, p. 263–283.

FISCHER, A. G., 1961, Stratigraphic record of transgressing seas in the light of sedimentation on the Atlantic coast of New Jersey: American Association of Petroleum Geologists Bulletin, v. 45, p. 1656–1666.

GALLOWAY, W. E., AND HOBDAY, D. K., 1983, Terrigenous Clastic Depositional Systems: Springer-Verlag, New York, 423 p.

HAYES, M. O., 1979, Barrier island morphology as a function of tidal and wave regime, *in* Leatherman, S. P., ed., Barrier Islands: Academic Press, New York, p. 1–28.

———, HULMES, L. J., AND WILSON, S. J., 1974, Importance of tidal inlets in erosional and depositional history of barrier islands: Geological Society of America, Abstracts with Programs, v. 6, p. 785.

HEREFORD, R., 1977, Deposition of the Tapeats Sandstone (Cambrian) in central Arizona: Geological Society of America Bulletin, v. 88, p. 199–211.

HICKS, S. D., 1981, Long-period sea level variations for the United States through 1978: Shore and Beach, v. 29, p. 26–29.

HOWELL, D. G., VEDDEER, J. G., MCLEAN, H., JOYCE, J. M., CLARKE, S. H., JR., AND SMITH, G., 1977, Review of Cretaceous geology, Salinian and Nacimiento blocks, Coast Ranges of central California: Pacific Coast Paleogeography Field Guide No. 2, Pacific Section, Society of Economic Paleontologists and Mineralogists, p. 1–46.

HUNTER, R. E., CLIFTON, H. E., HALL, N. T., CSASZAR, G., RICHMOND, B. M., AND CHIN, J. L., 1984, Pliocene and Pleistocene coastal and shelf deposits of the Merced Formation and associated beds, northwestern San Francisco Peninsula, California: Field Trip Guidebook No. 3, Society of Economic Paleontologists and Mineralogists, Midyear Meeting, San José, p. 1–29.

JELGERSMA, S., 1961, Holocene sea level changes in the Netherlands: Mededeelingen van den Geologische Stichtung, C-VI, no. 7, 100 p.

KENYON, N. H., BELDERSON, R. H., STRIDE, A. H., AND JOHNSON, M. A., 1981, Offshore tidal banks as indicators of net transport and as potential deposits: International Association of Sedimentologists, Special Publication No. 5, p. 257–268.

KRAFT, J. C., 1971, Sedimentary facies patterns and geologic history of a Holocene marine transgression: Geological Society of America Bulletin, v. 82, p. 2131–2158.

———, AND CHRZASTOWSKI, M. J., 1985, Coastal stratigraphic sequences, in Davis, Jr., R. A., ed. Coastal Sedimentary Environments, second edition: Springer-Verlag, New York, p. 625–663.

PHILLIPS, R. L., 1983, Late Miocene tidal shelf sedimentation, Santa Cruz Mountains, California, in Larue, D. K., and Steele, R. J., eds., Cenozoic Marine Sedimentation, Pacific Margin, USA: Pacific Section, Society of Economic Paleontologists and Mineralogists, Los Angeles, p. 45–61.

PLINT, A. G., 1983, Facies, environments, and sedimentary cycles in the Middle Eocene, Bracklesham Formation of the Hampshire Basin: evidence for global sea level change: Sedimentology, v. 30, p. 625–653.

REINECK, H. E., 1970, Marine Sandkörper, recent und fossil: Geologische Rundschau, v. 60, p. 302–321.

———, AND SINGH, I. B., 1980, Depositional Sedimentary Environments: Springer Verlag, New York, 549 pp.

RYER, R. A., 1977, Patterns of Cretaceous shallow-marine sedimentation, Coalville and Rockport areas, Utah: Geological Society of America Bulletin, v. 88, p. 177–188.

SCHOLL, D. W., AND STUIVER, M., 1967, Recent submergence of southern Florida: a comparison with adjacent coasts and other eustatic data: Geological Society of America Bulletin, v. 78, p. 437–454.

VAN HORN, M. D., 1979, Stratigraphy of the Almond Formation, east–west central flank, Rock Springs uplift, Sweetwater County, Wyoming: American Association of Petroleum Geologists Bulletin, v. 50, p. 2150–2175.

VAN STRAATEN, L. M. J. U., 1964, De bodem der Waddenzee, in Het Waddenboek: Nederland Geologische Vereningung, p. 75–151.

WEIMER, R. J., HOWARD, J. D., AND LINDSAY, D. R., 1982, Tidal flats and associated deposits, in Scholle, P. A., and Spearing, D., eds., Sandstone Depositional Environments: American Association of Petroleum Geologists Memoir 31, p. 191–245.

———, AND LAND, C. B., 1972, Field guide to the Dakota Group (Cretaceous) stratigraphy, Golden-Morrison area, Colorado: Mountain Geologist, v. 9, p. 241–267.

YOUNG, R. G., 1973, Depositional environments of basal Cretaceous rocks of the Colorado Plateau, in Fassett, J. E., ed., Cretaceous and Tertiary Rocks of the Southern Colorado Plateau: Memoir of Four Corners Geological Society, Durango, Colorado, p. 10–27.

PART V
QUATERNARY DEPOSITIONAL SEQUENCES

LATE QUATERNARY SEA-LEVEL FLUCTUATIONS AND SEDIMENTARY PHASES OF THE TEXAS COASTAL PLAIN AND SHELF[1]

ROBERT A. MORTON

Bureau of Economic Geology, The University of Texas at Austin, Austin, Texas 78712

AND

W. ARMSTRONG PRICE[2]

428 Ohio Street, Corpus Christi, Texas 78404

ABSTRACT: The coastal plain and continental shelf of Texas were sites of simultaneous erosion and deposition related to late Quaternary eustatic fluctuations in sea level. Geologic maps, deep borings, and seismic profiles from the area provide evidence of how the dominant sedimentary processes responded to changes in base level during the most recent (Sangamonian-Holocene) depositional episode.

The early Wisconsinan falling sea level and subsequent lowstand caused upstream river entrenchment and downstream deltaic progradation beyond the shelf edge. Later, deltaic sedimentation shifted landward in response to a middle Wisconsinan sea-level rise and then seaward in the late Wisconsinan as sea level fell to its lowest position. Carbonate reefs grew on a broad terrace between the major deltas during the initial postglacial rise in sea level. The continued sea-level rise (Holocene) and highstand resulted in erosion and retreat of deltaic headlands, progradation of interdeltaic barriers and strandplains, and aggradation of alluvial valleys, bays, and the inner shelf. Modern patterns of shoreline deposition resemble those of the preceding (Sangamonian) highstand.

Local and regional structures controlled the position and thickness of some late Wisconsinan and early Holocene deposits, such as river channels, sand ridges, and carbonate reefs. Lowstand deltas along the basin margin are several times thicker than their updip counterparts because of rapid subsidence and progradation into relatively deep water at the shelf edge. Landward of the shelf edge, however, thicknesses of depositional sequences and individual fluvial, deltaic, and barrier island sand bodies are comparable regardless of whether they were deposited under static or falling sea-level conditions. Apparently, thicknesses of these stable-platform deposits depended nearly equally on subsidence and water depth.

INTRODUCTION

Quaternary sediments of the northwestern Gulf of Mexico have been the subject of numerous investigations directed toward understanding how sedimentary basins respond to both global and regional fluctuations in sea level. The Gulf coast province is also where Barton (1930), Price (1933), Fisk (1939, 1944), Shepard and Moore (1960) and Bernard and LeBlanc (1965) mapped the lower coastal plain sediments and interpreted the physical processes that were responsible for the sedimentary record of the past 100,000 yrs. Since the pioneering efforts of these earlier workers, a wealth of additional information has become available regarding sedimentologic characteristics and regional distribution of late Pleistocene and Holocene sediments preserved on the Texas coastal plain and continental shelf (Fig. 1). Objectives of this paper are to summarize that information, to describe the physical properties and sedimentary facies of the shallow-water depositional complexes, and to place the depositional sequences in a stratigraphic framework controlled by late Quaternary changes in sea level.

Seismic profiles and foundation borings from the barriers and continental shelf provided geometric and sedimentologic information regarding the nearshore sediments that accumulated principally as a result of late Quaternary sea-level cycles. Distinct depositional sequences were recognized and interpreted on the basis of internal seismic reflections, terminations along sequence boundaries (Mitchum and others, 1977), lithology, geometry, and spatial variations in facies.

Most of the depositional sequences are composed of several lithologic units. Composition of these units was determined mainly by descriptions of borings rather than by seis-

mic characteristics, although seismic profiles can convey some lithologic information. For example, relatively thick layers of sand are commonly characterized by opaque seismic signatures that lack distinct internal bedding, and highly bioturbated mixtures of sand, shell, and mud may be indicated by transparent zones. Finer grained bedded sediments, on the other hand, commonly display distinct seismic reflections, including parallel and clinoform configurations.

Sequence boundaries mapped on seismic profiles may coincide with lithologic changes or with abrupt changes in water content and cohesive shear strength even if lithology is uniform. The decrease in water content and increase in strength are evidence of dessication and oxidation (subaerial exposure) or overconsolidation (prior burial). Regardless of their cause, abrupt changes in physical properties suggest the presence of disconformable surfaces (Fisk and McClelland, 1959).

CONCEPTS OF QUATERNARY SEDIMENTATION AND GENETIC STRATIGRAPHY

Sedimentation in the Gulf of Mexico during the Quaternary Period was affected by at least eight major glacio-eustatic cycles (Beard and others, 1982). Cycles were characterized by warmer and cooler paleotemperatures and by sea-level highstands and lowstands that were partly related to changes in the volume of continental ice sheets. These interdependencies were recognized by Fisk (1939), who explained the eroded valleys, river terraces, and depositional surfaces that comprise the coastal plains of Louisiana and Texas in terms of Pleistocene glacial and interglacial stages.

Fisk (1944) and subsequent workers have demonstrated that a repetitive sequence of erosional and depositional events accompanied each major eustatic cycle. As sea level gradually fell during glacial periods (Fig. 2), streams began downcutting and were confined to valleys that crossed the

---

[1]Publication authorized by the Director, Bureau of Economic Geology, The University of Texas at Austin.

[2]Deceased.

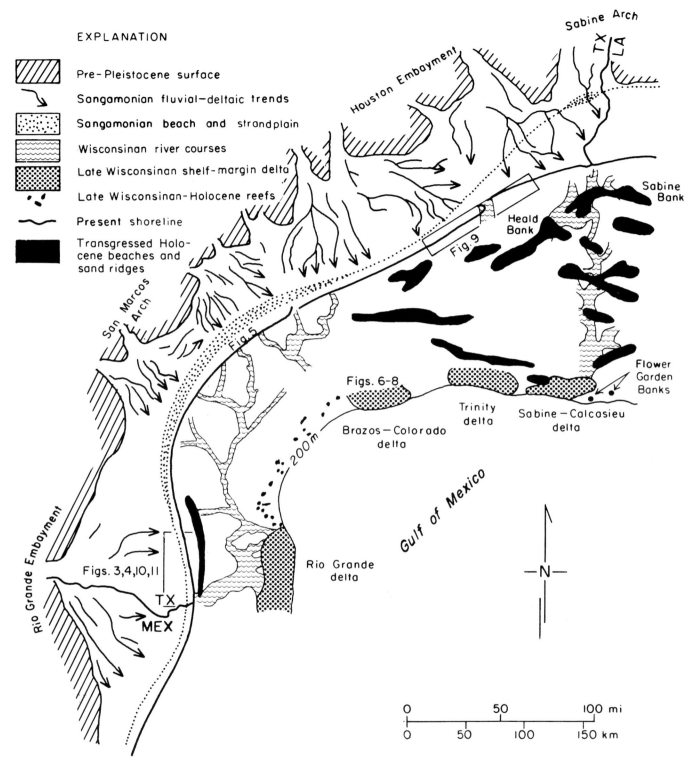

FIG. 1.—Tectonic elements and regional distribution of late Pleistocene and Holocene depositional systems, Texas coastal plain and continental shelf. Compiled from maps by Curray (1960), Winker (1979), and Suter and Berryhill (1985). Locations of other figures are also shown.

broadened coastal plan. Mature soil profiles and erosional topography having low relief formed on the exposed surfaces during sea-level lowstands, which coincided with maximum glaciation. When sea level was lowest, the shoreline was at or near the shelf edge. Because the lowstand shelf was extremely narrow or absent, major rivers

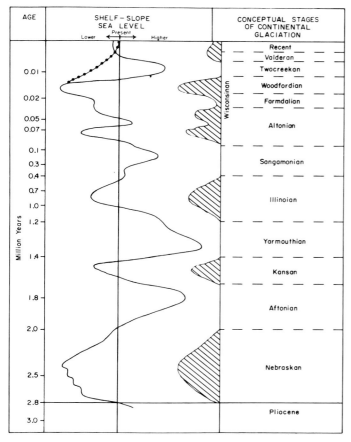

AGE	SHELF - SLOPE SEA LEVEL		CONCEPTUAL STAGES OF CONTINENTAL GLACIATION

FIG. 2.—Inferred Pleistocene sea-level fluctuations in the northwestern Gulf of Mexico and their relation to conceptual stages of continental glaciation in the northern hemisphere which began about 2.8 Ma. Derived by Smith (1965) from interpreted water depth and paleotemperatures and modified by Beard and others (1982). Average post-lowstand curve from Curry (1960), Ballard and Uchupi (1970), Nelson and Bray (1970), and Frazier (1974).

acted as point sources, discharging sediment directly onto the outer shelf and upper slope. During interglacial periods, sea level rose rapidly (Fig. 2) and entrenched valleys were inundated. The drowned valleys formed estuaries that eventually filled as the coastal plain was submerged and partially truncated by shoreface retreat. The eroded coastal plain became the continental shelf during sea-level highstands, which coincided with minimum extent of the ice caps.

Frazier (1974) refined and expanded these concepts of Quaternary cyclic sedimentation to include the timing of coastal aggradation, coastal progradation, and marine transgression, the latter being the transitional event that temporally separates depositional episodes and spatially separates depositional sequences. According to Frazier's terminology, progradation occurs when sea level is relatively stable or falling, aggradation both accompanies and follows progradation, and transgression represents the final phase of a cycle. Retrogradation is a term sometimes used to describe a transgression occurring when sediment supply is abundant but insufficient to prevent a gradual landward shift in sedimentary facies. When rates of deposition are

substantial, yet slightly less than the combined rates of subsidence and sea-level rise, an upward-fining vertical sequence forms that is the mirror image of a progradational sequence. Thick retrogradational sequences can be observed in Tertiary Gulf coast sediments deposited during eustatic rises in sea level lasting nearly a million years (Morton and others, 1985). Except for minor retrogradations accompanying brief relative rises in sea level, late Quaternary transgressions that terminated depositional episodes were characterized by low sediment influx and shoreface erosion because deglaciation decreased precipitation and rapidly increased sea level.

The conceptual relationships between relative sea level and sediment supply described by Curray (1964) are useful for illustrating how aggradation, progradation, and transgression determine the architecture of depositional sequences. Fluvial and strandplain aggradation and shoreface retreat predominate under conditions of rising sea level and low sediment supply, whereas river entrenchment and deltaic progradation predominate under conditions of falling sea level and high sediment supply.

These extremes of relative sea level and sediment influx, which approximate conditions during the most recent depositional episode, also help explain why within each depositional cycle aggradational deposits thicken landward, whereas progradational deposits thicken seaward (Frazier, 1974). The updip or landward portions of depositional sequences are composed chiefly of coastal plain sediments that were deposited by subaerial floods and vertical sediment accumulation. These aggradational processes maintain seaward gradients when sea level is constant and increase surface elevations in the face of a rising sea. The downdip or seaward portions of depositional sequences, on the other hand, are mainly composed of subtidal sediments that accumulate by lateral accretion. These progradational deposits initially form in extremely shallow water and on stable substrates that severely limit their thickness. Also, they progressively advance into deeper water and onto steep, unstable slopes that promote basinward thickening.

Depositional episodes (time units), depositional sequences (rock units), and hiatal surfaces that form the underlying and overlying sequence boundaries (Frazier, 1974) are now widely accepted concepts that, together with eustatic sea-level curves (Vail and others, 1977), serve as the basis for establishing regional stratigraphic frameworks within basins and global correlations among basins.

REGIONAL GEOLOGICAL SETTING

Major and Minor Depocenters

The principal Quaternary depocenter in the northwestern Gulf of Mexico was located near the shelf margin offshore from the Texas-Louisiana border where maximum thickness of Pleistocene sediments exceeds 3,500 m (Woodbury and others, 1973). Geology of the Pleistocene depocenter is complex owing to the interaction of rapid shelf-margin progradation, large fluctuations in sea level, propagation of enormous growth faults, mobilization of salt domes and shale ridges, and widespread deposition in deep-water environments (Woodbury and others, 1973; Caughey, 1975; Morton and others, 1985). These variables produced numerous inter-diapir basins, each experiencing slightly different histories and each containing slightly different sediment fill.

In the Pleistocene depocenter, thick, massive sandstones deposited in fluvial channels grade basinward into coarsening-upward deltaic and submarine fan deposits that accumulated beyond the shelf edge. Together these aggradational and progradational deposits advanced the shelf margin about 48 km near the Texas-Louisiana border and progressively lesser amounts in a westerly direction.

While fluvial systems of continental proportion supplied the Pleistocene offshore depocenter, coastal plain rivers associated with smaller drainage basins locally supplied deltas along the Texas coast (Fig. 1). Baseflow of Texas rivers was not augmented by glacial meltwater, and their sediment loads and discharge were greatly susceptible to climatic reductions in precipitation. The total volume of sediment delivered by these minor rivers was periodically increased, however, by higher fluvial discharge, accelerated degradation of uplands, and enlargement of drainage basins during extreme sea-level lowstands. As a result of these circumstances, shelf-margin delta complexes are two to three times thicker than stable platform deltas owing to slower progradation, faster subsidence, and deeper water near the shelf edge. These shelf-margin deltas (Fig. 1) range in size from 50 km wide and 60 m thick to 70 km wide and 180 m thick (Lehner, 1969; Suter and Berryhill, 1985). The Rio Grande depositional complex is the largest late Wisconsinan shelf-edge delta in the northwestern Gulf (Suter and Berryhill, 1985). The unusually great thickness and lateral extent of this delta are probably related to late Miocene epeirogenic uplift of basins in the Rio Grande Rift and attendant integration of drainage networks that rejuvenated deposition in the Rio Grande embayment.

Eustatic Fluctuations

Post-Sangamonian sea-level curves for the northwestern Gulf of Mexico (Curray, 1960, 1965; Ballard and Uchupi, 1970; Nelson and Bray, 1970; Frazier, 1974) were derived largely from depths and ages of features submerged on the continental shelf. Actual values give conflicting histories because dated features at different depths have similar ages and vice versa. These differences can be explained by crustal warping and local diapirism, but the curves are drawn as if isostatic and tectonic deformation was negligible.

The clastic margin of the Gulf coast basin is generally unstable; therefore, it may be necessary to establish a late Quaternary eustatic sea-level curve in a more stable area. In fact, Fisk and McFarlan (1955) and Poag (1973) concluded that details of the postglacial sea-level rise are obscure because of isostatic and tectonic instability. At least two studies (Walcott, 1972; Clark and others, 1978), however, suggest that post-Wisconsinan sea-level curves for the Texas shelf should be reliable, because the Gulf of Mexico lies within the zone of postglacial geoid adjustment separating global regions of emergence from regions of submergence.

Although details may differ considerably, sea-level curves for the Gulf coast clastic province generally have configurations that are comparable to those published for other regions. Most curves show that sea level began falling about 90.0 ka during early Wisconsinan glaciation and reached its lowest position about 75.0 ka (Fig. 2). This lowstand was followed by a moderate ($\approx$30 m) rise in sea level that reached mid-shelf during the middle Wisconsinan interstadial about 50.0 to 30.0 ka. The following late Wisconsinan glaciation caused an even lower drop in sea level that lasted until about 18.0 ka, when sea level began a rapid but irregular rise that lasted until about 4.5 ka. Since then, sea level has remained essentially constant (Fig. 2), although there may have been minor fluctuations having amplitudes of a few meters or less. None of the Gulf coast curves support a substantially higher than present sea level about 6.0 ka, as proposed by Fairbridge (1961), even though climatic reconstructions suggest that temperatures were warmer then than now (Smith, 1965; Fig. 2). The absence of emerged Holocene beaches in this area supports the theory of nearly uniform sea level for the past few thousand years and conforms with the relatively stable crustal response to glacial unloading predicted by Clark and others (1978).

Absolute ages of coastal plain and shelf sediments and correlation with eustatic cycles responsible for their deposition are still uncertain, mainly because the number, magnitude, and ages of Pleistocene sea-level changes are not precisely known and a wide range of good radiometric dates is unavailable. Recent studies incorporating biostratigraphic, seismic stratigraphic, and geochemical evidence indicate that (1) eustatic cycles were more numerous than previously thought, and (2) as many as four cycles occurred during the past 100,000 yrs (Beard and others, 1982). Planktonic foraminiferal assemblages, carbon and oxygen isotopes, and seismic sequences are currently being used to elucidate late Quaternary sea-level fluctuations in the Gulf coast basin.

Tectonic Elements

Principal tectonic features of the Texas coastal plain and inner continental shelf include the Rio Grande and Houston embayments that are bounded to the east by the San Marcos Arch and the Sabine Arch, respectively (Fig. 1). These four structural features affected late Quaternary nearshore sedimentation patterns by confining the largest fluvial-deltaic systems to the embayments.

Tectonic processes of greatest magnitude affecting the area are regional seaward tilting along the coast and corresponding uplift of inland areas (Doering, 1935; Fisk, 1939; Russell, 1940). The amount of structural warping is controlled by the isostatic adjustment to sediment loading. Price (1958), Bernard and LeBlanc (1965), and Winker (1979) estimated tectonic deformation of the lower coastal plain relative to a higher sea level by assuming that Pleistocene beach ridges were contemporaneous shoreline deposits. Distance between the Sangamonian strandline and extant shoreline (Fig. 1) roughly indicates the relative amount of tilting. Only minor downwarping (<1 m) occurred in southeast Texas, where post-Sangamonian deposition was minor; in contrast, substantial downwarping (>5 m) occurred near the site of principal deposition located within the Houston Embayment (Price, 1958; Winker, 1979).

Compared to the remainder of the Texas coastal plain, the Rio Grande Embayment was the most active site of late Quaternary sedimentation and downwarping. The moderately large rivers and deltas that occupied this subbasin (Figs. 3, 4) deposited a greater volume of sediment than contemporaneous fluvial-deltaic systems to the northeast. Gradual subsidence and attendant deposition by the ancestral Rio Grande are indicated by thickening of strata offshore and southward along depositional strike (Fig. 4). In contrast, sediment thickening is minor northeast of the San Marcos Arch, where changes in thickness of equivalent strata are imperceptible and structural attitude of beds is nearly horizontal. Apparently, nearshore portions of the Houston Embayment and Sabine Arch have been relatively stable or slightly uplifted during the late Quaternary, as evidenced by the location of depocenters away from this area, such as in south Texas and in south Louisiana.

Secondary structural features within the basin fill, such as deep-seated growth faults, shale ridges, and adjacent withdrawal synclines of Miocene age, controlled the position of several late Quaternary depositional complexes. Persistent extensional stresses within the sediment column kept shelf-margin fault zones active long after they were buried by thick sequences of coastal plain deposits. These faults, some of which intersect the sea floor, influenced the locations and orientations of some late Wisconsinan river channels, shoreline features, and carbonate reefs observed on the modern shelf. In offshore south Texas, mid-shelf reefs preferentially grew over structural highs and fault escarpments. Similarly, long segments of major fluvial systems flowed nearly parallel to the shoreline and shelf edge (Fig. 1), where the rivers coincided with structural sags (Berryhill, 1981) that formed between fault zones of early and middle Miocene age.

LATE PLEISTOCENE HIGHSTAND PHASES

Coastal Plain Aggradation

Pleistocene depositional surfaces that form the western Gulf coastal plain have been correlated and subdivided us-

FIG. 3.—Late Quaternary fluvial-deltaic systems deposited in south Texas during successive sea-level highstands. The Holocene Rio Grande delta overlaps the adjacent late Pleistocene delta. Onshore map units are modified from Brown and others (1980).

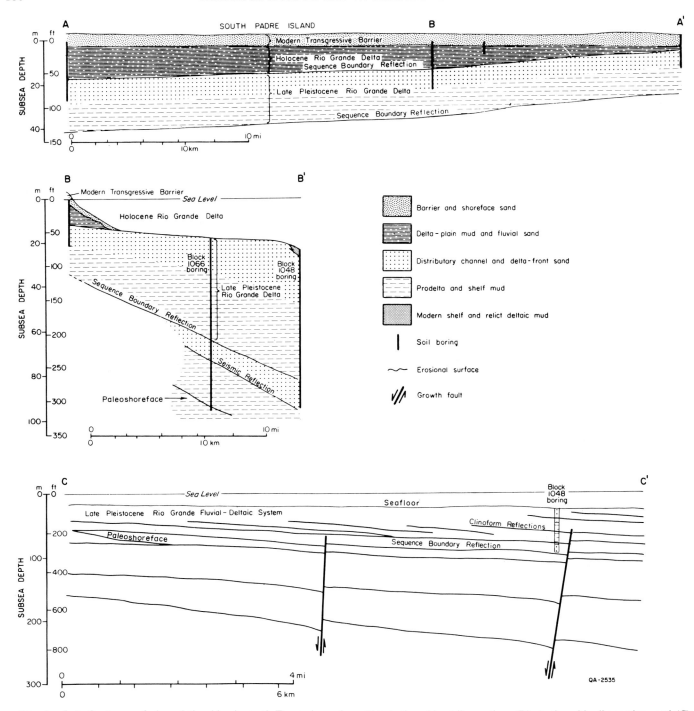

Fig. 4.—Late Quaternary facies relationships in south Texas shown by a (A) stratigraphic strike section, (B) stratigraphic dip section, and (C) high-resolution seismic profile. Locations of diagrams are shown on Figure 3. The cross sections were constructed using descriptions of shallow borings (Morton and McGowen, 1980) and other unpublished data. Increased seafloor gradient near Block 1048, which is interpreted as a paleo-shoreface, is shown in more detail in Figure 10.

ing morphological criteria such as elevation, slope, degree of dissection, and soil type (Barton, 1930; Doering, 1935; Fisk, 1939; Russell, 1940; Bernard and LeBlanc, 1965; Winker, 1979). These and other workers concluded that: (1) the surfaces dip seaward, and slopes progressively de-

crease toward the coast; (2) older surfaces have steeper slopes and pass beneath younger surfaces; (3) older surfaces occur at higher elevations and exhibit greater stream dissection; (4) oxidized soil profiles mark the upper surface of each deposit; (5) each depositional sequence represents a sea-level highstand; (6) each sequence was deposited disconformably on an older formation; and (7) extensive river-valley terraces merge downstream with equivalent delta plains.

The lower Texas coastal plain consists of nearshore sediments that aggraded during highstands of sea level. Coalescing mud-rich fans of the Beaumont Fm constitute the youngest Pleistocene highstand deposits that are exposed on the coastal plain. The Beaumont is assumed to be Sangamonian in age or about 120–130 ka (Fig. 2) because of its geomorphic characteristics and stratigraphic position.

The gradual seaward slope of the Beaumont surface (0.2 to 0.4 m/km) is evidence of the flat alluvial plains aggraded by the major coastal rivers (Barton, 1930). Physiographic features such as natural levees, abandoned channels, point-bar scrolls, and other depositional remnants are well preserved on the delta plain and alluvial plain surfaces. In Louisiana, Beaumont deposits are thought to be several hundred to 1,000 m thick (Russell, 1940), whereas along the upper Texas coast equivalent deposits exhibit two to three vertically stacked aggradational cycles that together are less than 30 m thick (Winker, 1979). Similar thicknesses are indicated for Beaumont deposits of the ancestral Nueces River that form the coastal plain of the middle Texas coast (Morton and McGowen, 1980; Fig. 5).

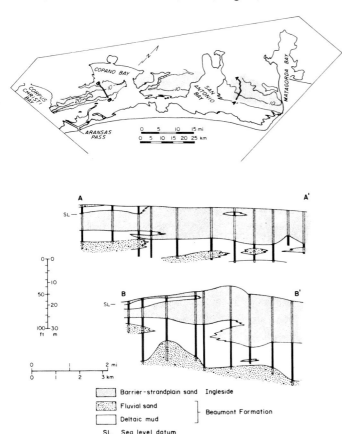

FIG. 5.—Stratigraphic dip sections that transect the Ingleside barrier-strandplain (modified after Winker, 1979). The interbedding of reworked marine sand and delta-plain mud indicates contemporaneous aggradation.

Deltaic Progradation

Aggradational alluvial plain deposits of Sangamonian age pass seaward into progradational fluvial-deltaic sediments deposited during the highstand and subsequent falling sea level. Near the Texas-Mexico border, the Beaumont Fm was deposited by both fluvial and deltaic-marine systems (Brown and others, 1980). Sediments of both systems (Fig. 3) are composed mainly of sand that respectively originated as meanderbelt and strandplain deposits. Correlative fluvial-channel and delta-front sands form the sea floor over most of the adjacent inner shelf (Figs. 3, 4). These tan and gray silty fine sands grade downward into stiff tan and gray silty clay and shelly clay. These prodelta-shelf deposits dip basinward at 1.5° to 2.0°. Measurements from soil borings and high-resolution seismic profiles indicate that the overall coarsening-upward prodelta and delta-front sequence is 15 to 80 m thick with thicknesses increasing offshore and toward the fluvial axis (Fig. 4A, B). Thickness of this shallow-water deltaic sequence is comparable to that of the San Bernard lobe of the Mississippi delta (Frazier, 1974). The Texas inner shelf is steepest near the Rio Grande, and this steeper seafloor slope is probably a reliable estimate of maximum basinward thickening that can be attributed simply to progradation without subsidence or a rise in sea level. The fact that late Pleistocene Rio Grande delta deposits are about twice the thickness predicted using present seafloor gradient (Fig. 4B) indicates that sediment accumulation depended slightly more on rate of subsidence than on depth of water.

Strike-aligned isopach patterns, as well as lateral continuity and abundance of sand (30%) exhibited by this delta system (Fig. 4A, B), typify wave-dominated deltas. The base of the progradational sequence (Fig. 4B) coincides with a strong seismic reflection (Fig. 4C). Offlapping stratigraphic relationships above the sequence boundary, which occur beneath much of the south Texas inner shelf, record the last Pleistocene depositional event. The top of the sand lithofacies also represents a sequence boundary that coincides with the Holocene-Pleistocene unconformity and is recorded in the subsurface as a lithologic boundary and a high amplitude seismic reflection (Fig. 4A). This surface formed as sea level fell about 50.0 ka and was modified during the last postglacial rise in sea level, which began about 18.0 ka. As the former coastal plain and entrenched valleys were transgressed, the upper surface of the sand lithofacies was reworked by waves and longshore currents. The resulting marine facies override the coastal plain sequence of thick fluvial-channel and delta-front sands that grade laterally and landward into floodbasin and delta-plain muds (Morton and McGowen, 1980).

Barrier-Strandplain Aggradation and Progradation

Late Pleistocene strike-fed systems formed between the major highstand deltas where restricted influx of fluvial sediments allowed the accumulation of thick barrier and strandplain sands. The Sangamonian strandline sand, known as the Ingleside barrier-strandplain (Figs. 1, 5), was first described by Price (1933). It exhibits accretionary beach ridges and contains a nearshore marine fauna like the adjacent modern barriers.

Remnants of the Ingleside shoreline can be traced from northeastern Mexico to southwestern Louisiana (Price, 1958; Fig. 1). Along its extent, it displays the same morphogenic features as the modern Texas coast, including barrier islands, strandplains attached to the mainland and erosional beaches seaward of alluvial plains (Winker, 1979). Paleogeographic reconstructions of the Gulf shoreline during the Miocene also indicate that strandplains typically formed during regressive periods of high sediment supply and stable or falling sea level, whereas barrier-lagoon systems preferentially formed during major transgressions associated with rises in sea level.

The Ingleside strandline of the central Texas coast (Fig. 5) consists of a broad (16 km wide) strike-aligned sand body that was deposited under wave-dominated marine conditions perhaps as much as 120 ka. The sand was supplied by moderately sinuous rivers that meandered across the coastal plain and emptied into the Gulf 8 to 25 km inland from the present shoreline (Fig. 1). There the sand was sorted by waves and transported by longshore currents until it was deposited along the prograding beach and shoreface.

Sands of the Ingleside barrier-strandplain attained a maximum thickness of about 25 m (Fig. 5). They interfinger with deltaic muds (Beaumont Fm) in a landward direction and thin in a seaward direction. Their downdip limit is uncertain, but they have been encountered in borings beneath modern barriers along the central Texas coast (Wilkinson and others, 1975; Morton and McGowen, 1980). The nearshore marine deposits are typically coarse- to fine-grained, yellow to brown sand or dark gray shelly sand that is intercalated with brown mud. They overlie hard, blue to gray, sandy clay containing carbonate concretions. Winker (1979) interpreted the Ingleside as a multistory beach-shoreface sequence because of its great thickness and its interbedded relation with deltaic muds of the Beaumont Fm (Fig. 5). The Ingleside is dominantly an aggradational deposit that formed contemporaneously with deltaic deposition during a highstand in sea level. The last phase, however, was progradation related to a fall in sea level that caused some of the coastal plain deltas to advance beyond the Ingleside shoreline. Remnants of these slightly younger deltas are preserved in the Houston Embayment (Fig. 1).

LATE PLEISTOCENE LOWSTAND PHASES

Shelf-Margin Progradation

Sedimentary phases of the Wisconsinan glacial stage included river entrenchment, integration of drainage networks, and subsequent deltaic progradation across the shelf and down the upper slope as base level was lowered. Seven depositional sequences that accumulated during this lower sea level and preceding lowstands are recognized on the basis of seismic profiles and foundation borings from near the shelf edge (Figs. 6, 7). Geologic ages of the youngest sequences are inferred from their stratigraphic position in conjunction with the most recent sea-level changes (Fig. 2); however, absolute ages of the underlying sequences are unknown. They are judged to be late Pleistocene sediments,

considering that the base of the Pleistocene is about 518 m below sea level (600 msec two-way travel time) in this area.

Sequence 1.—

The oldest depositional sequence penetrated by outer shelf borings is composed of one or two lithologies arranged in several different successions depending on location. Beneath Block A-76, sequence 1 consists of three lithologic units (Fig. 7). The lowermost unit is characterized by very stiff gray clay interbedded with silt. This mud unit is overlain by gray clayey sand that grades upward into medium to coarse sand containing gravel and shell fragments. The sand unit, which is about 12 m thick, grades basinward into and is overlain by very stiff to hard gray clay containing sand laminae and shell fragments.

Sequence 1 typically exhibits high amplitude, continuous, and parallel seismic reflections. Although multiples of shallower reflections interfere with the internal stratification, it appears that some strata terminate in a toplap relationship with the upper sequence boundary (A on Figs. 7 and 8A). This upper boundary is disconformable partly because of local structures associated with a graben over the Brazos Ridge (Fig. 8A), which is a deep-seated middle Miocene fault zone with large displacement and numerous antithetic faults. The attitude of strata above the lower sequence boundary is uncertain because the quality of data deteriorates with depth. Vertical lithologic successions, lateral facies relationships, and seismic signatures suggest that sequence 1 was deposited as a regressive-trangressive couplet. Upward coarsening of the lower two units indicates progradation of a deltaic complex during a former sea-level lowstand. The overlying unit of fining-upward sediments was deposited during the subsequent transgression that accompanied subsidence and a relative rise in sea level.

Sequence 2.—

This sequence is composed entirely of very stiff gray clay containing silt laminae, sand lenses, scattered shell fragments, and cemented nodules. Sequence 2 is 20 to 25 m thick in a dowdip position but thins updip (Figs. 7, 8A). Seismic reflections within the sequence are low-amplitude discontinuous to wavy. The uniform gray color, presence of shell fragments, and sand-filled burrows indicate deposition in a prodelta-shelf environment. The upper sequence boundary (B) appears to be both conformable and disconformable with underlying strata depending on location (Figs. 7, 8A). Above and updip of the Brazos Ridge (Fig. 8A) the upper boundary is an erosional unconformity that, together with the cemented nodules and shelf fragments, suggests shoreface retreat during a rising sea level.

Sequence 3.—

The third depositional sequence can be subdivided into two lithologic units (Fig. 7). The lower unit is composed of light gray clayey and shelly fine sand that coarsens upward and grades laterally into gray sandy silt and silty clay containing sand lenses and shell fragments concentrated near the top. The lower unit is from 6 to 19 m thick; maximum thickness coincides with the sand-rich portion of the unit.

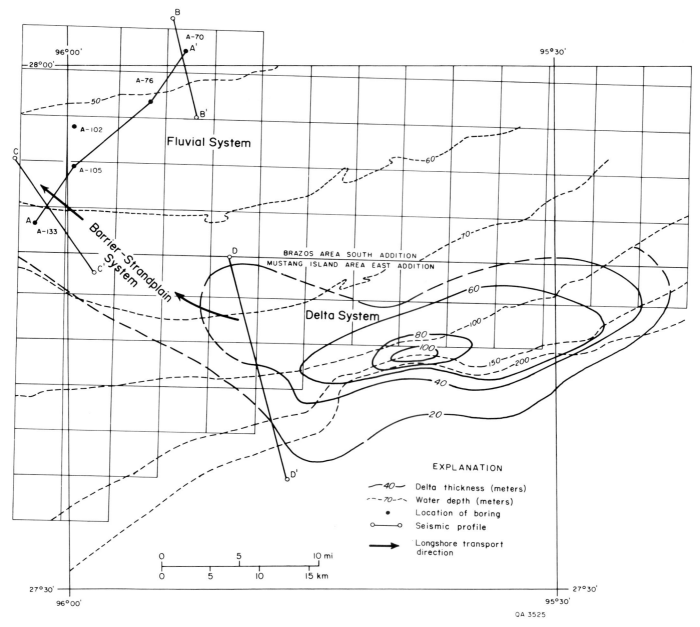

Fig. 6.—Locations of sediment borings and seismic profiles in relation to bathymetry and shelf-margin deltaic deposits. Delta isopach contours are from Suter and Berryhill (1985).

The upper lithologic unit consists of brown to gray silty clay containing sandy silt laminae, shell fragments, and cemented nodules. This fining-upward sequence is capped by a layer of tan or brown clay, which indicates an oxidizing environment and possible soil profile. Abrupt changes in engineering properties also coincide with the change in clay color. The lower boundary (B) is onlapped by sequence 3 (Figs. 7, 8A, B) that is locally thick because of a structural sag over shallow antithetic faults. High-amplitude internal reflections, which are continuous and parallel, terminate by toplap against the upper boundary (sequence boundary C in Fig. 8A).

Sequence 3 is a regressive unit exhibiting both coarsening-upward and fining-upward components. The coarser sediments were probably deposited as a distributary-mouth bar that merges downdip with prodelta and shelf deposits. The overlying finer grained and oxidized sediments appear to have a delta plain origin and represent the former base level of deposition. Overall, the deltaic sequence is 18 to 35 m thick. As expected, delta thickness is greatest near the distributary channel and decreases basinward (Fig. 7). Absolute age of sequence 3 is unavailable, but its stratigraphic position suggests deposition occurred during the early Wisconsinan falling sea level and lowstand.

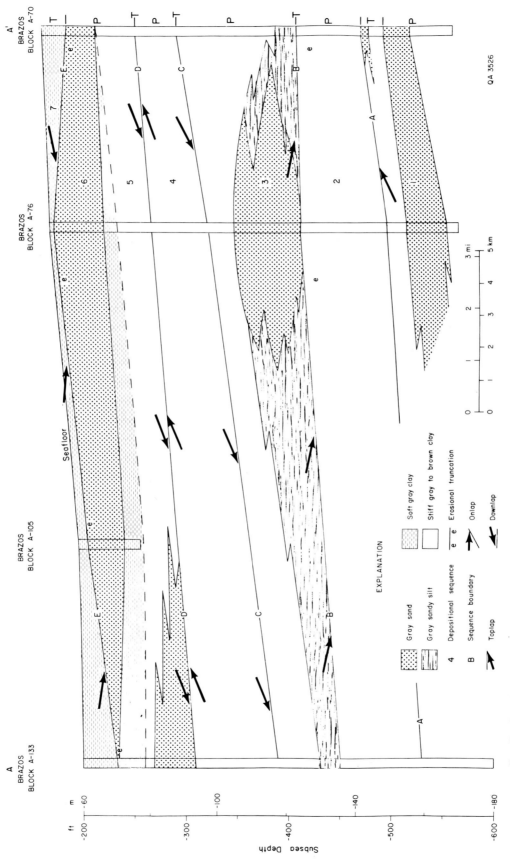

FIG. 7.—Late Quaternary depositional sequences preserved near the Texas continental shelf edge. The sequences reflect alternating progradation (P) and transgressive (T) episodes controlled by regression during sea-level lowstand and rapid transgression during rising sea level. Location of cross section is shown in Figure 6.

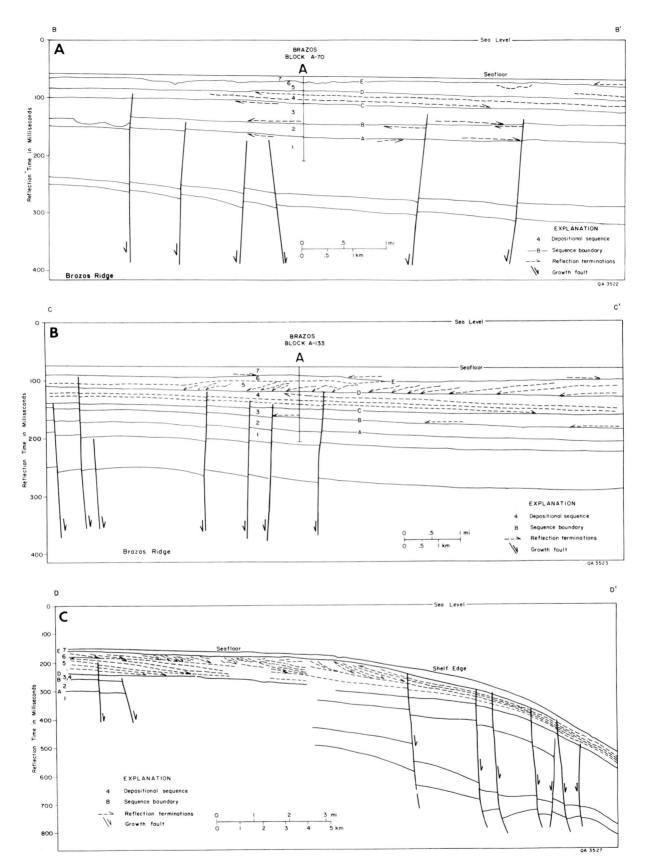

Fig. 8.—Interpreted high-resolution seismic profiles showing shelf-margin depositional sequences and sequence boundaries related primarily to fluctuations in sea level. Locations of seismic profiles are shown in Figure 6.

Sequence 4.—

The fourth sequence is composed entirely of stiff to very stiff brown, tan, or gray clay and silty clay containing silt laminae, sand lenses, and shell fragments. The brown colors, coarser sediments, and shell debris are generally concentrated near the top of the unit, suggesting progressively shallower water and higher wave energy.

Medium- to high-amplitude, low-angle clinoform reflections having uniform dips typify the internal stratification within the sequence (Fig. 8A, B). The clinoform strata downlap the lower sequence boundary (C) and display toplap relationships with the upper boundary (D in Figs. 7 and 8A, B). Basinward of Figure 8B, strata onlap the youngest clinoform reflections. Thickness of this regressive sequence increases basinward and ranges from 12 to 24 m. The downlapping seismic configurations, muddy lithology, and presence of shells all indicate a prodelta-shelf environment of a prograding shelf-platform delta located farther updip. Stratigraphic position of sequence 4 suggests that it may have been deposited during the middle Wisconsinan sea-level highstand.

Sequence 5.—

This sequence is composed of stiff gray clay interbedded with sandy silt and containing shell fragments. The mud-rich unit grades basinward into gray fine sand and silty sand (Fig. 7). The sand-rich unit is 12 m thick and displays coarsening-upward and fining-upward textural patterns. The relatively mud-free middle succession is well sorted in contrast to the overlying poorly sorted silty sand, which grades upward into firm silty clay containing sand laminae. Correlative strata from the eastern flank of the depocenter and in 200 m of water are composed predominantly of mud containing minor amounts of sand in the lower part of the progradational sequence (Sidner and others, 1978).

Stratal configurations in sequence 5 are related to lithology. The mud-rich unit to the northeast (Fig. 7) displays moderate-amplitude, continuous and parallel reflections that become low-angle clinoforms in a basinward direction (Fig. 8C); the clinoforms downlap the lower sequence boundary near the shelf edge. Strata within the sand-rich section also baselap the lower boundary, but in a landward direction (Fig. 8B). Broad, low-angle clinoforms that are present near the sand body crest progressively steepen landward and become irregular as the sandy unit thins and onlaps the underlying surface.

Sequence 6.—

Sequence 6 can be subdivided into two lithologic units. The lower unit is composed of soft to very soft gray clay and silty clay containing shell fragments and sand lenses. This mud unit grades upward into gray fine sand (Fig. 7) that is interbedded with silt and clay and contains some shell fragments and detrital organic matter. Seismic signatures for sequence 6 are low-amplitude wavy to discontinuous reflections near Block A-70 (Fig. 8A) that become sigmoid reflections farther downdip (Fig. 8C). In all cases the uppermost reflections are truncated by the overlying sequence boundary (E in Fig. 8B, C).

Sequences 5 and 6 comprise a single, large depositional complex. The locus of deposition outlined by isopach contours depicting a compound shelf-margin delta (Fig. 6) that attained a thickness of more than 100 m (Suter and Berryhill, 1985). Internal geometry and morphology of the lower sand suggest reworking of the delta flank and lateral accretion of sand transported northwestward by waves and strong longshore currents (Figs. 6, 8B). This delta-margin shoreface deposit was subsequently buried by prodelta mud and fluvial-channel or distributary-mouth bar sand of a younger delta lobe. Sand deposited near the channel mouth is as much as 16 m thick (Fig. 7, Block A-76).

The combined regressive unit (sequences 5 and 6) was probably deposited during a middle Wisconsinan falling sea level and subsequent late Wisconsinan lowstand that exposed the delta and promoted progradation of the shelf margin. The landward segment of the upper sequence boundary (E) probably represents the subaerial erosional unconformity formed during the most recent sea-level lowstand about 18.0 ka. Sparker profiles across the late Wisconsinan Brazos-Colorado delta (delta A of Suter and Berryhill, 1985) exhibit clinoform reflections associated with two depositional episodes (Fig. 8C) perhaps controlled by minor fluctuations in sea level. The steepened clinoforms near the shelf edge indicate greater slopes, but they may also reflect greater subsidence and sediment supply.

Sequence 7.—

Sequence 7, which is 1.5 to 11 m thick (Fig. 7), is mainly composed of very soft gray clay, sandy clay, or poorly sorted clayey sand containing shell fragments and organic matter. Overall, the sequence displays an upward decrease in abundance of sand. Sand-filled burrows as well as sand and silt laminae are common, even though mud is the predominant sediment type.

Strata within sequence 7 appear on seismic profiles as low- to high-amplitude parallel and continuous reflections that onlap the lower sequence boundary (E in Figs. 7 and 8). These transgressive shelf deposits are the depositional record of submergence and shoreface retreat that accompanied the postglacial rise in sea level. Therefore, the sediments would range in age from about 18.0 ka to present.

Discussion.—

Although the largest sedimentary volume in this series was deposited during progradational phases attendant with falling sea level and relative lowstands, the individual sequences document a cyclicity that was probably influenced by sea-level fluctuations. On the basis of vertical succession and interpreted depositional environment, it appears that sequences 1, 3, 5, and 6 are products of the lowest sea levels, whereas sequences 2, 4, and 7 are the result of relatively higher sea levels. Together the sequences also reveal paleogeographic relationships, such as proximity to a fluvial axis, as indicated by a greater proportion of sand (distributary-mouth bars) in the Block A-76 boring. At that location borings contain 37% sand, whereas at Blocks A-133 and A-70 they contain only 15 and 13% sand, respectively, in the upper 120 m of sediment. These sand percent values are also typical of proximal and distal deltaic deposits of Tertiary age encountered beneath the Texas coastal plain and continental shelf.

Formation of Carbonate Banks and Reefs

Coral reefs and displaced Tertiary strata encrusted by calcareous algae are located between the lowstand delta complexes (Fig. 1). These seafloor prominences were living reefs during late Wisconsinan postglacial rising sea level, when Gulf waters near the shelf edge were shallow, clear and possibly replenished by upwelling nutrient-rich basinal waters (Parker and Curray, 1956; Ludwick and Walton, 1957). The banks and reefs grew on firm substrates, such as clay mounds or strandline sands reworked from the shelf-margin deltas (Berryhill and others, 1976). Their locations and the locations of Wisconsinan fluvial channels on the broad interdeltaic platform were also partly determined by contemporaneous movement of diapirs and growth faults (Berryhill, 1981). Within the offshore diapiric province, the banks overlie salt domes, but southwest of the ancestral Brazos-Colorado delta (Fig. 1), they are associated with the Brazos Ridge structural trend (Fig. 8A, B). The carbonate banks are preferentially located on upthrown fault blocks or over-

lie the domal crest created by rollover into the master listric fault.

Most of the coral reefs died and became encrusted banks because they were unable to keep pace with sea-level rise. They remain as seafloor prominences and are slowly being buried by modern shelf muds transported in the nepheloid layer (Rezak, 1985). A few active reefs, such as Flower Garden Banks (Fig. 1), have continued to grow after the Holocene transgression because salt diapirism has kept the reef tops above the nepheloid layer. These active reefs rise more than 116 m above the sea floor and come within 19 m of the sea surface.

LATE HOLOCENE-MODERN HIGHSTAND PHASES

Valley Aggradation

During the late Wisconsinan sea-level lowstand, principal streams eroded valleys below the coastal plain (Fig. 9). Maximum entrenchment of as much as 40 m (Fig. 9) occurred near the present shoreline, which approximately coincided with the basinward limit of progradation during the Sangamonian highstand (Fig. 1). Depths of valley en-

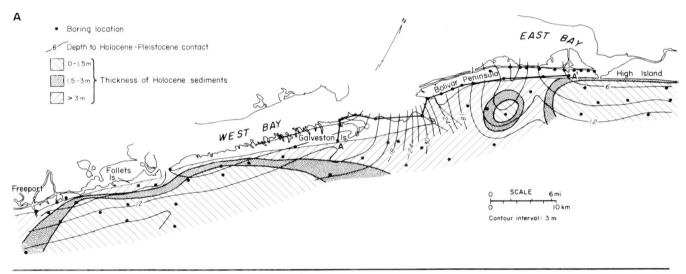

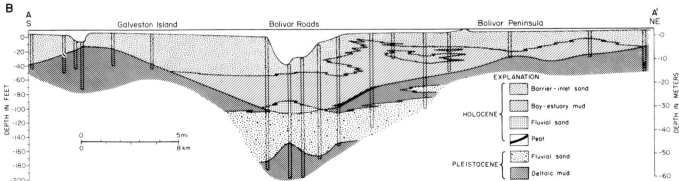

FIG. 9.—(A) Isopach map and (B) stratigraphic cross section showing the thickness and lateral extent of late Quaternary sediments along the upper Texas coast. Contours give depth to the Pleistocene-Holocene unconformity. Interpretations based on shallow subsurface data from Bernard and others (1970), U.S. Army Corps of Engineers (1972), and Williams and others (1979).

trenchment gradually decrease both landward and seaward from this point. Modern bays, which occupy the former entrenched valleys, are only partly filled because fluvial discharge and sediment transport decreased in response to climatic changes. The bay fill deposited during and after the Holocene rise in sea level (Fig. 9) is characterized by an onlapping transgressive sequence (Shepard and Moore, 1960; Nelson and Bray, 1970) that can be subdivided, from oldest to youngest, into three units: (1) regressive alluvial sands, (2) transgressive fluvial sands that grade upward into deltaic sands and muds, and (3) aggradational bay-estuarine muds. Some valley-fill sequences are overlain by a thin uppermost regressive unit where small bayhead deltas have prograded over the bay mud. Other valley-fill sequences are capped by regressive sands and muds deposited in barrier and inlet environments (i.e., Bolivar Peninsula, Fig. 9) or transgressive shelf-sand ridge complexes (i.e., Sabine Bank, Fig. 1).

Thickness and lateral extent of nearshore Holocene deposits are related to topography of the late Wisconsinan coastal plain and configuration of the Holocene sediment wedge. The oldest sediments penetrated beneath the upper Texas coast by shallow borings (Beaumont Fm) are composed of gray to brown, stiff to very stiff clay containing calcareous nodules (Fig. 9). Within the thick mud sequence is a laterally persistent layer of gray silty sand which has an irregular basal contact; the sand is as much as 20 m thick. The sand and surrounding mud are part of a thick succession of aggradational fluvial-deltaic deposits. These overcompacted late Pleistocene sediments are separated from the overlying Holocene sediments by an erosional unconformity having substantial local relief. Gray silty sands of the ancestral Trinity River occupy the valley floor. These fluvial sands are overlain by soft gray clay containing some shell fragments. A thin layer of peat, probably representing a fringing marsh, locally separates these estuarine and open-embayment deposits from the underlying Pleistocene mud. Nearshore marine muds were deposited as sea level rose, whereas overlying sandy sediments were deposited in barrier and tidal-inlet environments after sea level reached its present position.

Minor Sea-Level Fluctuations

Minor glacio-eustatic oscillations in sea level apparently last a few thousand years and have a range of a few meters. Several physical criteria document brief sea-level oscillations and temporary pauses in the general rise in sea level since the late Wisconsinan glaciation. Submerged features identified by irregularities in shelf bathymetry (Figs. 1, 10) offer evidence of intermediate stillstand positions. These shelf features, such as wave-cut terraces (also buried beneath Holocene bay fill), elongate shoals, and bank crests having similar elevations (Parker and Curray, 1956; Curray, 1960; Nelson and Bray, 1970), are the remnant expressions of former shorefaces, barrier islands, and reefs. Sabine Bank and Heald Bank (Fig. 1) are elongate shoals that comprise a shelf-ridge complex that is 10 m thick, 16 km wide, and composed predominantly of sand and shell (Nelson and Bray, 1970). Remnants of the oldest sand ridges coincide with the surface expression of a middle Miocene expansion fault zone. This relationship suggests that local relief along the faults may have contributed to ridge development by trapping sand on the downthrown (basinward) side of the faults.

Paleoshorelines formed during brief lulls or reversals in the Holocene transgression can be delineated by subtle variations in slope (Price, 1954) and abnormally high concentrations of coarse sediments (Curray, 1960; Morton and Winker, 1979). Steep slopes associated with reworked deltaic promontories (Figs. 1, 10) coincide with coarse sediment trends containing caliche nodules, rock fragments, and

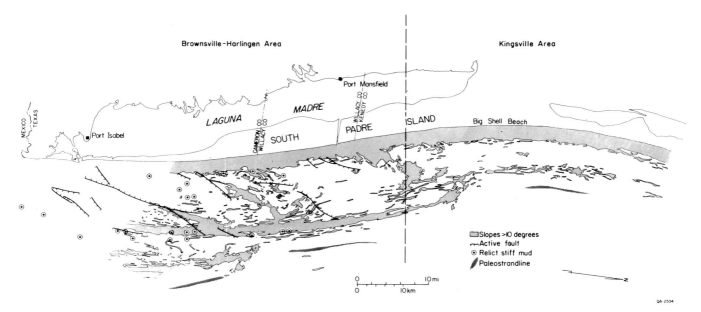

FIG. 10.—Slope map of the south Texas inner shelf illustrating the relationships among seafloor gradient, active faults, and paleostrandlines. Locations of near-surface relict stiff mud are taken from McGowen and Morton (1979).

brackish water mollusks. Together these trends delineate former beach and shoreface deposits that are submerged and partially buried by recent shelf sediments (Morton and Winker, 1979).

Fluvial Aggradation

Unusually thick sequences of fluvial sediments accumulated during the late Wisconsinan-Holocene eustatic cycle in the Mississippi and Brazos River alluvial valleys (Fisk, 1944; Bernard and others, 1970). The vertical transition from coarse-grained basal deposits to fine-grained alluvial-plain deposits in both valleys records the fluvial response to a fall and rise in sea level. During highstands or stable sea level, broad meanderbelt systems formed as a result of frequent channel avulsion and repeated occupation of former channels. Bernard and others (1970) reconstructed the late Quaternary depositional history of the Brazos River and subdivided the aggradational deposits into three units on the basis of former sea-level positions. The basal unit (late Wisconsinan lowstand deposits) exhibits a fining-upward succession 12 m thick; the middle unit (rising sea-level deposits) is 10 m thick and composed dominantly of sand that is distinguished from younger fluvial sediments only by radiocarbon ages. The top unit (modern highstand deposits) is 18 m thick and displays an upward decrease in grain size from coarse sand and gravel to clay. In most of the borings, total thickness of the fluvial sediments deposited since 18.0 ka is about 28 m, even though the estimated channel depth was only about 18 m below the floodplain.

Vertically stacked, fining-upward sequences also characterize fluvial sediments deposited by the Rio Grande since 7.0 ka (Fulton, 1975; Fig. 11). Periodic avulsion of river channels, construction of crevasse splays, and aggradation

of other floodbasin deposits were responsible for the shallowest depositional sequence of the Rio Grande. Apparently it formed in response to (1) gradual subsidence and (2) landward migration of the shoreline. Subsidence, due to shallow compaction or deep crustal loading, would reactivate fluvial channels and renew floodplain deposition. Shoreline retreat would also have the same effect as a relative sea-level rise and would cause flooding along the lower reaches of the stream. Both processes would produce thin overbank sediments and channel fills such as the youngest sequences preserved in the shallow subsurface (Fig. 11). These sand and mud deposits are as thick (18 m) as those of the Brazos River, but individual channels of the Rio Grande system are only 8 to 10 m thick. Dimensions of the ancestral Rio Grande are smaller than those of the Brazos River, because they represent channel size for the upper delta plain rather than for the alluvial plain. Furthermore, younger channels were shallower than older channels (Fig. 11), a chronostratigraphic relationship that commonly occurs where thin but areally extensive delta-plain sediments are deposited over older and more stable fluvial-channel sediments.

Deltaic Progradation and Transgression

In the Rio Grande Embayment, the base of the youngest progradational sequence coincides with the Holocene-Pleistocene erosional unconformity (Fig. 4, section B-B', and Fig. 11). Holocene fluvial-deltaic sediments overlying the unconformity can be subdivided into four lithofacies that together constitute a moderately thick regressive sequence (Fig. 11). Brown to gray clays of prodelta origin compose the basal lithofacies, which is 3 to 11 m thick. This unit grades upward into thin gray sands interbedded with sedi-

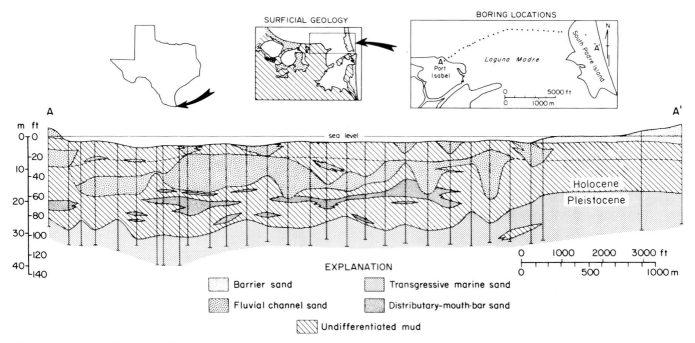

FIG. 11.—Stratigraphic section of late Quaternary fluvial-deltaic and barrier island sediments deposited in south Texas by the Rio Grande. Point A' in Figure 11 is the same as point A in Figure 4.

ments similar to the prodelta muds. These alternating sands and muds (second lithofacies) comprise the delta-front deposits that are as much as 7.5 m thick. Sediments above the distributary-mouth bar are relatively thick (11 m) and are composed either of brown to gray sandy clay and organic-rich clay or gray fine sand and sandy silt. These two lithofacies, which respectively originated in delta-plain and fluvial-channel environments, account for most of the Holocene Rio Grande fluvial-deltaic system. The thin progradational facies (prodelta and delta-front deposits) and thick aggradational facies (channel-fill and delta-plain deposits) are typical of fluvially dominated shallow-water deltas that build onto stable shelves constructed during a preceding regressive episode.

Holocene sediments deposited by the Rio Grande range in thickness from 1.5 m to nearly 30 m (Fulton, 1975; Fig. 11). Sediment thickness increases away from the overlapping contact with adjacent Pleistocene sediments and toward the river mouth (Fig. 4A), where subsidence was greatest and the entrenched valley was deepest. Sand concentrations in the thicker parts of the sediment wedge range from 20 to 50% depending on the thickness of channel-fill deposits. Aggradation of the upper delta-plain and fluvial channels accompanied valley filling and delta progradation across the inner shelf about 4.0 to 7.0 ka when the rate of sea-level rise diminished (Fulton, 1975; Morton and McGowen, 1980).

Morphologic and sedimentologic evidence suggests that the modern Rio Grande delta (4.0 to 7.0 ka) was located about 25 to 40 km seaward of its current position (Price, 1954; Morton and Winker, 1979; Fig. 10). Reductions in sediment load and discharge associated with a warmer, drier climate, however, caused subsequent delta abandonment and headland retreat that is manifested as shoreline erosion along the south Texas coast. Delta destruction was also accompanied by compactional subsidence, which contributed to formation of Laguna Madre, South Padre Island, and the adjacent wind-tidal flats about 2.0 ka (Rusnak, 1960).

Barrier-Strandplain Progradation and Aggradation

The rapid Holocene transgression resulted in an onlapping aggradational sequence of paralic sediments that were products of beach and barrier migration across the submerged coastal plain. Evidence for widespread transgressive barriers is provided by (1) morphology of the oldest subaerial shoreline deposits preserved in modern back-barrier environments and (2) presence of underlying mid-Holocene bay-lagoon deposits (Fisk, 1959; Shepard and Moore, 1960; Bernard and others, 1970; Wilkinson and others, 1975; Morton and McGowen, 1980; Fig. 9). These transgressive barriers became progradational barriers because sea level stabilized and, more importantly, because abundant sand for seaward accretion initially was available by transportation from updrift rivers, erosion of adjacent fluvial-deltaic promontories, and erosion of the adjacent inner shelf that was locally blanketed by sand. Most of these barriers prograded 1 to 2 km before reaching equilibrium with increased water depth, diminished sand supply, and a wave-dominated shoreface profile.

Thickness of the regressive barriers ranges from 10 to 16 m depending on location and relation with underlying facies. The thickest barriers, which are located in the interdeltaic embayment of the central Texas coast, are composed of vertically stacked sequences representing transgressive, transitional, and regressive depositional phases. Of the total barrier thickness, about 3 m were deposited during the transgressive phase, whereas about 3 m and 10 m were respectively deposited in subaerial (beach and barrier flat) and subtidal (shoreface) environments during the regressive phase. Abnormally thick (>16 m) barrier sequences are attributed to nearly coincident shoreline positions and the resulting superposition of barrier facies. Parallel beach ridges and the coincidence of barrier core thickness and shoreface depth (Fisk, 1959; Bernard and others, 1970; Wilkinson and others, 1975) strongly suggest that these barriers mainly grew by Gulfward accretion rather than by aggradation related to subsidence and/or sea-level rise. If recent rates of sea-level rise (Swanson and Thurlow, 1973) had persisted since barrier formation, then these features would be submerged beneath 12 m of water because the rates of submergence greatly exceed the rates of barrier aggradation. The progradational barriers are composed of gray to brown silty to clayey sand containing some shell fragments. They thin laterally along depositional strike (Fig. 9) and merge with extant transgressive barriers that are 3 to 5 m thick and overlie muddy sediments of bay-lagoon or delta-plain origin (Figs. 4, 11). All the barriers are currently aggrading as a result of periodic storm washover and eolian processes that temporarily accelerate during droughts.

Shelf Aggradation

Surficial sediments of the Texas continental shelf are primarily (1) reworked and mixed terrigenous and biogenic clastics that represent relict and palimpsest sediments deposited before or during the post-Wisconsinan transgression, and (2) modern sands and muds deposited chiefly by storm processes. Relict sediments covering broad areas of the shelf are firm, oxidized muds and sandy muds with root casts. These delta-plain deposits are exposed at the sea floor or underlie a thin veneer of shelf mud along the upper coast and offshore from the ancestral deltas (Curray, 1960; Morton and Winker, 1979). In these same areas, muddy to well-sorted sand and gravel deposits are interpreted as relict shorefaces, beaches, and sand ridges (Fig. 1) because they are similar to modern transgressive beach and shoal deposits. Relict sediments in the interdeltaic embayment are commonly indurated with carbonate cement and composed of crossbedded sandstone, micritic limestone, and shelly mudstone. These rocks have been variously interpreted as eolian, lacustrine, and lagoonal deposits that aggraded on the arid coastal plain before it was transgressed (Hayes, 1967; Thayer and others, 1974).

Holocene and modern sediments deposited seaward of the advancing shoreface are only a few centimeters to a few meters thick over much of the shelf (Fig. 9), except between the late Wisconsinan deltas and landward of the reefs (Fig. 1) where they are as much as 45 m thick (Berryhill and others, 1976) and they disconformably overlie an erosional surface that is stratigraphically equivalent to sequence boundary E (Figs. 7, 8). At least the upper few meters of these aggradational nearshore deposits are composed of intercalated and bioturbated sand and mud; the predominance of either constituent depends mainly on water depth and distance from the shoreline. Percent sand and the number of discrete sand layers are highest along the shoreface and over the ancestral deltas; elsewhere mud predominates (Berryhill and others, 1976). The sedimentologic charcteristics and young age of these shelf sediments suggest episodic deposition related to storm processes that periodically transported shoreface sands basinward below normal wave base (Hayes, 1967; Berryhill and others, 1976; Morton, 1981). The shelf deposits aggraded as the adjacent barriers prograded shortly after sea level reached its present position. The substantial thickness of these paralic sediments above the late Wisconsinan unconformity indicates that rates of middle and outer shelf sedimentation can be significant during highstands of sea level.

DISCUSSION AND CONCLUSIONS

Shallow subsurface data from the Texas coastal plain and continental shelf are useful for evaluating the effects of local tectonism and relative sea-level fluctuations on position, thickness, and lithology of late Quaternary depositional sequences. Extreme climatic fluctuations drastically and simultaneously altered sea level and sediment supply, causing markedly different responses in depositional architecture. Most depositional sequences that formed as a result of these glacio-eustatic cycles are highly asymmetrical. Glacial stages were characterized by a gradual fall in sea level, increased precipitation, and increased sediment yield that produced sequences with thick progradational facies and thin aggradational facies (Figs. 4, 7). Interglacial stages, on the other hand, were accompanied by rapid rises in sea level, reduced precipitation, and abrupt decreases in sediment supply that caused rapid retreat of the shoreline and shoreface erosion, resulting in a ravinement surface. Sequences deposited in a rising sea or at highstand typically exhibit thin progradational facies and thick aggradational facies (Figs. 5, 11).

Attempts to correlate each depositional sequence with a eustatic cycle would be unsatisfactory, because the number of sequences in the upper 150 m of sediment near the shelf margin exceeds the number of significant late Pleistocene eustatic fluctuations in sea level. This discrepancy indicates that deltaic processes and shifting sites of deposition controlled some relative sea-level changes, whereas others were clearly the result of eustatic fluctuations.

The surficial influence of deep structural features is apparent when the locations of late Wisconsinan and Holocene submerged barriers, drowned reefs, and buried channels are compared to underlying growth faults, shale ridges, salt diapirs, and withdrawal synclines. Progradation onto the upper slope and displacement by growth faults cause a two- to threefold expansion of mixed fluvial- and wave-dominated deltas near the shelf margin. Landward of the contemporaneous fault zone, however, thicknesses of individual sand bodies and of entire depositional sequences

are comparable whether their position on the shelf was related to rising or falling sea level.

Progradational sequences deposited in neritic environments are 18 to 60 m thick (Figs. 4, 5, 7, 11), but nominal thicknesses ranging from 25 to 30 m are typical of many cyclic sequences (Figs. 7, 11). These latter thicknesses are about twice the water depth of the lower shoreface, which suggests that stable-platform deposition depends nearly equally on relative sea-level changes and seafloor slope even though rates of subsidence determine the thickness of basin fill over long periods of geologic time.

ACKNOWLEDGMENTS

Data for this study were acquired in conjunction with the Submerged Lands Project funded in part by the Bureau of Economic Geology, State of Texas, and Minerals Management Service. The Texas Department of Highways and Public Transportation, Mobil Oil Company, and Cities Service Oil Company kindly provided most of the soil boring descriptions; the high-resolution seismic profiles were obtained in cooperation with the U.S. Geological Survey. Special thanks are extended to C. D. Winker, who assisted with the initial compilation and integration of data. The reviews by Bill Galloway, Dag Nummedal, and John Suter greatly improved the clarity and content of the manuscript.

REFERENCES

BALLARD, R. C., AND UCHUPI, E., 1970, Morphology and Quaternary history of the continental shelf of the Gulf coast of the United States: Bulletin of Marine Science, v. 20, p. 547–559.

BARTON, D. C., 1930, Deltaic coastal plain of southeastern Texas: Geological Society of America Bulletin, v. 41, p. 359–382.

BEARD, J. H., SANGREE, J. B., AND SMITH, L. A., 1982, Quaternary chronology, paleoclimate, depositional sequences and eustatic cycles: American Association of Petroleum Geologists Bulletin, v. 66, p. 158–169.

BERNARD, H. A., AND LEBLANC, R. J., 1965, Resume of the Quaternary geology of the northern Gulf of Mexico province, in Wright, H. E., Jr., and Frey, D. G., eds., The Quaternary of the United States: Princeton University Press, Princeton, p. 137–185.

———, MAJOR, C. F., JR., PARROTT, B. S., AND LEBLANC, R. J., SR., 1970, Recent Sediments of Southeastern Texas, a Field Guide to the Brazos Alluvial and Deltaic Plains and the Galveston Barrier Island Complex: University of Texas at Austin, Bureau of Economic Geology, Guidebook 11, 132 p.

BERRYHILL, H. L., 1981, Map showing paleogeography of the continental shelf during the low stand of sea level, Wisconsin glaciation, Corpus Christi 1° × 2° quadrangle: U.S. Geological Survey, Map I-1287-E, 1:250,000.

———, SHIDELER, G. L., HOLMES, C. W., HILL, G. W., BARNES, S. L., AND MARTIN, R. G., 1976, Environmental studies, South Texas Outer Continental Shelf, Geology: National Technical Information Service Publication PB-251 341, 393 p.

BROWN, L. F., JR., BREWTON, J. L., EVANS, T. J., MCGOWEN, J. H., WHITE, W. A., GROAT, C. G., AND FISHER, W. L., 1980, Environmental Geologic Atlas of the Texas Coastal Zone, Brownsville-Harlingen area: University of Texas at Austin, Bureau of Economic Geology, 140 p.

CAUGHEY, C. A., 1975, Pleistocene depositional trends host valuable Gulf oil reserves: Oil and Gas Journal, v. 73, part 1, p. 90–94; part 2, p. 240–242.

CLARK, J. A., FARRELL, W. E., AND PELTIER, W. R., 1978, Global changes in postglacial sea level: a numerical calculation: Quaternary Research, v. 9, p. 265–287.

CURRAY, J. R., 1960, Sediments and history of Holocene transgression, continental shelf, northwest Gulf of Mexico, in Shepard, F. P., Phleger, F. B., and Van Andel, T. J., eds., Recent Sediments, Northwest Gulf of Mexico: American Association of Petroleum Geologists, Tulsa, p. 221–266.

———, 1964, Transgressions and regressions, *in* Miller, R. L., ed., Papers in Marine Geology, Shepard Commemorative Volume: MacMillan Press, New York, p. 175–203.

———, 1965, Late Quaternary history, continental shelves of the United States, *in* Wright, H. E., Jr., and Frey, D. G., eds., The Quaternary of the United States: Princeton University Press, Princeton, New Jersey, p. 723–735.

DOERING, J., 1935, Post-Fleming surface formations of coastal southeast Texas and south Louisiana: American Association of Petroleum Geologists Bulletin, v. 19, p. 651–688.

FAIRBRIDGE, R. W., 1961, Eustatic changes in sea level, *in* Ahrens, L. H., Press, F., Rankama, K., and Runcorn, S. K., eds., Physics and Chemistry of the Earth, v. 4: Pergamon Press, New York, p. 99–185.

FISK, H. N., 1939, Depositional terrace slopes in Louisiana: Journal of Geomorphology, v. 2, p. 181–200.

———, 1944, Geological investigation of the alluvial valley of the lower Mississippi River: U.S. Army Corps of Engineers, Mississippi River Commission, Vicksburg, Mississippi, 78 p.

———, 1959, Padre Island and the Laguna Madre flats, coastal south Texas: Louisiana State University, Second Coastal Geography Conference, Baton Rouge, p. 103–151.

———, AND MCCLELLAND, B., 1959, Geology of continental shelf off Louisiana: its influence on offshore foundation design: Geological Society of America Bulletin, v. 70, p. 1369–1394.

———, AND MCFARLAN, E., JR., 1955, Late Quaternary deltaic deposits of the Mississippi River: Geological Society of America Special Paper 62, p. 279–302.

FRAZIER, D. E., 1974, Depositional episodes: their relationship to the Quaternary stratigraphic framework in the northwestern portion the Gulf basin: University of Texas at Austin, Bureau of Economic Geology, Geological Circular 74-1, 28 p.

FULTON, K. J., 1975, Subsurface stratigraphy, depositional environments, and aspects of reservoir continuity—Rio Grande delta, Texas: Unpublished Ph.D. Dissertation, University of Cincinnati, 314 p.

HAYES, M. O., 1967, Hurricanes as geological agents: case studies of hurricanes Carla, 1961, and Cindy, 1963: University of Texas at Austin, Bureau of Economic Geology Report of Investigations 61, 56 p.

LEHNER, P., 1969, Salt tectonics and Pleistocene stratigraphy on continental slope of northern Gulf of Mexico: American Association of Petroleum Geologists Bulletin, v. 53, p. 2431–2479.

LUDWICK, J. C., AND WALTON, W. R., 1957, Shelf-edge calcareous prominences in northeastern Gulf of Mexico: American Association of Petroleum Geologists Bulletin, v. 41, p. 2054–2101.

MCGOWEN, J. H., AND MORTON, R. A., 1979, Sediment distribution, bathymetry, faults, and salt diapirs, submerged lands of Texas: University of Texas at Austin, Bureau of Economic Geology, 31 p.

MITCHUM, R. M., JR., VAIL, P. R., AND SANGREE, J. B., 1977, Seismic stratigraphy and global changes in sea level, part 6: stratigraphic interpretation of seismic reflection patterns in depositional sequences, *in* Payton, C. E., ed., Seismic Stratigraphy-Applications to Hydrocarbon Exploration: American Association of Petroleum Geologists Memoir 26, p. 117–133.

MORTON, R. A., 1981, Formation of storm deposits by wind-forced currents in the Gulf of Mexico and the North Sea: International Association of Sedimentologists Special Publication 5, p. 385–396.

———, JIRIK, L. A., AND FOOTE, R. Q., 1985, Depositional history, facies analysis, and production characteristics of hydrocarbon-bearing sediments, offshore Texas: University of Texas at Austin, Bureau of Economic Geology, Geological Circular 85-2, 31 p.

———, AND MCGOWEN, J. H., 1980, Modern depositional environments of the Texas coast: University of Texas at Austin, Bureau of Economic Geology, Guidebook 20, 167 p.

———, AND WINKER, C. D., 1979, Distribution and significance of coarse biogenic and clastic deposits on the Texas inner shelf: Gulf Coast Association of Geological Societies Transactions, v. 29, p. 306–320.

NELSON, H. F., AND BRAY, E. E., 1970, Stratigraphy and history of the Holocene sediments in the Sabine-High Island area, Gulf of Mexico, *in* Morgan, J. P., and Shaver, R. H., eds., Deltaic Sedimentation, Modern and Ancient: Society of Economic Paleontologists and Mineralogists Special Publication 15, p. 48–77.

PARKER, R. H., AND CURRAY, J. R., 1956, Fauna and bathymetry of banks on continental shelf, northwest Gulf of Mexico: American Association of Petroleum Geologists Bulletin, v. 40, p. 2428–2439.

POAG, C. W., 1973, Late Quaternary sea levels in the Gulf of Mexico: Gulf Coast Association of Geological Societies Transactions, v. 23, p. 394–400.

PRICE, W. A., 1933, Role of diastrophism in topography of Corpus Christi area, south Texas: American Association of Petroleum Geologists Bulletin, v. 17, p. 907–962.

———, 1954, Dynamic environments: reconnaissance mapping, geologic and geomorphic, of continental shelf of Gulf of Mexico: Gulf Coast Association of Geological Societies Transactions, v. 4, p. 75–107.

———, 1958, Sedimentology and Quaternary geomorphology of south Texas: Gulf Coast Association of Geological Societies Transactions, v. 8, p. 41–75.

REZAK, R., 1985, Local carbonate production on a terrigenous shelf: Gulf Coast Association of Geological Societies Transactions, v. 35, p. 477–483.

RUSNAK, G. A., 1960, Sediments of Laguna Madre, Texas, *in* Shepard, F. P., Phleger, F. B., and Van Andel, T. J., eds., Recent Sediments, Northwest Gulf of Mexico: American Association of Petroleum Geologists, Tulsa, p. 153–196.

RUSSELL, R. J., 1940, Quaternary history of Louisiana: Geological Society of America Bulletin, v. 51, 1199–1233.

SHEPARD, F. P., AND MOORE, D. G., 1960, Bays of central Texas coast, *in* Shepard, F. P., Phleger, F. B., and Van Andel, T. J., eds., Recent Sediments, Northwest Gulf of Mexico: American Association of Petroleum Geologists, Tulsa, p. 117–152.

SIDNER, B. R., GARTNER, S., AND BRYANT, W. R., 1978, Late Pleistocene geologic history of Texas outer continental shelf and upper continental slope, *in* Bouma, A. H., Moore, G. T., and Coleman, J. M., eds., Framework, Facies and Oil Trapping Characteristics on the Upper Continental Margin: American Association of Petroleum Geologists, Studies in Geology 7, p. 243–266.

SMITH, L. A., 1965, Paleoenvironmental variation curves and paleoeustatics: Gulf Coast Association of Geological Societies Transactions, v. 15, p. 47–60.

SUTER, J. R., AND BERRYHILL, H. L., JR., 1985, Late Quaternary shelf-margin deltas, northwest Gulf of Mexico: American Association of Petroleum Geologists Bulletin, v. 69, p. 77–91.

SWANSON, R. L., AND THURLOW, C. L., 1973, Recent subsidence rates along the Texas and Louisiana coasts as determined from tide measurements: Journal of Geophysical Research, v. 78, p. 2665–2671.

THAYER, P. A., LAROCQUE, A., AND TUNNELL, J. W., JR., 1974, Relict lacustrine sediments on the inner continental shelf, southeast Texas: Gulf Coast Association of Geological Societies Transactions, v. 24, p. 337–347.

U.S. ARMY CORPS OF ENGINEERS, 1972, Texas Coast Hurricane Study: Galveston District, U.S. Army Corps of Engineers (not consecutively paginated).

VAIL, P. R., MITCHUM, R. M., JR., AND THOMSPON, S., III, 1977, Seismic stratigraphy and global sea level, part 4: global cycles of relative changes of sea level, *in* Payton, C. E., ed., Seismic Stratigraphy-Applications to Hydrocarbon Exploration: American Association of Petroleum Geologists Memoir 26, p. 83–97.

WALCOTT, R. I., 1972, Past sea levels, eustasy and deformation of the earth: Quaternary Research, v. 2, p. 1–14.

WILKINSON, B. H., MCGOWEN, J. H., AND LEWIS, C. R., 1975, Ingleside strandplain sand of central Texas coast: American Association of Petroleum Geologists Bulletin, v. 59, p. 347–352.

WILLIAMS, S. J., PRINS, D. A., AND MEISBURGER, E. P., 1979, Sediment distribution, sand resources, and geologic character of the continental shelf off Galveston County, Texas: U.S. Army Corps of Engineers, Coastal Engineering Research Center, Miscellaneous Report 79-4, 159 p.

WINKER, C. D., 1979, Late Pleistocene fluvial-deltaic deposition, Texas coastal plain and continental shelf: Unpublished M.S. Thesis; University of Texas at Austin, 187 p.

WOODBURY, H. O., MURRAY, I. B., JR., PICKFORD, P. J., AND AKERS, W. H., 1973, Pliocene and Pleistocene depocenters, outer continental shelf, Louisiana and Texas: American Association of Petroleum Geologists Bulletin, v. 57, p. 2428–2439.

LATE QUATERNARY SEA-LEVEL FLUCTUATIONS AND DEPOSITIONAL SEQUENCES, SOUTHWEST LOUISIANA CONTINENTAL SHELF

JOHN R. SUTER

Louisiana Geological Survey, Coastal Geology Program, P.O. Box G, University Station, Baton Rouge, Louisiana 70893

HENRY L. BERRYHILL, JR.

U.S. Geological Survey, P.O. Box 6732, Corpus Christi, Texas 78411

AND

SHEA PENLAND

Louisiana Geological Survey, Coastal Geology Program, P.O. Box G, University Station, Baton Rouge, Louisiana 70893

ABSTRACT: Interpretations of over 20,000 line km of single-channel, high-resolution seismic-reflection profiles, coupled with nearshore vibracores and logs of industrial platform borings, provide the data base for determining the history and stratigraphy of late Quaternary sea-level fluctuations on the southwest Louisiana continental shelf. Regional unconformities, formed by subaerial exposure of the shelf during glacio-eustatic sea-level falls and modified by shoreface erosion during ensuing transgression, serve as markers to identify the boundaries of depositional sequences. Unconformities are recognizable on seismic profiles by high-amplitude reflectors as well as discordant relationships between reflectors.

Within the upper Quaternary section, six depositional sequences have been recognized. Five of these are related to glacio-eustatic fluctuations, involving sea-level fall close to, or beyond, the margin of the continental shelf. Three of these fluctuations culminated in the deposition of shelf-margin delta sequences. Extensive fluvial channeling characterizes the regressive phase of these sequences. Transgressive phases are marked by infilling of fluvial channels, floodplain aggradation, truncation, or deposition of sand sheets, depending upon sediment supply and rate of sea-level rise. Sequences 4 and 5 are correlated with the late Wisconsinan glacial stage and Holocene transgression. The upper portion of sequence 5 consists of an early Holocene Mississippi delta complex. Abandonment and transgression of this delta are responsible for the formation of sequence 6. Although these deposits cover a smaller area, this demonstrates that deltaic processes can produce sequences similar to those driven by glacially-controlled sea-level changes.

INTRODUCTION

Regional setting.—

The study area on the southwest Louisiana continental shelf is located between 94°W and 92°W longitude, extending from just west of the Texas-Louisiana border at Sabine Pass to the western end of Vermilion Bay, Louisiana (Fig. 1). Throughout much of the Quaternary, this area was the principal depocenter for terrigenous clastics in the northwestern Gulf of Mexico (Woodbury and others, 1973), resulting in as much as 6,000 m of Quaternary section (Frazier, 1974). During the Holocene, the locus of deposition has shifted eastward to the modern Mississippi delta, causing the cessation of major sedimentation in southwest Louisiana.

Glacio-eustatic fluctuations have played a major role in the development of the Quaternary stratigraphy of the continental shelf. Multiple falls of sea level (Figs. 2, 3) have resulted in the expansion of the coastal plain and formation of widespread fluvial and deltaic facies, eventually culminating in the deposition of thick deltaic wedges at the shelf margin (Fisk, 1944, 1956; Lehner, 1969; Sangree and others, 1978; Sidner and others, 1978; Winker, 1982; Winker and Edwards, 1983, Suter and Berryhill, 1985). Ensuing transgressions submerged, reworked and redistributed the lowstand deposits (Curray, 1960; Frazier, 1974), often forming broad sand sheets and shoals. Given sufficient sediment supply, deltaic complexes can prograde across the shelf during a phase of local sea-level rise or stillstand, as has the modern Mississippi delta (Coleman and others, 1983), producing similar stratigraphic signatures.

The conceptual framework is well established, but details of the interactions of sediment supply and fluctuating sea level to produce depositional sequences are not clearly understood. The objectives of the present paper are to examine the late Quaternary sediments on the southwest Louisiana continental shelf in order to delineate the depositional sequences, determine their relationship to sea-level fluctuations, and suggest a possible chronostratigraphic framework.

Data base.—

Over 20,000 line km of single-channel, analog high-resolution seismic reflection profiles constitute the major data base for this investigation. Three types of seismic profiling systems were used: 400-joule minisparker, ORE Geopulse* (a uniboom-type system), and 3.5-kHz subbottom profiles. The lower frequency minisparker provided better penetration, thus enabling study of older units, whereas the 3.5-kHz system has superior vertical resolution and greater detail in the upper sediments. Geopulse profiles were available in limited areas of the inner continental shelf but generally provided excellent penetration and resolution. Data were collected in grid patterns ranging from 1 km × 1 km in nearshore areas to 5.5 km × 5.5 km in others (Fig. 1). Conversion of acoustical travel time to depth was made using a sound velocity of 1,500 m/sec, which is accurate in the water column and upper sediments. Geometries of depositional sequences and facies were determined by mapping major reflectors, and analysis of reflection configuration and character permitted some lithologic interpretations using procedures outlined by Mitchum and others (1977). Information on lithology and sedimentology was obtained from numerous widely spread proprietary platform borings

---

*Use of brand names does not constitute endorsement by the U.S. Geological Survey.

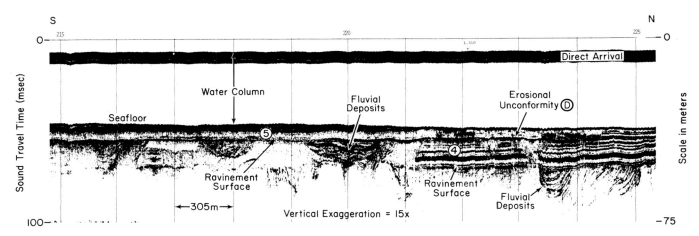

FIG. 9.—3.5-kHz subbottom profile showing ravinement surfaces separating sets of fluvial channel fill of sequences 3 and 4, which truncate pre-existing lowstand and transgressive deposits. Unconformity D coincides with ravinement surface at the right of the diagram and lies at the base of scouring at the left. Unconformity C is not visible. For location, see Figure 15.

depositional sequences. Where the scoured base of the channel forms the lower boundary of subaerial erosion, and the truncated top of the channel or estuarine fill represents a transgressive erosion surface, the sequence boundary was picked at the base of the channel fill. Thus, the channels are incised during the sea-level fall that cuts the lower sequence boundary and are filled during the succeeding sequence. The implication of such a choice is that all of the channel fill is transgressive, which is incorrect. Part of the channel fill represents lowstand deposition, whereas the remainder corresponds to deposition under rising sea-level conditions. During early postglacial periods, meltwater may increase flow by several times in rivers whose drainage basins include glaciers (Emiliani and others, 1975). Together with increased sediment supply from erosion of glacial deposits, this suggests that much of the coarse fill within the

valley sequences relates to the early stages of the transgression (Fisk, 1944). Consistent determination of the timing of a particular fluvial channel deposit, however, is not considered practicable. Although a fluvial system cut during a glacio-eustatic fall and submerged during sea-level rise has time-transgressive fill, the base of channel scour has chronostratigraphic significance, because all sediments above it are younger than those below it.

The ravinement surface forms an easily identifiable reflector which could be used as a sequence boundary. This choice would result in the separation of transgressive deposits in the channel fill from the overlying deposits of the same transgression. As the use of either method results in some inconsistency, the concepts of Vail and others (1977, 1984) were employed to designate the depositional sequence.

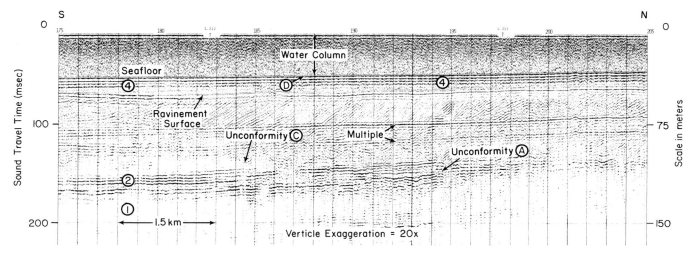

FIG. 10.—Minisparker profile of a large sequence 3 fluvial channel. Letters designate unconformities and numbers designate sequences discussed in text. Large-scale, high-angle clinoform reflection patterns represent point bar accretion, the dominant channel-fill type in fluvial facies of sequence 4. Attenuation of sound energy as well as multiples of overlying sequences obscure base of channel and sequence 3, unconformity B in this profile. For location, see Figure 13.

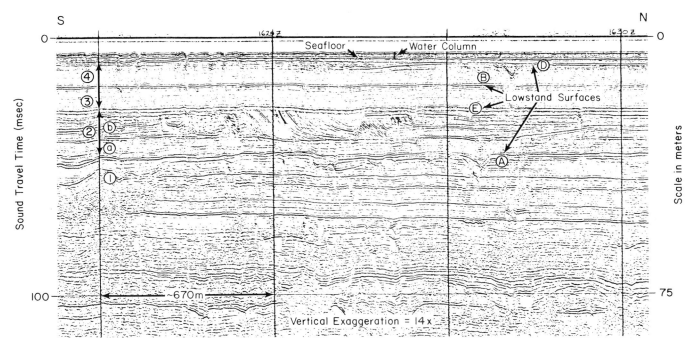

FIG. 11.—Geopulse seismic profile taken in very shallow water near Cameron, Louisiana. Letters and numbers refer to unconformities and sequences discussed in text. All unconformities designated by letters represent lowstand surfaces. A, B, and D have been modified by ravinement, whereas E was buried by progradation of upper sequence 2 deposits. Deposits designated a and b within sequence 2 represent period of transgression and aggradation, respectively, following sequence 1 lowstand. Note well preserved low-angle clinoform reflectors and multiple surfaces within 2b, representing overbank sediments associated with small meandering coastal plain stream. Unconformity C pinches out seaward of this profile, so that correlative boundary between sequences 3 and 4 is to be found within a continuous sequence of root-mottled, interbedded, reddish-brown and tan clays and silts, representing floodplain deposits of both sequences 3 and 4. A thin veneer of sandy Holocene silt rests on top of unconformity D.

DEPOSITIONAL SEQUENCES

Depositional sequence 1.—

Seismic characteristics of depositional sequence 1 are shown in Figures 8, 10, 11, and 12. Unconformity A, the upper boundary of sequence 1, is a prominent, high-amplitude reflector on minisparker profiles (Fig. 8), and most of the energy penetrating to that depth is reflected. In addition, extensive fluvial downcutting occurred during the lowstand, and attenuation of sound energy in the channel fill increases the difficulty of resolving sequence 1 sediments. Platform borings document a succession of stiff, interbedded gray and tan clays beneath unconformity A in non-channelized areas. Upper sediments of sequence 1 are visible on the nearshore Geopulse profiles (Fig. 11).

Shelf margin deltas found at levels of −400 m/sec offshore of south Texas, upper Texas (Sidner and others, 1978), and Mississippi-Alabama are believed to represent low-

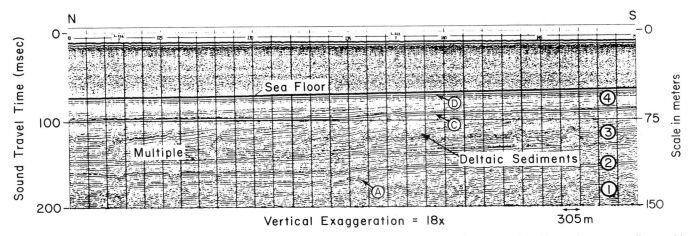

FIG. 12.—Minisparker profile of a sequence 3 shelf-phase delta deposit. Letters and numbers refer to unconformities and sequences discussed in text. Toplap pattern of clinoform reflectors in sequence 3 is seen to be erosional truncation on corresponding 3.5-kHz profile. For location, see Figure 12. Modified from Suter and Berryhill (1985).

stand deltas associated with this sequence. Because of the great thickness of overlying deposits, as well as structural deformation, the deltas were not recognized in southwest Louisiana. Due to the recognition of shoreline withdrawal to the shelf margin, unconformity A is a type 1 unconformity, modified by ravinement in interfluvial areas.

Depositional sequence 2.—

Unconformity A forms the lower boundary of depositional sequence 2. Fluvial channel fill is an extensive facies in the lower part of sequence 2 throughout much of the area. This facies, mapped as a regional sand by Roemer and Bryant (1977), is characterized by complex acoustic reflection patterns and channel forms. Platform borings through this deposit showed 60 m of coarse to fine sand with occasional gravel. The system is believed to be analogous to the valley-fill system of the modern Mississippi River (Suter, 1986).

Unconformity B, the reflector forming the upper boundary of sequence 2, is an erosional truncation surface on the outer shelf (Fig. 8). Low-angle clinoform reflectors beneath the unconformity indicate progradation, and channels are found within the sequence, although these are neither as numerous nor as well developed as in overlying and underlying sequences. Sequence 2 does not contain shelf-margin delta deposits. Landward, unconformity B could only be traced for some 30 km north of Figure 8 before becoming unresolvable due to coincidence with acoustic multiples. It is visible, however, on nearshore profiles (Fig. 11). Vibracores showed that the reflector is the result of an erosional contact between a 1-m-thick shelly sand with a brackish water fauna (*Rangia sp., Crassostrea sp.*) and underlying root-mottled, oxidized sandy silts and clays that grade downward into laminated gray clays representing floodplain and deltaic deposits of sequence 2.

Depositional sequence 3.—

Once the transgression had ceased, increased glaciation and renewed sediment supply caused resumed progradation. An extensive series of shelf-phase deltaic deposits (Suter and Berryhill, 1985) were deposited (Fig. 12) covering much of the shelf (Fig. 13). Thickness of these deltas reached as much as 25 m, with areal extents of over 6,000 km². Seismically, these deposits are characterized by low-angle, oblique, parallel to shingled clinoform reflectors in dip sections and subparallel to low-angle clinoform reflectors in strike sections. The clinoforms dip toward the southwest. The toplap pattern of the reflectors indicates progradation during a relative stillstand or slow relative fall of sea level. Lithologic descriptions from platform borings indicate interbedded sands, silts, and clays typical of delta plain deposits. Abrupt updip termination of the deposits indicates that initially sea level fell rapidly from a highstand to about −40 m, at which level deposition of the shelf-phase deltas began.

As sea-level fall continued, large fluvial systems were cut into the subaerially exposd shelf, producing the drainage patterns shown in Figure 13. These erosional surfaces cover 21 percent of the study area and have 60 m of relief near the shelf margin. The major extrabasinal system near

the western margin of the area is interpreted as a possible former position of the Mississippi River.

Contemporaneous with the fluvil channels and shelf-phase deltas are extensive shelf-margin deltas recognized by high-angle clinoform reflectors in dip sections (Fig. 14). Deltaic deposits in this sequence have been considerably deformed by diapirism, faulting, and mass transport of sediments (Fig. 14). Although maximum thickness of the deltas could not always be determined, the deposits exceed 150 m in thickness in several places (Fig. 13). In relatively undeformed sequences, the tops of the deltas occur at −300 msec, approximately −225 m.

Unconformity C, the upper boundary of sequence 3, is a prominent high-amplitude reflector, mappable from the shelf margin to the nearshore zone. In the western portion of the area, this surface loses its distinct character as an erosional unconformity and appears to merge with conformable reflectors at subsurface depths of 5 m in water depths of 15–20 m. Farther east, ringing on the minisparker profiles and lack of penetration through thicker overlying sediments on the 3.5-kHz data preclude an accurate assessment, although a similar situation is judged to prevail. The transgression which formed the ravinement surface that modified unconformity C was produced by a high sea level lower than that of today.

Depositional sequence 4.—

Rising sea level terminated shelf-margin delta deposition of sequence 3 and began transgression of the lowstand deposits. The primary feature of this transgression was erosion, as evidenced by truncated deposits (Figs. 9, 10). Submergence of fluvial systems during transgression caused by glacio-eustatic rise is believed to produce a predictable sequence within the channel fill: regressive alluvial sands and transgressive alluvial sands grading upward into deltaic sands and muds capped by aggradational estuarine deposits. Only the lower portion of this succession is preserved in sequence 4. Channel fill in the major rivers in the western part of the area is characterized by high-angle clinoform seismic reflectors, which are interpreted as epsilon crossbeds or point bar accretion surfaces. Channel fill is as much as 60 m thick and as much as 20 km wide, whereas individual channels are calculated to have widths of over 1 km and depths greater than 30 m. Reflection patterns within the channel fill seems to document a multistory sand body (Fig. 9), although near the shelf margin, individual sands reach 60 m in thickness. Platform borings through the channel fill typically show coarse-grained sediments, often fining upward from gravel to fine sand. Very little fine-grained material is preserved, and the tops of the channels are commonly truncated (Figs. 9, 10). Pervasive truncation of sequence 3 deposits indicates a relatively slow transgression.

Following the transgression, the sea again withdrew to the shelf margin. The deposits of this regressive phase are the youngest encountered at the shelf margin and can be interpreted as late Wisconsinan, oxygen isotope stage 2, on the basis of stratigraphic position. Such an age designation is strengthened by an 11.7 ka radiocarbon date for a cypress stump from the outer shelf (Suter and Berryhill, 1985).

Again, extensive fluvial-deltaic facies were deposited

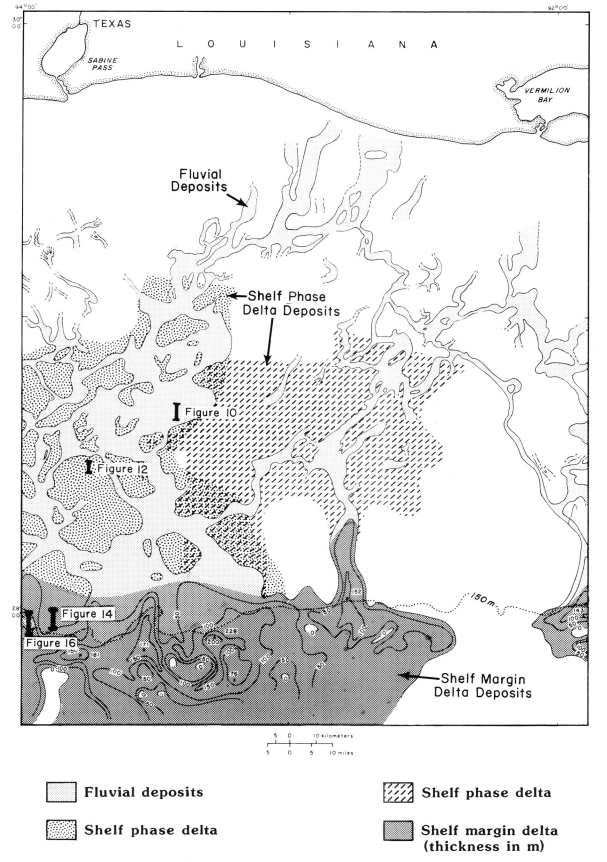

FIG. 13.—Map showing extent of sequence 3 fluvial channels, shelf-phase deltaic deposits, and shelf-margin deltaic deposits.

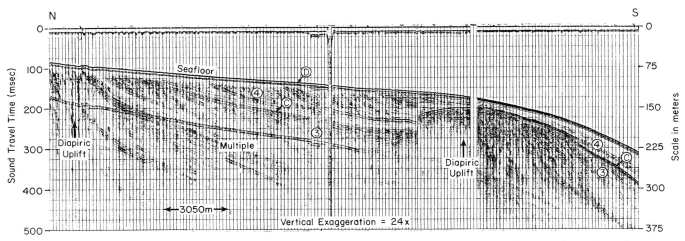

FIG. 14.—Minisparker profile showing shelf-margin delta deposits of the last two lowstands of sea level. Letters and numbers refer to unconformities and sequences discussed in text. Note the deformation of deltaic deposits by diapiric uplift, a significant process in southwest Louisiana. For location, see Figure 13 (modified from Suter and Berryhill, 1985).

during the lowstand. One important difference between these deposits and those of the underlying sequence 3 is the lack of a well preserved shelf-phase delta sequence. This condition is attributed to a very rapid sea-level fall, resulting in relatively thin deposits.

The drainage pattern for the fluvial systems of this sequence covers 29% of the map (Fig. 15). The more intricate pattern, as compared to Figure 13, is partly an artifact of the seismic profiling technique. The deeply buried sequence 3 fluvial systems are often beyond the penetration range of the high-frequency 3.5-kHz subbottom profiler, whereas the shallower channels of sequence 4 are fully recorded. Consequently, profiles having a higher resolution are available for mapping the younger channels. By late Wisconsinan time, the locus of deposition for the area had shifted eastward, where the largest fluvial system is located (Fig. 15). Although its lateral extent is not as great as that of the older system in sequence 3 (Fig. 13), individual channels have roughly comparable dimensions to those of the older rivers and have similar reflection character. This system is also interpreted as a former Mississippi River drainage (Suter and Berryhill, 1985).

Shelf-margin delta deposits of sequence 4 cover as much as 5,000 km^2 and are more than 160 m thick. During late Wisconsinan time, rapid sea-level withdrawal did result in sediment bypassing the shelf, in accordance with seismic stratigraphic models (Vail and others, 1984). Toplap of oblique tangential reflection patterns, typical of most undeformed shelf-margin deltas (Fig. 16), indicates that much of the deposition of these features occurs during the lowstand itself. Progradation is largely a function of relative rates of sediment supply and sea-level change (Curray, 1964; Coleman and others, 1983), but thickness of progradational

deposits is a function of water depth, relative sea level, and subsidence. Thus, during a slow eustatic fall with high sediment supply, relatively thin deltas such as the shelf-phase deltas of sequence 3 are deposited (Figs. 12, 13), but when sea level is stabilized, thicker sequences form. The thickest progradational deposits are formed during periods of base level stability and progradation into the deeper water near the shelf margin. This can be accomplished by the formation of lowstand deltas or by progradation of a highstand delta across the shelf, such as that of the modern Mississippi River.

In several areas along the shelf margin, a number of localized, buried submarine troughs occur (Fig. 17). These features have been active during the last several lowstands of sea level. Original length of the largest trough was about 90 km, width around 16 km, and depth reached 305 m (Berryhill, 1981). Reflection characteristics suggest that the trough originated by a combination of erosional scour and retrogressive failure of the shelf edge, similar to the origin proposed by Coleman and others (1983) for the Mississippi canyon.

The greater resolution of the profiles in the upper sediments allows features that relate to short-term sea-level fluctuations during the lowstand to be distinguished, which may be related to glacial advances and retreats (Winker, 1982; Suter and others, 1984; Suter and Berryhill, 1985). These features include vertically stacked lobes of shelf-margin deltas, composite fluvial systems, disconformable surfaces at the shelf margin, and intertongued transgressive and regressive deposits. A maximum of three vertically stacked lobes was recognized in the shelf margin deltas, indicating two sea-level fluctuations following lowstand and preceding final transgression.

FIG. 15.—Map of southwest Louisiana showing the extent of fluvial channels cut and shelf-margin deltas deposited during the last lowstand of sea level. Largest channel systems of this age are located in the eastern portion of the map area. Note the development of east-west orientation at three different areas on the shelf. These represent estuarine systems formed during sequence 5 transgression. Modified after Suter and others, (1985a).

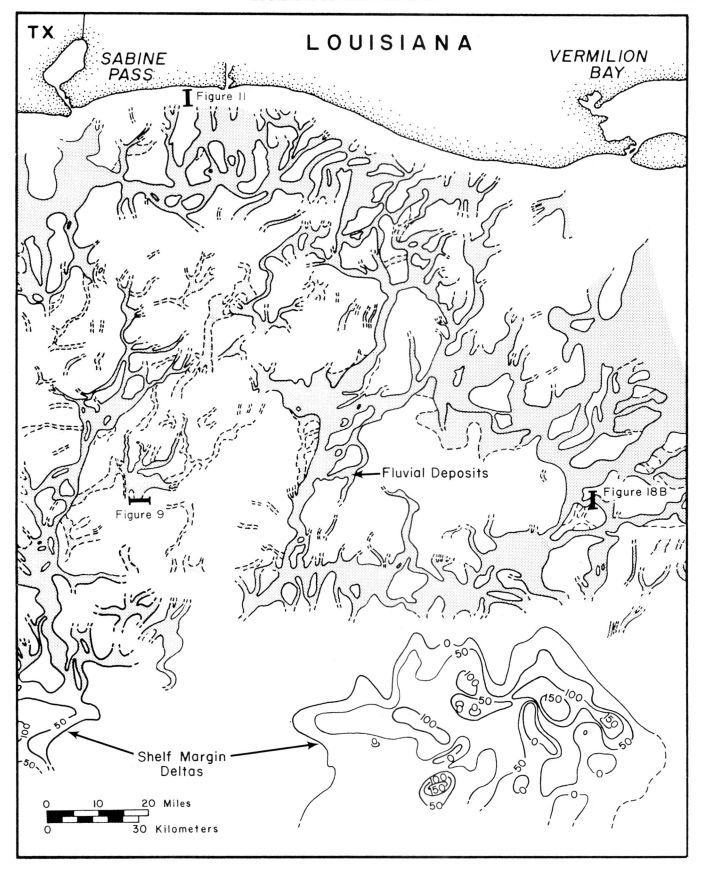

TX

LOUISIANA

SABINE PASS

VERMILION BAY

Figure 11

Fluvial Deposits

Figure 18B

Figure 9

Shelf Margin Deltas

0   10   20 Miles

0   30 Kilometers

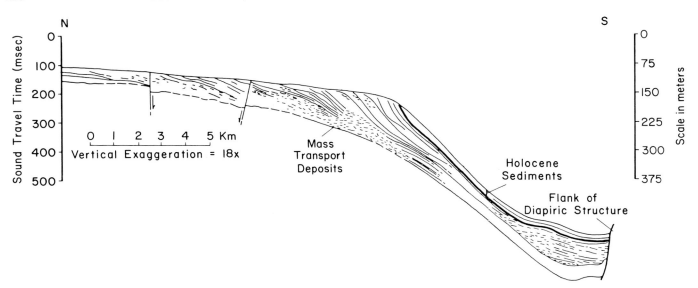

FIG. 16.—Line drawing from a minisparker profile, located just west of 94°W longitude, showing the oblique-parallel to oblique-tangential clinoform reflection pattern typical of shelf-margin deltas in the northwest Gulf of Mexico. Toplapping reflectors were seen to be erosionally truncated on corresponding 3.5-kHz line. Reflection pattern indicates steady progradation during stable sea-level lowstand. Chaotic facies indicate penecontemporaneous mass transport of sediments (after Suter and Berryhill, 1985).

Depositional sequence 5.—

Rising sea level at the close of the late Wisconsinan stage marked the beginning of the Holocene transgression, which differed from that of the immediately preceding transgression in several important aspects. Considerable erosion of late Wisconsinan lowstand deposits occurred along the outer shelf (Figs. 17, 18A,B), submergence of fluvial channels produced extensive estuarine deposits (Fig. 19), and multiple, shore-parallel sand bodies were deposited at various positions on the continental shelf (Figs. 19, 20).

The wave-cut terrace (Figs. 17, 18A) is one manifestation of outer shelf truncation. Cutting of this terrace probably began by shoreface erosion during an early stillstand in the Holocene transgression with a sea level of −90 to −80 m. This feature is also present offshore of Mississippi-Alabama and south Texas (Suter and Berryhill, 1985). The deepest occurrence of the terrace corresponds to Frazier's (1974) figure of −91 m for the late Wisconsinan lowstand.

Fine-grained sediments were deposited on the outer shelf during the transgression (Fig. 17). These deposits drape some of the shelf-margin deltas and cover the wave-cut terrace along the outer shelf. Transgressive sediments are very thin in the western part of the area, forming a condensed section of Vail and others (1984), but thicken considerably eastward, reaching a thickness of 15 m (Fig. 20).

Evidence of transgressive erosion can be seen throughout the shelf in a number of different settings. Aggradational fluvial deposits were particularly susceptible, with results ranging from minor erosion of overbank deposits to complete planation of levees (Fig. 18B). At several elevations on the shelf, slightly increased gradients mark truncation surfaces which may be preserved shorefaces.

The drainage pattern in Figure 15 shows several east-west-oriented systems similar in size to modern bays and lagoons along the Texas and Louisiana coastlines. Sediments contained within these features are characterized seismically by disorganized, chaotic to high-angle clinoform reflectors overlain by conformable, parallel to subparallel reflectors which onlap channel margins. High-amplitude mounded reflectors representing oyster banks and/or reefs are often found at various levels in the fill (Fig. 19). This succession represents the transition from fluvial to estuarine deposition during rising sea level. Platform borings through these deposits confirm this interpretation, showing soft interbedded clays, silts, and sand with high shell content. A vibracore taken in an estuarine deposit near shore showed oysters in growth position.

Lagoonal systems depend upon stable or rising sea level and the existence of barrier shorelines to provide shelter from the effects of waves. The existence of barriers and lagoons implies the existence of tidal inlets, raising the possibility that some of the channel deposits mapped in Figure 15 represent inlet fill. Transgressed tidal inlets have been recognized on the Atlantic shelf (Kumar and Sanders, 1974; Hine and Synder, 1985) and on the Lousiana shelf (Penland and Suter, 1983; Penland and others, 1985; Suter and Penland, 1985) and can form an extensive facies. The tendency of inlets to reoccupy old fluvial and distributary channels, and similar seismic facies for inlet fill, made differentiation difficult. Channels found within estuarine sequences (Fig. 19) could be inlet fill as inlets tend to form by downcutting into estuarine sediments during transgression.

Reworking of the late Wisconsinan deltas produced a transgressive sand sheet across much of the shelf (Curray, 1960; Frazier, 1974). A series of east-west-oriented sandy shoals occurs at several elevations (Figs. 19, 20) (Curray, 1960; Frazier, 1974; Nelson and Bray, 1970). These deposits vary from 24 km by 6 km on the outer shelf to over 90 km by 10 km for the Sabine Bank trend on the inner

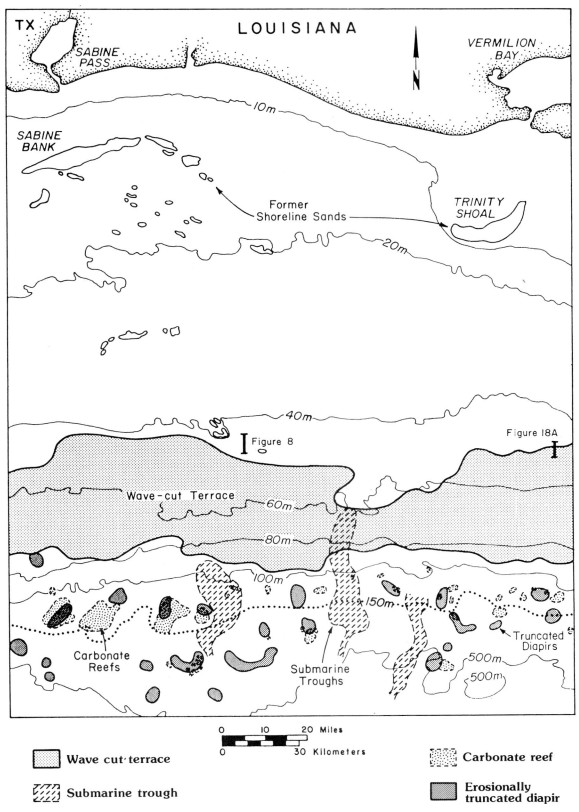

FIG. 17.—Map of features showing evidence of former lowered sea level.

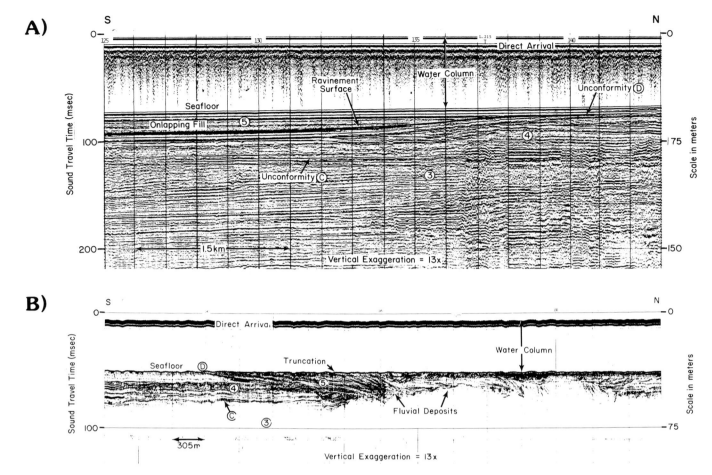

FIG. 18.—Examples of transgressive erosion on the outer shelf: (A) Minisparker profile across wave-cut terrace in sequence 4 sediments during stillstand in Holocene transgression. (B) 3.5-kHz subbottom profile of truncated sequence 5 fluvial sediments.

shelf (Fig. 20). Most of the deposits are 3–5 m thick but reach over 6–7 m in some areas (Suter and others, 1985a), showing geometric similarities to modern barrier islands as well as to inner shelf shoals found associated with the abandoned lobes of the modern Mississippi delta (Penland and others, 1985).

Considerable discussion prevails about the nature of the Holocene transgression. Fairbridge (1961) believed the transgression was episodic, including regressive as well as transgressive phases, whereas Shepard (1963) argued for a smoothly asymptotic rise. The deposits on the southwest Louisiana shelf seem to support an episodic transgression.

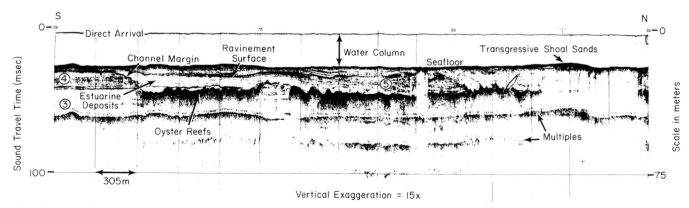

FIG. 19.—3.5-kHz subbottom profile showing transgressive estuarine sediments developed in a sequence 5 fluvial channel, with overlying transgressive sand shoals. Note sharp base of sand deposits. For location, see Figure 20.

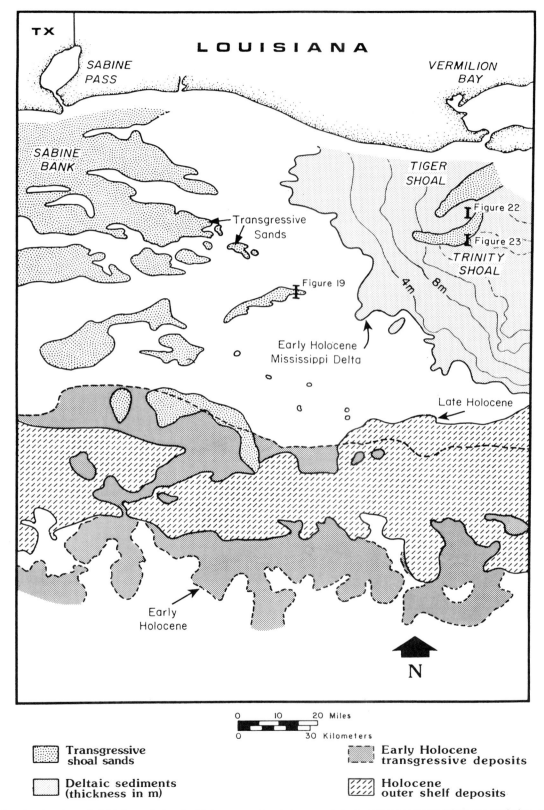

FIG. 20.—Map showing deposits laid down during the Holocene sea-level rise, sequence 5, and subsequent deltaic progradation, sequence 6 (after Suter, 1985).

The shoals have been interpreted as shoreline or nearshore sands representing stillstand positions during the Holocene transgression (Curray, 1960; Nelson and Bray, 1970; Frazier, 1974; Gagliano and others, 1982). Frazier (1974) reported four distinct strandlines at levels of −90 m, −53 m, −42 m, and −16 m, with corresponding ages of 17.0, 12.96, 9.46, and 8.5 ka, respectively, based on radiocarbon dates of surf-zone and nearshore fossils and brackish marsh peats. He correlated the stillstand intervals directly with continental glacial advances.

Only three lagoonal trends are recognizable in this study (Fig. 15), so that the four strandlines of Frazier (1974) could not be a simple matter of barrier island-lagoonal association. In fact, more than four distinct trends of shoals are present on the shelf (Fig. 20). Possibly, the original formation of some of these deposits was related to downdrift transport of coarse material from the early Holocene Mississippi delta, meaning that the shoal age trends would be associated with both "eustatic" and local events, making a confused picture. Gagliano and others (1982) classified the shoals into a number of different coastal landforms but appear to have discounted the effects of shoreface erosion and ensuing landward migration of barriers, a process affecting Holocene Mississippi delta inner-shelf shoals (Penland and others, 1986; Suter and others, 1985b). Ship Shoal has migrated landward as much as 1.5 km in the last 100 yrs, based on repetitive bathymetric surveys (Penland and others, 1986). In addition, some shoals may have formed as marine sands, never representing coastal barrier facies at all. Reflection patterns for many of the shoals (e.g., Fig. 19) indicate a sharp basal relationship with underlying sediments, rather than the gradational one expected for an in-place drowned coastal barrier. Until a thorough coring study tied to the regional seismic data can be made, interpretations of the depositional environments of the shoals and their direct correlation to sea-level changes is problematic.

In the northeastern portion of the study area lies an abandoned complex of the Holocene Mississippi delta (Fig. 20) deposited some 6.0–10.0 ka (Frazier, 1967). Within the study area, sediments of this delta extend some 110 km onto the shelf and reach a thickness of 15 m. East of the area, these deposits reach a maximum thickness of about 42 m (Frazier, 1967). This feature, part of the oldest of the early Holocene Mississippi deltas that form a significant platform farther to the east, probably formed during a stillstand in the Holocene sea-level rise (Frazier, 1974). In dip sections, the deposit is characterized by low-angle, oblique, parallel seismic reflectors that are similar to the shelf-phase deltas in sequences 2 and 3. Subtle changes in angular relationships result from stacking of multiple lobes within the complex. Platform borings through the delta record very soft to firm gray clay interbedded with sands, silts, and shell material. Channels seen in the seismic profiles (Fig. 21) exhibit much different geometries and seismic facies from those interpreted as fluvial in the underlying sequences and are believed to represent distributaries.

The chenier plain, which forms much of the current shoreline of southwest Louisiana, is also a prograding unit, although it consists of alternating transgressive and regressive deposits. The chenier plain has prograded some 30 km in 3,000 yrs and reaches a thickness of 7–8 m (Byrne and others, 1959; Gould and McFarlan, 1959). Recent sedimentation from the Atchafalaya delta has initiated a new phase of chenier plain progradation.

Depositional sequence 6.—

Avulsion of the Mississippi River resulted in abandonment and transgression of this delta complex around 6.0 ka (Frazier, 1967), creating a new depositional sequence. In the shallow-water early Holocene Mississippi deltas, the thickness of the transgressive phase is often nearly equivalent to the deltaic progradational package (Penland and others, 1985). Trinity Shoal (Figs. 17, 20, 22) is a transgressive sand body associated with the deltaic facies in this area. The shoal is 5–7 m thick, 36 km in length, and 5–10 km wide. On seismic sections, the shoal sand consists of parallel to low-angle clinoform reflectors. The occurrence of channel features within the shoal sand body itself suggests the presence of tidal inlets, indicating that Trinity Shoal may retain characteristics of an earlier existence as a barrier shoreline (Suter and others, 1985b).

DISCUSSION

Chronology of sequences.—

The absolute age of each depositional sequence and its exact correlation with late Quaternary sea-level fluctuations

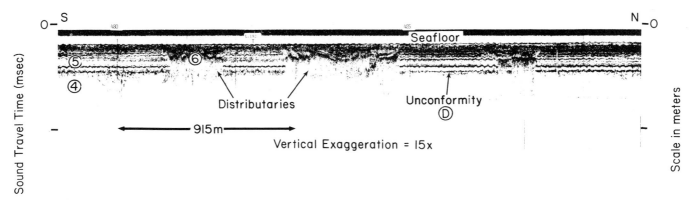

FIG. 21.—3.5-kHz subbottom profile showing distributaries associated with early Holocene Mississippi delta. For location, see Figure 20 (after Suter, 1986).

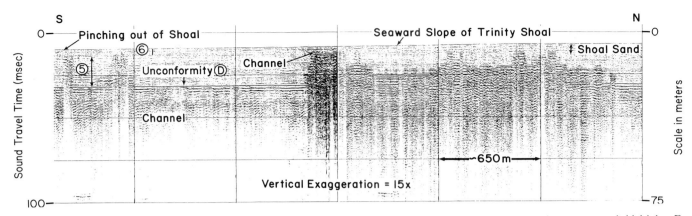

FIG. 22.—Geopulse profile showing seaward slope of Trinity Shoal. Channel within shoal sand body is interpreted as a preserved tidal inlet. For location, see Figure 20 (after Suter and others, 1985a).

cannot be provided due to an absence of samples for dating, as well as uncertainties in global sea-level chronology (Butzer, 1983). A relative chronostratigraphic curve for the sequences is shown in Figure 23. Sidner and others (1978) and Beard and others (1982) have provided stratigraphic frameworks for late Quaternary deposits in the northwest Gulf of Mexico. Sidner and others (1978) found two major stages of shelf-margin outbuilding, dating the intervals of paleontologically and isotopically as beginning 350 ka and 80 ka. Beard and others (1982), employing geochemical, paleontological, magnetic, and seismic techniques, found four glacio-eustatic cycles in the last 100,000 yrs of the Quaternary section (Fig. 2). Sea-level curves developed from oxygen isotopes from deep-sea cores, tropical coral terraces, and related fauna (Shackleton and Opdyke, 1973; Bloom and others, 1974; Shackleton, 1977; Fairbanks and

Matthews, 1978; Aharon, 1983; Williams, 1984) show even larger numbers of fluctuations (Fig. 3).

Considerable margin of error exists in assigning ages to the sequences in the late Quaternary sediments on the southwest Louisiana continental shelf and in attempting to correlate these marine deposits with continental glaciations (Fillon, 1984). Based on stratigraphic position and comparison to published chronologies, the sequences seen in the high-resolution seismic profiles can be interpreted with increasing confidence as the relative age decreases. Sequence 1 is interpreted to represent the lowstand associated with the last full glacial period, oxygen isotope stage 6 (Illinoian?). The Sangamonian interglacial period, oxygen isotope stage 5, corresponds to the basal portions of sequence 2, whereas the regressive upper part of sequence 2 represents the beginning of building outward in the Wis-

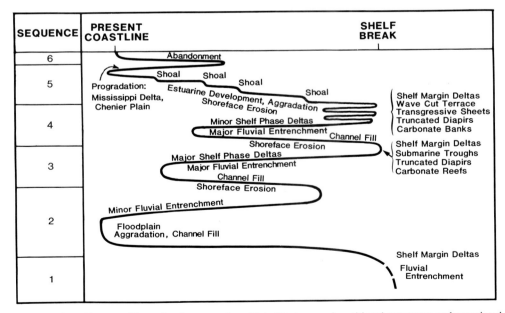

FIG. 23.—Relative chronostratigraphic curve illustrating interpretation of late Quaternary depositional sequences and associated facies. Fluctuations within Holocene transgression are from Frazier (1974). See text for discussion of problems with Holocene curve.

consinan glacial stage, oxygen isotope stage 4. Sidner and others (1978) dated the progradation at 80 ka, whereas Beard and others (1982) give a date of 60 ka for this event, which they correlated with the early Altonian glacial substage. Sequence 3 then brackets early Wisconsinan transgressive and regressive deposits, the middle and late Altonian of Beard and others (1982), oxygen isotope stage 3, and sequence 4 represents middle Wisconsinan transgressive and late Wisconsinan sea-level withdrawal, oxygen isotope stages 3 and 2. The Holocene transgression, oxygen isotope stage 1, and progradation and abandonment of the early Holocene Mississippi delta are represented by sequences 5 and 6.

Magnitude of sea-level fluctuations.—

Despite intensive research by many investigators, the extent of sea-level lowering at the time of the last glacial maximum is still a matter of dispute, given at -120 ± 60 m (Bloom, 1983). Shackleton (1977) used oxygen isotope data to estimate the magnitude of late Wisconsinan sea-level fall at as much as 160 m. The magnitude of lowering for the northwest Gulf of Mexico has been variously estimated at -140 m by Fisk and McFarlan (1955), -120 m by Curray (1960), and -91 m by Frazier (1974). Recent work on the Atlantic shelf (Dillon and Oldale, 1978; Blackwelder, 1980) suggests a maximum lowering of about -80 m, although Belknap and Kraft (1981) advocated a figure of greater than -100 m.

Sea-level fall during a glacio-eustatic cycle is a function of a number of factors, including the absolute water-volume change due to ice formation, the tectonic setting and neotectonics of the area in question, and the ratio of subsidence and sea level. Variable effects of geoidal deformation (Morner, 1976) and isostasy indicate that for the continental shelf, as for the many "eustatic" curves developed from coastal data (Bloom, 1977), each area may have its own relative sea-level curve.

Erosional and depositional features beneath the southwest Louisiana shelf strongly suggest sea-level fall to the vicinity of the shelf margin during the last glacial maximum. Shelf-wide erosional unconformities, buried fluvial systems, and deltaic deposits at the shelf margin indicate a maximum lowering of -120 to -130 m compared with present sea level. This figure is obtained by measuring the depth at the brows of six late Wisconsinan shelf-margin deltas throughout the Gulf of Mexico from south Texas to Mississippi-Alabama (Suter and Berryhill, 1985). Further support for sea-level lowering of this magnitude comes from the occurrence of carbonate reefs and banks with shallow-water fauna and erosional truncations at the tops of diapirs found at depths of as much as -150 m (Poag, 1973; Suter and others, 1984).

Although shoreline withdrawal to the vicinity of the shelf margin can be documented, correction for change in the elevation of the shelf margin since the lowstand must be made. Factors affecting this correction are the rate of shelf-margin subsidence due to sediment loading, tectonic subsidence, and hydro-isostasy or the weight of the water column. These have been studied and modeled (Bloom, 1967; Walcott, 1972; Chappell, 1974; Clark and others, 1978).

Bloom (1967) estimated that as much as one-third of the depth of a feature could be due to hydro-isostatic subsidence. Walcott (1972) indicated that the Texas-Louisiana area has been relatively stable since the last glacial maximum, and that depths of shelf features would reflect eustatic movements. Chappell (1974) calculated a maximum lowering for the Gulf of Mexico at about -130 m. Clark and others (1978), however, calculate that a lowering of about -103 m for the Atlantic continental shelf would result in a predicted sea level in the Gulf of Mexico at the last glacial maximum of about 120 m below the present. This is in close agreement with the observed values of -120 to -130 m found in this study.

Another problem in sea-level research is the question of the maximum Farmdalian, or middle Wisconsinan, oxygen isotope stage 3, highstand (Saucier, 1977; Bloom, 1983). Many researchers along the Gulf and Atlantic coasts of the United States (e.g., Curray, 1960; Milliman and Emery, 1968; Frazier, 1974) presented evidence that sea level rose to near its present position sometime during the middle Wisconsinan, based on radiocarbon dating of peats and marine and estuarine shells. Thom (1973) carefully reviewed the available data and concluded that most of the supporting dates were invalid. Saucier (1977) reviewed a number of features along the northern Gulf coast which he cautiously suggested represented middle Wisconsinan transgression. Bloom (1983), in the most recent review of the question, rejected the concept of a middle Wisconsinan highstand near or above present sea level, estimating its position at no more than -40 m. Recently, however, Goy and Zazo (1986) reported a possible middle Wisconsinan sea level above the present in Western Spain, based on $^{230}U/^{234}Th$ dates, and Gonzalez and others (1986) used radiocarbon dates to document such a sea level in Argentina. A study of Virginia barrier islands by Finkelstein and Kearney (1986) presented evidence for a middle Wisconsinan sea level within 2 m of its current position, based on radiocarbon dates of lagoonal deposits.

Ravinement by middle Wisconsinan shoreface erosion can be seen to pinch out at depths of about -20 m on the southwest Louisiana shelf, so that the associated shoreline was considerably seaward of the present shoreline but well landward of one that would correspond to a sea level of -40 m. Sea-level rises associated with the earlier interstadial events in the early Wisconsinan appear to have come closer to present sea level than did that of the middle Wisconsinan. Bloom and others (1974) found an early Wisconsinan interstadial sea-level maximum at -15 m in New Guinea; thus, our older unconformity C could correspond to this period. Alternatively, as the coral terrace sea-level curves show several interstadial maxima at around -15 m in early Wisconsinan time, unconformity B could also correspond to one of these periods, as the levels are a closer match.

Preservation potential.—

The question of preservation potential is fundamental to the interpretation of the depositional sequences. Fischer (1961) suggested that preservation was a function of the depth of shoreface erosion as transgression progressed.

Belknap and Kraft (1981) cited the rate of relative sea-level rise as being most important to preservation, with rapid rise favoring greater preservation. This idea has been adopted in interpreting the sequences shown in this paper.

Each of the transgressions studied has its own erosional signature. Sequences 2 and 3 have relatively thick transgressive sediments, sequence 4 shows extensive truncation of pre-existing deposits and little or no estuarine development, and sequence 5 shows extensive truncation, estuarine development, and pervasive sand-shoal deposition. Sequence 6 shows fairly complete preservation of underlying deltaics, with reworking of coarse-grained materials into sand shoals. The most pervasive erosion appears to have occurred during sequence 4, truncating channel-fill deposits and aggradational sediments down to the deltaic deposits of sequence 3. Alternatively, little or no aggradational or estuarine deposits may have formed, although this is considered less likely. The lack of sand shoals in sequence 4 is puzzling but may be attributable to erosion by shelf currents during transgression or subaerial erosion in the subsequent lowstand.

The preservation potential of the shoals in sequences 5 and 6 is intriguing. Shoals in the western part of the area have been subjected to shoreface erosion and landward migration, reworking at least their upper portions. These will likely be subaerially exposed during the next sea-level fall and will suffer further erosion. Trinity Shoal, by contrast, has excellent preservation potential due to its impending burial by the newly active Atchafalaya delta.

Regressive facies suffer from shoreface erosion upon transgression, but the majority of prograding sequences can be preserved if subsidence and burial occur. Shelf-margin deltas exhibit excellent preservation potential, whereas the shelf-phase and stillstand deltas have a greater percentage of their total section reworked.

Preservation potential of fluvial deposits is variable. Transgression of levee and upper floodplain deposits produces truncation (Figs. 9, 10, 17), whereas burial results in excellent preservation (Fig. 11). Basal channel-fill facies have the greatest preservation potential.

CONCLUSIONS

High-resolution seismic reflection profiles, supplemented by platform borings and vibracores, document that the stratigraphy of the southwest Louisiana continental shelf is the result of a number of glacio-eustatic and isostatically driven sea-level fluctuations. The major conclusions of this study are as follows.

(1) Five depositional sequences related to glacio-eustatic fluctuations have been identified in the upper Quaternary section of the southwest Louisiana continental shelf. Sequence boundaries are formed by regional unconformities consisting of lowstand surfaces modified by shoreface erosion during transgression. Throughout much of the area, the ravinement surface has eroded into lowstand deposits, so that these two types of unconformity coincide on one surface. Separation of the two occurs in valley-fill sequences, where the base of the channel scour represents the lowstand unconformity and the truncated top of the channel fill is a ravinement surface. On some areas of the outer shelf, the lowstand surface, ravinement surface, and condensed interval can coincide.

(2) A sixth depositional sequence has been formed by abandonment of an early Holocene complex of the modern Mississippi delta.

(3) Sequences formed by glacio-eustatic fluctuations are characterized by sea-level fall close to or beyond the shelf margin, prolonged subaerial exposure of the shelf, and extensive fluvial erosion. Depending upon the rate of sea-level fall, deposition of relatively thin (<40 m), widespread shelf-phase deltas may or may not occur. These deposits will be reworked by fluvial processes upon subaerial exposure of the shelf. Fluvial erosion can result in widespread drainage networks covering as much as 30% of the area. Incised valleys are as much as 60 m deep and 50 km wide, with individual channels having dimensions greater than 35 m in depth and 1 km in width. The thickest deposits in the sequences are found at the shelf margin, where progradation of deltas at lowstand can produce accumulations over 160 m in thickness and 5,000 km^2 in area. Upon sea-level rise, transgression results in the aggradation of the coastal plain and the filling of the incised valleys. Much of the deposition within the valleys may be in response to the increased runoff and sediment load from early postglacial melting and erosion of glacial deposits. Continuing sea-level rise causes formation of estuaries within drowned valleys, followed by truncation by shoreface erosion as transgression continues.

(4) The depositional sequence produced by Holocene deltaic progradation covers a smaller area but reaches similar thickness on the shelf. Progradational deposits resemble those in glacio-eustatic shelf-phase deltas but lack the regional subaerial exposure surfaces and extensive fluvial facies. Abandonment and transgression of the delta have produced shelf shoals comparable to those formed during the transgression of the Pleistocene deposits farther west. The shoals associated with the Holocene deltaic complexes probably have a higher preservation potential than those on the non-deltaic portions of the shelf due to impending burial by the newly active Atchafalaya delta.

(5) Three times during the late Quaternary, sea level was at or near the shelf margin. On the basis of stratigraphic position, these withdrawals are tentatively correlated with the Illinoian(?), oxygen isotope stage 6; early Wisconsinan (late Altonian), oxygen isotope stage 4; and late Wisconsinan, oxygen isotope stage 2. A fourth sea-level drop that did not reach the shelf margin is correlated with the early Wisconsinan (early Altonian), oxygen isotope stage 4. For the late Wisconsinan, measurements of erosional features on shelf-margin deltas throughout the northwest Gulf of Mexico suggest a maximum sea-level lowering of 125 m to 130 m. Clinoform reflectors of older deltaic deposits are found farther seaward, suggesting that sea-level lowering during their deposition was to similar levels. With one exception, sea-level rises associated with the transgression cannot be fully determined, as their erosional surfaces pass under the modern shoreline. The ravinement surface correlated with middle Wisconsinan, isotope stage 3, transgression pinches out at a current depth of −20 m.

ACKNOWLEDGMENTS

The authors gratefully thank all the organizations and individuals who contributed to this research. The U.S. Geological Survey (USGS) and the Louisiana Geological Survey (LGS) provided support, geophysical data, and vibracores. Access to platform borings was obtained through McClelland Engineers from Atlantic Richfield, Conoco, Gulf, Chevron, and Mobil. John West, Doug Owen, Jim McFarlen, Jim Ray, and Jack Kindinger of the USGS, and C. Lee Black, Steve Rabalais, and Wilton DeLaune of the Louisiana Universities Marine Consortium helped collect Geopulse seismic data. Karen Westphal of the LGS and Paula Kolda drafted the illustrations, and Karen Ramsey, Delores Falcon, and Lyn Louden of the LGS typed the manuscript. This paper is a contribution to the International Geological Correlation Program Project No. 200: Sea Level Correlation and Applications.

REFERENCES

AHARON, P., 1983, 140,000-yr isotope climatic record from raised coral reef in New Guinea: Nature, v. 304, p. 720–723.

BEARD, J. H., SANGREE, J. B., AND SMITH, L. A., 1982, Quaternary chronology, paleoclimate, depositional sequences, and eustatic cycles: American Association of Petroleum Geologists Bulletin, v. 66, p. 158–169.

BELKNAP, D. F., AND KRAFT, J. C., 1981, Preservation potential of transgressive coastal lithosomes on the U.S. Altantic shelf, in Nitrouer, C. A., ed., Sedimentary dynamics of Continental Shelves: Elsevier, Amsterdam, p. 429–442.

———, AND ———, 1985, Influence of antecedent geology on stratigraphic preservation potential and evolution of Delaware's barrier systems: Marine Geology, v. 63, p. 235–262.

BERRYHILL, H. L., JR., 1981, Ancient buried submarine trough, northwest Gulf of Mexico: Geo-Marine Letters, v. 1, no. 2, p. 105–109.

BLACKWELDER, D., 1980, Late Wisconsin and Holocene tectonic stability of the United States mid-Atlantic coastal region: Geology, v. 8, p. 534–537.

BLOOM, A. L., 1967, Pleistocene shorelines: a new test of isostasy: Geological Society of America Bulletin, v. 81, p. 1477–1493.

———, 1977, Atlas of Sea Level Curves: Cornell University, New York (not consecutively paginated).

———, 1983, Sea level and coastal morphology of the United States through the late Wisconsinan glacial maximum, in Wright, H. E., and Porter, S., eds., Late Quaternary Environments of the United States, v. I: University of Minnesota Press, Minneapolis, p. 215–229.

———, BROECKER, W. S., CHAPPELL, J. M. A., MATTHEWS, R. K., AND MESOLELLA, K., 1974, Quaternary sea level fluctuations on a tectonic coast: new ^{230}Th/^{234}U dates from the Huon Peninsula, New Guinea: Quaternary Research, v. 4, p. 185–205.

BUTZER, K. W., 1983, Global sea level stratigraphy: an appraisal: Quaternary Science Reviews, v. 2, p. 1–15.

BYRNE, J. V., LEROY, D. O., AND RILEY, C., 1959, The chenier plain and its stratigraphy, southwestern Louisiana: Gulf Coast Association of Geological Societies Transactions, v. 9, p. 237–260.

CHAPPELL, J., 1974, Late Quaternary glacio- and hydro-isostasy on a layered earth: Quaternary Research, v. 4, p. 429–440.

CLARK, J. A., FARRELL, W. E., AND PELTIER, W. R., 1978, Global changes in post-glacial sea level: a numerical calculation: Quaternary Research, v. 9, p. 265–287.

COLEMAN, J. M., PRIOR, D. B., AND LINDSAY, J. F., 1983, Deltaic influences on shelf edge instability processes, in Stanley, D. F., and Moore, G. T., eds., The Shelfbreak: Critical Interface on Continental Margins: Society of Economic Paleontologists and Mineralogists Special Publication 33, p. 121–137.

CURRAY, J. R., 1960, Sediments and history of Holocene transgression, continental shelf, northwest Gulf of Mexico, in Shepard, F. P., Phleger, F. B., and Van Andel, T. H., eds., Recent Sediments, Northwest

Gulf of Mexico: American Association of Petroleum Geologists, Tulsa, p. 221–266.

———, 1964, Transgressions and regressions, in Miller, R. L., ed., Papers in Marine Geology, Shepard Commemorative Volume: MacMillan Press, New York, p. 179–203.

DILLON, W. P., AND OLDALE, R. N., 1978, Late Quaternary sea-level curve: reinterpretation based on glacio-tectonic influence: Geology, v. 6, p. 56–60.

EMILIANI, C., GARTNER, S., LIDZ, B., ELDRIDGE, K., ELVEY, D. K., HUANG, T. C., STIPP, J. J., AND SWANSON, M. F., 1975, Paleoclimatologic analysis of late Quaternary cores from the northeastern Gulf of Mexico: Science, v. 189, p. 1083-1088.

FAIRBANKS, R. G., AND MATTHEWS, R. K., 1978, The marine oxygen isotope record in Pleistocene coral, Barbados, West Indies: Quaternary Research, v. 10, p. 181–196.

FILLON, R. H., 1984, Continental glacial stratigraphy, marine evidence of glaciation, and insights into continental-marine correlations, in Healy-Williams, N., ed., Principles of Pleistocene Stratigraphy: International Human Resources Development Corporation, Boston, p. 149–207.

FINKELSTEIN, K., AND KEARNEY, M., 1986, The geomorphic, chronologic, and stratigraphic relationships between late Quaternary inner and outer barrier islands, Cape Charles, Virginia (abs.): Society of Economic Paleontologists and Mineralogists Annual Midyear Meeting, Raleigh, p. 36.

FISCHER, A. G., 1961, Stratigraphic record of transgressing seas in light of sedimentation on Atlantic coast of New Jersey: American Association of Petroleum Geologists Bulletin, v. 45, p. 1656–1666.

FISK, H. N., 1944, Geological investigation of the alluvial valley of the lower Mississippi River: U.S. Army Corps of Engineers, Mississippi River Commission, Vicksburg, 78 p.

———, 1956, Nearsurface sediments of the continental shelf off Louisiana: Eighth Texas Conference on Soil Mechanics and Foundation Enigineering Proceedings, 36 p.

———, AND McFARLAN, E., JR., 1955, Late Quaternary deltaic deposits of the Mississippi River: Geological Society of America Special Paper 62, p. 279–302.

FRAZIER, D. E., 1967, Recent deltaic deposits of the Mississippi River: their development and chronology: Gulf Coast Association Geological Societies Transactions, v. XVII, p. 287–315.

———, 1974, Depositional Episodes: their Relationship to the Quaternary Stratigraphic Framework in the Northwestern Portion of the Gulf Basin: Texas Bureau of Economic Geology, Geologic Circular 74-1, 28 p.

GAGLIANO S. M., PEARSON, C. E., WEINSTEIN, R. A., WIDEMAN, D. E., AND McCLENDON, C. M., 1982, Sedimentary studies of prehistoric archaeological sites: criteria for the identification of submerged archaeological sites of the northern Gulf of Mexico continental shelf: Coastal Environments, Inc., Baton Rouge, 120 p.

GONZALES, M. A., WEILER, N. A., AND GUIDA, N. G., 1986, Late Pleistocene transgressive deposits from 33 S.L. to 40 S.L., Argentina, in Pirazzoli, P. A., and Suter, J. R., eds., Late Quaternary Sea Level Changes and Coastal Evolution: Journal of Coastal Research, Special Issue no. 1, p. 39–48.

GOULD, H. R., AND McFARLAN, E., JR., 1959, Geologic history of the chenier plain, southwestern Louisiana: Gulf Coast Association of Geological Societies Transactions, v. 9 p. 261–270.

GOY, J. L., AND ZAZO, C., 1986, Western Almeria (Spain) coastline changes since the last interglacial, in Pirazolli, P. A., and Suter, J. R., eds., Late Quaternary Sea Level Changes and Coastal Evolution: Journal of Coastal Research, Special Issue No. 1, p. 89–94.

HINE, A. C., AND SNYDER, S., 1985, Coastal lithosome preservation: evidence from the shoreface and inner continental shelf off Bogue Banks, North Carolina: Marine Geology, v. 63, p. 307–330.

KUMAR, N., AND SANDERS, J. E., 1974, Inlet sequence: a vertical succession of sedimentary structures and textures created by the lateral migration of tidal inlets: Sedimentology, v. 21, p. 491–532.

LEHNER, P., 1969, Salt tectonics and Pleistocene stratigraphy on continental slope of northern Gulf of Mexico: American Association of Petroleum Geologists Bulletin, v. 53, p. 2431–2480.

MILLIMAN, J. D., AND EMERY, K. O., 1968, Sea levels during the past 35,000 years: Science, v. 162, p. 1121–1123.

MITCHUM, R. M., JR., VAIL, P. R., AND SANGREE, J. B., 1977, Seismic stratigraphy and global changes of sea level, part 6: stratigraphic interpretation of seismic reflection patterns in depositional sequences, *in* Payton, C. E., ed., Seismic Stratigraphy-Applications to Hydrocarbon Exploration: American Association of Petroleum Geologists Memoir 26, p. 53–62.

MOORE, W. S., 1982, Late Pleistocene sea level history, *in* Ivanovich, M., and Harmon, R. S., eds., Uranium Series Disequilibrium: Application to Environmental Problems: Clarendon Press, Oxford, p. 481–496.

MORNER, N. A., 1976, Eustasy and geoid changes: Journal of Geology, v. 84, p. 123–151.

NELSON, H. F., AND BRAY, E. B., 1970, Stratigraphy and history of the Holocene sediments in the Sabine-High Island area, Gulf of Mexico, *in* Morgan, J. P., ed., Deltaic Sedimentation, Modern and Ancient: Society of Economic Paleontologists and Mineralogists Special Publication 15, p. 48–77.

PENLAND, S., AND SUTER, J. R., 1983, Transgressive coastal facies preserved in barrier island arc retreat paths in the Mississippi River delta plain: Gulf Coast Association Geological Societies Transactions, v. XXXIII, p. 367–382.

———, ———, AND BOYD, R., 1985, Barrier island arcs along abandoned Mississippi River Deltas: Marine Geology, v. 63, p. 197–233.

———, ———, AND MOSLOW, T. F., 1986, The Holocene Geology of the Ship Shoal Region, Northern Gulf of Mexico: Louisiana Geological Survey, Coastal Geology Bulletin No. 1, 95 p.

POAG, C. W., 1973, Late Quaternary sea levels in the Gulf of Mexico: Gulf Coast Association Geological Societies Transactions, v. XXIII, p. 394–400.

ROEMER, L. B., AND BRYANT, W. E., 1977, Structure and Stratigraphy of Late Quaternary Deposits on the Outer Louisiana Shelf: Texas A & M Technical Report, College Station, 169 p.

SANGREE, J. B., WAYLETT, D. C., FRAZIER, D. E., AMERY, G. B., AND FENNESSY, W. J., 1978, Recognition of continental-slope seismic facies, offshore Texas-Louisiana, *in* Bouma, A. H., Moore, G. T., and Coleman, J. M., eds. Framework Facies and Oil Trapping Characteristics of the Upper Continental Margin: American Association of Petroleum Geologists, Studies in Goelogy No. 7, 87–116.

SAUCIER, R. T., 1977, The northern Gulf coast during the Farmdalian substage: a search for evidence: U.S. Army Corps of Engineers, Miscellaneous Paper Y-77-1, 30 p.

SHACKLETON, N. J., 1977, Oxygen isotope and paleomagnetic evidence for early northern hemisphere glaciation: Nature, v. 270, p. 216–219.

———, AND OPDYKE, N. D., 1973, Oxygen isotope and paleomagnetic stratigraphy of equatorial Pacific core V28-V2381: oxygen isotope temperatures and ice volumes on a 10^5 year and 10^6 year scale: Quaternary Research, v. 3, p. 39–55.

SHEPARD, F. P., 1963, Thirty-five thousand years of sea level, *in* Essays in Honor of K. O. Emery: University of Southern California Press, Los Angeles, p. 1–20.

SIDNER, B. R., GARTNER, S., AND BRYANT, W. R., 1978, Late Pleistocene geologic history of Texas outer continental shelf and upper continental margin: American Association of Petroleum Geologists, Studies in Geology No. 7, p. 243–266.

SUTER, J. R., 1985, Northwest Gulf of Mexico continental shelf sands I: southwest Louisiana, *in,* Berryhill, H. L., Moslow, T. F., Penland, S., and Suter, J. R., Shelf and Shoreline Sands, Northwest Gulf of Mexico: American Association of Petroleum Geologists Short Course Notes, p. 5-1-5-53.

———, 1986, Buried late Quaternary fluvial channels on the Louisiana continental shelf, USA, *in,* Pirazzoli, P. A., and Suter, J. R., eds., Late Quaternary Sea-Level Changes and Coastal Evolution: Journal of Coastal Research Special Issue No. 1, p. 27–37.

———, AND BERRYHILL, H. L., 1985, Late Quaternary shelf margin deltas, northwest Gulf of Mexico: American Association of Petroleum Geologists Bulletin, v. 69, p. 77–91.

———, AND PENLAND, S., 1985a, Environments of sand deposition, southwest Louisiana continental shelf: Gulf Coast Association of Geological Societies Transactions, v. XXXV, p. 495–503.

———, AND PENLAND, S., 1985, Cat Island Pass, Louisiana, USA: a microtidal transgressive inlet, *in* Abstracts of the Symposium on Modern and Ancient Clastic Tidal Deposits: International Association of Sedimentologists, Utrecht, the Netherlands, p. 132–133.

———, ———, AND BERRYHILL, H. L., 1984, Stratigraphic evidence for sea level changes, Louisiana continental shelf (abs.): Society of Economic Paleontologists and Mineralogists Midyear Meeting, San José, p. 79.

———, ———, AND MOSLOW, T. F., 1985b, Trinity Shoal: a reworked deltaic barrier on the Louisiana continental shelf: American Association of Petroleum Geologists Bulletin, v. 69, p. 309–310.

SWIFT, D. J. P., 1975, Barrier island genesis: evidence from the central Atlantic shelf, eastern U.S.A.: Sedimentary Geology, v. 14, p. 1–43.

———, 1976, Coastal sedimentation, *in* Stanley, D. J., and Swift, D. J. P., eds., Marine Sediment Transport and Environmental Management: John Wiley and Sons, Inc., New York, p. 255–310.

THOM, B. G., 1973, Dilemma of high interstadial sea levels during the last glaciation: Progress in Geography, v. 5, p. 167–246.

VAIL, P. R., HARDENBOHL, J., AND TODD, R. G., 1984, Jurassic unconformities, chronostratigraphy, and sea level changes from seismic stratigraphy and biostratigraphy, *in* Schlee, J. S., ed., Interregional Unconformities and Hydrocarbon Accumulation: American Association of Petroleum Geologists Memoir 36, p. 129–144.

———, MITCHUM, R. M., JR., TODD, R. G., WIDMEIR, J. M., THOMPSON, S., III, SANGREE, J. B., BUBB, J. N., AND HATELID, W. G., 1977, Seismic stratigraphy and global changes of sea level, *in* Payton, C. E., ed., Seismic Stratigraphy—Applications to Hydrocarbon Exploration: American Association of Petroleum Geologists Memoir 26, p. 49–205.

WALCOTT, R. I., 1972, Post sea levels, eustasy, and deformation of the earth: Quaternary Research, v. 2, p. 1–14.

WILLIAMS, D. G., 1984, Correlation of Pleistocene marine sediments of the Gulf of Mexico and other basins using oxygen isotope stratigraphy, *in* Healy-Williams, N., ed., Principles of Pleistocene Stratigraphy Applied to the Gulf of Mexico: International Human Resources Development Corporation, Boston, p. 65–118.

WINKER, C. D., 1982, Cenozoic shelf margins, northwestern Gulf of Mexico: Gulf Coast Association of Geological Societies Transactions, v. 32, p. 427–448.

———, AND EDWARDS, M. B., 1983, Unstable progradational clastic shelf margins, *in* Stanley, D. J., and Moore, G. T., eds., The Shelfbreak: Critical Interface on Continental Margins: Society of Economic Paleontologists Mineralogists Special Publication 33, p. 139–157.

WOODBURY, H. O., MURRAY, I. B., JR., PICKFORD, P. J., AND AKERS, W. H., 1973, Pliocene and Pleistocene depocenters, outer continental shelf, Louisiana and Texas: American Association of Petroleum Geologists Bulletin, v. 57, p. 2428–2439.

PART VI
SEQUENCE-BOUNDING UNCONFORMITIES

STRATIGRAPHIC RECORD OF QUATERNARY SEA LEVELS: IMPLICATIONS FOR MORE ANCIENT STRATA

JAMES M. DEMAREST, II

Exxon Production Research Company, P.O. Box 2189, Houston, Texas 77001

AND

JOHN C. KRAFT

Department of Geology, University of Delaware, Newark, Delaware 19716

ABSTRACT: The stratigraphic record of Quaternary transgressions due to glacio-eustatic rise varies as a function of sediment supply from rivers to the paralic realm. Extremes from low to high sediment supply are represented by the Atlantic and Gulf coasts of the United States, respectively.

The vertical sequence produced by these transgressions at the low sediment supply end of the spectrum consists of paralic and fluvial lithosomes erosionally truncated by shoreface retreat and overlain by shelf marine lithosomes. The lithosomes produced in the landward portion of the paralic realm are commonly preserved, whereas the lithosomes from the more shoreward part are less likely to be preserved. Thus, beach facies are rarely incorporated into the transgressive stratigraphic record, except as a peak sea-level deposit preserved by abandonment. Erosional truncation of the paralic section produces a unique stratigraphic surface, the ravinement surface, which exhibits many of the physical characteristics of a major break in deposition. The surface is then overlain by nearshore to offshore shelf facies in a deepening-upward succession.

When encountered in the stratigraphic record, the ravinement surface is likely to be interpreted as a depositional sequence boundary. When this occurs, a continuous cycle of deposition during transgression is not recognized. When a ravinement and its associated facies are properly interpreted, a complete cycle of transgression and regression in response to changing sea level can be recognized.

INTRODUCTION

In this paper we will examine the stratigraphic record of Holocene and Pleistocene transgressions caused by rising sea level. The emphasis will be on those aspects of transgressive stratigraphy important to recognition and interpretation of similar depositional sequences in the ancient rock record. Toward this end, we will develop a generalized vertical sequence model for transgressive stratigraphy and will present several variations that are frequently encountered.

Our view of stratigraphy formed during transgression, based on Holocene and Pleistocene analogs, is limited by lack of access to much of the geologic record of these transgressions. The most accessible strata are those Holocene sections now evolving landward of the beach in barriers and lagoons. Extensive coring and sampling have produced a detailed picture of the facies associations within the paralic realm. Much less is known about the continental shelf. The critical zone of transition from paralic to marine realm is perhaps the most inaccessible environment for study due to the high energy and extreme temporal variation of events and processes within this setting. Understanding transgressive deposits in the ancient rock record, however, is largely dependent on our understanding of the processes of deposition and erosion along the shoreface.

Definitions

Transgression is the migration of the shoreline in the landward direction. We restrict the use of this term to regional, long-term migration of environments and use the terms progradation and retrogradation for fluctuations on a local scale due to variations in sediment influx. Although the direction of movement of the shoreline is the reference for transgressions, beach deposits do not have to be present in a transgressive sequence. All sediments which are deposited during a regional landward shift in the shoreline are considered transgressive. This implies that a transgressive depositional sequence is also a time-stratigraphic unit requiring time-stratigraphic subdivision of the rock record.

Paralic realm is used to refer to the entire area from the shoreline landward to the limit of tidal or marine influence, whichever is farther landward. Beach face deposits are not included in the paralic realm as these are dominated by marine processes and are therefore more closely associated with marine deposits. Ebb-tidal deltas are likewise not included in the paralic realm. The shoreline thus becomes a clear line of demarcation between paralic and marine environments.

Eustacy is a world-wide change in the level of the sea surface with reference to the center of the earth. Relative sea-level change is change in the level of the sea surface with reference to a geodetic datum. This change is mainly the combined effect of eustacy, tectonic subsidence and compaction of the pre-existing sediment column.

In our usage, each of these terms has application on different spatial and temporal scales from global to local and long-term to instantaneous. Short-term sedimentation responds to relative seal-level change and shifts in transport paths in the form of progradation and retrogradation. Regional, longer term deposition and erosion are a response to relative sea-level change in the form of transgression and regression. Sedimentary systems do not respond directly to eustatic change.

Depositional versus Erosional Transgressions

The stratigraphic section produced during transgression is dependent on the rate of sediment supply and the rate of relative sea-level rise. Extremes of possible sediment influx rates for the same rate of relative sea-level rise produce dramatically different vertical sequences (Fig. 1).

The mid-Atlantic shelf of the United States has experienced a transgression driven by rising relative sea level from 18.0 ka to the present. Due to the low sediment supply from rivers, this transgression has been dominated by retrogradational processes of deposition and erosion. The history of shoreline movement is one of nearly continuous landward retreat, although rates of retreat may have been quite

TRANSGRESSIVE STRATIGRAPHY

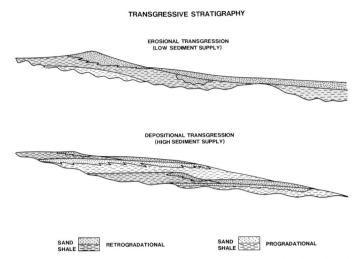

FIG. 1.—Distribution of progradational and retrogradational sand and shale facies within erosional and depositional transgressions. Erosional transgressions are dominated by retrogradational deposition during shoreface retreat, whereas depositional transgressions are dominated by progradational deposition. Both types of transgressions produce predominantly coarsening-upward depositional packages.

variable. The source of sediment to the beach is almost entirely from reworked pre-existing strata ranging in age from Cretaceous to Pleistocene. This type of transgression is called an erosional transgression (Curray, 1964; Swift, 1968).

During the last 18,000 yrs, a general transgression of the Mississippi delta has occurred, because each progradational delta lobe has not reached as far seaward as the previous one. The stratigraphic record of this transgression consists of progradational delta lobes (tens of meters thick) separated by retrogradational sediments (rarely more than tens of meters thick; Frazier, 1967; Penland and Boyd, 1982). More time can be represented by the thinner retrogradational section than by the thicker progradational section. This type of transgression has been termed a depositional transgression by Curray (1964) and Swift (1968).

Sediment supply is the most important factor in the difference between these two types of transgression. Low sediment supply erosional transgressions produce stratigraphic units that result predominantly from processes of retrogradation, whereas high sediment supply depositional transgressions are dominated by processes of progradation. The vertical sequence developed by erosional transgressions is difficult to recognize without a good understanding of the products of shoreface retreat.

QUATERNARY TRANSGRESSIVE SEQUENCES OF THE DELMARVA PENINSULA

During the Quaternary, glacio-eustatic fluctuations have resulted in numerous transgressions of the continental shelves. On the Delmarva Peninsula (Fig. 2), these fluctuations have produced shoreline trends recording the peak sea-level position of the beach (Fig. 2). Through mapping of crosscutting relationships of geomorphic features associated with shorelines and dating of fossil shell material associated with shoreline trends, Demarest and Belknap (1980) produced

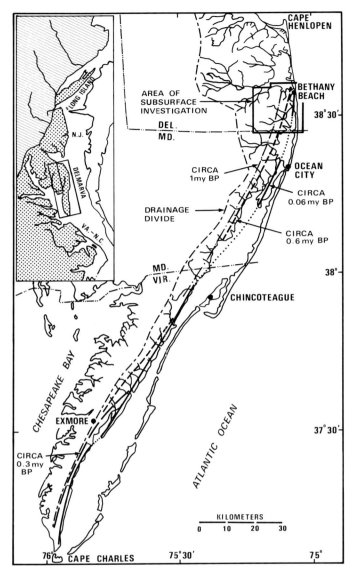

FIG. 2.—Location map to area where Quaternary shoreline development has been studied. Shoreline trends are indicated with approximate ages (Demarest and Belknap, 1980). Cross section in Figure 3 is based on Holocene stratigraphy north of Bethany Beach. Cross sections in Figures 4, 5 and 6 are from box labelled "Area of Subsurface Investigation."

an age model for the shorelines. This model indicated the ages of the peak sea-level events to be between 1.2 Ma and present. Since only six high sea-level events, including the present shoreline, appear to be recorded, not all ice-volume minima indicated in the $\delta^{18}O$ isotope record (Shackleton and Opdyke, 1973) produced sea levels high enough to cause transgression to this area and/or some shorelines were removed by later transgressions. The glacio-eustatic rise during the last 18,000 yrs has brought the present shoreline landward to where it is eroding older shorelines in southern Delaware and to a position just offshore of the older shorelines farther south on the Delmarva Peninsula (Demarest and Leatherman, 1985).

The stacking pattern produced by multiple abandoned

shorelines has created a Quaternary stratigraphic package, the Omar Fm of Jordan (1962), that becomes progressively younger in the seaward direction. We hesitate, however, to refer to the Omar Fm as regressive, since each vertical sequence within the unit was deposited during a transgression.

In eastern Sussex County, Delaware, detailed stratigraphic analyses of the Omar Fm by Demarest (1981) and Demarest and others (1981) have shown the extent of these Quaternary shorelines and have documented the transgressive origins of each shoreline trend. Dating of the shorelines was accomplished by Belknap (1979), using amino acid racemization in fossil mollusks recovered from outcrops and cores in the area. Little or no retrogradational section appears to occur seaward of the shorelines. These shorelines do not represent progradational pulses in an overall transgression but shorelines that were abandoned due to rapid fall in relative sea level. This is a different preservation mechanism than that in the "overstepping" model (Sanders and Kumar; 1975, Rampino and Sanders, 1981), where a barrier is partially preserved by a rapid rise in sea level causing a rapid landward shift in shoreline position.

Through comparison of Holocene transgressive vertical sequences (Fig. 3), where the depositional mechanisms and timing are well documented (e.g., Kraft, 1971; Kraft and others, 1973; Kraft and Belknap, 1975; Belknap and Kraft, 1981; Belknap and Kraft, 1985), with vertical sequences observed in the Pleistocene shorelines, the evolution of the Pleistocene shorelines can be obtained. Widely spaced "jet wash" borings were first obtained to get fast coverage over a large area. These data, in combination with water well logs and other published and unpublished data from the area, allow general stratigraphic interpretation to be compiled at minimal expense in time and capital. Three Pleistocene shorelines, the White Neck, Cedar Neck and Bethany, were thus identified (Demarest, 1981; Demarest and others, 1981; Fig. 4). A program of detailed vibracoring in critical locations was conducted to establish correlations and "calibrate" the environmental interpretations based on "jet wash" borings. Vibracoring was carried out along profiles ap-

proximately perpendicular to the paleoshoreline trend every 100 to 300 m along each profile to establish the detailed facies correlations necessary for comparison of Holocene vertical sequences and lithosome geometry. Two such profiles, Cedar Neck South (Fig. 5) and Miller Creek (Fig. 6), show the distribution of facies within the Cedar Neck barrier system. In both sections, the transgressive origin is clearly indicated by the gradual migration of barrier and back-barrier environments over lagoonal environments. The sedimentary structures, grain size, bioturbation, unit thickness, and lithologic contacts can be directly compared to similar features observed in Holocene transgressive deposits where depositional mechanisms can be observed. From our experience in these Quaternary deposits, it is possible to describe a generalized transgressive vertical sequence.

Transgressive Vertical Sequence

In order to simplify and organize our study of transgressive vertical sequences, lithosomes produced by migrating transgressive environments have been divided into three broad realms: (1) fluvial (F), (2) paralic (P), and (3) marine (M) (Fig. 7). During transgression, lithosomes from each of these realms, when formed and preserved, follow in succession with fluvial at the base and marine at the top. Within each realm, environments which produce the individual lithosomes are interrelated and have highly variable interfingering contacts. For this reason, the vertical succession of environments within a realm is variable and, when different from that shown, it is not necessarily an indication of discontinuous transgression or multiple depositional sequences. When the vertical succession of depositional realms occurs out of order, it is an indication of discontinuous transgression within the vertical profile. The following discussion summarizes the results of numerous studies of coastal stratigraphy with emphasis on those aspects pertinent to interpretation of ancient sequences.

Fluvial realm.—

Two environments produce the lithosomes most commonly encountered within the fluvial realm. As rising sea level elevates the stream profile, stream beds commonly aggrade their valleys, producing stream-bed deposits (F-1, Fig. 7) at the base of the transgressive interval above the underlying sequence boundary. As sea level continues to rise, freshwater swamps or bogs (F-2, Fig. 7) may form. Freshwater swamps form at or above sea level, whereas the stream-bed sands form slightly above sea level or well above sea level. Lithosomes formed in the fluvial realm usually are confined to the basal part of the incised valley and have a lenticular, discontinuous geometry. Freshwater swamps may persist in an area during rising sea level long enough to rise out of the incised valley into the interfluvial areas, particularly in areas of high freshwater runoff or low tidal range. When this occurs, the freshwater swamp (F-2) lithosome may become tabular (Fig. 4) but would otherwise be lenticular, similar to stream-bed sands. Fluvial realm lithosomes rarely are encountered in the subsurface in the study area due to their confinement to valleys and/or to the lack of deposition of these lithosomes. In other settings,

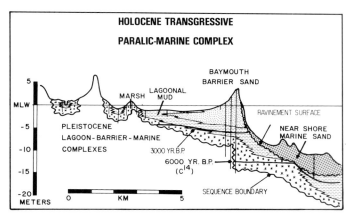

FIG. 3.—Cross section of Holocene deposits north of Bethany Beach, Delaware. Holocene sequence consists of transgressive paralic deposits erosionally truncated to the east and overlain by nearshore strata (after Kraft, 1971).

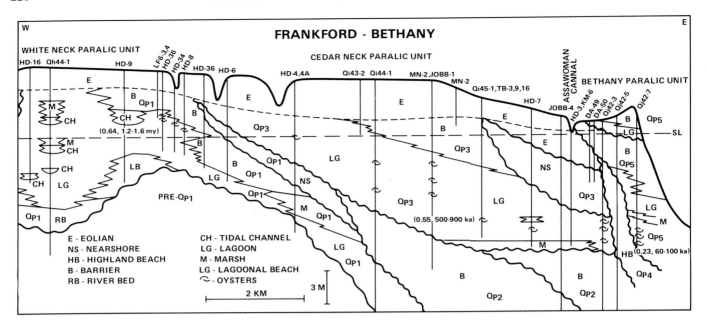

FIG. 4.—East-west cross section along latitude 38° 35′ N within area of subsurface investigation. Environment, facies and ages are indicated. Pattern is one of transgressive deposits stacked horizontally in an overall progressively younger seaward direction. The entire Quaternary package is in the Omar Fm (Jordan, 1962) and is composed of several transgressive paralic units. Exposed near the surface are the White Neck (circa 1.2 ma), Cedar Neck (circa 0.6 ma) and the Bethany paralic units (circa 0.08 ma) (from Demarest, 1981).

particularly ones where river sediment supply is greater, fluvial lithosomes may occur more frequently.

Paralic realm.—

The depositional record of transition from the fluvial to the paralic realm can be gradational or sharp depending on the facies succession. We have found it useful to subdivide the paralic realm informally into two groups of depositional environments: distal and proximal. Distal refers to those environments which are not directly influenced by barrier or baymouth processes of deposition and erosion, whereas proximal refers to those environments which are directly influenced by, or are an intergral part of, the barrier or baymouth dynamics. This distinction is useful to make, but a

sharp separation is impossible. The order in which the paralic lithosomes are listed in Figure 7 is generally from distal to proximal and is thus the order in which they stack during transgression. Due to the variability of the environmental distribution in the paralic realm, however, the vertical succession produced by the paralic environment is not fixed. When lithosomes occur in an order other than those listed in Figure 7, one should not necessarily infer an associated change in shoreline migration direction. This can only be inferred by observation of the position of the paralic to marine transition through time.

The paralic realm contains five general environmental settings. Coastal marsh (P-1) is the salt- or brackish-water equivalent to the freshwater swamp (F-2) of the fluvial realm and commonly gradationally overlies the freshwater swamp

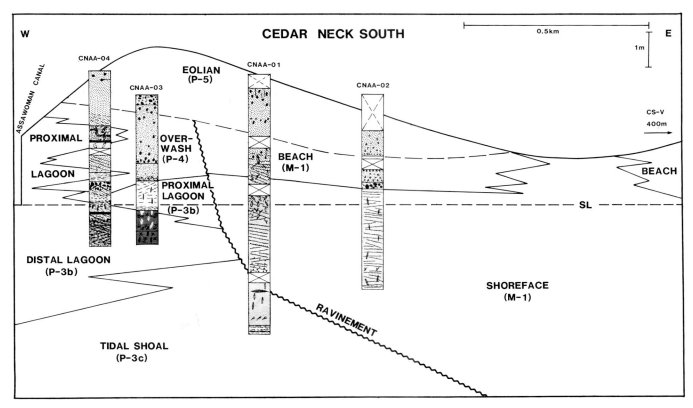

FIG. 5.—Cedar Neck South cross section along the northern portion of the Cedar Neck paralic unit just west of Bethany. Unit is dominated by transgressive overwash and inlet processes with ravinement surface, representing most landward position of shoreline prior to abandonment. Shoreface sands in cores CNAA-01 and CNAA-02 are local deposits of a prograding beach deposited during initial stage of falling sea level after peak interglacial level between 500 ka and 900 ka (from Demarest, 1981).

lithosome. Coastal marsh, when present, represents the leading edge of the paralic realm during transgression. It is commonly found on interfluves covering wide areas. Coastal marsh can also form in more proximal settings of the paralic realm and thus is not diagnostic of the basal part of the transgressive section. P-1 along with F-2 combine to form thick tabular lithosomes when at the base of the transgressive section, whereas P-1 is generally thinner and more laterally discontinuous when not at the base of the succession.

Overlying the coastal marsh or lower sequence boundary when marsh and fluvial lithosomes are missing, paralic shoreface (P-2) lithosomes can form lenticular or "shoestring" sand bodies. Paralic beach sediment textures are influenced strongly by source textures because little transport and winnowing occur. The tendency is for these deposits to be fine-grained, except near coarser source materials, and to be thin, laterally discontinuous bodies. They commonly grade vertically and laterally into tidal flat (P-3a), estuarine/lagoon (P-3b), or tidal shoal or channel (P-3c) deposits. Paralic beach deposits also can form on the back side of barriers.

Distal paralic deposits are primarily restricted to P-1 and P-2 with the P-3 (a–c) representing transitional facies. Tidal flat, estuarine/lagoon, and tidal shoal or channel are grouped as components of the P-3 subenvironment because they can occur in any vertical order and commonly repeat vertically.

P-3 lithosomes are usually the thickest of the paralic deposits and typically grade from one to another. Channel sand deposits (P-3b) are usually lenticular in shape and commonly have erosional bases. Also, they are commonly encased in estuarine/lagoonal shales. Where the paralic deposits are formed in a large estuary with no barrier across the baymouth, tidal shoal and channel lithosomes will cap the paralic portion of the transgressive vertical sequence. Where the paralic realm is formed by a barrier beach with abundant, migrating inlets, tidal channels may cut deeply into more distally formed lithosomes and may deposit tidal channel and shoal lithosomes. These deposits may cap the paralic section or may be overlain by the back-barrier overwash deposits.

Where the paralic environment is the result of a barrier system enclosing a lagoon, back-barrier overwash sand (P-4) will overlie the transitional facies and is a diagnostic indicator of the proximity of the barrier beach. This facies generally will have a gradational base with lagoonal facies (P-3b) below. As the barrier system migrates landward, the overwash process transports sand to the back side of the barrier onto the back-barrier flat and into the lagoon. When this occurs, an overall coarsening-upward sequence toward the top of the paralic lithosomes will result.

Capping the paralic vertical sequence are eolian sands (P-5). Under conditions unusual today, the back-barrier flat

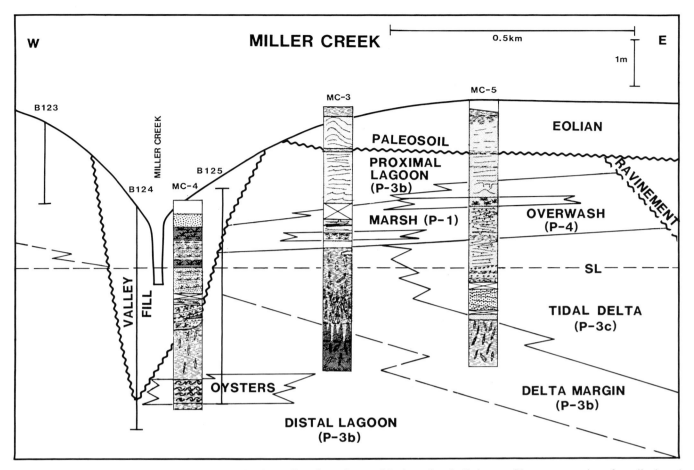

FIG. 6.—Miller Creek cross section across Cedar Neck paralic unit southwest of Bethany Beach, Delaware. Uppermost portion of paralic deposits consists of overwash sands in Cores JMD-MC-3 and JMD-MC-5. Lower part of Core MC-5 is dominated by flood-tidal delta deposits. The position of the ravinement surface is inferred from presence of overwash and normal distance from shoreline that overwash is found in the Holocene. This position also corresponds to the position of a change in slope in the land surface associated with the seaward edge of this unit (Demarest, 1981). Core JMD-MC-4 penetrated a valley-fill sequence that was depopsited in an incised valley which eroded into the Cedar Neck trend and is probably several hundred thousand years younger, possibly between 60 and 120 ka (from Demarest, 1981).

can become extensive enough to produce thick lithosomes of eolian sands. This is most likely in areas with strong onshore winds and/or an arid climate (for example, South Padre Island, Texas).

The complete vertical sequence produced by the paralic environment typically exhibits a fining-upward section (P-2 and P-3) from the lower sequence boundary to the transition from distal to proximal lithosomes (P-3), then a coarsening upward with increasing influence of barrier and/or baymouth processes as the more proximal facies (P-3, P-4, and P-5) are deposited. This vertical sequence is preserved intact when preserved by abandonment due to a peak sea-level event as seen in the Delmarva Peninsula. When transgression causes the marine realm to override to paralic realm, the paralic lithosomes are eroded and overlain by transgressive marine deposits.

Marine realm.—

The transition from a paralic to a marine realm is erosional due to the process of shoreface retreat. Erosional truncation of the paralic section produces the ravinement surface (Stamp, 1922; Swift, 1968), which exhibits many of the physical characteristics of an unconformity but does not represent a sequence boundary. This surface has also been referred to as a transgressive surface (Ryer, 1977) and it is a diastem (Weimer and others, 1985). The ravinement surface exhibits bedding truncation below, rip-up clasts, gravel or shell lag above, and a dramatic change in lithofacies, paleo-water depth and paleoenvironment. In addition, lithosomes have no direct geometric or interfingering relationship across the ravinement surface. Temporally, the ravinement is a time-transgressive erosion surface. Fluvial and paralic deposits found below the ravinement are deposited contemporaneously with marine strata above the ravinement surface formed earlier and farther seaward (see also Nummedal and Swift, this volume). In addition, the ravinement surface does not represent a sudden shift in depositional environment or catastrophic change in shoreline position; rather, it is the product of the gradual landward migration of an erosional shoreface. The ravinement sur-

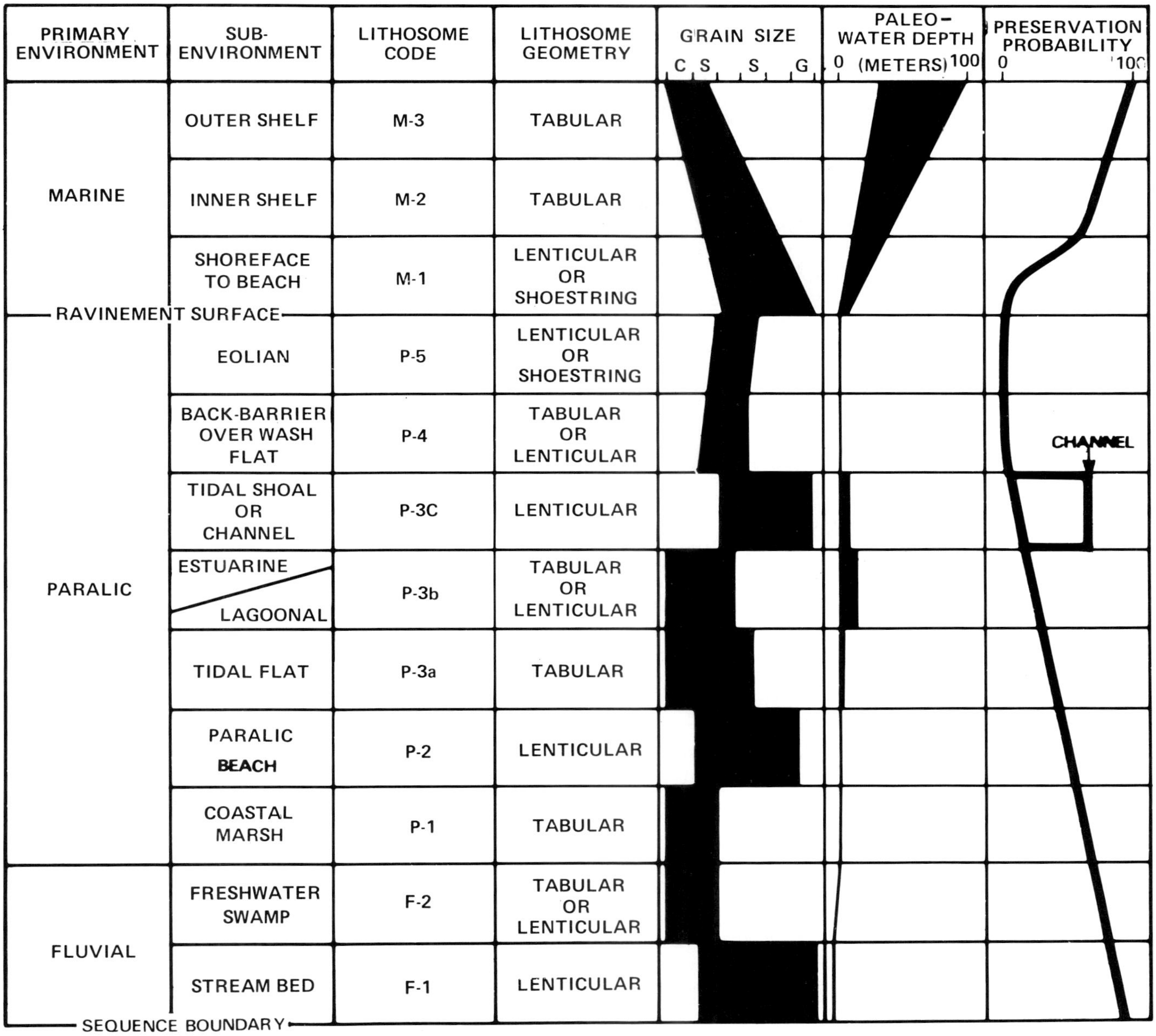

PRIMARY ENVIRONMENT	SUB-ENVIRONMENT	LITHOSOME CODE	LITHOSOME GEOMETRY	GRAIN SIZE C S S G	PALEO-WATER DEPTH 0 (METERS) 100	PRESERVATION PROBABILITY 0 100
MARINE	OUTER SHELF	M-3	TABULAR			
	INNER SHELF	M-2	TABULAR			
	SHOREFACE TO BEACH	M-1	LENTICULAR OR SHOESTRING			
— RAVINEMENT SURFACE —						
PARALIC	EOLIAN	P-5	LENTICULAR OR SHOESTRING			
	BACK-BARRIER OVER WASH FLAT	P-4	TABULAR OR LENTICULAR			CHANNEL
	TIDAL SHOAL OR CHANNEL	P-3C	LENTICULAR			
	ESTUARINE / LAGOONAL	P-3b	TABULAR OR LENTICULAR			
	TIDAL FLAT	P-3a	TABULAR			
	PARALIC BEACH	P-2	LENTICULAR			
	COASTAL MARSH	P-1	TABULAR			
FLUVIAL	FRESHWATER SWAMP	F-2	TABULAR OR LENTICULAR			
	STREAM BED	F-1	LENTICULAR			
— SEQUENCE BOUNDARY —						

FIG. 7.—Classification system for transgressive lithosomes as they occur vertically. See text for discussion of classification and its use.

face represents an erosional facies change similar to the surface produced at the cut bank of a meandering stream and therefore does not represent a regional boundary between time-stratigraphic depositional units.

The potential for misinterpretation of the ravinement surface as a major unconformity separating deposits of different depositional sequences is great due to the dramatic vertical change of lithofacies. Paleo-water depths can change from near sea level below the surface to lower shoreface or deeper above it, tempting one to interpret a catastrophic flooding or transgression; however, gradual transgression is known to produce the same vertical sequence (Kraft, 1971; Belknap and Kraft, 1981).

As the shoreface migrates landward, the upper portion of the profile experiences net erosion. Deposition may occur during fair weather conditions, but the sediments produced are ephemeral, being removed during storms. Under high wave-energy conditions, after the fair weather sands have been removed, erosion of the paralic section occurs, progressively moving the shoreface profile higher and more landward in response to rising sea level. The deposits that become incorporated as part of the transgressive vertical sequence above the ravinement surface are dependent upon the width of the zone of net erosion. Where the zone is narrow, shoreface deposits may be preserved, and where the zone is wider, sediments farther offshore will immediately overlie the ravinement surface. The wider the zone of net erosion, the farther offshore the first sediments above the ravinement will be deposited and the more dramatic the surface will later appear in terms of change in paleoenvironment. A wider zone of net erosion does not imply deeper erosion of the paralic lithosomes. In fact, the opposite may be the general relationship, as implied by Belknap and Kraft (1981, 1985).

Shoreface deposits (M-1, Fig. 7), when present, tend to be discontinuous and consist predominantly of lower shoreface sands directly overlying either paralic deposits, where preserved, or the underlying sequence boundary. Linear sand shoals of upper shoreface sands also are formed during transgression (Stubblefield and others, 1984; Swift and others, 1984), and these may or may not be preserved below lower shoreface sheet sands. Inner shelf (M-2, Fig. 7) sheet sands, storm-graded beds and silty shales normally are present above the shoreface sands and graded beds, and silty shales can develop above the shoreface sands and grade upward into outer-shelf shales (M-3, Fig. 7) if the transgression persists long enough.

Probability of occurrence and preservation.—

The classification scheme shown in Figure 7 illustrates the vertical sequence which would develop if all depositional environments present occurred in succession at a single location during transgression. All environments are not likely to occur in a single vertical sequence, and the preservation of deposits produced by some environments is more likely than others. Therefore, the probability of preservation is also plotted in Figure 7. The preservation potential of a particular deposit is controlled by the distance and elevation of the associated environment relative to the shoreline, as well as the areal extent of the environment. In addition, our own experience adds some empiricism to the probabilities.

Deposits that have the highest preservation potential are those produced at the greatest distance from the shoreline, especially when deposited within incised valleys (Belknap and Kraft, 1985; Weimer and others, 1985), with a few exceptions. This distribution of preservation is directly related to the energy distribution during transgressions. The farther from the surf zone an environment occurs, the more likely the deposits are to be incorporated into the final vertical sequence. Distal paralic and fluvial environments produce deposits that have a good probability of being buried deeply enough to be under the ravinement surface as the shoreface migrates landward. Marine deposits produced farther offshore are less likely to be removed by major storms than deposits produced closer to shore.

Two important exceptions are deep estuaries and tidal channels such as inlets. Deep estuaries may produce fine-grained deposits in a position proximal to a barrier. In this setting the deposition may be deep enough to be untouched by erosional shoreface retreat. Tidal inlets, on the other hand, can scour out deep passes in the paralic deposits under the barrier. Tidal inlet fill can then be deposited below the level of ravinement scour. The shallower a channel erodes, the lower the probability for preservation of tidal channel deposits. Only the basal channel and lag deposits of the inlet

fill have potential to be preserved. The uppermost part of the channel fill will almost never be preserved by a continuously retreating shoreline system (Kumar and Sanders, 1974) but may be preserved in an abandoned barrier shoreline.

One of the most common vertical sequences produced during transgression is that produced by the overwash barrier. This type is illustrated in the Cedar Neck and Miller Creek cross sections. Core JMD-MC-03-80 (Fig. 8) illustrates this vertical sequence. The upper sandy portion of this vertical sequence is produced by the overwash processes in a position proximal to the shoreline. In the Cedar Neck barrier this sequence was preserved because the shoreline was abandoned during falling sea level prior to migrating beyond the core site of JMD-MC-3 (Fig. 9). If transgression had continued, the sandy proximal part of the section would be lost to shoreface erosion, putting deposits of the marine realm (M-1 or M-2) immediately on top of distal lagoon deposits (P-3a and b). This general vertical sequence is usually observed due to the widespread nature of paralic lagoonal deposits and the dominant overwash nature of high wave-, low tidal-energy coasts. This same vertical sequence conceivably could be produced by a barrier with inlets where the inlets are shallow compared to the depth of shoreface erosion. For this to occur, a small tidal prism (shallow inlet) would have to be combined with a low-angle shoreface. Under these conditions, inlets may form, but they would not remain open for long and the coast would therefore not be dominated by inlets. If the vertical sequence in Figure 9 is observed over a wide area, it is generally safe to interpret it as having been produced by a shoreline dominated by overwash. Although the base of the transgressive sequence is shown to have a coastal marsh peat (P-1), it is also possible to have fresh-water swamp peat (F-2), stream-bed sands (F-1) or lagoonal beach (P-1). In addition, distal lagoon deposits can sit directly on the basal unconformity.

Where tidal inlets do dominate the coastal system, a vertical sequence containing inlet-fill sands under the ravinement surface is likely to occur. As the inlet or tidal-delta channels migrate along the barrier, they scour out all or most of the paralic deposits which underlie the barrier. A sharp erosional base is thus formed between the tidal channel sands (F-3c) and estuarine/lagoonal muds (P-3b). The Miller Creek cross section illustrates these relationships. The Cedar Neck shoreline appears to be a combination of inlet and overwash as core JMD-MC-5-80 (Fig. 10) did encounter tidal inlet sands. The upper part of the tidal channel would be eroded during shoreface retreat and would be overlain by shoreface or inner-shelf sands and muds (Fig. 11). For this reason, the salt-marsh peats seen over the tidal-delta deposits are not likely to be preserved, except when the shoreline is abandoned. Since inlets tend to open, migrate along the beach and close again, tidal channel sands may be discontinuous lenses under the ravinement surface or, if inlets migrate rapidly, they may form a continuous sheet of complexly interfingered sands below the ravinement surface.

Spit systems, which prograde laterally into the mouths of large estuaries, can produce a vertical sequence identical

JMD-MC-03-80
Elevation 3.66 m (12.0')

Lat. 38°30'47" Long. 75° 06'17"
Eastern corner of intersection
of DEL 362 and DEL 363.
Bethany Beach, Del. 7.5'
Quadrangle (SW ¼)

METERS

Soil — 0
EOLIAN

(Paleosoil?) — 1
EOLIAN

— 2

OVERWASH
MARSH
OVERWASH — 3

PROXIMAL
LAGOON — 4

— 5
DISTAL
LAGOON

— 6

Peaty SAND

Orange mottled F SAND with distorted laminae
and some organics (roots)

Gray Sandy SILT with organic specs

White F SAND, finely laminated with heavy
minerals, organic specs (roots?), occasional
silty laminae and M sand laminae

(same as above)
L Gray F SAND, structureless.
Brown Peaty VF SAND
M Gray F SAND, structureless

D Gray SILT-CLAY with VF SAND in burrows
80% burrowed, no preserved structures,
fining down, individual burrows more distinct
toward base.

(grading)

VD Gray Silty CLAY with some burrows filled
with Silt or VF Sand.

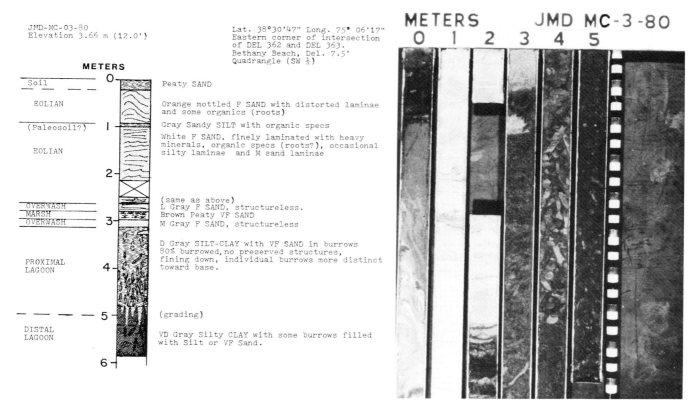

METERS   JMD MC-3-80
0 1 2 3 4 5

FIG. 8.—Core JMD-MC-03-80. Location, lithology and interpretation are indicated. This core is an example of an overwash-dominated vertical sequence and was used as part of the cross section in Figure 6. Presence of marsh peats at 2.8 m depth indicates deposition at sea level where an overwash flat was colonized by marsh flora and fauna. Vertical sequence is overall coarsening upward and shallowing upward, whereas vertical succession of environments is conclusive evidence of deposition during landward migration of shoreline toward this location. Thus, the sequence is transgressive. If transgressions had continued, the upper part of the sequence would have been eroded and overlain by marine sands.

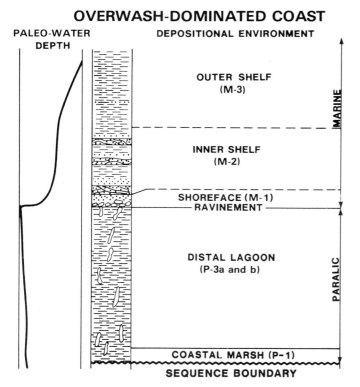

OVERWASH-DOMINATED COAST

PALEO-WATER DEPTH

DEPOSITIONAL ENVIRONMENT

OUTER SHELF (M-3)

INNER SHELF (M-2)

SHOREFACE (M-1)
RAVINEMENT

DISTAL LAGOON (P-3a and b)

COASTAL MARSH (P-1)

SEQUENCE BOUNDARY

MARINE

PARALIC

to the inlet-dominated coast. A spit filling the opening to an estuary represents the updrift end of a migrating inlet, only in this case the inlet is very wide. From a process point of view, they are very similar and therefore the resulting deposits are similar. A major difference will be the more open-marine fauna in the estuarine deposits below the tidal channel sands. The sands will also tend to be more continuous and wide-spread as spits represent major sinks for sand within the coastal system.

Where deep, wide incised valleys are being transgressed, a variance on the barrier-coast vertical sequence will develop. We call this a "mega"-estuary vertical sequence. Large estuaries commonly have barrier island coasts along the estuarine shorelines with expansive coastal marsh and freshwater swamps behind them. As the flooding of the estuary due to rising sea level continues, these estuarine shorelines migrate landward. Part of the vertical sequence produced by such a setting is seen in core JMD-DCAD-5 (Fig. 12) from an area south of the Miller Creek cross section. Ex-

FIG. 9.—Complete transgressive vertical sequence expected by an overwash-dominated coast. Overwash sands shown in JMD-MC-3 (Figs. 6, 8) are not preserved, as the ravinement processes erode the upper part of the paralic section. A deepening upward from ravinement through shoreface (M-1), inner shelf (M-2) and outer shelf (M-3) is shown in its entirety, although the total marine succession would rarely be developed.

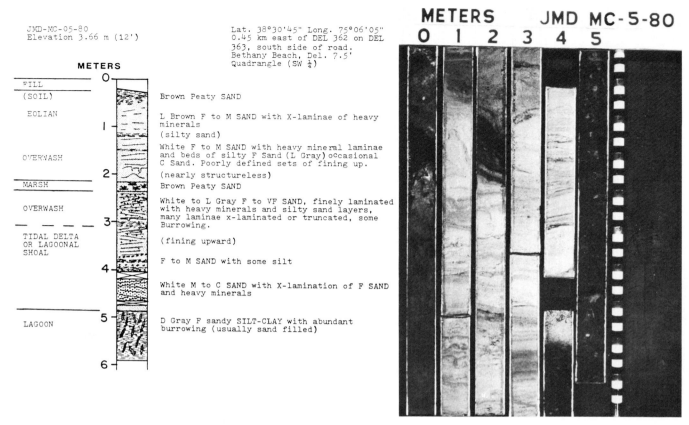

FIG. 10.—Core JMD-MC-05-08. Description, location and interpretation are shown. The marsh at 2.2 m is the same marsh within overwash sands encountered in JMD-MC-o3 (Figs. 6, 8). This vertical sequence indicates the succession of lithologies produced by an inlet-dominated shoreline and serves as an example of the bases for the generalized vertical sequence shown in Figure 11. Distal lagoon at base of core to 4.8 m is overlain by tidal deposits which filled a tidal channel. The channel-fill or tidal-delta deposits are fining upward and are overlain by overwash sands. This core was used in the construction of the Miller Creek cross section shown in Figure 6.

tensive oyster bioherms in creek banks and cores from the area show as much as 15 m of extensively bioturbated estuarine muds. Lagoonal muds commonly lie directly on top of Miocene sand or have intervening paralic beach and marsh deposits, as seen in JMD-DCAD-5 (Fig. 12). The vertical succession of coastal marsh deposits followed by paralic beach deposits is commonly reversed.

As the transgression continues, the complete vertical sequence that would be generated by a "mega"-estuary could contain several paralic successions from distal to proximal overlain by open estuarine muds and tidal shoal sands (Fig. 13). The overall sequence will coarsen upward as the mouth of the estuary approaches with its associated tidal shoals, channels, and spit.

Most estuaries have shallow shoals near the mouth, which are eroded as the open-marine deeper water environment migrates over them. As a result, an erosional surface can still be produced even though no shoreface was present. The process producing this surface is the same as if a shoreface was present, and a widespread erosional surface can be produced, so the surface can be called a ravinement surface. Evidence of erosion can be minimal, and commonly a bioturbated surface of stalled sedimentation is seen be-

tween estuarine tidal shoals and marine sands. A deepening upward from this point is clear evidence of a continuing transgression. "Mega"-estuaries tend to produce the thickest transgressive paralic sections preserved below the ravinement surface or inner-shelf shoals.

In contrast to the "mega"-estuary sequence, the thinnest transgressive vertical sequence is produced by the beach against headland or highland beach. In this situation, no fluvial or paralic deposits are preserved below the ravinement. Shoreface retreat erodes into sediments below the underlying sequence boundary, making the sequence boundary and the ravinement surface coincident (Fig. 14). Where the highland material is sandy or gravelly, shoreface sands (M-1) and thinner shelf sands may form and be preserved. If no sands are present in the highlands or transported along shore, however, marine shales (M-2 and M-3) may overlie the basal sequence boundary and ravinement surface.

Preservation of paralic deposits below the ravinement is controlled primarily by pre-existing topography and rate of sea-level change. Belknap and Kraft (1981, 1985) observed that a thicker, more widespread transgressive paralic section was preserved under the ravinement surface on the outer shelf than on the inner shelf during the Holocene transgres-

INLET/SPIT-DOMINATED COAST

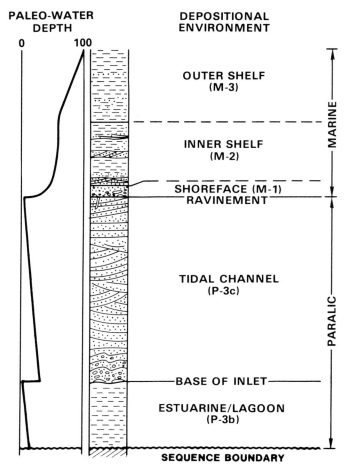

FIG. 11.—Generalized vertical sequence of inlet/spit-dominated coast where estuarine/lagoonal shales are overlain by a fining-upward tidal channel deposit of inlet-fill or tidal-channel sediments within a flood-tidal delta. Thus, when transgression continues beyond that shown in core JMD-MC-05-08 (Fig. 10), the upper part of the sequence is eroded during shoreface retreat and is overlain by a deepening-upward marine section that may or may not be fully developed, as shown here. Abrupt changes in paleo-water depth occur at erosional base of tidal channel and at ravinement surface. A rise in relative sea level is required to explain this vertical sequence. A gradual rise throughout the sequence development is sufficient with no need for abrupt rises at the surfaces which show abrupt deepening.

sion of the United States Atlantic shelf. They attributed this primarily to the faster rate of relative sea-level rise during the earlier part of the transgression. Demarest and Leatherman (1985) have hypothesized that much of the shelf seaward of the youngest Pleistocene highstand shoreline had the geomorphology of an abandoned shoreface prior to transgression, rather than an incised dendritic drainage pattern seen landward of the youngest shoreline. The relative flatness and shallow seaward-dipping configuration of this surface, over which the Holocene transgression occurred, would have caused much wider paralic realms to develop

than we see today. A wider paralic realm would allow greater rise in sea level prior to shoreface migration over the paralic realm, producing thicker paralic deposits. This, coupled with the shallower erosion of the shoreface during more rapid relative sea-level rise in the early Holocene (Belknap and Kraft, 1981), would produce greater preservation of paralic deposits than has occurred recently during the last stage of transgression (Belknap and Kraft, 1985).

Coastal erosion of pre-existing strata in areas where the ravinement and the underlying unconformity are coincident is the source of coarse sediment for beach development along the Delmarva Peninsula (see Kraft and others, this volume). When the mouths of rivers are drowned by rising sea level, sediment supply to the coastal system is controlled by the total area over which the underlying sequence boundary crops out along the shoreface. If the rate of sea-level rise remains constant as sediment supply increases, the rate of transgression decreases, reducing the amount of erosion along the shoreface and thus reducing the sediment supply through shoreface retreat. Thus, a dynamic equilibrium is established where outcrops along the shoreface feed sediment to the coastal zone at a rate that is in equilibrium with the rate at which new sediment is needed to maintain the shoreface profile during rising sea level. This process of dynamic equilibrium means that, in the absence of river sediment supply to the beach, the ravinement surface must be coincident with the basal unconformity in some places but cannot be coincident everywhere throughout the transgression. Thus, paralic deposits should be produced during transgression, particularly in incised valleys, and should be preserved at least locally and may be preserved over wide areas. Introducing sediment from river sources will serve to slow the rate of transgression and increase the potential for preservation of paralic sediment. Sediments not preserved as fluvial or paralic deposits are redeposited in the marine realm, making it difficult to envisage conditions where transgressions would not produce at least a transgressive marine sedimentary record.

IMPLICATIONS FOR MORE ANCIENT STRATA

Determination of depositional history is dependent on proper interpretation of two fundamental aspects of vertical sequence, *time* and *environment*. The vertical succession must be subdivided into time-stratigraphic units, which represent a relatively conformable succession of sediments separated by significant hiatuses or shifts in depositional system, or both. This fundamental unit or building block has been termed a depositional sequence (Mitchum and others, 1977). Second, the strata within the depositional sequence must be interpreted in terms of paleodepositional environments. The interpretation of paleoenvironment is usually accomplished through the application of a depositional model, which describes the predicted succession of lithofacies within a general environmental setting. Unfortunately, the interpretation of time and environments is not an independent endeavor. "Significant" time breaks are commonly picked, based on disruption in the succession of facies predicted using a depositional model. In addition, the

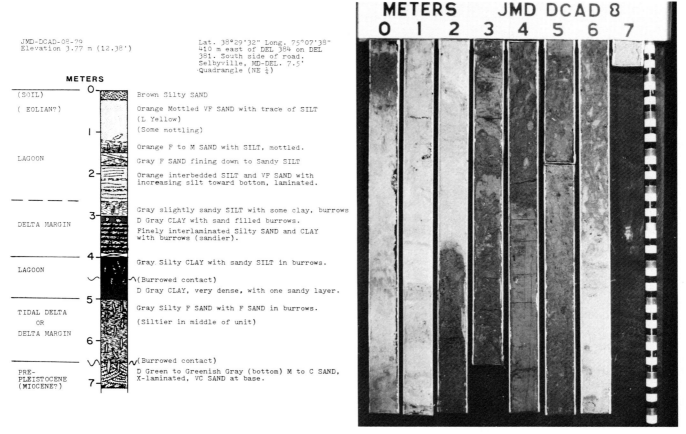

Fig. 12.—Core JMD-DCAD-08-79. Description, location and interpretation are shown. This core is from south of the Miller Creek cross section (Fig. 6) and represents deposition in a large estuary which is dominated by estuarine shoals, mud flats and oyster bioherms. Extensive oxidation of the upper 2.6 m has occurred during soil formation. The sequence boundary at the base of the Cedar Neck paralic unit was penetrated at 6.5 m where Miocene sands are encountered. This unconformity represents several million years of hiatus but shows no evidence of erosion or soil formation. In addition, it is extensively burrowed with Miocene sands being reworked upward to 1 m above the unconformity. The overall estuarine sequence is coarsening upward slightly, but much internal variation is present.

model applied to the vertical sequence is dependent on where the "significant" time breaks are thought to be.

Traditionally, initial subdivision of the rock record is based on evidence of erosion, non-deposition or dramatic change in depositional setting across a surface over a large geographic area, or on evidence of sub-aerial exposure. The normal sources of such evidence are lithology, sedimentary structures, biostratigraphy (age and environment), and diagenetic alteration. These criteria are not infallible and can lead to erroneous conclusions. Our experience after many years of subsurface and surface investigation of Quaternary deposits of the east coast of the United States is that (1) major time breaks or hiatuses within the vertical sequence typically are lithologically indistinct, and (2) the most consistently recognizable and lithologically distinct erosional surface and dramatic vertical change in environment occur at the ravinement surface, which is not a major hiatus. During these field studies, the normal criteria used to distinguish Holocene from Pleistocene deposits in cores have been compaction contrasts, oxidation, and ^{14}C dating. Radiometric ages commonly are the only certain way of distinguishing Holocene from Pleistocene sediments, even with

continuous, high quality cores through the Holocene-Pleistocene sequence boundary, where the age difference may be as much as 1 million years. Sequence boundaries within Pleistocene deposits are not identifiable based on radiometric dating, compaction or diagenetic alteration. Within the Pleistocene section, interpretations are completely dependent on a vertical sequence model for distinguishing one depositional sequence from another and for inferring the time-stratigraphic significance of stratal discontinuities.

The ravinement surface as seen in Holocene deposits (Belknap and Kraft, 1985; Kraft and others, this volume) is typically distinct physically, is characterized by evidence of substantial erosional scour, lag deposits and burrowing, and is laterally correlatable over a wide area. It also shows a sudden vertical change in depositional environment from paralic to marine. When the ravinement is coincident with the sequence boundary at the base of the transgressive deposits, there is no problem of interpretation. Where they are not coincident, however, the ravinement surface can be more easily identified and appears to be a more geologically significant surface.

Thus, our experience casts doubt on the traditional cri-

"MEGA"-ESTUARY

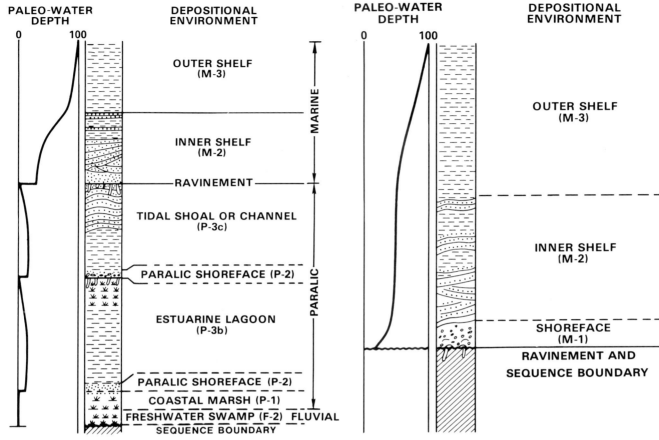

HIGHLAND BEACH

FIG. 13.—Generalized vertical sequence of "mega"-estuary depositional sequence. This sequence is observed in part in Figure 12 and has also been encountered in part in Delaware Bay. Where transgression continues to completion, the estuarine shoals are overlain by tidal shoals deposited near the mouth of the estuary; the shoals are eroded by the ravinement surface and are overlain by inner-shelf shoals. Preservation of estuarine mouth shoals will be highly variable, as will development of inner-shelf sands. Where shorelines are well developed along the perimeter of the estuary, paralic beach sands and scour surfaces as well as marsh deposits can develop at the base or within the estuarine shoals. Vertical changes in paleo-water depth show sudden deepening into the marine deposits, although relative sea-level rise was gradual and continuous throughout development of the sequence.

FIG. 14.—Generalized vertical sequence of a highland beach. This sequence is produced where the lower sequence boundary is topographically high relative to other areas or where erosion during shoreface retreat is deep. This sequence shows the ravinement surface and the sequence boundary as coincident. Evidence of the type of shoreline present has been removed by shoreface retreat, and a deepening-upward marine sequence from the ravinement-sequence boundary is indicated. Laterally, the ravinement and sequence boundary are expected to diverge, preserving an intervening paralic section.

teria for recognizing time-stratigraphic depositional sequences and has implications for the application of depositional models to the interpretation of more ancient vertical sequences, where paralic and nearshore marine deposits are vertically stacked through a succession of transgressive and regressive cycles.

To illustrate this point, we can look at a hypothetical vertical sequence (Fig. 15) consisting of two shallowing-upward sequences based on paleontologic and paleoenvironmental analyses. Two erosional surfaces occur in the section, one at 3.5 m and another at 8.0 m. The upper erosional surface is associated with a major change in depositional environment from paralic to lower shoreface and thus a

"sudden" deepening of paleo-water depth. The general succession of paleoenvironments from 0 to 8 m is from lower shoreface, fluvial channel or beach deposits overlain by paralic sediments. The erosional surface at 3.5 m is not associated with any major change in lithofacies. The cross-laminated sand just below the erosional surface at 3.5 m could be interpreted as fluvial channel or beach, whereas the cross-laminated sand above 3.5 m is of fluvial channel origin with an erosional base. Above 8.0 m, a thin lag is followed by a relatively thick section of sands deposited just above wave base (lower shoreface), followed by upper shoreface cross-laminated sands. These are, in turn, conformably overlain by paralic lagoon or delta-plain interdistributary shales and peats. The entire section is capped by alluvial plain floodplain sands.

Interpretation of this section is dependent on the signif-

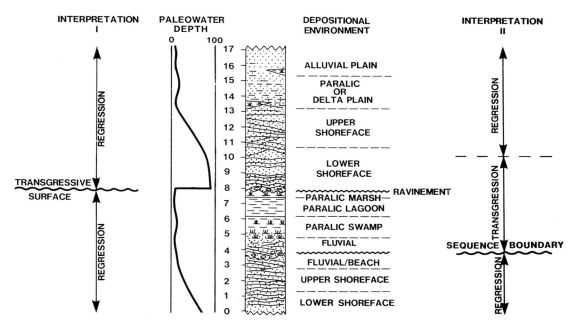

Fig. 15.—A hypothetical vertical sequence is shown with two possible interpretations based on differing vertical sequence models. The relative merits of these interpretations are discussed in the text.

icance attached to the two erosional surfaces and the depositional model applied. In interpretation I (left side, Fig. 15) a regressive or progradation model is used, and the erosional surface at 8.0 m is interpreted to represent a sequence boundary, using the dramatic change in palevironment and "sudden" deepening with little or no deposition as evidence. In this interpretation the erosional surface at 3.5 m is considered a minor shift in channel position, since no major paleoenvironmental change is associated with the erosion.

In interpretation II (right side, Fig. 15), the erosional surface at 3.5 m is interpreted as a sequence boundary between regressive deltaic deposits below and transgressive fluvial/paralic deposits above. The erosion at 3.5 m would be interpreted as having been caused by a lowering of relative sea level, resulting in down-cutting of streams. The fluvial/paralic deposits are then produced during rising base level during a later relative sea-level rise. The paralic deposits from 3.5 to 8.0 m are then eroded during shoreface retreat, producing a ravinement as the transgression continues. A conformable transition into a subsequent regressive deltaic deposit caps the section.

Neither of these interpretations can be proven correct, except through detailed mapping in outcrop or closely spaced cores, and therefore each must be carried as a working hypothesis. In interpretation I, the ravinement surface and sequence boundary are interpreted as the same surface. A regressive unit is overlain by a subsequent regressive section with no intervening transgressive deposits. This implies that (1) transgressive paralic and marine deposits will be found in lenses where the ravinement and the unconformity separate or that (2) the transgression was so rapid that there was no time for deposition of a transgressive section. The first situation is possible and is expected, based on modern

analogs. The second situation is highly unlikely, as it is difficult to have shoreface erosion during coastal retreat with no deposition of eroded material.

In interpretation II, a regressive section extends 3.5 m above the base. This is followed by a transgressive fluvial unit, a transgressive paralic unit, the ravinement surface, and transgressive marine units. Transgressive marine deposits are conformably overlain by regressive marine shoreface/deltaic deposits. This interpretation is compatible with known processes of transgression and regression and requires no catastrophic rates of sea-level change or shoreface retreat. Increased marine influence above 3.5 m records the onset of transgression in the area of the vertical section. In addition, the transgressive paralic/fluvial section can be expected to vary in thickness between zero and tens of meters, and transgressive marine sands can be expected to coarsen landward and become more discontinuous and may thicken in lenses oriented parallel to shore. The sands would be expected to continue down-dip, just above the ravinement surface.

To illustrate our point further, two examples of stratigraphic sections from the literature will be examined for the possible occurrence of transgressive vertical sequences and ravinement surfaces. As we have not remapped or examined the sections in the field, we do not claim that the interpretations we present are correct. Our discussion is intended to show how the vertical sequence model presented here may be applied to interpreting ancient strata.

Detailed logs from the Cretaceous Falher A sequence in Alberta, Canada (Fig. 16; Cant, 1984) show stacked transgressive and regressive fluvial, paralic, and marine deposits. Cant (1984) has interpreted environments of deposition and has recognized a transgressive nearshore sand near the base of the sequence overlying paralic shales and coals.

FALHER A SEQUENCE, ALBERTA CANADA

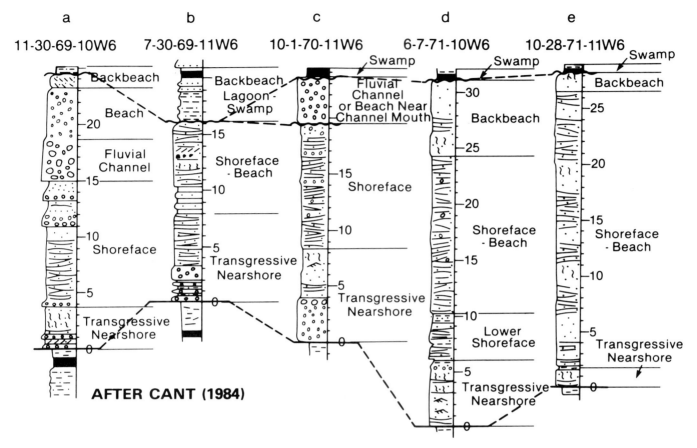

FIG. 16.—Measured sections of the Falher A sequence, Cretaceous of Alberta, Canada, after Cant (1984). Based on the transgressive vertical sequence model presented here, we would interpret the dashed horizon at 0 m to be a ravinement surface within a transgressive sequence and the dashed line near the top of the sequence as a basal unconformity over which a subsequent transgression occurred.

The contact is correlated in Figure 16 with the lower dashed line and occurs at 0 m in each of the logs. There is little doubt that the surface represents a ravinement surface, as a beach must have migrated through the area prior to deposition of the transgressive nearshore sands. The question arises as to whether the underlying shales are part of the same sequence as the sands or whether the ravinement in this area is coincident with the unconformity over which the transgression occurred. The vertical sequence of depositional environments as described in logs a through e (Fig. 16; Cant, 1984) is consistent with what would be predicted based on the transgressive vertical sequence model presented here. Using this model, we would not interpret the ravinement surface at 0 m as a sequence boundary. Instead, we would propose that the section from the base of the paralic deposits below the illustrated sections to the top of the transgressive nearshore sands represents the entire transgressive section. The section from the top of the transgressive deposits to the top of the shoreface-beach and fluvial section would represent a regressive section ending at the upper dashed line at the base of the next paralic shale.

This upper surface is a likely candidate for another sequence boundary, representing a hiatus and fluvial bypassing in this area as progradation progressed farther seaward. The upper boundary of the Falher A sequence is another ravinement surface and may be within a transgressive section which starts at the base of the paralic shales. The only change from Cant's (1984) interpretation is the inclusion of the lagoonal swamp deposits in the base of the transgressive part of the sequence rather than at the top of the regressive section.

Two implications arise from this discussion of the Falher A sequence. First, if the application of our model to the placement of lagoonal deposits is appropriate, then a rise in relative sea level during transgression is required to put transgressive lagoon over regressive fluvial channel or beach deposits, followed by marine sands as seen in section c (Fig. 16). The rise in relative sea level could thus be the driving force for the change from regression to transgression.

Second, if the sequence boundary is at the base of the lagoonal deposits, then it is inappropriate to define the Falher A stratigraphic section as bounded by the ravinement

LITHOFACIES

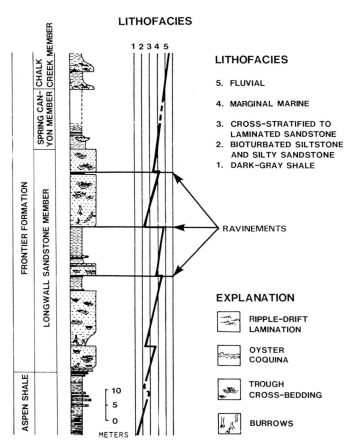

LITHOFACIES

5. FLUVIAL

4. MARGINAL MARINE

3. CROSS-STRATIFIED TO LAMINATED SANDSTONE

2. BIOTURBATED SILTSTONE AND SILTY SANDSTONE

1. DARK-GRAY SHALE

RAVINEMENTS

EXPLANATION

RIPPLE-DRIFT LAMINATION

OYSTER COQUINA

TROUGH CROSS-BEDDING

BURROWS

FIG. 17.—Composite vertical sequence of the lower portion of the Frontier Fm, Cretaceous of Utah, after Ryer (1977). In this composite section, the ravinement surfaces are located based on paralic/fluvial to marine transition across a sharp erosional surface and are possible within transgressive sequence. See text for further discussion.

surfaces at 0 m and at the top of the illustrated sections in Figure 16. A more appropriate subdivision would be at the sequence boundary over which the transgressions occurred, so that the Falher A only includes genetically related strata. Application of the transgressive vertical sequence model in this way explains the data presented for the Falher A section but results in a somewhat different view of the depositional history and may result in different regional correlations and reconstructions.

Another example of application of our model can be illustrated using the Cretaceous Frontier Fm of Utah. The Frontier Fm consists of stacked progradational coastal units with facies ranging from offshore dark gray shales to fluvial sandstones separated by disconformities which represent minor or major shifts in shoreline position (Fig. 17; Ryer, 1977). Many of the disconformities are described as "transgressive surfaces" and are considered the only record of rapid transgression between progradational units. Of the 26 disconformities identified, 14 occur between paralic or fluvial deposits (lithofacies 4 or 5; Fig 17; Ryer, 1977) and marine sands or shales (lithofacies 1, 2 or 3; Fig 17; Ryer, 1977). Thus, 14 of the surfaces produced by landward shifts in shoreline position are ravinement surfaces and may not

represent sequence boundaries. The same discussion in reference to the Falher A section (Fig. 16) applies to the Frontier Fm (Fig. 17). Application of the transgressive vertical sequence model to the Frontier Fm of Utah may indicate that more of the section has been deposited during a transgression than previously interpreted.

CONCLUSIONS

Thus far, this discussion has concentrated on erosional transgressive vertical sequences exemplified by the Holocene and Pleistocene shorelines on the east coast of the United States. The general vertical sequence and important variations commonly observed have been presented. Of particular importance is the process of shoreface retreat that produces the ravinement surface which can easily be mistaken for a major hiatus. This can result in misinterpretation of ancient depositional history. In addition, care must be taken not to infer that abrupt vertical changes in depositional environment across erosional surfaces necessarily represent abrupt horizontal changes in environments of deposition in time. In particular, the ravinement surface between paralic and marine lithosomes, although physically abrupt in a vertical profile, does not imply an instantaneous change in shoreline position. Only through testing the application of several depositional models, including an erosional transgression model, can a ravinement surface be distinguished from a sequence boundary when the surfaces are not coincident.

Depositional transgressions, formed where rivers supply sediment to the coast during transgressions, experience alternating cycles of progradation and retrogradation which combine to form a transgression. The Holocene Mississippi River delta exemplifies such a depositional transgression. Close examination of the retrogradational phase of many of the delta lobes by Frazier (1967, 1974) and Penland and Boyd (1982) shows that the retrogradational section produced during abandonment of a lobe is nearly identical to that produced during erosional transgression on the east coast of the United States. Marine sands tend to be thick and continuous as shoreface retreat reworks stream-mouth bar sands. Interdistributary bays tend to fill with thick paralic organic-rich mud or peat during retrogradation. Transition from retrogradation to progradation and vice versa is conformable in both paralic and marine environments. Only the ravinement surface produced during retrogradational shoreface retreat forms a sharp, erosional contact over a wide area. Again, this surface should not be mistaken for a hiatus between depositional sequences or between progradational cycles, although locally it may be coincident with the depositional sequence boundary.

The retrogradational phase of a depositional transgression and the entire erosional transgression produce vertical sequences by the same processes and therefore result in similar successions. Only the temporal and spatial aspects of the deposits distinguish one as retrogradational and the other as transgressive. As a result, it is reasonable to consider the vertical sequence presented here as that produced by retrogradation in general, independent of whether or not it occurs during retrogradational phases of erosional or depositional transgression or general regression. The occurrence of variations in vertical sequence will be different under each type of retrogradation and the temporal significance of the vertical sequence will vary. Thus, only after general mapping and detailed correlations can a retrogradational vertical sequence as described here be interpreted as representing all of an erosional transgression, a phase of depositional transgression or a small interruption during a general regression.

ACKNOWLEDGMENTS

This paper has benefited from discussions with many colleagues, including R. B. Biggs, D. F. Belknap, H. W. Posamentier, P. R. Vail, and G. R. Baum. The field work was conducted between 1978 and 1981, with equipment and support from the Department of Geology, University of Delaware. Field assistance was provided by numerous graduate students at the University of Delaware, particularly W. H. Hoyt. The manuscript was reviewed by D. F. Belknap, K. T. Biddle and other anonymous reviewers. Their many helpful suggestions are greatly appreciated. We also thank Exxon Production Research Company for support in preparing this paper.

REFERENCES

BELKNAP, D. F., 1979, Application of amino acid geochronology to stratigraphy of Late Cenozoic marine units of the Atlantic coastal plain: Unpublished Ph.D. Dissertation, Department of Geology, University of Delaware, Newark, 580 p.

———, AND KRAFT, J. C., 1981, Preservation potential of transgressive coastal lithosomes on the U.S. Atlantic Shelf: Marine Geology v. 42, p. 429–442.

———, AND ———, 1985, Influence of antecedent geology on stratigraphic preservation potential and evolution of Delaware's barrier system: Marine Geology, v. 63, p. 235–262.

CANT, D. J., 1984, Development of shoreline-shelf sand bodies in a Cretaceous epeiric sea deposit: Journal of Sedimentary Petrology, v. 54, no. 2, p. 541–556.

CURRAY, J. R., 1964, Transgressions and regressions, in Miller, R. L., ed., Papers in Marine Geology, Shepard Commemorative Volume: Macmillan Press, New York, p. 175–203.

DEMAREST, J. M., 1981, Genesis and preservation of Quaternary paralic deposits on Delmarva Peninsula: unpublished Ph.D. Dissertation, Department of Geology, University of Delaware, Newark, 240 p.

———, AND BELKNAP, D. F., 1980, Quaternary Atlantic shoreline on Delmarva Peninsula—chronology and tectonic implications: Northeastern Section, Geological Society of America, Abstracts with Programs, v. 12, no. 2, p. 30.

———, BIGGS, R. B., AND KRAFT, J. C., 1981, Time-stratigraphic aspects of a formation: interpretation of surficial Pleistocene deposits by analogy with Holocene paralic deposits, southeastern Delaware: Geology, v. 9, p. 360–365.

———, AND LEATHERMAN, S. P., 1985, Mainland influence on coastal transgression: Delmarva Peninsula: Marine Geology, v. 63, p. 19–33.

FRAZIER, D. E., 1967, Recent deltaic deposits of the Mississippi River: their development and chronology: Gulf Coast Association of Geological Societies Transactions, v. 17, p. 287–315.

———, 1974, Depositional episodes: their relationship to the Quaternary stratigraphic framework in the northwestern portion of the Gulf basin: Texas Bureau of Economic Geology, Geological Circular 74-1, 28 p.

JORDAN, R. R., 1962, Stratigraphy of the Sedimentary Rocks of Delaware: Delaware Geological Survey Bulletin 9, 51 p.

KRAFT, J. C., 1971, Sedimentary facies patterns and geologic history of a Holocene transgression. Geological Society of America Bulletin, v. 82, p. 2131–2158.

———, AND BELKNAP, D. F., 1975, Transgressive and regressive sedimentary lithosomes at the edge of a late Holocene marine transgression: IXme Congress International de Sedimentologie, Nice, 1975, p. 87–95.

———, BIGGS, R. B., AND HALSEY, S. D., 1973, Morphology and vertical sedimentary sequence models in Holocene transgressive barrier systems, in Coates, D. R., ed., Coastal Geomorphology: State University of New York Publications in Geomorphology, p. 321–354.

KUMAR, N., AND SANDERS, J. E., 1974, Inlet sequence: a vertical sequence of sedimentary structures and textures created by the lateral migration of tidal inlets: Sedimentology, v. 21, p. 491–532.

MITCHUM, R. M., JR., VAIL, P. R., AND THOMPSON, S., III, 1977, Seismic stratigraphy and global changes of sea level, part 2: the depositional sequence as a basic unit for stratigraphic analysis, in Payton, C. E., ed., Seismic Stratigraphy—Applications to Hydrocarbon Exploration: American Association of Petroleum Geologists Memoir 26, p. 53–62.

PENLAND, S., AND BOYD, R., 1982, Transgressive depositional environments of the Mississippi River delta: a guide to the barrier islands, beaches and shoals in Louisiana: Guidebook No. 7, Geological Society of America Annual Meeting, New Orleans, 223 p.

RAMPINO, M. R., AND SANDERS, J. E., 1981, Evolution of the barrier islands off southern Long Island, N.Y.: Sedimentology, v. 28, p. 37–47.

RYER, T. A., 1977, Patterns of Cretaceous shallow-marine sedimentation, Coalville and Rockport areas, Utah: Geological Society of America Bulletin, v. 88, p. 177–188.

SANDERS, J. E., AND KUMAR, N., 1975, Evidence of shoreface retreat and in-place "drowning" during Holocene submergence of barriers, shelf off Fire Island, New York: Geological Society of America Bulletin, v. 86, p. 65–76.

SHACKLETON, N. J., AND OPDYKE, N. D., 1973, Oxygen isotope and paleomagnetic stratigraphy of equatorial core V28-238: Quaternary Research v. 3, p. 39–55.

STAMP, L. D., 1922, An outline of the Tertiary geology of Burma: Geology Magazine v. 59, p. 481–501.

STUBBLEFIELD, W. L., McGRAIL, D. W., AND KERSEY, D. G., 1984, Recognition of transgressive and post-transgressive sand ridges on the New Jersey continental shelf, in Tillman, R. W., and Siemers, C. T., eds., Siliciclastic Shelf Sediments: Society of Economic Paleontologists and Mineralogists Special Publication 34, p. 1–23.

SWIFT, D. J. P., 1968, Coastal erosion and transgressive stratigraphy: Journal of Geology, v. 76, p. 444–456.

———, McKINNEY, T. F., AND STAHL, L., 1984, Recognition of transgressive and post-transgressive sand ridges on the New Jersey continental shelf—discussion, in Tillman, R. W., and Siemers, C. T., eds., Siliciclastic Shelf Sediments: Society of Economic Paleontologists and Mineralogists Special Publication 34, p. 25–36.

WEIMER, R. J., PORTER, K. W., AND LAND, C. B., 1985, Depositional modeling of detrital rocks: Society of Economic Paleontologists and Mineralogists Core Workshop No. 8, 252 p.

TRANSGRESSIVE STRATIGRAPHY AT SEQUENCE-BOUNDING UNCONFORMITIES: SOME PRINCIPLES DERIVED FROM HOLOCENE AND CRETACEOUS EXAMPLES

DAG NUMMEDAL

Department of Geology and Geophysics, Louisiana State University, Baton Rouge, Louisiana 70803

AND

DONALD J. P. SWIFT

Department of Oceanography, Old Dominion University, Norfolk, Virginia 23508

ABSTRACT: Sequence stratigraphic concepts are powerful tools in the analysis of the evolutionary history of sedimentary basins. The criteria used in the identification of depositional sequences differ for outcrop and subsurface data sets because of scale differences in stratal continuity and spatial resolution. This paper documents sedimentary and stratigraphic characteristics of sequence boundaries and the overlying transgressive succession of depositional systems. By emphasizing the sedimentology and the different patterns of systems stacking above the sequence boundaries, this paper aids in identifying these key stratigraphic boundaries in outcrop.

The key stratigraphic surfaces encountered in shallow marine sedimentary sequences are: (1) subaerial unconformities, cut by episodes of sea-level fall, and representing a significant hiatal break; and (2) diastems, surfaces representing relatively short interruptions in sedimentation. Most diastems in shallow marine and coastal settings are associated with transgressions and may be loosely grouped as "transgressive surfaces." Diastems include the ravinement diastem, which is formed by transgressive shoreface retreat, channel-base diastems, and various marine erosion diastems.

Subaerial unconformities of regional or interregional extent and their correlative marine unconformities and conformities serve as boundaries of depositional sequences. The depositional architecture between the sequence boundary and the overlying transgressive surface, e.g., the ravinement diastem, is controlled by the relief of the coastal plain and the rate of transgression.

Transgression of a coastal plain previously dissected by an episode of significant sea-level fall will produce shore-normal estuaries and shore-parallel lagoons. The resultant stratigraphic succession will be characterized by an inner-shelf sand sheet above back-barrier deposits and "ribs" of fluvial and estuarine sediments filling former subaerial valleys. This architecture characterizes the Holocene stratigraphy of the United States Atlantic and Gulf shelves, and the basal Cretaceous strata (Oak Canyon Mbr of the Dakota Sandstone) of the San Juan basin in New Mexico.

In rapidly subsiding basins, such as the Holocene Mississippi Delta region of the Gulf Coast basin and the western foredeep area of the Cretaceous Interior Seaway, relative sea-level fall may be insignificant or nonexistent. Consequently, the sequence boundary may be a rather subtle unconformity, or even a conformity. Nevertheless, the transgressions will cause erosional shoreface retreat, the cutting of ravinement diastems and formation of offshore erosion surfaces. These surfaces generally are of limited spatial extent and are discontinuous in the stratigraphic record, yet, they form distinct lithostratigraphic breaks and may easily be mistaken for sequence boundaries. Time lines cross these transgressive surfaces, but they do not cross sequence boundaries.

The Coniacian strata of the San Juan basin provide an example of a sequence boundary and associated transgressive depositional systems formed in response to a relatively small sea-level fall and subsequent rise in a rapidly subsiding basin. A mid-Coniacian sea-level fall, detectable across the entire Western Interior Seaway, caused the western coastal plain rivers to return to grade by depositing a coarse fluvial sandstone (Torrivio Mbr of the Gallup Sandstone), enhanced the bypassing of fines, and intensified storm-induced coarse-grained sediment transport onto the distal shelf (Cooper Arroyo and basal Tocito Sandstones). The subsequent transgression resulted in shoreface retreat by destruction of distributary mouth bars of the Torrivio Mbr, formation of offshore linear shelf sand ridges above the ravinement diastem (Tocito Sandstone ridges), the deposition of a series of transgressive sand bodies in back-barrier settings (e.g., flood-tidal deltas of the Borrego Pass Sandstone), and rapid accretion of low-energy fluvial facies (Dilco Coal Mbr of the Crevasse Canyon Fm). Individual ravinement surfaces underlie many Tocito Sandstone ridges and separate them from regressive facies, but these surfaces may be of limited areal extent and are probably not connected to a single regional unconformity. The ravinement surfaces and the transgressive Tocito sandstones climb progressively higher in the section relative to the mid-Coniacian sequence boundary as one moves updip (paleo-landward).

INTRODUCTION

Sequence stratigraphy has recently experienced rapid development because of the common availability of seismic reflection data in numerous sedimentary basins. Only very recently, however, have the concepts developed in seismic stratigraphy been applied to depositional sequences in outcrop. The extension of sequence stratigraphic analysis to outcrop data promises to improve greatly our understanding of the processes associated with sequence boundaries and related stratigraphic surfaces. Also, using outcrop data, it is possible to document precisely the architecture of the depositional systems within the genetically related strata referred to as the depositional sequence. One of the key challenges in modern sedimentology is to develop such predictive models for depositional sequence architecture, and to help define the larger scale patterns of order which seem to exist in the Phanerozoic stratigraphic record.

As a first step in such modeling, this paper documents

the sedimentary and stratigraphic characteristics of shallow marine and coastal sequence boundaries and the architecture of the overlying transgressive sequence of depositional systems. By emphasizing the sedimentology and the different patterns of systems stacking above the sequence boundaries, the paper is specifically designed to aid in identification of these key stratigraphic surfaces in outcrop. The paper also attempts to explain the observed depositional systems architecture of the transgressive part of the depositional sequence in terms of the physical sedimentary processes which operate in coastal and shallow marine environments.

The definition of a depositional sequence is based on the analysis of deep reflection seismic records where the spatial resolution is on the order of tens of meters. This study of depositional sequences—in outcrop—has revealed a very complex picture. Sequences are not simply "conformable successions of strata"; they have a hierarchial internal structure. Strata are indeed the fundamental building blocks, but sequences of strata form lithosomes (Wheeler and Mallory, 1953) distinguished by different lithologies and stratigraphic patterns (Fig. 1). Assemblages of laterally adjacent process-related lithosomes, in turn, make up depositional systems (Fisher and McGovern, 1967). During the interactions of subsidence, sediment input, and sea-level change, depositional systems are progressively stacked forming depositional sequences. These stacks are bounded above and below by unconformities and correlative conformities: the sequence boundaries.

BASIN DYNAMICS AND DEPOSITIONAL SYSTEMS ARCHITECTURE

Depositional sequence boundaries are defined as "unconformities or their correlative conformities bounding (essentially) conformable successions of strata" (Vail and others, 1977, p. 53). Where unconformable, boundaries of depositional sequences are generally considered to be cut by subaerial erosion during periods of relative sea-level fall. Depending on the position of the lowstand shoreline relative to the edge of the continental shelf, Vail and others (1984) differentiate between type 1 and type 2 boundaries. Type 1 boundaries form when sea level falls below the shelf edge and fluvial systems become incised across the former

shelf (Fig. 2). Type 2 boundaries are associated with shoreline advance to some intermediate position on the shelf. Because the shelf gradient generally is less than the equilibrium slope of the coastal plain, shoreline displacement to a mid-shelf position is commonly not associated with significant fluvial entrenchment of shelf strata (Pitman, 1982).

Type 1 and 2 sequence boundaries have been described from the passive margins of the Atlantic and Gulf coasts. The Holocene-Pleistocene boundary along these margins represents a type 1 sequence boundary. Variants of both types of boundaries also occur in the Cretaceous foreland basin of the United States Western Interior. A third type of sequence boundary, formed by punctuated sea-level rise without intervening periods of fall, may also occur in the rapidly subsiding Western Interior foreland basin.

This diversity of sequence boundaries is a consequence of the tectonic setting. During the Cretaceous, thrust-plate loading with attendant flexural subsidence, plus rapid first-order sea-level rise of probable global scale, resulted in high rates of relative sea-level rise along the overthrust western margin of the basin. During the Santonian, Campanian and early Maastrichtian, subsidence accelerated in the central and southern portions of the basin, attaining rates unlikely

STRATUM

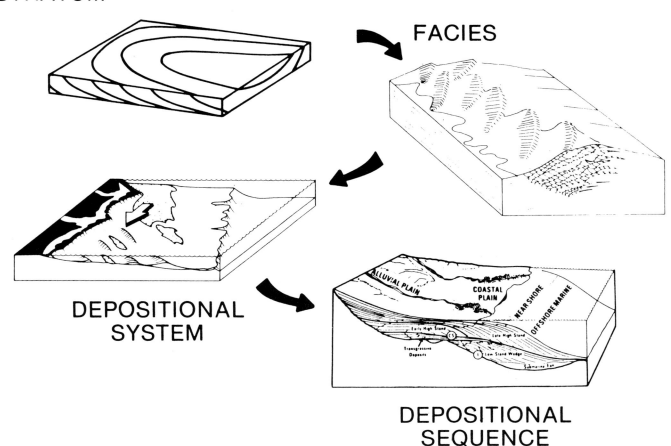

FIG. 1.—Hierarchy of stratigraphic units from individual strata to depositional sequence.

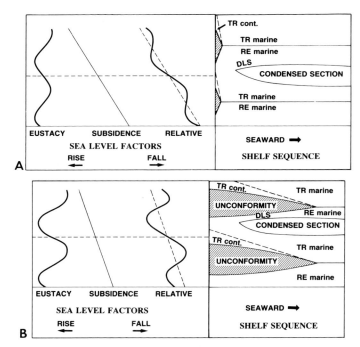

FIG. 2.—Formation of depositional sequence boundaries as a function of subsidence rate and amplitude of absolute (eustatic) sea-level fluctuations. Time increases vertically in both diagrams. The idealized shelf stratigraphic sequences on the right are adapted from Vail and others (1984) and refer to settings where the subsidence rate increases offshore. (A) Rapid subsidence and low-amplitude eustatic signal. The relative sea-level curve will consist of only slight falls (or stillstands) separated by periods of rapid rise. The sequence bounding unconformities (cross-hatched) will extend only a short distance offshore. The marine section will consist of a lower regressive and upper transgressive part, probably separated by a distinct lag associated with shallow-water reworking of shelf sediments at the onset of the transgression. The condensed section will attain its maximum landward extent at the time of maximum flooding. The regressive strata will downlap onto the condensed section (DLS: downlap surface). (B) Slow subsidence and high-amplitude eustatic signal. The relative sea-level curve will consist of periods of significant fall and rise. Major subaerial unconformities are cut during fall; their farthest seaward extent is attained at the time of maximum rate of sea-level fall. The transgressive depositional systems above the sequence boundary will be divided into continental and marine by a major transgressive surface (TR: the ravinement diastem).

to be exceeded by eustatic sea-level variation during this apparently ice-free period (Kominz and Bond, pers. commun.; Cross and Pilger, 1978). Under these circumstances, eustatic fluctuations may only have resulted in variation in the rate of relative sea-level rise without associated periods of sea-level falls (Fig. 2).

Because the basin was hinged along the cratonic eastern side and subsided most rapidly along the western overthrust margin, eustatic sea-level change would have different signatures across the basin. Eustatic falls would have translated into major relative falls of sea level along the cratonic eastern margin where type 1 or 2 unconformities might have developed as boundaries separating highstand deposits. Unconformities resulting from such sea-level falls on the eastern margin might pass into conformities within the clastic wedges of the rapidly subsiding western margin. Alternatively, subtle sea-level falls along the western margin may

have produced regrading coastal plains and coarse shelf strata. Thus, a major eustatic sea-level lowering might result in a relative sea-level fall on the eastern margin sufficient to cause incision of the drainage system, while farther west the relative sea-level fall would be smaller and less likely to cause incision.

In the extreme case, the eustatic fall would fail to lower sea level along the western margin; it would merely suffice to slow the relative rise, possibly inducing shoreline progradation. When the rapid rise resumed, the subaerial surface that had built seaward would still be aggrading as the surf cut back across it. During this phase, it would be reshaped by shoreface erosion as a surface of ravinement. This surface is one of many "transgressive surfaces" discussed in this paper. Because of their time-transgressive nature and the short interval of time generally associated with their formation, the transgressive surfaces are not sequence boundaries. The conformable equivalent of the erosional sequence boundary would lie at some depth beneath this transgressive surface. The Cretaceous transgressions discussed all appear to have followed episodes of relative sea-level fall. Our data are currently inadequate to evaluate the extreme case of continuous relative sea-level rise.

THE SUBAERIAL EROSION SURFACE

Subaerial Erosion of Holocene Shelves

Present shelves along the United States continental margin were subaerially exposed at the latest Wisconsinan sea-level lowstand (Curray, 1965; Milliman and Emery, 1968). Integrated drainage networks extended across this shelf (Swift and others, 1980) and probably graded to canyon heads or shelf-edge deltas (Swift, 1976; Suter and Berryhill, 1985). The channels of major rivers were deeply incised, e.g., the Mississippi River (Fisk, 1944), the Susquehanna and its tributary the Potomac River (Knebel and others, 1981), and the Delaware River (Sheridan and others, 1974).

During this period of shelf emergence, the channel network dissected an exposed, weathered surface subjected to a long interval of pedogenic processes. The soils, however, were generally eroded off the interfluves by shoreface retreat during the subsequent Holocene transgression (e.g., Demarest and Leatherman, 1985). Much valley-floor soil was eroded by scour of migrating fluvial and estuarine channels. Thus, while rooted soil horizons in shelf sediments are diagnostic indicators of sea-level lowstands (Weimer, 1984), their preservation potential is low. Rooted paleosols may be present at sequence boundaries, but they will be limited in their areal extent to the preserved flanks of the subaerially eroded valleys.

The geometry of the valley network is significant because it directly controls the isopach pattern of the depositional systems preserved between the valley floor (the sequence boundary) and the first overlying transgressive surface (commonly the ravinement surface). Suter and others (this volume) have mapped a complexly anastomosing pattern of valley fills extending for 200 km across the late Pleistocene-Holocene shelf off southwestern Louisiana. All valleys are essentially dip-oriented (to the southwest toward

the late Pleistocene depocenter). Individual fluvial and estuarine depositional systems preserved within the transgressed valleys on the western Louisiana shelf range in
thickness from 10 to 50 m and can extend for tens of kilometers in width.

An isopach map of Holocene sediments on the shelf off
Delaware illustrates a somewhat different valley-fill pattern
(Belknap and Kraft, 1985, fig. 9; see also Kraft and others,
this volume). The ancestral Delaware River valley forms
the central northwest-southeast-trending axis of the fill
flanked by the dendritic pattern of the tributary fills. The
maximum Holocene valley-fill thickness is in excess of
40 m. As noted by Belknap and Kraft (1985), the Holocene
fill is entirely removed by marine erosion in the many areas
on the inner shelf which represent interfluves on the transgressed coastal plain.

Subaerial Erosion in the Cretaceous Western Interior

Significant erosional relief is evident in Aptian, Albian
and early Cenomanian unconformities in the Denver, Powder River and San Juan basins. The local relief at the base
of the late Albian J Sandstone of the Dakota Group in the
Denver basin is about 50 m (Weimer, 1984, modified from
data in Haun, 1963, and Matuszczak, 1976). This relief
was probably cut by a major sea-level fall about 97 ma.
The isopachs of the J Sandstone in the Denver basin (Weimer, 1984, fig. 17) and the Muddy Fm of the Powder River
basin (Stone, 1972, fig. 10) indicate that both of these hy-
drocarbon-rich sandstones filled lowstand, incised valley
systems.

The J Sandstone crops out in the Dakota Hogback along
the western flank of the Denver basin. Measured sections
along this outcrop belt from Denver north to the Wyoming
State line further illustrate the late Albian valley-floor unconformity. Local relief along this outcrop belt is in excess
of 40 m (MacKenzie, 1971). Rooted and weathered zones,
indicative of paleosols, are commonly associated with the
unconformity surface.

The basal unit of the Dakota Sandstone in the San Juan
basin, the Cenomanian-age Oak Canyon Mbr, is also characterized by large-scale erosional relief at the base. The
regional relief along the southern and eastern margins of
the basin, from El Morro on the flank of the Zuni uplift to
the Chama basin near the Colorado State line, is about
35 m. A wide valley dissected underlying Jurassic strata
between Cub and Regina (Fig. 3; Aubrey, 1986).

MARINE EROSION SURFACES

The Ravinement Surface

The shoreface has been described as a surface of equilibrium formed in response to the wave and current regime
(Bruun, 1962; Schwartz, 1967; Swift, 1976; Niedoroda and
others, 1985; Everts, this volume). As sea level rises, the
shoreface profile translates upward and landward through a
process of erosional shoreface retreat. The ravinement surface cut by this process will physically rise toward the basin
margin. It will also become younger in the same direction.

In an early analysis of the problem of preservation of the

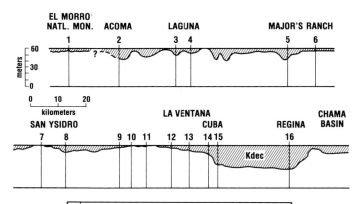

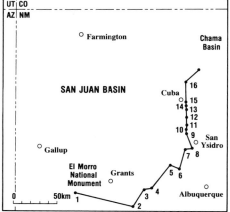

Fig. 3.—Simplified cross section of the lowermost member of the Dakota Sandstone in the San Juan basin: the Encinal Canyon Mbr (Kdec).
Modified from Aubrey (1986).

costal lithosomes, Fischer (1961) recognized that the thickness of the preserved section would be a function of the
depth of shoreface erosion relative to the thickness of the
coastal plain deposits above the sequence boundary. Following Fischer's concepts, Belknap and Kraft (1981) concluded that the preserved coastal stratigraphic section is a
function of the rate of sea-level rise, the antecedent topography and the depth of the shoreface. This latter parameter,
in turn, is determined by the power expended by waves,
and storm and tidal currents.

It is particularly important to recognize that the ravinement surface is not simply a surface of erosion; it is a surface of sediment transfer: sediment eroded from the shoreface by storm currents is commonly redeposited above the
ravinement surface farther seaward. In a regime of a continuously rising sea level, the sediment redeposited above
the ravinement surface may be preserved, because it lies
beneath the steadily climbing seaward limb of the equilibrium profile.

Because of its genesis as a surface of sediment transfer,
time lines commonly cross the ravinement surface. In contrast, time lines do not cross a sequence boundary. The
diachronous nature of the ravinement surface is illustrated
in Figure 4A. Storms occurring while the barrier is in position 1 (sea level 1) will concurrently deposit back-barrier
washover fans at B1 and inner-shelf storm sands at S1. At

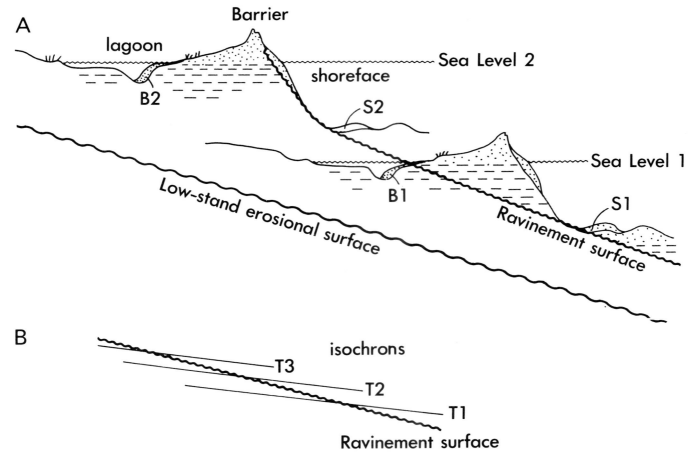

FIG. 4.—Origin of the diachronous nature of the ravinement surface. (A) Storms occurring while the shoreline is at sea level position 1 may concurrently deposit back-barrier strata at B1 and inner-shelf strata at S1. When sea level has risen to position 2 and the shoreline has moved a corresponding distance landward, the ravinement process has truncated the original barrier superstructure but preserved the back-barrier facies at B1. New inner-shelf strata, at S2, are younger than their immediately subjacent back-barrier facies at B1, but these latter units are coeval with S1, located above the ravinement surface farther seaward. (B) In a generalized sense the chronostratigraphic surfaces along the leading edge of a transgression will dip toward the basin, but at a lower angle than the ravinement surface. Consequently, time planes do cut this erosional surface.

a later time, when sea level has risen to position 2, the barrier will have moved a corresponding distance landward. The ravinement process will now have truncated the original barrier superstructure but preserved the washovers at B1. New inner-shelf sands, immediately above B1, at S2, are younger; B1 is time-equivalent to S1, yet the two deposits are now located on opposite sides of the ravinement surface. The same argument holds for other back-barrier environments. In a generalized sense, isochronous surfaces along the leading edge of a transgression will dip toward the basin at a lesser angle than the ravinement surface (Fig. 4B). Consequently, time planes cross this erosional surface.

Shoreface depth along coasts of moderate- to high-wave energies are relatively constant over great distances. Where the shoreline consists of estuary mouths or tidal inlets, the shoreface includes the seaward slope of the ebb-tidal delta complex. Thus, the shoreface is continuous, as is the resulting ravinement surface. During transgression, the ravinement surface becomes a regionally level surface of con-

siderable extent. Because of distinct lithologic contrast between the back-barrier and inner-shelf depositional systems, the ravinement surface becomes a sharp lithologic boundary in the stratigraphic record (see Demarest and Kraft, this volume).

Classification of Erosional Surfaces

Multiple erosional surfaces of varying extent are produced during a coastal transgression. Any of these surfaces may truncate any other, and any of them may remove the lowstand subaerial surface and locally replace it as the sequence boundary. To avoid confusion in discussions of erosion surfaces contained within coastal and marginal marine stratigraphic sections, we propose formal definitions for such surfaces. Two classification systems can be devised, one based on the temporal extent of the associated hiatus, and another based on the physical genesis of the surface. Both systems are presented and used throughout the paper.

In the time classification scheme there are two types of surfaces (unconformities and diastems) and many subtypes.

Unconformity.—

An unconformity is a substantial break or gap in the geologic record where a rock unit is overlain by another that is not next in stratigraphic succession (Bates and Jackson, 1980). Unconformities may be of subaerial or submarine origin.

An *inter-regional unconformity* is an unconformity resulting from erosion and non-deposition during global (eustatic) fall of sea level, hence interregional in its occurrence (Vail and others, 1977).

Diastem.—

A diastem is a relatively short interruption in sedimentation involving only a brief interval of time (Bates and Jackson, 1980). We recognize the following distinct diastems in this paper.

(a) *Channel diastem:* a local surface of erosion resulting from the lateral migration of a channel floor (Weimer, 1984). Because of lateral migration, the diastem is diachronous, on a time scale commensurate with that of the channel migration.

(b) *Marine deflation diastem:* a local surface of erosion resulting from marine scour. Marine deflation diastems commonly form in swales between shelf sand ridges.

(c) *Offshore marine erosion diastem:* a surface resulting from regional marine erosion. Such erosion surfaces may form on shelves subject to accelerating storm or tidal currents.

(d-1) *Marine ravinement diastem:* a regional marine erosion surface produced by erosional retreat of the shoreface (Stamp, 1921; Swift, 1968). The ravinement diastem generally is diachronous. Where a transgressive surface truncates previously subaerial interfluves or other coastal headlands, the ravinement diastem replaces the sequence boundary. Where back-barrier facies or bay fills are truncated, the ravinement diastem lies above the sequence bondary and generally represents only a short chronostratigraphic interval (see Demarest and Kraft, this volume).

(d-2) *Bay ravinement diastem:* a local ravinement diastem cut by the landward retreat of a bay shoreline. This is preserved only in basins subsiding rapidly enough to prevent its removal by the retreating shoreface. It commonly overlies most channel diastems and must underlie the marine ravinement diastem.

The preceding definitions are based primarily on the time scale of the hiatus associated with the erosional surface and only secondarily on the mechanism of formation. It is helpful also to consider a classification based on formative mechanisms.

Subaerial erosion surface.—

A subaerial erosion surface is a surface cut by subaerial weathering and erosion during periods of lowered sea level.

Transgressive surface.—

A transgressive surface is a surface cut by wave and current action in the marine environment. Subcategories are (a) *ravinement surface,* and (b) *offshore marine erosion surface.*

In regressions where the shoreline does not retreat as far as the shelf edge (type 2 unconformity; Vail and others, 1984), the subsequent transgression will produce a marine erosion surface of dual origin. As the shoreface is driven back over the surface of subaerial exposure, a ravinement surface results, as discussed above; however, the adjacent offshore sea floor may also erode. This erosion occurs because the rate of sediment input drops as sea level begins to rise and deltaic coasts turn into sediment-trapping estuaries or lagoonal coasts. The hydrodynamic regime does not undergo a parallel change. Because of low sea level and generally shallow shelf waters, wave- and current-induced winnowing is effectively removing fine sediments which are no longer replaced from terrigenous sources. Coarse "lags" may be the result, and the offshore marine erosion surfaces are expected to be paired with nearshore ravinement surfaces.

TRANSGRESSIVE FACIES ARCHITECTURE

Holocene of the Atlantic and Gulf Margin

Estuary and back-barrier stratigraphy.—

Coastal encroachment onto a sequence boundary during an interval of relative sea-level rise does produce onlap. If the rate of relative sea-level rise exceeds the coastal sedimentation rate, the onlap will be associated with a transgression, i.e., a landward movement of the shoreline (Curray, 1964); however, regressive facies successions, deposited when coastal sedimentation exceeds relative sea-level rise, are also associated with basal onlap.

In a situation of transgressive coastal onlap, the coastal and marginal marine strata will ultimately be truncated by the retreating shoreface, producing a ravinement surface. The depositional systems architecture between the sequence boundary and the ravinement surface is controlled by the relief on the transgressed coastal plain (Demarest and Kraft, this volume). Transgression of a coastal plain previously dissected by an episode of falling sea level will produce estuaries (shore normal) and flanking back-barrier lagoons and marshes. The consequent stratigraphy will be characterized by an inner-shelf sand sheet above back-barrier deposits and "ribs" of fluvial and estuarine sediments filling former subaerial valleys. This is the character of the type 1 sequence boundary. Locally, the sequence boundary and the transgressive ravinement surface will be separated by tens of meters of sediments deposited during sea-level lowstand; in other areas the two surfaces may be merged.

The thickest lowstand depositional systems are formed and preserved in the deepest entrenched valleys. They consist of a vertical sequence of fluvial, bay-head delta, open-estuary, and estuary-mouth facies, generally arranged with the major axis of the system oriented in the direction of the regional dip. This generalized fluvial-estuarine depositional systems architecture is supported by a model proposed by Nichols and Biggs (1985), based on their own investigations in Chesapeake Bay and on studies by Jouanneau and Latouche (1981) in the Gironde estuary of France.

The lower Potomac River, a western arm of Chesapeake

Bay, is filled with as much as 40 m of Holocene sandy and silty fluvial and bay sediments. This material unconformably overlies a late Wisconsinan valley floor cut some 34 to 54 m below present sea level (Knebel and others, 1981). The sandy and silty fluvial strata became the substrate for extensive oyster reefs and mounds which formed on the now buried bay margin. The last few thousand years of near stillstand in sea level have caused infilling of the central bay channel by clay and silty clay.

The depth to the late Pleistocene valley floor (basal Holocene sequence) beneath Matagorda Bay on the central Texas coast is also about 50 m (Wilkinson and Byrne, 1977). Borings through the flanks of this bay (south Lavaca Bay) demonstrate the existence of a 35-m-thick, fining-upward sedimentary sequence, interpreted to represent a succession of fluvial sand and gravel, bay-head delta sand and silt, and open-bay muds. The channel base is deeply scoured into the Pleistocene substrate. The bay-head deltaic facies consists of interbedded discontinuous sand bodies and mud. Depending on the location, the bay mud is overlain either by the modern, regressive bay-head delta or by sandy spits built off some bay-margin headlands (Wilkinson and Byrne, 1977). Nearly identical vertical facies successions are documented in transgressed valley fills on the Atlantic shoreface of Delaware (Kraft and others, this volume, and Demarest and Kraft, this volume).

This thick estuarine-fill sequence contrasts sharply with the much thinner Holocene sequence documented by Morton and Donaldson (1973) for Wachapreague Lagoon on the outer coast of Virginia, and the study of Virginia back-barrier facies presented by Finkelstein and Ferland (this volume).

Transgressive shelf stratigraphy.—

The regional ravinement surface is recognized in numerous coring and high-resolution seismic reflection studies on continental shelves. On the United States mid-Atlantic shelf, the ravinement surface is typically buried by a discontinuous "surficial sand sheet" 0 to 10 m thick (Swift and others, 1972; Hollister, 1973; Pilkey and others, 1981). The sand sheet has a ridge-and-swale topography impressed upon it. Locally, the swales have been deepened by storm-current erosion. In these areas the ravinement surface does not occur at the topographic base of the ridge; it is instead truncated some distance up on the ridge flank (McKinney and others, 1977; Stubblefield and others, 1975). The back-barrier strata have the nearly flat, regional ravinement as their upper surface. Their lower surface, the subaerial erosion surface, has some tens of meters of relief.

Rapid lateral changes in coastal and inner-shelf environments produce a wide variety of transgressive depositional systems architecture. Some systems are very complex, and all require the proper placement of the ravinement surface in order to derive the correct interpretation. The six schematic stratigraphic sequences presented in Figure 5 are inferred from specific Holocene examples along the United States coast for the purpose of illustrating the most common types.

The "classic" transgressive shallow-marine facies pattern is based on findings by Curray (1960), Gould and McFarlan (1959), and Swift and others (1972). Common to these studies is the recognition of the Pleistocene subaerial surface (sequence boundary) overlain by back-barrier (lagoonal) mud and peat, shoreline sand and inner-shelf mud (Fig. 5A). A ravinement surface separates the shoreline sand and the shelf sediments.

Stahl and others (1974) documented the transgressive systems architecture at Beach Haven ridge on the inner New Jersey shelf. This ridge formed at the base of the shoreface of a retreating barrier complex, possibly from sand deposited in an ebb-tidal delta. A regional erosion surface, the ravinement surface, separates the shelf marine sand of the ridge complex from the underlying silty sand of probable back-barrier origin. The back-barrier deposits, in turn, overlie mud which occupies a coast-parallel tidal channel cut into both Pleistocene and Miocene strata. The Holocene sequence boundary is the erosional base of this channel (Fig. 5B). This is an example where a channel-base diastem has locally replaced the regional subaerial surface as the sequence boundary. Note also that this inferred depositional history has produced a coarsening-upward sedimentary sequence beneath the ravinement surface. This sequence contrasts with the fining-upward transgressive succession present in Lavaca Bay on the Texas coast (Fig. 5C). The latter environment was controlled by a sediment source at the landward side of the bay, the receding bay-head delta.

Recently, more detailed studies of the Beach Haven ridge by Miller and Dill (pers. commun.) and by Figueiredo (1983; see also Niedoroda and others, 1985) have documented a highly variable transgressive stratigraphy in the area. The northeast-southwest-trending, 5-m-thick ridge overlies a channel complex, probably fluvial, which trends to the southeast, essentially down the regional coastal plain gradient. This vertical juxtaposition of coastal plain and marine facies implies the presence of an intermediate ravinement surface. A vertical stratigraphic section of a vibracore through the Beach Haven ridge-and-channel complex demonstrates stacked fining- and coarsening-upward sequences (Fig. 5D). The ravinement surface is located within the upper coarsening-upward part of the sequence, separating two sand bodies of only subtle differences in lithology.

Preservation of inferred flood-tidal deltas, tidal channel and lagoonal fills beneath Holocene sand ridges is well documented on the inner New Jersey continental shelf (Figueiredo, 1983). Moreover, regional studies on the southeastern United States continental shelf have concluded that lagoonal peat and remnant lagoonal fauna are widespread across much of the area, implying that barrier islands and their associated environments must have existed across much of the shelf. These barrier complexes have migrated landward during the Holocene transgression (Swift and others, 1985; Niedoroda and others, 1985; Sheridan and others, 1974; Pilkey and others, 1981; Field, 1980).

The common preservation of Holocene tidal channels and flood-tidal deltas beneath the ravinement surface on the Atlantic shelf implies that at least two additional vertical facies successions above a type 1 sequence boundary would be expected in the rock record. If a landward tidal channel is overriden by a flood-tidal delta during a transgression, a combining fining-upward and coarsening-upward succes-

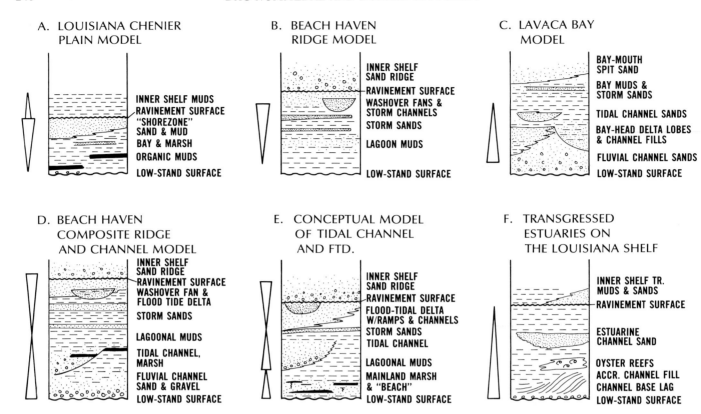

A. LOUISIANA CHENIER PLAIN MODEL
- INNER SHELF MUDS
- RAVINEMENT SURFACE
- "SHOREZONE" SAND & MUD
- BAY & MARSH
- ORGANIC MUDS
- LOW-STAND SURFACE

B. BEACH HAVEN RIDGE MODEL
- INNER SHELF SAND RIDGE
- RAVINEMENT SURFACE
- WASHOVER FANS & STORM CHANNELS
- STORM SANDS
- LAGOON MUDS
- LOW-STAND SURFACE

C. LAVACA BAY MODEL
- BAY-MOUTH SPIT SAND
- BAY MUDS & STORM SANDS
- TIDAL CHANNEL SANDS
- BAY-HEAD DELTA LOBES & CHANNEL FILLS
- FLUVIAL CHANNEL SANDS
- LOW-STAND SURFACE

D. BEACH HAVEN COMPOSITE RIDGE AND CHANNEL MODEL
- INNER SHELF SAND RIDGE
- RAVINEMENT SURFACE
- WASHOVER FAN & FLOOD TIDE DELTA
- STORM SANDS
- LAGOONAL MUDS
- TIDAL CHANNEL, MARSH
- FLUVIAL CHANNEL SAND & GRAVEL
- LOW-STAND SURFACE

E. CONCEPTUAL MODEL OF TIDAL CHANNEL AND FTD.
- INNER SHELF SAND RIDGE
- RAVINEMENT SURFACE
- FLOOD-TIDAL DELTA W/RAMPS & CHANNELS
- STORM SANDS
- TIDAL CHANNEL
- LAGOONAL MUDS
- MAINLAND MARSH & "BEACH"
- LOW-STAND SURFACE

F. TRANSGRESSED ESTUARIES ON THE LOUISIANA SHELF
- INNER SHELF TR. MUDS & SANDS
- RAVINEMENT SURFACE
- ESTUARINE CHANNEL SAND
- OYSTER REEFS
- ACCR. CHANNEL FILL
- CHANNEL BASE LAG
- LOW-STAND SURFACE

FIG. 5.—Stratigraphic columns from selected Holocene marginal marine settings. The figures are generalized representations of detailed core and seismic data in the referenced sources. (A) Vertical sequence through the transgressive half of the Holocene Louisiana chenier plain. The sequence is coarsening upward through the shore-zone sands, truncated by a ravinement surface (inferred) and overlain by inner-shelf mud. The column represents a deposit about 10 to 15 m thick. Data from Gould and McFarlan (1959). (B) Vertical sequence through the Beach Haven ridge complex, New Jersey. The sequence boundary (top of Pleistocene and Miocene strata) is overlain by mud infilling an abandoned tidal channel. Interbedded washover sand increases in abundance upward as a transgressive barrier moved closer to the section. The barrier superstructure was removed by the retreating shoreface and replaced by a ravinement surface. This surface is overlain by an inner-shelf sand ridge. The overall sequence is coarsening upward. Data from Stahl and others (1974). (C) In contrast to case B, the Holocene fill of Lavaca Bay on the central Texas coast consists of a simple fining-upward sequence. Immediately above the sequence boundary (the scoured top of the Pleistocene lowstand surface), there is fluvial sand in the bay axis. This is followed by a fining-upward succession of bay-head delta and open-bay mud, representing the continued landward (more distal) migration of the river-mouth spit. Continued sea-level rise may truncate this spit by the retreat of a bay ravinement. Data from Wilkinson and Byrne (1977). (D) Combined fining- and coarsening-upward sequence inferred for part of the Beach Haven ridge complex from seismic profiles and vibracores. The sequence boundary is the erosional base of a large, probably fluvial, channel. The channel fill is fining upward, from gravel to fine sand. The mid-section channel in this column is hypothetical. Its base is a diastem. The overlying coarsening-upward column is identical to that shown in (B). Data from Miller and Dill (pers. commun.). (E) Conceptual model of two fining-upward sequences representing mainland "beach"-to-lagoon and tidal-channel fill, overlain by a coarsening-upward sequence of a flood-tidal delta, a ravinement surface and an inner-shelf sand ridge. Generalized after observations on the Texas, North Carolina and Delaware coasts. (F) Inferred vertical lithologic column based on interpretation of seismic reflection patterns in Holocene estuary fill on the western Louisiana continental shelf. A basal channel lag, at the sequence boundary, is overlain by accretionary beds of a sandy(?) channel fill, oyster reefs, bay mud and a ravinement surface. The ravinement may be capped by either transgressive sand or mud. Column constructed from data in Suter (1986).

sion would be predicted (Fig. 5E). The ravinement surface would be within the coarsening-upward part of the succession. Alternatively, a tidal inlet channel cutting into its associated, landward, flood-tidal delta would produce a coarsening-upward sequence abruptly truncated by a channel diastem. This would be overlain by a subtly fining-upward channel-fill sand and then finally truncated by a ravinement surface.

A different estuarine systems architecture is encountered across the late Pleistocene-Holocene boundary on the Louisiana outer continental shelf. Rapid relative sea-level rise converted the Louisiana shelf valleys into estuaries during the earliest Holocene. Some of the estuary fills consist of

as much as 25 m of combined lateral accretion facies (point bars of active meandering channels), aggradational facies (overbank and abandoned channels) and mounded oyster reefs (Fig. 5F; Suter and others, this volume).

Cretaceous: Dakota Sandstone of the San Juan Basin

Sections through the Dakota Sandstone in the San Juan basin provide an excellent example of both the facies and architectural variability encountered in Cenomanian estuarine and back-barrier sequences. As previously discussed, a major sea-level fall 97 ma caused incision of the J Sandstone in the Denver basin into the Skull Creek Shale. The incision of the Cretaceous Huerfano drainage (MacKenzie and Poole, 1962) into Jurassic rocks exposed on the San Juan basin coastal plain was probably a correlative event.

Four exposures of the Oak Canyon Mbr of the Dakota Sandstone along the eastern and southern flanks of the San Juan basin document the facies variability associated with a type 1 sequence boundary. The sites are: Bernalillito Mesa, White Mesa, Deadman Rock, and Tierra Amarilla.

Bernalillito Mesa is one of the best exposures of the Dakota Sandstone in the southern San Juan basin (Figs. 6, 7). From base to top the exposed units are: the Jackpile Sandstone (Upper Jurassic, member of the Morrison Fm; Jm); a basal Cretaceous transgressive lag, the only coarse-grained Oak Canyon unit at this section (Kds; Fig. 8A); a brackish to marine dark shale interval assigned to the Oak Canyon (Kdoc); the Cubero Tongue (Kdc), a second shale unit, assigned to the Clay Mesa Shale Tongue of the Lower Mancos (Kmc); and the topmost sandstone, the Paguate Tongue (Kdp).

A detailed stratigraphic section has been measured on the southeast flank of the Bernalillito Mesa (Fig. 9). A brief description of key sedimentological aspects of this section follows.

Unit 1, from 0 to 2.4 m, is a trough crossbedded, poorly sorted, pebbly, kaolinitic subarkose with a mean grain size of 350 μm. This is the Jurassic Jackpile Sandstone.

Unit 2, from 2.4 to 3.1 m, is a very coarse, pebbly sandstone (mean size: 1,000 μm with pebbles as large as 3 cm), overlying the Jackpile with a sharp, uneven erosional contact (Fig. 8A). The unit is about 20% burrowed with trough crossbeds, indicating a southward paleoflow direction. This unit is lithostratigraphically assigned to the basal part of the Oak Canyon Mbr of the Dakota Sandstone.

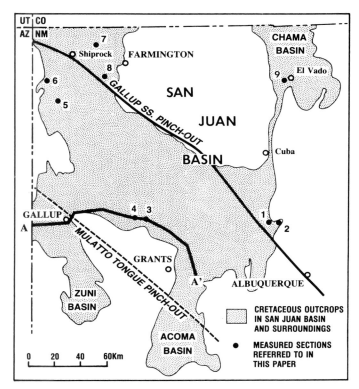

FIG. 7.—Location map of the measured sections in the San Juan basin referred to in this paper. Location of seaward pinchout of the regressive Gallup Sandstone and overlying transgressive Mulatto Tongue of the Upper Mancos Shale are from Molenaar (1983b) and field work by the authors.

FIG. 6.—Bernalillito Mesa in the southeastern San Juan basin, New Mexico (sect. 1, Fig. 7). The stratigraphic units in this mesa are: Jm (Jurassic, Jackpile Sandstone Mbr of the Morrison Fm); Kds (basal Dakota "lag," properly included in the newly defined "Encinal Canyon Mbr"; Aubrey, 1986); Kdoc (Oak Canyon Mbr of the Dakota Sandstone, here a marine shale tongue); Kdc (Cubero Tongue of the Dakota Sandstone, a regressive shelf sandstone); Kmc (Clay Mesa shale tongue of the Mancos Shale); and Kdp (Paguate Tongue of the Dakota Sandstone, another regressive shelf sandstone). Arrow denotes location of measured section in Figure 9.

Unit 3, from 3.1 to 18.0 m, is a dark gray silty shale, black in the lower 5 m. Thin detrital coal laminae and sulfur stains are abundant in the lower part. Upsection, the shale changes from a fissile to a blocky-fracture pattern, and the percentage of interlaminated coarse silt and very fine sand increases. Small burrows and casts of small pelecypod valves are present near the top of the unit. This unit is assigned to the upper Oak Canyon Mbr of the Dakota Sandstone. The basal shales were probably deposited in a brackish, restricted marine embayment. The environment is inferred to have become more fully marine upward. Units 4 through 9 in Figure 9 are all fully marine shelf deposits not directly related to the discussions of the sequence boundary in this paper.

At White Mesa the transgressive sandy facies of the lower Oak Canyon Mbr are much better developed (Fig. 10). As at Bernalillito Mesa, unit 1 is the Jackpile Sandstone. Unit 2, from 14.6 to 18.5 m, is the lower Oak Canyon Mbr. The base of this unit, the basal Cretaceous sequence boundary, is a sharp, erosional contact (Fig. 8B). The contact is overlain by a very coarse, pebbly, poorly sorted, carbonaceous, trough crossbedded sandstone. It contains as much as 5% chert pebbles and mud clasts. Measured axes of trough cross-stratified sets indicate a paleoflow direction to the east-southeast. This very coarse sandstone is about 1 m thick at the measured section, but varies greatly along the outcrop, suggesting channel fills. Low-angle accretion beds can be

FIG. 8.—Lithologic characteristics of the basal Dakota Sandstone in the southeastern San Juan basin. (A) Pebbly sandstone on top of the K/J contact 5 km east of Bernalillito Mesa. This unit represents the transgressive lag formed as the Cenomanian shoreface retreated across an "interfluve" highland composed of Jackpile Sandstone (white sandstone in middle of picture). (B) Contact between basal Dakota Sandstone and the Jurassic Jackpile Sandstone member of the Morrison Fm at White Mesa (at head of person on the right). The 2-m-thick basal Dakota Sandstone at this section is interpreted as back-barrier facies. (C) Sandstone, shale and coal infilling a channel in the back-barrier facies of the basal Dakota Sandstone at White Mesa. (D) Dakota Sandstone facies at Deadman Rock on the north rim of the Acoma Valley. From the base up the lithologic units are: Jm (Jurassic, Brushy Basin Mbr of the Morrison Fm); Kds (basal Oak Canyon fluvial sandstone); Kdol (lower Oak Canyon; estuary-fill shale and overlying marginal marine sandstone); Kdou (upper Oak Canyon marine shales) and Kdc (Cubero Tongue of Dakota Sandstone, a regressive tongue of shelf sandstone).

observed north of the line of section and an abandoned channel is seen in cross section in Figure 8C. Within the channel a coarse sandstone is overlain by about 3 m of interbedded fine sandstone, carbonaceous shales and coals. Burrows, including *Skolithos,* are present but not common within these sandstones.

This stratigraphic unit is interpreted as the basal Oak Canyon Mbr on the basis of stratigraphic position and lithologic relationship to the Oak Canyon stratotype near the Jackpile mine north of Laguna (Owen, 1966; Owen and Siemers, 1977). Environmentally, the Oak Canyon Mbr at this outcrop is thought to represent coastal plain channels, possibly tidal, which were abandoned and overlain by back-barrier marsh during rising sea level. Ultimately, sandy washover fans covered the marsh. Continued transgression and shoreface retreat truncated this back-barrier sequence.

The burrowed top of unit 2 (Fig. 10) is interpreted as a ravinement surface. Above unit 2 this section consists entirely of shelf shales and sandstones.

The White Mesa section has preserved a much thicker back-barrier sequence than did the Bernalillito Mesa, suggesting the existence of coastal plain relief. At the Deadman Rock overlook of the Acoma Valley, the lower Oak Canyon strata become very thick, suggesting that the exposure represents a location much closer to the axis of a relatively deep coastal plain valley (Fig. 8D). The lower Oak Canyon Mbr at Deadman Rock consists of medium- to coarse-grained, crossbedded channel sandstones overlain by organic-rich shales. The upper Oak Canyon Mbr (Kdou) is separated from the lower Oak Canyon by a burrowed ravinement surface. Marine shales of the basal Cubero Tongue overlie this ravinement surface.

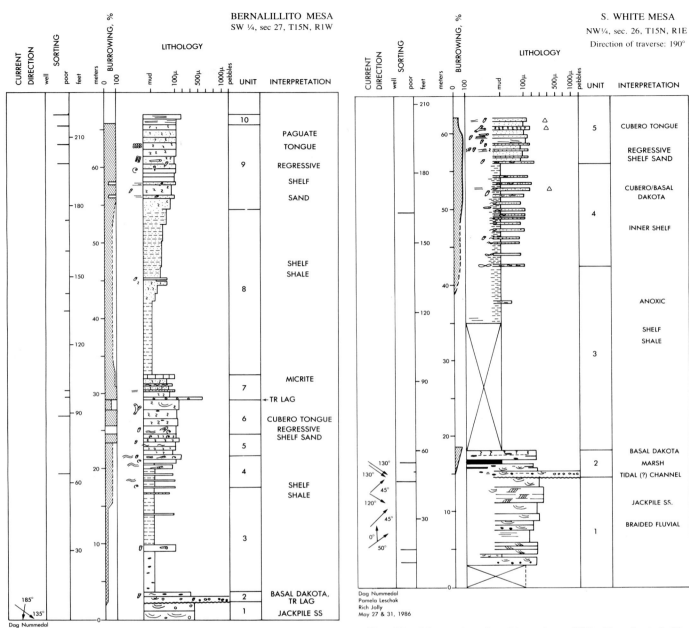

FIG. 9.—Measured stratigraphic section at the southeast corner of Bernalillito Mesa (sect. 1, Fig. 7). The section is self-explanatory. See text for discussion of units and Figure 16 for symbols legend.

FIG. 10.—Measured stratigraphic section at White Mesa (sect. 2, Fig. 7). See text for discussion of units and Figure 16 for symbols legend.

This succession records a classic transgressive estuary fill, similar to the Lavaca Bay model (Fig. 5C), overridden by marine strata as a consequence of shoreface retreat. Because of the dominance of back-barrier over channel sandstones in this outcrop, it probably represents the flank, rather than the axis, of a filled valley.

A roadcut along United States Highway 84 south of Tierra Amarilla in the Chama basin contains thick basal Oak Canyon carbonaceous fluvial sandstones and associated thin (overbank?) shales. It is interpreted as a possible example

of an axial basal fluvial deposit of a transgressive estuary-fill sequence. This outcrop, however, has not yet been studied in detail.

The Oak Canyon Mbr of the Dakota Sandstone is inferred to represent a series of transgressive estuary fills separated along strike by elevated "interfluves" of Jurassic rocks. At the interfluves the transgressive strata are very thin and consist essentially of the basal transgressive lag, such as at Bernalillito Mesa. The transgressed valleys off Delaware and Texas, which are discussed above, are good Holocene analogs to the lower Oak Canyon Mbr. The basal sequence boundary of the Upper Cretaceous marine strata in the San Juan basin thus constitutes a type 1 sequence boundary.

Cretaceous: the Coniacian of the San Juan Basin

A regional unconformity formed across the southern part of the Western Interior basin during the middle Coniacian. In the eastern and central part of this Cretaceous basin, the unconformity separates the Carlile Shale (below) from the Niobrara Fm (above; Hattin, 1964; Kauffman, 1983; Pratt and others, 1985). The following discussion will evaluate the development of strata bordering the equivalent unconformity in the San Juan basin.

From the latest Turonian through the early Coniacian, a major strandplain depositional system, the Gallup Sandstone, prograded across the southwestern San Juan basin (Molenaar, 1983b). Based on macro-invertebrate biostratigraphic zonation, the upper marine Gallup Sandstone tongues are of early Coniacian age (zones of *Prionocylus quadratus* through *Inoceramus erectus:* Molenaar, 1983b; Kauffman, 1983; Hook and others, 1983; King, 1974). The vertical stacking of successive tongues of the Gallup Sandstone (Fig. 11) and the lack of internal unconformities imply that deposition of most of the marine Gallup Sandstone occurred during an interval of continuous relative sea-level rise along the southwestern seaway margin. Local sediment supply was sufficient to maintain Gallup progradation.

Above the Gallup Sandstone and its seaward correlative Lower Mancos Shale lie the Crevasse Canyon Fm (depositionally updip) and the Tocito Sandstone (Fig. 12; McCubbin, 1969; Campbell, 1979; Molenaar, 1983b). The equivalent unit at El Vado, New Mexico, on the eastern flank of the San Juan basin is the Cooper Arroyo Sandstone (King, 1974). An unconformity separates the Gallup Sandstone and equivalent offshore shales from the Tocito and Cooper Arroyo sandstones (Molenaar, 1983b). The age and duration of the hiatus associated with this unconformity has bearing on its mode of origin. At the western margin of the basin (Shiprock area of New Mexico), the unconformity represents, at most, one ammonite zone: the zone of *Scaphites preventricosus* of earliest middle Coniacian age (Dane,

ZONE	STAGE		SOUTHWEST SAN JUAN BASIN	CENTRAL AND EAST SAN JUAN BASIN
36	UPPER		MULATTO TONGUE OF UPPER MANCOS SH.	MULATTO TONGUE OF UPPER MANCOS SH.
		CREVASSE CANYON FM.	BORREGO PASS SANDSTONE / TOCITO SANDSTONE	TOCITO SANDSTONE
37	MIDDLE		TORRIVIO MBR.	COOPER ARROYO SS.
	CONIACIAN		?	
38	LOWER	GALLUP SS. ↑	non-marine GALLUP SANDSTONE	Hiatus
39			Marine GALLUP SANDSTONE	
				?
40	UPPER TURONIAN		LOWER MANCOS SHALE	JUANA LOPEZ MBR. OF LOWER MANCOS SHALE
41				

FIG. 12.—Time-stratigraphic nomenclature chart for Upper Turonian and Coniacian rocks in the San Juan basin. The numbered faunal zones are those of Molenaar (1983b). The precise age range of the units is still uncertain; therefore, there are no lines separating them. The tentative ages are from: Molenaar (1983a, b), Dane (1960), King (1974), and Hook and others (1983).

1960; Molenaar, 1983b). At El Vado, New Mexico, and in southeastern Colordo the hiatus appears to represent three *Inoceramus* faunal zones: *I. erectus, I. lusatia* and *I. deformis* (King, 1974). These zones span all of the early and most of the middle Coniacian age. Hence, the duration of the hiatus increases seaward. This unconformity probably correlates with the same sea-level fall which produced the Carlile-Niobrara unconformity on the eastern seaway margin.

Two additional observations suggest that local relative sea level fell after deposition of the uppermost marine Gallup Sandstone: (1) extensive incision of fluvial channel sandstone of Torrivio affinity into the marine Gallup Sandstone at Pinedale (Molenaar, 1977), and (2) erosion of thick intervals of the Lower Mancos Shale at the base of many subsurface Tocito sand bodies in the northwestern San Juan basin (McCubbin, 1969).

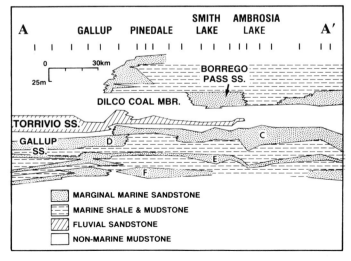

FIG. 11.—Stratigraphic cross section along the southern margin of the San Juan Basin along line A-A' in Figure 7. From Molenaar (1983a, fig. 14).

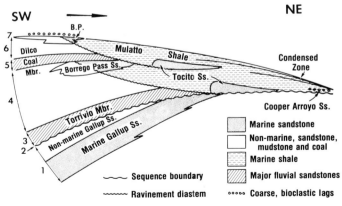

FIG. 13.—Proposed architecture of the transgressive part of the Coniacian depositional sequence in the San Juan basin. The middle Coniacian sequence boundary is at the base of the Torrivio, basal Tocito and Cooper Arroyo sandstones. The Borrego Pass Sandstone and Tocito Sandstone bodies higher in the section are related to a set of discrete, stair-stepping ravinement surfaces, possibly caused by short-term regressive-transgressive cycles superimposed on the general Coniacian transgression.

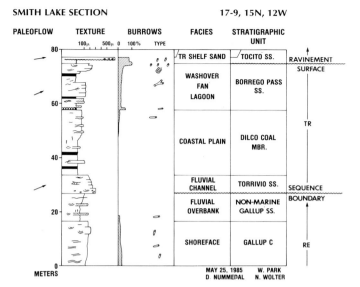

SMITH LAKE SECTION   17-9, 15N, 12W

FIG. 14.—Stratigraphic section from the Gallup through Tocito sandstones at Smith Lake (sect. 4, Fig. 7). The Gallup records regression across the Coniacian coastal plain. The base of the Torrivio Mbr is interpreted as the sequence boundary. A transgressive section of distal coastal plain streams (Dilco Coal Mbr) and back-barrier washover fans (Borrego Pass Sandstone) overlies the boundary. A ravinement surface separates these continental facies from the overlying Tocito shelf sand ridge facies. Compare vertical textural trends to those shown in Figure 5D.

The early middle Coniacian lowstand was followed by an extensive transgression which deposited the Tocito Sandstone, the Dilco Coal Mbr of the Crevasse Canyon Fm, the Borrego Pass Sandstone and the Mulatto Tongue of the Upper Mancos Shale (Fig. 12). This is the T3 transgression of Molenaar (1983b). The Dilco Coal Mbr is interpreted as transgressive coastal plain marsh and distal fluvial facies. The overlying Borrego Pass Sandstone consists largely of fluvial deposits, flood-tidal deltas and tidal channel facies formed behind a transgressive barrier island shoreline (Nummedal and Tillman, 1986).

The Coniacian rocks of the San Juan basin described above illustrate the architecture of marginal marine transgressive stratigraphy and the relationship between sequence boundaries and the transgressive ravinement diastem. A schematic representation of the inferred architecture is presented in Figure 13. The model is consistent with (1) the architecture of Holocene transgressive depositional systems discussed earlier in their paper, (2) numerous measured sections through Coniacian strata on the southern and western flanks of the San Juan basin (e.g., Fig. 14), and (3) the regional cross sections published by Campbell (1979) and Molenaar (1983a). Rapid subsidence and high sediment supply on the southwestern margin of the basin caused the landward dip in time lines.

During time 1 (Fig. 13) the Gallup strandplain and its associated offshore Lower Mancos Shale were characterized by progradation. The strandplain was buried updip by distal fluvial facies (non-marine Gallup Sandstone). The middle Coniacian sea-level fall caused transport of coarse sand far out onto the Mancos shelf (time 2). At time 3 sea-

level rise resumed, and direct fluvial sediment supply to the shelf ceased. Wave and storm-current action reworked the coarse upper part of the Lower Mancos Shale into a lag (the Cooper Arroyo and basal Tocito sandstones). The major hiatus beneath the Cooper Arroyo Sandstone at El Vado (King, 1974) and at the base of the Tocito Sandstone in the Horseshoe oilfield (McCubbin, 1969) suggests that there was topographic relief on the Mancos shelf at the time of the sea-level lowstand. Maximum erosion probably occurred at the regional seafloor highs. The resumption of local sea-level rise in the middle Coniacian also initiated aggradation of the fluvial systems depositing the Torrivio Mbr of the Gallup Sandstone.

The Coniacian transgression also caused erosional shoreface retreat with excavation of the distal portions of the Torrivio and Gallup sand bodies (distributary mouth bars?, channel sands, and upper shoreface facies). The released sand was partitioned between seaward transport onto shelf sand ridges (the main bodies of the Tocito Sandstone) and landward transport into transgressive barrier islands and back-barrier sandbodies. The two depositional systems would be separated by a ravinement diastem as explained in Figure 4. The preserved back-barrier facies constitute parts of the Borrego Pass Sandstone Mbr of the Crevasse Canyon Fm. Continued transgression during time 4 aggraded the distal fluvial systems, producing the Dilco Coal Mbr of the Crevasse Canyon Fm. Continued reworking of the barrier systems ultimately carried the Borrego Pass sand bodies far updip of their original shoreface source location. Petrographic similarity of the Tocito and Torrivio sandstones further supports the proposed relationship between these two units (I. Bergsohn, 1987, pers. commun.).

Multiple disconformities in the transgressive lower Niobrara Fm in Colorado (Fisher and others, 1985) suggest that the Coniacian transgression was punctuated. Consequently, at time 5, during a period of sea-level stillstand or minor fall, the shoreline would again have prograded, and additional terrigenous mud would have been supplied to the Upper Mancos Shale. Moreover, regressive shoreface sand would have buried the ravinement surface (Demarest, 1981; Demarest and others, 1981). The Borrego Pass Sandstone should therefore be expected to contain both transgressive and regressive sand bodies. Fluvial systems would be expected to have built seaward onto the prograding strandplains. At time 6 sea-level rise resumed, the latest regressive sand bodies would again be truncated by erosional shoreface retreat, a new ravinement surface formed, another Tocito sand ridge nucleated on the adjacent shelf, and a new Borrego Pass sandbody began its landward migration.

These processes were repeated multiple times during the punctuated Coniacian transgression, and a series of stacked Tocito and Borrego Pass sand bodies formed. Note that the resulting ravinement surfaces are separated from each other and detached from the basal sequence boundary. On the outer shelf individual time lines merge into a condensed section because terrigenous sediment supply was limited. Even during the short-term regressions included in this model, the seaward limit of the prograding clastic wedge would be fairly close to shore.

This interpretation is consistent with the observations of Campbell (1979), who has shown that on the northwestern margin of the San Juan basin, Tocito sand ridges are distributed in stepwise fashion across the eroded surface of the Gallup strandplain as they climb stratigraphically toward the west. This distribution is most easily explained as the consequences of modulations of the Coniacian transgression by high-frequency shoreline oscillations. Thus, the Tocito sand ridges are sub-tongues of the transgressive upper half of the Gallup clastic wedge, just as the lower, regressive Gallup contains successive tongues. The basal Gallup tongues, deposited during the regression, are as much as 30 m thick (Molenaar, 1983a), whereas the tongues of the upper transgressive phase are much thinner. Tocito sand ridges are plano-convex lenses which locally attain 15 m in thickness, but where they attach to the main body of littoral sandstone, they are commonly 5 m or less thick.

Given the asymmetry, two models for the architecture of the Coniacian transgressive surface in this area are possible. In one, the basal regressive facies of the high-frequency oscillation is thinner than the depth of shoreface erosion, so that it is destroyed as the transgression is resumed; only the resulting debris pile, namely the sand ridge, is preserved. The transgressive surface branches repeatedly with gently dipping second-order erosion surfaces extending from the main surface into the overlying shale. In the second case, shown in Figure 13, the high-frequency regressive tongues are thicker than the depth of shoreface erosion and are partially preserved. In this case, there is no main erosion surface, only the second-order surfaces, rising in stair-step fashion toward the basin margin. This latter model is consistent with the data presently by Campbell (1979) and represents our preferred explanation for the Tocito stratigraphy. Further work is needed, however, to test the veracity of this model.

Toward the end of the Coniacian transgression, the Dilco coastal plain had aggraded sufficiently to become a very low-gradient coastal plain characterized by extensive fine-grained depositional environments. Transgressive shoreface retreat across this coastal plain failed to release significant amounts of sand, and the formation of Borrego Pass and Tocito sand bodies ceased. This is consistent with the observation that the youngest, and most landward, Tocito sandstones include thin lags consisting of abundant molluscan fragments.

Detailed measured stratigraphic sections document the sedimentologic attributes of the facies within the lower transgressive half of the Coniacian depositional sequence in the San Juan basin. The section at Smith Lake northeast of Gallup documents well the depositional systems of the updip (landward) part of the sequence. A section at the Hogback oilfield near Shiprock illustrates the facies succession near the Gallup shoreface pinchout.

Smith Lake section.—

This 80-m-thick section contains Coniacian strata which extend from the base of the C tongue of the Gallup Sandstone to the top of the Tocito Sandstone (Fig. 14). The section was also measured by Molenaar (1983a, sect. 45).

The Gallup C tongue consists of 16.4 m of moderate to well-sorted quartzose sandstone coarsening upward from a mean size of 125 μm at the base to about 200 μm near the top. Stratification is subhorizontal with a few troughs near the top. Sparse burrows, probably *Ophiomorpha,* are scattered throughout the unit; the total abundance of burrows decreases upward. The unit is inferred to represent a prograding shoreface deposit.

Overlying the Gallup Sandstone is a 10.4-m interval of mudstones and muddy sandstones with abundant coal fragments. Trough cross-stratified lenticular sandstones account for about 20% of the section. The unit is inferred to represent fluvial overbank and crevasse splay(?) facies and is assigned to the nonmarine member of the Gallup Sandstone. It is considered to be part of the continued regressive development of the Gallup coastal plain.

The base of the overlying unit, the Torrivio Sandstone, is erosional. The mean grain size at its base is 300 μm, with well-rounded quartz grains and abundant mud clasts, some as large as 3 cm in diameter. Mean grain size generally decreases upward through the unit, reaching 175 μm at the top. Beds are mostly trough cross-stratified with an east-northeasterly paleoflow direction.

The Torrivio Mbr of the Gallup Sandstone is interpreted as a fluvial channel complex, resting unconformably on the underlying nonmarine Gallup and directly on the erosionally truncated uppermost Gallup shoreface tongue at some locations.

Above the Torrivio Mbr is a 24.6-m-thick section of the Dilco Coal Mbr (Fig. 14). At its base the Dilco Coal Mbr is characterized by interbedded organic-rich mudstones and coals. Some coal beds are nearly 1 m thick. Ripple-laminated, muddy sandstone beds increase in abundance upward; the mean sandsize coarsens upward from 80 μm at the base to about 125 μm near the top. Some of these sandy beds are rooted and burrows increase in abundance upward. Distinct bentonites, suitable for regional correlation, are present within the Dilco Coal Mbr. The Dilco Coal Mbr is interpreted as deposits of lower coastal plain high-sinuosity streams. Rapid aggradation characterized the coastal plain during this middle to late Coniacian transgressive interval, both because of a probable absolute sea-level rise in the seaway and rapid subsidence in front of the Sevier thrust belt.

The Borrego Pass Sandstone overlies the Dilco Coal Mbr at the Smith Lake section. The Borrego Pass Sandstone is 17 m thick and consists of two sandstone bodies separated by a mudstone unit and coals about 3 to 5 m below the top. The lower sandstone unit consists of interbedded fine and very fine sandstones (85 to 150 μm) arranged in a generally coarsening-upward succession. Wave and combined flow ripples are common; burrows occupy from 10 to 30% of the rock volume and include *Ophiomorphia* and *Thalassinoides.* These units are interpreted as deposits of distal flood-tidal deltas or washover fans.

The fine-grained unit of the Borrego Pass Sandstone consists of intensely burrowed, organic-rich sandy mudstones and coals overlain by wavy-bedded siltstones. This unit is inferred to represent low-energy lagoonal sedimentation removed from sites of active washover or tidal delta sedimentation.

The upper Borrego Pass Sandstone is somewhat coarser than the underlying units. It coarsens upward from 150 μm at the base to 250 μm near the top. Both upper and lower contacts are sharp; burrows average about 10% by volume at the base. Ichnogenera include *Ophiomorpha* and *Arenicolites*. The coarsest bed near the top contains large soft-sediment deformation structures (Fig. 15A) and a broad, shallow, fining-upward channel fill with trough cross-stratified sandstone about 1.5 m thick. The top of this unit is intensely bioturbated both within and outside the channel margins. The burrowing is clearly unrelated to, and post-dates, the channel formation. This upper unit of the Borrego Pass Sandstone is an excellent example of a washover fan deposit. In fact, all the sedimentary attributes described here are identical to those observed along the margins of hurricane channels scoured through the fan behind Corpus Christi Pass on the south Texas coast by Hurricane Allen in 1980 (Nummedal, 1982; Maynard and Suter, 1983).

The intensely burrowed upper surface represents the abandonment of active washover sedimentation. Above this surface is a 1-m-thick unit of inferred lagoonal shale. This shale is capped by a 1-m-thick medium to coarse (250 μm–750 μm), trough crossbedded, glauconitic, 20% burrowed, pebbly sandstone (Fig. 15B). This sand unit is the updip equivalent of the Tocito Sandstone. It is interpreted as a transgressive, inner-shelf lag formed just seaward of the base of the eroding shoreface. This thin, landward, lag facies of the Tocito Sandstone is ubiquitous above the Borrego Pass Sandstone in the region between Gallup and Grants. Locally, the lag consists mostly of molluscan fragments. The lack of Tocito ridges in this area may be a function of insufficient sediment supply and a very shallow, embayed inner shelf at this stage close to the time of maximum Mulatto transgression. The ravinement surface, which occurs at the base of this coarse lag, separates the shelf facies of the Tocito Sandstone from the underlying lagoonal shales.

The stratigraphic succession described at Smith Lake corresponds closely to the transgressive stratigraphy at the Beach

FIG. 15.—Facies characteristics of stratigraphic units adjoining the Upper Coniacian transgressive surface in the San Juan basin. (A) Large-scale soft-sediment deformation structures at the 75-m level of the Smith Lake section (Fig. 14). This facies is interpreted as a back-barrier storm washover fan. (B) Coarse pebbly sandstones and bioclastic lags are characteristic of the landward Tocito Sandstone. Photograph shows the Tocito Sandstone at the top of the Smith Lake section (Fig. 14). Scale in centimeters. (C) Location of measured section at the Hogback oilfield. Photograph can be related directly to section in Figure 16. Numbered units correspond to those used in Figure 16. (D) Intraclasts ("burrow clasts") at the Mancos-Tocito contact in the Hogback oilfield. These clasts are lcoated at the basae of the Tocito Sandstone wherever this is a marine erosion surface. Scale in centimeters.

FIG. 15.—(E) Sharp angular contact at the base of the Tocito Sandstone exposed at Rattlesnake Anticline. Note truncation of thin, storm-deposited sand beds in the Mancos Shale (at right).

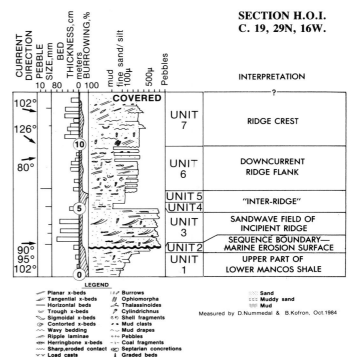

FIG. 16.—Measured stratigraphic section through the Mancos Shale and the Tocito Sandstone at the Hogback oilfield (sect. 8, Fig. 7). Note the coarsening upward of the Mancos Shale beneath the marine erosion surface (due to shoaling and steepened coastal plain stream gradients) and the great thickness of the Tocito Sandstone compared to that at the more landward Smith Lake section (Fig. 14). See text for discussion of stratigraphic units. The symbols legend used in this figure also applies to the other graphic logs in this paper.

Haven composite ridge-and-channel model (Fig. 5D). The facies succession between the sequence boundary and the ravinement surface is nearly identical, except that the transgressive section at Smith Lake is much thicker due to the rapid sedimentation and subsidence in the thrust belt foredeep. This matching of facies successions lends additional confidence to the assignment of a sequence boundary at the base of the Torrivio Mbr of the Gallup Sandstone, and it clearly assigns the Dilco Coal Mbr to the transgressive part of the Coniacian depositional sequence.

The Tocito Sandstone lag at the Smith Lake section clearly is younger than the Borrego Pass Sandstone immediately below; however, some basinward Tocito Sandstone ridges are probably time-equivalent with the Borrego Pass sandstones described here. Consequently, the time lines cross this ravinement surface as schematically portrayed in Figure 4.

Hogback oilfield section.—

This section is typical of the Tocito Sandstone facies immediately offshore from the Gallup shoreface pinchout. The measured section (Fig. 16) is depicted in Figure 15C.

Unit 1, 0 to 2.0 m, consists of interbedded, bioturbated fine sandstone and sandy siltstone generally coarsening upward from 70 μm at the base to 500 μm at the upper contact of the unit. Thin beds of form-discordant ripple-bedded sets are preserved. Burrowing ranges from more than 75% by volume at the base to about 30–50% near the top. This unit is assigned to the upper part of the Lower Mancos Shale. The rapid upward coarsening took place in response to an influx of coarse fluvial material from the "Torrivio channels" as sea level fell.

Unit 2, 2.0 to 2.1 m, is coarse, poorly sorted sandstone (mean grain size in excess of 700 μm with individual pebbles as large as 3 mm). The unit also contains abundant aggregate intraclasts (Fig. 15D). The basal unit boundary is sharp and disconformable. The intraclasts observed at the measured section form a continuous base beneath the Hogback oilfield ridge throughout the area of its exposure. Many

of these clasts appear to be cemented burrows, reworked from the Mancos Shale and concentrated at the disconformity as a basal lag (Singh, 1985). These "burrow clasts" are a diagnostic marker for the Mancos-Tocito contact in many areas. Where exposed, the basal Tocito Sandstone contact is commonly sharp; occasionally, it is also distinctly angular (Fig. 15E). These sharp ridge bases are interpreted as ravinement surfaces or (probably more commonly) marine deflation diastems formed by acceleration of storm currents on the upcurrent flank of an incipient ridge.

Units 3 through 7 are subfacies of the Tocito Sandstone shelf sand ridge. The ridge complex consists of two sand bodies separated by 1 m of sandy mudstone (unit 4). The sandstone units are coarse- or medium-grained, glauconitic, cross-stratified, and burrowed by shallow marine trace fossils including *Ophiomorphia, Asterosoma,* and small *Skolithos*-like burrows. Bioclasts are common, particularly thick *Inoceramus* shell fragments. The thick, tabular crossbedded sets in unit 3 indicate a paleoflow direction toward the east-southeast, i.e., nearly parallel to the crest of the Tocito sand ridge in the Hogback oilfield (Nummedal and others, 1986).

Spontaneous potential and resistivity wire-line logs through ARCO's Navajo #4 well in the Horseshoe oilfield (Fig. 17) demonstrate that there are two stacked Tocito reservoirs in that area, and that the lower sandstone locally overlies the Juana Lopez calcarenite with a sharp erosional contact.

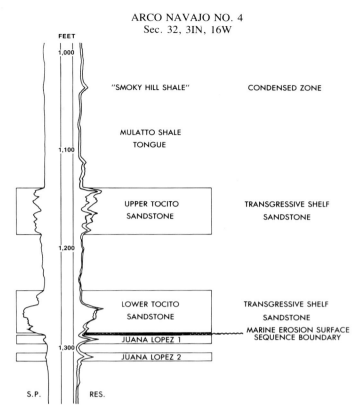

ARCO NAVAJO NO. 4
Sec. 32, 3IN, 16W

FIG. 17.—Subsurface logs through the Tocito Sandstone interval at ARCO Navajo #4 in the Horsehose oilfield (sect. 7, Fig. 7). There are two stacked Tocito Sandstones in this oilfield; the lower one erosionally overlies the Juana Lopez Mbr of the Mancos Shale.

This implies that the upper part of the Lower Mancos Shale interval, which is present at the Hogback oilfield, has been eroded beneath the Horseshoe field. Regional subsurface studies by McCubbin (1969) documented this erosion quite well. The upper Tocito sand body has a gradational contact with the Mancos Shale, suggesting continuous shelf aggradation consistent with the model proposed in Figure 13.

Detailed surface to subsurface correlations of the Tocito-Gallup complex along the western margin of the Four Corners platform have been established by Campbell (1971, 1979). The section demonstrates the stratigraphic climb of successive series of Tocito Sandstone ridges toward the basin margin. Campbell documents discontinuous erosional surfaces beneath the landward parts of each ridge.

SUMMARY AND CONCLUSIONS

Correct interpretation of the history of sedimentary basins requires an understanding both of the origin of the sedimentary facies and the mechanisms which formed erosional surfaces within the stratigraphic record. A formalized approach to such integrated basin analysis is provided through sequence stratigraphic concepts. In this paper we have attempted to apply sequence stratigraphy to rocks on the outcrop scale by focusing attention on the physical and stratigraphic sedimentary characteristics of the sequence boundaries, the overlying transgressive erosional surfaces

and the depositional systems architecture produced during the transgression. The use of modern and ancient analogs has reinforced the interpretations because they provide data on different scales.

The geometry of a shallow marine sequence boundary is a function of the depositional relief of the transgressed coastal plain. This geometry, in turn, controls the thickness of the resulting lowstand and transgressive deposits. This is illustrated in isopach patterns of Holocene transgressive systems on the United States Atlantic and Gulf shelves and many Cretaceous examples from the Western Interior (J Sandstone, Muddy Sandstone and Encinal Canyon Mbr of the Dakota Sandstone). Transgression of these deeply dissected coastal plains has produced a depositional systems architecture characterized by inner-shelf sand sheets above back-barrier deposits and "ribs" of sediments filling former sub-aerial valleys.

The transgressive systems of a depositional sequence are bounded below by the sequence boundary (both subaerial and submarine portions) produced at the time of rapid sea-level fall. They are bounded above by a condensed section formed at the time of maximum flooding (peak transgression). Within the transgressive depositional systems there are a number of erosional surfaces here labeled "transgressive surfaces." These surfaces include ravinement diastems, channel diastems, marine deflation diastems, offshore marine erosion diastems, and bay ravinement diastems. Such surfaces represent short time intervals of missing strata and are generally time-transgressive (diachronous).

The generalized vertical succession of facies within a transgressive estuarine depositional system is modeled after studies in Chesapeake Bay, the Gironde estuary, the Potomac River, and Texas and Louisiana coastal bays. Such systems consist of an upward sequence of fluvial facies, bay-head delta, open-estuary and estuary-mouth facies truncated by a marine ravinement diastem and overlain by inner continental shelf linear sand ridges or mud. Six different "type sections" were derived from an array of Holocene examples.

The application of this transgressive depositional systems model accounts for the observed variability within the basal Dakota Sandstone of the San Juan basin. Cretaceous transgressive strata associated with interfluves are very thin, consisting essentially of a basal erosional lag, such as at Bernalillito Mesa. Moreover, the sequence boundary and the transgressive ravinement surface are merged. Within deeply entrenched Cretaceous valleys, such as at Deadman Rock or Tierra Amarilla, the sequence boundary at the base of the valley fill is separated from the transgressive ravinement diastem by a complete succession of fluvial and estuarine facies as described above.

The San Juan basin is sufficiently far from the eastern margin of the basin for eustatic sea-level falls to have been at least partly compensated by subsidence. Base-level lowering during less severe sea-level falls would have been relatively slight, and the widened coastal plain may have regraded by subaerial deposition and insignificant stream incision. The Coniacian sea-level fall may have been such an event. Consequently, the transgressive systems architecture of the Coniacian depositional sequence differs in fundamental ways from that of the basal Dakota Sandstone.

We infer that the lower marine Gallup Sandstone tongues were deposited in a regime of relative sea-level rise. As the rise slowed, and then reversed, the coastal plain was regraded with coarse, gravelly sand (Torrivio Sandstone Mbr of the Crevasse Canyon Fm). Shoaling on the storm-dominated adjacent shelf enhanced the bypassing of fines and facilitated the dispersal of coarser sand (Cooper Arroyo Sandstone). As transgression resumed, the Dilco Coal Mbr was deposited behind a retreating barrier island complex, components of which were intermittently preserved as parts of the Borrego Pass Sandstone. Submarine erosion restructured the coarser shelf sand deposits into Tocito sand ridges. High-frequency oscillations of the shoreline during the retreat caused intermittent progradation, shoreface retreat, and the formation of multiple sand ridges separated by a series of stair-stepping ravinement surfaces. The entire transgressive sequence of coastal plain and inner-shelf depositional systems is more than 60 m thick along the southern flank of the San Juan basin.

The development of new sequence stratigraphic concepts and their application to the Upper Cretaceous strata of the San Juan basin provide interpretations which differ significantly from those advanced in earlier studies of these rocks.

ACKNOWLEDGMENTS

The authors gratefully acknowledge financial support from ARCO Oil and Gas Corporation, Cities Service Oil and Gas Company, the Gulf Coast Section of SEPM and the Department of Geology at Louisiana State University. Participants in a Gulf Coast Section-SEPM-sponsored field trip to the San Juan basin in December of 1986 contributed much to the final articulation of many of the ideas here put forth. Special thanks are extended to John Barwis, Jim Demarest and Robyn Wright for being particularly effective "devil's advocates." Jim Demarest, Roderick Tillman, Ivo Bergsohn, Pam Leschak, Tim Fleming and Niels Wolter provided constructive reviews of the manuscript.

REFERENCES

AUBREY, W. M., 1986, The nature of the Dakota-Morrison boundary, southeastern San Juan Basin, in Turner-Peterson, C. E., ed., A Basin Analysis Case Study: The Morrison Formation, Grants Uranium Region, New Mexico: American Association of Petroleum Geologists, Studies in Geology 22, p. 93–104.

BATES, R. L., AND JACKSON, J. A., 1980, Glossary of Geology: American Geological Institute, 751 p.

BELKNAP, D. F., AND KRAFT, J. C., 1981, Preservation potential of transgressive coastal lithosomes on the U.S. Atlantic shelf: Marine Geology, v. 42, p. 429–442.

————, AND ————, 1985, Influence of antecedent geology on stratigraphic preservation potential and evolution of Delaware's barrier systems: Marine Geology, v. 63, p. 235–262.

BRUUN, P., 1962, Sea level rise as a cause of shore erosion: Journal of Waterways and Harbors Division, American Society of Civil Engineers, v. 88, p. 117–130.

CAMPBELL, C. V., 1971, Depositional model—Upper Cretaceous Gallup beach shoreline, Ship Rock area, northwestern New Mexico: Journal of Sedimentary Petrology, v. 41, p. 395–401.

————, 1979, Model for beach shoreline in Gallup Sandstone (Upper

Cretaceous) of northwestern New Mexico: New Mexico Bureau of Mines and Mineral Resources, Socorro, Circular 164, 32 p.

CROSS, T. A., AND PILGER, R. H., 1978, Tectonic controls of Late Cretaceous sedimentation, Western Interior, USA: Nature, v. 274, p. 653–657.

CURRAY, J. R., 1960, Sediments and history of Holocene transgression, continental shelf, northwest Gulf of Mexico, in Shepard, F. P., Phleger, F. B., and van Andel, Tj. H., eds., Recent Sediments, Northwest Gulf of Mexico: American Association of Petroleum Geologists Special Publication, p. 221–266.

————, 1964, Transgressions and regressions, in Miller R. C., ed., Papers in Marine Geology, Shepard Commemorative Volume: Macmillan, New York, p. 175–203.

————, 1965, Late Quaternary history, continental shelves of the United States, in Wright, H. E., and Frey, D. G., eds., The Quaternary of the United States: Princeton University Press, Princeton, p. 723–735.

DANE, C. H., 1960, The boundary between rocks of Carlile and Niobrara age in the San Juan Basin, New Mexico and Colorado: American Journal of Science, Bradley Volume, v. 258-A, p. 46–56.

DEMAREST, J. M., 1981, Genesis and preservation of Quaternary paralic deposits on the Delmarva Peninsula: unpublished Ph.D. Dissertation, University of Delaware, Newark, 240 p.

————, BIGGS, R. B., AND KRAFT, J. C., 1981, Time-stratigraphic aspects of a formation: interpretation of surficial Pleistocene deposits by analogy with Holocene paralic deposits, southeastern Delaware: Geology, v. 9, p. 360–365.

————, AND LEATHERMAN, S. P., 1985, Mainland influence on coastal transgression: Delaware Peninsula: Marine Geology, v. 63, p. 19–33.

FIELD, M. E., 1980, Sandbodies on coastal plain shelves: Holocene record of the U.S. Atlantic inner shelf off Maryland: Journal of Sedimentary Petrology, v. 50, p. 505–528.

FIGUEIREDO, A. G., 1983, Submarine sand ridges: geometry and development, New Jersey, U.S.A.: Unpublished Ph.D. Dissertation, University of Miami, Coral Gables (not consecutively paginated).

FISCHER, A. G., 1961, Stratigraphic record of transgressing seas in light of sedimentation on the Atlantic coast of New Jersey: American Association of Petroleum Geologists Bulletin, v. 45, p. 1656–1666.

FISHER, C. G., KAUFFMAN, E. G., AND VON HOLT WILHELM, L., 1985, The Niobrara transgressive hemicyclothem in central and eastern Colorado: the anatomy of a multiple disconformity: in Pratt, L. M., Kauffman, E. G., and Zelt, F. B., eds., Fine-Grained Deposits and Biofacies of the Cretaceous Western Interior Seaway: Evidence of Cyclic Sedimentary Processes: Society of Economic Paleontologists and Mineralogists Midyear Meeting, Golden, Field Trip Guidebook No. 4, p. 184–198.

FISHER, W. L., AND McGOWEN, J. H., 1967, Depositional systems in the Wilcox Group of Texas, and their relationship to the occurrence of oil and gas: Gulf Coast Association of Geological Societies Transactions, v. 17, p. 105–125.

FISK, H. N., 1944, Geological Investigations of the Alluvial Valley of the Lower Mississippi River: U.S. Army Corps of Engineers, Mississippi River Commission, Vicksburg, 78 p.

GOULD, H. R., AND McFARLAN, E., JR., 1959, Geologic history of the Chenier Plain, southwestern Louisiana: Gulf Coast Association of Geological Societies Transactions, v. 9, p. 261–270.

HATTIN, D. E., 1964, Cyclic sedimentation of the Colorado Group of west-central Kansas: Kansas Geological Survey Bulletin 169, p. 205–217.

HAUN, J. D., 1963, Stratigraphy of Dakota Group and relationship to petroleum occurrence, northern Denver Basin, in Geology of the Northern Denver Basin and Adjacent Uplifts; Guidebook, Rocky Mountain Association of Geologists, p. 119–134.

HOLLISTER, C. D., 1973, Atlantic continental shelf and slope of the U.S.: texture of surface sediments from New Jersey to southern Florida: U.S. Geological Survey Professional Paper 529 M, 23 p.

HOOK, S. C., MOLENAAR, C. M., AND COBBAN, W. A., 1983, Stratigraphy and revision of nomenclature of Upper Cenomanian to Turonian (Upper Cretaceous) rocks of west-central New Mexico, in Hook, S. C., compiler, Contributions to Mid-Cretaceous Paleontology and Stratigraphy of New Mexico—Part II: New Mexico Bureau of Mines and Mineral Resources, Socorro, Circular 185, p. 7–28.

JOUANNEAU, J. M., AND LATOUCHE, C., 1981, The Gironde Estuary: Contributions to Sedimentology 10, Schweitzerbartsche Verlagsbuchhandlung, Stuttgart, 115 p.

KAUFFMAN, E. G., ed., 1983, Depositional environments and paleoclimates of the Greenhorn tectono-eustatic cycle, Rock Canyon Anticline, Pueblo, Colorado: Penrose Conference on Cretaceous Paleoclimates, Field Excursions Guidebook, 98 p.

KING, N. R., 1974, The Carlile—Niobrara contact and lower Niobrara strata near El Vado, New Mexico: New Mexico Geological Society Guidebook, 25th Field Conference, Ghost Ranch, New Mexico, p. 259–265.

KNEBEL, H. J., MARTIN, E. A., GLENN, J. L., AND NEEDELL, S. W., 1981, Sedimentary framework of the Potomac River estuary, Maryland: Geological Society of America Bulletin, v. 92, p. 578–589.

MACKENZIE, D. B., 1971, Post-Lytle Dakota Group on west flank of Denver Basin, Colorado: The Mountain Geologist, v. 8, p. 91–131.

———, AND POOLE, D. M., 1962, Provenance of Dakota Group sandstones of the Western Interior, *in* Symposium on Early Cretaceous Rocks of Wyoming and Adjacent Areas: Wyoming Geological Association, 17th Annual Field Conference Guidebook, p. 44–61.

MATUSZCZAK, R. A., 1976, Wattenberg Field: a review, *in* Epis, R. C., and Weimer, R. J., eds., Studies in Colorado Field Geology: Colorado School of Mines Professional Contribution 8, p. 275–279.

MAYNARD, A. K., AND SUTER, J. R., 1983, Regional variability of washover deposits on the south Texas coast: Gulf Coast Association of Geological Societies Transactions, v. 33, p. 339–346.

McCUBBIN, D. G., 1969, Cretaceous strike valley sandstone reservoirs, northwestern New Mexico: American Association of Petroleum Geologists Bulletin, v. 53, p. 2114–2140.

McKINNEY, T. F., DEALTERIS, J., CHOO, Y., STAHL, L., AND RONEY, J., 1977, Offshore sediment processes and responses near Beach Haven—Little Egg Inlet, New Jersey: Proceedings, 15th Coastal Engineering Conference, Honolulu, July 1976, p. 1899–1948.

MILLIMAN, J. D., AND EMERY, K. O., 1968, Sea levels during the past 35,000 years: Science, v. 162, p. 1121–1123.

MOLENAAR, C. M., 1977, The Pinedale oil seep—an exhumed stratigraphic trap in the southwestern San Juan Basin, *in* Fassett, J. E., ed., Guidebook of San Juan Basin III, Northwestern New Mexico, p. 243–246.

———, 1983a, Principal reference section and correlation of Gallup Sandstone, northwestern New Mexico, *in* Hook, S. C., compiler, Contributions to Mid-Cretaceous Paleontology and Stratigraphy of New Mexico: New Mexico Bureau of Mines and Mineral Resources, Socorro, Circular 185, p. 29–40.

———, 1983b, Major depositional cycles and regional correlations of Upper Cretaceous rocks, southern Colorado Plateau and adjacent areas, *in* Reynolds, M. W., and Dolly, E. D., eds., Mesozoic Paleogeography of West-Central United States: Rocky Mountain Section of Society of Economic Paleontologists and Mineralogists, p. 201–224.

MORTON, R. A., AND DONALDSON, A. C., 1973, Sediment distribution and evolution of tidal deltas along a tide-dominated shoreline, Wachapreague, Virginia: Sedimentary Geology, v. 10, p. 285–299.

NICHOLS, M. M., AND BIGGS, R. B., 1985, Estuaries, *in* Davis, R. A., ed., Coastal Sedimentary Environments: Springer-Verlag, New York, p. 77–186.

NIEDORODA A. W., SWIFT, D. J. P., FIGUEIREDO, A. G., AND FREELAND, G. L., 1985, Barrier island evolution, Middle Atlantic Coast, USA, part II: evidence from the shelf floor: Marine Geology, v. 63, p. 363–396.

NUMMEDAL, D., 1982, ed., Sedimentary Processes and Environments of the Louisiana-Texas Coast: Geological Society of America Annual Meeting, New Orleans, Field Trip Guidebook, 92 p.

———, AND TILLMAN, R. W., 1986, Flood-tidal deltas in the Coniacian Borrego Pass Sandstone, New Mexico (Abs.): Society of Economic Paleontologists and Mineralogists, Midyear Meeting, Raleigh, p. 84–85.

———, SWIFT, D. J. P., AND WRIGHT, R., 1986, Depositional sequences and shelf sandstones in Cretaceous strata of the San Juan Basin, New Mexico: A Field Guide for the 7th Annual Research Conference of the Gulf Coast Section of Society of Economic Paleontologists and Mineralogists, 162 p.

OWEN, D. E., 1966, Nomenclature of Dakota Sandstone (Cretaceous) in the San Juan Basin, New Mexico and Colorado: American Association

of Petroleum Geologists Bulletin, v. 50, p. 1023–1028.

———, AND SIEMERS, C. T., 1977, Lithologic correlation of the Dakota Sandstone and adjacent units along the eastern flank of the San Juan Basin, New Mexico: *in* Fassett, J. E., ed., New Mexico Geological Society Guidebook, 28th Field Conference, San Juan Basin III, p. 179–183.

PILKEY, O. H., BLACKWELDER, B. W., KNEBEL, H. J., AND AYERS, M. W., 1981, The Georgia Embayment continental shelf: stratigraphy of a submergence: Geological Society of America Bulletin, v. 92, p. 52–63.

PITMAN, W. C., 1982, The effects of sea level changes on the stratigraphy of the continental margins: Proceedings of the Joint Oceanographic Assembly, 1982, Dalhousie University, Nova Scotia, 22 p.

PRATT, L. M., KAUFFMAN, E. G., AND ZELT, F. B., 1985, eds., Fine-Grained Deposits and Biofacies of the Cretaceous Western Interior Seaway: Evidence of Cyclic Sedimentary Processes: Society of Economic Paleontologists and Mineralogists Midyear Meeting, Golden, Colorado, Field Trip Guidebook No. 9, 249 p.

SCHWARTZ, M. L., 1967, The Bruun theory of sea-level rise as a cause of shore erosion: Journal of Geology, v. 75, p. 76–92.

SHERIDAN, R. E., DILL, C. E., AND KRAFT, J. C., 1974, Holocene sedimentary environments of the Atlantic inner shelf off Delaware: Geological Society of America Bulletin, v. 85, p. 1319–1328.

SINGH, I. B., 1985, Burrow clasts—a source of intrabasinal coarse clastic grains (Abs.): Society of Economic Paleontologists and Mineralogists Midyear Meeting, Golden, Colorado, p. 83.

STAHL, L., KOCZAN, J., AND D. J. P. SWIFT, 1974, Anatomy of a shoreface-connected ridge system on the New Jersey shelf: implications for the genesis of the surficial sand sheet: Geology, v. 2, p. 117–120.

STAMP, L. D., 1921, On cycles of sedimentation in the Eocene Strata of the Anglo-Franco-Belgium Basin: Geological Magazine, v. 58, p. 108–114.

STONE, W. D., 1972, Stratigraphy and exploration of the lower Cretaceous Muddy Formation, northern Powder River Basin, Wyoming and Montana: The Mountain Geologist, v. 9, p. 355–378.

STUBBLEFIELD, W. L., LAVELLE, W. J., AND SWIFT, D. J. P., 1975, Sediment response to the present hydraulic regime on the central New Jersey shelf: Marine Geology, v. 107, p. 469–477.

SUTER, J. R., 1986, Late Quaternary facies and sea level history, southwest Louisiana continental shelf: Unpublished Ph.D. Dissertation, Louisiana State University, Baton Rouge (not consecutively paginated).

———, AND BERRYHILL, J. L., JR., 1985, Late Quaternary shelf-margin deltas, northwest Gulf of Mexico: American Association of Petroleum Geologists Bulletin, v. 69, p. 77–91.

SWIFT, D. J. P., 1968, Coastal erosion and transgressive stratigraphy: Journal of Geology, v. 76, p. 444–456.

———, 1976, Continental shelf sedimentation, *in* Stanley, D. J., and Swift, D. J. P., eds., Marine Sediment Transport And Environmental Management: Wiley, New York, p. 311–350.

———, KOFOED, J. W., SAULSBURY, F. P., AND SEARS, P., 1972, Holocene evolution of the shelf surface, central and southern Atlantic shelf of North America, *in* Swift, D. J. P., Duane, D. B., and Pilkey, O. H. eds., Shelf Sediment Transport: Process and Pattern: Dowden, Hutchinson and Ross, Stroudsbourg, Pennsylvania, p. 499–574.

———, MOIR, R., AND FREELAND, G. L., 1980, Stream net of the New Jersey shelf of North America during Quaternary lowstands: subaerial, submarine and buried valleys: Geology, v. 8, p. 276–280.

———, NIEDORODA, A. W., VINCENT, C. E., AND HOPKINS, T. S., 1985, Barrier island evolution, middle Atlantic shelf, USA, part I: shoreface dynamics: Marine Geology, v. 63, p. 331–361.

VAIL, P. R., HARDENBOL, J., AND TODD, R. G., 1984, Jurassic unconformities, chronostratigraphy and sea level changes from seismic stratigraphy and biostratigraphy, *in* Schlee, J. S., ed., Interregional Unconformities and Hydrocarbon Accumulation: American Association of Petroleum Geologists Memoir 36, p. 347–363.

———, MITCHUM, R. M., JR., TODD, R. G., WIDMIER, J. M., THOMPSON, S., III SANGREE, J. R., BUBB, J. N., AND HATLELID, W. G., 1977, Seismic stratigraphy and global changes in sea level, *in* Payton, C. E., ed., Seismic Stratigraphy-Applications to Hydrocarbon Exploration: American Association of Petroleum Geologists Memoir 26, p. 49–205.

WEIMER, R. J., 1984, Relation of unconformities, tectonics, and sea level changes, Cretaceous of Western Interior. U.S.A., *in* Schlee, J. S., ed., Interregional Unconformities and Hydrocarbon Accumulation: American Association of Petroleum Geologists Memoir 36, p. 7–35.

WHEELER, H. E., AND MALLORY, V. S., 1953, Designation of stratigraphic units: American Association of Petroleum Geologists Bulletin, v. 37, p. 2407–2421.

WILKINSON, B. H., AND BYRNE, J. R., 1977, Lavaca Bay—transgressive deltaic sedimentation in central Texas estuary: American Association of Petroleum Geologists Bulletin, v. 61, p. 527–545.

SUBJECT INDEX

SUBJECT INDEX